WRITER'S DIGEST
UNIVERSITY

A MULTIMEDIA EDUCATION
IN WRITING AND PUBLISHING

D0521310

FROM THE EDITORS OF WRITER'S DIGEST

WRITER'S DIGEST
BOOKS

WritersDigest.com
Cincinnati, Ohio

For more resources for writers, visit www.writersdigest.com/books.

To receive a free weekly e-mail newsletter delivering tips and updates about writing and about Writer's Digest products, register directly at http://newsletters.fwpublications.com.

14 13 12 11 10   5 4 3 2

Distributed in Canada by Fraser Direct
100 Armstrong Avenue
Georgetown, Ontario, Canada L7G 5S4
Tel: (905) 877-4411

Distributed in the U.K. and Europe by F+W Media International
Brunel House, Newton Abbot, Devon, TQ12 4PU, England
Tel: (+44) 1626-323200, Fax: (+44) 1626-323319
E-mail: postmaster@davidandcharles.co.uk

Distributed in Australia by Capricorn Link
P.O. Box 704, Windsor, NSW 2756 Australia
Tel: (02) 4577-3555

Library of Congress Cataloging-in-Publication Data

Writer's digest university / from the editors of Writer's Digest. -- 1st ed.
     p. cm.
 Includes bibliographical references and index.
 ISBN 978-1-59963-137-0 (pbk. : alk. paper)
 1. Authorship--Marketing--Handbooks, manuals, etc. 2. Authors and publishers--Handbooks, manuals, etc. I. Writer's digest.
 PN155.W74 2010
 808'.02--dc22   2010020785

Edited by Melissa Hill
Designed by Terri Woesner
Cover designed by Claudean Wheeler
Production coordinated by Mark Griffin & Debbie Thomas

TABLE OF CONTENTS

INTRODUCTION by Jane Friedman, WD Contributor and former Director of Content & Community Development

PART I
GETTING STARTED: HOW DO I ...

PART II
FORMATTING & SUBMITTING YOUR WORK

PART III
MINDING YOUR BUSINESS

PART IV
EVERYTHING AGENTS

PART V
LISTINGS

APPENDIX

> "Sit down and put down everything that comes into your head and then you're a writer. But an author is one who can judge his own stuff's worth, without pity, and destroy most of it."
>
> —*Colette (1873–1954)*

It's not polite to start a conversation with a negative remark, but in the case of this handbook and guide, it's important to get it out of the way.

You will be rejected.

The good news is that every published author has been rejected many times over. What makes a successful writer? The steps he then takes after rejection.

It's important to start talking about rejection right away because most of us have dreams of being published or otherwise discovered, as if these things happen once we produce good enough work.

The truth is, however, that writers with strong marketing skills and ordinary work are more likely to get published than writers with ordinary marketing skills and excellent work.

This guide attempts to give you the 3 keys to publication:

- A clear idea of what makes any work suitable for sale

- How to professionally package and present your work for sale

- The most appropriate markets open to a sale

If you're completely new to writing and publishing, then take a look at Part I for a general overview of writing techniques and genres. If you already have work that's ready to market, then Part II will help you prepare it properly. Parts III and IV go into more advanced information about the business end of publishing, especially once you start making sales. The good news is that many things in the publishing world are a matter of common sense, and politeness and professionalism go a long way toward covering up any amateur mistakes you might make.

This guide does not recommend specific agents, editors, or publishing companies, though we do list hundreds of opportunities for you to pursue in Part V. These listings are fully vetted by the staff of Writer's Digest and are legitimate, traditional publishing companies that pay writers for their work, or do not ask for payment to publish.

The main benefits of this book and accompanying DVD are:

- Learning the basics of how to get published in any genre

- Understanding what it means to be a professional writer and conduct business in an ethical way

- Developing the right expectations of editors, agents, and other publishing professionals whom you'll deal with

- Avoiding the typical (and sometimes disastrous) beginner mistakes that can sabotage your efforts to get published

- Access to the most up-to-date market information, including agents, book publishers, and magazines

Make sure you take advantage of the full value of this package by viewing the online seminars and registering for your free subscription at WritersMarket.com, which gives you access to more than 8,000 markets—updated daily—as well as a regular featured markets report.

THE CRITICAL NEXT STEPS

Let's go back to the earlier point: It's not that you get rejected that counts. It's what you do afterward. So … what do you do?

1. Keep trying. Of course you should keep trying. Persistence is essential. But most importantly, you should keep writing. Once you finish a manuscript, the first thing you should do is start work on another project. Why? Because it helps create distance and perspective from the project you just finished—which will inevitably need to be refined and approached with a more critical eye once you begin to market it.

Don't neglect this step! You need to be able to evaluate your work from a sales perspective, and with as little emotional attachment as possible. This often only comes with time, or with the assistance of a good editor or critique partner.

2. Develop relationships and connections with people who can help you. More progress than you might think will depend on the willingness of others to help you and advise you. One of the most effective ways to develop relationships is to attend conferences and meet other writers, as well as editors and agents.

One of the most difficult aspects of getting published is trying to query cold. But once you've established a relationship with an editor or agent, then it's no longer a cold contact, but a person who may be compelled to pay attention because you made a good impression on them. Or, if you develop good connections with published authors, they can offer hard-won advice, even referrals to agents, if they believe in your work.

3. Don't get bitter. I meet many writers who ask, often at a moment of frustration and desperation, "Read my writing and tell me if I should keep trying."

I empathize if you're looking for some reason to continue in the face of rejection. It's tough to continue doing something when you receive no recognition or encouragement for it.

What I find is that most reassurances, while offering a boost to a writer's ego, are ultimately external and fleeting. A writer needs an essential fire inside, or an attitude, that carries them the distance.

Strive for an attitude and approach that's defined by:

- Seeking feedback from smart people (avoid defensiveness and protectiveness)

- Loving the writing process and the meaningfulness of what you're doing (it can't be about just the money)

- Taking advantage of every possible growth opportunity (not resistant to change)

- Being in control of your own destiny (not waiting to be discovered)

You'll experience frustrations, and sometimes disagree with the feedback or direction you receive along the way. But take note of everything, take away what is useful and suitable for your core mission, and ignore the rest.

My hope is that every writer I meet will not ask, "Read my work and tell me what to do," but "This is my mission, how can I improve and grow?"

Stay passionate. Stay persistent.

Read more of Jane's advice for writers at her blog, There Are No Rules (http://blog.writersdigest.com/norules)

PART I
GETTING STARTED: HOW DO I ...

CHAPTER 1

HOW DO I KNOW IF I HAVE WHAT IT TAKES?

One of the biggest problems that plagues beginning writers is self-doubt. Whether that doubt results from age, gender, profession, lack of experience, or limited education, it creeps into the minds of beginning writers and often dampens hope and hinders progress. Unfortunately, self-doubt doesn't go away with experience, age, or even success. Writers will always wonder if they have what it takes; even after a long career of publishing, you may wonder if you've been faking it all along.

The answers in this chapter provide a starting point for thinking about some of these existential problems, but many of the final answers will be unique to you and will change over time. Writers tend to have opposing views on the role self-doubt plays in the creative life. Sylvia Plath said, "The worst enemy to creativity is self-doubt," while Sidonie-Gabrielle Colette said, "The writer who loses his self-doubt, who gives way as he grows old to a sudden euphoria, to prolixity, should stop writing immediately."

This chapter also addresses questions that relate to setting up life as writer—the tools, space, and time that you will need. Again, the answers to these questions often depend on knowing the best way to remove distractions and allow for productive writing time. All writers work a little differently, and no one way is best.

What does it take to become a writer?

Mostly passion and persistence—the passion to write and the persistence to keep writing in the face of failure. Curiosity and an awareness of human behavior are also signature qualities of successful writers. Knowledge about the publishing industry can be vital and helps you avoid frustration and wasted time.

I'm interested in writing but not sure I have the aptitude for it. Are all good writers born with writing talent?

Certain writers may be born with more talent than others, but writing is mostly learned through practice; talent often boils down to having the discipline to write regularly and frequently. Anyone with the energy and willingness to develop as a writer can learn the craft and become successful at it. It's also possible for a talented and gifted writer to lack the energy and persistence necessary to publish with any degree of success.

How can I be sure I really have creative writing ability?

You'll never be sure. It's best to believe in yourself and keep moving forward. Most writers cycle between periods of self-doubt and periods of confidence.

How can I decide whether to write fiction or nonfiction?

Look at what you most enjoy reading, and see if that leads you to an answer. Many talented writers have made names for themselves in both fiction and nonfiction, so it's not necessary to limit yourself to one or the other.

What causes writer's block, and how can I combat it?

Ask twenty writers what causes writer's block, and you'll probably get twenty different answers. The causes of writer's block usually don't have anything to do with writing but rather are connected to factors that distract writers, keeping them from concentrating on the craft.

Look at your work and see if you're actually ready to begin writing; it may be that you haven't done all your preliminary work yet. Step away from the work and try to look at it objectively. You may not have a clear understanding of how you want it to turn out. You may be writing it one way, when you know subconsciously that it would be better if it were treated some other way.

Some say a writer should make sure he wants to write about his current subject; if you're trying to make yourself write about something you just don't like, your mind could be rebelling.

Anxiety about the quality of one's writing is frequently cited as a cause of writer's block. Novelist Dean Koontz claims this is easily solved: "Read a novel by a really bad writer whose work you despise, and tell yourself, 'If this junk can get into print, publishers will fight one another for the rights to my book.'"

What's the best book I could write to make sure I'd be published?

The best book you can write is your best book. In other words, your best shot at selling a book to a publisher is to write about what you want to write about, and write it as well as you can. It doesn't necessarily matter what's currently selling; the book business is full of unknowns and the unexpected. Choose whatever interests you, and hopefully others will be informed, inspired, or entertained by what you've written.

What is the best market for writers? What sells most easily?

There is no such thing as one best market, since so much depends on the type of writing each individual writer does. A market is good for a particular writer if he writes the kind of material that market needs.

I'm only interested in writing nonfiction. Is there any reason I should read fiction?

Nonfiction writers should be familiar with fiction techniques, as they're often used in nonfiction. The most successful nonfiction writers use dialogue, suspense, characterization, description, and emotion—all part of the fiction writer's craft—in their work. In fact, a writer should be able to learn from the study of any good writin, be it fiction, nonfiction, poetry, or script.

I sometimes wonder if I write fast enough. Are there any standards I can measure my writing speed against?

It's said Marcel Proust would spend three or four days working on a single paragraph. In contrast, Jack Kerouac is said to have written *On the Road* in a single protracted session at the typewriter. It's best for each writer to set his own goal, since writing speed varies with the individual. When setting your daily quota of pages or words, you should make it a little higher than you think you might be able to reach, so you can have something to shoot for. Consider that if you wrote one page per day, you'd have a book-length work in a year.

Some days I just don't feel like writing. Are there any secrets or formulas for disciplining oneself to write regularly?

Discipline can separate the would-be writer from the published writer. You should think of yourself as a professional and regard your writing as any other job. Techniques that make the writing task seem easier include (1) finding the time of day when you think best and writing during those hours, (2) dividing a project into easily accomplished parts, so the entire job doesn't loom above you, and (3) choosing a writing time when distractions are few.

I work at home and sometimes have trouble starting work at the beginning of the day. How can I overcome this problem?

One good way to begin is to edit or revise work that's already been written. Some writers deliberately stop a writing session in the middle of a thought, section, or sentence, so they will know exactly where to resume the next day and will be less likely to procrastinate. Browsing through writing magazines or reading a chapter from a how-to book on writing can also put you in the mood. (Reading about writing is an important part of your workday, but know when to stop reading and start writing.)

A few months after one of my article ideas was rejected by an editor, a similar article appeared in that magazine. This has also happened when an entire manuscript was rejected. How can I protect myself from editors who steal my ideas?

Beginning writers (and sometimes established ones) are quick to suspect their ideas have been stolen by editors. Such assumptions are almost always false. Since a magazine often has three months or even one year of lead time between an issue's creation and its publication, the published piece was probably written or assigned before you even wrote your query letter. Unless the published article uses, word-for-word, the same paragraphs and sentences as the rejected work, there is no proof of editorial piracy. The truth is that the better your understanding of the market, the greater the chance of similarities between your ideas and published articles or manuscripts.

Writers also frequently ask how they can protect their ideas from other writers. When fellow writers gather and talk shop, a writer will casually mention a piece he's working on. Months or years go by, and another writer ends up doing an article or book on the same idea. This other writer hasn't intentionally stolen from you and may not even remember that you were working on the same idea, since most writers get ideas from many different sources including newspapers, magazines, books, television, films, neighbors, and co-workers. Once you've discussed your idea with others, you've put it out where others can get at it—consciously or unconsciously. (Ideas can't be copyrighted.) A good rule is: Don't discuss a work in progress with other writers if you fear it being stolen.

I'm fourteen years old. Am I too young to get my stories published?

You're never too young to submit your work for publication. Editors everywhere are looking for good writing. If a fiction editor is sent a short story that is compelling and entertaining, or a magazine editor is sent a feature story that is direct and informative, he wouldn't pass just because the writer is young. (And how would he know unless you told him?)

That said, a young writer is likely to face a tougher challenge breaking into an adult publication market than an older writer would. This has nothing to do with age, and everything to do with experience. Writers who are twenty to thirty years older than you are going to have ten to twenty more years of trying-to-get-published experience under their belts. They're likely to have a more developed sense of what a query letter should look and sound like, what markets accept what kinds of pieces, etc. Although this information can be researched and learned by anyone, it is something that is only fully understood with practice.

So, get started now. The earlier you dive in and try, the sooner your chances of success will manifest themselves. Do not be discouraged if your writing is not accepted at first. Rejection is a fact of the writer's life, and every writer of every age must face it.

I recently retired, and I've found the time to write. Am I too old to begin?

You're never too old to start writing.

Do writers who live in New York or Los Angeles have an advantage over those who live in other parts of the country?

No matter where you live and write, you must be able to turn out quality work, and external environment is only part of what enables you to do so. Top-quality writing attracts the attention of editors everywhere, no matter where it originates.

I'm intrigued by the idea of being a writer; but, having no experience, I'm afraid to get my feet wet. Can you give me ideas for basic, challenging writing projects I could do to get some practice?

One often overlooked but excellent way to get practice is by writing letters to the editor. Everyone has ideas and opinions, but the ability to get them down on paper in an organized and concise manner is the mark of a good writer. Although you won't receive a response from the editor, you can compare what you wrote to what was printed to see how your copy was edited to exclude repetition, awkward sentences, and wordiness.

Many clubs and local organizations use volunteer writers to create newsletters and to handle publicity. Any such writing is excellent training and bolsters your confidence; it also gives you published work for your portfolio.

Some editors won't consider my work unless I can show them clips of my previously published work. But how can I get clips if I can't get published without them?

This seeming catch-22 situation is not new to writers. But you can get published without clips. You have several options.

First, if you have a strong idea for a publication that accepts first-time writers, then clips become a nonissue. So seek out those publications, brainstorm a stellar idea, and send it their way.

Another way to obtain publishing experience is by writing for free. Some writers will argue that you should not write for free—that your work deserves pay—but writing for local school, community, or group newsletters without pay is charitable, as well as smart. The main reason editors want to see your clips is to confirm that you can actually write. A nonpaying published clip confirms this as well as a paying one does.

Finally, if you have a spectacular idea for a magazine, but the magazine only deals with previously published writers, send a complete manuscript to break in. Some publications state that they do not accept complete manuscripts, but if you have an idea that interests them and no clips to show them that you know your writing stuff, sending the complete article may be the only option. The editors will forgive you for breaking their rules if you send a killer complete manuscript their way.

Friends love hearing me tell stories and say I should write a book. Should I?

Unless you have a passion for writing, you should probably ignore your friends' advice. As Heather Sellers says in *Page After Page*, "Writing is a ton of work. It's exhausting. You can hardly do it when you are tired—it's that hard to do well. It's a way of life, and you have to really look inside yourself. It's like cleaning house—fun to have finished, less fun to do. Writing is not always the answer. It's not always right to say to people, 'Yes, you have a great story. You should write it.' Maybe you should write. Maybe not."

What does it mean to be professional?

A writer who is professional has a firm grasp of the skills of his craft, understands the techniques required for writing successful fiction or nonfiction, and constantly strives to improve. Professionals study markets before submitting their work, so they know their audiences and the needs of specific editors, making their acceptance rate higher. When a professional receives a rejection slip, he realizes that his manuscript is a product for sale and that there was not a need for the product in that particular market at that time. Therefore, he proceeds by looking for another suitable market, or by analyzing the strengths and weaknesses of the work itself.

Most importantly, professionalism is an attitude. For the beginning writer, it means professional presentation of queries and manuscripts, a thorough study of the markets, and the ability to deliver assigned work on time.

It seems every topic I want to write about has already been covered. How can I use my idea without duplicating another writer's work?

You're unlikely to duplicate another writer's work simply by using the same idea. Even if you use the exact same idea, you're sure to execute it differently. Writers have different styles, attitudes, voices, and approaches, and it's nearly impossible for two writers to execute the same idea in the same way or with the same slant.

Where do writers get their ideas?

From the world around them. Look at your experiences, your family, your workplace, your home, your reading, the newspaper, the television, and the places you've been. Things you're familiar with can provide a gold mine of ideas and make more viable stories than things you know little about. For instance, suppose a responsible woman in your office just didn't show up for work for an entire week. Would you wonder during that week what had happened to her? Where she went? Whether she would come back? Constantly ask yourself questions. If an idea comes to you, write it down immediately. It may never pass through your mind again. Keep in mind that most ideas need to gestate for a while before you develop them.

MATTERS OF PERSONAL PREFERENCE

Is it a good idea to keep a journal?

A journal can be invaluable to a writer, since it records ideas, impressions, and anecdotes for future use. Even if your journal entries never get into print, journal writing can help your career by instilling in you the habit of writing regularly.

Julia Cameron popularized journaling in her best-selling book *The Artist's Way*, in which she advocates doing "morning pages" (writing a few pages, no matter what the quality, first thing in the morning). Some writers have found this advice to be life changing, while others, such as Pulitzer Prize winner Richard Russo, have scoffed at journal keeping. It's a matter of what works for you.

If I want to work on my writing in my spare time, would it be better to hold a job completely unrelated to writing?

Unfortunately, there's no simple answer to that question. Some writers find that doing any sort of writing, even if it's not related to their personal work, sharpens their skills and is infinitely preferable to any other sort of work. Other writers find that holding down a writing-related job makes it more difficult to devote energy to writing at home. There's no way to know unless you try it.

How much time should I put into developing my skills? Should I write every day?

You should devote as much time as possible to writing if you expect to accomplish very much. Most serious writers put in time every day; other writers, especially novelists, have intense work cycles when they write all day every day for several months to finish a project, then take a period of time off.

I find it difficult to find enough time to write. What should I do?

Never say you don't have enough time to write. You make time for the things you care about; if you care about writing, you will make time.

Is it in my best interest to write only about a specific topic and build a reputation in that field, or should I write about what interests me at any given time?

It's probably best, at least early in your career, to play the field. By doing so, you'll have the opportunity to sample different types of writing to determine which brings you the most satisfaction and success. Many writers who specialize continue to write on other topics in which they're interested, even after they've established a name for themselves in one field. If a specialist limits his writing to one field, he runs the risk of being without an outlet for his work should that market go sour, or of being so closely associated with it that his credibility in other fields is weakened.

TOOLS AND EQUIPMENT

No avocation in the world has as little start-up expense as writing. Ideas, energy, a scrap of paper, and a pencil are all a beginner requires. As your skill develops, only a few more tools are necessary to create work that is properly formatted and looks professional.

I'm trying to keep expenses to a minimum. What equipment and supplies do I need to get started?

All you need to begin is paper, pens, and access to a computer and printer, though your equipment needs will expand with your success. If you plan to become a freelance writer, a telephone and daily access to e-mail and the Internet will become essential—both are your connection to clients and research resources.

If you become a career writer, a good, sturdy office file will become necessary. Many writers have tried to do without a file cabinet, but sooner or later have realized the need for organizing correspondence, old manuscripts, financial records, etc. Once you begin getting paid for your work, you may need an accounting software program like QuickBooks to keep track of your finances.

I don't use computers. Will an editor accept work typed on a typewriter?

Probably not. If you produce a manuscript with a typewriter, you won't be able to submit it as an electronic file, and very few (if any) editors will be willing to rekey your work—it's costly and time consuming. Editors will also be turned off by your inability (or refusal) to use computers.

Should I buy a desktop computer or a notebook?

What type of writer are you? Are you frequently traveling, on the go? Do you prefer to work outside of the home, in coffee bars or parks? Or do you want to frequently move your computer between many rooms of your house? Would you like to use it on research trips to the library or bookstore? If the answer to any of these questions is yes, you may prefer a notebook. If you write only at home or in an office setup, or if you can only get work done without distractions, then consider a desktop model. A desktop model is likely to be more expandable (upgradeable) and less expensive than a notebook.

What word-processing software should I use?

Ask yourself how fancy you'd like it to be. For basic writing that requires minimal or no professional layout, you can get away with bare-bones text editors. Text editors are very simple programs that come with your computer, such as TextEdit (for Mac) and WordPad (for Microsoft Windows). This software will allow you to edit, save, and print your work, but it's not recommended for formatting and submitting professional queries and manuscripts. Professional work requires that you have additional capabilities, such as margin settings, paragraph formatting, running heads, and page numbering. For this, you need a program like Microsoft Word.

Most writers and businesses—whether using Macs or PCs—use Microsoft Word. Word files are highly compatible between platforms and versions, meaning that a manuscript created using an older version of Word on a Mac, for instance, will still be readable by a newer Word program on a PC. Microsoft Word won't set you back more than a couple hundred dollars, and it might even come packaged with your computer.

If you prefer not to use Microsoft products, or if you just want free, downloadable word-processing software that's more powerful than a basic text editor, look for OpenOffice.org (www.openoffice.org).

What extras should I look for when purchasing a computer?

Today's computers have several times the capacity that most writers require. Any new, off-the-shelf computer is guaranteed to have the essentials you need to start writing, e-mailing, surfing the Internet, and sharing photos. Unless you (or your children) have a video-game hobby—or you plan to use or store lots of photos, music, or movies—don't worry about speed, hard-drive size, or memory when buying a new machine.

If you have a writing archive on older disks—such as the 3.5″ disks that are becoming obsolete—be aware that many new computers don't come with any disk drive except a CD/DVD drive. However, even if you do buy a computer that doesn't have the right disk drive, you can typically buy an external disk drive to plug into your computer.

For writers with archived material on older disks, consider transferring your files (which will likely become damaged and inaccessible over time) to writeable CDs or DVDs, or other available media—such as flash memory sticks, external hard drives, and even iPods. Most flash memory sticks are small enough to fit in your pocket, and they plug right into your computer. External hard drives are a good choice if you have an enormous amount of information to store or archive. (iPods are external hard drives that are designed and sold as music players.) Do realize that transferring material from very old floppy disks might require professional help.

If all this sounds confusing, consult with a young person or computer geek in your social circle. She'll help you find the best option for your situation. In general, you should keep at least two or three copies of your important work on separate media. Think about how much you would miss if your current working copy suddenly disappeared.

Is it necessary to have a portable audio recording device? What kind should I get?

Many writers find audio recorders useful in a variety of situations. Recording an interview allows you to concentrate on your subject, the surroundings, and the questions you want to ask. Using a recorder is a good way to verify quotes and can help establish credibility with editors. You can also use it to record your impressions and ideas when driving home from an interview.

The model you choose should have a built-in microphone, a tape counter (so you can note points in the tape where the interviewee makes important comments), and a telephone adapter (to record interviews conducted via the telephone).

Are stationery and business cards necessary for a writer? How elaborate should they be, and how can I obtain them?

Printed stationery is not necessary for a beginner, but as you develop—and especially as you publish—you may want to accompany your professional manuscripts with professional letterhead. It doesn't need to be elaborate or expensively designed. Most office-supply stores and quick-print shops offer standard imprinted letterheads in a variety of type styles, colors, and paper quality.

Business cards can enhance your image as a professional writer and help you network; you generally give them to potential clients, editors, agents, people you interview, people you meet at writers conferences, etc. When you're just starting out, you don't need to invest very much to have a business card made. A chain print shop can create, print, and cut a hundred black-and-white, one-sided business cards for about fifty dollars.

WHERE TO FIND OUT MORE

Books

Page After Page: Discover the Confidence and Passion You Need to Start Writing and Keep Writing—No Matter What! by Heather Sellers, is the perfect inspiration book if you're a nonwriting writer.

The Artist's Way: A Spiritual Path to Higher Creativity, by Julia Cameron, helps you find the discipline to write every day.

Writing Down the Bones, by Natalie Goldberg, brings a touch of Zen to the writing life.

Bird by Bird: Some Instructions on Writing and Life, by Anne Lamott, tackles the toughest psychological questions of the writing life, with wit and verve.

How to Be a Writer, by Barbara Baig, helps you practice the skills that allow you to communicate clearly and powerfully on the page.

The Productive Writer, by Sage Cohen, helps you establish order out of chaos as you arrange your work space, set and clarify goals, manage your submissions, and organize your writing time.

Websites

Author Holly Lisle (www.hollylisle.com) maintains a great collection of articles and information for writers, particularly those just starting out.

In A Newbie's Guide to Publishing (www.jakonrath.blogspot.com), author J.A. Konrath shares what he's learned in his career and provides links to about three hundred recommended writing blogs.

CHAPTER 2

HOW DO I GET PUBLISHED?

Getting published is a step-by-step process of (1) researching the appropriate publications or publishers for your work, (2) reading their submission or writers guidelines, and (3) sending a query letter. The query letter is the primary tool for writers seeking magazine or book publication. A nonfiction writer with an article or book idea can elicit, through a query letter, the interest of an editor and sometimes even the particular slant an editor prefers. For fiction writers, a query letter attempts to persuade an editor or agent to request a full or partial manuscript for review. The questions and answers in this chapter will fully explain the query letter and its advantages.

RESEARCHING THE MARKET

Do all magazines and book publishers read unsolicited manuscripts or accept unsolicited queries?

No. Publications that accept unsolicited manuscripts or queries usually indicate that in their listings in *Writer's Market*, on their website, or in their guidelines. Some places only accept material submitted by agents. With few exceptions, no agent or editor will accept a complete manuscript on first contact; you have to query first.

Are there any rules concerning which editor or department should receive requests for submission guidelines or writers guidelines?

Always look online first or in *Writer's Market* for guidelines. If you absolutely can't find them, then resort to mail. Write on the outside envelope, in the lower left corner, "Request for Submission Guidelines," and address the envelope and the letter to the editor of the publication. (If you don't know the editor's name, just address the request to "The Editor.") Your request will be routed quicker and get a faster response with the corner notation.

I am interested in having my book published. However, I've had no experience with these things. Where do I start?

Use a market guide (such as *Writer's Market* or *Novel & Short Story Writer's Market*) to find places likely to be interested in your particular book, or check the library or bookstores to find books similar to your own, and note who the publishers are. The listings in the market guides will tell you what to submit, where to submit it, and how to submit it. Send an SASE with every submission.

How can I find out which publishers are most likely to be interested in a new novelist?

There are several ways. You can research publisher listings through a market guide and look at the percentage of new writers they publish; you can read magazines like *Booklist*, *Writer's Digest*, and *Publishers Weekly*, which periodically give profiles of first novelists and information about their books; or you can browse through the fiction shelves at the bookstore or library and look at author bios, then note the publishers of first-time novelists. One company particularly known for its support of new novelists is MacAdam/Cage, an independent book publisher based in San Francisco. They still read unagented manuscripts.

MAGAZINE QUERIES

Do editors usually choose pieces from the slush pile to publish in their magazines and, if so, how frequently do they choose from the pile?

If an editor works at a publication that accepts unsolicited submissions, then the answer to the first question is yes, they do use pieces from the slush pile—but only if the queries fit the bill. This means that the queries should first and foremost exhibit that the person querying the publication is familiar with the content of the publication. The query should also reflect that the person has read the publication's guidelines. Guidelines are important because they let the freelancer know what sections of the magazine are open to freelance submissions and what sections are not.

In addition to being on target, the query needs to be fresh and creative. Editors see lots of queries by lots of writers who all present the same article ideas. Make your idea stand out in that slush pile by finding a new slant on a topic of interest to the publication.

How frequently are queries from the slush pile actually assigned?

That depends on how often editors see queries like those described above, and it depends on the publication's inventory of articles. If a publication has its editorial lineup for the upcoming year well in hand, as well as a significant number of unused articles, that particular publication may not be purchasing many articles. It is "overstocked." If this is the case, then no matter how on target your query is, the publication may be unwilling to purchase it for fear it will sit in its yet-to-be-published files for an unreasonable length of time.

What information should a query letter contain for a magazine article?

The information in a query letter serves two purposes. It should convince the editor that your idea is a good one for her publication's readership, and it should sell you as the best writer to turn out a good article on the subject. The query letter should contain an alluring (but concise) summary of the article's central idea and the angle or point of view from which you intend to approach it. Outline the structure of the article, giving facts, observations, and anecdotes that support the premise of the article. Don't give too many facts; the idea is to leave the editor wanting more. The letter should tell the editor why the article would be important and timely, and it should present a convincing argument for why the article would fit into this particular magazine.

You should also give the editor some indication of why you think you could write a good article on this particular subject. Share some sources of information and describe any special qualifications you may have for developing the idea. For example, if you are proposing an article on a topic in which you have some professional expertise, you should mention that. Samples of your published work will also help the editor see what you can do. The close of the query can be a straightforward request to write the article. You might also specify an estimated length and delivery date. If photographs are available, mention that, too. Don't discuss fees or request advice.

These are guidelines, of course, not a hard-and-fast pattern for a query letter. Good query letters are as individual as the writers who send them and as unique as the ideas that are proposed.

How long should a query letter be?

Most successful query letters run only one page. Two or three pages of single-spaced typewritten copy is more than a busy editor wants to read. If that much copy is needed to give an editor the gist of the article, you probably have failed to focus on a specific angle.

I have no previous publications, but I don't want to hurt my chances of having my article accepted by admitting that to an editor. How much must my query letter tell about my background?

If you've never been published before, it's best to ignore the subject of past credits and discuss instead your qualifications to write the article at hand. Discuss only those aspects of your background that relate to your subject. If you're proposing an article about how small businesses use computers, for example, mentioning your computer knowledge through education or employment would be a plus. What's important to an editor is not how many articles you've had published, but how much promise is shown by your query letter. Even if you've never published anything, a thorough and professional approach to the query letter will allow you the same chance to sell an article as someone who has a few articles in print.

Should I include two or three samples of my work when sending a query letter?

It's always a good idea to include a few clips of your previously published articles. If an editor is not familiar with your work, looking at other pieces you've written is one way she can familiarize herself with your abilities and the quality of your work. The articles you send with your query ideally should be of the same category as the article you are proposing; a suggestion for an article on easy house painting could be bolstered by your published article on how to reupholster furniture. Even if the clips you send differ from the type of article you're proposing, send only your best published articles. Showing insignificant clips to the editor of a major publication could defeat your purpose. If you are dissatisfied with something you wrote, chances are the editor will not be too impressed with it either.

How do I obtain clips or tearsheets of my work?

Publishers frequently furnish free contributor copies, tearsheets, or clips to freelance writers. If none of these are offered or provided, you may offer to buy copies of the issue your work appeared in from the publisher.

Do I always have to query before sending a manuscript, or are there times when querying isn't necessary?

For certain types of articles, editors prefer to see the finished manuscript rather than a query. For example, personal experience articles, humor, nostalgia, and editorial opinion pieces rely so much on the writer's personal style that reading the finished product is the best way an editor can assess their acceptability for her publication. Articles requiring extensive research, however, are best attempted after an editor has responded favorably to a query. That saves the writer time, since the editor may prefer a different approach to the subject than the one the writer originally had. If you have any doubts, check *Writer's Market* for the specific magazine's policy on various types of articles.

It seems so presumptuous for a beginning and unpublished writer to query first. How much attention would be paid to a beginner?

A busy editor would much rather read a query to decide whether she's interested in a certain idea than plow through a lengthy manuscript for the same purpose. From the writer's standpoint, think of the savings in postage and wear and tear on the manuscript. What is presumptuous is the writer who disregards an editor's stated request to query first and deluges the editor with completed manuscripts. Editors pay as much attention to beginners as they do to professionals, as long as the query letters are professionally written and the ideas are suitable to the magazine's readership and the editor's needs.

Is it okay for me to submit more than one idea at a time to the same magazine?

Submitting more than one idea at a time means you're making a multiple submission, and this practice is generally not preferred. Due to space limitations in a good query letter, it is difficult to fully develop more than one idea at a time, and it's easier for editors to contend with only one idea per letter. However, some magazines, like *National Geographic*, request that writers send a letter containing several one-paragraph ideas. If the editors find any idea promising, they request a more detailed two-page outline. Look in *Writer's Market* or send for a magazine's writers guidelines to find out what a particular editor prefers.

If a magazine's masthead lists an editor and a managing editor but no articles editor, who should get my unsolicited manuscript?

Since it is the editor's job in most cases to determine what stories are assigned and to whom, as well as what will be printed in a particular issue, you should send your manuscript to her. At most magazines, the managing editor is concerned more with the actual production of the magazine.

A magazine bought and published seven articles I submitted over the last several years. Each check was accompanied by a letter encouraging me to submit more of my work. Should I continue to enclose a SASE?

Continue to enclose an SASE unless the editor specifically tells you it's no longer necessary. However, you needn't enclose an SASE if you are sending an article that you have written on assignment, after having queried the editor.

Do magazines accept free contributions? I have written an inspirational essay that carries a message and do not feel that I should accept money to have it reach the public.

If it is a magazine's policy to pay for material it uses, you should not offer your contribution for free. Don't be misled into thinking that just because it's free, an editor will use it. If, in the editor's estimation, it's worthy of being printed, she will automatically pay for it (and you can send the check to your favorite charity). If it doesn't seem publishable to her, then the fact that it's free will not persuade her to use it.

When an editor requests samples of my writing, is it sufficient to send a copy of the first page of a six-page published article, or must I send the complete article?

A photocopy of the complete published article is preferable so the editor can see how you handle not just the opening, but the examples, transitions, and the conclusion.

Unsolicited manuscripts should always be sent with a SASE, but what about solicited manuscripts?

Editors should pay the freight for their own solicitations. But if you query a magazine and an editor says, "Okay, let me see it on spec," include a SASE. That's not a solicited manuscript.

What should I do if a magazine tells me they would like to keep my query letter for future consideration? I had planned several other slants to the story that might interest other publications.

Write to the editor, acknowledging your interest in her future consideration but indicating your intentions to query elsewhere with different versions of the story in the meantime.

When a magazine specifies "contributions cannot be acknowledged or returned," how long must a contributor wait before submitting the item to another magazine for consideration?

That's up to you, but you should give the magazine enough time to consider your work—about eight to ten weeks is usually reasonable.

A magazine recently published an article strikingly similar to one I have been trying to sell to the same magazine for some time. What can I do about this?

First, don't assume that the idea was stolen by the editor and given to someone else to write. One frustrating fact of a writer's life is that you're often beaten to publication by someone with the same idea—sometimes even using the same words. But you're not forced to forget about selling your idea elsewhere, because many articles are published on the same subject in a variety of publications within a two- or three-year period. If your article is well written and hits the right magazine at the right time, publication of the other article will not be a deterrent to publication of yours.

I submitted a query to a magazine's top editor. The assistant to the editor replied: "Although we can't use this idea, we'd like to see more of your work." Now I have another idea for that magazine. Do I now correspond with the assistant or with the top editor?

Direct all future ideas or manuscripts to the person from whom you received the last correspondence. Top editors rarely are the first to review incoming manuscripts. It's best to submit to an articles editor or associate editor.

It's not unusual for a single publishing company to produce several magazines with similar editorial content. Will my manuscript automatically be considered for use in all the magazines, or should I submit to each one separately?

Unless otherwise noted in *Writer's Market* or in a magazine's guidelines, you should query each magazine separately. This allows you to personalize your submission—addressing it to the proper editor, mentioning a previously published article you admired, etc.

I submitted a seasonal article idea too late and received a rejection slip. Should I resubmit to that same market in about four months?

Seasonal queries should be submitted at least six months ahead of schedule. Some editors prefer queries at least one year ahead of season. If you receive a rejection for seasonal material with a note stating "received too late," resubmit it again in plenty of time for the editor to consider it for next season. See *Writer's Market* for publications' policies. "Received too late" may also mean that it is not good enough to keep on file for the following season.

After I have received a favorable reply to a query, how soon will the editor expect the manuscript?

If an editor gives you a favorable response on an article idea and doesn't specify a deadline, ask for one.

GENERAL ETIQUETTE

I'm going to New York with my husband to a convention at just about the time I'll have my book finished. Would it be to my advantage to visit agents there with it?

No, it is not to your advantage and would likely kill your chances with that agent. Never go knocking on doors—it is considered rude, obnoxious, and unprofessional. Neither agents nor editors want personal visits from potential authors (and sometimes they don't even want visits from their established authors, especially unannounced visits).

Is there any situation in which I can query by telephone?

Very few, especially for beginning writers, but check the submission guidelines to see if phone queries are accepted. In almost all cases, you should query by mail or e-mail. A written query allows the editor to examine the proposal at her convenience, and to show it to her associates for their opinions. An editor is better able to judge the merits of an idea if it's in tangible, written form than if it's related to her over the telephone.

To the writer, the time and energy required to develop a carefully written query or proposal seems a large investment, especially when a telephone call might sell the editor on an idea with far less effort. However, a phone call interrupts the editor's workday and forces her to answer without proper time to think the matter through. Except in rare instances, an unexpected phone query usually receives either a no (whether deserved or not) or a response which puts you back at square one: "We're willing to look at it if you send a detailed query by mail." If you receive a negative response by phone, you have closed the door to a query that might have been considered more carefully had it come by mail. Once you have sold an editor several articles, or otherwise have an established relationship, she may be more receptive to phoned queries.

What about fax queries?

The fax is falling out of favor, especially with the proliferation of e-mail. It's best not to use a fax to communicate with an editor unless the submission guidelines clearly state that fax queries are accepted.

What about e-mail queries?

The number of publications that accept e-mail queries is growing as more publications find that it saves them time and money. The benefit to writers is that it can improve overall response time and make it easier for you to track submissions. The key is to first ascertain how a particular editor or publication prefers to receive electronic submissions, if it accepts them. Just as you would for a paper query, you must do your homework to determine the best way to reach a particular editor. Check the publication website or submission guidelines and see if they have a policy on e-mail queries. Sometimes you will be asked to complete and submit a form from their website or to use a specified format for your e-mail query. Follow such instructions to the letter. If no such instructions are given, then follow the rules for any good query letter.

I have an e-mail address for an editor who works for a publisher that states it doesn't accept e-mail queries. May I e-mail this editor anyway with a query?

You can give it a try, though most industry professionals frown on the practice. There is some merit to e-mailing an agent or editor a very succinct description of your project and an offer to send more information. Such an e-mail should be only a few sentences long so it will not look like a time investment to read or consider. The worst that can happen is that you'll receive no response, which almost always means the editor or agent was not interested—and then you have your answer. Do not try to follow up or badger the editor via e-mail.

If I e-mail a query to a magazine publisher that requires clips, what's the best way to provide them?

You can approach this in a few ways. You could post your clips on your personal website, if you have one, and give the editor the site URL. If you don't have a site, you could attach your clips as a PDF file, but only if the editor accepts attachments. If neither of those options are feasible, you could fax the clips or send them through the mail. Try to find out if the editor has a preference for any of these options.

How soon can I follow up a query letter if I don't get a response? Should I phone?

If you've not heard from the editor or agent after a month (or after the response time indicated in the market listing in *Writer's Market*), don't hesitate to send a brief follow-up note. The note should describe the query (or include a copy) so the editor or agent can readily identify it, and should simply ask whether she's had time to consider it. Be sure to include the date of the original query, since some offices file unsolicited queries and manuscripts by date of arrival. If your follow-up note does not elicit a reply, then assume the editor or agent is not interested and move on. You should not phone.

Is it permissible to submit a query to two different editors (at two different publications) at the same time?

Yes, but do keep in mind that if you make simultaneous submissions to editors, you'll face the possibility of having more than one editor ask to see or purchase the material. This might be flattering to your ego, but it can also be incredibly awkward and can irritate editors (and agents as well).

In the case of a book, it can be preferable to have many editors vying for the same material so that you get the best possible advance and contract, but it's much better to have an agent handle that situation than to attempt to negotiate it yourself.

I've noticed that many publishers in New York will not accept unsolicited submissions, even if you query first. What's that all about?

Many of the largest publishing houses have stopped reading manuscripts that come in directly from authors—it's just too much work and hassle to go through the hundreds they would receive each week. Instead, editors have come to rely on agents to bring them quality work that fits their needs. So if you dream of being published by a big house, you'll have to get an agent to represent you.

Should I send with my query photocopies of one or two friendly rejections I've received from previous editors?

Absolutely not—near misses do not work in your favor! However, if an editor who rejected you provided a referral to someone else, you might mention it—but avoid stating the fact you were rejected. Simply say, "Joe Editor said you might be a good fit for my project."

I have several questions for various departments of a magazine, dealing with a query, my subscription, and other facets of their business. Is it okay to write just one letter?

Such a practice can save you postage but can also try an editor's patience. Honoring all those requests takes a lot of time (making photocopies, routing to various departments). It's best to send separate letters. Not only will doing so ensure that your requests get to the right people, it will make the editor look more kindly on you in the future.

Is it okay to send editors to my website?

If you are sending an e-mail query and wish to provide clips of your work via your personal Web page, you may do so if the editor accepts clips this way. Otherwise you should provide everything the editor needs to make a decision in your query letter. Do not force editors to view or print your manuscript or proposal from your site, unless it involves something very unusual (like a portfolio of art or demonstration of your Web design work). If you do provide your website address in your query, make it part of your letterhead or business card, or otherwise ensure it is peripheral to the main point of your query. Keep in mind that many editors and agents will search for you on the Web anyway to see what turns up.

While most how-to books about freelancing advocate specifying rights for sale on manuscripts, others claim this is a mark of amateurs. What is the accepted practice?

Most magazine or journal editors will assume you're offering first North American rights unless you specify otherwise, so it's not necessary to spell it out in the query. Once you're given an assignment, you'll want to get a contract or letter that spells out rights, payment, deadlines, and so on. If you're querying a publication that's known for buying reprints or buying all rights (according to its writers guidelines or market listing), and that's not what you're offering, then you should make that clear up front.

BOOK QUERIES

What does a novel query look like?

A novel query gives a brief overview of your novel's protagonist, plot, and setting, while also giving a little bit of information about yourself; a good novel query does not exceed a page. Do not query until you have a completed manuscript! An editor will not accept your work based on a partial manuscript if you're an unpublished or unknown writer.

A novel query usually includes five elements: (1) why you're querying this particular editor or agent, (2) your novel's title, genre, and word count, (3) a concise 100- to 200-word description of your novel's characters and plot, (4) a brief bio, and (5) a closing.

This may not sound like enough information for an editor to know whether or not she's interested in your novel, but it is. Your concise description of your novel, or its hook, should spark sufficient interest for the editor to request the first three chapters or complete manuscript. Most beginning writers make the mistake of giving too much detail (and boring detail at that) and attempting to mention every plot device and minor character. Focus on your main character (the protagonist), that character's conflict, the setting, and whatever sets your story apart from the rest. That's it.

Don't forget to establish why this particular editor or agent would be interested in your work—perhaps she's published work similar to your own, or you read an interview that described her interests, and she seemed like a good match. Whatever the case, let her know you've done your research and haven't blindly sent the exact same query to dozens of others.

It doesn't matter in which order you tackle the five elements of a novel query, though you should put your best foot forward. If your connection to the editor or agent is strong (you've met at a conference, for instance), that should go first. Perhaps your hook is so riveting that it should serve as the opening. If you have impressive credentials, a strong record of publication, or a prestigious writing degree, you might start with that.

Can I include the first few chapters of my novel manuscript with my query?

No, unless the submission guidelines indicate that's what you should do. However, if you want to tuck in the first five pages, that's almost always acceptable—especially when you're confident about the quality of those pages.

Should I send a synopsis with the query?

If editors or agents request a synopsis with your query, they're probably looking for a quick summary of your entire novel. Synopsis lengths vary, but a few pages is typical. Sometimes agents or editors ask for an outline when what they really want is a synopsis. Or, when asking for an outline, an agent or editor may want a chapter-by-chapter outline (a synopsis of each chapter). When in doubt, ask.

Is it acceptable to submit copies of my book manuscript simultaneously to different editors?

Yes, but it's a good idea to advise the editors that you've done so. Don't worry about offending editors with a simultaneous submission; most of them assume that's the case anyway and wouldn't expect you to give them an exclusive submission unless requested.

I have sent several query letters to different publishers to see if they're interested in my book, and I received a letter from a publisher who said she would like to see the material immediately, so I sent

it to her. In the meantime, I've received answers to all my letters, all saying they are interested and would like to see the material. What's the best way to answer these letters?

You should write the other publishers to say that another editor is considering and enclose a copy of the manuscript. This will either heighten their interest or turn them off completely, depending on the editor.

Is it proper to indicate in a query letter that my novel is the first of a series?

Yes, but your query should focus only on the first book in that series—don't attempt to give a rundown of every title you have planned.

If an editor keeps my manuscript a long time, does that mean she likes it? Or am I setting myself up for disappointment by thinking that?

You'll probably be disappointed. It takes most editors anywhere from two days to six months (or longer!) to comment on a manuscript. Check *Writer's Market* for a publication's stated response time. If that time passes without any report, it's possible that your manuscript passed one editor's approval and is now being read by the other editors. However, it could also mean that your manuscript is buried under a pile of submissions or that the editor is out of the office or even that your manuscript was lost in the mail. So it's best not to get your hopes up. If you still haven't received word two to four weeks beyond the stated response time, write the publication (include a SASE) and ask for an update. If that letter receives no response, move on.

I have an idea for a nonfiction book that I want to write. What should I do first?

You don't have to write the manuscript for a nonfiction book before you query publishers. You can write a book proposal first. The book proposal is a very in-depth analysis of your book project, sometimes as long as a hundred pages, that details the book's contents, the book's market or audience, and your qualifications to write the book and sell it. You also must explain how your book is different from or better than others that have been published on the same topic. The most comprehensive guide to writing a nonfiction book proposal is *How to Write a Book Proposal*, by Michael Larsen.

As you're preparing your book proposal, you will likely become familiar with publishers known for publishing books on your topic. To further research publishers (or agents), use a book like *Writer's Market* or *Guide to Literary Agents* to compile a list of who would be best suited to be your publisher or agent. Or check libraries and bookstores to see who has published books that are similar to what you want to write. You might only find a few suitable publishers if you're writing on a very specialized topic, or you might find dozens if your topic has general appeal. Once your proposal is fully complete, send out queries (or your complete proposal—check submission guidelines) that detail why there's a need for your book. After that, it's up to the editor or agent to decide whether she is interested in your book.

Is it okay to send my book proposal to editors on first contact, without querying first?

Generally you'll be okay if you send the proposal first without querying—many editors need to see the entire proposal anyway to make a decision. However, it's always wisest to consult the submission guidelines first and make sure you won't be breaking an editor's or agent's cardinal rule.

I'd like to query publishers with an idea that is extremely timely. If they take several months to reply, the material I have researched and collected will become outdated. Do you have any suggestions to speed up the process?

For starters, make sure you query many publishers at once and make sure you're querying the right people. Nothing wastes more time than sending your material to inappropriate publishers. If your topic is extremely timely, you may want to look for writers conferences where you can set up an appointment with an appropriate agent or editor to discuss your idea. Keep in mind, though, that most traditional publishers take one or two years to get a book to market.

WHERE TO FIND OUT MORE

Books

Writer's Market, published annually by Writer's Digest Books, contains information on more than four thousand places to publish your work, plus query letter and submission tips.

Novel & Short Story Writer's Market, which is also published annually by Writer's Digest Books, is the most comprehensive resource on where to publish your fiction; it includes many nonpaying markets that *Writer's Market* does not list.

In *The American Directory of Writer's Guidelines*, about 1,600 magazine editors and book publishers explain what they're looking for. This resource differs from *Writer's Market* in that it offers unedited self-descriptions of what publications are looking for.

Give 'Em What They Want, by Blythe Camenson and Marshall J. Cook, is a complete guide to writing novel queries, synopses, and outlines, as well as to how the publishing process works.

The Writer's Guide to Queries, Pitches & Proposals, by Moira Allen, is a solid query-writing guide and includes some valuable extras on securing an agent, syndicating your work, and other topics of interest to aspiring writers.

The Writer's Digest Guide to Query Letters, by Wendy Burt, gives tools to master the essential marketing tool for any writer: the query letter.

The Writer's MarketGuide to Getting Published, by the Editors of Writer's Digest, gives the inspiration and instruction needed to achieve long-term success in an ever-changing industry.

Websites

Miss Snark (www.misssnark.blogspot.com), a blog by a literary agent, features excellent commentary and Q&A on the querying process, and also occasional query letter critiques.

Evil Editor (www.evileditor.blogspot.com), a blog by a book editor, offers novel query critiques.

MediaBistro (www.mediabistro.com), offers excellent articles and online workshops about querying, particularly for magazines.

Carol Denbow provides writing, publishing, and marketing advice at A Book Inside: How to Write and Publish a Book (www.abookinside.blogspot.com)

CHAPTER 3

HOW DO I WRITE A SUCCESSFUL NOVEL?

After ten years of writing, Janet Evanovich decided to get serious about getting published. She had three novels written, all of which had been submitted to and rejected by dozens of publishers and agents. So she decided to abandon those projects and try genre writing. Her first effort was rejected, but her second manuscript was accepted, and she was on her way to becoming the best-selling author of the Stephanie Plum mystery series.

Becoming a published novelist is mostly a matter of talent, persistence, and luck. First, you have to write very well—well enough to stand out against the competition—and then you have to send and resend your material until it reaches someone who appreciates it as much as you do. It takes drive and determination, and many years of dedication to the craft. Most first efforts don't find publishers; it's your second, third, fourth, or even tenth effort that finds a home.

This chapter can't possibly answer every novel-writing question a beginner has, but it introduces you to the most common issues and topics that concern novelists. To develop confidence as a novel writer, it takes practice, and maybe a few fiction-writing technique books to help you identify your weaknesses and show you how to improve.

QUESTIONS OF GENRE

In my quest to submit my work, I have stumbled across a problem. I'm having trouble categorizing my work. What is the difference between commercial, mainstream, and literary fiction?

In general, fiction is divided into literary fiction and commercial fiction (also called mainstream fiction). There aren't any hard and fast definitions for one or the other, but there are some basic differences, and those differences affect how the book is read, packaged, and marketed.

Literary fiction is usually more concerned with style and characterization than commercial fiction. Literary fiction is also usually paced more slowly than commercial fiction. Literary fiction usually centers around a timeless, complex theme, and rarely has a pat (or happy) ending. Good examples of literary fiction are books by Toni Morrison and John Updike.

Commercial fiction, on the other hand, is faster paced, with a stronger plot line (more events, higher stakes, more dangerous situations). Characterization is generally not as central to the story. The theme is very obvious, and the language not as complex.

The biggest difference between literary and commercial fiction is that editors expect to make a substantial profit from selling a commercial book but not necessarily from selling literary fiction. Audiences for commercial fiction are larger than those for literary fiction. Tom Clancy, John Grisham, and Stephen King are all prime examples of commercial fiction authors.

One of the easiest ways to determine whether your work is literary or commercial is to ask yourself, "Is my book more likely to be read in college English classes or in the grocery checkout line?"

What is a genre novel?

The term genre is generally used to describe fiction that has certain expectations and conventions; some specific genres are romance, mystery, horror, science fiction, fantasy, and westerns. Genre novels must adhere to the styles, conventions, and tropes of their category in order to meet readers' expectations. For example, readers of mysteries assume any novel in that genre will start with a crime or threat of a crime, provide clues and possible motives throughout the story, and conclude with a resolution of the problem (the criminal being brought to justice, the evil plan being thwarted). Readers of romance expect to encounter a hero and heroine who feel intensely attracted to each other, undergo some sort of conflict that complicates their relationship, and resolve that complication so the romance can flourish (and, often, result in marriage). In order to understand the conventions of each genre, you should read several books in that category and note the similar structures, plot devices, and character types within them.

I have dabbled in creative writing for many years but have never published anything. I am ready to get serious. Are there particular genres of fiction that are easier for new writers to break in to?

Before looking into which markets are easiest to break in to, first consider what you enjoy reading, what you enjoy writing, and what you write well. The single most important factor determining whether you succeed (and get published) is the quality of your writing. Ultimately, if you want to get published, a good story well written is key. If you're passionate about your subject matter, that level of engagement will come through in your story, and your enthusiasm can help you get through the tough patches when you lack confidence, inspiration, or fresh ideas.

If you must look strictly at marketability, the romance genre would be the place to break in. Statistics from a 2004 Romance Writers of America study show that romance novels comprise 55 percent of paperback book sales in the United States, and 40 percent of all fiction sold is romance. (Comparatively, the mystery/thriller genre comprises 30 percent of all fiction sold, and so-called general fiction comprises about 13 percent.) Within the romance genre, contemporary romance is the most popular subgenre, with 1,438 titles (of 2,285 romance titles) published in 2004. So statistically, contemporary romance offers the greatest opportunity to break in. But again: Write what you love, and write the best book you can, and worry about publication later.

My novel crosses a number of genres—I call it a romantic thriller fantasy that will appeal to readers in a number of genres. But editors tell me that I have to stick with one genre. Why?

29

You may be able to find a publisher willing to take a risk on your cross-genre book, but most agents and editors look for stories they can easily target to a specific audience. Without a firm categorization, your book is a difficult pitch to store buyers, and it's a difficult sell to readers. While you may think crossing genres makes the audience bigger, the market usually proves that interest in cross-genre books is limited—unless you find yourself in the midst of a cross-genre trend. (At the time of this book's publication, literary fiction was fond of incorporating fantasy or supernatural elements, such as in *The Time-Traveler's Wife*, by Audrey Niffenegger.) It's best to push the boundaries of a genre—and stay well within it—rather than struggle to find a publisher for a cross-genre work.

When pitching a cross-genre work to an agent or editor, you can increase your chances of success by aligning it with the one genre that's at the heart of your story—or by identifying the one audience that would be most interested in it. (Does your novel appeal mostly to romance readers, mystery readers, science-fiction readers, etc.?)

What is a novel-in-stories?

A novel-in-stories is a book-length collection of short stories that are interconnected. (One of the very first examples of this genre is *The Canterbury Tales*; a more recent example is *The Girls' Guide to Hunting and Fishing*, by Melissa Bank.) A novel-in-stories overcomes two key challenges for writers: the challenge of writing a novel-length work, and the challenge of publishing a book-length work of unrelated short stories. (Few publishers are willing to publish a short-story collection from an unknown writer.) So, the novel-in-stories helps you sell a story collection like you would a novel—as long as the interconnected nature of the stories is strong and acts as a compelling hook. Another advantage to novels-in-stories is that they afford you the opportunity to publish pieces of your novel in a variety of literary magazines, which might attract the attention of an editor or agent. (Editors and agents often troll literary publications looking for new talent to publish or represent.)

CRAFT AND TECHNIQUE

What is a protagonist?

The protagonist is the main character of a story, the one the author spends the most time exploring or developing and the one whose conflict moves the plot along. The protagonist may also be the story's first-person narrator, although this is not always the case.

What is point of view?

Point of view refers to the perspective from which the story is told. There are three traditional points of view:

First-person narration. The narrator—often the protagonist—tells the story from his perspective (using I), and the information given to the readers is filtered through this character.

Examples are *The Adventures of Huckleberry Finn*, by Mark Twain, and *The Catcher in the Rye*, by J.D. Salinger.

Third-person omniscient. The story is narrated by an all-knowing voice that does not belong to any one character but instead gives readers access to the thoughts, feelings, and motivations of all characters. The narrator refers to the characters using third-person pronouns. Examples are *The Old Man and the Sea*, by Ernest Hemingway, and *Brave New World*, by Aldous Huxley.

Third-person limited. The story is narrated by a removed voice that does not belong to any one character but focuses on a single character and only gives the readers access to the thoughts, feelings, and motivations of that focused character. The narrator refers to the characters using third-person pronouns. An example is *Of Mice and Men*, by John Steinbeck.

There's also second-person point of view, which is rarely used and a tough one to make work. For a successful example, see *Bright Lights, Big City*, by Jay McInerney.

Many books use different points of view for different chapters or sections, but this is difficult to do in a seamless and unobtrusive way.

I'm writing a novel about two central characters. How do I decide which to use as my viewpoint character?

If you're using third-person point of view, you can include the viewpoints of both. When both of your central characters become viewpoint characters, you can more easily develop subplots and suspense, as well as the personalities and histories of those characters. Care must be taken to switch viewpoints only at scene changes—never within a scene (unless you're an absolute master).

I keep reading warnings not to switch viewpoints in the middle of a scene, but I can't find any information on how to detect accidental shifts. What's wrong with switching viewpoints, anyway?

The reader needs time to shift gears as the viewpoint of the story changes; switching viewpoint frequently creates an effect similar to having several people speaking to you at once. Confusion is the probable outcome. Also, consider: Through how many viewpoints do you see the world? Only one, of course. You cannot see into any mind other than your own; you can only know as much about other people as is indicated by their actions and what they tell you.

You can detect a shift in viewpoint by counting the number of characters who share their thoughts or opinions within a scene. Remember: If you're sticking to one viewpoint per scene (which you should), then you should relate only one viewpoint character's thoughts, feelings, or observations. Keep in mind that revealing a character's thoughts and feelings doesn't always take the direct form of Sally thought or Sally felt. A viewpoint is present in any statement of a thought or observation, like "How had the apartment become so filthy and disgusting, especially Jack's room ..."

Viewpoint is one of the most complicated aspects of fiction writing, sometimes difficult even for advanced writers to grasp. If you're committed to writing novels, you should read up on viewpoint—*Characters, Emotion & Viewpoint*, by Nancy Kress, would be a good start.

I am writing a novel about a fourteen-year-old ballerina. She is telling the story. I am concerned about reader identification. Will adult readers identify with a leading character of this age?

It's rare, but adult readers can identify with younger heroes and heroines. But look closely at your work: Are you really writing young adult fiction? YA novels can be just as complicated and meaningful as adult work, and there's no disadvantage to writing for that market; it can sell as well as adult fiction. A publisher might issue and market your novel within that genre anyway, whether you think of it as young adult fiction or not.

Editors tell me my dialogue passages are too long, but I'm only telling it the way it is in real life. What's wrong?

You're probably doing too much in the way of "telling it the way it is in real life." You must refine your dialogue so that you present the reader with only the essence of reality. Conversation in real life is never as pointed as writers present it in fictional dialogue. Readers will be bored by dialogue that recounts the polite rituals and trite conversations that are a part of everyday life. Compress and focus your dialogue so that your characters get right to the point when they talk. All dialogue should either advance the plot, characterize the people, or both. If it doesn't do these things, it's not effective or necessary.

My writing teacher says dialogue has to do more than just let characters talk. What does he mean?

Besides the fact that good dialogue positively affects pacing—makes a novel easier to read by relieving the reader from long descriptive passages—it also effectively characterizes and adds to the reality of the speakers. It can take the place of long, tedious character descriptions. What a character says about himself and how a character speaks about others should give clues to his personality, emotions, attitudes, opinions, and desires. In addition to revealing character, good dialogue must also advance the plot by giving information that heightens conflict or by building tension between characters.

An editor said my exposition in the first chapter is too long. Can you tell me how much exposition I should have?

You've heard the old writing directive Show, don't tell; think of exposition as the telling part of writing—the scene-setting explanation that provides backstory, context, or description. The reason writing instructors caution against too much telling is that readers are generally more interested in and engaged by showing. For this reason, economy of language in exposition is key: Everything in your exposition should have a purpose, whether it is to give tone or mood, to describe the setting and time, to characterize, or to provide necessary background. One thing beginning writers often forget is that background information doesn't have to come in the first paragraphs of the novel. The reader doesn't need to know the backstory just yet, and you're likely to lose him quickly if you start with a long, uninteresting history. However, if you start off with an interesting situation that grabs the reader's attention, he will demand explanation. Then breaking into the flow of the plot is more easily justified.

I've heard editors say how important it is for a character to be well rounded. What makes a character well rounded?

Well-rounded characters are distinctly individual; you come to understand their motivations, flaws, emotional traits, and other distinctive qualities. These can be related through a character's actions, his reactions to situations and other characters, dialogue, and also through narrative. A flat character, in contrast, usually carries only one distinguishing trait or might act predictably or according to stereotype.

A friend read the first draft of my novel and suggested that I write a prologue. When writing a novel, is it necessary to have a prologue?

Unless your audience will be confused by the details of your story, there's no need to include a prologue in your novel.

How important is research in the novel?

Many beginning writers know a novel is a work of imagination but seem unaware that the factual material in a novel must be as accurate as that in a nonfiction work. The fiction writer uses the same research tools as the nonfiction writer—particularly sources on the period he is writing about, whether he's writing a Regency romance or a novel set in 1930s New York. And the research must be carefully woven into the story, not dropped in awkwardly in a way that interrupts the flow. Study good novels to see how research is integrated, or read interviews with novelists to see how they approach it.

Identifying research needs is a very project-specific task. The best time to do this is during the initial outlining stage. As you add each scene, make a note of any research required to complete that step. Managing the results of your research requires good note taking and leaving yourself a retraceable path back to the source. For information gleaned from printed sources, make a photocopy of the material itself and be sure to note the source title, publisher, publication date, the page numbers (if they don't appear on the copy), and where you physically located the source. Keeping this information right on the copy will help you document your work and locate the source again, should that become necessary. If you're doing research online, print out relevant pages and make sure that the website appears on your printout. Bookmark any sources you think you'll return to often.

What kind of planning should I do before I start to write a novel?

Planning methods vary greatly among writers, who often modify their systems as they gain experience and maturity. Some are satisfied with a brief summary of the plot, the character's conflict, and the resolution. Others may put together as many as fifty or a hundred pages of detailed charts of action, character, and environment sketches. (This is usually referred to as outlining.)

Writers who advocate outlining say that it cuts down on wasted time and endless revision because you understand your characters at the outset and can produce a logical plot. But writers against outlining say it inhibits creativity and inspiration, and even prevents them from finding the true line through the story. You'll have to decide for yourself what makes sense for you. Perhaps it would be useful to begin with an outline but give yourself permission to go off script and revise your original outline if you get new and better ideas once you start writing.

What makes up a chapter in a novel? How do I separate scenes within a chapter?

Exactly what and how much goes in to a chapter is up to the individual author. Chapter divisions are an author's means of organizing the major events and developments in his novel and can provide easy transitions in time, place, or point of view. Many writers (and agents) like to have a cliffhanger at the end of every chapter that keeps people reading and on the edge of their seat.

Changing scenes within a chapter can be accomplished by a simple paragraph change, using a transitional phrase like The next morning, she … . Or it can be accomplished by leaving blank lines between paragraphs, a technique especially helpful when the scene change also involves a change in viewpoint.

What are some common beginner mistakes that I might learn to avoid?

In *Writing for the Soul*, Jerry Jenkins points out a major mistake that plagues nearly every beginning writer: including too many details of ordinary life that don't contribute to character or plot. For instance, if your character backs his car into a garbage truck, just state it. There's no need to lead up to it with your character's movements to leave the house, walk to the car, open the door, slide in, turn the key—unless these movements are highly unusual and somehow make a significant contribution to character. Otherwise, cut to the chase and don't go overboard on the showing. (Writers, after hearing Show, don't tell one too many times, can err in the other direction.) Jenkins also points out how ordinary life scenes, even if written well, fall into cliché territory that you're better off avoiding. He advises, "Don't begin with the main character waking to the alarm clock; don't allow your character to describe herself in the mirror; don't make future love interests literally bump into each other at first meeting."

At the sentence level, most writers go overboard on the adjectives and adverbs. Instead, you should favor concrete nouns and action verbs. A book like *The Elements of Style* can teach you and show you what this looks like.

What about flashbacks?

It's best to avoid flashbacks, because they prevent the story from moving forward. But carefully considered and implemented, they can add texture and meaning. Look to some of the resources at the chapter's end to learn how to handle them effectively.

WORKING WITH IDEAS

I've got a couple of good ideas for a mystery, but I'm not quite sure how to go about getting them into novel form. What should I do?

First, learn the techniques, style, and conventions of the genre, and read widely from classic mysteries (Arthur Conan Doyle, Agatha Christie) to contemporary bestsellers (Sue Grafton, Harlan Coben). You want to understand what popular writers are doing, though it would be a mistake to closely imitate them—you're not likely to sell your mystery unless it has a fresh voice or approach.

Many mystery writers find detailed plot outlines to be useful, but be careful that you don't become so wrapped up in the intricacies of the puzzle that you neglect to build a strong theme or well-rounded characters. Like all fiction (and most nonfiction), your mystery must have a human element to it.

Some basic elements of mystery stories are described in *Writing and Selling Your Mystery Novel* by Hallie Ephron and *How to Write a Damn Good Mystery* by James N. Frey.

I have had a novel in mind for almost ten years. My insurmountable problem is that I need to skillfully covering many years without confusing the reader. What should I do?

Decide exactly how many years the story really needs. If the same basic story can be told in five years rather than fifteen, by all means choose the shorter period. Remember that, for dramatic purposes, you can telescope events that might, in real life, be spread over a long period.

Regardless of how much time the story spans, you must be discriminating in your choice of detail. Don't include anything that does not keep the action moving forward toward the climax. Avoid all irrelevancies and descriptions for description's sake. Develop important incidents in full scenes. But information of minor significance can sometimes be handled by brief transitional summaries that link the highlights together. Flashbacks can help a story make a time leap, but use this technique sparingly because too much hopping back and forth between the past and present can wreak havoc with readers' time sense.

I have a very broad-stroke idea for a story. Can you share some tips as to how to evolve concept to story line?

One of the best quick-stroke plotting tools comes from the 1945 (yes, 1945) *Writer's Yearbook*. It's what author John Nanovic calls the Triple-O method. For every story concept, identify in one or two words these three things: object, obstacles, outcome. If you can't name all three, you don't have a story; if you can, you have the backbone of your plot.

QUERIES AND SUBMISSIONS

I have a novel in the works, but it is months from completion. When should I send query letters to publishers? Is it ever too soon to send one?

With your first novel, don't send a query letter to agents or editors until the work is complete. You need to be able to demonstrate that you are capable of finishing a novel. Many writers can craft a strong fifty or one hundred pages, but can't go the distance, which is why agents and editors in general aren't interested in a first novel until it's done.

Some of the agents I plan to query ask for a synopsis. What is a synopsis and why does an agent need one?

A synopsis is a complete summary of your novel that's supposed to help sell it. Synopsis length varies tremendously, so you should try to find out the agents' preferences on length before sending one. If in doubt, make yours one to two pages single-spaced, or three to five pages double spaced, and go from there. (If you find yourself writing three or four different lengths of synopses to please three or four different editors, consider it good practice for your writing skills.)

What makes synopses so difficult to write (at least for most authors) is that the shorter ones require you to leave out the majority of the story and usually quite a few characters. To make them lively and interesting, the synopses are generally written in present tense, third person; they should read almost like a novel and carry the same tone (humorous, dark, mysterious, etc.) as your actual manuscript. They rarely feature dialogue.

A basic synopsis will give the opening hook, sketch out the key characters, describe the plot's high points, concentrate on the core conflict, and reveal the ending. Evan Marshall, in his book *The Marshall Plan for Getting Your Novel Published*, says "To achieve conciseness, you must write as clean and tight as you know how. Don't do what many writers do and try to keep boiling down your actual novel again and again until it's short enough. Instead, learn to write in a synoptic style—read a section or chapter of your novel and simply retell it, as you might describe a great book or movie to a friend."

Like query letters, synopses should not include editorialization, such as "in a thrilling turn of events" or "in this heartbreaking scene."

Are an outline and a synopsis the same thing?

The term outline is often used interchangeably with synopsis. Sometimes, though, an editor or agent is looking for a chapter outline when he asks for a synopsis. A chapter outline makes each chapter its own story and takes a few paragraphs to describe each chapter. Never submit an outline unless an editor asks for it. (Fewer and fewer want them these days.)

I am writing a novel, and realized a long time ago that it may be too long to publish as one book. In a heartrending decision, I managed to separate my novel into four smaller books. Do I need to finish the entire work (all four books) before I query an agent for the first of them?

Your first book should be strong enough to stand alone without the other three, and if it's complete, you can begin querying right away. It doesn't hurt to have all four finished, but as long as you have one finished and outlines of the rest of the books in the series, you should be okay.

I've heard that it's impossible to sell a book longer than 100,000 words. Is this true?

There's some truth to the fact that the longer your manuscript, the more challenging it is to sell it. Publishers prefer novels that are in the 80,000- to 120,000-word range, depending on the genre. Once you start getting into the 150,000-word or 200,000-word range, an editor or agent is going to think twice before making an investment.

Word count becomes even more crucial when writing in a genre with rigid conventions, such as category romance. Publishers that issue romance series have strict limitations on how long each book can be, so you should write to fit their specifications and not consider yourself an exception.

I'm an unpublished novelist and don't have any fiction-related writing credentials to mention in my query letter. What should I say about myself if I lack publications?

If you have any writing education, or any way to reveal the seriousness or quality of your writing, you can mention those factors instead. Maybe you have a degree in writing, took a writing workshop under a noted author, or have won awards. Or perhaps the manuscript you're shopping around is actually the sixth unpublished novel you've written—that's actually a positive thing because agents and editors know that you learn, grow, and mature each time you finish a novel-length manuscript. Another tactic is to mention any experience you have that relates to the novel you're writing. For instance, if you're pitching a legal thriller, and you have a legal background, you definitely want to mention it. But the best remedy for writers with no quality credentials is to summarize their novel in a way that sounds unique, interesting, and compelling.

How much detail should I get into when describing my novel in the query letter?

Not much. The agent or editor only needs a taste of your novel's plot and protagonist to know whether he wants to read a partial or complete manuscript. Most successful novel queries are only a page long, single spaced. The description of your novel should take only a couple of paragraphs, and no more than half your query. The very best queries contain a mini-synopsis that isn't more than a couple hundred words. In *Writing the Breakout Novel Workbook*, agent Donald Maass says, "Long plot summary overwhelms the person getting the pitch."

According to Maass (a literary agent who represents novels exclusively), your mini-synopsis should describe your protagonist, your protagonist's problem/conflict, the setting, and the one thing that sets your novel apart from all the rest. He warns, "So many novels sound ordinary and unoriginal, like I have read them before. Probably I have. There are no new stories, after all, just new ways of telling them. And that is what I'm interested in. What is your new angle on it? What is the twist or turn in your novel that no one sees coming? Yes, give it away! Why are you saving it?"

What are some major mistakes that people make when writing novel queries?

Don't put so much hype in the letter that you come across as amateurish. Predicting your book's climb up the best-seller lists, comparing yourself to Stephen King, or claiming you've got the next Da Vinci Code on your hands—all of these tactics will only put off the editor or agent. Similarly, refrain from editorializing the description of your novel. The agent or editor shouldn't have to be told your novel is thrilling or romantic or heartbreaking. Your description should show or reflect these qualities.

Also avoid caps, exclamation points, and exaggeration, as well as adjectives, superlatives, and anything more than a word or two on your theme. Keep a professional tone and avoid acting like a salesperson. Concentrate on the story, and you'll win over agents and editors.

Final word of warning: Don't claim your mother (or child or spouse or friend) absolutely loves your work. (However, if you have an endorsement from a best-selling author who loves it, mention that!)

Is it okay to compare my writing style to that of another author?

Agents and editors disagree on this point, but one thing's for sure: It's not to your advantage to compare yourself to a mega best-selling author. The best comparisons are those that indicate your writing style, your story's themes, or the overall feel of your work. Sometimes it's better to mention specific book titles that evoke the same style as yours, or to mention authors that would be familiar to the agent or editor you're querying. (It's wonderful if you can compare your work to a book that the agent or editor recently represented or edited.)

Is it okay to include the first chapter or so with my query?

Unless the submission guidelines ask for that first chapter (or more), don't include it. However, if you think your first five pages are really outstanding, there's no harm in slipping them in with your query letter. (But no more than five!)

WHERE TO FIND OUT MORE

Books

Writing the Breakout Novel and *Writing the Breakout Novel Workbook*, by Donald Maass, provide excellent instruction on how to write a novel, for both beginning and advanced (published) novelists.

You Can Write a Novel, by James V. Smith Jr., coaches and encourages you through a simple writing plan.

The First Five Pages, by Noah Lukeman, helps you discover how agents can spot a manuscript's flaws in the first five pages, and learn how you can fix those flaws in your own work.

The Plot Thickens, by Noah Lukeman, is a follow-up to *The First Five Pages* and concentrates on effective plotting for your novel.

Book in a Month, by Victoria Schmidt, leads you through a proven 30-day novel-writing system without the intimidation factor.

The 90-Day Novel, by Sarah Domet, is a practical guide for committed writers that leads the reader from brainstorming to outlining to a first draft.

The Complete Handbook of Novel Writing is a compilation of the best articles on novel writing from *Writer's Digest* magazine, *Writer's Market*, and other sources.

How to Write a Damn Good Novel, by James N. Frey, is a longtime favorite of writers that focuses on the basics of storytelling.

Your First Novel, by Ann Rittenberg and Laura Whitcomb, is a guide for first-time novelists, written by an agent and author team.

The Marshall Plan for Novel Writing, by agent Evan Marshall, offers a very detailed, systematic plan for writing your novel, complete with worksheets and tables. Great for people who love to outline and do a lot of preplanning.

The Elements of Fiction Writing series and the Write Great Fiction series by Writer's Digest Books focus on specific elements of fiction writing, such as character, plot, dialogue, setting, and description. Invaluable if you find yourself struggling with a weakness in a particular area of fiction writing.

CHAPTER 4

HOW DO I SELL MY NONFICTION BOOK?

Writers do their best work when they write what they love. Unfortunately, love is sometimes not enough when it comes to writing and selling nonfiction books—you have to understand what will sell and how to sell it. This chapter will help you understand how to bring about that transformation.

Do you have to be an expert on something to get a nonfiction book published?

Usually some level of expertise is necessary to produce a successful nonfiction book, especially for fields such as health, self-help, or parenting, where no one will trust your advice without recognized credentials. Your background must instill trust in the readership. (Would you, as a reader, trust a health care book by an author with no medical degrees or experience in the health care field?) However, some types of nonfiction, especially biographies, historical surveys, and creative nonfiction/memoir, can be written by anyone who has good research skills plus organizational and writing abilities.

In writing a nonfiction book, is it advisable to try to first publish single chapters as magazine articles?

Previously published articles can certainly be used to sell a book idea. They show the editor your abilities and that your idea is a marketable one. If you do sell your book chapters as articles first, make sure you don't sell all rights to the material. One warning, however: Some book manuscripts are rejected because they are simply a collection of articles. A successful nonfiction book has a definite focus and thread of continuity that runs from beginning to end. After the book is published, you might want to write related articles—or sell excerpts—to help promote it.

What is narrative nonfiction?

Narrative nonfiction tells a true story using fictional techniques and is meant to be entertaining. An example of narrative nonfiction is *Seabiscuit*, by Laura Hillenbrand.

What is prescriptive nonfiction?

Prescriptive nonfiction usually gives advice, rules, or directions on how to do something or achieve something. The book you're reading now is prescriptive nonfiction. Usually there is less emphasis on writing or literary quality in a prescriptive guide, and the emphasis is on the quality of information or instruction. The book sells based on the benefit to the reader, for example, losing weight, making money, or knitting a sweater.

Do I have to write the manuscript first before querying agents and editors with my nonfiction book idea?

For the majority of nonfiction book ideas, you should prepare a book proposal first. A book proposal argues why your book idea will make a salable, marketable product, and if the editor is convinced by your proposal, she'll offer you a contract and advance to write the book. (Remember: The opposite is true for first-time novelists; you always complete the novel first, then query and receive a contract.) The querying and submission process for book proposals is the same as fiction; you send a query, then submit your book proposal if invited, though some agents or editors will take a book proposal on first contact. Check their submission guidelines.

Sometimes it's better to complete the manuscript first. If you're an unpublished writer, you may be better off completing your book first so that agents and editors see that you're able to pull off your idea successfully. Another consideration is whether or not your nonfiction book will primarily inform or entertain. If you're writing a prescriptive nonfiction book meant to inform, then you're selling it based on the quality of your idea, its market potential, and your expertise; having a completed manuscript is of less importance. If you're writing a memoir that will succeed based on its literary merit or entertainment value, then it becomes more important to have a completed manuscript that shows your writing strengths and ability to construct a narrative.

I published my own nonfiction book, and now I'd like to query commercial publishers about a second edition, but how can I approach them about this idea?

There are two ways you can approach this. One way is to submit a copy of your book to several publishers along with a concise description, its market potential, and the sales record you achieved on your own. Include any other information likely to convince them to invest in your project (such as your marketing plan), as well as copies of notable reviews and special promotional contacts you may have.

If your book didn't sell many copies, and you consider your self-publishing attempt a big mistake, then don't send a copy of the book. Query the publisher as if it were a new project, and if your manuscript is requested, send a printout of the word-processed manuscript (not the typeset book)—as well as the proposal.

Do I need an agent to sell my nonfiction book?

It depends. Consider these factors:

1. Are you writing a book that you believe has significant commercial value?

2. Do you want to publish with a New York house, or does your project merit a large advance (at least $20,000 or more)?

3. Do you need the expertise and knowledge of an agent to get your proposal into the right hands?

If the answer to any of these questions is yes, then you probably should look for an agent.

Projects that don't require agents include scholarly works that should be published by a university press; regional works that are likely to be published by a regional or independent press; a work with little commercial value; or a work that has a specialized audience and would work well with a specialized press. For many specialized or niche books (which include scholarly or regional works), you're often better off approaching publishers on your own, particularly if those publishers are small and specialized themselves. Of course, always check to make sure the publishers you're querying take unsolicited queries and submissions.

THE BOOK PROPOSAL

If I have a completed nonfiction manuscript, do I still need to write a proposal to accompany it?

Yes, it's a smart idea. The editor or agent will want to know your target market for the book, your marketing platform and promotion plan, and any other information that shows why your book will sell.

How long is a book proposal and what should it contain?

Book proposals vary in length, format, and content, depending on the project; a strong proposal will cover, at the very least, these areas:

Target market. Who's the audience for your book? How big is that audience? What evidence do you have that your book will sell to that audience? Editors and agents look for quantifiable proof that a market exists for your book and that it will sell. If you're an expert in a particular field, and you know your market well, this may be a very easy task. But if you don't have a clear idea of your audience, or if you've been generalizing your market as "everyone who likes a good read," then it's probably time to do some market research. Look for studies, reports, magazine and newspaper articles, books, and anything else that shows your book idea can be sold and marketed successfully to a well-defined audience.

Competitive title analysis. What books currently on the market are similar to yours? What are the strengths and weaknesses of these competing titles? Why is yours different, better, or unique? Many editors and agents will know the biggest competitors to your book, but they need to hear from you why your project is a needed addition to the market. Show how your book fills a gap or brings something new to the table. It could relate to content, presentation of content, format and packaging, comprehensiveness, price, illustrations or special features. Your book must have a special angle or hook that sets it apart from the other books on the shelf. Why would someone choose your book over a competitor's?

Author bio. You must convince agents and editors that you're the perfect author for the book. Don't simply attach a resume; tailor your bio and background to the book idea you're proposing. Show how your expertise or experience has given you the perfect platform from which to address your target audience. If you have no background or expertise in the subject area you're proposing to write about, you have a tough battle ahead. Look for other strengths that may help give you credibility or sell books: established connections to experts or to your target audience, a strong online presence or following, and previous success in marketing and promoting yourself and your work.

Marketing plan/marketing platform. Your marketing platform is your unique space in your field that allows you to market, promote, and sell your book. It's your reach into the marketplace, including your personal and professional network, your website, your e-newsletters or e-mail list, your regularly published articles or columns, your positions within national or regional organizations, speaking engagements, media experience, and so on. A strong marketing plan details how you plan to make your audience aware of your book and should build upon the strengths of your platform. For instance, "As president of the National Widget Guild, my book will be featured in the monthly Widget Guild newsletter that reaches fifty thousand readers."

Chapter outline and sample chapters. If your manuscript is not complete, you'll need to include a chapter outline that describes your book's content. You should also include a sample chapter or two. Write a chapter that showcases the very best material in your book and not something like the introduction.

After you have all of these elements ready, you should write an overview (several pages long) to begin the proposal; it should tie together the most persuasive or important elements of your proposal and summarize why the book is needed, who the market is, and why you're the perfect author for it.

As mentioned before, length can greatly vary, but even the most simple proposal usually runs a dozen pages, longer if an extensive outline or sample chapters are included. Very detailed proposals can run one hundred pages or more.

Proposal writing is an art, and the best ones demand careful research, careful writing, and careful revision. Be sure to read a good sample proposal or two before embarking on your own. *How to Write a Book Proposal*, by Michael Larsen, has several proposal examples, not to mention excellent and in-depth instruction on writing a compelling book proposal.

I think I have a good idea about my audience, but I'm not sure how to collect meaningful information about them or the market. What kind of information should I be looking for?

Here are some questions that should help spark some ideas.

As far as your potential market, what's your book about and what's at stake here? How serious is the problem or issue? How far-reaching? Usually you can find news articles online through simple keyword searches, or ask your librarian to help you research information on your topic.

Who's affected by the issues in your book? What age are they, how much money do they have, what's their education level? Where do they shop? What organizations or clubs do they belong to? Where are they likely to live in the country? In what type of setting? Is your audience growing or dwindling or stagnant? Does the economy affect your market? Does technology affect your market? Offer any facts or figures that show trends favoring your book sales.

How much thought should I put into the book title? I hear that publishers just change it anyway.

While it's true that the publisher will likely change your book's title, you should still create an effective title that captures people's attention and identifies the book's audience, benefit, or purpose. Usually you want your book title to be positive and empowering, and to convince book buyers that it will solve their problems or otherwise benefit their lives.

Can I include clippings, illustrations, or photos along with my proposal?

Yes, include any supporting materials, as long as they look refined and professional. You can attach them at the end, and include a page serving as a brief table of contents if you have more than a few supporting documents. Or, if using a pocket folder, put the main proposal on the right-hand side and put your supporting documents on the left-hand side.

How can I find the sales of competing titles?

You can try to interpret Amazon rankings or look at a book's reprint record (on the copyright page) to determine its popularity or endurance, but you won't be able to find its sales numbers. Publishing houses do have access to an online resource, Nielsen BookScan, that gives sales information that's said to account for about 70 percent of a book's sales. But this resource is not available to the general public; publishers pay very high subscriber fees to get access.

If you're trying to figure out what the best-selling books are in a particular category, check how many copies the chain bookstores keep in stock on the shelf; more than one or two copies at a time is the mark of a fast seller. Also, sometimes a high number of Amazon reviews can tip you off to a particularly favored or popular title.

While my nonfiction book proposal is circulating among publishers, may I sell parts of it as magazine articles?

Yes, you can sell parts of your book as magazine articles; it is not likely to affect the chances of getting your book published and may even help a little. Just make sure that you're only selling first rights. (You should ensure that in any case.) If you do subsequently find a publisher, make it clear to them, before signing a contract, that portions have been previously published.

You should not sell portions of your book as magazine articles after you're contracted with a publisher unless you receive permission. Usually your book contract stipulates who has the right to sell serializations, and how the proceeds will be divided between publisher and author.

TROUBLESHOOTING YOUR BOOK IDEA

My nonfiction book was rejected by an editor who said it wasn't authoritative enough. What does that mean, and how can I solve the problem?

The editor might mean that you have not researched the topic adequately or that you have not used your research wisely. Or he might be saying that you are not qualified to write about the subject and would lack credibility with readers.

If you lack credentials or qualifications to write your book, you could try finding a well-known expert in the field to endorse your book or write an introduction. You could also include more material in your book from experts (interviews, quotes, and other references).

What are some other common rejection reasons for a nonfiction book?

Many prospective authors (usually beginners) don't bother writing a book proposal, especially if they have a completed manuscript—or they write a few pages describing their book without any discussion of the target market or their marketing platform. Never assume your project is the exception to the rule because of its compelling or timely nature, and don't submit your idea to numerous publishers without any care or attention. Example: "I know that ABC Publishing House doesn't usually consider books in this subject area, but this is such a compelling book, I thought you should see it anyway." A few other tips:

- Pitch only the book you know has a firm and identifiable spot in the marketplace. Don't assume that the editor or agent will make exceptions for your project, or that someone will figure it out later. Unfortunately, excellent proposals sometimes get rejected because the book's market is just too small for a publisher to pursue.

- Don't skimp on the competitive title section—editors can tell when you haven't done your homework. (Also, knowing the competition and its strengths/weaknesses should help you better write your own proposal.) Whatever you do, don't claim there are no competitors to your book. If there are truly no competitors, then your book is probably so unusual it won't sell.

- Editors of nonfiction aren't looking to acquire finely written manuscripts; they're looking to acquire a powerful selling handle. Your proposal should deliver a promise of a book that will fly off the shelves and make the publisher a profit. (Exception: Editors of narrative-driven nonfiction, such as memoir and popular biography, do look at the writing as the first consideration, though the selling handle still matters just as much. It's no good to have great writing on a subject no one is interested in.)

- An incredibly common problem with many book ideas is that they're too general and broad, without a unique angle or hook. For example, if you wanted to write a book on losing weight and titled it "How to Lose Weight Fast," it would be much too generic to interest anyone. Or if you wanted to write a book on how children can cope with parents who have Alzeihmer's, you would need to find a special angle or unique hook that sets the book apart from the many competitors already on the shelf.

- Similarly, many aspiring writers want to do a book based on their own personal experience of overcoming a problem or investigating a complex issue, without any expertise or credentials. Sometimes such books are thinly disguised memoirs, written more for the author's psychological benefit than for a reader's benefit. Remember: Just because you experienced it doesn't mean you can write a salable book about it.

MEMOIR

I've written a memoir about my military service. It includes 280 letters to my mother, illustrations of the times, and my recollections. I wrote it for my family, but friends say it warrants publication. What course should I follow to find out?

Many people who write life stories or memoirs—which are of primary interest to family and friends—decide to self-publish with a print-on-demand (POD) company. There are a couple of reasons for taking this approach. First, you can publish your work right away, and you don't have to go through the time-consuming process of looking for an agent or publisher who might reject your work because it's not marketable enough. Second, going the POD route is relatively inexpensive and will allow all friends and family, as well as future generations, to cherish your life and history in a lovely book that can be kept on the shelf for years to come.

However, if you think your work might be marketable to the general public, and you're willing to spend some time writing a book proposal and looking for an agent, you may want to consider the traditional publishing route.

How do I know if my memoir is salable or marketable?

It's probably safe to assume that your memoir is not salable unless you're confident of several things. First, your writing must be outstanding. If your memoir is your very first book or very first writing attempt, then it may not be good enough to pass muster with an editor or agent. Second, you must have a compelling and unusual story to tell. If you're writing about topics that affect thousands and thousands of people that's not necessarily in your favor. Alzheimer's memoirs or cancer memoirs, for example, are very common, and will put you on the road to rejection unless you're able to prove how yours is unique or outstanding in the field. Third, you must have a marketing platform. If you have a way to sell your memoir, on your own, without a publisher's help, then your book is more likely to be attractive to an editor or agent.

What's the difference between autobiography and memoir? When reviewing publisher and agent listings regarding what they specialize in, I often see biography/autobiography and memoir as separate topics. To me, they're basically the same.

It's true that in some general contexts, memoir and autobiography can be used interchangeably. However, when publishing houses note a difference, they're making the following distinction: Autobiography focuses on the writer's entire life, whereas memoir focuses on a certain aspect of it. As Susan Carol Hauser explains in *You Can Write a Memoir*, autobiography focuses on the chronology and timeline of a life. Memoir takes an in-depth look at one or more themes in a life, rather than an in-depth look at an entire life.

WHERE TO FIND OUT MORE

Books

How to Write a Book Proposal by Michael Larsen, now in its third edition, has instructed writers on how to craft nonfiction book proposals for more than twenty years.

Write the Perfect Book Proposal: 10 That Sold and Why, by Jeff Herman and Deborah Levine Herman, offers ten examples of book proposals and why they succeeded.

Nonfiction Book Proposals Anybody Can Write, by Elizabeth Lyon, is another helpful resource on the craft of book proposals.

Thinking Like Your Editor—How to Write Serious Nonfiction and Get It Published, by Susan Rabiner and Alfred Fortunato, is a publishing insider's look at why certain nonfiction ideas get accepted and why others don't; most of the book is devoted to the craft of nonfiction and working with an editor and agent.

Publish Your Nonfiction Book, by Sharlene Martin and Anthony Flacco, goes beyond query letter and proposal basics to give you a broader insider understanding of what the publishing industry is really like and how to navigate it successfully in order to ensure a long-term career.

Damn! Why Didnt I Write That?: How Ordinary People Are Raking in $100,000.00 or More Writing Nonfiction Books & How You Can Too!, by Marc McCutcheon, is a combination pep talk/how-to guide that offers encouragement to amateur writers who want to support themselves (and their families) by writing.

CHAPTER 5

HOW DO I WRITE AND SELL MY ARTICLES?

The wonderful thing about magazines is that there are just so many of them—by some counts, more than twenty thousand in North America alone. The terrible thing about magazines is that there are just so many of them. Each of them has a different audience, a different style, and a different voice—and different requirements of their writers.

The trick to selling your work to any of these magazines is matching the article to the magazine. In other words, to sell an article to a magazine, you have to do a little market research. Professional writers recognize that magazines are as individual as people are and that they have to know what stirs readers' interests and what bores them. This chapter will cover the ins and outs of how to do that effectively and what problems you might encounter.

TYPES OF ARTICLES

How many different kinds of articles are there?

Dozens. Articles most commonly published today include interviews and how-to, personal experience, inspirational, humorous, investigative, personal opinion, travel, technical, and new product articles.

- How-to pieces teach the reader how to do something, such as find a job, build a bookcase, or fix a leaky faucet. They usually focus on step-by-step instruction and sometimes include photographs or illustrations.

- A personal experience piece relies upon the writer's personal experience to entertain and inform about a larger issue applicable to everyone (for example, finding reliable child care).

- An inspirational piece is meant solely to inspire and motivate the reader by telling of a challenge overcome or a lesson learned. Sometimes the word inspirational also refers to pieces of a religious nature.

The other popular article types—interview, humorous, investigative, personal opinion, travel, technical, and new product—are fairly self-explanatory. As with all article types, their focus and slant should closely match the interests and attitudes of the magazine's readership. For more instruction on different magazine article types and how to write them, read *The Writer's Digest Handbook of Magazine Article Writing*, edited by Michelle Ruberg.

In college we wrote what teachers referred to as essays, but I don't see many markets for essays. What's the difference between an essay and a magazine article?

An article is usually based on facts uncovered in research and/or interviews and manifests itself in forms like the personality sketch, the investigative report, or the how-to. It will have a particular slant, but any opinion will be backed up with quotes, anecdotes, and statistics. While they are often entertaining, articles are usually meant to educate and inform.

In its original sense, the essay was meant to express opinion, to be persuasive, or to be interpretive. It is marked by a more personal treatment of the subject matter, which may or may not interest a wide audience. Although an essay may require research, the information is used along with subjective ideas, whereas an article remains fairly objective. More recently, newspapers have printed interpretive essays. These pieces are really extensions of the news story, analyzing the background of a political event. Editorials, humor pieces, and inspirational articles could all be considered essays.

What is a feature?

The term feature usually refers to those articles appearing in a magazine that are not columns or part of a regularly appearing department. Feature articles run longer than columns and department pieces, get featured on the cover, and are grouped together in what is called the editorial well, which is at the magazine's center.

What is new journalism?

New journalism is a school of article writing that uses fiction techniques to relate an event or story that is factual; it's a form of journalism that also involves the writer's own feelings about his subject, as opposed to what is termed objective journalism.

What is a think piece?

A think piece is usually an article that has an intellectual, philosophical, provocative approach to its subject.

I have known some very ordinary people who have done some very unusual things in their lives. Is there a market for articles about these people? It seems I only read stories about famous people.

Your stories may not interest editors of major magazines, but they may very well sell to local newspapers and possibly to a specialized consumer magazine or trade publication. The only way to find out is to look through *Writer's Market* until you find some magazines interested in buying the human-interest nonfiction you want to write. Make sure you study a magazine thoroughly before you decide to query or send a manuscript to its editor.

An editor said that he thought part of my article would work better as a sidebar. What does he mean?

Sidebars are short articles that accompany longer features. They're boxed off and titled separately from the rest of the article and may even be set in a different typeface. Sidebars are used to add information to the article or to take an in-depth look at a topic that is related to the main article but is too tangential to be included in it. For example, an article on a papal visit to the United States might have a sidebar summarizing the city-by-city heavy security precautions. Other kinds of sidebars include historical notes, tables of statistics, and how-tos.

What subjects are taboo in magazines?

It depends. Magazines with taboo topics often mention them in their submission guidelines. You just have to do your research. Try the magazine's website or *Writer's Market*.

MATCHING ARTICLE TO MARKET

Is it better to have a specific market in mind when writing an article or to write the article first, then look for a market for it?

It is usually better to write with a specific market in mind so that your writing will match the publication's style and tone, and be directed toward its particular readership. Writers trying to earn a living as freelancers study potential markets before starting to write; this increases potential sales.

However, you can write an article and then look for a suitable market. Make sure you carefully research the market before you submit anything. Editors do not appreciate writers who bombard them with material that is obviously not aimed toward their audience.

Most experienced freelancers will query a market before writing an article specifically for it, and write only on assignment. That is, they only write articles that have been assigned to them based on a query.

How do I obtain sample copies of magazines not sold locally?

First, check the magazine's website and see if there's any way to order sample copies online, or look for a general e-mail address for inquiries. If there's no way to contact the publication via e-mail or through an online request form, try calling the customer service number, if it exists. As a last resort, snail mail a request to the magazine, along with a SASE, and offer to pay for a sample copy. Some magazines charge, others don't.

How can I find back issues of a magazine?

Check the magazine's website. Most of them explain how they handle back issues of their publication. If not, look closely at the fine print in the magazine's masthead. Most explain how you can order back issues either by phone or snail mail.

What is meant by the slant of a magazine article?

A writer slants his article when he specifically gears it to a particular magazine's audience. Finding the proper slant demands in-depth market study to determine the subject matter and style an editor is interested in, and the kind of audience his magazine is intended for. Carefully review several issues of a magazine you wish to write for, analyzing the articles. Are there mostly opinion pieces? Factual features? Personality profiles? What's the tone of the articles? How about the average length? Close observation of the advertisements will give you an idea of the average age and socioeconomic status of the readers, as well as some of their hobbies and interests. By studying the market, you'll be able to present an editor the kind of article he wants, thereby greatly increasing your chances of making a sale.

I have an idea for an article that would be perfect for a home decorating magazine. However, I found that the magazine published a similar article several years ago. Does this mean it won't be interested? Should I try other magazines instead?

You can still query the magazine, but emphasize your piece as an update of the previous article or suggest new ideas and angles. Many magazines must cover the same topic in many different ways in a very short time; for instance, *Cosmopolitan* has at least one article about how to improve your sex life in every issue, but its angle or hook is different every time. Find a unique angle or hook to your idea that will distinguish it from other pieces that may have recently run.

Where can I find a listing of markets where a beginner can break in?

Look for magazines with smaller circulations and lower payment rates. While the editors will not be less demanding about the quality of material they accept from freelancers, you may not have as much competition.

What are literary magazines?

Literary magazines (or journals) are small-circulation publications that print political, literary, and often unorthodox material that might not otherwise be published. They represent creative writers interested in fine literary quality and are read by writers, editors, and students of literature. Since these publications make little or no profit, payment for published work is usually no more than a contributor's copy or a subscription to the magazine.

Is there some way I can find out about upcoming community and corporate events that I can use as possible subjects for freelance articles?

Large companies, universities, and nonprofit groups schedule a variety of events that can be grist for the freelancer's mill. Most public relations departments of large organizations maintain mailing lists and notify interested persons of upcoming events. Convention and visitor bureaus of large cities can also inform you when special-interest groups and professional organizations will be holding conventions in your area. All you have to do to start receiving information is contact the organization and ask—as a professional freelance writer—to be placed on its mailing list.

COMMON ARTICLE PROBLEMS

I've done very little writing, but I'd like to write an article about working mothers—especially those with small children. I know several in my neighborhood and am impressed by what they manage to accomplish in a day's time. But whenever I begin to write, I quickly run out of things to say—after only a page or two. What's my problem?

It seems that you have a fairly solid interest in your subject, so your problem might be a lack of ample research. Have you really talked to these women about their trials, the advantages and disadvantages of their two-career situation? Another problem may be that you do not have a clearly developed angle for your article. Instead of merely making random comments on how working mothers cope, you could perhaps better interest your readers by including specific tips on how they could manage their own time better, secure cooperation of other family members, etc. A writer who knows enough about his subject will never be at a loss for words: Ideas, anecdotes, facts, and angles will come easily. Begin by formulating a solid outline and strive for smooth transitions between ideas. Take plenty of time to plan, research, and write your piece; rushing things will result in disorganized and unclear writing. And it's a good idea to write such a piece with a particular publication in mind. That way, you can tailor your story to the magazine's style, tone, and readership.

An editor rejected my article, saying he uses a more anecdotal style in his magazine. What does that mean?

Used in article writing, an anecdote is a brief human-interest story illustrating a point. Although each anecdote is complete in itself, it should be relevant to the purpose of the article. Anecdotes can serve to hold reader interest by breaking up a lot of factual material. They can be used to add insight to the personality of someone discussed or featured in an article, to act as a transition from one topic to another, or to provide a grabber of a lead in a news or feature article.

A good interview will easily yield anecdotes. Ask your subject open-ended questions like "What person influenced you most in life and how?" or "What was your greatest opportunity?" or "What do you consider the most important decision in your life?" Through such inquiries, you will learn much about the forces that guide and shape the person. If you are writing about someone not available for interview, talk to people who know him and get them to discuss incidents involving your subject, and his personal characteristics.

Often writers use anecdotes stemming from personal experience, which can be appropriate and useful, but don't overdo it. It only takes a couple of anecdotes before you're writing an article that's more about yourself than the topic at hand.

Do the anecdotes I use in my articles have to be true?

If you're going to mention people's names, then you'd better stick to real-life facts; however, if you want to make up an anecdote to illustrate a point, then you might preface it with something like: "It's the sort of town where something like the following could easily happen … " or "There's a rumor going around that …" This way the point can be made without giving the erroneous idea that the incident actually did take place. The secret of good anecdotes is witnessing a real occurrence and describing it in such a way that your interpretation gives it new dimension and significance.

I sent an article to a magazine and got back a rejection with the comment "Too general—no peg." What does that mean?

It means that you did not concentrate on one specific aspect of your topic, and the article was too general for the audience of that magazine. Most article ideas lend themselves to several pegs, each one of which could be developed into a separate article. For instance, an article on buying a computer could be geared toward the needs of a college student, a family with children, a self-employed businessperson, a teacher, or a corporation—five different article possibilities (or pegs) that could end up in five different magazines, each with a different audience.

WORKING WITH EDITORS

When a magazine published my article it was completely changed from my version, although they used my facts. Does this mean they didn't like my writing and only wanted to use my research? I know they needed to shorten it, but I was surprised to see it changed so much from the way I submitted it.

An editor will often change syntax, clean up grammar, and rearrange ideas to make an article clearer and more easy to read. If the article is longer than the specified number of words, it will be cut. Editorial space is limited. The editor may be forced to do a lot of rewriting, even though the article may contain valuable information, because he knows that it does not conform to reader expectations or the personality of the magazine—editors edit to make you sound better relative to the rest of the magazine. You can avoid severe editing of your work by studying the slant and style of the magazine to which you are submitting. Look closely at the printed version of your article and analyze the reasons for changes. And it wouldn't hurt to drop the editor a note and ask why the changes were made. He will probably be frank with you, and you may learn something from the experience.

I've written a magazine article for which I've taken some photographs as possible illustrations. How do I submit a manuscript-photo package?

If you've already been given an assignment and the editor is expecting the photographs, then choose a couple of your best shots and include them with your manuscript. If she's not expecting the photos—or if you're simply querying or submitting on spec—then don't send the photos; just let the editor know they're available.

I sold a piece to a magazine, and it was a year before it was published. When it was published, they spelled my name right, but that was about all. The style was hacked apart until there was no style. What's more, facts were altered, so the reader was bound to get an impression different from what I intended. How much can my story be edited or changed without my permission?

Ethically, an editor should discuss any significant changes with you, especially if they affect the intent of your piece. Some editors will show galley proofs to authors; others will not. You might ask to see galleys at the time the piece is purchased. If you don't like what you see on the galleys, you can ask to have your original meaning restored or the manuscript returned to you for submission elsewhere. But be sure you aren't mistaking tight editing for changes in meaning, as beginning writers sometimes do. Most of the editor's changes are to make the story more readable—not different.

An article I recently sold was heavily edited, distorting the meaning of some of the opinions and quotes contained in it. Can I ask for the right of article approval on any future sales?

It might not be a good idea to make such a request in your query letter, since such preconditions might turn off the editor. The question can be raised when you submit your article; simply state that if the editors make any changes—in terms of content, not copyediting revisions—that you would like the opportunity to see the final edited copy before publication.

Can a magazine change the title of my story?

Just as the editor has the right to make editorial changes, so too does he have the right to change your title. Some editors might consult you first, but titles are changed routinely for a variety of reasons. If the editor changes your title in a way that distorts your meaning, you certainly have cause to complain.

A magazine editor assigned an article to me, based on a variation of an idea I queried him about. When I got into the actual research, I found the article wasn't going to produce what the editor was looking for. There just wasn't enough solid information available to support the editor's thesis. What's the best way to handle this?

Let the editor know right away what the problem is. The editor will either abandon the idea and pay you a kill fee, or suggest some contacts who may be able to supply you with what the editor is searching for. Editors, as well as writers, sometimes have to admit that a certain idea has to be temporarily abandoned.

Is one editor liable for another editor's commitment? When an editor assigns something to a writer or offers payment for a manuscript, then leaves the magazine staff, is the replacement editor liable for that assignment or payment?

There are no rules on this one. Often it depends on the terms of departure for the editor. If he is fired, chances are his replacement or his former manager will want to disregard his editorial thinking—perhaps that was the reason for his dismissal. If he was promoted or transferred, or if he otherwise departed on good terms, there is likely to be more transitional grace, and old projects and commitments may be honored. The writer should summarize the situation in a letter to the new editor, including copies of all correspondence. The new editor then will be in a position to judge whether he wants to keep the writer on assignment or kill the idea. Whether a kill fee will be paid depends on whether a kill fee was part of the original agreement and how far the writer has gone with the idea. Most editors will be fair with the writer. But when a magazine staff changes, it is often because the publisher is unhappy with earlier staffers—and it can signal a new editorial direction for the publication.

What does it mean to be a contributing editor?

Contributing editors are writers who regularly sell articles to a magazine. Being named as a contributing editor usually gains the writer no additional money or special favors, but is prestigious in that it indicates that the writer knows how to successfully (and repeatedly) write for and sell to that magazine. It also gives her more visibility, in that her queries, suggestions, and manuscripts are given red-carpet treatment (they are read sooner and acted on more quickly than unsolicited mail). Contributing editors have more clout when arranging interviews, and the title may give the writer more credibility when she wants to break in to other markets.

What exactly does a magazine correspondent do? How can I get a job as a correspondent?

Magazine correspondents usually work on assignment, conducting interviews, making phone calls, and doing all sorts of other research for articles that are sometimes initiated by the magazine and written by staff writers. The results of this legwork are usually submitted as a research report and are incorporated into articles of larger scope. The correspondent may also be able to initiate, research, and write articles of his own for the magazine. He's in a better position than the regular freelancer, because his editors know the quality of his work and are more willing to consider it for publication.

To get a job as a correspondent, you usually must have a substantial track record as a writer and be able to demonstrate a wide knowledge of and interest in the subjects you write about. These jobs are normally obtained with a particular magazine after the writer has had several pieces published in that magazine.

What do editors call the small descriptive phrase or sentence that usually appears under the main title of an article?

Some editors call it a subhead, and others a deck. This phrase or sentence is designed to pique the reader's interest in reading the article or story by telling just a little bit about the subject matter.

MARKETING YOUR WORK

Is there any danger a writer might get too many articles going at the same time?

Planning your production time—whether you are a part-time or full-time freelance writer—is important. If deadlines are too close together, you may be inclined to rush through an article without sufficient research, eliminate some important interviews, or turn out a draft that really needs better organizing and rewriting. You will be judged by your readers and editors on what appears under your byline, so give only your best effort to each assignment.

I have written a human interest article that I think would be perfect in the Sunday supplement magazine in our local newspaper. How many weeks in advance should I make my submission if I have a particular Sunday in mind?

It would be wise to submit your piece several months (or more) before the date you would like to see it published. This gives the editor plenty of time to make a decision concerning your article, and, if it is accepted, to ask for revisions or prepare accompanying artwork.

Writers should consider lead time (the time between submission and publication) when writing articles that are time sensitive. For a monthly magazine, you should submit your work no less than five or six months in advance of the issue date. A magazine's lead time for seasonal articles is usually listed in *Writer's Market*.

I've written several articles for local newspapers and magazines, but I'm not sure I can write a national-interest article. How can I write something that will sell to a national publication?

Many topics of local and regional articles can be expanded to fit the needs of national publications. By examining how a local story relates to a national trend, or by using it as an example of that trend, a writer can create an article that will be attractive to a national magazine. Of course, you'll have to supplement your local information with related examples from national sources, which you'll have to uncover through research. You should also contact persons involved in the subject at a national level, obtain their viewpoints and comments, and add their quotes to your story.

I've come up with several ideas for articles, but I don't know enough about the topics to write about them. Do magazine editors purchase story ideas, or will writers more knowledgeable in a specific area buy the rights to use my ideas?

It may surprise you how little the average writer knows about a given topic before he begins to write about it. With some research and interviews with knowledgeable sources, you can learn enough about your subject to intelligently write the article yourself.

That said, magazine editors only purchase queries that pitch a written (or soon-to-be written) article, not ideas that will later be written by someone else. Writers who specialize in specific fields of information usually have so many ideas of their own that they don't purchase from others.

How can I find addresses of the daily and weekly newspapers to which I can submit articles of regional interest?

Editor & Publisher magazine publishes the *Editor & Publisher International Year Book,* an annual directory containing a comprehensive list of all the dailies worldwide and all the community and special interest U.S. and Canadian weeklies. The yearbook is available by mail or online at www. editorandpublisher.com.

TRAVEL WRITING

I just discovered the travel-writing field and am very excited about it. How can I get started in this field?

One way to get started in travel writing is to do some short travel features aimed at local newspaper and regional magazine markets. It helps if you have a general knowledge of newspaper and magazine article writing and some experience in freelance writing. If you're new to writing, check out *Travel Writing,* by L. Peat O'Neil.

At the beginning of your career, you will have to finance your trips out of your own funds. Later, when your name becomes known for travel pieces, the publications you write for will often pay your travel expenses. Payment depends on the newspapers, books, or magazines you write for and the degree to which you sell reprints of your articles.

You shouldn't quit your job to become a travel writer. You should work as a freelancer in that field until you have established enough credit with magazine and book editors to enable you to support yourself entirely from your writing income.

I want to do an article that will involve some travel expense to a nearby state. Will an editor reimburse me for these expenses as well as pay me for the article?

If you are fairly new to the business of freelancing and have not built up many writing credits, you will probably be expected to cover extra expenses yourself—but it never hurts to ask! Expenses may include travel, extensive research, photography, photocopying, and the like, and should be negotiated prior to accepting the assignment. An established writer can often get an advance from the editor to cover expenses, and, when writing on assignment, may even get a flat-out expense-paid trip to wherever, he needs to go. If you do have to cover your own travel expenses, keep receipts, and remember that travel expenses can be written off with your other business expenses as a tax deduction. Take full advantage of every trip by taking notes, being observant, taking photographs, and following leads that will open and enhance other writing projects, too.

I'm planning a trip to the Middle East next fall and am interested in doing some magazine article writing while I'm there. Is there any way I can get some assignments before I leave?

Unless you've written many articles in the past and editors know your name and your abilities, you probably won't be able to secure any definite assignments. However, if you are able to suggest in detail some of your ideas in a query letter, you may find a couple of interested editors who will consider your work on speculation. Make sure your ideas have sharply focused angles; general suggestions such as "I'd like to do an article about modern Arabia" will only label you as a novice and will yield few interested editors.

In a travel writer's newsletter I saw a reference to a fam trip. What does this term mean?

Fam trip is an abbreviation for familiarization trip: a trip a public relations agency for a country, hotel, or airline arranges so travel agents, travel editors, and travel writers can visit and become familiar with the amenities offered by the host country or firm: The PR agency and its client hopes that these trips will lead to subsequent travel articles and business. Transportation and lodging costs might be paid for travel agents and offered at a considerably reduced rate for editors and writers.

CONTRACTS AND PAYMENT

How much money can I expect to earn from a typical magazine article sale?

What magazines pay freelancers depends largely on what they can pay (in terms of circulation and advertising revenue), the length of the article in question, and the reputation of the writer. Paychecks can vary from a few dollars to thousands of dollars. With some publications, the fee paid is standard, and with others it is negotiable. Check the market listings in *Writer's Market* for the specific rates various magazines will pay for freelance material.

Should I set a price for my articles, or does the editor set the rate of pay? How do I determine my own pay scale?

Most magazines have a certain rate they pay writers, and they make an offer based on those standard rates. If you're a new writer and have never sold anything to the publication before, you can't expect to get more than that. Remember that sometimes, especially early in your career, a byline is more important than a check, since it bolsters your confidence, builds your reputation, and may lead to other sales.

If you're a well-established writer and think you might be able to negotiate a better rate because of your experience and value to a magazine, go ahead and suggest a higher rate than standard. What payment you finally receive will depend on your previous record, the locale, and your ability to negotiate.

If you are just getting started as a freelance writer, don't try to do too much bargaining with an editor. Take what he offers and give him the best piece of writing you can. If he wants you to rewrite, do it. It is important that you get quality work published. When you feel you have made enough sales to warrant it, you can begin to negotiate or set rates.

What happens when an article is accepted by a magazine? Does the writer get a check in the mail, or are there preliminaries to go through?

The writer is customarily notified of acceptance through a phone call or by e-mail. You may have to sign a contract, and you may be asked to make revisions or review proofs. If the magazine pays upon acceptance of an article, you will receive payment shortly after it is accepted. If the magazine pays upon publication, you'll have to wait longer.

What do the phrases payment on acceptance and payment on publication mean?

Both refer to the time the publisher begins the check-writing process. Payment on acceptance means the check is ordered after the editor accepts the article as ready for publication (that is, after the writer completes any necessary rewrites). The article may be filed and not edited or published for a period of time, but that does not affect the writer's payment.

Payment on publication means the check is not ordered until after the piece appears in print. At a newspaper, this is generally no more than a few days or weeks. The writer may not even notice a delay in receiving his check. At a monthly or quarterly magazine, however, publication may lag months—even years—after acceptance (depending on the size of the editor's manuscript inventory).

When a story is accepted with payment on publication, is payment to the writer assured?

Payment on publication is risky, though it is sometimes necessary to the beginning writer trying to get established. There is never a guarantee that an article will be published or paid for when it's accepted. Sometimes editors change their minds, and the piece is eventually returned to the author, neither used nor paid for. Most publications, though they may take a long time to actually publish the piece, will pay after publication. It doesn't happen too often that you don't get paid, so it's worth the risk if you want to get published. In the case of new markets, you have the risk that the magazine may fold (discontinue publication) after one or two issues are published, and you'll never be paid. If a magazine folds, you will not be paid, but you are free to submit that material to other markets.

What does payment in contributor's copies mean?

Contributor's copies is a term that means copies of the issue in which the contributor's work appears. A magazine that pays in copies (as it is also phrased) offers writers no other remuneration than a copy of the magazine in exchange for the right to publish a work. This is why they are less elegantly called nonpaying markets.

What does it mean when a publisher listed in *Writer's Market* **says he'll accept a writer's work on spec?**

When an editor responds to a query letter by offering to look at the proposed work on speculation (on spec for short), she means she's interested in the article idea and will consider the finished article for publication. In her response, the editor will usually indicate a deadline, the desired word count for the article, and the terms of payment if it's accepted. However, agreeing to look at the work on spec in no way obligates an editor to buy the finished manuscript. Since an agreement on spec does not guarantee a sale, some freelancers will only write an article on assignment, with the editor giving a firm commitment to purchase the finished product; but beginning writers should celebrate an invitation to submit an article on spec. Often the editor will buy the finished manuscript—if it meets editorial specifications and is submitted within the time specified.

What's a kill fee, and when is it used?

A kill fee is a fee paid to a writer who has worked on an assignment that, for one reason or another, was not published. For example: A writer is asked (assigned) to write a 3,000-word article, but after he does the research and writes the 3,000 words, the editor decides the piece will not be published after all. The writer is then given a percentage or a flat fee as a kill fee. The amount of a kill fee is usually flexible and depends on the publication's policy. It's rare for an editor to offer a kill fee to a writer whose work is not familiar to him or to a writer who hasn't previously worked for him. The writer is, after receiving the kill fee, permitted to submit the manuscript to other markets for possible sale. A writer should not expect to receive a kill fee unless this provision is specifically covered in the original assignment.

I want to submit a how-to article to a magazine that pays by the word. The problem is that I spend much more time on the charts and diagrams that accompany the article than I spend on the actual writing. In fact, my articles often contain very little copy. What should I do?

The magazine will most likely consider payment for graphics separately from that for the article itself, depending on the quality of the graphics. Often an editor must have his staff redo the artwork. You might write and ask this particular editor for an answer to your question.

I submitted an article to a magazine that ceased publication with the issue in which that article appeared. I was never paid for the article. Can I submit it to other publications?

Since the publication never paid for your article, although it was published, you are legally free to use it elsewhere. Be sure to inform the editor who buys the article of the circumstances under which it was originally published.

After submitting a 2,000-word article to a magazine, I received a letter of acceptance saying the editor was buying 500 words of the article at five cents a word, with a check for twenty-five dollars enclosed. Is this a usual procedure?

A publisher who is not able to use a full article may offer to buy a part of it from the writer. If the writer accepts, then he agrees to the terms. The balance of the article can be sold by the writer, since he still owns the rights to that material.

What is the difference between selling one-time rights and first North American rights?

If you sell first North American rights to a magazine, you are guaranteeing that it will be the first publisher of your article in the United States and Canada, but you are not restricted from selling it to other North American publishers after that initial publication (or to publishers on other continents before publication). One-time rights can be sold to any publication, regardless of whether it's the first to print the story, but that publication can't run the story more than once.

Once in a while I sell a story that the magazine pays for, yet I never see it in print—even though the editor said he would send copies of the issue containing it. What's going on?

Sometimes magazine editors forget to send copies of stories they published to the original authors. Write a note to each of the editors asking for a copy of your story, if it has been published. In some cases, editors leave or editorial policies change, and although stories are bought, they are not used. Many magazines keep a large inventory of manuscripts, so your piece may not have run. Be patient.

What's the going rate for a magazine column?

What a magazine will pay a columnist varies greatly with the size of its circulation and the eminence and expertise of the writer. A small magazine might pay a couple hundred dollars (or less), while a large-circulation magazine may pay thousands. Although payment is usually on a per-column basis rather than per word, the editor will usually specify desired column length. If you have an idea for a column for a small magazine, send a query along with a six sample columns to the editor, explaining why you think the column would benefit his readers.

Will a magazine's libel insurance protect me from libel suits for articles I write?

It depends on the publisher. Many major magazine publishers have libel insurance that can be applied to a freelancer at the discretion of the publisher, and in most cases the publisher will extend coverage to protect the writer. But if the publisher feels the writer has been negligent in preparing the material, she may decide to let the writer get himself out of the situation. Many publishers have no coverage for freelance writers.

If an article involves investigative reporting and/or a potential lawsuit, a freelancer should consider asking the magazine about freelance insurance when negotiations are underway for such an assignment. The writer should ask the publisher the circumstances under which he would be covered if his article caused any libel action. But don't count on a publisher's insurance bailing you out of hot water if you haven't properly researched and written your article. Accuracy is still the best insurance against libel.

My magazine article was published four months ago and I haven't received payment for it. What recourse do I have? How can I get the editor to pay me?

If the magazine's policy is to pay on publication, you might expect to receive payment within sixty days after publication. You should never be expected to wait longer than ninety days. If you still haven't received a check, send a follow-up letter requesting the specific amount of payment. Give the editor all the details—whether the manuscript was submitted on speculation or assignment, the date of original submission, the date and title of the published piece. If that doesn't work, you can try appealing to a publication's accounting department or senior executives.

In a worst-case scenario, write the Better Business Bureau. Also, send a letter with all the above-mentioned information to *Writer's Market*, which will notify its readers to be wary of dealings with this publication. You might also try the National Writers Union. There is no additional recourse but to sue, which can result in a net financial loss because of legal fees, unless you can take your case to a nearby small claims court.

REPRINTS AND RESELLING

Freelancers who discover the magic of multiple markets and reprint sales often also discover the difference between being a working writer and a working, selling writer. Reselling is often the best way to achieve the maximum return on a minimum investment.

What rights to my story should I sell to a magazine so that I may also sell it to a number of other magazines?

Although most editors will specify the rights they want to purchase, you might be successful in negotiating the rights purchase. Try to sell one-time rights or first rights, which leaves the whole gamut of reprint and second rights open for you.

How do I indicate in my query that my article submission has been previously published?

Simply offer reprint rights and give the name and date of the publication in which the material first appeared.

Many magazines buy first or second rights—I know what first rights are, but what are second rights?

Second rights mean simply that an editor buys (typically for a lower price than you originally received) the right to publish an article, story, or poem that has already appeared in another publication.

When a publisher buys first or second rights, it usually means he will consider material that has been sold before as well as original material. Some editors want to buy both first and second rights—which is the right to publish the manuscript first, and then reprint it either in another publication, in an anthology, or in the same magazine several years down the road (when the audience is new). If the publication does want to purchase second rights in addition to first rights, restrict the rights it buys to nonexclusive second (or reprint) rights, so that you can sell the article again as well.

I sold first and reprint rights for an article to a magazine. Can I sell reprint rights to another publication, or must I wait until the first magazine has used its reprint rights?

It is permissible to sell reprint rights to the second publication. The only exception would be if you sold the first magazine exclusive reprint rights for a certain period of time. Then you would have to wait until the article was reprinted before reselling.

If I sell first rights to a magazine article, does a certain amount of time have to pass before I sell reprint rights to a second publication?

Unless otherwise specified in your contract, the piece you sold may be resold immediately after the first publication publishes it. Actually, you can sell reprint rights any time after you sell first rights, but the second magazine may not publish the article until the owner of the first rights has done so.

What will I get paid if my article is reprinted in another publication?

Assuming you sold only first rights to the original publisher, the reprint publisher will either make an offer or ask the writer to suggest a fee. This payment will be a per-word rate or a flat fee, which could be, for example, 50 percent of what the publication would pay for an original article.

Can I reuse the basic research for one article I sold to a magazine by rewriting and reslanting the original article, adding new interviews and quotes to it, and selling it as original material to another magazine?

Research always belongs to the writer, and you are free to rewrite, reslant, and resell articles based on that research as many times as you can. In fact, you owe it to yourself to try for as many sales as possible. Look for different angles, different spins you can give your research to write an article for another publication. One caution: Don't send rewritten articles to publications with slants similar to the one you originally sold to, unless they accept reprints or material from competing markets.

Under what conditions may I not resell a work?

You may not sell a published work to another publication if you sold all rights to the piece to the first publication. If the first-rights purchaser has not yet published your manuscript, then you can only sell second rights to a publisher if he agrees to hold off his publication until the holder of first rights has printed the work. You cannot sell a piece that was written as work made for hire. Some people find old pieces of writing and try to have them published under their own name; even if the piece of writing in question is not covered by copyright and is in the public domain, this practice is ethically wrong.

A public service newspaper column I write in connection with my job has the potential to become a regular syndicated feature. After it has been printed for the purpose of my job, can I sell it elsewhere?

Companies generally feel that the writing produced as a part of a person's job falls under work-for-hire category and belongs to the company rather than to the writer. However, it's possible that you might be able to work out an agreement with your employer allowing you to have outside use of the material.

A magazine article a publication rejected was slanted so specifically that I can't find another market. How can I make the article marketable elsewhere?

Change the slant. Although your particular arrangement of the facts in your article isn't salable to other magazines, revision and rewriting could make it suit the slant of another publication. For example, an article about stress tests with a slant toward executives could be sold to an airline magazine; with the same research, another article could be written for a sports magazine with a slant toward how stress tests can improve sports performance. In any rewritten article, open the piece with the specific tie-in to that magazine's readership. Amplify the point with extra quotes and information you've gathered through additional research.

Several times in the course of my writing career, newspapers have written me for permission to reprint my articles. I've always given my permission, but I've never been paid for this use of my material. Should I request payment when this happens, or should I just be content with the publicity?

If you've never brought up the subject of payment, that's why the newspapers haven't paid you! As long as you give permission without asking for payment, the newspapers aren't going to volunteer to pay you.

I have contributed a great deal of material—free—to our local natural history group's mimeographed magazine. Is it permissible to sell some of these articles? If so, is it necessary to tell the prospective buyer the details about how it has been used?

You are free to make whatever use of it you wish. It would be ethical to advise prospective buyers where and when the articles first appeared.

In such magazines as **Reader's Digest,** *do the editors select the articles from perusal of various magazines, or do authors submit printed articles they believe are suitable for reprint?*

Editors usually select the articles for reprinting, but an author may submit tearsheets to bring his material to their attention. For a magazine's editorial requirements, see its website.

I have sold some verses and articles to a British magazine and would like to sell them to American publications also. Can I still offer first North American rights? Should I mention that these items have already been printed in Britain?

Yes, you can sell to American publications, but check your British contract—there might be restrictions. Tell the American publications of the previous sale.

For several years I have edited a newsletter for a club (I am a member). I may want to gather all the material and publish it in a small book. Each issue is published with the notice "Permission to reprint material from this newsletter is granted provided proper credit is given." May I legally gather and print my material without permission from the club? I intend to make it clear that the material came from the newsletter.

Yes, you can. But in the interest of good relations, you'll probably want to mention it to the other members.

I recently sold a novel idea for a party invitation to a leading children's magazine. Do the rights purchased by the magazine prohibit me from selling the invitation elsewhere—to a greeting card company, for instance?

That depends on what the terms of your agreement were. If the magazine bought only first or one-time serial rights, you can resubmit. If you don't know what rights the magazine bought, drop a note to the editor and clarify this point before you submit your idea to another company. Although ideas themselves cannot be copyrighted, the particular presentation of the idea—in this case, a party invitation—is covered by copyright.

One of my stories was published in a nonpaying magazine. Can I sell it to a paying magazine?

Yes, but the fact that your first "sale" was to a nonpaying magazine does not change the fact that you granted the nonpaying magazine first rights. A publication can still acquire rights to your manuscript without paying you for them—your compensation was publication.

A magazine that recently folded had accepted several of my pieces. The pieces were never published. Can I remarket them?

If the material was not paid for, you are free to market it elsewhere. If, however, the magazine paid for the work, the company that owned the magazine may choose to sell the rights to publish to another investor, who may resurrect the magazine under its original or other name. The deciding factor, then, is whether the material was purchased. If it was, contact the magazine owner and request that the rights be reassigned, in writing, to you.

WHERE TO FIND OUT MORE

Books

The Writer's Digest Handbook of Magazine Article Writing, edited by Michelle Ruberg, is a comprehensive guide to the craft.

The Complete Idiot's Guide to Publishing Magazine Articles, by Sheree Bykofsky, Jennifer Basye Sander, and Lynne Rominger, has the weight of New York literary agent Sheree Bykofsky's experience behind it.

How to Publish Your Articles, by Shirley Kawa-Jump, is a solid guide for beginners.

The Best American Magazine Writing is an annual collection of the best articles from magazines across the United States.

The Writer's Digest Guide to Query Letters, by Wendy Burt, has what every writer needs to master the essential marketing tool: the query letter.

Websites

MediaBistro (www.mediabistro.com) offers news, advice, and tips primarily for freelance writers at magazines. The best info is subscriber based but well worth the money.

Ed (2010) (www.ed2010.com) is a community of young magazine editors that offers advice, networking events, and constantly updated postings of journalism gigs.

The Freelance Writing Jobs Network (www.freelancewritinggigs.com), a blog network and community for freelancers, offers plenty of job leads plus tips and advice on everything from fair pay to health care.

Writer Gazette (www.writergazette.com) has writing-related articles, freelance job postings, tips, contests, resources, and a section of magazines to pitch.

CHAPTER 6

HOW DO I WRITE AND SELL SHORT FICTION?

The competition for publishing short fiction—especially in popular magazines and journals—is fierce, and the days when a fiction writer could earn a living writing short stories are long gone. Only a select few magazines—such as *The New Yorker*, *Harper's*, and *Esquire*—publish literary short fiction. To get an acceptance letter from one of these publications, you'll need to be writing at the level of John Updike and Alice Munro (and even then it's tough).

On the other hand, there are hundreds, if not thousands, of small-circulation literary journals and magazines (and online zines) that actively publish new writers and will give your work a fair chance. This chapter gives you an overview of what it takes to write successful and publishable short fiction.

CRAFT AND TECHNIQUE

I like to write short stories, but people say the things I write are not exactly stories. How can I find out what a short story is?

A traditional short story (with a beginning, a middle, and an end) features a character who meets with conflict either within himself, with another character, or with some other force outside of himself. The conflict and its resolution should change the character. It is this change, for better or worse, that makes a story.

Consider, for example, a story about two young boys on a Saturday afternoon fishing trip. If the author tells us about the nice time they had looking for the right spot along the bank to cast their lines, and the large number of fish they caught before they trotted happily home, would it be a story? Not unless one of the boys, who always thought of himself as a coward, had to muster his courage to save the other boy after he fell into the rushing river. Here, a character is in conflict with what he sees as his own limitations, and he learns that he can go beyond them—the series of incidents has become a story.

Look closely at what you've written. Does your story contain character conflict, change, and growth, or are you just relating a series of events that involve one or more characters? That may be the difference between what you've written and what a story is.

What is the difference between crisis and climax in a traditional short story?

The crisis in a short story arises from conflict that leads to a turning point. After a series of obstacles, the major character experiences a dark moment in which he sees no way to solve the problem. Then there is a moment of revelation as the character figures out everything. The climax normally follows the crisis and represents the most intense point in the story line. The story should end shortly thereafter.

What is a story theme? Is it any different from a story problem?

Writers disagree on the exact definitions, but here's one explanation: A theme is the message an author imparts to his readers through the plot and characters in his story. The writer starts with an idea, and as his story develops, it is influenced by his own philosophy or observation of the human condition. This is his theme. A story problem is the vehicle by which an author presents his theme. For instance, the problem facing Dorothy in *The Wizard of Oz* is getting home to Kansas. Through her trials and adventures in the Land of Oz, she realizes her folly in wanting to run away from home in the first place, and finally decides "there's no place like home," which is the overall theme of the story.

I'm having trouble coming up with fresh ideas for my fiction. What are some ways I can jog my imagination?

First of all, you should read widely—not just novels and short stories but magazines and newspapers. Something in a factual article might spark an idea. If something makes you think "I wonder what kind of person would do something like that," chances are you could use it as a starting point for your next story. Sometimes meeting an interesting person, recalling an event that happened to you at work, or remembering a daydream (or nightmare) can be a catalyst.

Another way to come up with new ideas is to listen to what people say—on the street, in a restaurant—and jot in your notebook any interesting pieces of dialogue. Remember: A good writer is also a good listener.

Your own life experiences can also provide the foundation for a short story or novel, but you must be careful to avoid becoming trapped by the facts. Remember that you're telling a story and that what was really said or what really happened will have to be modified (or ignored altogether) in the interest of creating readable dialogue and an entertaining plot.

Many writers have found that events in history and the classics of literature can be retold in modern surroundings: Othello as chairman of a corporation or a Napoleon figure as president of the United States, are only two of the many possible twists.

Above all, remember inspiration doesn't always strike like a flash of lightning. Ideas tend to ripen slowly, starting from a single impression or bit of information. The more opportunities you give your imagination, the greater the chance ideas will come to you.

I have a story in mind involving several character types, but I'm having trouble coming up with a strong plot. What can I do about this?

Most fiction is based on what the characters do. Interesting, believable characters create the atmosphere and conflict necessary for a successful short story or novel. Every story must have a basic conflict. By carefully examining your characters—their backgrounds, likes, dislikes, beliefs—you can get ideas about how to set up conflict. Ask yourself questions: What does the main character want? What obstacles might interfere with his goals? How do the characters relate to one another? Once you've set up the basic conflict, you can begin to outline the action of the story. If you're still having problems developing your story's plot, you may want to read *20 Master Plots*, by Ronald B. Tobias, which discusses twenty plots that recur in all fiction.

What is the difference between a plant and a false plant in a story?

A *plant* is something (a person, place, object, or fact) that the writer presents early in a story so when it is used later, it won't seem unrealistic or like too much of a coincidence. For example, imagine you're reading a short story in which a cowboy's horse has just died; the character is sun-parched and dying of thirst himself as he traverses the desert of the American Southwest, but is saved when he suddenly comes to an old deserted homestead that has a spring close by. Wouldn't you be bewildered? Where did that house and spring come from? A good writer will find a way to plant them earlier in his story, thus getting rid of the contrived coincidence.

The false plant is something deliberately placed by the author that ultimately has no connection with the conclusion or resolution of the conflict in the story. Introducing innocent suspects with viable motives in a mystery is a common use of this device. False plants must always be adequately explained somewhere in the story. If the writer of that cowboy short story mentioned an old homestead with a spring close by and didn't put it to some use later in the story, he would have placed what is called a dangling plant. These can be annoying to the reader and should be avoided.

How can I effectively create a character in the limited space of a short story?

Try to determine what is so unique about him that warrants a story. Find a single fact that sets him apart and gives him a recognizable trait. Then portray him in one sentence. Though difficult to write, one-line character descriptions can be extremely incisive.

Character traits should not be thrown at the reader but rather should be woven gradually into the story. A writer should let dialogue, actions, and reactions be the defining features of a particular character.

I have often wondered whether a man can write effectively about a woman, and vice versa. What is the practice among successful writers?

There is significant proof in literature that a writer can successfully portray a member of the opposite sex. Look at what Flaubert did with Madame Bovary, what Margaret Mitchell did with Rhett Butler, and what Tennessee Williams did with Blanche DuBois, to name just a few. The ease with which a male writer can slip into the consciousness of a female character and vice versa depends ultimately on the individual writer and how much insight he has into the workings of human nature, regardless of gender.

In dissecting a short story, how does a writer go about isolating a scene? To me, the scenes seem somewhat continuous. I fail to see any sharp dividing line in a taut story.

Whenever the action moves to a different setting, that's automatically a new scene. If, for example, a story opens in a young couple's kitchen, then moves to an incident in the husband's office, these two different settings constitute two different scenes. But suppose the story is a short-short in which all the action takes place in the kitchen. In that case, look for a division in time. A story may begin with the husband and wife in the kitchen at breakfast time, then jump to five o'clock, when the wife is preparing dinner. This is a device used often. For example: "Jim stomped out during breakfast without finishing his coffee. As Ellen prepared dinner, she thought of the silly argument they had had early that day."

When writing a short story, are you supposed to italicize everything that is spoken or thought?

Use quotation marks for dialogue spoken by story characters. Styles vary for denoting a character's thoughts: Some use quotation marks, some put a character's thoughts in italics, some merely set them off with a comma and capitalize the first letter, and some make no special designation at all if it's clear that the thoughts are the narrating viewpoint character's.

An editor told me I should strive to present a single viewpoint in my short story. Why should I? How do I decide whether third person or first person is better?

In a short story, strong reader identification with one of the characters is very important and is easily disrupted when the author employs a multiple viewpoint. Suspense and continuity are often lost in the transition from one viewpoint to another. For these reasons, short stories told from more than one viewpoint are rarely successful. The choice between first and third person should be made with the plot and characters in mind. Using first person can be subjective, and first-person point of view lends itself well to strong emotion and fast reader identification. Third person, on the other hand, is useful if your plot and characters demand objective treatment.

One of the editors who rejected my story told me he liked the basic idea very much but the whole story was much too complicated. How can I simplify it?

If you have too much going on in your story, it may be because you've tried to incorporate too many characters or incidents. You have to decide who the story is about and focus your narrative on that character and his problem. All other characters should be a part of the story you build around the major character. You may have to reduce arbitrarily the number of characters (to three or four at the most) and restructure your plot from there. The result should be greater simplicity and unity.

I submitted my story to an editor, and he returned it, saying it was too slow paced. What is he talking about?

If your story is too slow paced, you are giving too little attention to action and dialogue that moves the story toward the problem and its resolution. Editors often complain that stories written by beginners don't even start until page five of the manuscript. If the reader must watch the main character wake up, light a cigarette, make coffee, and start breakfast before he learns what the problem in the story is, the story is too slow. Since word space is so limited in short stories, the opening scene (as well as every other scene) should be short on exposition and quick to provide action and dialogue that engages the reader and is pertinent to the story's end.

The transitions in my stories never seem to work. How can I handle them without being abrupt or taking too much time?

Scene transitions involve changes in time, place, and emotion; the key to smooth transition is to link the old with the new. In the last paragraph of a scene, preferably the last sentence, indicate the present place and time period, and if possible, imply the new ones. Then the first sentence in the new scene can establish the time lapse and change of place. Note these points in the following example: "She hoped the Crandalls wouldn't like her antiques. But that must wait until tomorrow, she reminded herself, and tried to get some sleep. The next morning, worry about the Crandalls completely left her mind when … ."

How do I detect rambling in my story? A teacher told me I was rambling at some places where I thought description was necessary.

Examine the passages your teacher marked and evaluate them for their relevance to the story. Be able to define the purpose of each episode and descriptive passage. If you can't determine a function for each part, either discard it or rewrite it. If you determine that the information really is necessary, your teacher's assessment that it rambles is a sign that it should be incorporated into the story more subtly. For instance, can your spelled-out characterization be compressed into the character's actions or her dialogue? Every passage must perform three or four functions at the same time: advance the plot, add to the characterizations, introduce background information, and so on. Being able to write this concisely takes practice, but in the long run, your stories will be better.

When an editor says my story has loose ends, what does he mean?

It means the story has unresolved complications, lingering questions, or problematic inconsistencies. You may need to add or omit incidents, or merely add a phrase that refers to an earlier part of the story. Your story needs to be unified in time and action, and the course of events must be logical. For instance, don't introduce some line of plot action for which the reader expects some meaning in the story and then arbitrarily drop it. It only confuses and annoys the reader.

Looking at the short story I've written, I can see that the conclusion is weak and unconvincing. How can I fix it?

Endings can be the most difficult element of short story writing, since an ineffectual one (or the wrong one) will make the story dissatisfying and unpublishable. Is your ending too obvious? Is the outcome exactly what a reader would expect from your characters and plot? Your problem may be that you failed to plan for your ending before you started writing the story or, conversely, that you overplanned and stifled the real story. If you were hoping something would come to you as the story progressed, and nothing did, your ending undoubtedly seems irrelevant or illogical.

At this point, you have a few options. Your solution could involve going back to the beginning of the story and doing some replotting. Make your major character's decision a difficult one rather than an obvious one. Or use the conflict structure to misdirect your reader, leading him to expect a different ending than what you finally give him. Changes like these must be incorporated into the whole story, for if you merely tack on an ending, it will remain inappropriate and weak because it is not justified by the rest of the story. Ask yourself what you're trying to communicate to the reader through your story. Revisiting your themes might shed some light on the proper conclusion. If you still can't create a convincing and emotionally powerful ending, then it's possible you may need to set the story aside and begin work on something else. Sometimes distance from the material and fresh eyes are all you need to realize what's missing or to gain new insight into where your story should go.

I'm taking a course in short story writing and my teacher keeps noting "overstatement" in my stories. But he's never given me a solid definition of the problem.

Your teacher may be referring to what others call overwriting or purple prose. Redundancies, an excess of adjectives and adverbs in descriptive passages, or an overplay of emotion can all be considered overstatement. Passages that seem contrived or that just don't fit the tenor of the story may be overwritten. While overstatement is most easily spotted by someone other than the writer, you should develop the skill of recognizing and correcting this flaw, which would obviously hinder publication.

Why aren't true-life experiences the best model for planning a story? How could I possibly improve on the way it really happened?

True-life experiences often make a good skeleton for a short story, but they usually need to be dramatized before they will interest others. If the basic action of your story needs a lot of exposition, which it invariably does, you may need to invent action and dialogue to get it across more effectively. Readers will be bored by a straight narrative explanation. If your characters are based upon people you are acquainted with, chances are you don't know them as well as a writer of fiction must know his characters. In order to provide them with sufficient motivation, you may have to provide traits that make them unique and worthy of the reader's sympathies. Plot may need changes in time span and in order of events so that it effectively moves the story along.

DECIPHERING STORY TYPES

Fiction requirements of many magazines specify "no contrived stories." What do they mean by these terms?

By contrived, editors usually mean plots in which the action is constructed in an artificial, implausible way. For example, if a character purposely sets fire to a barn to kill the man inside, that's a credible, well-motivated act. But if a fire happens to break out in the barn for no reason other than the obvious one of helping the author dispose of the man inside, that's contrived.

Many guidelines state "no vignettes or slice-of-life pieces." What does that mean?

A slice-of-life story or vignette is usually one that depends less on plot for its interest than on mood and atmosphere and the detail with which the setting (and its effects on the characters) is described. It is a seemingly unselective presentation of life as it is, a brief, illuminating look at a realistic rather than a constructed situation, revealed to the reader without comment or interpretation by the author.

How long is a short-short story compared to a short story?

The average short-short story is from 500 to 1,500 words long, and the short story runs from 2,000 to 7,000 words. Individual publishers may have varying requirements, which would be listed in *Novel & Short Story Writer's Market*.

Besides the obvious one of length, are there differences between short stories and short-short stories?

Plot in a short story is limited to a small chain of events. In a short-short, it is confined to a single power-packed incident that gives the story its thematic value. There is no room for extensive character development, and the writer doesn't try to do more than focus intensely on one truth of life that may or may not be new to the reader. Good subjects for short-shorts include changes in parent-child or husband-wife relationships, a child's awakening to some facet of life, or an individual's reevaluation of his role in society.

It's hard to draw the line between short stories and novels, since there are also novellas. Just what are the differences in length, subject matter, and form in all of these types of fiction?

Although there are no set rules of length, the short story usually runs 2,000 to 7,000 words. Long stories, which are more difficult to sell, generally run 8,000 to 15,000 words. Novellas will range anywhere from 20,000 to 50,000 words. Herman Melville's *Billy Budd* and Ernest Hemingway's *The Old Man and the Sea* are examples of this genre. Novels are the longest type of fiction. The novel's structure is similar to that of a short story in that it presents a series of conflicts and temporary obstacles leading to a climax in which the major conflict is resolved or accepted as unsolvable. The difference lies in the fact that the novelist has more time and word space to develop his plot, subplots, and characters, and can more easily change the viewpoint of the narrator.

MARKETING YOUR STORIES

Should I send a query for my short stories?

Because of the nature of short fiction, editors rarely expect to be queried about it. Most editors prefer to receive the complete manuscript.

There are very few magazines that contain stories. Magazines print mostly articles. Who buys stories today?

While a few major magazines still have active fiction markets, the majority of markets for short stories aren't on the newsstand. You should look to literary magazines and journals, which are listed in *Novel & Short Story Writer's Market*.

How do literary magazines differ from general publications?

Literary magazines or journals are publications with limited circulation—generally of five thousand or less—that offer writers a vehicle of expression not found in commercial magazines. They aim for an audience of writers, editors, and students and teachers of literature. Their contributors are usually writers striving for literary excellence. T.S. Eliot, Flannery O'Connor, and John Gardner all received their early attention by having their work published in literary magazines.

Literary magazines are often sponsored by universities or nonprofit organizations, and do not rely on general public support; hence, their editors don't have to compromise the ideals of their publications toward a popular or commercial taste. A literary magazine can be centered on a specific theme or can be eclectic—open to work on any idea. Pay is usually low or nonexistent; contributing authors are often paid with copies or subscriptions to the magazine.

Do book publishers put out collections of short novels and stories that haven't previously been published?

Yes, but rarely. In the case of an unknown writer, the publisher is usually reluctant to start off with a short-story collection; novels are greatly favored. Many university presses and small presses hold competitions for short-story collections; first prize is almost always publication of the collection.

My local bookstore has a very limited supply of magazines, and I can't afford to send away and pay for a lot of sample copies. How can I find out what kinds of stories magazine editors consider good so I can read and learn from them?

There are several anthologies published annually that will give you a good overview. *The O. Henry Prize Stories* (with earlier editions published under the title *Prize Stories: The O. Henry Awards*) and *The Best American Short Stories* reprint stories that have appeared in magazines like *The New Yorker, Redbook,* and leading literary magazines. *The Pushcart Prize: Best of the Small Presses* reprints stories from some of the smaller magazines that you wouldn't find in most libraries. Each anthology prints a list of the magazines from which they selected stories. You can also check magazines' websites, which often offer sample editions or representative stories in their electronic archives.

WHERE TO FIND OUT MORE

Books

Novel & Short Story Writer's Market lists more than a thousand places to publish your stories, and includes interviews and articles on the craft and business of fiction writing.

The Art of the Short Story: 52 Great Authors, Their Best Short Fiction, and Their Insights on Writing, edited by Dana Gioia and R.S. Gwynn, is a massive anthology and an excellent resource for learning the craft.

Writing in General and the Short Story in Particular, by former Esquire fiction editor L. Rust Hills, is one of the best instructional guides to the craft; the author cuts right to the chase and tells you exactly what to do and what not to do.

Websites

Flogging the Quill (http://floggingthequill.typepad.com) is guaranteed to improve the art and craft of your storytelling.

The Writer's Resource Center (www.poewar.com) offers hundreds of articles on the craft of fiction, as well as poetry and freelancing.

Writesville (www.writesville.com) is run by an aspiring fiction writer who shares what he's learned so far.

CHAPTER 7

HOW DO I PUBLISH MY POETRY?

Robert Graves once remarked, "There's no money in poetry, but then there's no poetry in money either." And so writers continue their pursuit of the perfect poem even though the rewards often are only psychological.

THE MARKET FOR POETRY

I've written poems over the years, and everyone tells me the same thing—that I have a gift and a way with words. How do I get started publishing my poems?

Your best bet is to pick up the latest version of *Poet's Market*. It lists current publishers and what they're looking for, as well as tips for submitting your work. Also look for *The Directory of Poetry Publishers*, which lists thousands of publishing opportunities for poets of all skill levels. *Poets & Writers*, a bimonthly publication, is filled with markets, contest announcements, and calls for poetry manuscripts. The Internet can provide information on poetry markets as well; use search terms such as poetry markets and publishing poetry.

I have been published in three books from the poetry.com site. But I was wondering how I would go about getting my poems sold or getting them all published as a book?

It's important to remember that there aren't a lot of poetry book publishers, and those publishers want poets with proven track records. That's why the best way to start is by submitting your poems to literary magazines and building up a strong publishing history. Also keep in mind that anthologies like the one you mention often aren't considered viable publishing credits. Your work needs to appear in a variety of magazines that publish good examples of the kind of poetry you write. *Poet's Market* lists magazines and publishers you can check out, as well as contests.

Only when you've published about fifteen poems in different magazines is it time to think about collecting them in a single volume. You may have a better chance of publishing a chapbook, which is a soft-cover booklet of about twenty-four pages. There are many more chapbook publishers than book publishers when it comes to poetry.

Is poetry.com a legitimate place to publish poetry? I'm not too sure if my work is good or if they are just selling books, memberships, and awards to me.

At the very least, the site's claims are truthful (they do what they say they'll do), but Poetry.com is widely known for accepting nearly every poem submitted.

I don't see much poetry published in magazines these days. Does anyone buy poetry?

Few editors buy poetry in the sense that they pay cash for it. However, there's much poetry being published if you know where to look. In print, literary journals and magazines produced by colleges and universities or by small presses or individuals publish poetry, as do a few major publications like *The Atlantic* and *The New Yorker*. (In fact, literary journals devote a large percentage of their pages to poetry.) The Internet is another source of poetry publication, offering many online journals as well as special sites where poets can post their work and comment on each other's poems.

Most literary magazines offer contributors a copy or two of the issue in which their work appears. Magazines like *The New Yorker*, and some of the more prestigious literary journals, do pay cash, but competition makes acceptance of your work very difficult. Often online publications offer no payment at all, except for publishing credit and the value of a poet's work being available to a worldwide readership.

I want my work to be read, so why should I publish my poetry in an obscure literary magazine? Shouldn't I aim for bigger markets?

Literary publications only seem obscure when compared to the mass-circulation publications that fill the racks at the supermarkets and bookstores. True lovers of poetry know where to find literary magazines, and they turn to them for the best poetry being written today. Serious poets do place their work in these magazines—so much so that submitting work to the best of the literary journals is highly competitive. However, don't assume the smaller magazines, even those that are truly obscure, are beneath your consideration. The editors of these journals are dedicated to the art of poetry and are delighted to give exposure to promising poets; plus the journals themselves are often visually interesting and artistic. Publication in literary magazines can offer exposure to a knowledgeable and appreciative audience, and make an attractive showcase for your work.

I have a book manuscript of over three hundred poems, and I'd like to see it published and available in bookstores. How can I make this happen?

First, three hundred poems is a lot for a first volume of poetry. It's nearly unheard of for a book-length manuscript of unpublished poetry to be accepted (unless you're a celebrity). Most poets start out by submitting their poems to magazines. Doing so helps them build a publishing history and enables them to show a book editor that their work has been accepted and appreciated in its own right.

Second, your dreams are precious to you, but you need to bring them in line with the realities of the publishing world. Few major publishers accept or consider poetry manuscripts, and those that do focus on poets with major reputations. Even university presses and small presses known for publishing poetry can be tough for beginners to break in to (although some may sponsor competitions to publish a first book of poetry).

As for bookstore placement, you won't find much shelf space dedicated to poetry (at least relative to fiction and nonfiction), and that space is dominated by offerings from the bigger publishers and the poets you probably read in school. Books of poetry rarely make it to the best-seller lists because the reading audience for poetry is small and specialized.

Serious poets don't expect to get rich and famous. They work hard at their craft, relish communicating with readers, and celebrate their triumphs. (For some poets, breaking in to a prestigious literary journal may be the highlight of their careers.) If you're hoping for more from your writing, particularly in terms of money and notoriety, seek out a different form of writing.

SUBMITTING POETRY

What are typical submission guidelines for poetry?

Guidelines usually indicate what kind of poetry the editor or publisher is looking for, how many poems to submit, the length of the poem, whether to submit by regular mail or e-mail, payment, response times, and similar information. In addition, especially where contests are involved, the magazine or publisher may outline exactly how the manuscript should be prepared (for instance, whether to include a cover sheet or whether the poet's name should appear on the manuscript pages). Submission guidelines may appear in the magazine or on a website, or may be available for a self-addressed stamped envelope (SASE).

I want to submit some poems to a magazine. How should I prepare my manuscript?

Set your word-processor margins to one inch. At the top of the sheet, type your name, address, phone number, e-mail address, and line count in the right corner. Drop down about six lines and type the title of your poem, either centered on the page or flush with the left margin. (Titles may be initial capped or in all capital letters.) Drop down two more lines, and begin your poem flush with the left margin; never center the lines of your poem in the middle of the page.

Most editors prefer poems to be single spaced, with double spacing between stanzas. Type only one poem per page, even if your poem is very short. For poems longer than one page, type your name in the upper left corner of subsequent pages; on the next line, type the poem title, the page number, and either "continue stanza" or "begin new stanza," depending on how your poem breaks between the pages.

How do I prepare my poems if I want to submit them by e-mail?

First, make sure the publication accepts e-mail submissions. Check guidelines, market listings, or the magazine's website to see how the editor wants electronic submissions formatted. Many editors forbid attachments, and they may automatically delete any e-mail that arrives with an attachment. For those editors, paste your poems into the body of the e-mail. For editors who do not mind attachments, format your document the same as you would if you were submitting it by regular mail. If you're including a cover letter, you can insert it at the beginning of your e-mail, whether you're pasting poems into the body of your message or attaching a document.

Take note of any special requirements an editor may have regarding e-mail submissions, such as whether to paste only one poem at a time in a message, whether an attachment should be in Word or another format, and what to put in the subject line. (Editors use the subject line to screen for spam and to direct the submission to the appropriate departmental editor; they can be very picky about what appears there.)

A growing number of magazine websites provide online contact forms for electronic queries as well as submissions. Depending on the form, you can paste your poem(s) into a field or load your manuscript from your hard drive. Click a button and your work is submitted.

How do I figure the number of lines in my poem? Do I count the title and the spaces between stanzas? Do I also include a word count for my poem?

The standard method is to count only lines of text in a poem and to not include the title or the spaces between stanzas. Sometimes magazine guidelines state to include spaces between stanzas, but this doesn't happen often. However, if magazine or contest guidelines mention it specifically, be sure to include spaces in your line count. You don't need to provide a word count for your poem unless guidelines ask for it.

How many poems should I submit to a magazine at one time?

It's best to follow a magazine's guidelines, but an average number is three to five poems per submission. More than five poems overloads the editor, but less than three doesn't really give the editor a sense of your abilities or a wide enough selection of poems from which to choose.

Do I need to include a cover letter with the poems I submit to a magazine?

There was a time when a cover letter wasn't expected with a poetry submission. However, many modern editors appreciate the personal touch of a cover letter. Such a letter shouldn't be long; it's simply a polite introduction of yourself and your work. List the poems you're submitting, and briefly mention something about yourself (publishing credits are fine if you keep them short). It's also nice to comment on the magazine in some way so the editor knows you're familiar with the publication. Editors often indicate their preferences regarding cover letters in submission guidelines and market listings.

Is it okay to submit my poetry to more than one magazine or journal at the same time?

For some editors, simultaneous submissions are fine; for others, they're taboo. Check submission guidelines or market listings. If you submit the same poems to more than one publication at a time, keep careful records to avoid confusion. If a poem is accepted by one publication, you must notify the other editors that the poem is no longer available for consideration. Failure to do so is unprofessional and discourteous and can be harmful to future poet/editor relationships.

When is a poem considered "previously published"? If I post one of my poems on a website, is that the same as publishing it? Is the poem considered published if I print it in a wedding program that's distributed to a limited number of people?

If your poem has appeared in print for public viewing—in a magazine or journal, anthology, postcard, or broadside—it's considered published. (A broadside is like a poster with a poem on it.) Your work is also considered published if it appears in a collection such as a chapbook, even if you self-publish the chapbook and distribute it only to friends and family.

In theory, publishing also includes printing your poem in a program for a private ceremony or event, such as a wedding, funeral, or anniversary. However, some editors may not be as strict about this type of publishing. If you want to submit a poem you've published in this way to a magazine, let the editor know in your cover letter so she can decide up front whether the previous publication matters. To be safe, don't submit a poem you've printed in a program or similar publication to a contest when the guidelines stipulate you must send an unpublished entry.

Opinions differ as to whether posting a poem on a website constitutes publishing it. For instance, some experts say if you post your poem to a forum where others can offer criticism, it doesn't count as publication, especially if the forum requires membership to participate. On the other hand, if you post your poem specifically to be read and enjoyed by an online audience (even on your own website), or if you have a poem accepted by an online journal, you should consider the poem published.

My poem won a prize in a competition. I received a cash award, but the poem wasn't published in any way. Is the poem still considered unpublished?

Yes, as long as your poem doesn't appear in print, it remains unpublished. It wouldn't hurt to mention the award in your cover letter if you submit the poem to a magazine, just to let the editor know the poem has already won some acknowledgment and might be worth extra attention.

When editors say they'll consider traditional forms of poetry, what do they mean?

They mean they'll consider poetry other than contemporary free verse, including poetry that rhymes or adheres to a fixed form. Traditional fixed forms include sonnets, villanelles, terza rima, Japanese haiku, ghazals, and American cinquain. The term traditional may mean different things to different editors, so it's best to study a particular publication before submitting work.

In market listings, many editors say they don't want greeting card poetry. What does this mean?

When editors speak of greeting card poetry, they're referring to poetry that has more in common with greeting card verse than serious poetry. Some of the characteristics of greeting card poetry include cliché topics, high sentimentality, sing-song rhythms, and predictable rhyme words and patterns.

BOOKS AND CHAPBOOKS

What's the difference between a book and a chapbook of poetry?

A book of poetry is usually more than fifty pages long and may be hardbound or softbound. Most modern poetry books are slim volumes of seventy-five to one hundred pages, although collected works of better-known poets may be much longer.

A chapbook consists of approximately twenty-four to fifty pages (shorter lengths are most common). It's usually 5" × 8" (digest size), saddle stapled, with a soft cover—although chapbooks can have any dimension and style of binding. (Some are even published within literary magazines.) Chapbooks are often most successful when the poems have a theme or are connected in some way to create an overall effect, rather than being a batch of disjointed poems gathered for the sake of collecting them in one place. Poets usually publish chapbooks of their work before pursuing book publication.

Are book and chapbook manuscripts formatted the same way as manuscripts sent to magazines?

Some of the same guidelines apply, including making sure your name and the title of your manuscript are at the top of each page, and typing only one poem to a page. You would also want to number your pages successively, include a credits page that lists where poems were originally published, and provide a title page and table of contents. Unlike fiction and prose manuscripts, poetry book or chapbook manuscripts usually aren't double spaced.

However, different publishers may have different guidelines. This is especially true in book/chapbook contests, where submission guidelines may state that a poet's name shouldn't appear anywhere in the manuscript, that a cover letter should be provided, or that the pages should be clipped or bound a certain way. Never submit a manuscript to a publisher or competition without carefully reading the guidelines.

I'm putting together a list of publishing credits for my chapbook manuscript. A couple of my poems appeared in anthologies. Does this kind of publication count in the same way magazine publication does?

Yes, a list of publishing credits should indicate where every poem to be included in the chapbook previously appeared in print. For an anthology, list the title of the collection, the publisher, the copyright date, the title of your poem, and even the page on which your poem appeared, so the publisher has all the background information. And don't forget to make sure you have the right to reprint your poem in your own chapbook. Some anthologies, especially those that acquire all rights, may require written permission to reprint the poem. Sometimes poets wait until a chapbook or book manuscript has been accepted for publication before pursuing reprint rights.

However, it never hurts to plan ahead and make sure everything is in place legally before you submit your manuscript.

I've had several poems accepted by literary magazines. Now I want to include those poems in a collection and submit it to publishers. Do I have to consult the magazine editors before I reprint my poems? What if an editor says I can't use my poetry?

First, check to see what kind of rights the magazines acquired when they published your poems. Many literary journals acquire first rights, meaning you own those poems again once the magazine has published them.

Often a magazine will simply say the copyright reverts to the poet upon publication of the poem. In such cases, you don't have to get permission to reprint your poems. Some editors may request you contact them for permission as a courtesy, or stipulate that in reprinting a poem you must give proper credit to the magazine. If you have any doubts, write to the editor and request written permission to reprint the poetry in your collection.

If any of the magazines acquired all rights to your poetry, you face a different situation. The purchase of all rights means the magazine controls the poems and may use them as it wishes, including producing the poems as postcards or reprinting them in their own anthologies, without notifying you. If you wish to use these poems in your collection, you must contact the magazine's editor and get formal permission in writing. If an editor refuses to grant you permission, you may have to negotiate for reprint rights, perhaps paying a reprint fee. You may even face the possibility of cutting that poem from your collection if an agreement can't be reached.

POETIC CRAFT

I have many thoughts and emotions I'd like to express in poetry. I've kept a journal for many years, but I can't seem to get from prose writing to poetry writing. Any suggestions?

If you've never studied the techniques of writing poetry, consider taking a class, or at least read some books on the subject to help you understand the differences between poetry and prose. Try *The Art and Craft of Poetry*, by Michael J. Bugeja; *The Poet's Companion*, by Kim Addonizio; or *Writing Metrical Poetry*, by William Baer. Your librarian or bookseller can also make good suggestions.

You also should be reading lots of poetry to improve your ear and help you distinguish between the characteristics of poetry and prose. Read classic as well as modern poets to develop a rounded appreciation of what poetry is (and isn't).

What's the difference between free verse and blank verse?

Blank verse is unrhymed iambic pentameter; that is, five sets of two syllables (an unstressed syllable followed by a stressed syllable) per line, and the lines do not rhyme. Free verse is free of meter—nothing is counted or measured (such as accents or syllables)—it has no predetermined pattern or fixed form, and lines can be of any length.

I get very confused by poetic forms—the different types of sonnets, what a villanelle is, and so on. Should I memorize them?

You could memorize the forms that interest you the most; if you frequently write in a certain form, such as sonnets, you may automatically learn them. Memorizing all poetic forms would be daunting, though.

There are many helpful books that define as well as explore poetic forms. These include *The Poetry Dictionary*, by John Drury, and *Writing Metrical Poetry*. Keep such resources handy for when you forget the difference between a Shakespearean and Petrarchan sonnet, or the word order in a sestina.

When I show my family and friends my poetry, which is all free verse, they tell me, "That's not poetry! It doesn't have any rhythm. It doesn't rhyme." What can I tell them?

You can try to explain that there are no rules about poetry having rhythm or rhyme. Tell them how modern free verse has rich roots going back to the nineteenth century and Walt Whitman, whose poetry was influenced by the long lines of Biblical verse. Help them understand free verse is not simply prose broken into lines; it encompasses many poetic elements, such as imagery, diction, alliteration, and enjambment.

What is light verse? What are some markets for it?

Light verse is poetry written to amuse and entertain, rather than to impart any deep literary message. Although it may comment wryly on a serious topic, light verse evokes a laugh or at least a chuckle. It often rhymes and may employ a playful rhythm pattern. Usually light verse does not find a home in serious poetry magazines. Check conventional and commercial publications to see if they have a need for light verse to use as filler material. Sometimes there are categories for light verse in contests sponsored by state poetry societies or in the annual competition of the National Federation of State Poetry Societies (www.nfsps.com).

I think some of my poems would make good song lyrics, but I can't write music. How can I get some of my poems put to music?

It's important to understand that poetry and song lyrics are two completely different things. Song lyrics are meant to be sung rather than read on the page or recited as poetry. Song lyrics usually make use of repetition in a way poems don't (for example, returning again and again to a particular hook phrase in the chorus or refrain). Also, the syllable structures (or meter) and rhyme schemes in song lyrics usually repeat in exactly the same way from verse to verse.

To create lyrics from your poems and have them set to music, your best approach would be to collaborate with a musician. If you're not in contact with someone who can write publishable music, seek musicians in your area and approach one of them about collaborating. Make sure you're aware of a particular songwriter's talent with melody before you get in touch. Also beware of song sharks, unscrupulous people who advertise that they'll set your lyrics to music, for a fee. Many of them are interested only in profit for themselves and will accept lyrics that have no chance of earning any money for the writer. Don't pay anyone to set your words to music. It's better to collaborate with a songwriter/musician and allow a reputable publisher to decide whether your work is good.

What are some reasons poems don't get accepted by editors?

Some are related to the quality of the poem itself, others to things like editorial bias, the volume and quality of competing submissions, and other issues.

Never send a poem unless you're confident it's your best work. Review it with a critical eye. Is your poem fresh and original, reflecting imaginative insight and language even when treating a worn-out subject? Have you let it "cool off" before revising it and sending it out (that is, have you left the poem alone for a few days or even weeks, then reread it for awkward wording, weak lines, and other flaws)? Have you read your poem out loud (if only to yourself) so you can judge how it sounds? Have others read your poem and provided feedback? Are you reading lots of other poets' work so you can sharpen your ear and fine-tune your own poetry?

Even if your poem is well written and highly polished, there are many reasons why it may be rejected. It may not be right for the journal (a quality that's hard for editors to explain sometimes). It may be too similar to another the magazine has accepted recently. Maybe the editor just doesn't like your style (editors are human and have their preferences, too). Or the editor may love your poem but has to pick and choose from an abundance of good poetry.

Consider the quality of your poetry first. Once you're certain you're submitting your best work, take rejections in stride and try to be patient. Eventually your poem and the right editor will find each other.

I always get printed rejection slips or form letters when my poems are returned, never any feedback. Does that mean my work isn't any good?

Generally, printed notices mean the editors don't have time to comment personally on the poetry they reject. Form rejection slips or letters may seem cold, but editors turn to them out of necessity. Between reading through piles of submissions and struggling to meet deadlines, editors are swamped. Take the form rejection as it's intended—as a simple "no thanks, not for us"—and send your poems out to the next publication. There are many reasons besides poor quality for rejecting work. As long as you're confident your poems are as good as they can be, keep them circulating to editors.

RIGHTS AND PERMISSIONS

I've had a poem accepted by an online literary journal. The editor says the journal retains archival rights to my poem when it's published. What does this mean?

Archival rights are the rights to make your poem available online indefinitely. Ask the editor if the archival rights are nonexclusive; if they are nonexclusive, the journal does not claim to be the only online publication that can publish and archive your poem.

Most online literary journals (and many print publications with associated websites) archive work electronically as content of a current or past issue, as a sample of that content, or as Web-exclusive content that doesn't appear in a print edition. There are other kinds of rights an online publication may acquire when accepting your poems. These include first electronic rights (you would be free to reprint your poetry in any medium after it first appears in the online publication); one-time electronic rights (which doesn't specify a time limit for usage but does allow you to submit your poetry to other markets); nonexclusive electronic rights (such rights may be requested indefinitely, but you're able to republish your work electronically at any time); and exclusive electronic rights for a specified amount of time (you grant a publisher exclusive use of your work for a specific period, usually three to six months, after which the publisher has the nonexclusive right to archive your poetry indefinitely). Always know what rights you're granting to an online publisher before agreeing to have your work printed.

Our weekly newspaper started a poetry column and invited contributions. I've contributed several poems and enjoyed seeing them in print. A friend tells me I've lost all rights to the poems I've published in the newspaper. Would I be able to sell them to a magazine? I hate to lose these poems, as someday I might want to put them in a book.

Check with the editor who accepted the poems. If the newspaper itself is not copyrighted, you still own rights to your work under the general copyright law. If the newspaper does acquire rights, find out what kind. Only in the case of the newspaper acquiring all rights would you lose ownership of your poems. Even then, you may be able to negotiate for permission to include them in a collection of your work.

If you own the rights to the poems, you may only submit them to magazines that consider previously published work. Inform the editor of the magazine where and when the poems first appeared.

A few years ago, I had a volume of poetry published at my own expense. Fortunately, the books sold well. Now I would like to submit some of these poems to magazines, but I've hesitated to do so as I'm not sure if this is permissible.

As long as the poems appeared only in the book you self-published, you own the rights and are free to submit the poems to magazines. However, keep in mind many editors may not be interested in previously published poems, especially those that have appeared in a book that has been available for some time. Target only magazines that say in their market listings or guidelines that they consider previously published work, and be clear in your cover letter that certain poems already appeared in your self-published volume.

I've written and sold a poem based on an idea I'm not sure was original. Is such borrowing considered unethical?

Ideas can't be copyrighted, so basing your poem on another's idea isn't unethical. As long as the idea is expressed in your own words and voice, and you present a fresh take on the idea, it's neither stealing nor copying.

If my poetry is published in other formats—such as greeting cards, calendars, or broadsides—do I retain my copyright?

It depends on who is using the work and what kind of legal agreement you enter into. Personal expressions publishers (greeting card publishers) and calendar publishers often buy all rights to a work they purchase for product use. That means you give up any ownership of that piece of writing; and in this case, you probably wouldn't be able to get permission to reuse it. The company may want to use it again on a future card or calendar, and it has purchased the right to do so. If a small press publishes a broadside or postcard using your work, it will probably acquire first rights or one-time rights, meaning that once the broadside or other product has been published, rights to the poem revert to you. You can then include the poem in a future collection of your work (provided you confirm any permissions requirements and provide publishing credit in your manuscript).

There are operations that will print your poem on T-shirts, coffee mugs, plaques, and other merchandise for a price; you can also work with a printer yourself to create such items. In such circumstances, you're basically paying someone to print the poem for you. You're not selling your work to the operation or printer for their own business use, so you retain all rights to the poem.

WHERE TO FIND OUT MORE

Books

Poet's Market provides how-to material on preparing and submitting manuscripts, identifying markets, and relating to editors.

Creating Poetry, by John Drury, and *The Art & Craft of Poetry*, by Michael J. Bugeja, are accessible guides to writing poetry that provide a strong foundation in the craft.

Writing Metrical Poetry, by William Baer, is an introductory course to writing formal poetry (as opposed to free verse).

The Poetry Dictionary, by John Drury, explains poetry terminology.

The Practice of Poetry: Writing Exercises From Poets Who Teach, by Robin Behn and Chase Twichell, is a popular collection of ninety writing exercises for poets.

Poemcrazy: Freeing Your Life With Words, by Susan G. Wooldridge, is an inspirational guide to writing poetry.

The Poetry Home Repair Manual: Practical Advice for Beginning Poets, by Ted Kooser, provides practical, accessible guidance for poets of all skill levels.

In the Palm of Your Hand: The Poet's Portable Workshop, by Steve Kowit, helps readers hone their writing skills through lessons and exercises.

Websites

The Academy of American Poets site (www.poets.org) offers poet profiles, poems, essays, podcasts and audio clips, resources, the National Poetry Map, and much more.

The website of the Haiku Society of America (www.hsa-haiku.org) includes membership information, contest announcements, and submission guidelines for their journal, *Frogpond*.

The National Federation of State Poetry Societies (www.nfsps.org) is the umbrella organization for affiliated state poetry organizations. Their website includes NFSPS contest guidelines, contact information and links for state societies, and an online edition of their quarterly newsletter, "Strophes."

The Poetry Foundation website (www.poetryfoundation.org) offers a unique search function, Poetry Tool; a daily round-up of poetry-related news; a wide range of features and book reviews; *Poetry* magazine's online content; and much more.

The Poetry Society of America site (www.poetrysociety.org) includes membership information, PSA contest guidelines, links, and features from their journal, *Crossroads*.

JPiC Forum for Writers (http://jpicforum.info) features debate, discuss, and critique work from poets around the world.

MoonTown (www.moontowncafe.com) is a network with thousands of poets where you can read, listen to, and watch poetry of all kinds.

Wild Poetry Forum (www.wildpoetryforum.com) is an uncensored forum that allows poets to share and workshop their work.

CHAPTER 8

HOW DO I BREAK IN TO CHILDREN'S WRITING?

In his National Book Award speech, Isaac Bashevis Singer gave a number of reasons why he began to write for children, and one of them was "Children read books, not reviews. They don't give a hoot about critics." If a book is boring, children won't read it just because an adult says they ought to. If a book is interesting and enjoyable, they can't wait to tell their friends. Beginners who want to write for young readers must know what children are like today, and not write only from their own childhood memories. When you successfully capture their emotions and dreams, you'll find young readers eager for stories, articles, and books.

GETTING STARTED

I've written stories for adults for many years and would like to try writing for children. Can you give me some general advice concerning the differences between writing for children and writing for adults?

When it comes to the basics of producing a good story, there isn't much difference between writing for children and adults. You must work in the same way to create believable characters with plausible motivations, and strong plot is still important in stories for all age groups. Conflict and emotion must be integrated into the story. The difference is that all of these things must be accomplished with simplicity and with subject matter geared to young readers. Children's books are also more age specific within the genre. Books popular with seven-year-olds, such as Barbara Park's Junie B. Jones series, will not be very entertaining to twelve-year-olds, who would be more interested in Cecily von Ziegasar's Gossip Girl books.

You must be well aware of the problems and attitudes of children, so you can incorporate them realistically into your stories. The complexities of characterization increase with the age of the reader, to the point that stories written for teenagers differ from adult stories only in the age of the characters and the kinds of situations the characters face. Try to put yourself on the level of your readers so you don't inadvertently talk down to or patronize them. The best way to get a feeling for how stories for children are written is to read lots and lots of them.

What are the most common age groups for which children's publishers produce books?

Generally, children's fiction and nonfiction fall into one of these five categories: board books for prereaders, picture books for preschool to age eight, easy readers for emerging readers ages five to eight, middle-grade books for ages nine to eleven, young adult (YA) books for ages twelve and up.

What are the differences between a picture book, a picture storybook, and a chapter book?

A picture book is a book for meant for younger children (prereaders or beginning readers). It features pictures on every page and tells the story through both the text and the pictures. A picture book can include anywhere from zero words to 500 or 1,000 words, but shorter is generally better. They are almost always thirty-two pages long, including copyright page, title page, etc., which means they include about twenty-eight pages of text and art).

A picture book can have many forms. Concept picture books promote an understanding of the children's world; these books include ABC books and books about giving up a blanket or getting a new baby sister. Concept books can also be novelty books; for example, one might be printed in the shape of a truck or duck, or contain some other gimmick, like pop-up embellishments or tabs to pull. A picture book can be fiction or nonfiction. It can be contemporary or historical. It can be sweet or sentimental or educational or funny. It can be written in prose or verse. Almost anything goes.

A storybook is also for younger children. A storybook may be longer than a picture book (perhaps double the word count, forty-eight pages) but doesn't have to be. A storybook may be a retelling of a folktale or fairy tale, a fantasy story, or a contemporary story, but it will always be fiction. A storybook may not be as dependent on illustrations as a picture book. It has a plot with a main character, and generally that character encounters a problem, works out the complications, and finds a solution.

A chapter book is for young readers who have moved up from picture books and easy readers, but are not quite ready for novels. These books may include illustrations, but the story is told solely through the text. Chapter books are generally forty to eighty pages in length and can run anywhere from 1,500 to 10,000 words, depending on the publisher. They're intended for young readers who can sustain interest through a longer plot, and they may be the first books kids pick out for themselves at the library.

I'm working on a middle-grade novel and I'm worried it's too long. What's the appropriate length for middle-grade and young adult novels?

There are no set-in-stone rules when it comes to the length of middle-grade and young adult novels. It varies from publisher to publisher and project to project. Middle-grade novels can range from 10,000 to 30,000 words, and young adult novels can range from 25,000 to 50,000. Recently, though, the Harry Potter series and Christopher Paolini's Inheritance trilogy have offered page counts exceeding what anyone thought middle-grade readers could handle. And YA novels-in-verse, which have grown in popularity in recent years, offer familiar page counts but spare text.

The Society of Children's Book Writers and Illustrators (SCBWI) offers length guidelines in terms of the appropriate number of manuscript pages for various genres (meaning the number of

How Do I Break in to Children's Writing?

pages a writer would submit to a publisher). For fiction, they suggest middle-grade page counts range anywhere from 40 to 150 manuscript pages and YA from 175 to 200 pages.

Consult listings in the current edition of *Children's Writer's & Illustrator's Market* for information on both fiction and nonfiction word counts for various publishers. Also consult submission guidelines for individual publishers that interest you. Spending some time in a children's bookstore looking at mid-grade and YA titles from a number of publishers is a good exercise as well.

It's unlikely your work will be automatically rejected if your submission exceeds a publisher's guidelines by few thousand words. However, if they generally publish mid-grade books that are around 25,000 words and you send them 65,000, you'll likely get a quick rejection. Try your best to stay in the ballpark, but also do what's appropriate for your story.

What kinds of subject matter are most popular in novels for young readers?

The interest areas of young readers are limitless. They enjoy contemporary, fantasy, mystery, historical novels, and more—trends in subject matter for children's books often reflect trends in adult publishing. Realistic treatment of current themes, including conflict with siblings or peers, dating and relationships, and struggles with school or family situations, interests both middle-grade and YA readers. Contemporary YA novels often delve into edgier material, including sexual situations and drug use. Books written for middle-grade and YA readers are often geared either for boys or girls, and the protagonist is generally several years older than the reader. It is best to keep adult involvement in children's novels to a minimum, allowing the protagonists to solve their problems without adult intervention.

I am interested in writing children's stories for elementary school children. Where can I obtain a suitable word list for these stories?

Publishers of trade books for leisure reading by children do not use formal vocabulary lists. Don't hesitate to use a big word in a children's story if you think it's the best word, as long as young readers can ascertain the meaning through the context of the story. After all, books are great tools for increasing young readers' vocabularies.

Publishers of textbooks for the primary grades often have formal restrictions on vocabulary. Consult individual educational publishers for vocabulary requirements. You might also refer to *The Children's Writer's Word Book*, by Alijandra Mogilner, which includes a dictionary of words and the grade levels for which they are appropriate.

CRAFT AND TECHNIQUE

I've always wanted to write for children, and I've got some ideas for stories. I thought I'd start out writing picture books, since they're nice and short. Can you offer some tips for writing them?

Don't let the length of picture books fool you—writing them is difficult. You have very few words—not to mention a limited vocabulary—in which to tell your story. You've also got to keep in mind that a good part of a picture book story is told in the pictures. Some picture books have no words at all. Picture books top off at about 1,000 words, but for editors and readers, shorter is better.

The text of picture books is generally only twenty-eight pages. (There are thirty-two total pages, a few of which are taken up by endpapers, the title page, copyright page, etc.) Creating a book dummy is often a helpful exercise for picture book writers. Breaking up your text into twenty-eight pages can help you identify many problems in your manuscript. Ask yourself a few questions as you go through your mock-up: Is there an illustratable action on each spread? Is there a beginning, a middle, and an end? Are you writing out details that could be expressed through the illustrations? Is the text too long? Read and study as many picture books as you can get your hands on to help in your learning process.

I see a lot of rhyming picture books in the stores, but I've heard editors at conferences discourage submitting rhyming text. What gives?

Indeed there are a number of rhyming picture books on the market. They are fun to read aloud and kids enjoy them. And new writers seem to gravitate toward rhyming stories. Rhyme is difficult to write, however. As one editor put it, you're either Seuss, or you're so not Seuss. Anyone can write a rhyming text—only a select few authors can write a great rhyming text. And nothing will get your picture book manuscript rejected quicker than bad rhyme. If you write in rhyme, be sure to read your work aloud (better yet, have someone new to the manuscript read it to you) to observe places where the rhyme or rhythm is awkward or forced. Rhyme should feel good coming off your tongue; it should flow. Again—read. Pick up rhyming books by master rhymers like Mary Ann Hoberman, Sarah Weeks, and Lisa Wheeler.

I've tried to write biographical pieces for children's magazines, but I can't seem to get the total picture of the subject's life into a short article that children would understand. Any suggestions?

One of the hardest things about writing biographies for children is deciding what to leave out. This is especially true when the writer is confined to the length of a magazine article. When researching your subject, pick out one important event and focus the entire article on it. You might concentrate on some childhood experience, if you are lucky enough to find information on it. Then your ending can state what this child grew up to do that made him famous. Lacking any good information on your subject's childhood, it's still a good idea to open the article with a reference to his early years in order to let young readers know that these famous people were children once, too. Then focus the article on an incident important in your subject's adulthood—probably the one that made him famous—but keep it simple. Force yourself to delete anything extraneous, remembering that children don't have the conceptual framework to remember historical details.

And it's okay, when working with the basic facts, to create conversations and incidents that will best dramatize them. However, don't devise anything that would not be in keeping with the character of the subject or times.

I've been trying to sell a children's fantasy with no luck at all. What could be wrong with my book?

Fantasy for young readers has enjoyed a resurgence in popularity thanks to authors like J.K. Rowling, Christopher Paolini, and Phillip Pullman. But fantasy is difficult to write because it demands that you make the unbelievable believable. If you are just starting out as a children's writer, you may need practice writing here-and-now stories before you attempt to write fantasy. A solid understanding of the techniques for establishing plot, character, setting, and viewpoint are necessary, because a fantasy story must be as logical as any other story. It must give the illusion of reality.

It may be that the kind of fantasy you're writing just isn't in vogue in the current marketplace. The market for stories like the classical fairy tales of Hans Christian Andersen and the Brothers Grimm is nearly nonexistent today; also, few fantasies today feature inanimate objects, like in classics such as *The Little Engine That Could.*

It seems like a lot of what makes up adult mystery novels, such as crime, violence, and suspense, just doesn't belong in children's mysteries. What elements can be included?

You are right in assuming children's mystery editors shy away from descriptive violence—especially murder. Most juvenile mysteries contain elements of humor along with the hair-raising suspense that makes the story effective. Tight plotting and a fantastic climax are important, as is a main character that is actively involved in solving the problem of the story. To learn of current subject matter and techniques used in writing children's mysteries, read and analyze books from that section of your bookstore (for the most current topics and techniques) or public library.

GETTING YOUR STORIES PUBLISHED

I've written a few short stories for children and would like to get them published. The problem is, I don't know how or where to sell them. What would you advise?

Markets for your work can be found in *Children's Writer's & Illustrator's Market.* Children's magazines are geared to specific age levels and publish both fiction and nonfiction. Get some sample copies of magazines you think might be prospects for your stories and read a few issues before you submit your manuscripts to the editors. Also, be sure to visit their websites—most children's magazines have websites offering sample stories and tables of contents, writers guidelines, theme lists, and more.

Should I include illustrations with my picture book manuscript when I submit it to publishers?

No, the publisher will choose the illustrator. Writers do not need to find an illustrator or offer illustration suggestions. If your story will be unclear without illustrations—you have included pages where the story is told entirely by the picture, for instance—include illustration notes within your text.

I'm collaborating on a picture book with an illustrator. How should we go about submitting our material once we've gotten our project together?

Partnering with an illustrator is not recommended, particularly for first-time authors. As stated above, publishers prefer to match up authors and illustrators for picture book projects. It's very difficult to get manuscript-illustration packages by collaborators accepted by publishers. (Professional illustrators who also write do better in this arena.) If an editor does not like part of the package, the whole package will likely be rejected. It's best to submit your manuscript on its own.

I have an idea for a series of children's books. How would I sell this series to a publisher?

It can be difficult, particularly for newer authors, to sell a fiction series to a publisher right out of the gate. You might try querying publishers about the first book in your series and mention that you have ideas for subsequent books with the same characters. Once you sell the first book and it shows good sales numbers, publishers will be open to capitalizing on that and may be willing to continue with sequels. You might also consider contacting a book packager. These companies often produce series for trade publishers. Book packagers are marked with a special icon in Children's Writer's & Illustrator's Market.

Do I need an agent to get my children's book published?

No, you don't. There are a number of children's publishers who accept unsolicited manuscripts and query letters from children's writers, so whether to pursue an agent is up to you. Working with an agent, however, can help get your work to editors much more quickly than going through the slush pile. And an agent may get you a better contract than you could get on your own. But if you're a creative type who is also comfortable marketing your work and negotiating contracts, you can pursue publication on your own.

For listing of agents who handle children's material, see Children's Writer's & Illustrator's Market and Guide to Literary Agents. There is also a list of agents available to members of the Society of Children's Book Writers & Illustrators (www.scbwi.org).

WHERE TO FIND OUT MORE

Books

Children's Writer's & Illustrators Market offers more than seven hundred listings for book publishers, agents, magazines, and art representatives.

You Can Write Children's Books and You Can Write Children's Books Workbook, by Tracey Dils, are excellent guides for beginners writing for children.

Children's Writer's Word Book, by Alijandra Mogilner, is a comprehensive reference on what words are appropriate throughout the grade levels and also what topics and issues are taught in each grade.

Writing & Selling The YA Novel, by K. L. Going, covers everything from plot, setting, characters, and dialogue to revision and approaching publishers.

Writing Picture Books, by Ann Whitford Paul, covers researching the picture books market, creating characters, point of view, plotting, and tips on writing rhyme.

Websites

Write4Kids (www.write4kids.com) offers one of the biggest online collections of free how-to information for children's writers.

Kid Magazine Writers maintains an online magazine for children's writers at www.kidmagwriters.com.

The Purple Crayon, a resource site run for children's writers by a children's book editor, is at www.underdown.org.

SmartWriters (www.smartwriters.com) is dedicated to providing professional information to children's writers.

Cheryl Klein (www.cherylklein.com) is a repository of in-depth writing and publishing advice by a senior editor at Scholastic's Arthur A. Levine Books.

Cynsations (cynthialeitichsmith.blogspot.com) offers a wealth of resources for children's and YA writers, including an exhaustive archive of editor, agent, publisher, publicist, and art director interviews.

Society of Children's Book Writers & Illustrators (www.scbwi.org) is the must-join organization for anyone who wants to publish material for young readers. The site includes an online community, and much of the site's useful information is available for nonmembers, too.

CHAPTER 9

HOW DO I MARKET MY SCRIPTS?

Some of the pitfalls of scriptwriting were pinpointed by Hubert Selby Jr. in a *New York Times* article: "A couple of years ago a network was going to do a series on the Ten Commandments," he recalled, "and I wrote one of the two-hour segments. The entire project was ultimately cancelled, probably because it was too radical. But the thing that really amused me was the fact that the network only took five of the Commandments with an option on the other five. That, my friend, is television."

While many other types of work can be successfully marketed directly by the writer, scripts usually require the intermediary of an agent to make it to the producer. In fact, breaking in to Hollywood almost always requires that you know someone who knows someone; trying to make it as an outsider will likely lead to frustration and failure. This chapter is provided as a resource for writers who might have a passing interest in what scriptwriting entails or how it works, but it doesn't even begin to scratch the surface of the movie and TV industry; you'll need to seek other resources for a real beginner's education; preferably, you should take a course.

SCRIPT MECHANICS

What's the proper way to type a movie or TV script?

It's too complex to describe here; you should look for a sample script and reference a book on scriptwriting. If you plan to spend any amount of time scriptwriting, you should invest in scriptwriting software, such as Final Draft, Movie Magic Screenwriter, or Dramatica Pro.

I am writing a screenplay for the movie industry and need to learn more about the camera shots.

Your best bet would be to study some actual movie scripts to get a feel for how this is done. Look online for websites that sell scripts or let you view them for free—Simply Scripts (www.simpl scripts.com) is a good place to start. Alternatively, several publishers produce books that contain the complete scripts of both classic and contemporary movies.

Usually it's not desirable to include production technicalities (such as camera angles) in a script you're selling on speculation. Those details will be added by the production staff after the script is purchased.

BREAKING IN TO SCRIPTWRITING

Is it crucial for scriptwriters to find an agent?

It is not crucial to obtain the services of an agent; you can always try sending query letters directly to producers and ask them if you can submit your script. But you're likely to have an easier time if you find an agent, especially if you live outside the Hollywood community and have little opportunity to make connections with the people who would be interested in your work.

Under what conditions will television producers look at a script submitted directly by the writer rather than through an agent?

If you submit your script with a signed release form and indicate that it is registered with Writers Guild of America (WGA), you might be able to get a producer to look at it. The release form makes it clear that you understand your idea may not be new to the producer, and the company is under no obligation to you if, although your script is rejected, a similar idea appears later on television. To avoid having the script returned unopened, be sure to type "Release Form Enclosed" on the outside of the envelope.

How can a writer register a script?

The Writers Guild of America (www.wga.org) can register your script for a fee. Registering simply verifies that you were the author of that particular script on that particular date. The registration comes in handy if a similar story is produced later and you wish to challenge the other author, the producer, or the agent.

I would like to propose a series concept to a television network. How do I go about doing that while protecting my idea?

First, unless you are famous or are willing to pay millions of dollars for the production of a new series, no one in Hollywood will consider working with a first-time screenwriter on a new series concept. This is why almost every television writer breaks in to the business by writing and selling a spec script (an original script for a current show).

Additionally, the only way to be taken seriously as a first-time scriptwriter is to write a complete script—not an outline, synopsis, or a page of ideas. Network executives, producers, and directors receive countless query letters and phone calls from amateurs who think they can sell their ideas. Unfortunately, this is not how it works in Hollywood. Ideas, no matter how wonderful they sound to you, are a dime a dozen. If you give the same idea to a dozen writers, you'll get a dozen completely different scripts. What matters in this business is the execution of that idea—the specific character traits, dialogue, and plot turns that make a script into a movie or TV show. Here's an example: "A sports team made up of players without a shred of athletic talent struggles to overcome far superior opponents. Through perseverance and blind luck, the team transforms from an underdog to a contender." Is this the idea behind _The Bad News Bears_, _Major League_, or _Necessary Roughness_? The answer: all three.

What's worse is that there are nine thousand professional screenwriters and tens of thousands of aspiring writers throwing out ideas every year. With those kinds of numbers, similarity of ideas is inevitable. In the business, it's called simultaneous creation. We all watch the same TV shows, movies, news broadcasts, and plays. We all read the same books, magazines, and newspapers. When multiple people are exposed to the same stimuli, they develop very similar ideas. Your friends and family might think you have an original idea, but there are tens of thousands of other creative souls out there, and at least one of them has had the same idea.

This also explains why you cannot copyright ideas. Copyright does not protect ideas or concepts. New scriptwriters worry about having their ideas stolen all the time. Since you cannot copyright your idea and can only copyright the way in which you tell the story, I highly recommend writing a complete script before you hand over an idea. Your script is your key to the front door of Hollywood.

What is the difference between a synopsis and a treatment?

A synopsis is a short, concise summary of the story. A treatment is a scene-by-scene explanation, indicating specific action, motivation, possible special effects, etc. It provides a fuller interpretation of the script's potential. Established writers can sell a script on the basis of a treatment, but beginners must have a complete script if they wish to make that important first sale.

I've cruised around the various websites that advertise "coverage" for as low as forty-nine dollars to ninety-nine dollars or more. What is coverage? How does it aid in selling my screenplay?

When you submit a script to a producer, the producer or a professional script reader will write coverage. Coverage is a one- or two-page synopsis of your script, detailing what does and doesn't work. This gives a producer or studio executive a quick sense of the screenplay without having to read it. Coverage is usually broken down into five categories—premise/concept, characterization, dialogue, story/structure, and set/production values.

A screenwriter might want to pay someone to write coverage for her script so she has a second opinion about what does and doesn't work in the script before she submits it to a producer. If you submit a bad script to a producer and the producer writes negative coverage, your name is placed "in the system" and you may never be able to submit another script to that producer.

Generally, coverage is very critical. Producers and professional readers are looking to separate the good from the bad, and no one wants to risk her career on a bad script.

Is it possible to make a decent living writing scripts that don't necessarily become movies?

Yes, it is possible, but few writers make a stable living doing such work. The only people who really make money on scripts that don't get produced are staff writers for television series and the lucky scriptwriters who are hired to develop novels, stories, and other material into scripts for producers.

If you live in or around Hollywood and can impress a producer with your writing skills, a producer may hire you to write a script based on material she purchases elsewhere; this is called a development deal. For example, if a producer purchases the rights to a best-selling book, the producer will hire a scriptwriter to develop that book into a script. In most cases, the scriptwriter will be paid for her services regardless of whether the script is produced.

Development deals usually pay from $30,000 to $500,000, depending on the experience of the writer. That said, the majority of development deals are given to scriptwriters close to Hollywood. So if you don't live in Southern California, make plans to move there.

An overall deal is one in which a scriptwriter is paid (usually in the low millions) to work exclusively with a single entity (a studio, a network, a producer, or a production company). Unfortunately, very few scriptwriters are able to land such a deal.

Is there a way I can submit story ideas to movie producers and directors without writing the entire script?

The only way to be taken seriously as a first-time television or screenplay writer is to write a complete script. There are plenty of scam artists out there who will try to sell you on the myth of "sell an idea, make a million bucks," but the only person getting rich off that myth is the scam artist.

For years I have dreamed about adapting my favorite novel into a screenplay for film. When do I require the original author's permission? How does one go about acquiring such permission? Does the original author have any rights to the screenplay?

Many amateur scriptwriters have dreams of adapting their favorite book (or even their own book) into a feature film. Unfortunately, few will ever be able to write an adaptation because of the way the film industry does business.

First, understand that even before a book is published, either the author's agent or the book's publisher will send the manuscript to production companies and studios all over the country. The initial goal is to make as much money as possible from the sale of the film rights. So, chances are, if a book has been even remotely successful, the film adaptation rights have already been sold.

Now, assuming the rights haven't already been sold, there are several things you need to consider. First, you have to find out who holds the rights. The author may have retained film rights, or the author may have turned them over to the publisher. Is the book or story in the public domain? The reason so many classical stories and novels are adapted into feature films is that the stories are in the public domain—anyone can adapt them to film or television.

If the story/book is not in the public domain, call the publisher and ask for the name of the writer's agent or attorney, whoever handles rights. After you have this information, call or write the person, explaining that you are interested in developing the work into a screenplay. That person will then tell you whether the work is already under option or otherwise unavailable for adaptation. If you're lucky, the representative will tell you that the work is available and you can begin negotiations.

If the book is new, the price will be high. If the book has been around for many years and has been rejected by multiple production companies and studios, the price will drop. Keep in mind, however, that you will probably have trouble selling the script if the book has already been rejected by many producers. If the book has been around for a while and no one has purchased rights, you may be able to convince the representative to give you a two-year option for free. This means that you have the rights to adapt the book for two years. If you are successful and sell the script, the representative will take a percentage of the sale price. If at the end of two years you are unable to make a sale, the rights revert to the original owner(s).

Once you have obtained option rights to the work, you can begin querying agents and producers. That said, you will have a much greater chance of success if you have a completed script ready for the agent or producer to review after she accepts your query.

Adaptations can be successful, but because of the rights involved, most scriptwriters have a greater chance of success with a completely original screenplay. Still, if you feel passionate about the story and are willing to put up with the possible legal headaches, adaptations can be great fun.

WHERE TO FIND OUT MORE

Books

Story, by Robert McKee, is one of the best-selling instruction books on the craft of screenwriting and is also helpful to fiction writers.

Making a Good Script Great, by Linda Seger, helps the beginning scriptwriter with characterization and script structure.

The Writer's Journey: Mythic Structure for Writers, by Chris Vogler, details the archetypes that are used over and over again in successful Hollywood movies.

The Screenwriter's Bible, by David Trottier, is an excellent starting point, especially if you don't know the terminology of Hollywood or how to format a script.

Screenwriting Formula: Why It Works & How To Use It, by Rob Tobin, shows how to get a script from the page to production.

The 101 Habits of Highly Successful Screenwriters: Insiders' Secrets from Hollywood's Top Writers, by Karl Iglesias, features interviews with 14 screenwriters, touching on such subjects as collaboration, schmoozing, discipline, Hollywood, and story pitching.

Websites

Alex Epstein publishes a detailed FAQ for beginning screenwriters at www.teako170.com/faq.html.

Done Deal Professional (www.donedealpro.com) allows you to find out, for a fee, who's buying what scripts. Offers some valuable free content as well.

The Artful Writer (http://artfulwriter.com) is a blog for professional screenwriters. Amateurs can learn a lot here.

The Hollywood Creative Directory (www.hcdonline.com) is an essential print and online directory for anyone looking to sell a script or find an agent.

Drew's Script-O-Rama (www.script-o-rama.com) is a massive database of scripts. If you want to write screenplays or teleplays, you have to read them.

CHAPTER 10

HOW DO I START A FREELANCE WRITING CAREER?

Freelance writers who think only in terms of articles, stories, poems, or books often overlook hundreds of other opportunities for using their writing skills, many of them in their own backyard. If you've been walking too narrow a path as a writer, broaden your horizons with some of the ideas suggested in this chapter. The range of writing opportunities open to you is limited only by your imagination.

GETTING STARTED

For many years, I've had a deep-seated desire to write, and I'd love to break in to the field and make enough money to support my family. How much money can I make freelancing?

A lot of money can be made by freelancing, but most writers receive fairly little income while they perfect their writing and marketing abilities. There are hundreds of full-time freelancers who make good livings but who started slow—freelancing on the side while holding down a day job. Your best bet is to begin with magazine articles, since the market is large and varied, and fodder for articles is everywhere.

How long does it take to become a competent professional freelancer?

There's no good answer to this question. Writers, even established ones, are continuously developing their skills, improving their style, and learning more about their writing, their markets, and the world. In that sense, you'll never stop striving to better yourself. A good test of your competence is whether your work is being accepted by publications or book publishers you respect. Being unpublished doesn't necessarily mean you don't have writing skills, but sales will probably make you feel more like a professional writer.

What are the advantages and disadvantages I might face as a full-time freelance writer?

There are many advantages to being a full-time freelance writer. You are your own boss. You control your working hours and, in a sense, the amount of money you make. You practice as a profession the thing you enjoy most. You may have much more opportunity to be creative than if you worked as a staff writer. You choose what you want to write about and get paid for learning something new through research. You can work at home, and if you're a parent, you can save on child-care expenses. In addition, the research involved in writing can bring you into contact with interesting, stimulating people.

On the other hand, most writers face innumerable rejections (and no income) before making their first sale. To avoid losing faith in yourself and your career at this stage, it helps if you are thick-skinned, self-confident, and persistent. Unlike a job in a company, freelance work does not bring regular paychecks in regular amounts. Further, you are responsible for collecting your own payments. You receive no fringe benefits, such as the insurance and retirement benefits that company employees receive. Being self-employed, you must spend part of your working time on administrative tasks like bookkeeping and filing income tax and social security forms.

Writers usually work alone, and this can be a disadvantage (depending on your personality), especially after a number of days without contact with your colleagues. If you're married, it's best to have a spouse who approves of your career and all it entails, since your irregular working hours and irregular income will affect him or her.

How are professional writers able to write enough to stay afloat?

Most writers are obsessively attracted to their work; that is, they have an inner urge to write. Professional writers find that the satisfaction their writing brings is enough to outweigh the deadlines, rejections, and other problems they face. On a more practical level, self-employed writers know that if they don't write, they don't eat, so they structure their work as though they had a regular job working for an employer. For example, self-employed writers begin at the same time every day (but not necessarily in the morning), produce the same number of words or pages each day, and establish a place (at home or away from home) to be used exclusively for writing. In addition, they make their working hours known to friends and family to minimize distractions. Finally, professionals get maximum mileage out of the work they produce; they resell articles, use one session of research to fuel two or more related pieces, and employ other tactics to maximize results.

How much should I earn as a writer before I can feel secure enough to quit my job and become a full-time freelancer? Can writers really make a living freelancing?

It's safe to start thinking about becoming a full-time freelance writer when your freelancing income over a period of several months equals or is greater than the salary earned on your regular job in that same time period. Plenty of writers have succeeded after breaking away from regular full-time employment, but the road to success isn't easy. You'll be better off if you enter into the venture with your eyes wide open to the disadvantages that you'll face. If you quit your job, you'll lose your steady income and all fringe benefits, like health and life insurance, retirement security, and paid vacations. You must also be prepared to discipline yourself to eight or more hours at the keyboard every day. It's not poor writing skills that defeat so many full-time freelancers, but a lack of economic preparedness.

Start planning your switch to self-employment about a year in advance. Begin to cut down on your spending, try to accrue about six months' income in your savings account, and, several months before the break, begin to step up your editorial contacts and magazine sales. A clear view of the difficulties to be encountered in the first months, some penny-pinching, and a lot of hard work are the keys to succeeding in the field of full-time freelance writing.

I'm not making as much money as I had hoped I would as a freelance writer. Can you suggest other sources of income that might utilize my skills as a writer?

There are many part-time, seasonal, or one-shot opportunities that will help you during the lean periods of your writing career. For example, a local advertising agency may need someone to write an annual report or do other types of staff-related work for clients. If your town is large enough to attract a convention, you might find out if any groups need someone to staff the press office and act as a liaison with the local media. Are there any local printers in need of competent writing, copyediting, or proofreading for themselves or their customers? If you've had enough experience, you might consider teaching journalism at the high school or community college level.

The first place you should look, though, is online. Many freelance opportunities can be found in your local area or across the globe—these days, it doesn't matter where you are located, as long as you can do a quality job by the deadline. See the end of this chapter for websites to help you get started.

NICHES

How does a writer get started in theater and movie criticism?

Start locally with a publication that doesn't have a staff critic. Don't expect to make much money (if any!)—do it because you love it.

Do I need special training to write book reviews?

You don't need special training, but you should know how to write interesting, brief reviews that editors will want to publish. Most local newspapers pay little or nothing for reviews, although the reviewer gets to keep the book. When contacting book review editors to see if they can use your work, enclose a sample review you've written of a relatively new book.

Do the publishers of comic books buy freelance material?

Different comic book publishers have different policies concerning the purchase of freelance material. Usually the editorial staff determines current needs, then assigns a story to a writer and designates its length. Beginners in the field often start by writing for fanzines—small, often amateur productions.

How can I get my comic strip published?

You can submit to newspaper markets yourself, or you can market your work to various national syndicates. It would probably be best to try to sell your strip to noncompeting local markets first. When submitting to a newspaper or syndicate, you should have finished art samples to submit and perhaps six months of ideas to carry on the strip.

Is there a market for freelancers interested in researching and writing other people's family histories? I'd like to try that kind of writing, but where do I find potential customers?

Most of the market for writing family histories comes from the elderly, so you could try placing ads in local newsletters to senior citizens or on bulletin boards in places you know they gather. If you make yourself known to area museums, librarians, and historians, they can refer inquiries to you.

Where can I find names and addresses of entertainers needing comedy routines?

Watch for rising young entertainers on TV comedy shows and contact these newcomers in care of those programs. You might also subscribe to *Variety*, the show-business newspaper that mentions the names and places where lesser-known comedians appear. Write the performers in care of the clubs where they appear.

I think I would do well as a technical writer. What steps should I take to break in to the field?

While the goal of creative writing is to entertain, the primary goal of technical writing is the accurate transmission of information. Technical writing, then, can be described as putting complicated information into plain language in a format that is easy to understand. The tone is objective and favors content over style. (This does not mean, however, that you should present the subject in a formal, stunted style.) Above all, technical writing should be concise, complete, clear, and consistent. The best way to achieve all these is to make sure your writing is well organized.

By far the biggest area for technical writers is the computer industry, though there are a wide variety of possible assignments, including preparation of customer letters, utility bills, owner manuals, insurance benefit packages, and even contracts (some states have laws requiring that contracts and insurance policies be written in simple English). In any technical field, writers who can bridge the gap between the engineers who design things and the customers who use them are in high demand.

Technical writers do not necessarily need formal training in the areas they cover. To the contrary, one of the greatest talents a technical writer brings to a project is the ability to take a step back from the technical details and see the subject from a different perspective than the engineers, scientists, and experts. Thus, a technical writer becomes familiar with a subject by interviewing experts, reviewing drawings, studying specifications, and examining product samples.

Technical writers themselves often shy away from the term freelance writer, preferring to be known instead as independent contractors or consultants. This probably has a lot to do with the fact that technical writers work mostly with corporations, where the term independent contractor sounds more impressive. It's very important to establish and maintain a high degree of credibility when working with firms.

The number of ways to enter the technical field are as varied as the people entering it. If you're cold-calling large companies, you'll want to contact the manager of technical communications or the manager of documentation. Local employment agencies may also be of service.

If you lack experience, build a portfolio by volunteering to write material for a nonprofit organization or offer to help your colleagues prepare reports and presentations. If you are interested in pursuing this type of work, it is probably a good idea to join the Society for Technical Communication (www.stc.org), where you can network to gain contacts in the industry. Many businesses hire writers from the STC talent pool.

Some books that might help you learn more about this field include *The Elements of Technical Writing*, by Gary Blake and Robert W. Bly, and *The Tech Writer's Survival Guide*, by Janet Van Wicklen.

What qualifications does a person need to write advertising copy?

There are two main reasons that an advertising agency or PR firm might hire freelance help. Sometimes expertise is needed, such as in writing about engineering, medicine, accounting, etc. Or the firm must produce a large volume of collateral material and find themselves in need of freelance help when the workload gets too heavy. This collateral material can take the form of a postcard, brochure, or direct-mail piece. Sometimes a company will look for someone who can shepherd a project from conceptualization to production. Other times they may only need simple copywriting.

Some large- and medium-size organizations may have their own in-house creative department in need of occasional (or not so occasional) assistance. Hospitals are especially open to freelance help because federal cutbacks and outside competition have forced them to walk a financial tightrope.

To land freelance assignments with an advertising agency or public relations firm, you usually need hard experience writing ad copy. However, a willingness to study what's already been produced and for whom, and to hit the streets asking for business, could get you copywriting jobs in a number of different areas. Small businesses, nonprofit groups, and industries that don't have advertising agencies usually rely on outside help for their advertising, and although they pay less than the big ad agencies, they are more willing to work with an inexperienced person.

To learn more about how to start writing copy for corporations, businesses, and organizations, consult two of the best-selling guides for copywriters: *The Well-Fed Writer*, by Peter Bowerman, and *The Copywriter's Handbook*, by Robert W. Bly.

How can I get started in ghostwriting?

When a book is ghostwritten, the person whose name appears on the book as primary author does little or none of the actual writing. She is merely a source of information—providing content,

How Do I Start a Freelance Writing Career?

background, information, and (hopefully) credibility. Typically, this person is a celebrity or someone well respected in her field of expertise. While she has the experience and the name recognition that can make for a best-selling book, she lacks professional writing credentials. As a result, the so-called author relies on a more experienced writer—a ghostwriter—to put her ideas into book form.

The ghostwriter gathers information for the book by interviewing the author, and will often conduct her own research and interview several other sources as well for background material. While each collaboration is different, the author usually will review the manuscript and possibly edit it for content. For their part, ghostwriters may be credited as a co-author or get no visible credit at all.

The arrangement that a ghostwriter walks into is inherently more complex than the typical relationship between a writer and publisher (which is already complex enough). It's easy for misunderstandings to arise between the so-called author and publisher, with the ghostwriter being caught in the middle. In one sense, the ghostwriter is a translator—taking what the author has to offer and trying to deliver what the publisher expects. The best way to diffuse potential conflict is to clearly map out in writing what each party expects from the arrangement.

There are a number of ways to break in to ghostwriting. One is to seek out a rising star in sports, entertainment, business, or politics. Publishers are often in search of new talent and new celebrities. Armed with a collaboration agreement and the right amount of talent, you can sell your services to a publisher.

Very often, successful executives or entrepreneurs look for writers who can help them self-publish a book of their own. The finished books are then distributed through their businesses to clients, co-workers, and relatives. This is a great way to get work and hone your talents, and possibly even make a name for yourself.

What are the markets for translations of foreign stories, articles, and books?

Few magazines are interested in translation material, but U.S. book publishers often issue translations of previously published foreign works (and vice versa). To find U.S. publishers of foreign works, look in *Writer's Market*.

I speak and read French and found a marvelous short story in a foreign magazine. I'd like to translate and sell the story to an American magazine. How do I do it?

If you have a facility with another language and would like to submit a translation of a foreign short story, you must write to the publication in which the story first appeared and get permission from the author and the publisher to do your translation. Whether you would be required to share payment from the American publisher with the original author and/or publisher depends on what arrangements you make with them. It's always best to clarify this point before you approach any American editor, so there is no delay if he is interested in your idea.

What qualifications do I need to write greeting card verse?

You need nothing more than the ability to study existing greeting card material and to provide appropriate copy to greeting card editors. Greeting card verse sells best if your ideas are original and carry a me-to-you message in a conversational tone. Enthusiasm is important, since writing verse for greeting card publishers is not as easy as it might seem. Companies that publish greeting cards can be found through the WritersMarket.com subscription service.

Are recipes copyrighted?

Simple lists of ingredients cannot be copyrighted, but the directions for how to make something from those ingredients can be copyrighted.

A friend of mine says hobby magazines are a good place to start getting published. Are they?

If you have ever designed a pattern for an embroidery project, made your own Christmas tree ornaments, or built a home darkroom, then craft, hobby, and handyman magazines might want to hear how you did it, step by step. Since these how-to articles are relatively simple to write (and you probably already subscribe to magazines that buy such pieces), many beginning writers find them an easy way to get started. Then you can move on to articles that require more research, organization, and writing skills.

Some authors rewrite unusual news stories to submit to other markets. Are there laws against using and reusing ideas culled from newspapers?

News items are facts open to anyone's interpretation, but feature articles usually have a specific angle or slant, and involve the research, selectivity, and interpretations of the individual writer. The expression of these elements is protected by the overall copyright on the paper or by the syndicate, if it is a syndicated feature. You may write a new article using the facts of the story, or use the original item to suggest a new slant and new research—in short, a new article.

FILLERS

What is meant by filler material? What is it used for?

A filler is any of a variety of short pieces of writing, including tips, anecdotes, short humor, recipes, proverbs, household hints, unusual trivia, brain teasers, puzzles, insightful quotes, and news clippings. Although editors originally used them to fill empty spaces at the ends of columns, fillers are now often used as regular magazine features. Because they are short and focus on one point, fillers are good practice for beginning writers and give novices a greater chance of being published.

One can find ideas for fillers anywhere, from daily reading to strange road signs. Everyday experiences often provide humor or helpful tips, but you may have to look hard at what's going on around you to see something worthwhile for publication. If you think you might like to write fillers, study the fillers in several magazines to get an idea of what editors are looking for, and go to it!

Some magazine editors say they buy anecdotes. What is an anecdote?

An anecdote is a short narrative slice of life, a description of a particular incident, usually biographical, autobiographical, or stemming from something the author has observed. Anecdotes may employ humor, dialogue, or unexpected endings to share insight or illustrate a point. Successful anecdotes will evoke laughter, surprise, sympathy, or some other emotional reaction on the part of the reader. Due to their brevity, they work quite well as fillers. Here is one of many good examples that can be found in *Reader's Digest*: "A woman who works for the state of Louisiana got a call from a man who paused when she told him the name of her agency. He then asked her to repeat it again. 'It's the Governor's Office for Elderly Affairs,' she told him again. There was another pause. 'For gosh sakes, sign me up,' he said. 'I didn't do too well when I was young.'" (This anecdote came from Smiley Anders of the *Baton Rouge Morning Advocate*.)

When writing an anecdote, make sure that your narration is uncomplicated and free from extraneous detail. Since description has to be short, every word used should be essential to the picture. The impact of the anecdote comes with a good punchy ending.

What is a newsbreak?

A newsbreak is a newsworthy event or item. For example, an opening of a new retail shoe store in a town might be a newsbreak for a shoe trade journal that publishes news items of new openings. Some publications (such as *The New Yorker*) use newsbreaks in a different sense—that is, to indicate a typo or an error in reporting that appears in a printed news story. Such newsbreaks—followed by tongue-in-cheek editorial commentary (known as a tag line)—are bought from contributors and used in publications as filler items.

Is it okay to submit identical fillers to several markets?

There's no reason why you can't, as long as you don't submit identical fillers to markets with common audiences. Editors of magazines with similar readerships don't want to see a filler they just bought from you published in a competitive magazine. You may want to indicate that the material is going to more than one publication at the same time by noting "This is a simultaneous submission to publications with differing readership."

I have written several anecdotes and other fillers, from my own personal experience. How can I find magazines that might be interested in buying these fillers?

Successful marketing is a combination of writing what you want to write and what magazine editors want to print. Read *Writer's Market* to find magazines that publish what you'd like to sell (anecdotes, for example) and then look at copies of those magazines to help you get a feeling for the style, content, and audience they cater to. Knowing what an editor is looking for before you send in your work will save you from the quick rejection you'd get if, for example, you sent your personal anecdotes to a political magazine that only publishes bureaucratic bloopers as fillers. Your chances of making a sale will be greatly enhanced if you are careful about deciding where to send your work.

How much money can I hope to get for my published fillers?

Depending on the magazine, the filler, and how it is used, the average payment can be nothing at all (except maybe free product), to a hundred dollars or more. Magazines that place a lot of emphasis on filler items pay several hundred dollars for a published item. See *Writer's Market* for payment rates.

Several months ago I sent a few jokes and a puzzle to a magazine. I have heard nothing from the editor so far. What kind of reply can I expect from the editor, and how long should I wait before inquiring?

Although some editors may hold a filler for six months before using it, if you have not received any sort of acknowledgment within two months, you should not inquire, but rather send your piece elsewhere. Due to the large volume of fillers that many editors receive, replying to individual contributors is often impossible. If you do receive a rejection slip, it may be very dry and to the point, or it may encourage you to keep trying.

GOING ONLINE

Ten years ago, freelance writers had to rely on market directories, personal contacts, and a bit of luck to find new opportunities and projects. Today, the Internet probably provides more opportunities for freelance work (and research and ideas) than you'll ever be able to pursue. It does take a critical eye, though, to ferret out the quality projects and information. Here are a few tips to help you get started.

Where do I find writing opportunities online?

When talking about online markets, we can divide the opportunities into several categories.

> **Print publications**. Most traditional magazines have online counterparts that publish original content. To find out if a print magazine does publish original online content, check its website or submission guidelines.

> **Electronic publications**. Online-only publications may not pay as much as print publications (or may not pay at all), but they can provide a beginner with good experience. Some online-only publications that pay for content are listed in directories like Writers Market.com.

E-newsletters. Many electronic newsletters accept content from freelancers. Check with the editors and see if they accept freelance material.

Corporate websites. It's easy to research companies and businesses that might need freelancers; those that are known for hiring freelancers usually have information posted especially for them.

Freelance writing sites. The most popular sites for freelancers contain market information or postings from people looking to hire writers and editors. The largest circulating e-newsletter for freelancers is Writers Weekly; sign up at www.writersweekly.com.

What's the difference between writing for the Web and writing for print?

People read copy differently online. They read more slowly, they scan, their eyes bounce around the screen. As a result, you must adjust your writing style to suit. Keep your writing focused and brief. If you drone on too long, readers will be tempted to click away. Break longer sentences into shorter sentences, and break stories into chunks, with catchy subheads.

FINDING A WRITING CAREER

Being a full-time freelance writer is a challenge, and many writers opt to use their writing skill to bring home a regular salary. People who seek full-time writing or editing jobs usually traverse one of two routes. They attend journalism school, or they acquire a good liberal arts background. There are exceptions, of course: Some start out in science and wind up in scientific or technical publishing; others turn from teaching to corporate communications.

What can a beginning writer do to get a job on a small newspaper staff?

Try to place some freelance features with the newspaper you'd like to work for, so the editor can see that (1) you know what a good feature is, and (2) you write well. You can also try supplying the editor with news items from a section of the newspaper circulation area that is not well covered. Show samples of your work that are similar to what the paper publishes.

I'd like to work on a newspaper but am having trouble finding any openings. What other similar career choices do I have?

The corporate world is always looking for people to edit and write company publications or run the PR machine. Charitable and nonprofit organizations also need grant writers, media people, and people with good communications skills. As long as there are words, you can find jobs. To fully explore your career options as a writer, take a look at *I'm an English Major—Now What?* by Tim Lemire. Even if you aren't an English major, this book can help you use your writing skills to find a career.

What are the advantages of working for a magazine versus working for a newspaper?

One of the major differences is that newspapers work against much shorter deadlines than magazines; deadlines are often a matter of hours for a newspaper as opposed to weeks or months for a magazine. A writer who doesn't work well under this kind of pressure is better off working for a magazine. The difference in deadlines means that magazine writers have a chance to develop their ideas into more in-depth articles, and newspaper writers must be concerned with quick, up-to-the-minute reporting.

What kinds of jobs are available in the book publishing industry?

Although duties vary with the size and scope of each publishing house, the jobs most often available are for editorial assistants, production assistants, and publicists. To learn the basics of book publishing jobs and the range of opportunities available, visit www.bookjobs.com, a site sponsored by the Association of American Publishers.

When looking for work in a publishing house, read the job postings at the Publishers Weekly site (www.publishersweekly.com), MediaBistro (www.mediabistro.com), and PublishersMarketplace (www.publishersmarketplace.com). The job descriptions and requirements should give you an idea of how much experience you need and what skills are expected.

WHERE TO FIND OUT MORE

Books

The Well-Fed Writer: Financial Self-Sufficiency as a Freelance Writer in Six Months or Less, by Peter Bowerman, provides helpful insight into how to earn money from corporate clients.

The Wealthy Writer: How to Earn a Six-Figure Income as a Freelance Writer, by Michael Meanwell, gives thorough information about the highest-paying freelance opportunities many freelance writers overlook. It offers invaluable tips on how to run your writing business, from marketing yourself to outsourcing work when you become too busy to take on every job you're offered.

Make a Real Living as a Freelance Writer: How to Win Top Writing Assignments, by Jenna Glatzer, is an excellent guide for novices considering the freelance life.

Ready, Aim, Specialize! Create Your Own Writing Specialty and Make More Money, by Kelly James-Enger, is a good guide for someone who is interested in a very specific subject area, like technology, business, or science.

How Do I Start a Freelance Writing Career?

The Renegade Writer: A Totally Unconventional Guide to Freelance Writing Success, by Linda Formichelli and Diana Burrell, tells you how to break the traditional rules of freelance writing, with style and panache.

The ASJA Guide to Freelance Writing: A Professional Guide to the Business, for Nonfiction Writers of All Experience Levels, by Samuel G. Freedman, includes contributions from members of the American Society of Journalists and Authors (ASJA) and will instruct you on all aspects of the freelance business.

102 Ways to Earn Money Writing 1,500 Words or Less, by I.J. Schecter, shows you the wide array of freelance opportunities available—and gives you everything you need to know to reap the benefits of a bustling writing career.

Websites

Absolute Write (www.absolutewrite.com) offers writing instruction and keeps tabs on upcoming contests and deadlines. Delivers two free e-newsletters, one specifically on markets, and has excellent message boards (Absolute Write Water Cooler).

WritersWeekly (www.writersweekly.com) is a popular place to learn how to make more money freelancing and to find new opportunities.

FreelanceWriting (www.freelancewriting.com) is a collection of resources for freelancers.

Ed (2010) (www.ed2010.com) is a community of young magazine editors that offers advice, networking events, and constantly updated postings of journalism gigs.

The Freelance Writing Jobs Network (www.freelancewritinggigs.com) is a blog network and community for freelancers offers plenty of job leads, plus tips and advice on everything from fair pay to health care.

Writer Gazette (www.writergazette.com) has writing-related articles, freelance job postings, tips, contests, resources and a section of magazines to pitch.

CHAPTER 11

HOW DO I CONDUCT EFFECTIVE RESEARCH?

American playwright Wilson Mizner said, "When you take stuff from one writer, it's plagiarism; but when you take it from many writers, it's research." Today's writer-researcher has at his fingertips not only the traditional resources of books, magazine articles, and directories of experts' names and addresses, but a host of new resources on the Internet that can save him hours of tedious manual searching.

It's been said a good writer doesn't have to know much; he just has to know people who do. Learning who these people are, how to find them, and what to ask them are among the basic tasks of a freelance or nonfiction writer. Fiction writers, too, need to verify facts presented in their works, maintain historical accuracy, and sometimes even discuss the personalities of their characters with psychologists. No matter what the subject of your article, story, or book (or even your poem), there's probably a source available that can help you add insight and authority to your manuscript.

Where should I start my research?

To find the most comprehensive up-to-date information on practically any subject, start with the Internet, where valuable resources await. Even if the information you need is not available online (or not verifiable online), you can search for the organizations, companies, libraries, museums, and other experts who can help you find or confirm that information. Basic starting places: The U.S. government site FedStats (www.fedstats.gov) features many government statistics and reports on specialized topics, and RefDesk (www.refdesk.com) is an essential bookmark for most researchers and librarians.

Second to the Internet should be the public library and librarians. Many accept phone calls from patrons asking research questions, so long as the questions are specific and can be answered quickly. Libraries at large universities are likely to have more resources available than your local library and are usually open to the public.

Other sources include businesses, organizations, and professional associations. Businesses routinely make information available through their public relations offices, and many trade associations and organizations can give you information or steer you to an expert in your topic. Most associations and organizations can be found online, and an individual association site will offer detailed information about the association and the services it offers.

How can I find contact information for authors and/or well-known persons for requesting interviews?

Book authors can generally be reached by contacting them through their publicists; the publicist's contact information (and specific instructions for contacting authors) can usually be found on the publisher's or author's website. The best way to locate contact information for anyone else is through an Internet search.

How can I get quotes from experts?

If you're having trouble finding an expert on your topic—say you need someone intimately knowledgeable with the effects of deforestation but don't have any contacts—use one of the many reference websites, such as ProfNet (www.profnet.com) or RefDesk, to find the right people. Also, JournalismNet has a page dedicated to finding experts online at www.people-searchpro.com/journalism/experts. If you already have an expert in mind, you should contact him by regular mail or e-mail, explain the subject matter of your article and the magazine for which you're writing, and ask your questions. Also, ask the experts to suggest other people who may be able to help you in your research.

How can I contact the author of a magazine article I recently read?

You can either write to the author in care of the magazine in which the article appeared, or you can e-mail the author directly. If you choose to write the author in care of the magazine, you can find the address of the magazine's editorial office on the magazine's masthead or contents page. Some publications have their subscriptions fulfilled at a different address, so be sure you write to the editorial address, not the circulation or advertising address. Most editors will forward mail addressed to contributing writers but will not give the home addresses of their contributors.

If you prefer to e-mail the author, check his bio at the end of the article for his e-mail address, or try an Internet search.

What's the difference between a primary source and a secondary source?

A primary source—or primary research—provides the writer with original, firsthand information. A primary source can be the writer's own experience and observation; another person (such as an interview subject); or personal papers, correspondence, diaries, or manuscripts relating to the person or subject being studied. Primary research is closer to the subject, and therefore preferable to secondary research, which is based entirely on what others have written in newspapers, books, or magazines about the primary sources. For instance, if your topic is former president Bill Clinton, a primary source would be a letter written by Clinton. A secondary source would be a book or article written about Clinton. If you use only secondary sources, you run the risk of a source's research being inaccurate or containing misquotations or other errors. Secondary sources should be used for gathering supporting information and background material for an article.

In doing a round-up article in which I quote the opinions of several different people, should I obtain the consent of the individuals included when the information is not obtained by interview?

While it probably isn't necessary to obtain permission to quote brief opinions from published sources, it's usually best to verify published quotes to avoid repeating another writer's error.

I'm writing a piece that requires a lot of research, and I don't know how to keep all my notes and sources straight. Is there a solution?

Every writer develops his own system of organization, so there is no right way to prepare your research. But it's important to develop some system to keep you from wasting time.

Generally you'll want to think through your article's requirements or elements from beginning to end and decide what kind of information you'll need—such as statistics, advice from experts, and illustrative anecdotes. Make a list of pertinent questions that must be answered in the course of the article, as well as secondary questions that are beneficial but not crucial. Decide what your probable sources are, and list them in the order in which you should consult them. Adjust your research plans to fit your schedule (how much time can you spend on this article?); budget (is the publisher covering any of your costs?); and the scope of the topic. Do your homework early, break everything into very small tasks that are easy to complete (and won't overwhelm you), and adhere to a schedule. As you gain experience, your system of research will develop, and you'll gain confidence and increase your ability to cut your research down to size.

When I'm finished researching an article, I have so much raw material I'm overwhelmed by the sheer bulk of it and don't know where to begin. How can I distill my research to a manageable size?

Most writers develop a very personalized way of dealing with research, but here's a step-by-step plan to help you get started. First, reduce the bulk of material you've gathered by getting rid of resources you aren't going to use anymore and taking notes on any material you've gathered from various publications (instead of keeping entire magazines and newspapers on your desk). Next, decide what information is essential to your article, and what's only tangentially related to your topic, filing the latter for future use. Then divide your material into subject categories. Some writers use highlighters to code the information, while others use card file folders, but many writers cut or copy and paste bits of information into computer files for saving or filing. (When you do a lot of copying and pasting into electronic documents—especially when you're taking copy from the Web—make sure you keep careful records of where the material came from; sloppiness can lead to plagiarism or just plain chaos when you're attempting to attribute sources.)

What are databases, and how can they be useful to a writer?

A database is a large collection of specialized information organized for rapid search and retrieval, and can save a writer tremendous amounts of legwork. One of the most well-known databases is

How Do I Conduct Effective Research?

LexisNexis (www.lexisnexis.com), which houses the world's largest collection of public records, opinions, legal documents, news, and business information.

The best databases are rarely accessible for free; you usually have to go through a library or university computer (or have a library membership or student ID) in order to access them. Don't let that discourage you; the benefits will far outweigh any inconvenience you might encounter, especially if you're seeking particularly specialized information.

I'm currently working on a novel set in the eighteenth century. How do I research it?

Start your historical research with a relatively simple book on that period or with a general history of the country in which you've decided to set your novel. Even if you're not writing about an actual historical figure, biographies can be a valuable source of information on the manners of the time.

To check on the customs, foods, clothing, and technology of the period, look for chat groups online or websites dedicated to the time period (in addition to any books). You're almost never the only one searching for information about a given topic, and you're likely to find someone generous enough to share the resources they found most helpful. If the Internet doesn't turn up anything useful, look to your librarian—he can be your best friend when in a time of resource need.

I'm doing some research using turn-of-the-century books and material from state archives, including some family papers. Since the material is a hundred years old, can I use it in my manuscript? Would it be covered by copyright?

The state archives should pose no problem for you if they aren't copyrighted. However, the family papers could possibly raise the question of invasion of privacy, if any members of the family are living. It would be a good idea for you to verify with any descendants whether they would object to your use of the material.

I'm researching an article, and some of my sources disagree on several points. What can I do about this?

One of the most difficult tasks in writing a nonfiction article or book is reconciling information received from different sources. In some cases, the writer's own research gives him enough knowledge about the subject to judge who is right. But other times, it becomes necessary for the writer to communicate the conflicting information to the conflicting sources, letting each answer the questions raised by the other. For example, if you were writing about the effects of cigarette smoke on nonsmokers, and two researchers gave you contradictory statements, you could call or write each and say "[Name], of [professional affiliation], disagrees with your position," quoting the other expert. Then ask, "Could you comment on that?" By including such comments in your finished piece, you allow readers to decide for themselves which source is credible. In some cases, both sources will be equally credible, and readers will come to the conclusion that enough research has not yet been done on the subject to reach a definitive decision.

Is it possible to overresearch an article?

When researching, it's usually better to wind up with too much information than not enough. The only way you can really overresearch an article is by using further research as an excuse to avoid actually writing the piece. In other cases, the trick is not to research less but to use your research wisely. Sometimes you'll end up with a stack of material several inches thick, and you'll realize you can never use it all. That's when you must begin the long process of weeding out information, choosing only the material most pertinent to your topic. Material not used in the article might shed some light on another angle of the subject or provide human interest. That material might be developed into a sidebar, a short feature appearing within an article, providing more depth or additional factual information that would not fit well into the body of the article. You could also use the extra material to write another article on the same subject, using a different approach and slanting it to another, noncompeting magazine.

Most books state on the copyright page: "No part of this publication may be reproduced, stored in or introduced into a retrieval system, or transmitted, in any form or by any means (electronic, mechanical, photocopying, recording, or otherwise), without the prior written permission of both the copyright owner and publisher." Does the warning mean I can't copy material for my private research without first contacting the publisher?

If the photocopy is for your research only, and you do not intend to reproduce the copied page in your article, then using the copy machine is as legal as taking notes. However, if you intend to quote much of the material verbatim in your manuscript, you will need permission.

Is there any way a library can find out if another library has a book I need?

Yes, if your library has access to the Online Computer Library Center (OCLC), a service which links the information centers of more than fifty thousand libraries in eighty-four countries and territories. OCLC allows its members to locate, catalog, and lend library materials. It provides libraries with catalog card index files, helps them exchange information, and lends books to member libraries. OCLC's central office, in Dublin, Ohio, keeps the location listings of library material. Its database contains material in hundreds of languages and dialects, and OCLC adds more than thirty thousand titles to its file every week. Visit their site at www.oclc.org.

ONLINE SEARCH

No doubt the Internet provides many wonderful shortcuts when conducting research. The challenge is sorting through a lot of junk to find meaningful information. Knowing a few good search sites and databases can save you a lot of time. A few helpful ones are listed below.

Cross-check information if you are not sure of the source. You can be fairly confident of the accuracy and fairness of information you uncover through academic, library, and government sites, but if you're looking at private or personal sites, always question the accuracy (even if several of these sites agree).

- Since 1995, RefDesk (www.refdesk.com) has been one of the best indexes of information available for free on the Web; every writer should bookmark it.

- AcademicInfo (www.academicinfo.net) is an online directory of twenty-five thousand handpicked educational resources.

- InfoMine (http://infomine.ucr.edu) is a database of scholarly Internet resource collections.

- LibrarySpot (www.libraryspot.com) includes a comprehensive listing of libraries, references, lists, and more.

- The American Library Association often issues a list of the best websites, which is always worth reviewing—visit www.ala.org.

WHERE TO FIND OUT MORE

Books

Since 1995, *The Craft of Research*, by Wayne C. Booth, Gregory G. Colomb, and Joseph M. Williams, has served as an essential guide to researching effectively, then incorporating the research into your writing.

Mastering Online Research: A Comprehensive Guide to Effective and Efficient Search Strategies, by Maura D. Shaw, provides the techniques and tools find information ranging from historical data to medical information to images and videos

Websites

In addition to the sites listed above, try these:

The Librarians' Internet Index (www.lii.org) allows you to search only websites that librarians trust.

Robert Niles's home page (www.robertniles.com/data) offers a helpful lists of research sites, divided by categories of interest.

If you feel overwhelmed by Internet searches, try taking a free online tutorial offered by UC Berkeley, Finding Information on the Internet (www.lib.berkeley.edu/TeachingLib/Guides/Internet/FindInfo.html).

CHAPTER 12

HOW DO I CONDUCT A STRONG INTERVIEW?

It's been said that a good interview is just like a good conversation. That's not so. In a good conversation, it's polite for the folks involved to ask questions of each other and to listen with equal interest to the answers. It's a time for mutual discovery and communication.

But an interview is a lopsided interaction. The interviewee probably doesn't care much about the person popping the questions, and the interviewer is probably doing more than simply enjoying herself. Interviewing is, after all, work.

It shouldn't feel like work, however, and that's what the interviews-are-conversations theory is all about. If a person being interviewed feels as if she is talking to an old friend, the interview is more likely to produce powerful anecdotes, colorful quotes, and revealing information. Yet, before a source feels comfortable with an interviewer, the interviewer has to relax—a tough trick for many beginners.

In an effort to calm your nervous stomach, what follows are general guidelines for planning and conducting fruitful interviews.

BEFORE THE INTERVIEW

What is the protocol for arranging an interview?

For an in-person interview, phone or e-mail the subject for an appointment. If the subject does not return your calls, send a short note introducing yourself, requesting an interview, and telling her you will call on a specific date to set up a meeting. Be ready to be flexible on the date and time of the interview. You will need to accommodate your subject's schedule. For a phone interview, follow the same procedure—but be prepared to conduct the interview on the spot should your subject say, "How about right now?"

What are the best places to conduct an interview?

Find a quiet setting where you can talk without frequent interruptions. Your subject's office—if she has one—can fit the bill, but may also be full of distractions. Office conference rooms, hotel lobbies and meeting rooms, libraries, parks, and quiet cocktail lounges are all good possibilities. Restaurants may prove too distracting to maintain the conversation (also, clattering silverware and the talking of other diners may render your tape recording indecipherable).

Should I query an editor before or after I ask the interviewee for her permission to be interviewed? And what should I do if I can't deliver an article because my interviewee wouldn't grant me an interview?

It is best to first get an editor's okay on an interview assignment before asking the subject for an interview. A subject is more willing to give you the time for an interview if she knows an editor is seeking the interview for her pages. But if a subject is willing to be interviewed without a commitment from an editor, you can also work that way. If a subject refuses to give you the interview, just drop a note to the editor and say that the interview was refused. Editors understand this. If a subject refuses the interview because you don't have an editor interested yet, then let the editor know. She may then give you a firm assignment for the interview.

How much research do I need to do for an interview?

The late historian Cornelius Ryan claimed that one of the rules of writing is "Never interview anyone without knowing 60 percent of the answers." He said that the person being interviewed has done her homework, so the writer should be equally prepared. Research is the best way to discover what you need to learn in the interview and the best way to learn it. It's always better to be overprepared than to run out of questions before you run out of time.

The main purpose of research is to enable yourself to talk and ask questions intelligently on any topic the interviewee raises. If you take the time to do your research, the interviewee can expect an intelligent discussion of the subject, which is always more interesting for an interviewee than talking to someone about a topic on which she is uninformed.

You should research the interviewee's background and any topics you think might be discussed. For a profile, prepare by interviewing around the subject, talking to friends, family, and co-workers to learn more about the person before you actually meet her.

Researching for an interview takes time, and you may not make use of even half the information you gather. But a thorough knowledge of the subject can help you craft good, specific questions and get the quotes that will make your work more lively and salable.

After I finish research for an interview, is it necessary to write a list of questions before the interview takes place? How many questions?

By deciding on a particular list of must-ask questions, the interviewer makes sure she doesn't conclude the interview without obtaining all the necessary information for the article. However, the interviewer should pursue any interesting path down which her subject wanders; the list of prepared questions is a set of boundaries, rather than a hard-and-fast road map. In John Brady's *The Craft of Interviewing*, freelancer Edward Linn says, "The list of questions and the logical sequence invariably disappear very quickly. If they don't, you're in trouble."

To decide on a list of questions, first choose your angle—or let your editor tell you what she has in mind. Then look at your research and decide what you must learn from the interviewee. The number of questions you need will vary depending on the topic of the article, the interviewee, and in some cases, the amount of time an interviewee allows. The more questions you prepare, though, the better chance of leaving the interview with the essential answers plus additional interesting information.

Structure the outline of the interview to follow a logical course. You might open with easy, mechanical questions, such as those that would establish the interviewee's relation to or view of the topic, then move on to knottier questions or more thoughtful probes, such as asking what she thinks about someone else's particular criticism of her actions or point of view. At the end, ask "Is there anything we've not talked about that you'd like to comment on?"

IN THE INTERVIEW

What are some good techniques to remember when I'm conducting an interview? How can I make sure the interview is productive and interesting for both myself and the subject?

First, try to build rapport with the interviewee. This serves two purposes: It not only makes your subject feel more at ease and more receptive to questions, it can help relax you and keep the interview flowing smoothly. Be a little formal at the start, rather than jumping into familiarity right away. (If you're doing an in-person interview, don't take liberties you wouldn't want a guest of yours to take, and remember that first impressions count, so dress professionally and avoid drawing attention to yourself.)

Don't talk too much at the outset. Encourage the interviewee to do as much of the talking as possible. Be flexible and follow the subject's lead. If an answer is very general, don't interrupt, but follow it up. Follow-up questions not only secure specific details and anecdotes, they reveal a lot about the interviewee's personality and bolster rapport by demonstrating your genuine interest in what she has to say. Reciting an anecdote you have previously heard about the subject will often nudge the interviewee into providing further human-interest comments, in turn giving you a good anecdote to use to open or close your article.

Don't overlook your article's need for specific details, anecdotes, and examples. You must request these comments directly. Ask such leading questions as: "Can you tell me about the first time that happened to you?" and "Do you remember a time that strategy worked for you?" When a subject rambles or is unclear, place the onus on yourself by saying "I'm sorry, but I don't quite understand that last point. Could you explain it for me?"

Sometimes when I'm setting up interviews for an article, I encounter people who are reluctant to talk about even the most innocuous of topics. The material isn't particularly controversial; they just aren't used to being interviewed and don't know what to do. How do I handle these shy interviewees?

People may be fearful of being misinterpreted or shown in an unfavorable light. Sympathy to the subject's quandary, friendly understanding, and professional performance on your part can overcome barriers.

Scholars and physicians can be reluctant subjects, since many of them view publicity as unprofessional. When faced with this attitude, point out the need for public information in the subject's area of expertise. Your interest and sincere enthusiasm can be the catalysts that spark the interviewee into sharing her knowledge.

Persistence pays off. If you become a more or less ubiquitous presence around a busy subject, you may find that she will make time for the interview in her packed schedule. John Brady tells of tracking down author Jessica Mitford at a university seminar. By "hanging around a lot," he found the right time to get the interview; although her schedule was filled each minute of the seminar, he drove her to the airport and got the interview on the way. Recommendations from the friends and co-workers of reluctant interviewees can also be an aid to getting the time with them.

If none of these techniques work and the interview is necessary to the story, tell the subject that her comments are crucial to the story and she probably will appear in the article anyway, but you'd rather get her opinions firsthand.

I'm not sure whether to take written notes or use a tape recorder when conducting an interview. What are the pros and cons of each?

Both methods have their good and bad points. Tape recorders and digital recorders allow an interviewer to concentrate on conducting the interview and observing the interviewee and the surroundings. They allow you to ask more questions in less time and concentrate more on the replies you receive, listening for possible follow-ups. If the subject matter is at all controversial, a recorded interview is your proof that an interviewee said what she said in the context being quoted. If you must interview a subject in a situation in which it would be difficult for you to take notes, such as over lunch, a recorder can be a real lifesaver. However, there's always the possibility the tape recorder will malfunction when you need it most. Also, some interview subjects are uncomfortable with recorders and will not talk as freely as with someone who unobtrusively takes notes.

Also, most reporters caution against relying too much on the recorder; they suggest augmenting it with some note taking. If you take notes, you can mark where in the interview a subject says something particularly provocative or relevant. Taking highlight notes is also insurance in case the recorder or tape breaks.

Keep your interview tapes and notes in a safe place after an article has been published. An editor may need them after publication if an interviewee claims, "I've been misquoted."

I would like to use a tape recorder when I interview. Should I ask the interviewee beforehand if she minds, or should I simply plop it down without a word, turn it on, and proceed with the interview as if it didn't exist?

It's more courteous to ask the subject first if she minds your using the tape recorder to make sure her statements are recorded as accurately as possible. Few interviewees will object.

I have a gadget that records telephone conversations. When I conduct a phone interview, do I have to inform the person that she's being taped?

Yes, that is always the safest course of action. Advising an interviewee that the conversation is being recorded for the sake of accuracy—and recording his agreement on tape—at the beginning of the conversation is the best defense against problems. No federal law prohibits taping of telephone conversations by either party as long as the taping is not being done for an illegal purpose.

TOUCHY TOPICS

How do I interview someone about information she might be reluctant to discuss?

Making the cross into sensitive territory can be a delicate process. You know you need the information but find it difficult to broach the subject without losing the interviewee's confidence. The tenuous path to sensitive information can be traveled only with patience and subtlety.

Each writer will find his own methods of dealing with each reluctant interviewee, but there are a few tried-and-true methods that will work in many situations. You could blame the question on someone else, as in asking an allegedly corrupt politician "There are those who claim you do some 'creative accounting' with the budget. Since you've heard these allegations, would you like to respond to your critics?" A playful approach—"Let me play devil's advocate"—can often place the question in a framework that makes it easier for your subject to answer. Prefacing a sensitive question with some praise for your interviewee can cushion the blow and make her more responsive.

Asking a question in a straightforward, matter-of-fact way, no matter how sensitive the topic, may elicit a response when all else fails. If the interviewee still does not respond, point out the gap in information and tell her that, in the eyes of the reader, silence can be more damaging, since it can lead to speculation on the answer.

The manner in which you cover sensitive material can influence how much information the interviewee will give you. If you do manage to extract a gem that has been under lock and key, don't make a big deal out of it; lack of restraint can cause your subject to say something like, "Oh, but maybe you'd better not print that." Just show normal interest, not wild delight that would worry or frighten your subject.

When a subject wants to talk off the record, should I accept or turn her down? Do anonymous sources lessen the quality of an article?

Within certain limits, using off-the-record sources can be helpful to a writer, but the writer should make sure she and her source understand the ground rules for their interview. There are two ways a source can talk off the record. She can request total anonymity, talking only to give the reporter background information; in such cases, the source is never to be quoted in the article. A source can also agree to talk "not for attribution." This means she is willing to give information for use in the article, but doesn't want her name mentioned; she can be quoted or paraphrased, but the material is attributed to "a source close to the scene," "a high-ranking official," "a veteran observer," or some other such tag.

Anonymous sources can provide the writer of an article with incisive, revealing information that he otherwise might not have been able to obtain. But there are dangers—identified sources make your article complete and credible. And anonymity can become an excuse for a subject to grind her particular axe without fear of retribution. Check what your anonymous sources tell you, and if a source gives you information, makes charges, or provides descriptions that she cannot document, ask her to go on the record.

If I only have a few minutes of an interviewee's time, how can I get the information I need?

A tight schedule makes an interview more difficult in a couple of ways. Not only do you have a time limit on getting the information, you must dispense with much of the preliminary conversation that can build rapport and goodwill with the interviewee. Cutting the chitchat must be done carefully, however; you don't want to seem abrupt or rude, which could affect the interviewee's receptiveness to questioning.

When you're interviewing under the gun, you should have your questions arranged in descending order of importance when the interview begins. This practice will ensure your getting as much pertinent information as you can in the time allotted. Take a gamble with your last few questions, making them more thought-provoking to interest the subject so she will permit the interview to run longer.

To supplement your brief notes, you can, at the end of the conversation, request a more detailed interview by e-mail (see later questions).

I need the opinions of average people for several articles I'm working on. Do I just walk up to people on the street and ask them? Do you have to name them in an article, or are you not supposed to name them?

Yes, many freelance writers just walk up to people at a shopping mall or other public place and ask if they can interview them briefly for some research material they are seeking. You can open the conversation by saying something like "I'm a freelance writer researching an article on [topic] for [name of magazine]. May I ask you a few questions?" Whether you name them in the article depends on how you write the article. For example, writing "Sally Jones, a twenty-year veteran teacher in inner-city schools, had this to say about merit pay increases in teacher salaries" might create more credibility than if you just referred to "One Chicago veteran teacher ..."

I can't afford to travel to conduct all my interviews in person. Can't I get the same information just as easily by phone or e-mail?

Telephone and e-mail interviewing prevent you from observing your subject's mannerisms and surroundings; for this reason, in-person interviews are usually best. Interviewing someone by telephone is the next best option, especially when you need only one key source and the subject is too far away for you to meet her in person before your deadline. Interviewing by phone can also be necessary when many sources are scattered far and wide. The practice even has a couple of advantages over face-to-face questioning: Many times, a subject will be willing to talk more freely if she can't watch you taking notes.

When interviewing by phone, always have your reference material nearby. If you use a recorder, advise the subject in advance. Remember the value of good telephone manners; be prepared to identify yourself and the publication for which you are writing, and also to answer some preliminary questions from a secretary or assistant to gain access to your subject.

At the end of the phone conversation, thank the subject and advise her that you might need to call again for follow-up questions or to fill in any gaps you find after you've transcribed your notes. Be sure to give the interviewee your phone number so she can reach you with any additional information or afterthoughts about your article.

So how about e-mail interviews? They're so easy and time efficient.

E-mail interviews can definitely save time, especially if you need to ask many people the same questions. For example, if you were writing an article on city spending on social programs and wanted to ask the members of the city council for their views, e-mail interviewing would be one way to get a lot of their opinions in a very brief time. This would also save you the expense of travel and long-distance telephoning.

To conduct an e-mail interview, first query your subjects. Your query should be personal, explaining the nature of your project and the name of the publication interested in your article. If you are contacting a number of people about the same issue, it's always better to personalize the e-mail query and the questions, based on what you know about your subject. Give your phone number, and tell interviewees to feel free to call you collect if a question needs clarification or talking to you is more convenient. Also indicate a deadline for response.

Examine the replies to see if follow-up questions are necessary or might provide additional, provocative answers, then e-mail the subject(s) with these questions immediately.

What are the drawbacks to e-mail interviews?

Purists say that e-mail interviews don't count, because they remove spontaneity and also permit intermediaries (such as a PR person or assistant) to respond to questions without you knowing. If you do an interview via e-mail, you're giving control over to your interviewee. Answers become pat and predictable—processed. As the interviewer, it's your job to pick up on voice inflections, to push through vague nonresponses, to ask the smart follow-up questions, and to be open to the synchronicity of the interview as it unfolds. If you're corresponding via e-mail, then you're giving up all those opportunities.

Use e-mail interviews to do quick surveys and gather lots of opinions in a short time—especially when your goal is to get a general feeling for what the majority (or minority) thinks about an issue. E-mail is also a useful tool for corresponding after the interview—maybe to double-check a fact or to ask a quick follow-up question; but don't rely on e-mail as your primary method for conducting interviews. Remember, too, do not bombard your source with dozens of pre- and post-interview e-mails. Doing so is absolutely unprofessional, and your source will likely form an unfavorable opinion of you.

If you're profiling a major figure, or if the very life of your story depends on the success of a particular interview, then you should try to do it in person, and if not, at least by phone. An in-person interview is mandatory if you're expected to deliver full, sensory detail about a person's behavior, manner, and appearance.

SOURCE CONCERNS

Should I ask my interview subjects to sign a release?

As a rule of thumb, no. If you identify yourself as a writer or reporter, and the subject agrees to speak with you, it is understood that she is consenting to the publication of her comments.

There are rare occasions—such as when your interview will involve extremely controversial or sensitive material—when you might wish to have the subject sign a release in which she agrees to the publication of her comments, gives you permission to edit the manuscript and sell it to an editor, and waives any right of inspection or approval of the edited manuscript.

If I write a profile, must I pay the subject?

Not usually. The question will rarely arise if you're interviewing a local businessman for a trade publication or a friend or neighbor for a crafts magazine. If it does, you should tell the subject that publications don't pay interview subjects, although they may provide complimentary copies of the article when it is published.

However, some writers and editors have paid for certain interviews and consider the practice a good investment. When a freelancer receives a request for payment to an interview subject, she should discuss it with the editor who gave the go-ahead for the piece.

I called to set up an interview for an article on which I am currently working, but the subject told me she'd only agree to see me if she could see her quotes before the article went to press. What should I do in a situation like this?

Unless this particular interview subject is essential to your article, it is best to tell her "Sorry, professional writers don't do that." That said, there are a few times when it is necessary for a writer to allow her interviewee to see the manuscript before it is printed. When dealing with scientific, technical, or medical topics, the writer may need the subject to check the facts and figures to make sure they are accurate. If the interviewee is your key source, then it may be necessary to agree to her review of the manuscript to get the interview. But the writer should make clear to any subject with whom she has such an agreement that the article is submitted for the interviewee's correction of factual material, not for her approval. It should be made clear to her that she is only proofreading the quotes, and that any alteration of the manuscript may be done only by the editor.

When I've interviewed thirty or forty people for an article, should I try to quote all of them, or at least as many as I can? Will they expect to be quoted in the article?

Not all the people you interview will appear in the finished manuscript. Some will be poor spokespersons; some will be misinformed and therefore useless; others will not be able to shed new light on the subject. Unless you are interviewing someone you know will be a key figure in the finished piece, you should make clear to each subject that you are interviewing a lot of people in order to obtain background information (as well as quotation) for the article, and that not all sources will be mentioned. If an interviewee later objects to not being quoted in the finished article, you can always say that there was a problem with limited space or that the article was heavily edited. If you anticipate this response from an interviewee, it's professionally polite to phone the subject in advance of the article's publication.

I recently tried to interview a celebrity, but her press agent insisted on ground rules, telling me that there were only certain topics her client would discuss. What do I do when this happens?

If you need the interview, you have little recourse but to accept the ground rules suggested. The rules are often self-serving and confine the interviewer, making it difficult for him to get the information he needs from his subject. However, while it may be necessary to agree to ground rules in order to get someone to grant an interview, the ground rules may not limit you in the interview itself. Your subject may simply be wary of discussing certain topics because of the way she has been handled by writers in the past. Once you begin the conversation, she may loosen up and discuss almost anything you wish. Agree to ground rules, and you may be surprised. Once your foot is in the door, the ground rules may go out the window!

Is it unethical to print information that a source has labeled off the record or not for attribution?

If you have taken information off the record or not for attribution, then you are obligated to keep it that way. Failure to do so can damage your reputation as a trustworthy writer and harm your chances of getting information from that source in the future.

Can a person I interview for an article be sued by a third party she mentions in the interview? Can the writer be sued for what the interviewee said?

The interviewee can be sued for libel or defamation by the third person. The writer and publisher of the interviewee's statements can also be sued. A writer, therefore, should not include such possibly libelous statements unless she can prove their truth if challenged.

What opportunities exist for a writer who doesn't like to interview people?

How Do I Conduct a Strong Interview?

Conducting interviews by e-mail is an alternative to the in-person interview and can be used to glean enough information from an expert or celebrity to develop a salable article. There are several kinds of magazine articles that don't necessarily require interviewing. Each of these can be completed with other types of research.

The how-to article demonstrates or explains to the reader how to accomplish something, such as woodworking projects or sewing different types of clothing. Illustrations or photographs are often an integral part of how-to articles.

The service article gives the reader information regarding the use or purchase of items, services, or facilities. An article discussing low-cost vacation spots or offering pointers on buying a used car would fit this category.

The personal experience article is designed to inspire, educate, or entertain. Writing about the experience of returning to college at age forty-five or making a career change are examples of this type of article. Your account of a personal struggle to get through a life-threatening experience or other conflict can also become a salable magazine article.

The think article analyzes facts, events, or trends as the writer perceives them. The writer presents informed opinions, drawing conclusions intended to persuade the reader. Think articles appear in newspapers on the op-ed page and in magazines such as *The Atlantic* and *Harper's*, where, of course, your opinions would have to be buttressed by those of experts you had researched in periodicals, books, and perhaps through personal correspondence.

Different aspects of historical events can be covered in a light manner for popular magazines, or through in-depth research for scholarly publications. Many editors indicate their lack of interest in "routine historical pieces," but a well-written historical piece related to a magazine's content can usually be sold, providing the slant is right and the approach is fresh and lively.

The travel article has two objectives: to inform the reader by way of facts and to enlighten her by way of impressions. This type of article requires a certain amount of preliminary research, and the writer must be perceptive enough to see the less conspicuous elements of the place she visits, such as the people, customs, and atmosphere. Photos are an essential part of most travel pieces.

The humorous article, although one of the most difficult to write, can be one of the most financially rewarding. However, many writers of humor attain success only after years of experience.

Is there any reason to keep interview notes and other research material after an article is finished?

Many writers keep old research material for several reasons: They may need to answer questions from editors, readers, or other writers who request information on the sources of the research, or they may want to use the research for future articles. You should save material for at least a year, or longer, depending on the type of research and how much further use you may have for it. Some newspaper reporters involved in investigative journalism, on the other hand, have developed the practice of destroying their notes once they have served their purpose. This prevents the notes from being subpoenaed if the reporter is questioned about his sources in an investigative piece.

WHERE TO FIND OUT MORE

Books

The Craft of Interviewing, by John Brady, was first released in 1977 and is still available. Excellent for beginning journalists, if you can get past the outdated nature of its research techniques and attitudes.

The Art of the Interview: Lessons From a Master of the Craft is by Lawrence Grobel, a famed Playboy interviewer, so it is rich in celebrity anecdotes if weak on the how-to. Gives a good glimpse of what an interviewer does.

Creative Interviewing: The Writer's Guide to Gathering Information by Asking Questions, by Ken Metzler, is an expensive textbook for serious journalists and contains strong how-to on the craft of interviewing.

How Do I Conduct a Strong Interview?

CHAPTER 13

Sommers, 1980
add
subtract
rearrange
substitute

HOW DO I REVISE?

The headmaster of an elementary school once commented, "I see four kinds of writing: (1) just plain bad, (2) correct but dead, (3) incorrect but good, (4) correct and good." The beginner's search for that last ideal is often a struggle.

The most common advice given by agents and editors is: Revise, revise, revise. Revision is what separates the serious writers from everyone else; professional authors revise their work multiple times—sometimes dozens of times. If you expect to get anywhere in your writing career, find an effective method of revising your work. (Check Janet Burroway's *Writing Fiction* for the method taught to nearly every creative writing student.)

This chapter answers a few of the most common revision and style questions. For more detailed discussions, read two classic books: *The Elements of Style*, by William Strunk Jr. and E.B. White, and *On Writing Well*, by William Zinsser.

What should I look for when revising my work? Is it possible to edit too much?

The process of editing is one each writer develops on his own, through experience, trial, and error. There is no definite number of drafts you should write before you can consider the manuscript finished. There are, however, some techniques that will probably prove helpful.

First of all, if your schedule allows it, set the work aside for a few days. After the writing has had a chance to cool, errors and awkward phrases will jump out. Once you do look at the work, try to cut it. Eliminate anything that isn't essential, as well as redundancies, irrelevancies, statements that are too obvious, unnecessary words, and circumlocution. (Don't worry about being too brutal; you can always put material back.)

Let the material rest again (for at least an hour or two), then read it aloud. This is probably the best way to discover awkward phrasings. If you stumble over something, fix it. Reading aloud also can tell you where you've cut too drastically, damaging the rhythm of the piece.

Assess the logical order of the remaining elements. Some writers use highlighters or colored pens to color-code the work's major elements to make sure the structure best suits the point they're trying to make. Next, check your word choices. Look for imprecise verbs and weak nouns that require too many modifiers. Finally, check for consistency of verb tense, verb agreement, punctuation errors, and misspellings.

It is possible to overedit. If, for example, you find yourself rewriting everything over and over, and seldom or never putting a manuscript in the mail, you might be using editing as a means of avoiding potential rejection. Most writers, though, are far more likely to be hurt by too little editing than by too much.

What should I look for when revising a novel?

Look for the weaknesses that most often cause rejection: unsympathetic or flat characters, unrealistic dialogue, slow pacing, a boring beginning, lack of voice, and bad or clichéd writing. You're probably wondering: How do I know if I have flat characters or a slow pace or any of these weaknesses? Show your manuscript to people you can trust to give their honest opinion, and if they all give you the same criticism, that's a red flag. You can also consult these two excellent how-to books, which give examples of good and bad writing: *The First Five Pages*, by Noah Lukeman, and *Self-Editing for Fiction Writers*, by Dave King and Renni Browne.

One last option is to attend a writing conference or workshop that offers a session or course on revision. Sometimes these sessions are very interactive and feature hands-on editing; other times they're lecture-based. Either way, they can help you spot and understand your weaknesses in a fraction of the time it would take you working alone.

What is a book doctor? Should I pay to have my book edited before submitting it?

A book doctor (as opposed to a copyeditor or proofreader) will read your book, looking for big-picture issues that need addressing, such as development, structure or organization, and flow. (When reading novels, they look at plot, character, pacing, and other elements vital to lively and salable fiction.)

An editor you pay will be more objective than a teacher, writing group member, friend, or spouse. They can help you fix what's wrong with your novel, though they cannot guarantee publication. They also can't turn bad writing or a clichéd story into a bestseller.

Check the track record of the editor you wish to hire. He should have a background in the particular field of your manuscript (novels, plays, etc.) and should, if asked, be able to provide a sample of a former critique to give you an idea of the nature, extent, and content of the criticism provided. Usually reputable book doctors or editors don't take on projects that they feel have no chance at traditional publication (if that's your goal).

Whether or not you should hire an editor is totally up to you, but most manuscripts do benefit from at least a line edit (or proofread) before submission. If an editor or agent has two manuscripts on his desk, and one needs a heavy edit, and the other looks polished and ready to go, it's not hard to know which one he'll prefer and be more likely to accept.

I recently queried an agent with the first twenty-five pages of my work. He responded personally with a note that my submission needs the help of a good editor. He gave me the name, address, and telephone number of someone he recommends. My question is, how do I go about contacting the editor? Do I send a letter, or contact him by telephone? I'm not sure what the etiquette is.

Send the editor a letter mentioning the agent's referral, and ask for some information, including a description of the type of editing he does, his rates, titles of books he's edited that went on to be sold to royalty-paying publishing houses, and references from other clients. Then, talk with those clients; ask them if they were happy with the editor's services. Determine if the type of editing that was done was the type you expect—was the work restructured or merely read for stylistic, grammatical, and typographical errors?

Do understand that editors edit. They are entitled to a fair fee for what they do. But editors aren't agents, and don't sell your work. Also, understand that working with a particular editor does not ensure that an agent or publisher will represent or buy your work. Be leery of agents or publishers who promise to represent or publish you if you work with a specific editor.

I need some advice on a manuscript I just finished. I'd like to consult a well-known author whose work I admire. What's the best way to approach him?

It would be an intrusion to send the author your unsolicited work. Of course, you can always write and ask for her advice, but don't send your manuscript unless you've received permission first. Many well-known writers who speak at writers conferences set aside time for individual questions and informal criticism, so it may be better to ask your questions in those situations.

STYLE

When an editor or teacher talks about my style, what does he mean?

Style refers to the way an author expresses his ideas. It's how he says something in his work, rather than what he says; style is form rather than content. Each writer's work has an individual style that's as unique as a fingerprint; this is true whether he writes novels, magazine articles, poetry, or plays. Good style need not be characterized by complex constructions and polysyllabic words; it is marked by a clear presentation and expression of ideas. A writer's personal style doesn't appear overnight. It takes time and practice to develop your own method of putting thoughts into words.

Would you explain the term depth *in the field of writing?*

Depth means many things to many editors. But perhaps the one interpretation they would all agree on is that a piece of writing that has depth has something important to say to readers. It avoids frivolity or top-of-the-head superficiality about the ideas presented; it requires thought on the part of the writer and the reader.

How can I improve my style?

Each writer has his own personal style, his own way of expressing his ideas, so there are no set rules or guidelines for improving style. Style should be natural for the writer, acceptable to the reader, and appropriate to the content of the piece. Good style can only evolve and be refined through the practice of writing and the study of good writing.

To improve style, read widely and determine what is good about a particular piece of writing. Evaluation by either a writing teacher or a professional editor is also helpful.

Several times I have come across the criticism of pedestrian writing. What is pedestrian writing?

The term *pedestrian*, when applied to writing, is definitely unflattering. It means the work is prosaic or dull. The Latin root *ped-* refers to the foot, and the usual definition of the noun pedestrian is "one who travels on foot," such as the common man (who presumably doesn't have a better way to travel). In connection with writing, the adjective means *common* or *ordinary*.

What does my writing teacher mean when he suggests that I loosen up my writing style?

The statement implies that you should decrease the formality of your writing and strive for a style that is more casual and easier to comprehend. Conventional idioms, slang, contractions (*he's* instead of *he is*), common words, and shorter sentences can achieve an informal style. Loosening up your style gives your manuscript a more conversational tone and makes it easier to read.

I recently read an article by a well-known fiction writer who said it isn't good to read other fiction writers. He stated that it confuses a writer's style and makes his work seem inferior. Is this true?

That view is not generally shared by most writers who have one love in common—the love of reading. If reading the work of others confuses a writer's style, then such a style was probably not individual enough or rooted deeply enough to begin with. (However, many fiction writers do avoid reading fiction while heavily involved in writing their own work, to avoid outside influence or distraction.) A beginning writer should expect to go through several phases of stylistic expression before she establishes the one that is her own.

At the bottom of a form rejection slip I received for an article, an editor had written, "Write more naturally." What does that mean?

It probably means your writing is stilted. Stilted writing can arise when you use "difficult" words rather than simple words. Or your writing may be convoluted—too complex, wordy, or intricate to understand easily—and not straightforward. Anything that draws attention to the structure of your language, rather than your meaning, may not read naturally.

A writing teacher said my writing lacked vigor. How can I make my writing more vigorous?

Make good use of the active voice: not, "the car was stolen by Bob," but "Bob stole the car." Instead of depending on adjectives and adverbs, write with strong, specific nouns and verbs. Avoid too many qualifiers like the words *very, little,* and *rather*. Cut away unnecessary words. *The Elements of Style* offers many guidelines and tips that make writing more strong and lively.

I seem to spend so much time on style that it takes forever to finish a manuscript. Is there such a thing as worrying too much about style?

If you spend all your time worrying about how to say something, you may never get it said. While it is important to write clearly and with appealing style, too much concentration on the technique of writing can create a roadblock that prevents you from finishing a piece. It's more important and helpful to get finished pieces into the hands of editors than it is to spend endless time refining the same manuscript over and over again. If the content is good, an editor will probably iron out stylistic problems.

If a particular section of your article or story bothers you, it's best to leave it alone for a couple of days or even weeks or months. If you look at one piece for an extended period of time, you can lose all perspective and find fault with even your best work.

Is it okay to use he *when referring to both sexes, or do I need to use* he or she?

You should avoid *he* as a generic pronoun. The word *they* is often used as a replacement, although it can be grammatically incorrect. For instance, if your original sentence is "Everybody does what he likes," you could edit it to read: "Everybody does what they like." This usage is frequent in conversation, but technically incorrect (everybody is singular, but they is plural) and may be inappropriate in writing.

Another option would be "Everybody does what he or she likes." Used extensively, however, *he or she* can become awkward. Some writers shorten it with a slash, but this only results in an equally distracting he/she or s/he. In many cases, rewriting the sentence can eliminate the need for the pronoun. Book publishers vary in their styles, but one commonly accepted solution is to alternate the use of he and she.

I've often seen The Chicago Manual of Style *referred to by editors. Just what is it and where can I find a copy?*

The Chicago Manual of Style (sometimes abbreviated as CMS) is an extensive volume that details the manner of preparing a manuscript according to the style guidelines developed by the University of Chicago Press. It gives guidelines for capitalization, punctuation, italicization, and much, much more. It is not designed to help you develop your own writing style. The word *Style* in the title refers to the way a manuscript is set up for typesetting. Your editor will not expect you to know CMS style or use it in your manuscript.

WHERE TO FIND OUT MORE

Books

Self-Editing for Fiction Writers, by Renni Browne and Dave King, is one of the most popular and useful guides to self-editing your fiction.

Getting the Words Right, by Theodore A. Rees Cheney, is a thorough guide on how to revise and rewrite any piece of writing.

Write Great Fiction: Revision And Self-Editing, by James Scott Bell, provides an exclusive four-draft plan that takes your writing from an organic draft though the rough draft to a final draft, and ultimately a polished story.

The Writing Group Survival Guide, by Becky Levine, presents the best way to create a respectful, productive critique group, from the important details of finding a group to running a critique meeting and building a group that will evolve with its members.

Websites

Author Holly Lisle offers a very detailed and systematic approach for revising your manuscript at http://howtoreviseyournovel.com/.

Critique Circle (www.critiquecircle.com) is an online workshop for writers of all genres and includes tools for manuscript progress, submission tracking, character generation, and more.

The Internet Writing Workshop (www.internetwritingworkshop.org) offers critiques delivered right to your e-mail inbox. The only cost is a minimum participation requirement.

My Writers Circle (www.mywriterscircle.com) has review boards for prose, poetry, and scriptwriting. Ask questions and get feedback, and have others critique your work.

DVD

So, Is It Done? Navigating the Revision Process, hosted by Janet Burroway, is a not-to-be-missed multimedia presentation that steps you through the revision process. Many noted authors share their own revision secrets. Visit www.erpmedia.net to purchase a copy.

CHAPTER 14

HOW DO I KNOW IF SELF-PUBLISHING IS RIGHT FOR ME?

Writers who get frustrated by the endless process of submission and rejection often look to self-publishing for satisfaction. Why waste countless months or years trying to please this or that picky editor—who will tear apart your work until it's unrecognizable—when you can easily get your book in print for a modest sum?

Self-publishing or print-on-demand (POD) publishing may afford you the chance to hold your book in your hands, but it will not get your book into stores or lead to many sales unless you're willing to put significant and persistent effort into marketing and promotion. Most self-published authors find that selling their book (or finding distribution) is just as hard—if not harder than—finding a traditional publisher or an agent.

To the credit of many who self-publish, they can be fiercely passionate about their work, and much happier and satisfied going it alone. But those who truly succeed (or profit) often devote years of their life, if not their entire lives, to marketing and promoting their work, and often set up small, independent presses of their own. In other words, they begin a publishing business.

Most people who self-publish simply want an easy, straightforward way to get their book into the world. Some people are disappointed by the results; others are happy with their decision. It all depends on your expectations. This chapter helps establish what expectations you should have as a self-publisher and whether it's the right path for you.

What is self-publishing?

If an author submits his book and it is published by Random House, Penguin, or another commercial publisher, then the editing, design, sales, promotion, production, and other facets of publishing they handle. If you self-publish your book, you in essence become your own Random House or Doubleday, and all the steps in publishing and marketing a book become your responsibility. You pay for the manufacturing, production, distribution, and marketing of your book, but you also keep all the profits. Each step involves considerable effort and expense with no guarantee of a positive return on your investment.

However, most self-publishers today do not have to make the sizable investment they would have even ten years ago. The advent of print-on-demand technology, which allows books to be produced one at a time, has revolutionized the face of self-publishing by eliminating the need for an expensive traditional press run. E-books also offer authors a lower cost way to get their work in front of readers. Now just about anyone has the time and money to self-publish his book, either on his own or through a subsidy or print-on-demand publisher.

What are subsidy publishers?

Subsidy publishers, sometimes called vanity presses, charge you to publish your book and will issue your book only if you pay for the printing or production costs. That's the difference between subsidy and commercial publishers. Commercial publishers are willing to take a chance on the books they publish, and profit from book sales alone, whereas subsidy publishers make most of their profits from the author.

Subsidy publishers will warehouse your book, fulfill and ship orders, and send you a royalty check based on your book's sales, just like a traditional publisher. And just like a traditional publisher, they share in the sales profits, since they're the ones paying for the cost of sales. However, subsidy publishers provide minimal sales and promotional effort. They usually agree to distribute copies of the book to reviewers and reprint rights buyers at other publishing companies, but these professionals usually ignore subsidy publishers' books. Consequently, publicity and sales prospects are not very encouraging.

What are print-on-demand publishers?

Print-on-demand (POD) publishers, such as Xlibris, iUniverse, and AuthorHouse, are the same as subsidy publishers, except they use print-on-demand technology. They rarely use traditional print runs, and your book is not printed or produced until it is ordered. Their up-front fees usually include the cost of getting your book set up in their system; any design, production, or editing work they do to prepare your book for publication; and other add-on services such as editing, marketing, promotion, advertising, etc. It's very affordable for most people to publish through a POD service, since the production cost plummets when you don't have to pay up front for a traditional print run.

Sometimes you can get your POD book stocked in a handful of bookstores if you approach them on your own, and some POD companies have relationships with bookstores that are willing to take selected titles. But this is not the norm. Although times are slowly changing, most bookstores have a bias against most POD publishers, since there's little or no quality control as far as the material they publish, the books often don't have the same quality look and feel as the traditional houses' titles, and few POD companies offer books on a returnable basis, which all bookstores expect.

I hear that self-publishing and POD publishing carry a stigma. Is this true? Are there ways to publish one's own works without the stigma?

There is a stigma associated with self-publishing; however, as self-publishing becomes more and more widespread and authors spend more time and effort creating a quality finished product, the strength of this stigma is getting weaker. When a subsidy or POD publisher accepts your work, they're not accepting it based on literary merit, marketability, or salability. They're accepting it and publishing it because you're paying them—and so anything goes, good or bad. Subsidy and POD publishers defend themselves by claiming that many books published by the traditional presses are poorly edited or are of poor overall quality. You can decide for yourself if this is a valid argument, but like it or not, the traditional presses still make the judgment calls and act as quality filters for the large majority of the reading public; either you have their stamp of approval or you don't.

Authors who take great pains to ensure their manuscript is properly edited and proofread, hire designers and layout artists to create their book's cover and interior, and carefully choose their book's production quality and specifications can and do create a product that is indistinguishable from the work of a traditional press. In fact, you can find many examples of stunning work that a traditional publisher wouldn't have been able to pull off. However, such a product does not come easily.

Today's "traditional" self-publishers—like those described in the last paragraph—sometimes frown upon the mass of writers rushing to POD services and online publishers that promise immediate publishing gratification on the cheap. They say many POD books and e-books aren't edited or designed well, and as a result, it casts a shadow on those self-publishers who produce quality books that rival or surpass traditional publishers' offerings.

However, a traditional printing is not right for every book, and you may not have the time, energy, or expertise to act as your own publisher, distributor, and warehouser. Many writers need the help of a fee-based publishing service. As POD technology develops, it makes it easier for these writers to create a quality product. Just be sure you know what to expect from it.

What kinds of projects are right for print-on-demand or subsidy publishing?

Family histories, memoirs, cookbooks, poetry—anything with limited market value or readership—are ideal candidates for POD publishing. POD can also be useful if you want to market and promote a very niche book on your website or via e-mail, and if you have excellent and direct connections to your target audience. (If you're in this type of situation, check out Lulu.com; it's completely free if you're happy with just an electronic version of your book. You pay when you want or need POD service.)

In general, you should seriously consider POD publishing only if:

- you know your book has limited potential in the marketplace (or holds little interest for mainstream publishers)

- you want to have the book published only for family and friends

- you want a few copies for personal promotional/marketing purposes

- you know how to sell and market the book on your own, direct to the consumer, and don't want to bother with the fuss of a traditional press run

- you want to get your out-of-print titles back into print

POD will disappoint writers with dreams of best-seller status who haven't had any luck breaking in to the traditional publishers. POD rarely leads to bookstore placement, best-seller lists, or media attention.

What are the biggest mistakes people make when using subsidy or POD services?

The biggest and most common mistake is not hiring a professional editor to review your work line by line. Mainstream publishers use an in-house editor, a copyeditor, a proofreader, and an indexer for each work they publish. If your book is full of errors, it will immediately lose credibility with readers. Don't rely on the subsidy or POD service to do the editing—they're not there to edit your work, and they pay little attention to its quality.

The second biggest pitfall for many self-published books is a poorly designed cover. Your book will not be taken seriously if it does not look professional and appropriate for your genre. Many authors make the mistake of designing their own covers or using artwork provided by family and friends who are not professional artists or designers. The cover of your book is often the number one sales tool, especially when it's sold primarily online. You want to make a positive impact and avoid an amateurish book cover. So make an investment in a professional designer, and get a cover that looks like it's from a traditional publishing house. It will lead to better sales because it will make a better first impression. (Note: Even if your POD or subsidy publisher provides a cover design as part of its services, sometimes what it produces isn't much better than what you could do yourself. Again, look to a professional who will do it right.)

I've heard that it's a good idea to self-publish your book first through a POD company, then shop it around to editors, agents, and readers as a kind of test run—that it shows you're willing to invest in your work. Is that true?

It can be useful to have a few POD copies of your book if you want to test-market it with your audience and peers. In general, this kind of test marketing works best when combined with a strong nonfiction book concept and a strong marketing platform. It's probably not a good idea if you're a novelist hoping to interest an agent or editor—you won't score any points if you use it as a pitching or querying tool.

Should I be worried about the publishing contract my POD company gave me to sign? What should I look for?

You should grant limited rights for print publication for a limited period. You want to be able to cut ties with the POD publisher upon written notice or have a defined time limit on its ability to print and sell the work. You should not give the POD company any of your subsidiary rights. Visit the Writer Beware site, at the end of this chapter, for more information on what to look for in POD contracts.

IF YOU'RE SELF-PUBLISHED

I have recently self-published my book. How can I get it stocked in bookstores?

You need to find a distributor. A distributor is essentially a middleman company that sells your book into major accounts such as Barnes & Noble. Getting a distributor can be just as difficult as securing a publisher—you have to convince them there's an audience for your book and that it's a quality work. A couple of the well-known distributors are Publishers Group West and Consortium. Distributors will ask you for a substantial discount (as much as 60 percent off retail price), then they will sell at discount to their accounts (usually at 50 to 60 percent off).

If you don't have a distributor, you are not likely to get your book into stores nationwide, though you may have some luck getting your local or regional bookstores to stock a few copies.

If I have a book published, have it copyrighted, and advertise and sell a few copies, will I later be able to offer it to a larger publisher, or do you think this would ruin my chances of selling it to a larger firm?

If you couldn't interest a larger publisher in your book before self-publishing it, you're not likely to find a buyer later unless you rack up significant sales on your own—usually several thousand copies for a novel, more for nonfiction. There are cases where a publisher will take on a successful self-published book, but the success stories make up a miniscule percentage of all the self-published books out there. If this is your goal, it's vitally important to promote and market your book so that you achieve the sales figures needed to get major publishers' attention.

If I have a self-published book that I'd like an agent to consider representing and selling to the traditional publishers, should I send him a copy of the book?

It depends on how proud you are of your self-published book and how successful it is. If you produced a remarkable book that sold well, you may want to send the book to the agent, especially if it's an attractive nonfiction book. (Query first, or follow the agent's guidelines.) If your book did not do well, or if it looks unprofessional, start all over again; pretend you never self-published the work. Most people who find themselves in this situation have self-published novels or children's books that sold a handful of copies; in such cases it's better to start fresh unless you have an unusual story to tell about the self-published book (for example, John Grisham read it and commented on how much he liked it).

E-BOOKS

What are e-books? Who publishes them?

E-books are electronic books that you download and read on your computer screen or on a handheld device. In the late 1990s, major publishers established divisions devoted entirely to e-books, but once the technology bubble burst, those divisions quickly evaporated.

At first, e-books have failed to capture the public's imagination, mostly due to the lack of a dominant format and user-friendly reading device. Now with the market bursting with the Kindle, iPad, iPhone, Sony Reader, Nook, and more, e-books are surging ahead to become a commanding force in the market.

Traditional publishers now routinely create e-book versions of their print books, and they also release some books in e-book-only formats. E-books also present an opportunity for self-publishing authors to reach a broad audience outside the confines and cost of print books.

Should I consider an e-book publisher for my work?

If you think an e-book publisher is a good fit for what you've written, and you like a particular e-publisher's offerings and services, this expanding market could be a good opportunity for you. Many reputable e-book publishers exist, though you shouldn't expect an advance or future riches by publishing through one. EPICon (www.epicauthors.com), an organization for e-book authors, is a good resource for learning the basics of e-publishing and to find reputable e-publishers. It hosts an annual conference, which is the best education any writer could have on the electronic publishing world.

E-books are a good opportunity for authors who have or are building an online following. Social networks make connecting with people in niche groups easy, and blogs provide a platform to promote your work. Both of these work hand in hand with e-book publishing. Publishing an e-book rather than a print edition can also keep overhead costs down for self-publishing authors.

As with any contract, make sure you carefully read the fine print before you sign with an e-book publisher. You don't want to give away every possible right, and it should be clear how often royalties will be paid. The EPICon site lists several red flags you should look for when reviewing an e-book contract.

What are the drawbacks to e-publishing?

The big and obvious drawback is that you may not have a print book to show people, and your book will probably not be stocked in brick-and-mortar bookstores. Distribution is often limited to the e-publisher's website, Amazon, and a few other sites. Some e-book publishers do offer print-on-demand services (or even traditional press runs) and can sell print editions of your book, but you're still unlikely to get any bookstore play. Also, some people in the publishing industry don't consider e-books published through e-publishers to be legitimate publishing credits; but this bias is changing rapidly as e-book formats and devices become more and more prevalent and sophisticated.

WHERE TO FIND OUT MORE

Books

The Complete Guide to Self-Publishing, by Marilyn Ross and Sue Collier, is a comprehensive guide to publishing your work, your way.

The Self-Publishing Manual, by Dan Poynter, is the best-known self-publishing guide on the market, authored by the acknowledged guru in the field.

The Indie Author Guide, by April Hamilton, is a hands-on, firsthand guide that equips you to edit, format, and market your self-published book.

The Fine Print of Self Publishing, by Mark Levine, examines and evaluates the contracts and services so you know what to avoid.

Websites

Writer Beware (www.sfwa.org/for-authors/writer-beware/pod), hosted by the Science Fiction and Fantasy Writers of America, has excellent information on POD publishing, as well as scam alerts on publishers and agents.

POD-dy Mouth (www.girlondemand.blogspot.com), now discontinued, is still helpful and informative for anyone who's considering print-on-demand.

The Small Publishers Association of North America (www.spannet.org) is a non-profit association of small publishers and self-publishers. Another good place to start to learn more about self-publishing and what it means to start a small press of your own.

Lulu (www.lulu.com) offers outstanding self-publishing services—not to be missed.

EPICon (www.epicauthors) is an organization for electronically published authors.

Fictionwise (www.fictionwise.com) is one of the most popular online e-book stores.

Publetariat (www.publetariat.com) is an online community and news hub built specifically for indie authors and small independent imprints.

Dog Ear Publishing (www.dogearpublishing.net/self-publishing-companies.aspx) offers excellent information to help you compare various services.

PART II:
FORMATTING & SUBMITTING YOUR WORK

CHAPTER 15

ARTICLES

There will always be a demand for articles in the writing market. Content that once went in newspapers is now going online. As one magazine folds, another prints its first issue. Articles can be on any topic—investigative pieces, features, interviews, travel writing, columns, sports, home and garden, lifestyle, art and music—there is a market for it all. Regardless of what type of article you want to write, you have to know how to properly submit to an editor or publisher, and how to format your work.

WHAT YOU NEED TO SUBMIT

The process of submitting articles begins with sending a query to an editor, continues through getting acceptance to write the article, and ends with submitting the article text itself. Barring some bumps along the way, the process is that simple.

Take note of the sequence: Query, acceptance, then writing. Before you write an article, you should sell it. That may sound backwards, but it is how the publishing world works. You can submit finished articles, but this is usually a recipe for disappointment. Most editors want queries before assigning articles. Even if an editor likes the idea for an article, he usually wants to provide some guidance before it is written. That can't happen if the article is already completed. Or it means major rewrites, and major headaches. Working on spec—meaning, submitting completed articles rather than simply the ideas for different stories—is usually an unprofitable habit for freelancers.

The query letter is the time-honored traditional method for selling an article. And that method is the one that editors and publishers prefer to use. As e-mail is quickly replacing snail mail as the main form of communication, the method of delivery and the average response time from an editor may be changing, but the overall process is not.

Another thing that hasn't changed: The query is your first impression with an editor. As you start to develop relationships with editors, pitching article ideas will get measurably easier. Correspondence becomes more informal. Your story pitches become less fleshed out. You're battle tested, so assignments come easier. But if you have no established relationship with an editor, remember to fall back on two things: professionalism and a darn good query letter.

QUERY LETTER

Submission Tips

The query should serve several primary purposes:

- Sell your idea through a brief, catchy description.

- Tell the editor how you would handle the lead and develop the article.

- Show that you are familiar with the publication and how your article would fit with it.

- Indicate why you are qualified to write this article.

When applicable—and when possible within space constraints—the query should also:

- State the availability of photography or other artwork. (If this is a key selling point, you should definitely include such information. If it's not, these details can be discussed when the editor contacts you about an assignment.) State how you'll be gathering the art, and whether you will take the pictures yourself or a third party will provide them.

- Provide a working title that succinctly and enticingly sums up your idea.

- Estimate the article's length. (It should be as long as you think is necessary to cover the topic, keeping in mind what is the typical length of pieces in the publication. Remember: The editor may think otherwise.)

- Outline possible sidebars.

- Summarize the supporting material, such as anecdotes, interviews, or statistics.

- State when the article will be available.

- Indicate if you are submitting this idea simultaneously to other publications.

A benefit for you as the writer is that preparing the query helps you define the project and develop a lead and a strategy for completing the assignment well before you actually have to do it. The downside is that a query letter can take longer to write, word for word, than the article itself.

Query letters are something of a genre unto themselves. Writing them successfully requires considerable attention to detail and tight editing to fit the one-page standard, which is a widely observed rule for article queries.

Formatting Specs

- Use a standard font or typeface, 12-point type. Avoid bold, script, or italics, except for publication titles. Arial and Times New Roman are fairly standard.

- Place your name, address, phone number, e-mail, fax, and website at the top of your letter, centered, or on your letterhead.

- Use a 1" margin on all sides.

- Keep it to one page. If necessary, separately attach a résumé or a list of credits to provide additional information.

- Use block format (no indentations, an extra space between paragraphs).

- Single-space the body of the letter and double-space between paragraphs.

Other Dos and Don'ts

- Do mention that you can send the manuscript on CD or via e-mail. Most finished articles will be sent as a Microsoft Word attachment. (Sending CDs to an editor comes in handy when dealing with high-resolution art that takes up a lot of memory.)

- Do address the query to a specific editor, preferably the editor assigned to handle freelance submissions or the section you're writing for. Call to get the appropriate name and gender.

- Do thank the editor for considering your proposal.

- Do include an SASE (self-addressed stamped envelope) or postcard for reply. State in the letter that you have done so, either in the body or in a list of enclosures. (Postcards are cheaper and easier. Get them printed in bulk.)

- Do mention previous publishing credits that pertain to the proposed article.

- Don't take up half a page listing credits of little interest to the editor. If you have extensive credits that pertain to the query, list them on an enclosed sheet.

- Do indicate familiarity with the publication. It's okay to make a positive comment, too, if it's sincere and appropriate, but don't get obsequious.

- Don't request writers guidelines or a sample copy in your letter. This clearly indicates you're not familiar enough to query. You should request guidelines before you send a query.

- Don't overpromise. If you can't deliver, it will soon become obvious to the editor.

- Don't tell the editor the idea was already rejected by another publication. Such full disclosure does you no good and isn't necessary.

- Do include clippings, especially when they're applicable to the idea you're proposing. No more than three are necessary, or even desirable.

- Do send copies, not originals, of your clippings. They can always get lost, even if you include an SASE. Editors assume photocopied clips are disposable; if you want them back, say so in your letter and make sure you include an SASE with sufficient postage.

- Don't discuss payment terms. It's premature.

ELECTRONIC QUERIES

Submission Tips

The digital age has brought an air of informality to communications between editors and writers, but manners have not been redefined. Communications with a new editor should still be formal and respectful whether you make contact by mail, fax, or e-mail. Once you've developed a relationship, you can afford to become less formal. Because the editor is familiar with your writing experience and ability to develop an article, you might pitch story ideas over the phone or in one- or two-sentence e-mails. But rarely will an editor make a judgment based on casual contact with a new writer.

Thus, the basic format, length, and tone of an electronic query shouldn't be much different than a query on paper, except that certain features of e-mails do dictate different strategies.

Formatting Specs

- Include the same information you would in a query on paper—your name and contact information. The biggest change is to include your contact information at the bottom left, under your signature, rather than at the top. Because an editor will have a limited view of your query in an e-mail window, it's a good idea to get right to the query text.

- Fill in the subject line of the e-mail with a description of your query. This gives you an extra selling line and can be a good place for the proposed title of your work. Don't be afraid to start the subject line with the word, *Query*.

- Follow the same format you would with a query on paper, including the date, salutation, and block paragraph format. Leaving out these formalities isn't unusual, but there's no good reason to do away with them just because it's an e-mail. The information could be useful to the editor, and it never hurts to be polite.

How to Include Clips With E-Mailed Queries

When you send an e-mail query, you can provide clips five ways. Pay attention to writers guidelines of the specific publication you are sending the query to in order to see if they would like to see clips in a particular fashion (for example, as links inside an e-mail query). There are no generally accepted standards for which is best, but the pros and cons of each method are described.

1. **Include a line telling the editor that clips are available on request.** If the editor requests them, you can then mail, fax, or e-mail the clips according to her preference. This is a convenient solution for the writer but not necessarily for the editor. The clips aren't available immediately, so you potentially slow the decision process by adding a step, and you lose any speed you've gained by e-mailing the query in the first place.

2. **Include electronic versions of the clips in the body of the e-mail message.** This can make for an awfully long e-mail, and it doesn't look as presentable as other alternatives, but it may be better than making the editor wait to download attachments or log on to a website. Also, since viruses are often transmitted as attachments to e-mails, editors may be leery of accepting e-mail attachments from you before they know who you are.

3. **Include electronic versions of the articles as attachments.** The disadvantage here is the editor has to download the clips, which can take several minutes. Also, if there's a format disparity, the editor may not be able to read the attachment.

4. **Send the clips in a separate e-mail message.** This cuts the download time and eliminates software-related glitches, but it clutters the editor's e-mail in-box.

5. **Hypertext links in the e-mail.** This may be the most convenient and reliable way for editors to access your clips electronically. If any of your stories are published online, simply include the links to those clips at the end of your e-mail. These provide a more accurate reading of what the editor can expect. If you have your own individual website dedicated to your writing career, include articles online that way.

Other Dos and Don'ts

- Don't use all caps or exclamation points in the subject line. These are among the dreaded earmarks of spam and may cause editors to summarily delete your e-mail.

- Don't submit an e-mail query unless you know it's welcome. Listings in *Writer's Market* or *Writer's Digest* will indicate whether electronic queries are accepted. If you can't find a listing, call the publication to check.

- Don't send an e-mail query to the editor's personal e-mail address unless expressly directed to do so. Many publications maintain separate e-mail addresses for queries.

- Don't insert clip art graphics or other images.

- Do attach or provide links to photos or graphics that have digital versions stored on your computer if their availability will help sell your article. They may take a long time to download, but the editor only needs to do it if she's interested.

- Do indicate how you'll make your clips and other supporting material available.

- Do turn off your spam filter if you use EarthLink. When an editor replies, she shouldn't have to confirm her existence as a human being just so you can get her response.

This is one of many letterhead styles you can use.

John Q. Writer
123 Author Lane
Writerville, CA 95355
johnqwriter@email.com
(323) 555-0000

January 30, 2009

Date flushed right

Jane Smith, managing editor
New Mexico Magazine
4200 Magazine Blvd.
Santa Fe, NM 87501

Always address the correct editor.

Dear Ms. Smith:

According to the Bible, it took God two days to create all living creatures. The way New Mexican Regina Gordon sees it, the 48 Hour Film Project involves the same amount of time—with an only slightly less complicated task.

Use a lead designed to hook and pique interest.

"Every second counts when you only have 48 hours to make a film." That's the motto of the 48 Hour Film Project (www.48hourfilm. com), a nationwide event that challenges local filmmakers to form teams and create four-minute movies—from script to set design to finished product—in forty-eight hours or less. Albuquerque hosted more than twenty teams in 2008.

All of these guerilla filmmakers report to one woman—the city's area producer, Regina Gordon, who must substitute passion, adrenaline, and insane amounts of coffee for sleep she certainly won't get. So what drives her and other participants to exhaust themselves like they do? I propose a 800-word short profile on Gordon along with New Mexico's involvement in the project for *New Mexico Magazine*. (I have already touched based with Gordon.) I believe that a Gordon feature would be a great fit for the "Introducing" section of your magazine. I would interview Gordon to hear anecdotes from last year's competition and discover what lies in store for this year as a sense of community for the project continues to build in the area.

Estimated word count

Targeting a specific section of the magazine shows you're familiar with the publication.

In 2003, I covered Philadelphia's involvement in the project for *Artspike* magazine. Thank you for considering this piece. My résumé and clips are enclosed.

Highlight qualifications quickly and effectively.

Be polite.

Respectfully,

Leave enough room here for your signature.

John Q. Writer

149

Articles

John Q. Writer
123 Author Lane
Writerville, CA 95355

March 24, 2009

Editors
Atlanta Journal-Constitution

Dear Sir/Ma'am:

I have an idea for newspaper article. I have a feeling that it would be a controversial and explosive story that would sell a whole bunch of copies—it's that good. What I want to do is give you some of my early thoughts, and if you're interested, we can talk some specifics over the phone (though bear with me; my cell phone gets bad reception).

This is what I'm thinking. I write an article on how the social networking juggernaut MySpace is affecting the dating scene in the ATL. Cool, huh? I know that I could have pitched this to *Atlanta Magazine* or even *People*, but I figured I would give you a shot. For the article, I would need some ideas for sources, and probably some upfront money to buy a laptop. At this point, I'm thinking the article will run about 5,000 words.

My writing influences are Stephen King, James Patterson, and Joe Eszterhas. I've blogged on MySpace plenty of times before and I also regularly comment on website forums and message boards, so I think I have the necessary experience to tackle such an article.

I'm offering a seven-day window on this query because I think that's fair. After all, this is a sizzling topic. Please get back to me right quick.

Peace,

John Q. Writer

No e-mail or phone number is included.

Address is missing.

Not targeting a certain editor shows you didn't even do the basic research to find an editor's name.

This simple grammatical error could have been caught with some proofreading.

Every query recipient wants to feel like you've picked this market for a reason, and arrogant talk like this will kill a query.

Why does this matter?

An editor doesn't need seven days. He'll just say no now.

There might be something here, but the idea is not fleshed out and there is no indication of how you would hook readers.

Always be humble. Adopting an attitude never works.

This proposed length is way too long for virtually any publication. Suggesting such an outrageous word count will torpedo your chances.

While you want to list credentials, something worse would be to list meaningless accomplishments.

It's not a bad idea to copy (CC or BCC) yourself on the e-mail to keep copies of all e-correspondence to editors.

You may capitalize key words in your subject line if you want to, but never use all caps.

TO: editor@fastcompany.com
CC: johnqwriter@email.com
SUBJECT: Query: Improving Attention the All Natural Way

August 13, 2008

Date flushed right

Kim Dearth, senior editor
brava
P.O. Box 45050
Madison, WI 53744-5050
kdearth@ericksonpublishing.com

Starting the subject line off with "Query" will help ensure your e-mail isn't mistaken as junk mail.

Dear Ms. Dearth:

I see on your editorial calendar that you'll be covering "Adult Attention Deficit Disorder" in your December 2008 issue.

Address a specific editor.

As a full-time freelance writer specializing in cognitive development, I'd like to propose an article to your upcoming issue. **"Pay Attention! Improving Attention the All Natural Way—With Brain Training"** would include the following:

Always explain your qualifications, but never brag.

The title and deck of the article are provided—making the editor's job easier.

1. Brain exercises that your readers can do at home to improve the three types of attention: selective, sustained, and divided.

2. The latest scientific research on brain training.

3. Quotes from a psychologist, a professional brain trainer in Madison, and an author.

General formatting rules—such as single-spaced paragraphs—remain the same.

I could fit the article to your desired word count.

My credentials include a B.A. in psychology and more than 1,000 published pieces including two nonfiction books for McGraw-Hill. I've written for countless parenting, health and women's magazines and currently work as a freelance editor for several publications.

Instead of putting your contact information at the top of an e-mail query, place it at the bottom. Only part of an e-mail will be visible in a computer window, so you need to get down to business fast.

If you have a working title, use quotations around it, or bold it, or both. If you can pique an editor's interest with the title alone, you're off to a good start.

Thank you for your time. I look forward to hearing from you.

Best,

John Q. Writer
123 Author Lane
Writerville, CA 95355
johnqwriter@email.com
(323) 555-0000
Clips available on www.johnqwriter.com

If you aren't mailing clips, make sure you have some work online that an editor can review.

This query fits on one printed page as well. Don't abuse the formlessness of e-mail to become verbose.

TO: editor@entrepreneur.com
CC:
SUBJECT: ARTICLE FOR FAST COMPANY MAGAZINE

Dear Editor,

I'm interesting in writing for you magazine. I have been working on an article on business ethics that I think will work well for *Fast Company*.

I have submitted this article to seven other business magazines but they have all passed on it. I hope you are interested in it. I expect to be paid three dollars per word for this article.

Thank you for your time and consideration.

Sincerely,

John Q. Writer

P.S. I'm attaching one of my published articles.

Don't type in all caps.

The simple research to find the editor's name wasn't done.

Typo. Be sure to read through your letter before you hit "Send."

Never say that the article has been rejected by other magazines.

Make sure your clip is actually attached—and in a format that's compatible with most computers.

This tells the editor nothing about your article.

This tells the editor nothing about your article. E-mail queries should be just as detailed as regular mail queries.

Never mention payment. A query is used to gauge interest in an article.

FOLLOW-UP LETTERS

Occasionally lines get crossed, mail gets lost, and plans change. And sometimes, editors are just plain rude. For whatever reason, your postcard or SASE is never returned, the article you submit never appears, or you don't get paid. You may need to follow up on a query, article submission, or payment. Here are some polite, gentle ways to go about it.

Submission Tips

When you haven't heard back from a publication within a reasonable time, such as sixty days or the reporting period cited in the listing in *Writer's Market*, send a brief, businesslike inquiry.

Formatting Specs

- As with queries, address it to the correct editor and use proper greeting and salutation, and letter format.
- Enclose a reply postcard or SASE (except in a follow-up on a late payment), in case your original was lost.

Other Dos and Don'ts

- Do be businesslike and polite.
- Do briefly explain the history behind your request (for example, "I sent you a query with a prepaid reply postcard on …").
- Don't be emotional or accusatory, or jump to conclusions about what happened.
- Do resubmit your query or invoice.

ARTICLE

What You Need to Submit

Compared to the query letter that leads up to the article, formatting the article itself is relatively easy. The style and approach of each article is different, of course, and beyond the scope of this book. However, the layout of the printed page and the information is relatively clear-cut. All you need is:

- A cover letter
- Your article

This section will guide you through the cover letter and the article itself.

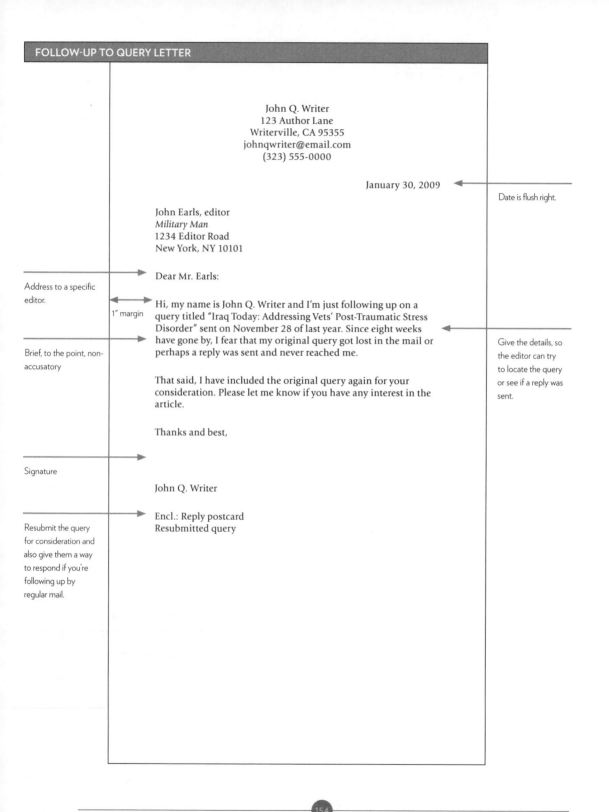

John Q. Writer
123 Author Lane
Writerville, CA 95355
johnqwriter@email.com
(323) 555-0000

January 30, 2009

Date is flush right.

John Earls, editor
Military Man
1234 Editor Road
New York, NY 10101

Address to a specific editor.

1" margin

Dear Mr. Earls:

Hi, my name is John Q. Writer and I'm just following up on a query titled "Iraq Today: Addressing Vets' Post-Traumatic Stress Disorder" sent on November 28 of last year. Since eight weeks have gone by, I fear that my original query got lost in the mail or perhaps a reply was sent and never reached me.

Brief, to the point, non-accusatory

Give the details, so the editor can try to locate the query or see if a reply was sent.

That said, I have included the original query again for your consideration. Please let me know if you have any interest in the article.

Thanks and best,

Signature

John Q. Writer

Encl.: Reply postcard
Resubmitted query

Resubmit the query for consideration and also give them a way to respond if you're following up by regular mail.

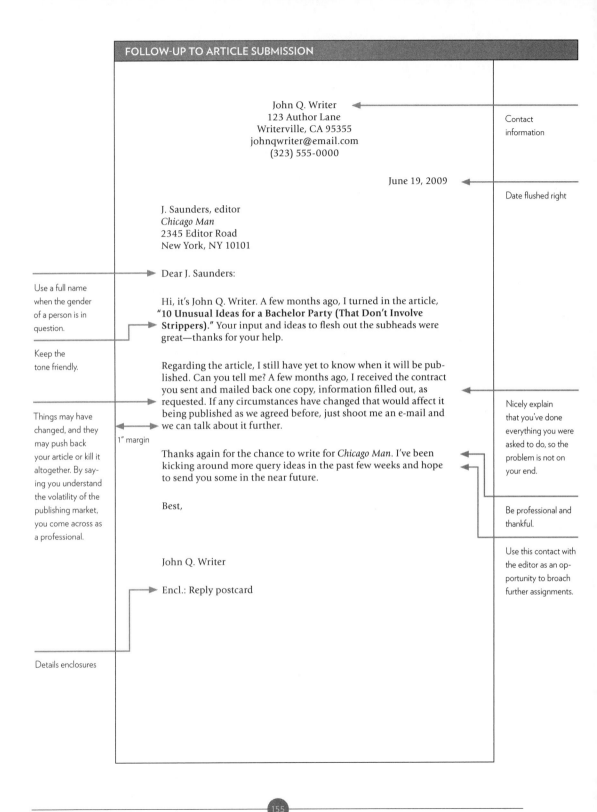

John Q. Writer
123 Author Lane
Writerville, CA 95355
johnqwriter@email.com
(323) 555-0000

Contact
information

June 19, 2009

Date flushed right

J. Saunders, editor
Chicago Man
2345 Editor Road
New York, NY 10101

Dear J. Saunders:

Use a full name
when the gender
of a person is in
question.

Hi, it's John Q. Writer. A few months ago, I turned in the article,
**"10 Unusual Ideas for a Bachelor Party (That Don't Involve
Strippers)."** Your input and ideas to flesh out the subheads were
great—thanks for your help.

Keep the
tone friendly.

Regarding the article, I still have yet to know when it will be published. Can you tell me? A few months ago, I received the contract
you sent and mailed back one copy, information filled out, as
requested. If any circumstances have changed that would affect it
being published as we agreed before, just shoot me an e-mail and
we can talk about it further.

Things may have
changed, and they
may push back
your article or kill it
altogether. By say-
ing you understand
the volatility of the
publishing market,
you come across as
a professional.

1" margin

Nicely explain
that you've done
everything you were
asked to do, so the
problem is not on
your end.

Thanks again for the chance to write for *Chicago Man*. I've been
kicking around more query ideas in the past few weeks and hope
to send you some in the near future.

Best,

Be professional and
thankful.

John Q. Writer

Use this contact with
the editor as an op-
portunity to broach
further assignments.

Encl.: Reply postcard

Details enclosures

COVER LETTER

Submission Tips

By the time you send the article, the editor should already know who you are and about the article. Use the cover letter to accomplish a few additional functions:

- Provide details that may be important in the editing and fact-checking process, including names, addresses, and phone numbers of sources.

- Inform the editor of the status of photographs and graphics that will accompany the article (whether they're enclosed or coming from another party).

- Provide information about how you can be reached for questions.

- Mention any details the editor should know in editing the manuscript, such as difficulty in reaching a particular source or conflicting data you received and how you resolved the conflict.

- Thank the editor for the assignment and express your interest in writing for the publication again.

Formatting Specs

- Use a standard font, 12-point type. Avoid bold or italics, except for titles.

- Put your name and contact information at the top of your letter, centered, or on your letterhead.

- Use 1" margins on all sides.

- Address the cover letter to a specific editor. (Call and get the appropriate editor's name and gender.)

- If you need more than a page, use it. The editor will need this information in handling your manuscript.

- Provide a word count.

- Provide contact names of sources if needed.

ELECTRONIC COVER LETTER

Submission Tips

Once an editor is interested in seeing your article, he may ask you to send the article via e-mail. Don't send the article by itself; just because you're using e-mail doesn't mean you should forgo a cover letter. The cover letter will provide the editor with valuable information regarding your article and should include the same information as one sent via mail.

The text of the cover letter should be submitted in the e-mail body. The article should be attached, preferably as a Microsoft Word document (.doc).

Formatting Specs

- Include the same information in your cover letter as you would in a paper cover letter—name, address, phone, fax, and website.

- Use the subject line to introduce the title of your article.

- Follow the same format you would with a paper cover letter, including date, salutation, and block paragraph format.

Other Dos and Don'ts

- Don't use all caps or exclamation points in the subject line.

- Don't insert clip art graphics or other images in your cover letter. Keep it simple.

John Q. Writer
123 Author Lane
Writerville, CA 95355
johnqwriter@email.com
(323) 555-0000

Contact
information

January 5, 2009

Elizabeth Cook
Food Processing
6789 Editor Ave.
Chicago, IL 60612

Some informality is
acceptable at this
point.

Dear Libby:

Enclosed is "Foods for (Shelf) Life" (1,500 words) for the March issue.

Photos should have arrived from the National Sunflower Association and USDA. If you don't receive them by the end of the week,
please let me know and I'll call to check on their status.

Provide information
about photography, if
you have it.

Tell how you can be
reached for ques-
tions when necessary.

1" margin

I'll be away on business from January 7–10, but I will be checking
voice mail daily. Feel free to leave any questions on my voice mail,
and I'll answer them on yours if I can't return the call when you're
in the office.

Here are the contact numbers for sources:

Many publications
require contact
names and numbers.
The cover letter is a
good place for this.

- Jeff Miller, agronomist with the U.S. Department of Agriculture, (716) 555-4322

- Pamela J. White, professor of food science at Iowa State
University, (515) 555-1224

- Larry Kleingartner, executive director of the National Sunflower Association, Bismarck, ND, (716) 555-3400

- Shin Hasegawa, a biochemist at the USDA's Agricultural
Research Service in Albany, CA, (510) 555-6070

It's always a good
idea to mention that
you are available
to do requested
changes.

Thanks again for the assignment. I look forward to working with
you again soon. As I mentioned before, let me know if this piece
needs any revisions or tweaks.

Best wishes,

Signature

John Q. Writer
Encl.: Manuscript, "Foods for (Shelf) Life"

If you're sending
an article through
the mail, consider
including a CD data
disk that contains the
article in electronic
format.

ARTICLE MANUSCRIPT

Submission Tips

Show you're a professional by submitting a clean, grammatically correct and properly spelled manuscript that hews as closely as possible to the style of the publication.

Formatting Specs

- Use a 1" margin on all sides.

- Don't number the first page.

- Include rights offered or negotiated and a word count in the top right corner of the first page.

- If you have one or more sidebars, indicate this in the top right corner of the first page, along with the word count for each sidebar.

- Put the working title in all caps or boldface and the subtitle underlined or in italic, centered, about one-third of the way down the page from the top margin.

- Skip one line and write "by" in lowercase, then skip another line and put your name. (If you're using a pseudonym, put that name in all caps, and then on the next line put your real name in parentheses.)

- Drop four lines and begin the article. Indent all paragraphs except the first one.

- Double-space the entire text of the story.

- Put a slug, a one- to two-word name, at the top left corner of the header in the second and preceding pages.

- Put page numbers (from page 2 to the end of the article) in the top right corner of the header.

- Use 12-point type.

- Optional: At the article's end, put a "–30–" or "–###–" notation. This is more of a relic in publishing than a necessity, but some writers feel insecure without it. It won't hurt to do it or leave it out.

- When sending an accepted article, be sure to include a copy of the article on disk or CD along with the hard copy.

Other Dos and Don'ts

- Do use paper clips in the top left corner of your manuscript (butterfly clips or paper clamps for articles of more than ten pages).

- Don't use staples.

- Don't clip, and especially don't staple, your cover letter to the manuscript.

- Don't use a separate cover page. It's pretentious for an article-length manuscript and wholly unnecessary.

- Don't justify text or align the right margin. Ragged right is fine.

- Don't insult the editor's intelligence or intentions by putting a copyright notice on the manuscript. It's copyrighted as soon as you write it.

- Don't use unusual fonts. A simple Times Roman will do fine.

- Do include suggested subheads in the body of your manuscript if the magazine's style is to use subheads; however, don't rely on subheads as a substitute for transitions. Subheads may need to be removed for layout or page composition purposes. Besides, they're an editor's prerogative. Don't count on them staying where you put them.

Winning Style Points

Virtually all newspapers and many magazines use some variation of Associated Press style. Other magazines and most books use *The Chicago Manual of Style* from the University of Chicago Press. Every freelancer should have the books *The Associated Press Stylebook and Libel Manual* and *The Chicago Manual of Style* on her shelf. *CMS* also provides useful general guidance on grammar and usage issues in addition to style points. Both books also offer online versions to which you can subscribe.

The most common style questions concern such areas as numbers, localities, abbreviations, and capitalization. Style manuals also cover such fine points as the difference in usage between *lawyer* and *attorney*. It's a good idea to at least skim through the style manuals to become familiar with the usage issues they cover, in addition to using them as references when unsure about a style issue.

Most publications have style rules of their own that deviate from whichever standard they use. Freelancers can't realistically be expected to know all the rules before first being published in a magazine, but try to be familiar with the publication's basic style standards.

Include contact information here.

John Q. Writer
123 Author Lane
Writerville, CA 95355
(323) 555-0000
johnqwriter@email.com

First North American Rights
Approximately 1,500 words

Provide a word count.

Title one-third of the way down the page

FOODS FOR (SHELF) LIFE
For advances in shelf life, researchers
increasingly change foods themselves

Underline or italicize the subhead or deck head.

by
John Q. Writer

Enhancing shelf life used to mean finding better preservatives. But food scientists increasingly are changing the food itself as

1" margin

they search for cleaner-reading labels, better taste, and stronger nutritional profiles to go along with improved shelf life.

Indent paragraphs except for the first one.

Researchers are modifying such basic foods as oils, beef, and fruit on the molecular or genetic level for the sake of preserving flavor or preventing spoilage.

One of the bigger changes in the next few years could be in oils for frying snacks and other foods. Research into high-oleic

Double-spaced text

versions of sunflower, soybean, and corn oils is bringing to market oils that offer extended shelf life for fried and other foods without requiring hydrogenation.

Shelf Life   5

Slug line at the
top left

Page number

A side benefit of the enzyme may be prevention of tumor forma-

tion. Separate studies at Baylor University and the University of

Western Ontario found the enzyme inhibited oral cancer tumors

in hamsters and human breast cancer cells in mice.

Vitamin E as Beef Preservative

Mark subheads
clearly.

Consumers also won't have to wait so long to see the benefits

from the addition of megadoses of vitamin E to the diets of beef

cattle.

Food processors have long used vitamin E as a natural

preservative in some foods. In recent years, agricultural research

in the U.S. and England has found that adding vitamin E to the

diets of both forage and grain-fed cattle one hundred days before

slaughter can increase the shelf life of the beef.

1" margin

In one study in Britain, among cattle given 1,500 interna-

tional units of vitamin E a day, compared with a natural diet sup-

plying 30–40 international units, shelf life was improved by two

to three days. In the U.S., inclusion of vitamin E in animal feed is

increasingly becoming standard practice as supermarket buyers

begin to specify it. Use of vitamin E cuts waste in the meat supply

chain by thirty dollars per head of cattle at a cost of only two to

three dollars per head, according to the USDA.

No need to mark
the end. Especially
avoid using "The
End" in nonfiction
articles. Use "—30—"
or "—###—" if you
feel the need.

SIDEBARS

Submission Tips

For sidebars included with articles, start the sidebar on a new page immediately following the last page of the main text. Don't include all the front-page information you put at the beginning of the main text. Simply use a header that says "Sidebar: (Same slug you used for the article)" in the top left corner and a word count in the top right corner.

Formatting Specs

- With the exception just noted, follow the same formatting specs used with the article manuscript.

- Don't number the first page of the sidebar, but do number subsequent pages, if there are any.

- Use the sidebar slug in the header of the second and following pages, along with a page number, in the same format as a regular article.

Other Dos and Don'ts

- Don't use staples to attach your sidebar page.

- Don't justify text or align the right margin.

- Do include suggested heads and subheads for your sidebar.

Contact
information

John Q. Writer
123 Author Lane
Writerville, CA 95355
johnqwriter@email.com
(323) 555-0000

First North American Rights
Approximately 1,500 words
Sidebars of 225 and 150 words

Indicate the sidebars
separately here as
part of the package.

Bold title

Timid Steps Toward Brave 'Nute' World

Title one-third
of the way down the
page

Italicized
subhead

Major food players get feet wet
but produce few patents so far

by

John Q. Writer

Nutraceuticals may have captured the interest and imagination of

major food companies. But at least based on patent activity, they

don't appear to have captured many research and development

dollars yet.

Double-
spaced text

Indent paragraphs
except for the first
one.

A Food Processing review of patents granted in the 1990s

shows that major food companies have received fewer than sixty

patents for nutraceutical products. One company alone, Procter

& Gamble Co., accounts for more than half of those. Even P&G,

however, denies it has a "nutraceutical" business.

That doesn't necessarily mean the food industry's R&D or

1" margin

patent activity in nutraceuticals is slack. But it does show that

Sidebar slug line on the first page.

Sidebar: Nutraceuticals   Approximately 225 words

Repeat the word count for the sidebar. If the sidebar goes more than one page, there's no need to repeat the word count on the subsequent pages. Instead, write "Sidebar Page 2" and so on.

Patents From Major Food Companies

Here's how the major food companies rank by number of nutraceutical-related patents, and a roundup of products for which they hold patents.

1. Procter & Gamble Co., 37

Psyllium and other cholesterol-lowering drinks and compounds, tea extracts, fortified drink mixes, enhanced bioavailability of nutrients and system for physiological feedback in administration of nutrients.

Double-spaced, just like manuscript text

2. Kellogg Co., 7

Psyllium and other cholesterol-lowering foods, improved iron fortification.

1" margin

3. Unilever NV, 4

Probiotic for treating irritable bowel syndrome, antioxidant tea extracts.

Source: U.S. Patent and Trademark Office, Food Processing Research

ELECTRONIC ARTICLE MANUSCRIPTS

Submission Tips

Submitting articles electronically isn't so much about what you do as what you don't do.

A certain amount of attention to detail is necessary to get the article's format across, but you don't have to try to design an article. That's a graphic designer's job.

More than likely, you'll submit your articles electronically as an attachment—preferably as a Microsoft Word document (.doc).

Formatting Specs

- Find out from the editor how she prefers to receive electronic files.

- Formatting is mainly a matter of removing potential glitches from your copy. For instance, don't put two spaces after a sentence. Typesetters automatically handle the space, and your extra spaces may need to be removed by an editor.

- Use the formatting function in your word processing software to double-space electronic files. Don't double-space by using hard returns, as the spacing could foul up production.

- If you mail a disk or CD, use the same kind of cover letter you would with a paper manuscript. Include a hard copy of the manuscript in the envelope as a point of reference if glitches appear in the electronic copy.

Other Dos and Don'ts

- Do ask for a confirmation receipt after you've sent a file to make sure it can be received. Electronic transfers can be unreliable, and deadlines for news publications are tight.

- Do note at the top of the file where you can be reached if you're not going to be close to the phone, especially if your editor is working on a daily deadline.

- Don't use "–30–" or "–###–" to mark the end of your article. In an electronic format, it's just another thing that will have to be removed.

- Do try to learn the style, especially with news publications. On tight deadlines, copy editors can get very testy about having to make style changes.

- Do include a suggested headline. It isn't necessary, and it probably won't fit, but it could be a starting point for the editor.

- Don't put any copyright information on the manuscript. It's copyrighted when you write it, and the editor knows this.

SUBMITTING PHOTOS AND GRAPHICS

Submission Tips

When submitting photos, graphics, and information graphic material for your article, give editors as much information as possible. Few things are as frustrating for an editor as scrambling to find artwork or a bit of information about it at the last minute.

Formatting Specs

- Provide suggested captions for photos on a separate page after your article.

- Captions should be brief, descriptive, action oriented, and in the present tense. Ultimately, caption writing is an editor's job, but she probably won't mind your help.

- Attach a form to the back of prints with key information.

- Use tape to attach the form to prints. Never use staples.

- Use a code on the margin of slides to identify them, corresponding to an information form. Put the slides in an envelope and then attach the envelope to the necessary form with tape or staples.

- If you would like the photo to be returned, provide a preaddressed, stamped mailer with sufficient strength and postage to get it through the mail intact. It's preferable to allow the publication to keep prints (when possible).

- If you have more than one photo or slide, use a coding system to keep captions and identifications straight.

- The most common and universal forms of electronic photos are JPEG and TIFF.

Other Dos and Don'ts

- Do make sure digital images are high resolution. The minimum requirement for most high-resolution images is 300 dpi (dots per inch), and the image should be at least 3" × 3" (8cm × 8cm) in size. The publisher's guidelines will indicate the resolution and size of the image required, as well as the preferred file format. Follow these guidelines! Do not refer editors to a website and ask them to copy the images; the resolution of these photos will not be high enough to reproduce a quality image.

- Don't send extremely large files via e-mail. If you have many high-resolution images, put the files on a disk or CD (ask the editor which format he prefers) and mail it to the editor along with a copy of your article.

Slug line for
the article

Double-
spaced text

Captions: Nutraceuticals

Photo A:

    Researchers at Procter & Gamble Co.'s Sharon Woods labora-

tory display tea beverage.

Credit: Procter & Gamble Co.

Use codes
with more than one
photo.

Photo B:

    Bill Mayer, president and general manager of Kellogg Co.'s

Functional Foods Division, discusses strategies for capitalizing

on the company's recent Food and Drug Administration approval

for health claims on psyllium-based cereals.

Credit: Andy Goodshot, The Associated Press

Always include a
credit, even when it's
simply the company
that provided the
photo.

Graphic

    Kellogg Co. wasted no time getting its health claims into ad-

vertising copy, placing this ad in women's and health magazines

within two weeks of FDA approval.

Reproduction
of an ad also needs a
caption for context.

SUBMITTING INFORMATION GRAPHIC MATERIAL

Submission Tips

Providing information graphics isn't part of your job as a writer, but providing the information that goes into those graphics is. Since *USA Today* debuted in 1982, information graphics—with or without articles attached—have become a staple of journalism.

If you and your publication have the know-how, one of the best ways to submit information graphic material is in the form of a spreadsheet. A variety of word processing and graphics programs can create simple graphics using spreadsheet information.

You can also submit your information in tabular form on a separate page appended to the end of your article.

Because of the hundreds of ways such information can be presented, you'll have to tackle each situation on a case-by-case basis. Here are a few simple formatting specs.

Formatting Specs

- Use a slug atop the printed page that links the graphic information to the article, for instance, "Graphic Information: Storyslug."

- Always include a line citing the source, even if it's only your own research (usually cited in the name of the publication, for instance, "Source: Your publication research").

- Take special care to double-check the numbers and make sure the column material is properly matched. A relatively simple miscue can render an informational graphic useless, ludicrous, or embarrassing.

Other Dos and Don'ts

- Do ask the editor if the publication has a preferred format for receiving information graphic material.

- Don't forget to cite the source of your information.

- Do put the story slug at the top of each page.

Story slug line

Graphic information: DTC-Direct

Table 1

New database and direct-response pharmaceutical drug marketing programs by year:

1999 108

2000 201

2001 258

2002 38 (through mid-February)

This could be used in a bar chart or a graph.

Source: John Cummings and Partners

Table 2

Top drug companies in database marketing:

1. GlaxoSmithKline

2. Merck

3. Pharmacia & Upjohn

4. Schering-Plough

Source: John Cummings and Partners

Cite the source of the information.

CHAPTER 16

NONFICTION BOOKS

Nonfiction books can be about any number of subjects—from a gigantic hardcover book featuring architecture to your run-of-the-mill diet book to a small pocket prayer guide. If it's true and it's a book, you can learn how to submit it to agents and editors. Note that unlike fiction, writers do not have to finish their nonfiction project prior to submitting work for consideration. Instead of writing the book's text and chapters, the all-important, complicated first step is composing a nonfiction book proposal, which will serve as a business plan for your book and its release.

CONCERNING MEMOIR

Memoirs are true-life stories, but they read like novels. They are nonfiction tales that employ common fiction devices, such as cliffhangers, character arcs, and a three-act structure. For this reason, memoir is treated like fiction.

WHAT YOU NEED TO SUBMIT

The first step in selling a nonfiction book is creating a book proposal. Typically the proposal will include a query letter, a detailed proposal, and at least one sample chapter. This all must be completed and reviewed—usually over the course of several months, by agents, editors, and business managers of the publisher—before the book writing begins in earnest. If you're writing out the entire book now, you should stop and start on a proposal instead.

For the writer, the proposal process begins with solid market research, which can prevent a considerable waste of time and energy. This means spending time in a bookstore and searching on Amazon.com for similar works to prove there is a market for your book. From the agent or editor's point of view, however, the process starts with the query. That's where this chapter will begin.

QUERY LETTER TO AN AGENT

Submission Tips

Most authors published by major commercial publishers are represented by agents. Establishing a relationship with an agent is often the first step toward selling your first book. Though you can present a proposal to an agent without a query, it makes more sense to query first. Inability to interest agents in your proposal is a strong sign that you need to rework or scrap your idea. When you send a query, be sure to check the agent's specific submission guidelines.

A query letter to an agent should:

- Make a convincing case for a compelling book concept

- Show why you are the person to write the book

- Outline the market potential for the book, including who the readers will be and what the competition is like

Sum up your concept in a single paragraph. It may seem impossible, but if you can't do it now, your agent won't be able to do it later when he pitches the book to a publisher. This may even be the same hook an editor uses to convince the committee that ultimately decides on your book. Later, it may be used by the publisher's sales rep to get your book into stores. Ultimately, a paragraph description will be used on the jacket to convince readers to buy it, generating the royalties that make this all a paying venture. So spend considerable time refining this concept.

A brief description of the market for this book is equally vital to your query. Why is it better than the competition? Why will it fly off the shelves?

The last paragraph of the query is an explanation why you are the perfect person to write this book. What qualifies you to write it? Are you a working professional in the field? This is also an important selling point of the book.

Formatting Specs

- The basic setup for a query to agents is similar to an article query.

- Use a standard font or typeface, 12-point type.

- Use 1" margins on all sides.

- Use block format—single-space the body; double-space between paragraphs.

- Use letterhead or type your personal information in the top right corner.

- Keep the query to one page.

Other Dos and Don'ts

- Do address an agent by name.

- Don't use "To whom it may concern" or other nondescript salutations.

- Do the basic research to find out what kinds of books the agent handles.

- Do summarize any relevant experience you have, especially in publishing books. (This query model assumes a first-time book author.)

- Do keep your query brief. As noted earlier, your pitch rides on three basic paragraphs.

- Do ask if the agent would like you to submit a full proposal. Indicate whether the proposal is ready now.

- Don't ask for proposal guidelines, though some agents offer them. Instead, express the confidence that you can handle a proposal on your own. After all, you bought this book.

- Don't fax or e-mail your query unless you have permission from the agent.

John Q. Writer
123 Author Lane
Writerville, CA 95355
(323) 555-0000
johnqwriter@email.com

Contact
information

July 5, 2009

Sabrina Smith
Smith & Smith Literary Agency
222 Forty-ninth St.
New York, NY 10111

Dear Ms. Smith:

Always address a
specific agent.

Single-
spaced text

When was the last time you tried selling an idea? Probably it was
the last time you had a conversation.

In today's economy, regardless of your career, selling ideas is what
you really do. And you do it in more directions than ever. Companies sell to customers, but they also sell ideas to suppliers. Employees pitch ideas to their bosses, and vice versa. In the modern
team-filled corporation, you may be selling your ideas simultaneously to a wide array of peers, bosses, and subordinates. Until
now, however, there was no definitive book on how to sell ideas.

The hook

1" margin

That's about to change. I am preparing a book, *Selling Your Ideas:
The Career Survival Strategy of the 21st Century*, to fill the void.
Hundreds of highly successful books have addressed sales tactics
for salespeople, and dozens of highly successful books address
persuasion skills for everyone else. But, up to now, no one has
addressed a book to cover the one sales job in which everyone in
corporate America engages—selling ideas. Unlike other sales and
persuasion books, *Selling Your Ideas* addresses everyone in business on a function-by-function basis. Because virtually anyone at
any walk of corporate life will be reflected in this book, the appeal is considerably wider than any previous work of its kind.

Differentiate this
book from the com-
petition.

Explain why
you should write this
book.

Included will be dozens of real-life case studies drawn from my
twenty years as a corporate executive, trainer, marketing consultant, and columnist for management publications. I would
be interested in sharing my detailed proposal with you at your
convenience.

A polite offer

Sincerely,

Signature

John Q. Writer

174

QUERY TO AN EDITOR

Do You Need an Agent?

When trying to sell a novel, you almost always need a literary agent. In nonfiction, however, it's more common to skip the agent and deal directly with a publisher. Books and ideas considered "small scope, small sales" are more likely to find a place with out the help of an agent. For example, a book about the role of Rhode Island in the Civil War is a project that has a small scope (a simple, regional appeal) that will likely have a small sales number (because of its limited audience). A book like this won't sell for much money, so an agent's 15percent commission would not be worth the effort.

Submission Tips

The goals and strategies for a query to a book editor are essentially the same as with an agent query. Both the agent and editor are looking for a marketable book. The book editor may play a role in shepherding the book through production—or at least hear about it when there are problems—so she may place a somewhat higher priority on the author's writing ability and track record in completing projects. Agents certainly care whether their authors have writing ability, but they're willing to work with or help find ghostwriters for books that are clear winners.

It pays to be familiar with the publishing house, its imprints, recent titles published, and how successful they've been. When possible, link your idea to a past success without portraying your book as a knockoff. This not only helps the book editor understand why your book will succeed but also helps the editor sell the idea internally. Publishers love nothing more than a proven formula for success and frequently shape new acquisitions along the lines of successful past ones. If you take this approach, do your homework. Misfiring by making an unsupported comparison or claiming a book was a success that really wasn't can hurt you badly. If you're not sure of your facts, you're better to forgo this tactic.

The easiest and most effective way to do the kind of research you need is by using the search engine of an online bookseller, such as Amazon.com. Not only do the search engines allow you to search by topic and publisher but some of them also tell you where the title ranks against all others in sales for that particular bookseller.

Of course, agents are the ones most likely to have the current information on publishing trends and to know the hot buttons of individual book editors, publishing houses and imprints, but if you think you can handle it on your own, or if your book's concept doesn't require an editor, go for it.

Formatting Specs

- Format your letter for an editor similar to that for an agent.
- Address your letter to a specific editor. Do the research in *Writer's Market* or call to find the appropriate editor for your query.

Other Dos and Don'ts

- Do keep your letter to one page.

- Do avoid rambling and wordiness, regardless of length.

- Don't overreach. Build a case for your qualifications based on reality.

- Don't come off as pompous, even if you do know everything about your topic.

- Don't fax or e-mail your query unless you have permission from the publisher or if submission guidelines state it is acceptable.

- Do show you're familiar with the publisher, possibly by comparing your book with other successful titles from the imprint.

- Do build your query on a strong, succinct concept, market insight, and a convincing reason why you're the right person to write the book. Ultimately the hook could be any of those three or a combination, but you need all three to build your case.

To: AMACOM BOOKS

New York City

Dear Editor,

I have written a great book on how to get a job in today's tight employment market. I think you'll want to add this book to your list and will be very happy when it sells like gangbusters.

Options today abound for those looking for work, but many folks don't know where to start—the newspaper, the Internet, friends, family, cold-calling, there are many ways to get a job that may seem confusing to most job seekers, they are not sure where to start and sometimes just give up before they really start and end up standing on the umemployment line and feel unfulfilled and unhappy and eventually those checks will run out, and where will they end up?

My book will tell readers where to start to find a job and how to best find a job that will make them happy. My book has been read by my many friends and family and they all said, wow, I wish I had this book when I was looking for a job, it really would have helped and I'd be much happier than I am now.

A book like this will hit the best-seller lists right away because it's the only one that tells it like it really is and doesn't kiss up to big corporations.

If you will send me your e-mail address I can e-mail you an electronic copy of the manuscript so you can see for yourself what a great book it is, and how we will be raking in the money on this one.

Thanks for your time, and I look forward to working with you!

Sincerely,

John Q. Writer
(323) 555-0000

This is set up like a memo, not a formal letter, and doesn't include any information on whom the letter is from, whom it is going to, or even the date.

Always address your queries to a specific editor that works with the type of book you're submitting.

Typo! Proofread your work

How will your book do this?
Be specific.

More bragging, with no information to back up such an outrageous claim.

Don't offer to send your book via e-mail. If the editor is interested, she will ask for more.

Be sure to include your address, phone number, and e-mail.

Boring! You need to capture the editor's interest. This is the time to sell your idea, not your book.

This is a rambling, run-on sentence that doesn't tell the editor needed information.

Editors don't care what friends and family think. State why you are the most qualified person to write this book and how you plan to differentiate it from the competition.

Being confident in your work is one thing—being arrogant and obnoxious is quite another.

ELECTRONIC QUERY LETTER TO AN EDITOR OR AGENT

Submission Tips

Many publishers and agents now accept queries via e-mail. Before you send a query off to a publisher or agent electronically, though, you must either have permission to send it via e-mail or make sure that the guidelines indicate that it is acceptable. Communicating with an editor or agent via e-mail should be just as formal and respectful as if you were sending it through the mail. The basic tone and format of the electronic query shouldn't be much different from a query sent on paper.

Formatting Specs

- Include the same information you would in a paper query, including your name, address, phone number, fax, and website. For e-queries, put your contact information at the bottom left of the e-mail. It isn't necessary to include your e-mail address in the body of the e-mail, though, since the editor can reply easily with the click of a button.

- Put a description of your book or its title in the subject line.

- Follow the same format you would with a paper query, including the date, salutation to a specific editor, and block paragraph format.

Other Dos and Don'ts

- Don't use all caps or exclamation points in the subject line unless the exclamation point is part of your book's title.

- Don't submit an e-mail query unless the publisher or agent specifically requests it, or if the guidelines clearly stated that it is acceptable.

- Don't insert clip art graphics or other images into your query letter. Keep it simple.

TO: submissions@smithsmith.com
CC:
SUBJECT: Got a Book 4 U

Put a brief description or the title in the subject line.

John Q. Writer
Writerville, CA 95355
johnqwriter@email.com

First of all, this contact information is incomplete. Secondly, it should appear at the bottom of an e-mail query.

March 3, 2009

Smith and Smith Literary Agency
222 Forty-ninth St.
New York, NY 10111

To Whom It May Concern:

Address your query to a specific agent.

I hope you are interested in nonfiction books about birds, because that is the type of book I have written. I would like to sell it to a publisher, which of course means that I need an agent.

Do your homework. Know what kinds of books an agent works with before sending a query.

Don't be obvious—an agent knows why writers need agents.

The subject of birds is a big one, but I know that my book stands out from all the others. People all over the country love to read interesting stories about these fascinating creatures, so the book will appeal to just about anyone who loves birds—they don't even have to be birdwatchers or nature enthusiasts. I've attached the first four chapters of my book and will send the rest at your request.

This tells the agent absolutely nothing about the book. Explain how your book differs from others currently on the market.

Don't send book chapters unless the agent asks for them. This is just a query.

I had such a good time writing about this, my favorite subject, over the past ten years. I am a bird enthusiast and even met my wife while on a birding expedition in the mountains of New England in 1999.

This is my first attempt at writing a book. I have written many articles that were never published on the subject so I thought it would be a good idea to put them all together in one book. I think that with the right editor's expertise and input this book has the potential to be a huge bestseller.

Don't point out your (or the book's) shortcomings. If it needs editorial help, you're not ready to send it to an agent.

Keep all your information focused on the book itself. Don't waste time with anecdotes that have nothing to do with the book.

Thanks,

John Q. Writer

Don't exaggerate. Be confident in your work, but don't overstate it.

BOOK PROPOSAL

What You Need to Submit

Like the article query, the book proposal is something of a genre in its own right. The differences are that it takes much more time and can vary considerably in length. A fully thought-out book proposal should include the following:

- Cover letter
- Cover page
- Overview
- Marketing information or business case
- Competitive analysis
- Author information
- Chapter outline
- Sample chapters
- Attachments that support your case

You really should send in a query letter before submitting a complete book proposal, but if your proposal is unsolicited, include an SASE or postcard for a reply.

Submission Tips

The thing agents and editors cite as most frequently lacking in book proposals is the marketing information. Authors often don't have a firm vision of whom the readers of the book will be and how to reach them, or they don't know what the competition is and how to differentiate their books from existing titles. It's strange that the marketing information is so often missing, because it's really where any author should start. Before you ever begin the painstaking process to create a book proposal, you have to know there's a market for your book. If you can't build a convincing business case for your book, go back to the drawing board. That's why, even if the marketing and competition information doesn't come first in the proposal lineup, you should prepare these sections first. In fact, you should do your homework on these sections before you query an agent or book editor to submit a proposal.

The other element that a proposal often lacks is the author's platform. This term, which has come to prominence in recent years, is defined as the author's avenues to sell his book to audiences that will buy it. In other words, what ability to do you have to market the book, sell the book, gain press for the book, and tap into its potential audience?

Read sample book proposals and seek out other books that help break down what makes up a winning proposal. Start with *Bulletproof Book Proposals* by Pam Brodowsky and Eric Neuhaus, and *How to Write a Book Proposal* by Michael Larsen.

Here is a piece-by-piece look at the elements of the proposal, along with some special instructions for book proposals sent electronically.

ELECTRONIC BOOK PROPOSAL

Submission Tips

Once you send a query and an editor is interested in seeing your proposal, she may ask you to send it via e-mail. The editor will indicate what format she prefers to receive files. Be sure to follow her guidelines.

- Don't forget the cover letter. Just because you're using e-mail doesn't mean you don't need to introduce your proposal.

- An electronic proposal should include the same components as a proposal sent via regular mail.

- Your cover letter may be included in the body of the e-mail. The additional elements of the proposal, including the cover page and overview, marketing/competitive analysis, author information, chapter outline, and sample chapters, should be sent as a file attachment unless the editor requests otherwise.

Formatting Specs

- Use the subject line of the e-mail to introduce the title of your book.

- Make it simple by keeping all the components together. It's not necessary to create a separate file each for the cover page, overview, marketing analysis, competitive analysis, author information, chapter outlines, and chapter samples unless the editor specifically requests them as separate files.

- A book proposal should follow the same format as a paper proposal, including a header and page numbers on every page. This will make it easy for the editor to keep everything in order when it's printed.

Other Dos and Don'ts

- Don't use all caps in your subject line.

- Don't submit a book proposal electronically unless the editor or publisher's guidelines specifically request it.

- Do send your proposal as an attachment of a Microsoft Word document (.doc) unless specified otherwise.

- Don't insert clip art graphics or images in your e-mail.

- Do proofread your work.

COVER LETTER

Submission Tips

Because so much information is included in the rest of the proposal, and because you should have already queried the agent or editor, the cover letter can be fairly brief. Don't use more than one page. Follow the same guidelines for submission to agents or book editors.

If you are submitting an unsolicited proposal, the cover letter should incorporate elements of the query letters provided earlier in this chapter, as well as introduce the proposal. The cover letter for a solicited manuscript simply serves to introduce a proposal and covers the following points:

- An introductory paragraph for the proposal

- An outline of the information included in the proposal

- A concluding paragraph politely seeking a response

Formatting Specs

- Use a standard font or typeface for the body of the letter, 12-point type.

- Letterhead is fine but not required. If you don't use letterhead, put your name, address, phone number, and e-mail in the top right corner.

- Use 1" margins on all sides.

- Keep it to one page.

- Use block format—single-space the body; double-space between paragraphs.

Other Dos and Don'ts

- Do address a specific editor.

- Don't start your pitch all over again in the cover letter. If your query made enough of an impression to spark interest, assume that the agent or editor remembers the book idea and who you are.

- Don't ask for advice or criticism regarding your proposal.

- Don't mention copyright information. What you've written is copyrighted, and you don't want to imply the agent or editor is out to steal your idea.

- Don't discuss payment or terms. It's still premature.

- Don't staple your cover letter to anything. Use a butterfly or clamp-style paper clip to hold the proposal elements together, leaving the cover letter alone in front.

John Q. Writer
123 Author Lane
Writerville, CA 95355
(323) 555-0000
johnqwriter@email.com

Contact
information

August 30, 2009

Date flushed right

Sabrina Smith
Smith & Smith Literary Agency
222 Forty-ninth St.
New York, NY 10111

Dear Ms. Smith:

1" margin

Continue to
address a specific
agent.

Enclosed is the proposal you requested for *Selling Your Ideas: The Career Survival Strategy of the 21st Century.*

Don't waste
time. Get right
to the point.

Included in the proposal are detailed market and competitive analyses, my biographical information, a complete chapter outline, and three sample chapters.

Brief preview

Single-spaced text,
block format

I hope after you've had a chance to review the proposal that you'll understand why I believe this book has so much promise. Please let me know if I can make any revisions or add any information to make the proposal more salable.

Offer to revise or
add on as necessary.

Thanks for your time. I look forward to hearing from you.

Sincerely,

Signature

John Q. Writer

Details
enclosures

Encl.: Proposal

COVER PAGE

Submission Tips

This is the same as the cover page you'll use with the ultimate manuscript. It includes the title, estimated word count, and either your contact information (if submitting directly to an editor) or your agent's contact information (if submitting through an agent).

Formatting Specs

- Contact information goes in the bottom right corner.

- Put an estimated word count (for the entire book, not for the proposal) in the top right corner. This is optional at this point, but it could be helpful

- Center the title, subtitle, and author's name in the middle of the page.

- Conventionally, the title is in all capital letters and the subtitle is uppercase and lowercase. If you want, use boldface for the title and italics for the subtitle.

Other Dos and Don'ts

- Don't include both your address and the agent's. Use one or the other.

- Don't use a header or number the title page.

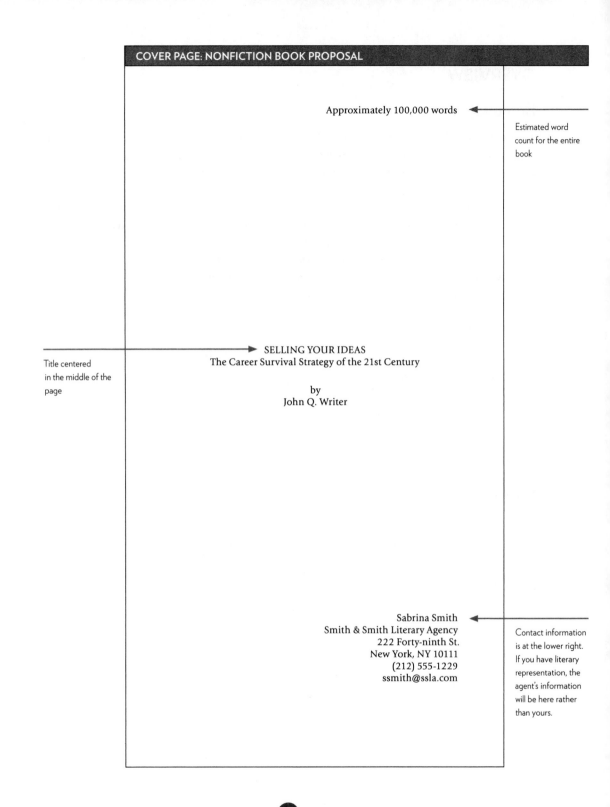

Approximately 100,000 words

Estimated word count for the entire book

SELLING YOUR IDEAS
The Career Survival Strategy of the 21st Century

by
John Q. Writer

Title centered in the middle of the page

Sabrina Smith
Smith & Smith Literary Agency
222 Forty-ninth St.
New York, NY 10111
(212) 555-1229
ssmith@ssla.com

Contact information is at the lower right. If you have literary representation, the agent's information will be here rather than yours.

185

OVERVIEW

Submission Tips

The overview is the place for your thirty-second sound-bite pitch. It incorporates elements of the concept, marketing and competitive analyses, and author information that is to be presented in the proposal, and ties them together convincingly, forcefully, and coherently. Even though it's a small element of the proposal, it's a powerful one.

The overview of the concept should be only one page. Use the same approach you used in the query to concisely explain the concept, but make it even more focused. Boil the pitch down to a single sentence, then use a paragraph or two to describe the contents of your book.

Resist the urge to give a blow-by-blow description of the rest of the proposal. No one needs a preview of a proposal. The overview is simply, to borrow from the corporate buzzword lexicon, "the top-line analysis," "the big picture," "the view from ten thousand feet."

Formatting Specs

- Begin numbering your proposal with this page. Place the page numbers in the top right corner.

- Use a slug in the top left corner of the header in this and succeeding pages.

- The slug should read "Proposal: Your Book Title Here."

- Center your heading, "Overview," and underline it.

- Double-space the text and use a 1" margin on all sides for the whole proposal.

Other Dos and Don'ts

- Do make sure the overview conveys a convincing hook, even though it's a freestyle exercise. Think of the overview as the speech the agent will make to the editor, the editor to the people on the editorial committee, the sales rep to the buyer, and the book jacket to the reader.

- Do write your entire proposal in the third person.

Selling Your Ideas / Writer   1

Header includes the title, your last name, and the page number.

<u>Overview</u>

Heading centered, one-third of the way down the page, and underlined

Selling Your Ideas is the sales how-to manual for the rest of us.

And it's long overdue.

No matter what you do, selling ideas is your job. And you do it in more directions than ever before. Companies sell to customers, but they also sell ideas to suppliers. Employees pitch ideas to their bosses, and vice versa. In the modern team-filled corporation, you may be selling your ideas simultaneously to a wide array of peers, bosses, and subordinates.

1" margin

Yet, among the thousands of sales how-to books, none has really been geared to help non-salespeople develop the fundamental skill of selling ideas—until now. *Selling Your Ideas* offers practical, time-tested strategies for all kinds of employees to sell all kinds of ideas to all kinds of audiences. Included will be dozens of real-life case studies drawn from corporate executive and marketing consultant John Q. Writer's twenty years as a corporate executive, trainer, marketing consultant, and writer.

Double-spaced text

The hook

Rather than relying on one-nostrum-fits-all approaches typical of sales and persuasion books, *Selling Your Ideas* takes a detailed approach to selling ideas within and outside the organization.

Write in the third person.

More information will follow.

Nonfiction Books

MARKETING ANALYSIS

Submission Tips

The marketing information section of your proposal answers that all-important question: Will this book sell? And it should answer the question in as much detail as possible. There are no limits on length here, beyond your ability to research and write. As with any part of your proposal, make this as tight and compelling as you can, and offer any facts or figures you can find to prove your book will be a hit.

The marketing analysis section covers the product (your book) and the consumers (its readers). The areas to cover in the analysis include:

- Who is the audience? Describe them. How big is the potential readership base? Is it growing? What are some important facts about the readership base that a marketer would want to know? What kind of media do they like? What organizations do they belong to? Where do they shop? Can you provide concrete numbers to prove that the audience is sizeable?

- What trends could affect the book? Why would the audience be growing, buying more books, or suddenly taking more interest in your book?

- Where, besides bookstores, could this book be sold? Are there special events, seasonal approaches, or other special channels through which this book can be sold?

- What information will the book provide? How will that appeal to readers?

- How will you approach the book? Will it have sidebars, callouts, interviews, pictures, charts, or other special features?

- What are the sources of information? What will the research be based on?

Closely linked to the marketing analysis is the competitive information that follows it. You may choose to combine these into a single section.

Other Dos and Don'ts

- Do write concisely and in the third person.

- Don't be too worried about the length. Take as long as you need to present all relevant marketing information.

- Do use charts, tables, and graphs if you have them.

Selling Your Ideas / Writer   4

Marketing Analysis

Heading centered, one-third of the way down the page, and underlined

Potential readers of this book include anyone who works, but it will especially appeal to upwardly mobile middle and upper managers who have the difficult job of selling in many directions

1" margin

at once. Because of the growing acceptance of such management philosophies and tactics as "empowerment," cross-functional teams, consensus building, and vendor-management quality efforts, these corporate soldiers have seen their roles change dramatically in ways that force them to sell their ideas more.

This is a market of more than 2.5 million people who are heavy book buyers. According to a recent report by the American Association of Middle Managers and the Business Executive Council (see attached report), middle managers buy an average of six management and career-related titles annually.

Full report is attached.

Special Distribution Opportunities

Subheads help clarify.

This book's special appeal opens additional distribution channels beyond bookstores. As a general-interest business book with wide application to a variety of consumers, including the small-office/home-office (SOHO) market, *Selling Your Ideas* should have the power to win shelf space in end-aisle displays at office superstores.

Double-spaced text

COMPETITIVE ANALYSIS

Submission Tips

The competitive analysis details what books are similar to yours, how they have done in the marketplace, and how your book is different and better than they are. There's no set format for handling this information, but it helps to begin with an overview of the genre or category into which your book fits, how that category is doing generally, and what the leading competitive titles are.

Then go into an analysis of the leading competitors, analyzing how those books have done and why yours is still needed. Even if the subject already has been covered, it may not have been covered for your audience, or the information may be hopelessly out of date because of changes in social mores or technology.

The traditional method for gathering this information is to visit a good-size bookstore, look for competing titles, and then research through Amazon.com and possibly BookScan (though this is a pay service) to see how the books are selling. Pay attention to how a competing book is similar to yours and how it is different. What is the print size of the book? Does it have illustrations or art of any kind? Is it told in a folksy, joke-filled manner?

Amazon.com provides a varied amount of information on books. You can compare sales rank, get commentaries from readers, and see what other books and authors are also popular with buyers of the title. You can't get information on total number of books sold, but if you combine some inside sales information from other authors with their Amazon.com ranking, you might be able to determine a ballpark estimate of how many copies a book has sold.

Other Dos and Don'ts

- Do use as much space as needed but write concisely.

- Don't critique the competing titles, but do point out what shortcomings they have that make room or create demand for your book.

- Don't contend that your book is so unique that it has no competition. Agents and editors will conclude that you didn't do enough research or that you are offering an idea so bizarre or unappealing that no book should be published. You can always find a comparable book if you try hard enough.

Header includes the title, your last name, and the page number.

Competitive Analysis

Heading centered, one-third of the way down the page, and underlined

Thousands of titles have tackled various aspects of selling or persuasion over the years, but none have directly tackled the subject of selling ideas to a wide range of constituencies inside and outside the corporation.

1" margin

Sales and persuasion titles are consistently strong performers. An analysis of titles listed by Amazon.com shows that more than fifty such titles have been published in the past year. They rank between 5 and 64,000 in sales for Amazon.com. In addition, analysis of older titles shows that the top twenty sales and persuasion books have a median ranking of 5,000, compared to 10,000 for the top twenty management theory books and 12,000 for the top twenty time-management books.

Double-spaced text

The four recent titles that come closest in subject to *Selling Your Ideas* have an average sales rank of 11,000.

Below is a detailed analysis of each title.

1) ***The Anatomy of Persuasion: How to Persuade Others to Act on Your Ideas, Accept Your Proposals, Buy Your Products or Services, Hire You, Promote You and More*** by Norbert Aubuchon. This book covers ground similar to *Selling Your Ideas*, but without the department-by-department, case study-based approach.

There is a lot of information you could include here, depending on how detailed you want to get. You can include the book's ISBN, publisher, and year of release, for instance.

AUTHOR INFORMATION

Submission Tips

The author information section is about you, but only in the context of what makes you the perfect person to write this book. Highlight any other information that makes you a salable author as well. This is not your life story; this is the story of how you will help the publisher sell books. It is the author platform.

Good points to include in the author information are:

- Teaching credentials (professors can often sell their books to their students and other professors).

- Organizational affiliations, groups you head, or any special audiences with whom you are connected and which could become channels for marketing the book.

- Previous publishing credits (including books, which show you can write one; articles, which show your expertise; and columns, which show a possible avenue of promotion).

- Any experience you have in other media (radio shows, TV shows, radio commentaries, websites, blogs—anything that shows you could promote your book effectively in a variety of media).

- Compelling personal history that could help generate publicity and get you booked on talk shows.

- Any of you blogs, websites, or newsletters that receive plenty of hits each day.

- Any public speaking engagements you do in front of large crowds.

Formatting Specs

- Double-space the text.

- Keep this to one page, regardless of how fascinating you are.

- Write this in the third person.

Other Dos and Don'ts

- Don't overreach. State your history and qualifications accurately.

- Don't provide information that's irrelevant to the book's marketing, such as the story of your life ("He was born in a small log cabin just outside …"). Family and other details that may be appropriate in a jacket blurb aren't necessarily helpful here.

Selling Your Ideas / Writer   12

Header includes
the title, your last
name, and the page
number.

Author Information

Heading centered,
one-third of the way
down the page, and
underlined

John Q. Writer has been selling ideas successfully both inside
and outside the corporation for more than twenty years. He is a
former senior vice president of sales and marketing for Hender-
son Steel Plating Corporation who now serves as a consultant on
customer service and marketing issues for more than two dozen
Fortune 500 corporations.

1" margin

He is also adjunct professor of business administration at
Colorado State University and former president of the Business
Executive Council, a 300,000-member-strong educational and
advocacy group for middle managers. He continues to serve as a
consultant on sales and marketing issues for the BEC, and he is
active in Mentors International, a nationwide network of mentors
and protégés.

Qualifications are
extensive without
bragging.

Double-
spaced text

Writer also writes a regular column on career planning for
Middle Manager magazine and hosts a call-in radio show on Denver public radio station WBZN-FM. He is also a frequent speaker
at business and trade organizations, having spoken at fifteen
events with a combined attendance of 25,000 over the past year.

Shows he has a fol-
lowing—several really.

Shows media savvy
and promotion skills.

Nonfiction Books

CHAPTER OUTLINE

Submission Tips

The chapter outline provides an extended table of contents for your book and includes a brief description of each chapter. This should not be in the classic outline format you learned in your high school composition class. Such an outline may help you write the book, but it's a little dry for the purposes of a proposal, which is meant to sell an editor on the merits of each chapter and show how it fits into the book.

Formatting Specs

- Describe one chapter per page.

- If the book is divided into parts as well as chapters, first list the part and part heading, then the chapter and chapter heading.

- Indent paragraphs and otherwise follow the same format as the rest of the proposal.

Other Dos and Don'ts

- Don't insert a new title page and start numbering all over again with the outline. The proposal is a single entity.

- Do describe how the chapter will unfold, including any sidebars, tables, charts, photos, or other illustrations that will be included.

- Don't approximate how many pages or photos you'll have in each chapter. Assuming you haven't actually written the book yet, it's impossible to know, and the information isn't likely to sway an editor.

Selling Your Ideas / Writer   15

Header includes the title, your last name, and the page number.

Chapter Outline / Table of Contents

Heading centered, one-third of the way down the page, and underlined

Part I: Getting Ready

Chapter 1: Overcoming Limitations

Whatever format you use, be consistent.

Use Arabic numerals to list chapters. Bold the title.

Every idea sold is sold by someone who has limitations. Those who sell well are aware of their limitations and overcome them. Dealing with limitations is the best way of developing self-confidence. This chapter explores strategies for self-assessment and overcoming limitations.

Use Roman numerals to separate large sections in a book table of contents. Underline the title.

1" margin

- How to sort out and leverage your best qualities
- Identifying your limitations
- How to evaluate and sharpen your presentation skills
- How to evaluate and improve written presentations
- Why and how to be a continuous student
- Selecting and developing mentors
- Selecting and developing confidants
- How mentors and confidants can help
- How mentors and confidants can hurt

Double-spaced text

SAMPLE CHAPTERS

Submission Tips

Agents and editors almost always want to see at least one sample chapter, even from established authors. If you've already written a book in the same subject area, you might get by without a sample chapter. Even then, however, some editors insist.

Most authors' natural inclination is to send chapter one, but some agents recommend against this. If chapter one seems too complete, they argue, it might be hard to make a case for the rest of the book.

Ultimately, the number of sample chapters and which ones to send is your judgment call. Look at the chapter outline. Which chapters are the most intriguing, or the most needed to make a case for the book? These are the chapters you should include. Submit up to three.

Formatting Specs

- Use the same formatting as the rest of the proposal. This is not exactly like manuscript format—it is a section of the proposal and should appear the same.

- After the first page of the sample chapter, continue using the header and page number as in the rest of the proposal. You need not indicate the chapter number or title in subsequent pages.

Other Dos and Don'ts

- Do center the chapter number and chapter title about one-third of the way down the page.

- Don't assume you must submit chapter one. Submit the most compelling chapter or chapters.

- Do submit a sample chapter that's already been published, if you can. For example, if your article in *Texas Parent* magazine can be a chapter in the book, submit the published article. It shows your writing style and proves that the idea has a market because it is published.

Selling Your Ideas / Writer   19

Header includes the title, your last name, and the page number.

The chapter is formatted like the rest of the proposal, not like a proper book manuscript.

Chapter 6

Heading centered, one-third of the way down the page, and underlined

Finding the Right Allies

Bold the chapter title.

You improve your chances of selling an idea significantly when you bring supportive constituencies on board early as advocates. Getting these early followers on board, however, can be difficult. Members of the group will carefully evaluate your idea and spot any weakness in your plan. Communication is the key to winning them over.

The best way to get any group within or outside the organization on board is by attaching your idea to their interests. If some element of your plan clearly works in the group's interest, you have a natural ally. But if nothing in your idea has any natural appeal to them, you need to find some way for the group to have ownership in your idea. Create a new piece of the plan or modify your idea based on input from the group. As the process continues, initial groups of followers add to the idea and start to sell what is now becoming their idea.

1" margin

Double-spaced text

What You Must Know About the Group

Subheads help break up copy.

Before you can approach the group with your idea, you need to understand some basic things about how it works. These include:

- Who are the leaders of the group, both the titular leaders and the actual ones?

Nonfiction Books

BOOK MANUSCRIPT

Submission Tips

The book manuscript is similar in most respects to the proposal format. This section begins with an explanation of the basics of the body of the manuscript, then looks at the specific requirements for various elements of the front matter and back matter.

You may end up submitting the manuscript in several stages to the publisher rather than in one installment, and you may not necessarily do this in sequential order.

Books, like newspapers and magazines, have become increasingly varied in design in recent years. Sidebars, callout quotes, subheads, and short pieces within chapters abound. No universal guidelines exist for handling these formats within books, so confer with your editor early on for guidelines.

Formatting Specs

- Use a 1" margin on all sides.

- Use a cover page.

- Don't number the title page. Begin numbering with the first page of the text of the book, which usually will be the introduction or chapter one.

- Use a header, with your last name or the title of the book.

- Double-space the entire text of the book.

- Use a 10- or 12-point standard font such as Times New Roman, Arial, or Courier.

- Put sidebars, captions, and other elements that fall outside the flow of the main chapter at the end of the chapter rather than within the body of the chapter. Design and space constraints will dictate their placement, and it's easier for editors and designers to have the elements in a single location.

- When sending an accepted manuscript, send a disk or CD containing the manuscript along with the hard copy.

- Feel free to use plenty of subheads and page breaks to add white space and break up what will be a very long document.

Other Dos and Don'ts

- Don't staple anything.

- Don't punch holes in the pages or submit it in a three-ring binder.

- Do keep an original copy for yourself both on your computer hard drive and on a separate storage medium kept in a secure place, such as a fireproof safe.

- Don't justify text or align the right margin.

- Don't put any copyright information on the manuscript. It's copyrighted when you write it, and the editor knows this.

ELECTRONIC BOOK MANUSCRIPT

Submission Tips

Some editors might ask you to submit your manuscript via e-mail or on a disk or CD. The editor can provide you with specific formatting guidelines indicating how she wants the manuscript sent and the type of files she prefers. Microsoft Word is the oft-used default.

Formatting Specs

- Use a 1" margin on all sides.

- Use a cover page.

- Remove any formatting that might cause potential glitches when the manuscript is typeset. Don't put two spaces after a sentence, and don't double-space electronic files by using hard returns.

- Put sidebars, captions, and other elements at the end of each chapter.

- Send the manuscript as an attachment unless the editor requests otherwise.

Other Dos and Don'ts

- Don't use all caps in your subject line.

- Don't submit a manuscript electronically unless the editor specifically requests it.

- Do ask for specific file format guidelines to make sure the editor can open your files.

- Don't justify text or align the right margin.

- Don't put any copyright information on the manuscript. It's copyrighted when you write it, and the editor is aware of this.

- Do follow up with an e-mail to verify that the editor has recieved you file.

Approximately 50,000 words

Rough word count
in the upper right
corner

THE 10 DIRTY LITTLE SECRETS TO DIETING

Title in all caps

Title centered, half-
way down the page

by
John Q. Writer

John Q. Writer
123 Author Lane
Writerville, CA 95355
(323) 555-0000
johnqwriter@email.com

If you don't submit
the manuscript
through an agent,
the contact informa-
tion in the lower right
corner will be your
own, including ad-
dress, phone number,
and e-mail.

Writer—*Make Your Woodworking Pay For Itself* 1

Header includes the title, your last name, and the page number.

Chapter 1
Shop Smarts—Saving Money and Space

Chapter and title centered, one-third of the way down the page

Before you find ways to make money by selling woodworking projects, it makes sense to study your workshop. Consider what tools you really need, and create a plan for acquiring them. Find ways to squeeze every penny you can out of the dollars you spend on wood, tools, and other supplies. The money you save by shopping smart and cutting waste adds substantially to the money you make. You don't have to pay tax on it, and it will make everything you sell more profitable. And, waste hurts the environment as much as your pocketbook.

1" margin

Double-spaced text

Use a line space to separate subheads in your text. Any white space is pleasing to the eye.

Equipment Basics—What You Really Need
Just which tools you need in your shop will depend on your projects. Few tools are absolutely essential if you are ingenious in finding a way around them, but there are some items most woodworkers would rather not do without.

Develop a consistent hierarchy for the heads.

Your Shop
How much room do you really need to set up shop? The answer always depends on what you do. A woodcarver may be able to work in the corner of a bedroom or basement. Some furniture makers may feel the need for a 1,000-square-foot workshop, plus additional room for milling and storing wood.

Nonfiction Books

FRONT MATTER

Submission Tips

The term *front matter* refers to a wide variety of items that fall between the cover and the body of the finished product. These include:

- Table of contents

- Dedication

- Epigraph or inscription

- Foreword

- Preface

- Prologue

- Acknowledgments

As books have become increasingly graphic, publishers largely have done away with such genteel niceties as lists of illustrations or photos, which could become a book unto themselves and take up space without conveying much useful information.

Tables of contents, on the other hand, have grown to become more detailed and complex, as publishers push for more page breaks, sidebars, and other nontraditional points of entry to appease readers with increasingly short attention spans.

One thing all front matter has in common is that it is not numbered as part of your manuscript. In some cases, publishers number these elements separately with Roman numerals in the actual book. Generally you don't need to worry about this unless you have a lot of front matter, or individual elements begin to span more than two pages. If your front matter is lengthy, number it using Roman numerals, or Arabic numerals and an altered slug that indicates the pages belong to the front matter.

Formatting Specs

- Generally front-matter pages are not numbered.

- Front-matter pages get slugs in the header.

- Heads for each element are centered.

Other Dos and Don'ts

- Don't get carried away with most of these elements. Readers routinely skip over them, and they take up space that should be devoted to the text of the book.

TABLE OF CONTENTS

Submission Tips

The table of contents is one of the first places a potential consumer goes to evaluate a nonfiction book. Publishers got wise to this fact, so now editors look for the table of contents to be more complete, descriptive, and compelling than ever.

Tables of contents in nonfiction books are as varied as the books they describe, so prescribing a slapdash formula for them is pointless. Many remain bare bones, merely listing the chapter titles and page numbers. Increasingly, however, the table of contents for many books looks like the chapter outline in the book proposal—no-holds-barred hucksterism aimed at doing the same sales job on the reader as the author and agent did on the editor. So keep that book proposal handy as you prepare the table of contents.

Formatting Specs

- Center the heading "Table of Contents" or "Contents" one-third of the way down the page.

- Provide extra-wide margins, at least 1.5".

- Don't number pages as part of the manuscript.

- Use a slug in the same place as the header in the rest of the manuscript.

- At the very least, include the chapter titles.

- Include such front-matter elements as prefaces, forewords, and prologues.

- Include back matter, such as the appendix or glossary.

- Don't include acknowledgments, dedications, and other short bits of front matter.

- Page numbers are the numbers as they occur in your manuscript. The numbers in the book will be different, of course, and impossible for you to predict.

Writer—*Make Your Woodworking Pay For Itself*

Header includes
your last name and
the title, but no page
number.

Table of Contents

Head centered,
one-third of the way
down the page, and
underlined

Indent second and
subsequent lines in
the same chapter.

1.5″ margin

Double-
spaced text

DEDICATIONS, EPIGRAPHS, AND INSCRIPTIONS

Submission Tips

These short pieces are all handled similarly from a format standpoint. A dedication is a short statement dedicating the book to a person or persons, often in combination with some expression of affection. An epigraph or inscription is a quote that sums up, signifies, or sets the tone for the book.

Formatting Specs

- Dedications and epigraphs are centered about one-third of the way down the page.

- Keep them to two or three lines.

- Don't put a heading above these to label them (for example, "Dedication").

- Don't number the page.

FOREWORD

Submission Tips

A foreword is a commentary or review of the book written by an expert in the field or someone familiar with the story of the book's creation. If the name and the review do not add something to the appeal of the book, they serve no function.

Formatting Specs

- Like the rest of the front matter, the foreword has a header but no page numbers.

- Use a heading, start about one-third of the way down the first page.

- The name of the foreword's author goes flush right at the end of the text, followed by his title and affiliation.

- Optional: The city and year where and when the foreword was written may go after the text, flush left.

Foreword: *Selling Your Ideas*

One way to keep front matter organized is by providing a slug line for the section. Whatever information you include in your header, make sure it's consistent throughout the front matter.

No page number

Foreword

Head centered, one-third of the way down the page

I was there when John Q. Writer had his first big idea in business. He returned from a sales call very excited, clutching a handful of napkins covered with notes, scribbles, and diagrams.

 I never understood how a sales rep came up with what would be known as the continuous casting process, but I quickly realized the power of his proposal. The engineers weren't used to taking cues from downy-faced salesmen just out of college. Good thing

1" margin

John already had an instinct for how to work the system. He had enlisted the help of his boss—me—and given me ownership of the idea at an early stage. Soon, I was using my contacts with junior-

Double-spaced text

level executives in the engineering department to find out if this idea truly had legs. By the time we made a formal presentation to the engineering department, we already had the support of key people in that organization. I watched John's career skyrocket after that day, and was witness to plenty more good ideas where the first came from. But more than just having good ideas, John learned quickly how to get other people to embrace them as their own. When he came into my office twenty-three years later with the idea for this book, I knew he had a winner. I know readers will come away armed with insights into how the system works and how ideas go from napkins to blueprints.

Pittsburgh, 2006

John Masterson
CEO, TronicCorp.

Date and location of the foreword flush left

Title and affiliation flush right

PREFACE, PROLOGUE, AND ACKNOWLEDGMENTS

Submission Tips

Formatting for each of these front-matter elements is very similar, though each serves a different purpose. The example here is a sample acknowledgments page, but the same formatting applies to the preface and prologue as well.

A preface explains the story behind the book—the reason it was written, the background, the unusual stories that were part of its creation. In other cases, a preface may serve as another pitch for the book, explaining why it's needed and how to use it. At least that's the theory. A preface sometimes gets muddled in with the purposes of an introduction or a prologue.

A prologue explains events or history that provide a context for the book. If you're writing a book that chronicles an event, for instance, the prologue might describe the events or forces that led up to that event.

The acknowledgments page is where you thank the folks who helped you put the book together. The preface and prologue may be optional, but the acknowledgments are not. It's virtually impossible to write a nonfiction book without someone's help, and it's impolite not to thank those people. Though this is front matter, it's among the last things you'll write.

Publishers and editors generally consider the introduction part of the body of the book. But in some cases, the book's introduction is treated as front matter, too, and handled the same way as these other elements.

Formatting Specs

- As with other front-matter elements, these are not numbered as part of the rest of the manuscript. They do, however, use headers.

- The introduction can be part of the main book, or it may be in the front matter.

- For each element, drop about one-third of the way down the page and use a centered heading.

- After the heading, drop an extra line, indent, and get started.

Other Dos and Don'ts

- Do include these elements if they add something to the book.

- Don't include prefaces or prologues just to appear impressive. This is the mark of an amateur.

- Don't forget anyone who helped in preparation of the book when you write the acknowledgments, unless they don't want to be mentioned. Keep a running file of names and ways that people helped so you don't have to scramble for this information at the end.

Writer—*Insiders' Guide to Greater Cincinnati*

Header includes the book title and your last name.

No page number

Acknowledgments

Heading centered, one-third of the way down the page, and underlined

Thanks to the many folks who provided tips and other assistance in the preparation of this book, particularly Gordon Baer for the back cover photo, Mary Anna Dusablon and Rita Heikenfeld for their insights on Cincinnati cuisine, and tipsters Julie Harrison, Michelle Howard, Bob Humble, Gail Paul, Irene Schaeffer, Joan Schaffield, Karen Tennant, Julie Whaley, and Joel Williams.

Among the librarians and public relations people who went out of their way to help include Alliea Phipps, who must operate the fastest fax/modem this side of the Alleghenies, and Bea Rose for her assistance in procuring photos of Albert Sabin.

Double-spaced text

Thanks to coauthor Skip Tate for his help, not least of which was writing half the book. Also thanks to editor Molly Brewster and to Beth Storie and the rest of the crew at The Insiders' Guides for making this possible.

Special thanks go to my wife, Glenda, for general forbear-ance and for again taking everyone but the dogs away for the oc-casional cramming to meet deadlines.

1" margin

BACK MATTER

Submission Tips

It's a dirty job, but somebody has to do it—that would be you. Back matter is that mostly unglamorous but necessary part of any nonfiction book that includes the endnotes, appendix, glossary, bibliography, epilogue, and index. You won't necessarily have all of these, but you should know how to handle each section.

The epilogue provides a final thought from the author, perhaps summing up the work's impact on the author or, in a revised edition, detailing changes that have occurred since or because of the book.

Endnotes are used mainly for scholarly manuscripts and business proposals, but they are sometimes included in other nonfiction books based on significant documentary research. They can be handy in eliminating the need to pepper the manuscript with attributions, allowing instead a quick reference to the endnote for anyone seeking the source of information. Endnotes may also be included in more scholarly articles. *The Chicago Manual of Style* is the definitive source on handling these and other back-matter issues.

The appendix is used for material that supports information or arguments in the book but which is too lengthy to include or would hamper the natural flow of the book. It's similar to the attachments found on a book proposal.

A glossary lists and defines special terminology used in the book, such as technical phrases, foreign words and phrases, and any other specialized lexicon or jargon.

The bibliography is a list of books cited in the manuscript, used in researching the manuscript, or otherwise useful as further reading. A bibliography with a brief commentary or review of significant titles and why they're helpful adds some value to an otherwise fairly dry formality. The bibliography may also be called "Recommended Reading" or incorporated into a section on "Resources" that includes information on websites of interest, events, or where to buy products related to the book's subject.

The index is a detailed listing of all the people, places, things, and concepts cited in the book, along with the page numbers. Generally, publishers hire professional indexers to prepare these.

Formatting Specs

- Unlike front matter, back matter is numbered as part of your manuscript.

- Back-matter pages take the same slug as the rest of the manuscript.

- All elements of the back matter start with a centered heading about one-third of the way down the page and are double-spaced.

- The format for the appendix and epilogue are the same as for front-matter elements, except that they are numbered as part of the manuscript.

- The details of these elements are easier to grasp by seeing them, so look to the models that follow.

Other Dos and Don'ts

- Do include these elements only if you have a good reason. As with front matter, you don't get any extra credit for having a well-rounded assortment of back matter. Except for the index, and at times the bibliography, none of these elements are indispensable.

Writer—*The Omega Plan* 332

Header includes the title, your last name and the page number.

Comments and Endnotes

Heading centered, one-third of the way down the page, and underlined

Chapter 1: Found: The Missing Ingredients for Optimal Health

1. The chart has been adapted from a chart that appeared in reference 10 above. It compares the number of patients who were free from cardiac death and nonfatal heart attacks.

1" margin

Double-spaced text

2. De Longeril, M., P. Salen, and J. Delaye. "Effect of a Mediterranean Type of Diet on the Rate of Cardiovascular Complications in Patients With Coronary Artery Disease." *J Amer Coll Cardiology*, 1996; 28(5):1103–8.

Indent each endnote.

3. Grady, D. "Unusual Molecule Could Be Key to Cancer Patients' Weight Loss," in *The New York Times*. Jan. 4, 1996, p. B10.

Authors, last name first

Journal title, year, volume, number

Writer—*Searching for Mary*   235

Header includes the title, your last name and the page number.

<u>Bibliography</u>

Heading centered, one-third of the way down the page, and underlined

Literature available on the subject of Marian apparitions is co-pious and of wildly varying quality and credibility. Of works consulted in the course of my research, most of which are listed below, a few stand out as superior tools for readers interested in plumbing the subject to greater depths.

Double-spaced text

Sandra Zimdars-Swartz's *Encountering Mary* has set the standard for balanced, scholarly treatment of the phenomena of popularity among communities of believers. If you read only one more book on the subject, this should be the one.

Commentary adds value to the listings.

No more succinct and helpful presentation of the Catholic Church's position in regard to claims of private revelation is to be found than in Benedict Groeschel's *A Still, Small Voice*.

Ashton, Joan. *Mother of All Nations*. San Francisco: Harper and

     Row, 1989.

Christian, William A., Jr. *Apparitions in Late Medieval and*

     Renaissance Spain. Princeton, N.J.: Princeton University

     Press, 1981.

Book citations flush left

Indent subsequent lines of multiple-line listing.

CHAPTER 17

SHORT STORIES

The market for short fiction consists of magazines, literary journals, anthologies, and some on-line websites. And, like novels, they can run the gamut of literature to genre tales to children's stories. The main difference between short stories and novels is length—short stories run anywhere from 1,000 to 20,000 words, whereas novels are much longer. Short stories are a medium all their own, and require a specific format and submission policy. Read on to learn how to submit your short stories to print and electronic publications.

WHAT YOU NEED TO SUBMIT

Submitting short stories is relatively simple. Unlike novels, where you typically need to submit a query letter as well as a few sample chapters and a synopsis, a short story require that you send only a cover letter and the story in its entirety.

COVER LETTER

Submission Tips

Your cover letter is important for two reasons: It lets the editor know who you are and how you write. This is different from a query because you are submitting the story along with the letter. The best cover letters contain three short paragraphs, in the following order:

- The introductory paragraph states the story's title, then hooks the editor with a brief description of the story.

- The biographical paragraph explains, in one or two sentences, a bit about yourself that is pertinent to the story, such as previous publishing credits, why you're sending it to this particular publication, or how a personal experience influenced your story.

- The concluding paragraph politely closes the letter.

While publication hinges on the story itself, a strong cover letter ensures your story gets a close read. Remember to keep it brief and to the point.

Formatting Specs

- Use a standard font, 12-point type. Avoid bold or italics, except for titles.

- Place your name and contact information at the top of your letter, centered.

- Use a 1" margin on all sides.

- Address the cover letter to a specific editor. Call to get the appropriate editor's name and gender.

- Keep it to one page.

- Use block format (no indentations, an extra space between paragraphs).

- Single-space the body of the letter and double-space between paragraphs.

- Give the story's exact word count.

Other Dos and Don'ts

- Do mention if your story has been—or will be—published in another publication.

- Do indicate familiarity with the publication. Make a brief positive comment about the publication. Be sincere but don't go overboard.

- Don't state that another publication has rejected your story.

- Don't ask for advice or criticism—that's not the editor's job at this stage.

- Don't mention anything about yourself that's not pertinent to the story, for instance that you're a first-time writer, that you've never been published, or how much time you've spent on the story. Your story must stand on its own merit.

- Don't bring up payment for the story. It's premature.

- Don't mention copyright information.

- Don't staple your cover letter to your story (a paper clip is okay).

- Don't fax or e-mail your cover letter and story unless you have permission from the editor or if submission guidelines state it is acceptable.

- Do thank the editor for considering your story.

- Do include an SASE (self-addressed stamped envelope) or postcard for reply, and state in the letter that you have done so. (Postcards are cheaper and easier. Get them printed in bulk.)

- Do state that you're able to send your story on disk, CD, or via e-mail, but this won't be necessary until the editor actually wants to publish your story.

ELECTRONIC COVER LETTER

Submission Tips

Before you send a cover letter and story to a publication via e-mail, make sure they accept electronic submissions by contacting the publication directly or checking out their writers' guidelines.

Formatting Specs

- Include the same contact information in your cover letter as you would in a paper cover, except do not include your e-mail address in the body of the e-mail, since the editor can easily click "Reply" to respond.

- Use the subject line to introduce the title of your story.

- Follow the same format you would with a paper cover letter, including the date, salutation, and block paragraph format.

Other Dos and Don'ts

- Don't use all caps or exclamation points in the subject line.

- Don't insert clip art graphics or other images in your cover letter. Keep it simple.

Contact information

John Q. Writer
123 Author Lane
Writerville, CA 95355
(323) 555-0000
johnqwriter@email.com

Simple return information, including phone number and e-mail. For e-correspondence, your contact info should be at the bottom left.

December 29, 2009

Date is flush right.

Address a specific editor.

Thomas Way
Thrills & Chills
666 Blood St.
New York, NY 11000

The publication's title is italicized.

Dear Mr. Way:

Enclosed is my short story, "Spitfire Sunday" (2,500 words). It's about Pastor Donald White, who spends every Sunday preaching hellfire and brimstone. But his little routine changes when atheist Katherine Condon comes to town. She doesn't just preach about perpetual suffering—she delivers it. The target of her latest sadistic crusade is none other than the preacher himself, as she kidnaps, tortures and prepares to set him ablaze just before the clock strikes midnight on Easter Sunday.

The first two sentences get right to the point.

I am a full-time pastor by day and part-time writer by night. My published stories have appeared in three mystery magazines (*Murderously Yours* 12/02, *Crime Pays* 1/03, and *Mystery Times*, 7/03). You are the first editor I'm soliciting with this story, and I will wait six weeks for your response before I approach another magazine. If you are not interested in the story, feel free to dispose of the manuscript, but please notify me with the enclosed SASE. If, however, you do want to publish it, I can send you an electronic version in a Microsoft Word attachment.

Single-spaced text

Makes request concisely

Thank you for considering "Spitfire Sunday." I look forward to hearing from you.

Sincerely,

Politely close the letter.

John Q. Writer

Signature

Encl.: Short story, "Spitfire Sunday"
SASE

Make sure you have the correct e-mail address.

It's not a bad idea to copy (CC or BCC) yourself to keep a record of all e-correspondence.

Since Toni could be male or female, take no chances and write out the full name.

Word count

Informs the editor that other publications are considering the piece.

Polite and short

Contact information goes at the bottom of e-mails.

TO: tgraham@cimarron.com
CC: johnqwriter@email.com
SUBJECT: Short Story Submission
March 2, 2009

Toni Graham
Cimarron Review
Oklahoma State University
205 Morrill Hall
Stillwater, OK 74078

Dear Toni Graham:

I am submitting my short story, "Things From Which You Can Never Recover" (6,465 words) for your consideration in *Cimarron Review*. The story is attached in a Microsoft Word document.

I am currently a freelancer for several newspapers and magazines, including the *Indianapolis Star*. Your website says you are seeking work with "unusual perspective, language, imagery, and character," and I think my story fits this description.

This is a simultaneous submission. As per your online guidelines, if I do not hear back within three months, I will assume the story was not a fit for *Cimarron Review*. Thank you in advance for your time and consideration.

Sincerely,

John Q. Writer
123 Author Lane
Writerville, CA 95355
(323) 555-0000
johnqwriter@email.com

State how the story is attached. Make sure the publication accepts e-mailed stories.

Give a reason for contacting this publication.

Let the editor know this magazine gets first dibs on publishing this story, and how long he'll wait for a response.

217

John Q. Writer
123 Author Lane
Writerville, CA 95355

No telephone number or e-mail.

December 29, 2005

The strange date is either a mistake or a clue that this letter has been copied and pasted many times—neither being a good sign.

Thomas Way
Thrills & Chills
666 Blood St.
New York, NY 11000

Hey Tommy,

Salutation is far too informal.

I have been a man of the pulpit for the last twenty-two years and I know about faith and evil and sin and redemption. I am also a published poet and fiction writer. I've had numerous poems published in our local paper and I write weekly stories for the church bulletin. I get lots of praise from my congregation for my stories, and other people in the community have made glowing remarks about my poetry.

Who cares? What qualifies them to give a valued opinion?

Every sentence in this paragraph begins with "I." Should begin with information about the story, not himself.

Anyhow, I've been working on this one short story for about five months now that I'd like your magazine to publish. It's about a minister who gets caught on fire and burned to death by a new woman in town that doesn't agree with his preaching practices.

Always a bad idea to tell the editor how much time you spent on the story. It's irrelevant.

Too colloquial

I'm sure you'll appreciate this story as it is based on some real people I have known and therefore it is based in reality but I made a lot of it up too. It'll scare the heck out of your readers.

Doesn't tell enough about the story, but does reveal the ending!

If for some reason you do not wish to publish this story, I would appreciate your wise and professional opinion about how to make it better.

Never ask for advice or criticism—that's not the editor's job at this stage.

Nowhere on this page does the writer mention the word count, the story's title, or the main characters.

Thank you for your time.

Sincerely,

John Q. Writer

Encl.: Manuscript
SASE

Even if the enclosed story is spectacular, the editor will be skeptical when reading it (if he bothers reading it after wading through this poor cover letter).

SHORT STORY MANUSCRIPT

Submission Tips

Establish yourself as a professional by following the correct short story format. A separate cover or title page is not necessary. Don't submit any materials that have handwritten notes on them. And as with all parts of your submission, make sure your work is revised and proofread.

Formatting Specs

- Use a 1" margin on all sides.

- Do not number the first page.

- Put your name and contact information at the top, centered, on the first page.

- Put the word count and rights offered in the top right corner.

- Put the story's title, centered in all caps, approximately one-third of the way down the page from the top margin.

- Skip a line and write "by" in lowercase, then skip another line and put your name in all caps. (If using a pseudonym, put that name in all caps, and then on the next line put your real name in parentheses.)

- Drop four lines, indent, and begin your story.

- Double-space the entire text of the story.

- Put a header at the top of every page (except the first) including the title, your last name, and the page number).

- Optional: Type "THE END" in all caps when the story is finished. (Some editors like this because it closes the story; others do not. It's your call.)

Other Dos and Don'ts

- Do use a paper clip in the top left corner to attach pages together (butterfly clamps work well for stories longer than ten pages).

- Do keep an original copy of the story for yourself.

- Don't put your social security number on the manuscript.

- Don't use a separate cover or title page.

- Don't justify the text or align the right margin. Ragged right is fine.

- Don't put a copyright notice on the manuscript. It's copyrighted as soon as you write it.

- Don't include your story on a disk or CD unless the editor asks for it.

- Don't use unusual fonts. A simple Times Roman, Arial, or Courier is fine.

- Don't e-mail or fax your story to a publication unless you have permission from the editor or if their submission guidelines say it is acceptable.

ELECTRONIC SHORT STORY MANUSCRIPT

Submission Tips

Make sure that the publication accepts e-mail submissions before you send your story in that way. Either get permission from the editor, or check to see if their submission guidelines allow it. Don't forget to include your cover letter in the body of your e-mail.

Send the story file as an attachment. You can also cut and paste the entire story below your electronic cover letter in the e-mail itself. This will allow the editor to see the story whichever way she wants.

Formatting Specs

- Before you send the manuscript, find out how the editor prefers to receive files.

- Follow the same formatting specs as a paper manuscript submission.

- If you are sending the manuscript via e-mail, send it as an attachment to your e-mail unless the editor requests otherwise.

Other Dos and Don'ts

- Don't use all caps in your subject line.

- Do ask for specific file format guidelines to make sure the editor can open your files.

- Don't use a separate cover or title page.

- Don't justify text or align the right margin.

- Don't put any copyright information on the manuscript. It's copyrighted when you write it.

- Don't put two spaces after sentences within the manuscript.

- Don't use hard returns to double-space the manuscript.

Contact information

John Q. Writer
123 Author Lane
Writerville, CA 95355
(323) 555-0000
johnqwriter@email.com

First North American Rights Only
2,500 words

The author has already discussed the rights with the editor. If you haven't, leave this blank.

Word count

Title is centered, all caps, one-third of the way down the page.

SPITFIRE SUNDAY

by

JOHN Q. WRITER

Name is centered, all caps.

Four lines between title and text

I was in a small white church south of Somerset, Kentucky, when I first heard the following words: "You will not love yourself until you love Jesus."

Indented paragraphs

Pastor Donald White was no ordinary preacher. He was intense, and moderation was not his game. He preached love but was full of hate. He hated women. He hated divorce. He hated gays. He hated mixed couples. He hated abortion-rights advocates. He hated unbaptized children. He hated sex. He certainly hated

Double-spaced text

the President of the United States. Yes, I'd say he pretty much hated everyone and everything. I'd honestly like to at least say he hated everything except Jesus, but that wouldn't be true. He didn't love Jesus; he only loved talking about Jesus.

1" margin

Anyway, a more self-righteous man I've never seen. He even ran for city council last year—and won—on the motto "You Can Only Go Right With White."

Writer/Spitfire Sunday   15

Header includes your name, the title, and the page number. Number all pages except the first.

As she poked and prodded him with that scalding hot branding iron, he danced amidst the flames, cursing and wailing at her.

"You shall not be torn between loving yourself and loving Jesus," he said. "For Jesus is life, and if you do not love Jesus, you cannot love your own life. You can hate me and torture me all you want. I know you're only doing it because you don't love Jesus. You don't love yourself!"

Katherine couldn't bear to hear one more word. She took the branding iron and pressed it to his mouth. He could not speak; he could barely scream. A look of horror fell over his face as he collapsed in the ring of fire. Then she pointed the gun at him. I thought she was finally going to shoot him, to put an end to this poor man's suffering. But she didn't. She dropped the gun, watched him burn, and smiled. Once his screaming stopped, Katherine picked up the pistol as if to finish the act, to make sure he'd be dead.

To my surprise, she put the pistol in her mouth and fired.

THE END

Optional, but perfectly placed if used

CHAPTER 18

NOVELS

N ovels are lengthy works of literary fiction—usually totaling 60,000 words or more. There are all sorts genres and types, from a paperback Harlequin romance to heavy literature to an installment in a mystery series. No matter what type it is, this chapter will provide guidelines for formatting a professional manuscript submission.

CONCERNING MEMOIR

Memoirs are true-life stories, but they read like novels. They are nonfiction tales that employ common fiction devices, such as cliffhangers, character arcs, and a three-act structure. For this reason, memoir is treated like fiction. If you're writing a memoir, follow the instructions in this chapter.

THE NOVEL PACKAGE

Before You Submit

Before you submit your novel to an agent or publisher, make yourself a checklist. First and foremost, you must finish the work. If you contact an agent and he likes your idea, he will ask to see some or all of the manuscript. You don't want to tell him it won't be finished for another six months. After it's complete, set it aside for a short time, then return with fresh eyes for revisions. Following your own rewrites and revisions, it's not a bad idea to have a trusted peer read over the story. Look for someone who is both skilled and honest. Some writers choose to hire an independent editor to critique their work. This route can be very effective—but know that freelance editors are not cheap. Always get a referral from a friend and ask for a free editing sample before signing a contract.

If your novel is complete and polished, it's time to write your query and synopsis. After that, you're ready to test the agent and editor waters.

What You Need to Submit

There are a few ways to submit your novel package to an agent or publisher, depending on the individual's submission guidelines. Some want only a query letter; others request a query letter and the complete manuscript; some demand a query letter plus three sample chapters and a synopsis; and still others request that you submit a query letter, a few sample chapters, an outline, and a synopsis. All want an SASE (self-addressed stamped envelope) with adequate postage, unless they request an electronic submission.

To determine what you need to submit, consult the current edition of market databases such as *Novel & Short Story Writer's Market*, *Writer's Market*, or *Guide to Literary Agents*. Or try the market's individual website. These sources have submission specifications that come straight from the editors and agents and tell exactly what to send, how to send it, when to expect a response, and other information unique to the agent or editor you will be soliciting.

Expect to send at least a query letter, a synopsis, and three consecutive sample chapters. These are the most important—and most requested—parts of your novel package. However, if you don't know whom you'll be soliciting and what they demand, try to have the following prepared before you start sending out submissions:

- A query or cover letter

- A synopsis

- At least three consecutive sample chapters

- A chapter-by-chapter outline

- An author biography

Rarely will you need to send them all in the same submission package, since each agent and editor has his own preferences. But you probably will need to use each of them at one time or another, so prepare everything before you actually start submitting your novel. Always include an SASE if you're sending your submission through the mail.

QUERY LETTER

Submission Tips

A query letter has two functions: to tell the agent or editor what you have to offer, and to ask if she is interested in seeing it.

Though you can send the query letter attached to a novel package, many agents and editors prefer you send the query letter either by itself or with a synopsis and a few sample pages from your novel. This is called a "blind query" or a "prepackage query," because you're sending it without having been asked to send it. No matter what you call it, it's your quick chance to hook the agent or editor on your novel.

If she likes your query, she'll call and ask for either specific parts of your novel package or the entire manuscript. Then she'll make her decision.

Some agents and editors prefer that you accompany your initial query letter with other parts of your novel package. If that's the case, include the required materials specified by the particular agent or publisher in the market database listing. When you accompany your query with your novel package, the query becomes your cover letter.

The query is the vital component to the submission, whether you submit the query by itself or with other material. Make it compelling, interesting, even funny—anything to make it outstanding to the agent or editor. And do it all in just one page. The query shows that you have a good grasp of your novel and can boil down the concept into a concise and compelling pitch. Although every winning query works its own magic, all good queries should contain the following:

- A grabber or hook that makes the reader want to get his hands on the actual novel

- One to three paragraphs about your novel

- A short paragraph about you and your publishing credentials (if you have any)

- A good reason you're soliciting the person you're soliciting (why this agent or publisher instead of another?)

- The length and genre of the novel

- A sentence or two about the intended audience

- An indication that an SASE is enclosed if you are sending it through the mail

Arguably the most important aspect of any query is the grabber, the hook that lures the reader into wanting to read your novel. Your grabber should be part of the paragraphs—the pitch—you devote to telling about the novel. Another good idea is to point out why your novel is different from all the others.

Then spend a few sentences telling about yourself; list your publishing credentials (if you have any), or toss in a personal anecdote that's pertinent to the novel (explain that you spent two years in the Peace Corps in Somalia if that's where your story takes place). Ideally what information you include in your bio paragraph shouldn't matter much because your pitch will have already hooked the agent. That said, if you don't have anything pertinentto say about yourself, skip this part and simply thank the agent or editor for her time.

Then, in another paragraph, mention why you're sending your query to this particular agent or editor. Feel free to allude to an author the publisher publishes (or the agent represents) whose work is similar to yours. Doing this is not just name-dropping, but also proof that you've done your research.

Finally, always include an SASE if you're sending your query through the mail.

Formatting Specs

- The basic setup for a query to an agent or publisher is similar to an article query or short story cover letter.

- Use a standard font, 12-point type. Avoid bold or italic except for titles.

- Use a 1" margin on all sides.

- Use block format (no indentations, an extra line space between paragraphs).

- Put your name and contact information at the top of your letter, centered, or in your letterhead.

- Keep the query to one page.

- Single-space the body of the letter and double-space between paragraphs.

- Catalog every item you're sending in your enclosures.

Other Dos and Don'ts

- Do state any previous publishing credits.

- Do tell if you're sending simultaneous submissions to other agents and editors.

- Do address your letter to a specific agent or editor. Call to get the appropriate name and gender.

- Don't fax your query.

- Don't mention that you're a first-time writer or that you've never been published.

- Don't spend much time trying to sell yourself. Your manuscript will stand on its own.

- Don't state that some other agent or editor has rejected your novel.

- Don't ask for advice or criticism—that's not the agent's or editor's job at this stage.

- Do summarize any relevant experience you have.

- Don't mention anything about yourself not pertinent to the novel.

- Don't bring up payment expectations.

- Don't mention copyright information.

- Don't staple your query letter to your manuscript.

ELECTRONIC QUERY LETTER

Submission Tips

Most publishers and agents now accept queries via e-mail. Before you send a query off to a publisher or agent electronically, however, you must either have permission to send it via e-mail or make sure that their guidelines indicate that it is acceptable. Communicating with a publisher or agent via e-mail should be just as formal and respectful as if you were sending it through the mail. The basic tone and format of the electronic query shouldn't be much different from a query sent on paper. Keep your query relatively short. Just because you're communicating via e-mail doesn't allow you to have a long query.

Formatting Specs

- Present the same information you would in a paper query, including your name and contact information. With e-mail queries, it's recommended to put your contact information at the lower left under your signature. Because the window to view the letter on a computer screen is not large, doing this allows the reader to jump right into your query. It isn't necessary to include your e-mail address in the body of the e-mail since the editor can reply easily with the click of a button.

- Put a description of your novel or its title in the subject line.

- Follow the same format you would with a paper query, including the date, salutation to a specific editor, and block paragraph format. See the tips for submitting a paper query; the same rules apply.

Other Dos and Don'ts

- Don't use all caps or exclamation points in the subject line.

- Don't submit an e-mail query unless specifically requested by the publisher or agent, or if their guidelines say that it is acceptable.

- Don't insert clip art graphics or other images into your query letter.

- Do maintain formal communication, just like you would in a paper query.

- Don't send your query letter as an attachment. Paste it into the e-mail body.

Dr. Doreen Orion
123 Author Lane
Writerville, CA 95355
(323) 555-0000
janeqwriter@email.com

Contact information

April 5, 2006

Date flushed right

Mollie Glick
Foundry Literary + Media
33 West 17th St. PH
New York, NY 10011

Always address your query to a specific agent.

Dear Ms. Glick:

Memoirs are the only kind of nonfiction treated like fiction because they read like novels. Memoirs require a query and synopsis.

I am a psychiatrist, published author, and expert for the national media seeking representation for my memoir titled, *Queen of the Road: The True Tale of 49 States, 22,000 Miles, 200 Shoes, 2 Cats, 1 Poodle, a Husband, and a Bus with a Will of Its Own*. Because you are interested in unique voices, I thought we might be a good match.

Books are *titled*, not *entitled*.

1" margin

When Tim first announced he wanted to "chuck it all" and travel around the country in a converted bus for a year, I gave this profound and potentially life-altering notion all the thoughtful consideration it deserved. "Why can't you be like a normal husband with a midlife crisis and have an affair or buy a Corvette?" I asked, adding, "I will never, ever, EVER live on a bus."

The author has done significant research on agents and chosen one for specific reasons.

A brief overview of the plot

What do you get when you cram married shrinks—one in a midlife crisis, the other his materialistic, wise-cracking wife—two cats who hate each other and a Standard Poodle who loves licking them all, into a bus for a year? *Queen of the Road* is a memoir of my dysfunctional, multi-species family's travels to and travails in the forty-nine continental states.

Use a quick, catchy hook with an entertaining but professional tone.

Include an author bio that demonstrates your platform and why you're the right author for this project.

As a psychiatrist, award-winning author (*I Know You Really Love Me*, Macmillan/Dell) and frequent media expert on psychiatric topics (including *Larry King, GMA, 48 Hours, The New York Times* and *People* magazine), my life has centered on introspection, analysis, and storytelling.

Single-spaced text, block format

I hope you are interested in seeing sample pages. If so, I would be most happy to send them to you via e-mail or regular mail.

Best wishes,

Signature

Dr. Doreen Orion

TO: jfaust@email.com
CC: janeqwriter@email.com
SUBJECT: Query – Murder on the Rocks

June 14, 2004

Jessica Faust
BookEnds, LLC
136 Long Hill Rd.
Gillette, NJ 07933

Dear Ms. Faust,

I enjoyed meeting you at the conference in Austin this past weekend. As I mentioned, I have had my eye on BookEnds for quite some time; when I discovered you would be at the conference, I knew I had to attend. We met during the final pitch session and discussed how the series I am working on might fit in with your current line of mystery series. Per your request, I have enclosed a synopsis and first three chapters of *Murder on the Rocks*, an 80,000-word cozy mystery that was a finalist in this year's Writers' League of Texas manuscript contest.

Natalie Barnes has quit her job, sold her house, and gambled everything she has on the Gray Whale Inn on Cranberry Island, Maine. But she's barely fired up the stove when portly developer Bernard Katz rolls into town and starts mowing through her morning glory muffins. Natalie needs the booking, but Katz is hard to stomach—especially when he unveils his plan to build an oversized golf resort on top of the endangered tern colony next door. When the town board approves the new development. The terns face extinction, and Natalie's Inn might just follow along. Just when Natalie thinks she can't face more trouble, she discovers Katz's body at the base of the cliff and becomes the number one suspect in the police's search for a murderer.

I am a former pubic relations writer, a graduate of Rice University, a member of the Writers' League of Texas, and founder of the Austin Mystery Writers critique group. I have spent many summers in fishing communities in Maine and Newfoundland.

If you would like to see the manuscript, I can send it via e-mail or regular mail. Thank you for your time and attention.

Sincerely,

Karen Swartz MacInerney
123 Author Lane
Writerville, CA 95355
(323) 555-0000
janeqwriter@email.com

Margin comments (left side):

Subject line contains the title and that it is a query.

Notes the personal connection and a reason to query me.

Establishes voice and a feeling for the book.

Karen's credentials are impressive. She's obviously been writing for a while and I really like the addition of her summers in Maine. It's a personal touch, but one that's perfectly related to the book.

In an e-mail query, your contact information should be at the lower left.

Margin comments (right side):

The word count is right there with the standards for cozy mysteries. Also, her description fits her genre. All too often submissions name a genre, but the description doesn't match the genre; a romantic comedy, for example, that didn't sound funny or a thriller that seemed less than thrilling.

Polite wrap-up; offers to send more.

Novels

John Q. Writer
123 Author Lane
Writerville, CA 95355
(323) 555-0000
johnqwriter@email.com

October 31, 2008

Contact
information

Date flushed right

Steven T. Murray, Editor-in-Chief
Fjord Press
P.O. Box 16349
Seattle, WA 98116

Dear Mr. Murray:

Address a
specific editor.

Plenty Good Room concerns the emotional struggles a thirteen-year-old African-American boy endures when his mother declares that he must leave his native Harlem and move down south (Florida) to live with a father he has never known. The three stages of the story show the young man's life: His time in New York and the events that subsequently lead to his mother's insistence that the father shoulder the remaining responsibility of rearing him; the not so clear-cut path he takes to become part of his father's life; and his life with his father and the ultimate unraveling of a dream he thought had come true.

The query jumps right
into the pitch, which is
perfectly acceptable.

Give a clear idea of
the overall structure of
the novel.

An effective pitch
shows map of the
novel.

The story is written entirely from the viewpoint of the teen protagonist (a la *Catcher in the Rye*) and is a first-person account replete with emotion and stingingly blunt dialogue. Despite the age of the protagonist, *Plenty Good Room* is not a children's book. The language is contemporary and often raw and unrelenting. The book is, however, a timely exposé on a young black male growing up in a single-parent home where the parent is too young, too inexperienced, and too poor to adequately parent and where the father is not at all involved.

1" margin

Single-spaced text,
block format

I have enclosed to the first twenty pages of my thirteen-chapter manuscript. Please notify me if you are interested in reviewing the complete text. Thank you for your consideration.

Sincerely,

Signature

John Q. Writer

Encl.: SASE

Details
enclosures

Get Published Books
P.O. Box 554
New York, NY 11584
(323) 555-0000

Contact information is misplaced— and incomplete.

October 15, 2009

Hi Mr. Editor—

Find out the name of a specific editor at the publisher who deals with the type of books you write.

I know that Get Published Books doesn't usually handle Western works, but I've written a book that will make us both a lot of money. I know you produce good work so maybe we can strike a deal on this special project. My book is like *The Da Vinci Code* of Westerns. Everyone in my writers' group thinks that *The Trail* is going to be a bestseller, and two women in my Weight Watchers group think it would make a perfect Oprah book.

It makes no sense to query a publisher if they don't represent the subject or genre you've written.

Fails to reveal a hook or plot or a reason to request the book. There is nothing here to indicate how this book will distinguish itself from the thousands of other similar books that have been published.

I grew up in New Mexico and have always struggled with my weight. I am a computer programmer by day, have two children (a boy and a girl) and have published several technical guides. I have written three novels and already have plans for two sequels, *The Frontier Rises* and *Lasso My Heart*.

References from people outside the publishing industry don't help your case.

I will be coming into New York next week and would like to set up an appointment with you so I can bring you the materials, and find out how much money I can reasonably expect to get paid for this project and what you can do to help make this a bestseller.

Broad claims

All best wishes,

John Q. Writer

Personal information is unrelated to your book

Don't mention pay- ment expectations. This is a query to assess a publisher's interest in your novel.

It's up to the agent to schedule a phone call or personal meeting, not you.

Talk about what you can do for the agent, not vice versa.

231

Novels

COVER LETTER

Submission Tips

A cover letter accompanying a novel package is a tightened version of a query letter.

Like the query, your cover letter lets the editor know who you are and what you have to offer. But, because so much information is included in the rest of the package, and because you should have already queried the agent or editor, the cover letter can be fairly brief.

With a cover letter, there's no need to explain why your book is worthwhile; you just need to introduce the material. Why spend a lot of space synopsizing your novel and telling about yourself when you've included a synopsis, three sample chapters, and an author bio? Of course, you still want to hook the editor or agent, but you don't need to go into as much detail as you would in a blind query letter.

A good rule of thumb is to keep your cover letter to three short paragraphs and organize it in the following order:

- The **introductory paragraph** states the novel's title, then hooks the editor with a brief description of your novel.

- The **biographical paragraph** explains, in one or two sentences, anything about yourself that's pertinent to the novel, such as previous publishing credits or why you're sending it to this particular agency or publisher.

- The **concluding paragraph** politely closes the letter.

Formatting Specs

- Use a standard font, 12-point type. Avoid bold or italic except for titles.

- Put your name and contact information at the top of the page, centered, or in your letterhead.

- Use a 1" margin on all sides.

- Address the cover letter to a specific editor. Call and get the appropriate editor's name and gender.

- Keep it to one page.

- Use block format.

- Single-space the body of the letter and double-space between paragraphs.

- Catalog every item you're sending in your enclosures.

Other Dos and Don'ts

- Do thank the editor.

- Do provide the novel's word count.

- Do mention whether you're soliciting other agents or editors.

- Do include an SASE or postcard for reply, and state in the letter that you have done so.

- Don't mention that you're a first-time writer or that you've never been published or that someone else has rejected your novel.

- Don't start your pitch all over again in the cover letter. If your query made enough of an impression to spark the editor or agent's interest, alluding to his request to see the package is enough. Your novel will stand on its own.

- Don't ask for advice or criticism—that's not the agent's or editor's job at this stage.

- Don't mention anything about yourself that isn't pertinent to the novel.

- Don't bring up payment; it's premature.

- Don't mention copyright information. What you've written is already copyrighted, and you don't need to imply that the editor or agent is out to steal your idea.

- Don't include your social security number.

- Don't staple your cover letter to your novel package. A butterfly or clamp-style paper clip can hold the package elements together, and the cover letter stands alone in front.

- Don't put a page number on the cover letter.

ELECTRONIC COVER LETTER

Submission Tips

If a publisher requests that you submit your book package electronically, don't forget to include the cover letter. Just like a paper cover letter, keep it brief, and stick to the format of an introductory paragraph, a biographical paragraph, and a concluding paragraph. Your cover letter should be pasted inside the e-mail body because it's your initial communication with the agent. You will attach your synopsis and other included materials, preferably as Microsoft Word (.doc) files.

Formatting Specs

- Present the same information you would in a paper query, including your name and contact information. The top center position is fine for this, though you can also put this information in a signature line at the end in an e-mail. It isn't necessary to include your e-mail address in the body of the e-mail, however, since the editor can reply easily with the click of a button.

- Put a description of your novel or its title in the subject line.

- Follow the same format you would with a paper query, including the date, salutation to a specific editor, and block paragraph format. See the tips for submitting a paper cover letter; the same rules apply, with the exception of including an SASE.

Other Dos and Don'ts

- Don't use all caps or exclamations in the subject line.

- Don't submit an e-mail cover letter and package unless the editor specifically requests you do so.

- Don't insert clip art graphics or other images into your cover letter.

- Do read the Dos and Don'ts listed for a paper cover letter submission; the same rules apply.

John Q. Writer
123 Author Lane
Writerville, CA 95355
(323) 555-0000
johnqwriter@email.com

March 2, 2009

Sam Sertz
A&B Publishing
187 72nd St., 5th Floor
New York, NY 10000

Dear Mr. Sertz:

In my novel, *Officer on the Run*, the town of Little Hills, Ohio,
gets a jolt when Police Chief John Murphy's body is found with a
bullet between the eyes and deep fingernail scratches down his
back. The primary suspects are women, particularly the Chief's
seven mistresses (he calls them his "Seven Deadly Sins"). But
none of their DNA matches the killer's. Is it possible that the
murderer could be none other than the man who's next in line for
the Chief's job, Lieutenant Robert Lieberman? It's up to detective
David Black to solve the case.

I am a published mystery writer whose short stories have appeared in *Over Your Dead Body* and *A Dime for Crime*. I am also a
prosecuting attorney, and I have brought my writing and professional interests together in *Officer on the Run*. The novel weighs in
at 70,000 words.

I think it will fit quite well with your successful series by Patty
Smith and your current bestseller *The CIA Murders* by Terry Clark,
both of which point to the continued popularity of detective
novels.

Thank you for considering *Officer on the Run*. I look forward to
hearing from you.

Sincerely,

John Q. Writer

Encl.: Contents page
Chapters 1, 2, 3
Synopsis
SASE

COVER PAGE

Submission Tips

The cover page includes the title, an estimated word count, and either your contact information (if you're submitting directly to an editor) or your agent's contact information (if you're submitting through an agent).

Formatting Specs

- If you're using an agent, put the agent's contact information in the bottom right corner and don't put your name and address on the cover. If you're submitting to an editor, put your contact information in place of an agent's.

- Put an estimated word count (for the entire book, not for the package) in the top right corner.

- Center the title, subtitle, and author's name in the middle of the page.

- Put the title in all capital letters and the subtitle in uppercase and lowercase. If you want to use bold for the title and italics for the subtitle, that's fine, too.

Other Dos and Don'ts

- Don't include both your contact information and the agent's. Use one or the other, depending on the situation.

- Don't use a header, or number the cover page.

- Don't fax or e-mail your package to a publisher or agent unless they specifically request it.

Always include the
novel's
word count.

70,000 words

OFFICER ON THE RUN
A Novel

by
John Q. Writer

Center the title
in the middle of the
page.

John Q. Writer
123 Author Lane
Writerville, CA 95355
(323) 555-0000
johnqwriter@email.com

Author's contact
information at the
lower right if the
package is going
to an agent. Use
the agent's contact
information if the
package is going to
an editor.

SYNOPSIS

Submission Tips

The synopsis supplies key information about your novel (plot, theme, characterization, setting), while also showing how these coalesce to form the big picture. Quickly tell what your novel is about without making the editor or agent read the novel in its entirety.

There are no hard and fast rules about the synopsis. In fact, there's conflicting advice about the typical length of a synopsis. Most editors and agents agree, though: The shorter, the better.

When writing your synopsis, focus on the essential parts of your story, and try not to include sections of dialogue unless you think they are absolutely necessary. (It is okay to inject a few strong quotes from your characters, but keep them brief.) Finally, even though the synopsis is only a condensed version of your novel, it must seem complete.

Keep events in the same order as they happen in the novel (but don't break them down into individual chapters). Remember that your synopsis should have a beginning, a middle, and an ending (yes, you must tell how the novel ends to round out your synopsis).

In a nutshell: You need to be concise, compelling, and complete.

THE SHORT SYNOPSIS VS. THE LONG SYNOPSIS

Since there is no definitive length to a synopsis, it's recommended you have two versions: a long synopsis and a short synopsis.

In past years, there used to be a fairly universal system regarding synopses. For every 35 or so pages of text you had, you would have one page of synopsis explanation. So, if your book was 245 pages, double-spaced, your synopsis would be approximately seven pages. This was fairly standard, and allowed writers a decent amount of space to explain their story. Write this first. This will be your long synopsis.

The problem is that sometime in the past few years, agents started to get really busy and they want to hear your story now-now-now. They started asking for synopses of no more than two pages. Many agents today request specifically just that—two pages max. Some may even say one page, but two pages is generally acceptable. You have to draft a new, more concise synopsis—the short synopsis.

Which do you submit? If you think your short synopsis (one to two pages) is tight and effective, always use that. However, if you think the long synopsis is much more effective, then you will sometimes submit one and sometimes submit the other. If an agent requests two pages max, send only the short one. If she says simply, "Send a synopsis," and you feel your longer synopsis is superior and your long synopsis isn't more than eight pages, submit the long one. If you're writing plot-heavy fiction, such as thrillers and mysteries, you will probably benefit from writing a longer synopsis.

Your best bet on knowing how long to make your synopsis is to follow the guidelines in the agency or publisher's listing.

Formatting Specs

- Use a 1" margin on all sides.

- Justify the left margin only.

- Put your name and contact information on the top left corner of the first page.

- Type the novel's genre and word count, and then the word *Synopsis* on the top right corner of the first page.

- Do not number the first page (but it is considered page one).

- Put the novel's title, centered and in all caps, about one-third of the way down the page.

- Drop four lines below the title and begin the text of the synopsis.

- The text throughout the synopsis should be double-spaced (unless you intend to keep your synopsis to one or two pages, then single-spaced is okay).

- Use all caps the first time you introduce a character.

- After the first page, use a header on every page. The header contains your last name, slash, your novel's title in all capital letters, slash, the word "Synopsis": Name/TITLE/Synopsis.

- Also after the first page, put the page number in the top right corner of every consecutive page, on the same line as the header. You can include this in the header.

- The first line of text on each page after the first page should be three lines below the header.

Other Dos and Don'ts

- Do keep in mind that this is a sales pitch. Make it a short, fast, exciting read.

- Do establish a hook at the beginning of the synopsis. Introduce your lead character and set up a key conflict.

- Do introduce your most important character first.

- Do provide details about your central character (age, gender, marital status, profession, etc.), but don't do this for every character, only the primary ones.

- Do include the characters' motivations and emotions.

- Do highlight pivotal plot points and reveal the novel's ending.

- Don't go into detail about what happens; just tell what happens.

- Don't inject long sections of dialogue into your synopsis.

- Do write in the third person, present tense, even if your novel is in the first person.

ELECTRONIC SYNOPSIS

Submission Tips

Some editors or agents might ask you to submit your synopsis via e-mail or on a disk or CD. The editor or agent can provide you with specific formatting guidelines indicating how she wants the outline sent and the type of files she prefers.

Formatting Specs

- Follow the same formatting specs used for a paper synopsis submission.

- When sending your synopsis via e-mail, put the name of your novel in the subject line.

- Send the synopsis as an attachment to your e-mail unless the editor or agent requests otherwise.

- Include your cover letter in the body of your e-mail, and your cover page and table of contents in the file along with the synopsis.

Other Dos and Don'ts

- Don't use all caps in your subject line.

- Don't submit a synopsis electronically unless the editor or agent requests it.

- Don't justify text or align the right margin.

Contact information on the top left corner of first page

John Q. Writer
123 Author Lane
Writerville, CA 95355
(323) 555-0000
johnqwriter@email.com

Mystery
70,000 words

Novel's genre and word length

Do not number the first page.

OFFICER ON THE RUN
Synopsis

Title is centered and in all caps.

Use all caps the first time a character is introduced.

Investigative officer DAVID BLACK doesn't know where to begin when he gets word Police Chief JOHN MURPHY is found dead on his bed—with a silver bullet between his eyes and half-inch nail marks running down his back. Black has to answer two questions: Who would kill the Chief, and why?

Establish a good hook, introduce important characters, and set up a key conflict

Double-spaced text

It turns out quite a few people aren't too pleased with the Chief. He'd been on the force for twenty-three years and no doubt made some enemies. All the townspeople called him Bulldog because he looked like a pit bull, and certainly acted like one.

Countless stories passed through City Hall about how the Chief wouldn't hesitate to roll up his cuffs and beat suspects into submission until they would confess to a crime. That was his method and it worked. He could take control of any person and any situation.

1" margin

Except his wife and his marriage. On that front, the Chief was completely out of control. He'd lost all affection for his wife, MARY, who was once the apple of his eye but now weighs 260 lbs.

Justify left margin only.

Writer/OFFICER ON THE RUN/Synopsis   2

Header includes
your name, the title,
the word *Synopsis*,
and the page
number.

Black interviews all seven women and finds no leads until MARLENE PRESTON, the Chief's "Seventh Deadly Sin," reveals how the Chief repeatedly would handcuff her arms and legs to four metal poles under the bleachers at the school football stadium. Marlene says she's never told anyone about any of it. Black then interrogates the six other "sins" to see if they had also been physically mistreated. They all say the Chief never tried anything like that with them.

Text begins three
lines below the
header.

Synopses are written
in third person, pres-
ent tense.

Black drinks himself into a stupor and pours out his problems to a young barmaid, SARAH, who just happens to be the best friend of the Police Lieutenant's daughter, KELLY LIEBERMAN. Sarah tells Black the Chief deserved to die and that he was a jerk, especially to Kelly. According to Sarah, the Chief used to talk dirty to Kelly and then warn her not to tell her father because LIEUTENANT LIEBERMAN was in line for a promotion.

Black interviews Kelly. She denies the Chief did anything but make a few lewd comments on occasion. When Black approaches Kelly's father, Lieutenant Lieberman says Kelly never mentioned a word about the Chief. Black returns to talk with Kelly and asks why she's never mentioned anything to her father. She says she's afraid he'd get upset at her for bringing it up. Black presses further, asking Kelly if the Chief ever did anything other than verbally harass her. Kelly says no.

In a long synopsis, a
new scene or twist
begins with the start
of a new paragraph.
There is not enough
room to do this in a
short synopsis.

Paragraphs are
short and fast reads,
mentioning only the
essentials of the story.

Black walks back under the bleachers to the spot where Marlene says the Chief repeatedly handcuffed her. There, he notices two sneaker shoestrings on the ground by the four poles Marlene pointed out. The strings had been tied in knots and then cut.

The genre of the novel is not mentioned here, nor is the word length. These elements should be included in the synopsis.

John Q. Writer
123 Author Lane
Writerville, USA 95355

Phone number and e-mail address are missing.

Officer on the Run

The title of the book should be in all caps, or at least bold and italicized.

Investigative officer David Black doesn't know where to begin when he gets word Police Chief John Murphy is found dead on his bed—with a silver bullet between his eyes and half-inch nail marks running down his back. Black has to answer two questions: Who would kill the Chief, and why?

The first time a character is introduced, the name should be in all caps.

The text should be double-spaced.

It turns out quite a few people aren't too pleased with the Chief. He's been on the force for twenty-three years and no doubt made some enemies. On the home front, the Chief was completely out of control. He'd lost all affection for his wife, Mary, who was once the apple of his eye.

A shorter synopsis is preferable, but this is too short and doesn't give enough information about the characters or the plot to make it compelling.

Black interviews all of the women that the Chief had affairs with, whom he called his "Seven Deadly Sins," and finds no leads until Marlene Preston, the Chief's seventh "sin." She reveals how the Chief repeatedly would handcuff her arms and legs to four metal poles under the bleachers at the school football stadium. Black drinks himself into a stupor and pours out his problems to a young barmaid, who tells him that the Chief deserved to die.

Pivotal plot points are glossed over—they should be highlighted.

The characters' motivations and emotions aren't conveyed at all in this synopsis, leaving the editor or agent to think, "Why should I care about these characters?"

Black continues investigating the Chief and uncovers all kinds of sordid details. The killer is revealed at the end, and it is a total shock and surprise to all, especially Black.

Be sure to reveal your novel's ending.

OUTLINE

Submission Tips

An outline is often used interchangeably with a synopsis, but for most editors and agents, there is a distinction. Whereas a synopsis is a brief, encapsulated version of the novel at large, an outline makes each chapter its own story, usually containing a few paragraphs per chapter. In short, an outline is a breakdown of the novel with a synopsis of each individually chapter.

Never submit an outline unless an agent or editor specifically asks for it. Fewer and fewer agents and editors want outlines these days. Most just request a cover letter, a few sample chapters, and a short synopsis or sometimes the entire manuscript. However, it's still something you will probably have to write sometime. Genre fiction editors often request outlines because genre books run for many pages and have numerous plot shifts.

Formatting Specs

- Use a 1" margin on all sides.

- Justify the left margin only.

- At the top left of every page, use a header with your last name, slash, your novel's title in all capital letters, slash, the word *Outline*: Name/TITLE/Outline.

- Put the page number in the top right corner of every page. This can be part of your header.

- Drop four lines below the header, then put the words *Chapter-by-Chapter Outline* centered and bold or underlined.

- Drop four more lines and type the chapter number.

- Drop two lines and put the chapter's title (if applicable) on the left margin and the number of manuscript pages that chapter runs on the right margin.

- Drop two lines and begin the text of the outline.

- Double-space the text throughout the outline.

- Use all caps the first time you introduce a character.

- Use a separate page for each chapter.

Other Dos and Don'ts

- Do keep in mind that your outline is an extended, more detailed, and structural version of your synopsis.

- Do explain the gist of each chapter.

- Do highlight pivotal plot points.

- Do provide a hook for each chapter.

- Do reveal how the chapter begins and ends.

- Do make sure each succeeding chapter picks up where the previous chapter left off.

- Don't include extended dialogue.

ELECTRONIC OUTLINE

Submission Tips

Some editors or agents might ask you to submit your outline via e-mail or on a disk or CD. The editor or agent can provide you with specific formatting guidelines indicating how he wants the outline sent and the type of files he prefers.

Formatting Specs

- Follow the same formatting specs as for a paper outline submission.

- When e-mailing your outline, put the name of your book in the subject line.

- Send the outline as an attachment to your e-mail unless the editor or agent requests otherwise.

- Include your cover letter in the body of your e-mail and your cover page and table of contents in the file along with the outline.

Other Dos and Don'ts

- Don't use all caps or exclamation points in your subject line unless their in the title of your book.

- Don't submit an outline electronically unless the editor or agent specifically requests it.

Writer/OFFICER ON THE RUN/Outline   3

CHAPTER-BY-CHAPTER OUTLINE

Header includes your name, the title, the word *Outline*, and the page number.

Indicate that this page is part of the chapter-by-chapter outline.

Chapter 3

Chapter number

Under the Bleachers at Campbell Field   14 pages

Chapter's title and number of pages it runs

Marlene takes Detective Black to a dark, concealed spot under the bleachers at the school football field, the same spot where the Chief used to take her. Marlene tells Black it was here that the Chief first came on to her, eventually handcuffed her, and threatened her to keep silent (which she did). Sure, everyone suspected they were having an affair, but nobody had a clue that it was entirely against her wishes.

Reveal how the chapter begins.

Justify left margin only.

Explain the gist of the chapter and highlight pivotal moments.

This all comes as a surprise to Black, who just assumed all the Chief's affairs were mutual. Black presses Marlene to tell him everything. She does. She even shows him where the chief would handcuff her arms and legs to the poles. About six inches from the ground around all four poles were rings showing where the paint chipped from the handcuffs grinding against them.

Double-spaced text

Dismayed, Black asks Marlene if she's ever told anyone else about this. She says, "Not a soul." Black wonders, could there be more?

1" margin

Reveal how the chapter ends.

Outline

CHAPTER-BY-CHAPTER OUTLINE

The header should also include the author's last name and the title of the book in all caps. It should also have page numbers in the top right corner of every page.

Chapter 3
23 pages

The chapter's title should be included here (if applicable).

Like in a synopsis, avoid stepping outside the story to expose the frame. Nix phrases like "This chapter begins ..." or "At the climax ..."

This chapter begins with Marlene Preston and detective Black. Marlene takes him to the bleachers and tells Black that this is where the Chief first came on to her against her wishes but he threatened her. Black is shocked. Marlene says she never told anyone about her affair with the Chief.

The text should be double-spaced.

How does the chapter end? What would make a reader want to move on to the next chapter?

This outline is too short to convey what happens in the twenty-three pages of this chapter. Pivotal moments should be highlighted and the character's motivations and emotions revealed.

AUTHOR BIOGRAPHY

Submission Tips

Your author bio is about you but only in the context of what makes you the perfect person to tell this story. Don't include any information that doesn't directly help the pitch. You may include educational information if you have an advanced degree, and your profession if it's pertinent to the novel. It's okay to say where you live and to whom you're married, but unless there's something strikingly unusual about your family, don't mention them. Definitely include any previous publishing credits. Keep your bio at less than a page.

Formatting Specs

- Use a header with your last name, slash, the novel's title in all caps, slash, the words *Author Biography*: Name/TITLE/Author Biography.

- Double-space the text.

- Write in the third person present tense.

- Keep it under one page. Standard length is 200–250 words.

Other Dos and Don'ts

- Don't mention your membership in any writers organizations, unless it can help promote your novel (for example, if you write a mystery, tell that you belong to the Mystery Writers of America).

- Do mention any publicity or promotion you've received, such as appearances on national TV or radio programs, or interviews in national magazines.

- Don't mention any "minor" publishing credits unrelated to your novel (for instance, that you had two poems published in your local paper).

- Don't spend too much time complimenting yourself.

- Do stick to the facts (don't exaggerate or lie).

- Don't include an author bio if you're a beginning writer with no publishing credits, and you don't have much to say regarding qualifications or credentials.

- Do write separate bios if you're collaborating with another author, but make sure both fit on the same page.

Header →

Writer/OFFICER ON THE RUN/Author Biography

About the Author

Reveal information
that's pertinent to
the novel. →

John Q. Writer has been a prosecuting attorney for Big Lake
County, Pennsylvania, since 1985. He garnered regional media attention during the late 1990s by winning the case that put all-star
Pittsburgh Steelers quarterback Warren St. Christofer in prison
for sexually harassing his sports agent.

Write in the
third person. →

Mr. Writer's writing credits include stories published in mystery magazines *Over Your Dead Body* and *A Dime for a Crime*, as
well as numerous articles in law-enforcement trade journals, such
as *Police Time, By the Book, Today's Attorney,* and *Beneath the Badge.*
← Mention previously
published material.

← Double-
spaced text

1" margin

He received his B.A. in Comparative Literature from Kent
State University and his law degree from Case Western Reserve.
Mr. Writer lives with his wife and three children in Allentown,
← Briefly tell about
yourself.

Keep the word count
between around
200–250 words. →

Pennsylvania. This is his first novel.

CHAPTER 19

CHILDREN'S WRITING

PICTURE BOOKS

Picture books are written for very young children to read or have read to them. They usually have very little text but plenty of illustrations to engage children. The text of a picture book is well organized and carefully constructed, since its audience has little experience with stories. Because picture books are often read aloud, and because children have an instinctual fondness for rhythm, poetic techniques such as alliteration, consonance, assonance, and onomatopoeia can enhance a picture book's story. Other techniques that appeal to children is a repeated anecdote, such as the one used in *The Three Little Pigs*, and a refrain, used in *The Gingerbread Man*. Vocabulary in picture books is simple, and sentence construction is likewise uncomplicated. Picture books often use the active voice and mimic speech patterns. Though picture books may rhyme, most publishers are not looking for rhyming books.

WHAT YOU NEED TO SUBMIT

A typical picture book contains around 150–1,000 words, running around thirty-two pages, with twenty-eight pages of text and illustrations. The rest of the book contains front and back matter, such as the copyright page and the title page.

The primary difference between submitting a picture book and an adult book is that you generally send the entire manuscript of your picture book, not just a proposal or a few sample chapters. Picture books are generally so short in length that it takes very little time to read the entire text and make a decision. Some publishers do accept and want query letters, though.

A common misconception among many new writers of picture books is that they must find illustrators for their work before they submit. This is absolutely not the case; in fact, most editors frown upon a writer and illustrator teaming up on a submission. Once a publisher accepts your material, the editor will select an appropriate illustrator for your project. So even if your sister-in-law or co-worker is an illustrator, it's best not to send their illustration samples with your manuscript. Most likely a publisher will not be interested in the whole package, and including those illustrations will only hurt your chances of getting published. Also, if you enclose unprofessional art samples with your manuscript, you're destined for rejection.

Even worse, the biggest taboo in picture book publishing is submitting finished artwork with the proposal. This is the unmistakable mark of an amateur—worse, an amateur who has not researched the field. The size, color, and method of printing the art can only be determined after a book is budgeted and designed. Your best bet is to write a great story, forget about the illustrations, make your query or cover letter professional, and submit your manuscript.

QUERY LETTER AND MANUSCRIPT

Submission Tips

Check each publisher or agent's specific guidelines before you send anything. An agent who represents "children's" or "juvenile" work may not present picture books, as well; she may just take on middle-grade and young adult work. Make sure before you send a submission.

The cover letter accompanying your manuscript should be brief and professional, yet friendly. It should interest the reader but not overdo it on cuteness or cleverness. Mention the title of the work you are sending, a few sentences about the material, and a brief summary of previous writing experience. If you don't have any previous experience, don't mention it and simply thank the editor or agent for her consideration.

And, even though the text for a picture book is short, publishers do not want you to submit more than one manuscript at a time.

Formatting Specs

Submit your picture book lines as double-spaced text, pushed left. If you have multiple lines on pages (rather than simply one line per page), feel free to use a blank line to signify page changes.

Other Dos and Don'ts

- Do obtain a copy of the publisher or agent's guidelines and follow them carefully.

- Don't include a sentence that says, "I read my work to my kids/grandkids/second-grade class and they loved it." This definitely does not sway an editor's opinion.

- Don't include unnecessary personal information in your query letter.

- Don't say, "I've always wanted to write for children." Although this may be true, it doesn't help your cause.

- Do research the publisher you are querying to make sure you are sending the type of book they publish (fiction, nonfiction, certain age groups, etc.).

- Don't recommend an illustrator for your manuscript. The editor will decide which illustrator she wants to use if she is interested in your book.

- Do indicate in your query letter any previous writing experience or credits you may have, as well as memberships in children's writing organizations such as the Society of Children's Book Writers & Illustrators (SCBWI).

- Don't send a query or manuscript via e-mail or fax unless a publisher or agent specifically requests it.

- Do include an SASE when sending a query or manuscript through the mail.

- Don't indicate page breaks and don't type each page on a new sheet of paper.

ELECTRONIC SUBMISSIONS

Before you send a query or manuscript to a publication via e-mail, make sure they accept electronic submissions by contacting the publication directly or checking out their writers' guidelines. Never send a query or manuscript via e-mail unless you have permission from the editor or the submission guidelines say it is acceptable.

Jane Q. Writer
123 Author Lane
Writerville, CA 95355
(323) 555-0000
janeqwriter@email.com

May 11, 2009

Goldie Locks
Just for Kids Books
34 Broadway
New York, NY 10019

Dear Ms. Locks,

One of the scariest moments in a small child's life is the first day he has to leave home to attend kindergarten. Helping kids become excited instead of apprehensive about their first day at school is what my picture book, *Ira's Big Day*, is all about.

Ira's Big Day follows six-year-old Ira Nelson as he prepares for his first day at kindergarten. His mother, father and older sister all help Ira plan for the big day—his mom lays out his new clothes, his dad gives him a brand-new knapsack filled with school supplies, and his older sister, Paige, tells him all about her first day in kindergarten. Ira asks the hard questions that most kids ask, and his loving and supportive family answers them honestly, thus helping Ira—and the reader—put his mind at ease.

I have been a kindergarten teacher for twenty-three years, and have seen firsthand the fears that children bring with them on their first day of school. I have had articles and stories published in *U.S. Kids*, *Jack and Jill*, *Highlights*, *Parenting* and *Teaching K-8* magazines, most of them dealing with first-day-of-school jitters and other anxieties that kids face in new environments.

Ira's Big Day is 900 words and complete. May I send you a copy of the manuscript? I have enclosed an SASE for your reply. Thank you for your consideration, and I look forward to hearing from you.

Sincerely,

Jane Q. Writer

Encl.: SASE

Contact information—name, address, phone number, and e-mail

Date flushed right

Address a specific editor.

Include a good, concise outline of the reasons behind your choice of topic.

1" margin

Outlines professional experience and publishing credits.

Indicate length of the manuscript (which falls within the typical length of a children's picture book) and that it is completed and ready for submission.

Signature

SASE enclosed for reply

Pitch gives a quick overview of the storyline and introduces the main characters.

Politely asks for permission to send the manuscript, indicates that an SASE is enclosed, and thanks the editor for her time.

Contact informa-
tion—name, address,
phone number, and
e-mail

Jane Q. Writer
123 Author Lane
Writerville, CA 95355
(323) 555-0000
janeqwriter@email.com

June 23, 2009

Date flushed right

Sandra Bernie
The Sandra Agency
111 Broadway
New York, NY 10001

Dear Ms. Bernie:

Address a
specific editor.

Enclosed is my 900-word picture book, *Ira's Big Day*, which follows six-year-old Ira Nelson as he prepares for his first day at
kindergarten. His mother, father and older sister all help Ira plan
for the big day—his mom lays out his new clothes, his dad gives
him a brand-new knapsack filled with school supplies, and his
older sister, Paige, tells him all about her first day in kindergarten.
Ira asks the hard questions that most kids ask, and his loving and
supportive family answers them honestly, thus helping Ira—and
the reader—put his mind at ease.

1" margin

Introductory para-
graph includes the
book's title, the word
count, the central
characters, and tells
what the story
is about.

Mention pertinent
personal information
and past publishing
credits.

I have been a kindergarten teacher for twenty-three years, and
have seen firsthand the fears that children bring with them on
their first day of school. I have had articles and stories published
in *U.S. Kids*, *Jack and Jill*, *Highlights*, *Parenting*, and *Teaching K-8*
magazines, most of them dealing with first-day-of-school jitters
and other anxieties that kids face in new environments.

Thank you for considering *Ira's Big Day*, and I look forward to
hearing from you.

Politely close
the letter.

Sincerely,

Jane Q. Writer

Signature

Encl.: Manuscript, *Ira's Big Day*
SASE

Detail everything
that is included in
the submission pack-
age. Omit the SASE
if you are sending
your manuscript via
e-mail.

Header with the author's name and the novel's title in all caps

Page number (on the same line as the slug line)

Writer/IRA'S BIG DAY   1

When Ira Nelson woke up on Sunday morning, he knew

this day was different. What was it? Was it his mother's birthday?

No, her birthday was the day after the Fourth of July. Was it his

dad's birthday? No, his birthday was just last month. His big sister

Paige's birthday? No, her birthday was easy to remember—it was

Justify left margin only.

on New Year's Day. So what was so different about this day? As Ira

sat up in bed trying to figure it out, he heard his mother calling

him from downstairs.

1" margin

"Ira, time for breakfast!" she said in a sing-song voice.

"We've got your favorite, eggs and bacon and bagels!"

Don't indicate page breaks.

"Come on Ira, we're hungry," yelled his big sister Paige.

"Woof," said Ira's dog Sparky.

Ira jumped out of bed and headed downstairs to the kitchen.

His mother would know what was so different about this day.

"Here's our sleepyhead," said Ira's dad. "Just in time for

breakfast." Ira took his seat at the end of the table, and

Sparky sat down at his feet.

"Mom," Ira said as he took a gulp of orange juice. "What is

today?"

Double-spaced text

"Sunday," his mother said.

"I know," said Ira as he took a bite of his bagel. "But what's dif-

ferent about today?"

"Different?" said his mom. "Oh, Ira, today's the day before you

start kindergarten!"

Ira felt funny. That's what was so different.

"I don't want to go to kindergarten," Ira said. "I want to stay

here with you and Sparky."

Children's Writing

MIDDLE-GRADE AND YOUNG ADULT BOOKS

Books written for children ages nine to fifteen are divided into two groups according to the readers' ages: books written for children twelve and younger are called middle grade (MG), and those written for children older than twelve are called young adult (YA). Nonfiction books for middle grade and young adults should reflect the age of the intended reader; obviously a book on science geared toward fifth graders would be much more simplistic than one written for high school freshmen. Make sure you know the educational level of the book's intended audience and write specifically for them.

The main character in a children's novel should be no younger than the age group of the book's intended audience. In fact, the character is typically a year or two older than the novel's oldest reader. Children like to read about the adventures of older kids.

MG novels tend to focus on topics such as friendships, neighborhood adventures, school rivalries, and bullying. These novels usually run between 20,000 and 45,000 words. YA novels revolve around characters involved in more complex plots and show more depth than those characters in middle-grade novels. YA books can deal with more adult subjects—such as violence, sex and drugs—whereas MG cannot. Also, YA novels employ a more sophisticated writing style, vocabulary, subject matter, and general treatment. They are typically 45,000–65,000 words.

In writing a YA novel, remember that this work will be read predominantly by young teenagers, since older teenagers are likely to read fiction written for an adult audience. Therefore, the plot and situations of the characters should be identifiable to the child of junior high school age. Reading children's novels and talking to public or school librarians are important steps toward understanding your audience.

WHAT YOU NEED TO SUBMIT

Middle-grade and young adult novels should be the submitted as a novel package, the same as an adult novel. Your MG or YA novel package should include a query letter and sample chapters, along with an outline and an SASE for a reply. See the discussion on "The Novel Package" in chapter eighteen for more on the requirements. For nonfiction books, follow the guidelines outlined the "Book Proposal" section in chapter sixteen.

QUERY LETTER AND MANUSCRIPT

Submission Tips

Check each publisher's specific guidelines before you send anything, and make sure that the children's publisher you are submitting to is interested in a mid-grade or YA book. Some children's publishers only work with picture books.

The query or cover letter accompanying your manuscript should be brief and professional, yet friendly. It should interest the reader but not overdo it on cuteness or cleverness.

Mention the title of the work you are sending, a sentence or two about the material, and a brief summary of previous writing experience. If you don't have any previous experience, don't mention it and simply thank the editor or agent for her consideration.

Don't send the entire manuscript at this point. Like with other novels, include an outline and sample chapters unless the editor or agent requests more.

Formatting Specs

To submit and format your mid-grade or young adult manuscript, see page 223 for the section on novel packages.

Other Dos and Don'ts

- Do obtain a copy of the publisher's guidelines and follow them carefully.

- Don't include a sentence that says anything such as, "I read my work to my grandkids and they loved it." This definitely does not sway an editor's opinion.

- Do indicate how your book is different from similar books on the market.

- Do indicate the word count of the book in your query letter.

- Do indicate the age group that your book is intended to reach.

- Do cite works from the publisher that you are sending your query to, if possible, to indicate where your work falls in the publisher's line. This shows your familiarity with the publisher's work and that you've done your homework and know the market.

- Do indicate in your query letter any previous writing experience or credits you may have, as well as memberships in children's writing organizations such as the Society of Children's Book Writers & Illustrators (SCBWI).

- Do indicate where you see your nonfiction book being used and marketed, if relevant (in the classroom, at home, sold through bookstores, or museum stores and catalogs.).

- Don't send a query or manuscript via e-mail or fax unless an editor or agent specifically requests it.

- Do include an SASE unless you are sending it via e-mail.

ELECTRONIC SUBMISSIONS

Before you send a query or manuscript to a publisher or an agent via e-mail, make sure they accept electronic submissions by checking out their writers' guidelines online. Never send a query or manuscript via e-mail unless you have permission from the editor or agent or if the submission guidelines say it is acceptable.

Subject line includes a brief description and the title of the book.

TO: submissions@williamson.com
CC: johnqwriter@email.com
SUBJECT: Query: Geology Rocks! Juvenile nonfiction submission

September 23, 2009

Pamela Potter
Williamson Publishing Company
Church Hill Road
P.O. Box 185
Charlotte, VT 05445

This paragraph shows that the author knows the publisher's mission and did his homework. He is offering something different from what's already on the market.

Dear Ms. Potter,

Address a specific editor.

Try to find fun, easy-to-understand geology activities that go beyond making baking soda and vinegar volcanoes. Imagine constructing your own periodic table while cooking *Igneous Edibles* or understanding how fossils by creating *Sponge Stones*.

Briefly outlines the author's experience in the subject.

For ten years I have researched, developed, and field-tested many hands-on geology activities. My experience is the basis for **Geology Rocks!** This manual of interconnected activities addressing conceptual geology:

Quickly outline on the content and goals of the book

- features innovative activities and uses inexpensive, everyday materials like candy and building blocks

- furnishes multiple, flexible ways to learn the same concept

- involves users in simulated geologic processes like cave formation

References books in the publisher's line where this book would fit in—this shows that the author knows the market.

Mention the age group the book is intended for.

Geology Rocks! emphasizes learning-by-doing. This single-subject book, aimed at children ages 7–12, would fit well with your Kaleidoscope Kids series. It would be appropriate for kids to use at home, for teachers planning lessons, and for professionals designing enrichment programs.s.

Outline potential uses and markets for the book.

The enclosed section, *Make Mine Metamorphic,* highlights the type of activities and information included throughout the book. I have also attached an outline. I look forward to hearing from you.

Contact information is at the bottom left in e-mail correspondence.

Sincerely,

John Q. Writer
123 Author Lane
Writerville, CA 95355
(323) 555-0000
johnqwriter@email.com

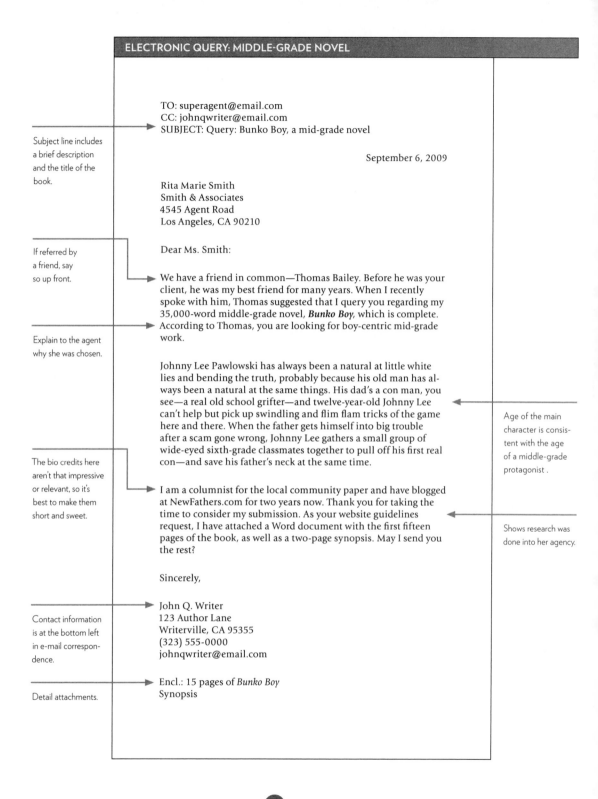

TO: superagent@email.com
CC: johnqwriter@email.com
SUBJECT: Query: Bunko Boy, a mid-grade novel

Subject line includes a brief description and the title of the book.

September 6, 2009

Rita Marie Smith
Smith & Associates
4545 Agent Road
Los Angeles, CA 90210

If referred by a friend, say so up front.

Dear Ms. Smith:

We have a friend in common—Thomas Bailey. Before he was your client, he was my best friend for many years. When I recently spoke with him, Thomas suggested that I query you regarding my 35,000-word middle-grade novel, *Bunko Boy*, which is complete. According to Thomas, you are looking for boy-centric mid-grade work.

Explain to the agent why she was chosen.

Johnny Lee Pawlowski has always been a natural at little white lies and bending the truth, probably because his old man has always been a natural at the same things. His dad's a con man, you see—a real old school grifter—and twelve-year-old Johnny Lee can't help but pick up swindling and flim flam tricks of the game here and there. When the father gets himself into big trouble after a scam gone wrong, Johnny Lee gathers a small group of wide-eyed sixth-grade classmates together to pull off his first real con—and save his father's neck at the same time.

Age of the main character is consistent with the age of a middle-grade protagonist.

The bio credits here aren't that impressive or relevant, so it's best to make them short and sweet.

I am a columnist for the local community paper and have blogged at NewFathers.com for two years now. Thank you for taking the time to consider my submission. As your website guidelines request, I have attached a Word document with the first fifteen pages of the book, as well as a two-page synopsis. May I send you the rest?

Shows research was done into her agency.

Sincerely,

Contact information is at the bottom left in e-mail correspondence.

John Q. Writer
123 Author Lane
Writerville, CA 95355
(323) 555-0000
johnqwriter@email.com

Detail attachments.

Encl.: 15 pages of *Bunko Boy*
Synopsis

February 2, 2009

Editor
Random House Inc.
Juvenile Books
201 E. 50th St.
New York, NY 10022

No contact
information

Dear Sir,

Should be addressed
to a specific editor.

Being professionally involved in the funeral industry through
contract work and having kids of my own has brought an interesting twist to my children's writing.

This is vague. What
is "contract work" in
the funeral industry?
What children's writ-
ing? Has the author
been published
before?

These experiences have allowed me to approach the subject of
death without being threatening to young readers. I have developed a series of stories involving the interaction of different dogs
with morticians and undertakers in a vast array of situations, including embalming, funeral planning, grief, and mourning, etc.

What age is specifi-
cally being targeted?

What is this series?
How long is each
book in the series?
Needs a lot more
detail.

If you are interested in a manuscript copy of one of these stories,
please contact me.

Publisher's guidelines
state that they re-
quest a copy of the
complete manuscript
with a query.

Thank you for your time.

Sincerely,

John Q. Writer

These are inap-
propriate subjects
for children's books,
which indicates that
the author knows
nothing about the
market.

At the very least, a
SASE should have
been included.

CHILDREN'S MAGAZINES

Writing articles for children's magazines is similar to writing articles for any other magazine—you have to know what audience a magazine serves and then write for that audience. There are hundreds of children's magazines for sale on newsstands and distributed in schools that are aimed at children of all ages and interests.

WHAT YOU NEED TO SUBMIT

Read as many back issues as you can of a magazine that you're thinking of submitting to so you can identify the magazine's "voice." Make sure you know what a publication's focus is before you submit anything. Don't send a short story or poem to a magazine that only publishes news stories for kids. In this and any other magazine market, you have to study what's out there so you don't waste your time submitting inappropriate articles and stories. Whether you are sending a story, article, or poem, your submission should be age appropriate and follow the publication's guidelines meticulously.

Submitting stories to children's magazines is much the same as submitting short stories; all you need to send in is a cover letter and the story in its entirety.

QUERY LETTER AND MANUSCRIPT

Submission Tips

Be sure to check each publisher's specific guidelines before you send anything. The query or cover letter accompanying your manuscript should be brief and professional, yet friendly. It should interest the reader but not overdo it on cuteness or cleverness.

Mention the title of the work you are sending, a sentence or two about the material, and a brief summary of previous writing experience. If you don't have any previous experience, don't mention it and simply thank the editor for her consideration.

Formatting Specs

To submit and format your story to a children's magazine, see specifications on article submissions in chapter 15.

Other Dos and Don'ts

- Do obtain a copy of the publisher's guidelines and follow them carefully.

- Don't include a sentence that says, "I read my work to my kids/grandkids/second-grade class and they loved it." This definitely does not sway an editor's opinion.

- Do indicate your familiarity with the publication. It's okay to make a positive comment if it's sincere and appropriate.

- Do indicate in your query letter any previous writing experience or credits you may have, as well as memberships in children's writing organizations such as the Society of Children's Book Writers & Illustrators (SCBWI).

- Do indicate if you are sending simultaneous submissions to other publications.

- Don't send a query letter or manuscript via e-mail or fax unless a publisher or agent specifically requests it.

- Don't discuss payment terms. This will be discussed if your manuscript is accepted.

- Do include an SASE if you're not using e-mail.

ELECTRONIC SUBMISSIONS

Before you send a query or manuscript to a publication via e-mail, make sure they accept electronic submissions by contacting the publication directly or checking out their writers' guidelines.

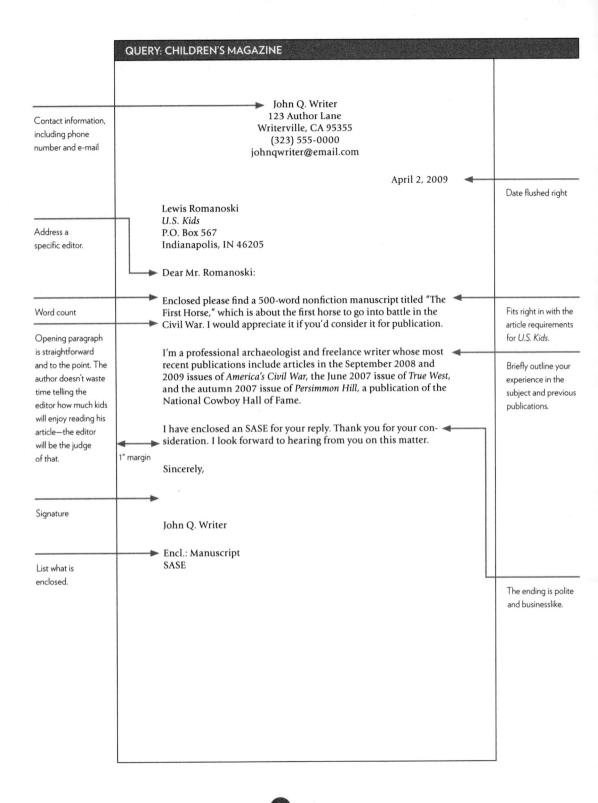

John Q. Writer
123 Author Lane
Writerville, CA 95355
(323) 555-0000
johnqwriter@email.com

Contact information, including phone number and e-mail

April 2, 2009

Date flushed right

Lewis Romanoski
U.S. Kids
P.O. Box 567
Indianapolis, IN 46205

Address a specific editor.

Dear Mr. Romanoski:

Enclosed please find a 500-word nonfiction manuscript titled "The First Horse," which is about the first horse to go into battle in the Civil War. I would appreciate it if you'd consider it for publication.

Word count

Fits right in with the article requirements for *U.S. Kids*.

Opening paragraph is straightforward and to the point. The author doesn't waste time telling the editor how much kids will enjoy reading his article—the editor will be the judge of that.

I'm a professional archaeologist and freelance writer whose most recent publications include articles in the September 2008 and 2009 issues of *America's Civil War*, the June 2007 issue of *True West*, and the autumn 2007 issue of *Persimmon Hill*, a publication of the National Cowboy Hall of Fame.

Briefly outline your experience in the subject and previous publications.

1" margin

I have enclosed an SASE for your reply. Thank you for your consideration. I look forward to hearing from you on this matter.

Sincerely,

Signature

John Q. Writer

Encl.: Manuscript
SASE

List what is enclosed.

The ending is polite and businesslike.

John Q. Writer
123 Author Lane
Writerville, CA 95355

Editor
U.S. Kids
P.O. Box 567
Indianapolis, IN 46205

To Whom It May Concern,

Young children love to use their imaginations. They will block out the world and use their imaginations. The simplest toy or object begins to talk and come alive. The mind of a child is a fantasy adventure. When told to keep busy or take a bath, their world comes alive with fantasy.

Please find enclosed my manuscript taken fro a picture book, titled *The Adventures of Sir Jerry in the Bath*. When Jerry takes a bath and brings some toys with him, the water and toys come alive. He becomes a fighter, protector, and then the hero. He lets his imagination run wild. It uses playful, humorous language and will appeal to a child's sense of fantasy.

I have submitted simultaneous submissions to *Highlights for Children*, *Humpty Dumpty's Magazine*, *Pockets*, and *Owl Magazine*. I have never been published before but my grandchildren just love my stories.

Sincerely,

John Q. Writer

Complete contact information should be included—name, address, phone number, and e-mail. Don't forget to include the date, too.

This is a dull, pointless opening. The space is better used to describe the manuscript that is being submitted, not obvious statements about children and imagination.

U.S. Kids is a magazine, so why is he pitching a picture book story? The author obviously doesn't know the market.

Include an SASE for a reply.

Should be addressed to a specific editor.

Watch out for typos! Spell-check wouldn't have caught this one.

There is no reason to list the names of other publications you are submitting to. The phrase, "This is a simultaneous submission" is enough.

Don't tell the editor that you've never been published, and don't tell him that your kids/grandkids/neighbors love your work! It screams "amateur."

CHAPTER 20

SCRIPTS

SCREENPLAYS

A screenplay is a script for a motion picture. They can be feature-length scripts for a typical movie, or a shorter script for a short film.

We all know what a novel looks like; we've been reading them most of our lives. But a screenplay is a different matter. You can't write a script in prose and then worry about the format later, once you are ready to submit. The format is such an integral part of a screenplay that it is necessary to first learn to use the parts of a script with a vocabulary of its own.

PARTS OF A SCRIPT

Screenplays have a specific industry-standard format. Most motion picture scripts run from 100 to 120 pages. Especially if you're a new writer, try to stick to that average page count. Figure on one minute of screen time for each manuscript page, in a Courier 12-point type (hence a 120-page script will run two hours). Scripts should include dialogue and action descriptions but few to no camera directions, no soundtrack suggestions, and no casting suggestions. Do not number your scenes, and always leave 1 to 1.5" margins at the top and bottom of each page.

A screenplay can be broken down into six basic parts. Here they are in the order they are likely to appear in your script:

- Transitions
- Slug line
- Action description
- Character cue
- Dialogue
- Parenthetical comment

Now let's take a closer look at each of these.

Transitions

Transitions simply indicate that a shot or scene is either beginning, ending, or shifting to another shot or scene. These include such directions as FADE IN:, FADE TO:, CUT TO:, and DISSOLVE TO:. Transitions appear in all caps and are flush with the right margin, except FADE IN:, which is flush with the left margin.

Slug Line

The slug line, also called a scene heading, sets the scene. It begins on the left margin and is written in all caps, with a double-spaced line before and after it. Most slug lines begin with either EXT. (exterior shot) or INT. (interior shot). After you determine whether the shot is outside or inside, identify the specifics of the shot, such as a particular building or house, and then if necessary, precisely where the shot takes place. With the slug line, organize the details by going from the general to the more specific. Each slug line typically ends with an indication of whether it's day or night. For example:

> INT. WOODROW WILSON ELEMENTARY SCHOOL—
> PRINCIPAL'S OFFICE—DAY

Note that there is no ending punctuation for slug lines.

Action Description

The action descriptions, also called narrative, are sentences or very short paragraphs that describe what happens during the scene. They should always be written in present tense. The text within the action descriptions begins on the left margin and is single-spaced, with regular capitalization. Do not justify the right margin. There should be one double-spaced line before and after the action text. If you have a lot of description, break up the text to leave some white space. Try not to allow a block of text to run more than five or six lines without a double-spaced break for the eyes (the more white space in a script, the better).

Character Cue

The speaking character's name—the character cue—should be typed in all caps, and should appear approximately 2.5" (or 5 tabs) from the left margin, quite close to the center. A double-spaced line should appear before the character's name, but there should be no double-space between the name and the dialogue, or between the name and the parenthetical comment (see below).

Dialogue

Dialogue should be in regular text (not all caps) and begin on the line below the speaking character's name. The left margin for dialogue is at at about 1.5" (or 3 tabs) from the left margin of the page, and the right margin is at about 2" from the right edge of the paper. This means dialogue will not touch the left or right edges of the page. Try to avoid large blocks of dialogue that run seven or more lines. If your character needs to say more than can be fit in seven lines, try adding some narrative—such as a visual cue—to break up the long speech. That will make the text more visually pleasing.

Parenthetical Comment

Parenthetical comments, also known as parentheticals, help the speaker of the dialogue know what emotion you intend for the delivery. Parenthetical comments are typically short (often a word or two), typed in regular text (not all caps), and set in parentheses. They appear one line below the character's name (and thus one line above dialogue). Parentheticals should look like this:

> CRAIG
> (panicking)
> I don't want to fight you, Russ.

> RUSS
> (re: Craig's nervousness)
> You should be scared.

Some screenwriters prefer not to use parentheticals and instead detail the emotion in a descriptive action line instead.

> Craig paces back and forth.

> CRAIG
> I've never been in a fight. Somebody tell me
> what to do.

Parentheticals are acceptable in a screenplay, but don't overuse them; try a descriptive line or an action beat to show emotion instead.

In addition to the aforementioned regular elements of your screenplay, you will probably find situations where you need some special formatting and cues. Here are some of the more common script tricks you can use in your screenplay.

Narrative Voice-Over

Some films have a first-person narrator who relates parts of the story to the viewer. If your script calls for voice narration, indicate it as such by typing "(V.O.)" next to the name of the character who is narrating. A scene with a voice narration should look like this:

INT. ROGER'S CHILDHOOD HOME—LIVING ROOM—DAY

Young kids are running around the room yelling and screaming at each other. The mother has no control over the situation.

> ROGER (V.O.)
> Mine wasn't what you'd call a typical childhood.
> With ten brothers and sisters running around, I
> never got the sense that I was unique. I was always
> just one of the boys. Mom spent her time trying to
> keep us from killing each other. Feeling special just
> wasn't possible. But she did the best she could.

Carrying Dialogue From One Page to the Next

Do your best not to make an actor (character) flip a page in the middle of dialogue. If, however, you can't avoid carrying a character's dialogue on to the next page, use the indicator "(MORE)" on the bottom of the first page and "(CONT'D)" next to the speaker's name at the top of the next page:

> ROGER
> I'm sorry, Marcia. I've tried and tried to please
> you but you never appreciate a damn thing I do.
> (MORE)

———————————— NEW PAGE ————————————

> ROGER (CONT'D)
> I just can't go on being your slave. You never
> clean up after yourself. Hell, you've never given
> me even a penny for the rent.

Having a Character Speak Off-Camera

In movies, characters often speak off-camera, and you'll probably write at least one scene in which this happens. When you have a character speaking off-camera, use "(O.S.)" (offscreen) next to the character's name. Let's say Roger is on camera in the bedroom while talking to Marcia, who is off-camera in the bathroom.

> ROGER
> Marcia, did you just say something? I thought
> I heard you say something.

> MARCIA (O.S.)
> I asked if you would bring me a towel. I'm soaking
> wet for God's sake. Are you deaf?

> ROGER
> What did you say?

Employing Continuing Shots

Although as a screenwriter you should refrain from giving camera directions (that's the director's job), you might want to tell part of your story with a series of camera shots without dialogue or narration. These kinds of "moving pictures" usually tell their own little story. They are often accompanied by a musical score and are used to quickly advance the plot. Try doing it like this:

SERIES OF SHOTS: ROGER AND MARCIA EXPLORE NEW YORK

(A) On a ferry to the Statue of Liberty.

(B) Eating hot dogs from a vendor on Times Square.

(C) Walking arm-in-arm through Central Park.

(D) Kissing outside the Guggenheim.

(E) Driving across the George Washington Bridge.

BACK TO SCENE

Another way to use continuing shots is with a montage. A montage is pretty much the same as a series of shots except it's used for a briefer sequence of shots and doesn't really have to tell its own story. A montage is formatted a little differently, with a double hyphen instead of letters in parentheses:

MONTAGE—ROGER AND MARCIA AT DISNEY WORLD

—They get their pictures taken with Mickey and Minnie.

—They ride Splash Mountain.

—Roger offers Marcia some cotton candy. She makes a mustache out of it and Roger eats it. They laugh.

END MONTAGE

With both a series of shots and montages, be sure to end with either "BACK TO SCENE" or "END MONTAGE."

Other Dos and Don'ts

- Do spell out numbers one through ninety-nine, but use numerals for 100 and over.

- Do spell out personal titles (Father Niehaus, Pastor Karl) except for Mr., Mrs., and Ms.

- Do spell out time indicators: eleven-thirty, not 11:30.

- Do spell out "okay," not OK or o.k.

- Do number your pages and put a period after the number. The page number goes at the top of the page, flush right, about four lines down.

- Do keep dialogue short.

- Don't use special effects directions, such as FX (visual).

- Don't use sound effects directions, such as SFX (sound).

- Don't use camera directions and camera angles.

- Don't number the first page.

- Don't number your scenes.

- Do leave 1 to 1.5" margin at the top and bottom of each page.

What follows are formatting specifications for your screenplay as well as a sample screenplay title page and a sample first page of a screenplay. Keep in mind you won't need to worry about nitty-gritty spacing format if you have professional screenwriting software.

Tab and Margin Settings

- Left and right margins: 1"

- Dialogue left margin: about 3 tabs, or 1.5" from left margin of the page

- Parenthetical comments: about 4 tabs, or 2" from left margin

- Character cue: about 5 tabs, or 2.5" from left margin

- Dialogue right margin: about 2" from the right edge of the page

- Transitions: flushed right (except FADE IN, which is flushed left)

- Page number followed by a period: top right corner

All Caps

- Type of shot (INT. and EXT.)

- Setting or scene location (ITALIAN RIVIERA)

- Time of day (DAY or NIGHT)

- The first time you introduce a character (JOHN walks in)

- The speaking character's name (PHIL), followed by dialogue

- Camera directions (PAN, CLOSE-UP, etc.)

- Important sound cues or objects (Ted hears a GUNSHOT in the hallway.)

- Scene transitions (CUT TO:, DISSOLVE TO:, etc.)

Single Space

- within dialogue

- within action/scene descriptions

- within camera directions, sound cues

- within stage directions

- between the character's name and dialogue

Double Space

- between the scene location and action/scene descriptions

- between the action/scene descriptions and the speaking character's name

- between the speeches of the different characters

- between the paragraphs of lengthy dialogue or action descriptions

- between dialogue and a new speaking character's name

- between dialogue and stage or camera directions

TITLE PAGE

Submitting Tips

Your title page will include the script's title, the author, whether or not the script is based on another source, and your contact information (if you have representation, it will include your agent's contact information instead).

Formatting Specs

- The title should be in all caps, centered, about one-third of the way down the page.

- Double-space twice, and type either "Written by," "Screenplay by," or just "by."

- Double-space again and type your name. (If your script is written with another person, use an ampersand between your names.)

- If your script is based on a novel or another source, drop six lines and type "Based on Novel's Title," drop two more lines and type "by" and "Author's Name."

- In the lower right corner, put your name, address, phone number, and e-mail, single-spaced, in regular text (not all caps).

- If you have an agent, put "Representation:", skip a line and put the agent's name, address, phone number, and e-mail instead of yours.

- In front of the title page, make sure you include a cover page that includes only the title and author's name.

- Preferred cover page paper is a white, cream, rust, or pale blue cover of card stock, 40 to 60 lb.

- Bind the pages in two brass brads, short enough so they don't cut through an envelope when mailed.

- Although your script should have three holes punched in it, only the first and third holes should have brads in them.

- Use a backing page with the same stock as the cover page.

Other Dos and Don'ts

- Don't put any pictures or artwork on your cover page.

- Don't use spiral or other machine-type bindings.

- Do register your script with the Writers Guild of America (WGA), but you don't need to put the WGA registration number on the cover page.

- Don't put the copyright symbol or even the word "copyright" on your work if you're sending it out. Agents and other professionals know your work is copyrighted.

OCTOBER SURPRISE

Script's title is in all caps, one-third of the way down the page.

Three lines between title and author

Written by

John Q. Writer

All this text is centered.

Six lines between author and original source material

Based on the novel *Because the Night*

by Evelyn Grimaldi

Tell if the script is based on a novel, and credit the author.

Representation:
Angela Ash
Big Time Agency
111 West Sun St.
Hunter, CA 90001
(323) 555-2222

Shows the writer has representation (includes agent's name, address, and phone number). This always goes in the bottom right corner.

1" margins on top
and bottom

WRITER / OCTOBER SURPRISE   13.

Use a header.
Include your name,
the script title, and
the page number.

EXT. POLICE PRECINCT—DAY

Civilians and police officers milling in and out. Down the
street walks BILLY VAN RAYNE, 20s, tall, powerful. He looks
at the police station, hesitating.

First time a character
is introduced, the
name is in all caps.

Slug line is in
all caps.

                              BILLY
                    Now or never.

Action description
(narrative) is single-
spaced and flush with
left margin.

He pulls something out of his pocket. It's a HANDHELD TAPE
RECORDER.

Capitalize key ac-
tions and objects.

                         VOICE (O.S.)
                    Need some help?

Left margin is at
1 inch.

Billy looks to see a BEAT COP, 30s, eyeing him suspiciously.

Signifies that
the character talking
is offscreen

                              BILLY
                    No thanks—I'm okay …

TITLE CARD: Washington, DC 1988

Use "Title Card" to
indicate when words
are superimposed on
the screen.

INT. POLICE PRECINCT—DAY—CON'T

The first person Billy sees is an obese DESK SERGEANT, who
is trying to answer questions. He is dealing with a Russian
SKINHEAD.

When one scene in
a location continues
directly into another,
use this abbreviation.

                         DESK SERGEANT
                    I don't know what else to tell you. You'll
                    have to go to the courthouse for further
                    instructions. After that—

Dialogue is single-
spaced (do keep
blocks of dialogue
short).

                              SKINHEAD
                         (in Russian)
                    I still don't understand you!

If writing dialogue
in another language,
write the English
translation and
indicate that the
dialogue is in another
language.

                    DESK SERGEANT (CON'T)
                    —we may be able to work something out.
                    That's all I can tell you. I'm very busy.
                         (calls out)
                    Next!

Parenthetical com-
ments are lowercase.

                         RYBAN

Don't leave "hangers."

1" margins on top
and bottom

274

SUBMITTING YOUR SCREENPLAY

After you finish your screenplay, it's time to submit it to a script manager, agent, or a production company. Ideally, you'll find a manager or agent to represent you—someone who knows the ins and outs of Hollywood. Having a good rep who believes in your work and is willing to go to great lengths to get it sold is invaluable. Almost every screenwriter in Hollywood has representation, and so should you.

Managers vs. Agents

Script agents have the ability to sell your work. They're the wheeler-dealers. They get 10 percent of what a writer makes for what they do. The problem is that agents are busy people who usually have a very full list of clients and a full plate of work each day. Getting them to read your work and sign you as a client is difficult. Script managers, on the other hand, specialize in working with new writers and grooming them. A manager will collect an additional 10 or 15 percent of money made by the writer.

Whether you seek a manager or agent, remember that you shouldn't have to pay any up-front fees for them to read your work. They make money when you make money.

The Value of a Rep

So, what is a good agent? Aside from being someone who believes in your work, a good agent knows who is working where, who has deals with whom, and who wants what. A good agent will direct your script to the most suitable producer and will negotiate payments on your behalf. Many beginning writers try to become a client at a major agency, but that's not always such a good idea. Newcomers often don't get much attention at major agencies. Your best bet is to find an agent who will appreciate your writing and do his best to champion it—no matter how large or small the agency. Just be sure the agent is a signatory of the WGA: signatory agents have signed and agreed to abide by industry rules and standards. All reputable agencies belong to the WGA; those who do not should be avoided.

Finding the Right Agent for You

A good way to acquire an agent who will appreciate your writing is to find one who represents material similar to yours. Seek out movies already made that are similar to your screenplay, and pay close attention to the credits. Write down the names of the writers or the story editors.

Once you get these names, call the Writers Guild of America, West (800) 548-4532, request to speak to the agency department, then ask which agency represents those writers or story editors. The agency department will grant your request if you have three names or fewer (no more). After you get the agency's name, consult the WGA's list of signatory agents to make sure that agent is a signatory. The WGA offers the list free on its website (www.wga.org).

Also check the following directories if you wish to do research on agents:

- *Screenwriter's & Playwright's Market*, published by Writer's Digest Books, contains detailed listings of hundreds of script agents and managers. It also includes a variety of insider information (profiles, interviews, articles) on marketing your work and getting your script in the right agent's hands. Its strength is detailed listings explaining what each rep is looking for and how to submit. (www.writersdigeststore.com)

- *Hollywood Representation Directory*, published by the Hollywood Creative Directory, offers probably the most complete list of agents and managers. It boasts seven thousand names and can be purchased as a book or an online directory. Its strength is in its sheer number of Hollywood insider contacts. (www.hcdonline.com)

Selling the Script Yourself

You may wish to shop your script to a studio or production company without first finding an agent. This will likely be difficult but it is still an option, and many first-time writers go this route. Fortunately, a few resources do exist for finding information about producers, studio executives, and other industry insiders. If you do decide to take this route, you should be well educated on who's doing what in Hollywood, because you'll need to make plenty of contacts and know which studies are looking for which properties.

If you want to stay tuned to the day-to-day operations in Hollywood, check out *Daily Variety* (www.variety.com) and *The Hollywood Reporter* (www.hollywoodreporter.com), both of which will keep you up on industry news. After you figure out which studio or production company you're interested in, call and ask for the story department, then ask for the name of the story editor. That's it. Don't ask to speak with the story editor—just get her name, then get ready to write your letter of inquiry.

QUERY LETTER

Once you know who to contact (agent, producer, or story editor), send him a query letter. Do not submit an outline, a treatment, or a script to anyone in the industry unless you've been asked to do so. He will return it because he can't look at anything ("unsolicited material") without a signed release form. In your query letter, say that you have written a script and would like him you're soliciting to consider it. Don't send a query letter unless you have the script written and polished. If he likes your idea, he may want to see the script immediately. Keep your query letter to a few short paragraphs (less than one page).

J. Michael Straczynski, in *The Complete Book of Scriptwriting*, suggests mentioning the following:

- That you know the films he produces (or the agency represents, if you're soliciting an agent).

- That you've written an original screenplay that fits in quite well with what he has been producing (or with an agency, representing) over the past few years.

- That you own the rights to the story.

- That you would like to submit your screenplay on a spec basis. (If you go into detail about the contents of your script, you'll ruin your chances of selling it.)

- That when you send your script you will enclose a standard release form or use the production company or agency's preferred release form.

- That you have writing credits or a professional background that qualifies you to write this screenplay. (If you've spent ten years as an attorney and your screenplay is a legal thriller, mention your background. Won awards? Say so.)

Basically, that's all you need to include in your query. Again, never send an unsolicited script, treatment, or synopsis to an agent, producer, or story editor—it will be returned, the package unopened. Producers and agents will not look at unsolicited scripts because they are afraid of getting sued for plagiarism. That's why you need to send the release form. Of course, mention your script idea in your query letter, but do so only in general terms.

Follow these formatting specifications when composing your query letter:

Formatting Specs

- Use a standard font, 12-point type (no bold or italic).

- Put your name and contact information in the top, centered, or in your letterhead.

- Use a 1" margin on all sides.

- Keep it to one page.

- Use block format (no indentations, an extra space between paragraphs).

- Single-space the body of the letter and double-space between paragraphs.

- Catalog every item you're sending in your enclosures.

Other Dos and Don'ts

- Do make the letter pointed and persuasive.

- Do include an SASE or postcard for reply, and state in the letter that you have done so.

- Do offer to sign a release form.

- Do offer to send the script.

- Do address your query to a specific agent, producer, or story editor. Call to get the appropriate name and gender.

- Don't mention that you're a first-time writer or that you've never sold any piece of writing.

- Don't tell how much time you've spent on the script.

- Don't ask for advice or criticism.

- Don't mention anything about yourself unless it's pertinent to the script.

- Don't bring up payment.

ELECTRONIC QUERY LETTER

Submitting Tips

Many agents, producers, and story editors now accept queries via e-mail. Before you send a query via e-mail, however, you must have permission to send it. The basic tone and format of the electronic query shouldn't be much different from a query sent on paper. Don't let the medium of e-mail let your query run long. Keep it at one page or less.

Formatting Specs

- Include the same information you would in a paper query, including your name and contact information. With e-mail queries, it's recommended to put your contact information at the lower left under your signature. Because the window to view the letter on a computer screen is not large, doing this allows the reader to jump right into your query. It isn't necessary to include your e-mail address in the body of the e-mail, however, since the editor can reply easily with the click of a button.

- Put "Query: (Your Title)" in the subject line.

- Follow the same format you would with a paper query, including the date, salutation to a specific editor, and block paragraph format.

Other Dos and Don'ts

- Don't use all caps or exclamation points in the subject line.

- Don't submit an e-mail query unless specifically requested by an agent, producer or story editor.

- Do read the Dos and Don'ts listed for a paper query; the same rules apply to electronic queries.

TO: mtaylor@hagency.com
CC: johnqwriter@email.com
SUBJECT: Query: October Surprise

June 19, 2009

Michael Taylor
The Hollywood Agency
123 Wilshire Blvd.
Beverly Hills, CA 90210

Dear Mr. Taylor:

My name is John Q. Writer and we crossed paths at the Writer's Digest Books Writers Conference in Los Angeles in May. After hearing the pitch for my feature-length thriller, *October Surprise*, you requested that I submit a query and synopsis. All requested materials are enclosed. This is an exclusive submission, as you requested.

Democratic U.S. Senator Michael Hargrove is breaking ranks with his own party to endorse a Republican for president. At the GOP national convention, he's treated like a rock star—that is, until he's abducted by a fringe political group and given a grim ultimatum: Use your live speech on TV to sabotage and derail the Republican nominee you're supporting, or your family back home won't live through the night.

The spec script was co-written with my scriptwriting partner, Joe Aloysius. I am a produced playwright and award-winning journalist. I will, of course, send a standard release form with my script submission. May I send you the full screenplay?

Sincerely,

John Q. Writer
123 Author Lane
Writerville, CA 95355
Phone (323) 555-0000
johnqwriter@email.com

It's not a bad to idea to copy (CC or BCC) yourself on your queries to keep a record of your e-correspondence.

Address a specific script manager. Use proper greetings and last names.

Some managers and agents want an exclusive look at queries (or most often, at the script itself). If you're submitting exclusively, make sure they know it so they will give your work a quicker look.

Include all contact information at the bottom left..

Include a reason for contacting the script manager.

Keep the pitch to one paragraph.

Be concise and honest about your credentials.

John Q. Writer
123 Author Lane
Writerville, CA 95355
(323) 555-0000
johnqwriter@email.com

Contact information
with address, phone
number, and e-mail

April 28, 2009

Date flushed right

Cynthia Picture
Story Editor
S&T Productions
1111 Movie Road
Hollywood, CA 90120

1" margin

Dear Cynthia Picture:

Address a specific
story editor. Using
"Ms. Picture" here is
also acceptable.

I've written a screenplay, *100K*, that I think fits in quite well with
pictures recently produced by S&T Productions (namely, *An Uncivil Action*, which shows the popularity of legal thrillers is growing). The script is 118 pages, and I do own the rights to the story.

Show you're familiar
with other scripts the
production company
represents, and mention the audience, the
script's length, and
state that you own
the rights to the story
in a short space.

Briefly tell the gist of
the script's story but
only in general terms.
The recipient will
know quite quickly if
the story falls in line
with what projects
she's looking for.

In *100K*, Cathy McTierney dies after the car she and her husband,
John, are traveling in wrecks during a blizzard. After John awakens from his coma, he's faced with another problem: Cathy's
mother and father are claiming vehicular homicide.

They think John killed Cathy for the $100,000 dollars she recently
inherited from her dying grandfather. A courtroom battle ensues.

I am a published writer whose articles have appeared in *Legal Times*
and other trade journals. I am also a prosecuting attorney. I have
brought my writing and professional interests together in *100K*. I
would like to submit my spec script for *100K* to S&T Productions.

Mention writing
credits and pertinent
professional background.

Single-spaced text,
block format

I will, of course, send a standard release form with my script submission. If S&T Productions has its own release form, please send
it in the enclosed SASE.

Politely close
the letter.

I look forward to hearing from you soon.

Sincerely,

Signature

John Q. Writer

Note enclosures.

Encl.: SASE

TO: submissions@filmfactory.com
CC:
SUBJECT: Story for you!

123 Author Lane
Writerville, CA 95355

Dear Story Editor:

After working on it for nearly ten years, I've just compleetd my very first screenplay. It's a story of my father's life growing up in the Great Depression on a farm in Iowa. I don't have a name for it yet.

The screenplay follows my father's life from his birth in a barn to raising eleven children on the same farm in Iowa. It is a story of epic proportions with lots of drama.

This is my first attempt at any kind of writing, but my father's life was so interesting that everyone in my family has always said it would make a great movie. Can I send you the script and you can tell me what you think about it?

I can see Haley Joel Osment playing my father as a boy and Russell Crowe playing my father as a man. Jessica Lange would be perfect as my long-suffering mother. Thank you very much for your time and I look forward to hearing from you soon.

Sincerely,

John Q. Writer

Include all your contact information, not just your address. And it should be at the bottom of an e-mail.

This looks like a form letter, as it's not addressed to any particular production company or to a specific person.

Never mention how much time it's taken you to write your screenplay, and don't mention that you're a first-time writer.

Never mention casting suggestions in your query.

Complete contact information should be included here—name, address, phone number, and e-mail.

Typo! Proofread your work.

Tells very little about the screenplay. What is the title of your screenplay? What makes this story compelling?

Don't ask for criticism or advice. The purpose of this query is to gauge interest in your screenplay.

Scripts

SCREENPLAY MANUSCRIPT

If your query letter does what you want it to, you'll receive a request for your script.

Before you do anything else, register your script with the WGA (you don't need to be a WGA member to do so). To register, contact the WGA (www.wga.org) and ask them to send you an application.

Then you need to get your script ready for submission. Print your script on standard three-hole, 20-lb. paper. Use heavy (40- to 60-lb. bond), colored stock paper (use cream, gray, rust or pale blue paper) for your cover/title page and your back cover. Bind your script with two brass paper fasteners (brads), one in the top hole and one in the bottom. Enclose a simple letter that says the requested script and release form are enclosed. Also include an SASE. Do not forget to sign and include the release form, and on the outside of the package's envelope be sure to write "REQUESTED RELEASE FORM ENCLOSED." Then send your script and wait four to six weeks for a reply.

OUTLINES AND TREATMENTS

Spec scripts are one way of getting noticed by a producer or agent, but outlines and treatments are also stepping-stones on the way to selling your full-length script. Both are summaries of your script, and both share the same format. The outline is a short precursor followed by a longer, more detailed (and more important) treatment. Although your script is composed mostly of dialogue, your outline and treatment cover the overarching story behind (and without) the dialogue and scene descriptions.

Outlines

An outline briefly synopsizes your script. You likely will not have to show anyone your outline, but you could be asked for one—if so, focus only on the major points of your story, keep the outline informal and write it in paragraph form. With an outline, less is more, especially when you use it as a pitch to sell your idea. You don't want to bore anyone, and the rule of thumb in Hollywood is that "high-concept" story ideas can be described quickly (ideally, one sentence) and are the most salable. The outline is an informal but crucial starting point from which you can successfully pitch your story idea, which leads to writing a compelling treatment, which ultimately leads to selling a script. Most outlines run to seven or more pages for a feature film. Rarely should your outline be more than 5,000 words.

Treatments

Unlike outlines, which tend to be a bit informal and more skeletal, treatments are carefully constructed, well-written summaries of your script (in fact, treatments are similar to a novel synopsis). You get to expand on the outline and go into more detail about your characters, settings, and plot twists. You can even weave some samples of dialogue into the narrative. Keep the number

---

of dialogue lines minimal, however, and be sure to inject them only at points where they can tell something significant about the character saying them.

A treatment for a motion picture feature might be ten to fifteen pages. No specific stipulations apply to the length of your treatment, but remember that shorter is usually better. (This is especially true with spec treatments. Keep them to less than ten pages.)

The two imperatives in formatting are that you double-space the text and write in present tense. Capitalize new characters as they are introduced. Tell the entire story front to back, like you're explaining it to your twelve-year-old nephew. Give away the ending. Don't be coy. And don't let the underlying framework show. Keep yourself out of the synopsis writing. Don't say "At the end of Act I ..." or "During the climax ..."

Ideally, your treatment should clearly delineate the major scenes in your script, with a new paragraph devoted to each scene or plot shift. You can break up your treatment by using subheads to denote when a new act begins—motion picture feature films consist of three acts. Doing so shows you've thought out the structure and timing of the script.

Why You'll Need an Outline and Treatment

Whether you're writing for television or the silver screen, to get your foot in the door you will need a sample spec script that showcases your talent as a writer. (That's why you must send a complete script after you have queried. A mere outline or treatment won't do because you still need to prove yourself as a writer.) If that spec script impresses the right person (hopefully, the producer), you might be invited to pitch ideas for other scripts. This is where knowing how to write an outline comes in handy: You use an outline to ensure you cover all the major points in your pitch. If your pitch is successful, you might get an assignment to write a treatment, and if that goes well, you might be asked to write the script.

To make sure you understand the process, let's walk through a hypothetical dream-come-true scenario. You've written a spec motion picture script called *The Summer of Love*, and you've been fortunate enough to get a producer at (since we're dreaming) DreamWorks to read your script. He loves it, but he refuses to buy it. Why? Because DreamWorks just bought a similar script called *1967*. However, he was so impressed with your writing that he wants you to come up with a few other movie ideas that he might consider optioning. You agree, come up with three ideas, write pitch outlines for each and make an appointment to pitch your story ideas to him. Your first two ideas don't go over so well, but your third one does. He tells you he'll talk to other producers and get back to you. A few weeks go by, and lo and behold, you get a call from the producer telling you that everybody at DreamWorks loves your idea, and DreamWorks would like to offer you a development deal, or a step deal. Are you interested? Of course.

You then sign a contract for the development or step deal, which means that you get a step-by-step commitment—and payment—from the producer as the deal goes through development. It works like this: The producer can stop the development of your script at any step in the process, but he must pay you for what you've already written. And because he's paid you for what you've done, he owns and can do what he wants with it.

What are the steps in a development deal? The first step is a treatment, next comes the first draft of a script, then a second draft, and finally the perfected script. Once the producer asks you to write the initial treatment for your story idea, he must pay you the negotiated fee for that step (step one) of the process. If, unfortunately, you turn in your treatment and DreamWorks doesn't like it, they have the option to drop you from the project and pass it on to other writers (you still, of course, get paid for the treatment).

If they do like it, however, you're asked to write (and get paid for) a complete draft of the script. Even if your final draft goes over well and you get paid lots of money for it, keep in mind that DreamWorks has the right to pass your script on to other writers to make improvements to it—that's just the way the business works. You'll still get the credit for the screenplay, of course, but your story could get changed quite a bit. So be prepared.

Formatting Specs

- Use a 1" margin on all sides.

- Justify the left margin only.

- Type your name and contact information at the top, centered, of the first page.

- Put the script's title, centered and in all caps, about one-fourth of the way down the page.

- Drop one line below the title and type "A Treatment by" or "An Outline by," centered.

- Drop one line and type your name, centered.

- Drop four lines and begin the text of the treatment.

- After the first page, use a header at the top left of every page containing your last name, slash, your script's title in all capital letters, slash, and either the word "Treatment" or "Outline": Writer/OCTOBER SURPRISE/Outline

- After the first page, put the page number in the top right corner of every consecutive page, on the same line as the slug line. Don't number the first page.

- The text throughout the treatment should be double-spaced.

- Use all caps the first time you introduce a character.

- The first line of text on each page after the first page should begin three lines below the header and page number.

Other Dos and Don'ts

- Do use present tense.

- Do write in the first person.

- Do keep in mind that you're writing a sales pitch. Make it a short, fast, exciting read.

- Don't number the first page (although it is considered page one).

- Do establish a hook at the beginning of the treatment. Introduce your lead character and set up a key conflict.

- Do introduce your most important character first.

- Do provide details about your central character (age, gender, marital status, profession, etc.), but don't do this for every character—only the primary ones.

- Do include characters' motivations and emotions.

- Do highlight pivotal plot points.

- Do reveal the story's ending.

- Don't go into too much detail about what happens; just tell what happens.

- Don't insert long sections of dialogue into your treatment.

ELECTRONIC SCRIPT SUBMISSIONS

It is rare for an agent, producer, or story editor to request your script via e-mail, but it might happen. If it does, make sure you get detailed guidelines as to how the script should be submitted and follow them meticulously.

No page number on
the first page

John Q. Writer
123 Author Lane
Writerville, CA 95355
(323) 555-0000
johnqwriter@email.com

Contact information,
centered at the top

SUMMER OF LOVE

An Outline by
John Q. Writer

Script's title is in all
caps and centered, .

Four lines between
author and the text

STEVE JENKEE, UCLA's leading student activist on race relations,

finds his mother, DR. JENKEE (UCLA's Director for Programs in

Peace & Justice and avid ally of blacks), has been murdered by an

African American. In a rage, Steve kills

1" margin

the murderer.

Use all caps the first
time a character
is introduced, and
introduce the most
important characters
first.

There are two major ironies to this script's central story:

1. That Dr. Jenkee, UCLA's Director for Programs in Peace
& Justice, who's been a champion of blacks and fighting
against racism since the early 1950s, would be killed by a
black student. Moreover, she must withstand violence (not
peace) and injustice (not justice).

Justify left
margin only.

2. That Steve Jenkee, who's been a leading activist against
racism, would actually commit the most atrocious act: murdering a person of the race he has been trying to advance
and protect.

Double-
spaced text

Notice how an out-
line is more informal
than a treatment.

No page number on the first page

John Q. Writer
123 Author Lane
Writerville, CA 95355
(323) 555-0000
johnqwriter@email.com

Contact information

SUMMER OF LOVE

A Treatment by
John Q. Writer

Script's title in all caps, centered, one-fourth of the way down the page

Four lines between the author and the text

Use all caps the first time a character is introduced, and introduce the most important characters first.

Justify left margin only.

1" margin

Incorporates a quote from the script.

It's 1967 and STEVE JENKEE, UCLA's leading student activist on race relations, doesn't know what to do when a crazed African-American student breaks into his mother's (DR. JENKEE) office and slits her throat, eventually killing her.

Steve can't figure it out and he's angry. Not only did his mother love and care for him, she was also UCLA's Director for Programs in Peace & Justice. She's been fighting for desegregation and against racism since the early 1950s. The murder just doesn't make sense. A white student murdering her would make sense (she was deemed the white man's enemy and the black man's Aunt Tom, even though she was white herself), but why would an African-American student kill her? After all, thinks Steve, "every African-American student and faculty member on campus loves mom." All, that is, but one. And now Steve is out to kill him.

The first paragraph establishes a hook by setting up a mystery and a conflict.

Use present tense.

Double-spaced text

Notice how a treatment (like a novel synopsis) tells the story instead of telling what the story is about, which is what an outline does.

287

TELEVISION SCRIPTS

Television scripts used for sitcoms, episodic dramas, soap operas, and television movies are very similar in format to a screenplay and follow many of the same steps to completion. After all, they both serve a visual medium. Although TV scripts follow a similar blueprint of film screenplays, each category of TV show has its own formatting quirks and differences, so it's crucial you observe sample scripts in the vein of the show you're writing or speccing.

SUBMITTING TELEVISION SCRIPTS

To get your television script through the Hollywood maze, you need to put it in the right hands. There are a few ways to go about this. The ideal way is to acquire an agent to represent you, but a few writers sneak through the cracks by contacting the production company first.

Before soliciting anyone, however, you should know a couple peculiarities about submitting scripts for television.

First, have more than one spec script ready to showcase. Some writers actually have a portfolio of scripts for each type of show they want to work on (if they want to write sitcoms, for instance, they'll have one script each for shows like *Two and a Half Men*, *The Office*, and *My Name Is Earl*).

Second, in choosing the shows you write spec scripts for, know that you probably will not be able to submit a script for the exact show you want to work on. It sounds crazy, but that's the way television works. So, if you want to write for *Criminal Minds* for example, you may break in by sending a *Without a Trace* script, or vice versa. You must do this because it reduces the chances of plagiarism lawsuits (plus the show's writers and producers might not be objective enough to fairly evaluate your writing). By submitting a similar type of script, you avert these problems while still demonstrating your writing skills in that medium. Writing a solid spec can also get you a job writing for a similar show. For example, if you write a spec for a fairly new, up-and-coming buddy-cop show, you may get picked up by a new show on another station that is trying to capitalize on the first buddy-cop show's popularity.

Whether you plan to solicit a production company or an agent, you must first target the show you plan to write for, watch it, and pay close attention to the opening and closing credits.

Contacting the Production Company

To contact the production company directly, look at the show's credits for the name of the production company and the producer or story editor. (Tape the show so you can pause it and get the correct names and spellings.) Then find the phone number and address of the production company, and send the producer or story editor a query letter.

The best way to find a production company's address is to call directory assistance. *The Hollywood Creative Directory* (www.hcdonline.com) is also a great place to locate the person you're looking for. This is the film and television industry bible, with the most complete, up-to-date information about who's who in film and TV development and production. It lists production companies, studios, and networks along with addresses, phone and fax numbers, and e-mail addresses. It also provides cross-referencing.

Contacting Agents

If you don't want to go directly to the production company, contact an agent who represents the show's writers. To do this, pay close attention to the show's credits to find the names of the writers or story editors. Once you get these names, call the Writers Guild of America, West (800) 548-4532, request to speak to the agency department, then ask which agency represents those writers or story editors. The agency department will grant your request if you have three names or less, so don't call with a long list of names.

After you get the agency's name, consult the WGA's list of signatory agents to make sure that agent is a signatory. The WGA offers the list free on its website (www.wga.org). Signatory agents have signed a membership contract agreeing to abide by industry rules and standards. All reputable agents belong to the WGA. A great place to start looking for reps is the book *Screenwriter's & Playwright's Market*, which lists managers and agents.

QUERY LETTER

After you've done your research and know how to contact the right agency, producer, or story editor, send a query letter. That's all you should send at this point; do not submit your spec script. In your query letter, say you'd like to write for the show and ask if the production company or agency is interested in new writers. J. Michael Straczynski, in *The Complete Book of Scriptwriting* (Writer's Digest Books), suggests mentioning the following:

- That you're enthusiastic about the show and have studied it.

- That you've written a spec script and would like to submit it. (Do not go into detail about the contents of your spec script—you'll definitely ruin your chances of writing for the show.)

- That when you send your spec script, you will enclose a standard release form or will use the production company or agency's release form.

- That you have writing credits or a profession that qualifies you to write for this show.

That's basically all you need to include in your query. Again, never send a spec script to an agent, producer, or story editor unless you are requested to do so. Do not mention any specifics about your story idea in your query letter or it will be returned immediately. They do this for legal reasons. Producers and agents refuse to look at unsolicited spec scripts and story ideas because they are afraid of getting sued for plagiarism. Just keep your query letter to a few short paragraphs and ask for permission to send your spec script.

Formatting Specs

- Use a standard font, 12-point type (no bold or italic).

- Put your name and contact information in the top right corner.

- Use a 1" margin on all sides.

- Keep it to one page.

- Use block format (no indentations, an extra space between paragraphs).

- Single-space the body of the letter and double-space between paragraphs.

- Catalog every item you're sending in your enclosures.

Other Dos and Don'ts

- Do include an SASE or postcard for reply, and state in the letter that you have done so.

- Do offer to sign a release form.

- Do offer to send the spec script.

- Do address your query to a specific agent, producer, or story editor. Call to get the appropriate name and gender.

- Don't mention that you're a first-time writer or that you've never sold any piece of writing.

- Don't spend much time trying to sell yourself.

- Don't tell how much time you've spent writing the script.

- Don't ask for advice or criticism.

- Don't mention anything about yourself not pertinent to the script.

- Don't bring up payment.

- Don't mention copyright information.

ELECTRONIC QUERY LETTER

Submission Tips

Many agents, producers, and story editors now accept queries via e-mail. Before you send a query via e-mail, however, you must have permission to send it. The basic tone and format of the electronic query shouldn't be much different from a query sent on paper.

Formatting Specs

- Include the same information you would in a paper query, including your name and contact information. With e-mail queries, it's recommended to put your contact information at the lower left under your signature. Because the window to view the letter on a computer screen is not large, doing this allows the reader to jump right into your query. It isn't necessary to include your e-mail address in the body of the e-mail, however, since the editor can reply easily with the click of a button.

- Put a description of your TV script or its title in the subject line.

- Follow the same format you would with a paper query, including the date, salutation to a specific editor, and block format. See the tips for submitting a paper query; the same rules apply.

Other Dos and Don'ts

- Don't use all caps or exclamation points in the subject line.

- Don't submit an e-mail query letter unless specifically requested by an agent, producer, or story editor.

- Don't insert clip art graphics or other images into your query letter.

- Do read the Dos and Don'ts for a paper query; the same rules apply.

Contact information (don't include the e-mail address if you're sending the query electronically)

John Q. Writer
123 Author Lane
Writerville, CA 95355
(323) 555-0000
johnqwriter@email.com

September 8, 2009

Date flushed right

Thomas Adams
Producer
Stellar Studios
1111 Inquiry Road
Hollywood, CA 90120

Get your query into the right hands.

Dear Mr. Adams:

I have completed a spec script for the show *Fringe*. I am a big fan of the new series and would like to write for the show. My spec script is titled "Perception."

1" margin

Don't go on too long or gush over how much you enjoy the show. Keep it short and sweet.

Single-spaced text, block format

I am the author of more than fifty magazine and newspaper articles—for both regional and national publications.

I will gladly send a signed standard release form with my script. If you would prefer that I use your company's release form instead, please send it in the enclosed SASE.

Politely close the letter.

Thank you for your time.

Sincerely,

Signature

John Q. Writer

Detail enclosures.

Encl.: SASE

TO: submissions@gilliganstudios.com
CC:
SUBJECT: I Love 30 Rock!

Jane Q. Writer
323-555-0000

To Whom It May Concern:

I just love the television show *30 Rock*, and I have a great idea for a story line for an upcoming episode. Can I send it to you? I think you'll really like it. I have a similar relationship with my coworker like Liz Lemon has with Jack, so I really understand what it's like. My husband told me I should write and submit an episode.

The episode I've written is from a real-life adventure that my daughter and I took on a road trip to visit our ailing aunt in the country. Our car trip was filled with witty banter, just like the characters on *30 Rock*, so I based the episode on that. Everyone in my family has read it and thinks it's just wonderful, if not better than the actual episodes that we see every week on *30 Rock*.

I have taken local writing workshops and while I have never been published, I think this is my big break into the land of television writing. Please give me a chance. I will send you the entire script. Since it's my first screenplay, any advice you can give on how to make it even better would be great!

I'm looking forward to working with you on this fabulous script.

Thanks!

Respectfully yours,

Jane Q. Writer

Include all of your contact information—name, address, phone number, and e-mail. It should be on the bottom left in an e-mail.

Be sure to address your query to a specific editor that works on the television show you are submitting your script for, and include the editor's address information.

Never say that your friends and family think your script is great. That means nothing to a story editor, and singles you out as an amateur.

Mention that you're willing to sign a standard release form.

Don't forget to date your letter.

Briefly state that you would like to write for a show and indicate that you have spec scripts ready to send; your family situation doesn't indicate to a story editor that you're qualified to write for it.

This paragraph should be used to outline your writing history and pertinent professional background. Explain why you are qualified to write for this show.

Don't mention that you're a first-time writer, and don't beg a story editor to read your script. And don't ask for advice or criticism!

Scripts

OUTLINES AND TREATMENTS

Outlines and treatments are also stepping-stones on the way to selling your script. Both are summaries of your script, and both share the same format. The outline is a short precursor followed by a longer, more detailed treatment. Although your script is composed mostly of dialogue, your outline and treatment cover the overarching story behind (and without) the dialogue and scene descriptions.

Outlines

An outline briefly synopsizes your script. You likely will not have to show anyone your outline, but you could be asked for one—if so, focus only on the major points of your story, keep the outline informal and write it in paragraph form. With an outline, less is more, especially when you use it as a pitch to sell your idea. The outline is an informal but crucial starting point from which you can successfully pitch your story idea, which leads to writing a compelling treatment, which ultimately leads to selling a script. Outlines for a half-hour sitcom run a few pages, while a television movie could be seven or more pages.

Treatments

Unlike outlines, which tend to be a bit informal and more skeletal, treatments are carefully constructed, well-written summaries of your script (in fact, treatments are similar to a novel synopsis). You get to expand on the outline and go into more detail about your characters, settings, and plot twists.

A treatment for a half-hour sitcom will probably run from four to six pages, whereas a treatment for an hour episodic drama might run six to nine pages, and one for a television movie might be ten to fifteen pages. No specific stipulations apply to the length of your treatment, but remember that shorter is usually better.

The two imperatives in formatting are that you double-space the text and write in present tense. Capitalize new characters as they are introduced. Tell the entire story front to back, like you're explaining it to your twelve-year-old nephew. Give away the ending. Don't be coy. And don't let the underlying framework show. Keep yourself out of the synopsis. Don't say "At the end of Act I ..." or "During the climax ..."

Ideally, your treatment should clearly delineate the major scenes in your script, with a new paragraph devoted to each scene. You can break up your treatment by using subheads to denote when a new act begins.

- Most sitcoms are divided into two acts, although a few are broken down into three acts. Some series use a teaser at the show's beginning or a tag at the show's conclusion.

- One-hour dramas typically have four acts; some shows also use a teaser at the show's beginning or a tag at the ending.

- Television movies contain seven acts. The act breaks coincide with the seven commercial breaks that typically occur during a two-hour time slot for movies on television.

SITCOMS: TWO APPROACHES

Sitcoms are unique in that they have two different formats, and you can tell which format each show will use by observing the show.

Shows that feature laugh tracks and are filmed on video (*How I Met Your Mother*, *Two and a Half Men*) have a distinct format that allows for a lot of white space (for handwritten changes and camera directions). A lot of what's written is in caps and double-spaced. There are good reasons for these differences, most notably that sitcom scripts often get revised up until the taping sessions (there are usually two sessions in front of live audiences, held on the same day), and sitcoms have directions for three cameras written alongside the script.

That said, know that many newer comedies now do not follow the old sitcom rules in that they have no laugh tracks and are shot on film from all angles (*The Office*, *30 Rock*, *My Name Is Earl*). These scripts follow a more screenplay-like approach. The dialogue is single-spaced and the narrative is in lower case, just like a screenplay.

If you're not sure which format to use, it's best to seek sample copies of the show's scripts online. Note: You're looking for scripts, not merely transcripts. This is a good idea in any case. The more scripts you read, the more you'll know how to handle transitions and the better you'll know one medium from the next.

SCRIPT STRUCTURE

Most sitcoms have only two acts, with three scenes per act (some shows use a teaser or a tag, which we'll discuss later). If your script is double-spaced, plan on about thirty seconds per script page. Consider that the viewing time of the average sitcom is about twenty-two to twenty-four minutes, so your script should be between forty and fifty double-spaced pages. Act titles are in all caps. At the end of the act, type "END OF ACT ONE," centered and underlined two or three spaces below the last line of the act. Some sitcoms break up their acts into scenes; some do not.

Teasers and Tags

Many sitcoms today begin with a teaser or end with a tag; some use both. A teaser is a short scene that airs at the beginning of the show, and a tag is a short scene that appears after the final act has been resolved. The tag almost always follows a commercial break and has the show's credits rolling alongside it. Both teasers and tags should run about two pages. Sometimes teasers and tags have little or nothing to do with that episode's story. For example, *The Office* almost always starts with a "cold open"—a short funny scene to get you laughing before introducing the conflict and storyline.

Page Numbers

Page numbers should appear in the top right corner of the page, flush with the right margin (about seventy-fikve spaces from the left edge of the page), about four lines from the top of the page, and followed by a period (for example, 17.).

Transitions

Transitions indicate that a shot or scene is either beginning, ending or shifting to another shot or scene. These include such directions as FADE IN:, FADE OUT, DISSOLVE TO: and CUT TO:. Transitions appear in all caps and are justified with the right margin (about seventy-five spaces from the left edge of the page), except FADE IN:, which is flush with the left margin (fifteen spaces from the left edge of the page). FADE OUT is used only at the end of an act and CUT TO: at the end of a scene (to indicate a new scene should begin). Some shows underline transitions.

Slug Line

The slug line (also called a scene heading) specifies the scene. It begins on the left margin (1" from the left edge of the page) and is written in all caps and underlined, with a double-spaced line before and after it. Your first slug line should appear two lines below FADE IN:. In sitcoms, the slug line will usually be INT. (interior shot), but occasionally you'll need to use EXT. (exterior shot). With the slug line, organize the details by going from the general to the more specific. End each slug line by indicating whether the action takes place during the day or at night. For almost every sitcom, the slug line typically contains three parts: INT. or EXT., the scene location and DAY or NIGHT. There is no ending punctuation for slug lines.

Your slug line will look like this:

INT. MARSHALL'S LIVING ROOM—NIGHT

Some shows have the character list for that particular scene in parentheses one line below the slug line:

INT. MARSHALL'S LIVING ROOM—NIGHT
(Patty, Marshall, Jane)

Action Direction

The action directions are sentences that describe specifics about what happens, when, where, how, and anything else that's important to the scene. The text within the action sentences begins on the left margin (1 inch from the left edge of the page), is single-spaced, in all caps, and should always be written in present tense (in some scripts, the action is in parentheses). Do not justify the right margin (which is at seventy-five spaces).

JONATHAN ENTERS THE DINING ROOM.

There should be one double-spaced line before and after the action description. If you have lots of description, break up the text to leave some white space—try not to allow a block of text to run more than four or five lines without a double-spaced break for the eyes (the more white space in a sitcom script, the better).

Character Cue

The speaking character's name (also called the character cue) should be in all caps and should appear approximately 2.5" (or 5 tabs) from the left edge of the page. A double-spaced line should appear before and after the character's name. The first time you introduce a character into the script (in the action or narrative), capitalize the character's name. If you're using the sitcom formatting where all narrative is already capitalized, underline the character's name instead.

> JACK
> I think I just saw Susan walk up the steps.
>
> Maybe she's coming up here.

Parenthetical Comment

Parenthetical comments, also known as *parentheticals*, help the speaker of the dialogue know what emotion or expression you intend with the delivery. A parenthetical is typically short (often a word or two), typed in all caps and appears either on the same line as the first line of dialogue or on a line by itself, not in all caps.

> VERONICA
> (EMBARRASSED) He really said I was cute?

Or:

> VERONICA
> (embarrassed)
> He really said I was cute?

Dialogue

Dialogue is double-spaced, typed in uppercase and lowercase text, and begins two lines below the speaking character's name. The left margin for dialogue is at approximately 1.5" (or three tabs), and the right margin of the dialogue approximately 2" from the right edge of the page. Do not justify the right margin.

Continuations

If you must continue dialogue from one page to the next, use what are called continuations, which are just the words (MORE) and (CONT'D). Use them like this: Put (MORE) under the last line of dialogue on the first page and (CONT'D) to the right of the character's name on the following page:

PAUL
Ira, if you don't knock before you come in here,
(MORE)

———————————— NEW PAGE ————————————

PAUL (CONT'D)
I'm going to sic Murray on you.

Using a Narrative Voice-Over

You will rarely need to use a narrative voice-over with sitcoms, but if you do, make sure you indicate it as such by typing "(V.O.)" to the right of the character's name:

CHARLIE (V.O.)
Wait a minute, now how did that happen?

Having a Character Speak Off-Screen

When you have a character speaking off-camera, type "(O.S.)" (off screen) to the right of the character's name. Let's say Jim is in the office in the hallway talking to Pam who's off hiding behind her desk.

JIM
You gonna stay like that all day?

PAM (O.S.)
Stop talking to me.

Other Dos and Don'ts

- Do keep dialogue short (break it up every four or five lines).

- Do spell out numbers one through ninety-nine, but use numerals for 100 and over.

- Do spell out personal titles except for Mr., Mrs., and Ms.

- Do spell out time indicators: eleven-thirty, not 11:30.

- Do spell out *okay*, not *OK* or *o.k.*

- Don't use any font other than Courier, 12-point.

- Don't justify right margins.

- Don't date your script.

- Don't include a cast of characters or set list page.

- Don't use camera directions and camera angles.

- Don't use special effects directions, such as FX (visual) or SFX (sound).

What follows are formatting specifications for your sitcom script as well as a sample script title page and sample versions of the first pages of two sitcom scripts.

Tab and Margin Settings

- Left and right margins: 1"

- Dialogue left margin: about 3 tabs, or 1.5" from left margin of the page

- Parenthetical comments: about 4 tabs, or 2" from left margin

- Character cue: about 5 tabs, or 2.5" from left margin

- Dialogue right margin: about 2" from the right edge of the page

- Transitions: flushed right

- Page number followed by a period: top right corner

All Caps

- Act and scene headings

- Act breaks

- All action/scene/stage directions

- Speech delivery (SLURRING)

- Transitions (FADE IN:, FADE OUT)

- Tags

- Teasers

- Slug lines (EXT. or INT., DAY or NIGHT)

- All descriptions

- Character names (except when part of dialogue or character list)

- Continuations (MORE or CONT'D)

- Act and show endings (END OF SHOW)

Single Space

- within action directions
- within scene descriptions

Double Space

- between scene heading and first lines of directions or scene descriptions
- between character's name and dialogue
- within dialogue lines
- between dialogue lines and directions or scene descriptions
- before and after transitions

ELECTRONIC SITCOM SCRIPT SUBMISSIONS

It is rare for an agent or story editor to request a sitcom script via e-mail, but it might happen. If it does, make sure you get detailed guidelines as to how the script should be submitted and follow them meticulously.

TITLE PAGE

Submission Tips

The title page includes the series title, the episode title, the author, and your contact information (this can be substituted with your agent's name and contact information if you have representation).

Formatting Specs

- The sitcom series should be in all caps, centered, about one-third of the way down the page.
- Drop one line and put the episode title in quotes.
- Drop four lines and type either "Written by" or just "by" (don't type the quotation marks).
- Drop one line and type your name.
- In the lower right corner, put your name and contact information, single-spaced, in uppercase and lowercase text. If you have an agent, type "Representation:", double-space, then put the agent's name and contact information instead of yours.
- In front of the title page, be sure to include a cover page that includes only the title and author's name.

- Preferred cover page paper is a white, gray, cream, rust, or pale blue cover of cardstock, between 40 and 60 lbs.

- The pages should be bound by two brass brads, short enough so they don't cut through an envelope when mailed.

- Although your script should have three holes punched in it, only the first and third holes should have brads in them.

- Use a backing page with the same stock as the cover page.

Other Dos and Don'ts

- Don't put any pictures or artwork on your cover page.

- Don't use spiral or other machine-type bindings.

See sample title page in the screenplay section earlier in this chapter.

1" margins on top and bottom

THE OFFICE

"BLACKBERRY ADDICTION"

A show such as *The Office*—one that has many camera angles and no laugh track—follows a format that is close to a screenplay. Find sample scripts of the show to help you.

ACT ONE

Act numbers are centered and in all caps. Sometimes acts are broken down into scenes (either A, B, C ... or 1, 2, 3 ...). *The Office* usually starts with a "cold open" before the credits play.

FADE IN:

INT. OFFICE—EARLY MORNING

MICHAEL WALKS IN THE DOOR. HE IS THE LAST ONE IN THE OFFICE.

> MICHAEL
> Good morning, everyone.

Episode title, centered and in quotes

HE SEES JIM USING A BLACKBERRY DEVICE.

> MICHAEL
> Hey! Cool phone. Is that a BlackBerry?

Transition in all caps

> JIM
> Uh, yeah, it is.

Scene slugs are pushed to the left and underlined.

The first time a character is introduced, underline the name.

> MICHAEL
> Kool Aid! Wow…
>   (re: Dwight)
> And Dwight, you've got one, too!

REVEAL: DWIGHT, USING HIS BLACKBERRY.

> DWIGHT
> Indeed, sir. With this, I shall be unstoppable.

> JIM
> Michael, you do know the entire office got them, right?

MICHAEL LOOKS AROUND TO SEE EVERYONE IN THE OFFICE PLAYING ON THEIR BLACKBERRIES. PAM. ANDY. KEVIN. EVERYBODY. A GLANCE TOWARD THE CAMERA REVEALS HE DIDN'T KNOW.

Single-spaced text

INT. OFFICE—MICHAEL'S OFFICE

MICHAEL IS TALKING TO SOMEONE VIA SPEAKER-PHONE.

1" margins on top and bottom

THE OFFICE / "BlackBerry Addiction"   2.

Use a header on all pages after the first one. Include page numbers.

MICHAEL
David, how come everyone in the office got a BlackBerry and I didn't?

Character cue is in all caps.

DAVID WALLACE (V.O.)
Michael, are you serious? We talked about this six months ago. I told you to buy one for work purposes and expense it. You told me later that you already went to the store and got it.

MICHAEL TALKING HEAD

MICHAEL TALKING TO THE CAMERA IN HIS OFFICE.

MICHAEL
The word "blackberry" can mean so many things. Like maybe a military code name. "Operation Black Berry." G.I. Joe, I believe that was. Or the food. Blackberries. Which is what I took it as.
       (beat)

Properly indent parenthetical.

They were delicious.

END OF ACT ONE

The end of an act or scene is centered and underlined. The next act or scene should begin on a new page.

***

V.O. signals voice-over, meaning that the character is speaking, but is not in the room. If someone offscreen is speaking, mark that with the abbreviation (O.S.) by the character cue.

Scripts

1" margins on top
and bottom

Series title in all caps
and centered

HOW I MET YOUR MOTHER

"AND THEN THAT HAPPENED"

ACT ONE

Each act or
scene begins on
a new page.

INT. 2029 LIVING ROOM—EVENING

(NARRATOR, DAUGHTER, SON)

In this version of
sitcom formatting,
characters in the
scene are listed
immediately after a
scene slug.

THE USUAL SUBURBAN HOME, THE SAME COUCH, THE
SAME TEENS. THE SAME NARRATOR TALKING.

Action line is in
all caps and single-
spaced.

NARRATOR (O.S.)
I know you've had a long day, but I've got

another great story to tell you.

THE KIDS ARE OBVIOUSLY BORED.

Left margin is 1".

NARRATOR (O.S.)
Just hear me out. Let me tell you about the time

Marshall and I went to the Mets game.

Dialogue is double-
spaced.

INT. TED AND MARSHALL'S APARTMENT—NIGHT

(MARSHALL, TED)

TED AND MARSHALL LOUNGE ON THE COUCH. HUGE
COUCH

The first time a
character is intro-
duced, the name is
underlined.

POTATOES. OPEN BAGS OF CHIPS AROUND THEM. THE
TV IS ON.

MARSHALL
I've never been more bored.

TED
I'm more bored than you are.

1" margins on top
and bottom

304

HOW I MET YOUR MOTHER / "And Then That Happened" 2.

Page number followed by a period, flush with right margin

MARSHALL

I'm too tired and bored to argue with you.

I mean, we're still watching *Dog the Bounty*

Hunter. Should I be worried?

TED
Oh no. I specifically remember the most boring

moment of our lives.

EXT. SHEA STADIUM—SEATS—DAY

Slug line is in all caps.

(MARSHALL, TED)

MARSHALL IS IN THE STANDS WATCHING THE GAME—
EATING POPCORN.

REVEAL: TED, SITTING NEXT TO HIM, WITH HIS WHOLE
VIEW BLOCKED BY A POLE. IN FACT, ONLY TED'S
SHOULDER IS VISIBLE.

MARSHALL
(LUCID) Wait a minute. This isn't the most

Character cue is in all caps.

boring moment of my life?

TED
(BEHIND POLE) What do you mean?

INT. TED AND MARSHALL'S APARTMENT—NIGHT

(MARSHALL, TED)
TED
I couldn't see anything!
MARSHALL
That was the most boring moment of *your* life,

sir. Let me tell you about mine.

***

Parentheticals are all caps. They can fall within dialogue or on a separate line.

ONE-HOUR EPISODIC DRAMAS

Structure

Your hour-long script will be approximately fifty pages long. Most one-hour dramas run forty-eight minutes, and as with the motion-picture format, you can average about one minute of viewing time per manuscript page. Nearly all hour-long dramas contain four acts that occur at roughly twelve- to fifteen-minute intervals (so your script should change acts every twelve to fifteen pages). The act breaks will correspond with the network's commercials, which occur about every thirteen minutes. Because networks want viewers to hang around through the commercial breaks, your story needs to have a cliffhanger or an emotional moment at the end of each act. Whether or not such a moment needs to be included in the last act depends on the individual show—does it typically end with a neat resolution or with something to carry over to next week?

One-hour episodic dramas share more in common with the formatting of screenplays than of sitcoms.

Transitions

Transitions simply indicate that a shot or scene is beginning, ending or shifting to another shot or scene. These include such directions as FADE IN:, FADE TO:, CUT TO:, and DISSOLVE TO:. Transitions appear in all caps and are justified with the right margin (1" from the edge of the page), except FADE IN:, which is flush with the left margin and should appear two lines below the act number. FADE OUT is used only at the end of an act (and is on the right margin).

Teasers and Tags

Many one-hour episodic dramas begin with a teaser or end with a tag; some use both. A teaser is a short scene that airs at the beginning of the show, and a tag is a short scene that appears after the final act has been resolved. The tag almost always follows a commercial break and sometimes has the show's credits rolling alongside it. Both teasers and tags should run about two pages. Sometimes teasers and tags have little or nothing to do with that episode's story.

Slug Line

The slug line sets the scene and specifies the shot. It begins on the left margin and is written in all caps, with a double-spaced line before and after it. Your first slug line should appear two lines below FADE IN:. Most slug lines begin with either EXT. (exterior shot) or INT. (interior shot). After you determine whether the shot is outside or inside, identify the specifics of the shot, such as a particular building or house, and then, if necessary, precisely where the shot takes place. With the slug line, organize the details by going from the general to the specific. End each slug line by indicating whether it's day or night. There is no punctuation at the end of the slug line. For example, your slug line might look like this:

INT. YMCA—MEN'S LOCKER ROOM—NIGHT

Action

The action descriptions (also called narrative) are sentences or very short paragraphs that describe specifics about what happens, location, the time of year, and anything else important to the scene.

The text within the action sentences begins on the left margin (seventeen spaces from the left edge of the page), is single-spaced (with regular capitalization), and should always be written in present tense. Do not justify the right margin (space seventy-five). There should be one double-spaced line before and after the action text. If you have lots of description, break up the text to leave some white space. Try not to allow a block of text to run more than five or six lines without a double-spaced break for the eyes (the more white space in a script, the better).

Character's Name

The speaking character's name (also called the character cue) should be in all caps and appear approximately 2.5" (or 5 tabs) from the left margin. A double-spaced line should appear before the character's name, but there should be no double-space between the name and the dialogue, or between the name and the parenthetical (see below). Note: The first time you introduce a character into the script, put that character's name in all caps. After the character has been introduced, use regular capitalization.

Parenthetical Comment

Parenthetical comments, also known as *parentheticals*, help the speaker of the dialogue know what emotion you intend for the delivery. Parenthetical comments are typically short (often a word or two), are typed in regular text (not all caps), appear one line below the character's name (and thus one line above dialogue) at space thirty-five, and are set in parentheses. A parenthetical should look like this:

PATTI HEWES
(antagonistic)
What in the hell's going on around here, Ellen?

Dialogue

Dialogue is typed in regular text (not all caps) and begins on the line below the speaking character's name (or one line below the parenthetical). The left margin for dialogue is approximately 1.5" from the left margin, and the right margin of the dialogue is about 2" from the right edge of the page. Do not justify the right margin. Try to avoid large blocks of dialogue that run seven or more lines. If your character needs to say more than can fit in seven lines, add a blank line space between the text so it's more visually pleasing.

In addition to the regular elements of your one-hour episodic script, you will probably find yourself in situations where you might need some special formatting and cues. Here are some of the more common script elements you might need to use in your script.

Carrying Dialogue From One Page to the Next

Do your best not to make an actor (character) flip to the next page in the middle of speaking. Sometimes, however, this cannot be avoided, and you must use what's called a continuation. To carry a character's dialogue onto the next page, use the indicator (MORE) on the bottom of the first page and (CONT'D) next to the speaker's name at the top of the next page:

> JOE
> I swear if I ever see you in this town again I'm going
> (MORE)

—————————————— NEW PAGE ——————————————

> JOE (CONT'D)
> to kill you.

Using a Narrative Voice-Over

If your script calls for a narrative voice-over, make sure you indicate it as such by typing "(V.O.)" next to the name of the character who is narrating. A scene with a voice narration should look like this:

> CAPTAIN SMITH (V.O.)
> Now how did she get into the apartment when the
> keys are inside?

Having a Character Speak Offscreen

When you have a character speaking off-camera, type "(O.S.)" (offscreen) next to the character's name. Let's say Steve is on camera in the kitchen while talking to Maggie who's offscreen on the back porch.

> STEVE
> Can you bring that old broom in here?

> MAGGIE (O.S.)
> What? You want me to put that filthy thing in our
> kitchen? You're crazy.

> STEVE
> I need it to sweep up all this flour I just spilled on
> the floor.

> MAGGIE (O.S.)
>
> Oh, you're pathetic.

Other Dos and Don'ts

- Do number your pages and put a period after the number.

- Do keep dialogue short (keep to seven lines per block, then insert a double space).

- Do spell out numbers one to ninety-nine, but use numerals for 100 and over.

- Do spell out personal titles except for Mr., Mrs., and Ms.

- Do spell out time indicators: eleven-thirty, not 11:30.

- Do spell out *okay*, not *OK* or *o.k.*

- Don't use special effects directions, such as FX (visual) or SFX (sound).

- Don't use camera directions and camera angles.

- Don't number the first page.

- Don't number scenes. This is done in the final stages of story editing, before the script moves into preproduction.

What follows are formatting specifications for your one-hour episodic script as well as a sample one-hour episodic script title page and a sample first page of a one-hour episodic script.

Tab and Margin Settings

- Left and right margins: 1"

- Dialogue left margin: about 3 tabs, or 1.5" from left margin of the page

- Parenthetical comments: about 4 tabs, or 2" from left margin

- Character cue: about 5 tabs, or 2.5" from left margin

- Dialogue right margin: about 2" from the right edge of the page

- Transitions: flushed right (except FADE IN, which is flushed left)

- Page number followed by a period: top right corner

All Caps

- Type of shot (INT. and EXT.)

- Setting or scene location (JOE'S ROOM)

- Time of day (DAY or NIGHT)

- The first time you introduce a character (JOHN walks in)

- The speaking character's name (PHIL), followed by dialogue
- Camera directions (PAN, CLOSE-UP, etc.)
- Important actions, sound cues, or objects (Ted hears a GUNSHOT in the hallway.)
- Scene transitions (CUT TO:, DISSOLVE TO:, etc.)

Single Space

- within dialogue
- within action/scene descriptions
- within camera directions, sound cues
- within stage directions
- between the character's name and dialogue
- between character's name and parenthetical
- between parenthetical and dialogue

Double Space

- between the scene location and action/scene descriptions
- between the action/scene descriptions and the speaking character's name
- between the speeches of the different characters
- between the paragraphs of lengthy dialogue or action descriptions
- between dialogue and a new speaking character's name
- between dialogue and stage or camera directions

ELECTRONIC ONE-HOUR EPISODIC DRAMA SCRIPT SUBMISSIONS

It is rare for an agent, producer, or story editor to request an episodic drama script via e-mail, but it might happen. If it does, make sure you get detailed guidelines as to how the script should be submitted and follow them meticulously.

EPISODIC DRAMA TITLE PAGE

Submission Tips

The title page includes the series title, the episode title, the authors, and the author's contact information (this can be substituted with your agent's name and contact information if you have representation).

Formatting Specs

- The name of the one-hour episodic series name should be in all caps, centered, about one-third of the way down the page.

- In the lower right corner, put your name and contact information, single-spaced, in regular text (not all caps).

- If you have an agent, put "Representation:," double-space, then put the agent's name and contact information instead of yours.

- In front of the title page, be sure to include a cover page with the title and author's name.

- Preferred cover page paper is a white, gray, cream, rust, or pale blue cover of cardstock, between 40 to 60 lb.

- The pages should be bound in brass brads, short enough so they don't cut through an envelope when mailed.

- Although your script should have three holes punched in it, only the first and third holes should have brads in them.

- Use a backing page with the same stock as the cover page.

Other Dos and Don'ts

- Don't put any pictures or artwork on your title page.

- Don't use spiral or other machine-type bindings.

See sample tiitle page in the screenplay section earlier in this chapter.

1″ margins on top
and bottom

1.

Page number
followed by a pe-
riod (flush with right
margin).

DAMAGES

"He Isn't Laughing Now"

Series title, episode
title, and act number
(underlined) are
centered near the
top margin.

Act One

FADE IN:

EXT. DOG PARK—DAY

Slug line is in
all caps.

Transition in
all caps

Dogs and owners everywhere. It's October, and many leaves
are falling. A YOUNG MAN we haven't seen before is in the
park, as well—except he seems to have no dog or purpose
there. Behind him appears PATTI HEWES, cool as ice, with
her dog in tow.

First time a character
is introduced, the
name is in all caps.

Action line is single-
spaced, upper and
lower-case text.

                    PATTI
          You're late.

                    YOUNG MAN
               (startled)
          Patti.

Properly indent
character cue.

                    PATTI
          You're late.

                    YOUNG MAN
          I know. I wasn't going to come. But I, uh,
          talked to Tom, and he answered … most of
          my questions. Listen, do we have to talk here?

Dialogue is single-
spaced. Keep blocks
of dialogue short.

                    PATTI
          What's wrong with here? You cynophobic?
               (He doesn't get it)
          Afraid of dogs?—

Parentheticals are on
a separate line.

Capitalize key ac-
tions, sound cues,
and objects.

The Young Man LAUGHS.

                    PATTI (CON'T)
          … No?

Double-space
between changes in
dialogue and action
lines.

                    YOUNG MAN

          Patti, you don't want to know what I'm

          afraid of.

Use this when the
same character's
dialogue is broken up
by action.

SOAP OPERAS

A finished soap opera script is the result of teamwork. Because soap operas must be cranked out five days a week, with multiple stories going at once to carry the drama from episode to episode (seemingly for perpetuity), a number of writers, producers, and executives are required to get the script in working order. The best way to keep up with such demand is the same way Henry Ford put together cars: division of labor. Soap scripts are an assembly line of sorts.

Here's how that assembly line works. The show's sponsor (usually a corporation, like Procter & Gamble) and the producers will meet with the show's head writer to create a yearlong, roughly sketched outline for the show. Then the head writer breaks that outline into specific weekly and daily outlines. Eventually, a short scene-by-scene synopsis (usually a paragraph or two per scene) is created for each episode; then the head writer sends the synopsis to various associate writers who write all the dialogue for a particular episode.

Most writers for soap operas are associate writers who pen the dialogue for individual episodes. The best way to become an associate writer is to send a spectacular spec script to the production company or to get an agent who represents the show's writers to also represent you. One other option is to find out if the show has an apprentice program for writers (the show's sponsor usually offers this program) and, if so, enroll in it. To see if the show you wish to write for offers such a program, contact the production company.

STRUCTURE

Most soaps run for an hour, with a few that run only a half hour. Either way, you can figure that the viewing time for a soap script is a little more than one minute per page. Therefore, a one-hour show script will run about seventy pages, and a half-hour show will be roughly thirty-five pages. Although commercial breaks will eat up some of this time, ignore them and write as if your show's either an hour or half hour. Unlike one-hour episodic dramas and sitcoms, which have a set number of acts, soaps work in a different way because they're continually running. A soap episode is more a series of scenes than one story episode delineated into a beginning, a middle, and an end.

Format

The script elements and formatting specifications for soaps are almost identical to those for motion pictures. There are, however, a few differences you should be aware of. The primary difference is that all action directions are capitalized, appear in parentheses, and get mixed in with the dialogue. Also, a soap script has practically no camera directions and relies heavily on dialogue.

One major problem with writing a spec script for a soap is that the formats vary so much from show to show. Many shows use the "standard" soap format shown on the following pages, but some opt for a format that looks more like a radio script:

JOHN: Would you please bring me some water?

MARY: I'm not your maid.

To determine what format the soap you want to write for uses, try to obtain back scripts from the production company. Finding the production company isn't too difficult. Contact them and say you want to write for the show and would like to obtain some back scripts. Offer to send an SASE with adequate postage. Making the call will pay off—it will be to your advantage to use the correct format for the show.

ELECTRONIC SOAP OPERA SCRIPT SUBMISSIONS

It is rare for an agent, producer or story editor to request a soap script via e-mail, but it might happen. If it does, make sure you get detailed guidelines as to how the script should be submitted and follow them meticulously.

1" margins on top
and bottom

DANCE OF THE HEART   5.

Page number
followed by a pe-
riod flush with right
margin.

FADE IN:

Transition is in
all caps.

HAROLD DANFORTH'S DEN. HAROLD IS SEARCHNG
THROUGH HIS DESK TRYING TO FIND THE RECEIPT
FOR THE NECKLACE HE BOUGHT FOR HIS MISTRESS,
ABIGAIL CHAMBERS. HIS WIFE, ELIZABETH DANFORTH,
WALKS INTO THE DEN.

Left margin is 1".

                    ELIZABETH
        (OPENS THE DOOR) Well hello, darling.
        (SLOWLY CLOSES AND LOCKS THE
        DOOR BEHIND HER)

Character cue
is in all caps.

                    HAROLD
        (NERVOUSLY CLOSES THE TOP DESK
        DRAWER AND LOOKS UP) Hi, dear.
        How are you? (LOOKS BACK DOWN AND
        STARTS SORTING THROUGH SOME
        PAPERS ON HIS DESK) I'm just in here trying
        to find that letter from the school board. Have
        you seen it? (KEEPS LOOKING DOWN,
        SHUFFLING THE PAPERS)

Action is in all caps,
surrounded by
parentheses (except
at the beginning
of a scene when
no parentheses are
required).

                    ELIZABETH
        (NOT RESPONDING, SLOWLY WALKS UP
        TO THE DESK AND JUST STANDS THERE)

                    HAROLD
        (NOT LOOKING AT HER) Dear? Have you
        seen it? (DISTRACTED KEEPS SHUFFLING
        THE PAPERS AND THEN LOOKS UP. HE
        SEES HER RIGHT IN FRONT OF HIS FACE)
        Ah! (SCREAMS) Damn, you scared me.

Dialogue is single-
spaced, upper and
lowercase text. Do
keep blocks of dia-
logue short.

                    ELIZABETH
        I did, did I? Well what do you have to be scared
        about? It's only me.

                    HAROLD
        (FLUSTERED) You just surprised me, that's all.
        (HESITATING, LOOKS DOWN AND SORTS
        MORE PAPERS) Where is that thing? I swear I
        saw it here this morning. It was right here.
        Where the hell could it be?

1" margins on top
and bottom

DANCE OF THE HEART   6.

                    ELIZABETH
          (CALMLY PULLS THE RECEIPT FROM HER
          LEFT SHIRT POCKET) Oh, could this be what
          you're looking for, darling? (SHE LETS IT HANG
          IN FRONT OF HIS FACE)

                    HAROLD
          (LOOKS UP, SEES THE RECEIPT, AND GRABS
          IT OUT OF HER HAND) Damn you. What the
          hell is this? (CRUMBLES UP THE RECEIPT)

                    ELIZABETH
          (STARTS TO CRY) You know damn well what it
          is, Harold. I suppose you bought that necklace for
          me. But why would you buy me anything? Why,
          you haven't bought me anything in years.

                    HAROLD
          (STANDS UP, WALKS AROUND THE DESK)
          Now dear. (TRIES TO HOLD ELIZABETH'S
          HAND)

                    ELIZABETH
          (PUSHES HIS HAND AWAY) Don't "now dear"
          me, Harold! For God's sake, just admit you're
          having an affair. Please! I swear, you're nothing
          but a weak, selfish, lying man. (SLAPS HIM AND
          WALKS AWAY. SLAMS THE DOOR ON HER
          WAY OUT)

                                        FADE OUT ←————————

                                                    Transition to
                    * * *   leave scene.

PLAY SCRIPTS

In general, there are three types of stage plays:

- The ten-minute play
- The one-act play
- The full-length play

Ten-minute plays are just that—they run ten pages and last ten minutes. They generally feature two or three characters in one setting and address one central conflict. One-act plays run twenty to sixty pages in length. Full-length scripts are 100 to 130 pages in length and usually feature two or three distinct acts, sometimes with an intermission. Using the following formatting specifics, plan on about one minute per page when performed out loud.

Despite the number of acts and pages a play possesses, all plays should follow the basic dramatic structure and have three overarching movements—a beginning, a middle, and an end. Here's a rough sketch of what the overall dramatic structure of your play should look like, as outlined in Jeffrey Hatcher's *The Art & Craft of Playwriting* (Writer's Digest Books):

Part One

Start of play

- Introduction of characters, place, time, setting, or exposition
- Introduction of the primary inciting event
- Initial point of attack or primary conflict
- Introduction of the central dramatic question

Part Two

- Characters embark on journey/struggle/search for answers/goals
- Conflicts with other characters, events, circumstances
- Characters reassess situations, respond to obstacles and challenges, plan new tactics, succeed, fail, attack, retreat, surprise and are surprised, encounter major reversals
- A crisis is reached
- Characters embark on an action that will resolve the crisis and lead inexorably to the conclusion

Part Three

- The major characters or combatants engage in a final conflict (climax)
- The character's goal is achieved or lost

- The central dramatic question is answered

- The actions suggest the themes or ideas of the play

- Following the climax is the resolution, in which a new order is established

- End of play

WHAT YOU NEED TO SUBMIT

Along with the stage play script, you need introductory pages, including a title page, an information breakdown page, act and scene breakdowns, and a cast of characters page.

TITLE PAGE

Submission Tips

The title page includes the name of the play, how many acts it contains, and your name and contact information (or the agent's name and contact information if you have representation). It also indicates if the play is based on a novel.

Formatting Specs

- The title should be in all caps, centered, about one-third of the way down the page.

- Drop four lines and type "A One-Act Play by," or "A Play in Two Acts by" or "A Play in Three Acts by" (depending on what you write).

- Drop four lines again and type your name. (If your play is written with another person, use an ampersand between your names.)

- In the lower right corner, put your name and contact information, single-spaced, in uppercase and lowercase text.

- If you have an agent, type "Representation:" skip a line and put the agent's name and contact information instead of yours.

Other Dos and Don'ts

- Don't number the title page.

- Do include your agent's name and contact information if you have representation.

- Don't submit your play via e-mail unless specifically requested.

THE SNOWFLAKE THEORY

Four lines between
title
and byline

A Play in Two Acts by

Nancy Gall-Clayton

If the script is based
on a novel, say so
here and credit the
author.

Nancy Gall-Clayton
123 Author Lane
Writerville, CA 95355
(323) 555-0000
johnqwriter@email.com

Your name and
contact information
goes in bottom right
corner, single-spaced
(or the agent's name
and contact informa-
tion if you have
representation).

INFORMATION BREAKDOWN PAGE

Submission Tips

The information breakdown page(s) of a play has several sections and purposes. It lists all the pertinent information about the play, from characters to scene breakdowns and the play's development. This information can cover one or two pages.

Listing Characters

Primary and secondary characters are listed, each with a brief description of the character. The description will be used mostly to help a director or producer in casting the part. Common aspects to include would be the character's age and any overarching characteristics (forexample, "grunge-loving, teen-angst-filled teenage boy"). This section can be broken down into primary characters and secondary characters if need be.

Time and Place

This section explains when the story takes place, whether it's present day Boston, or 19th-century London.

Scene Breakdown

Breaking down the acts and scenes helps producers and directors see how many scenes are in the play and the setting of each scene. Include the exact page count for each scene.

Notes

If you anticipate questions from readers, this is your chance to address them up front.

History of Awards and Development

In this section, elaborate on the play's past development. Has it received a staged reading? A workshop? Multiple workshops? If so, where? Has it placed in any contests? If so, was it a grand-prize winner, finalist, or semifinalist? What years? Make sure you include up-to-date information regarding the work's publishing and production history, if any. If you're contacting a theater in Colorado, for instance, can you tell them that the work has never been produced in the American West? That way, they understand it's not in consideration for a world premiere but rather for a regional premiere.

The Snowflake Theory

<u>CHARACTERS</u> (in order of appearance)

Marge Klein	A widowed Jewish woman, 58, primed to reinvent herself
Rebecca Klein	Marge's daughter, 40 (DOB = 1963), never married and doesn't mind, 17 weeks pregnant in Act I
Clark Klein	Marge's son, 33 (DOB = 1970), has been in a fog for years (or so it seemed), but is emerging
Violet Sample	Clark's girlfriend, non-Jewish, 20s, couldn't be less—or more—right for the Kleins, a fan of vintage clothes and fun hair colors
Harris Samuels	A rabbi, 57, he knows humor can heal

<u>TIME & PLACE</u>
February–April 2003. A city in the Midwest: Marge's kitchen and Harris's office.

<u>SCENE BREAKDOWN</u>
Act : Scene 1, Marge's kitchen, Wednesday, February 26, 2003, pages 1–35
Scene 2, Rabbi's office, the next day, page 35–50
Scene 3, Marge's kitchen, the next evening, pages 51–59
Scene 4, Marge's kitchen, two days later, pages 59–70

Act II: Scene 1, Marge's kitchen, a few minutes later, pages 71–88
Scene 2, Marge's kitchen, the next evening, pages 88–94
Scene 3, Marge's kitchen, eight weeks later, pages 94–106

<u>NOTES</u>
The several lines of Aristophanes' *Lysistrata* quoted in this play come from a version originally published in 1912.

<u>HISTORY OF AWARDS AND DEVELOPMENT</u>
The Snowflake Theory was presented as a staged reading at "Beyond the Borscht Belt: The Jewish Theatre Festival" at the Jewish Community Center in Columbus, Ohio, and the Ohio State University Hillel Foundation on October 26 and 27, 2008 and at ScriptFEST at Southern Appalachian Repertory Theatre on October 24, 2008. Previously, it was a Finalist for the Southeastern Theatre Conference Charles M. Getchell Award and a Semifinalist for the Dorothy Silver Playwriting Competition. This play has never been produced or published.

Side annotations (left):

The title is at the top, centered, bold, and italicized.

Keep character information to a minimum.

Character names flushed left

1" margin

Depending on the length of your notes and play history, this information can go more than one page—but keep it to two pages maximum.

Side annotations (right):

The "Characters" section is sometimes broken down into two subsections: primary characters and secondary.

Explain if the play has any readings, workshops, or productions.

SCRIPT PAGES

After the introductory page(s) comes the play script itself. The script pages include the following information, which should be formatted as specified.

Dialogue

Following the scene description, double-space and begin the dialogue. Formatting the dialogue is simple. The speaking character's name appears in all caps, centered. Dialogue starts from the left margin on the line below the character's centered name and should be in regular uppercase and lowercase text and single-spaced.

Parenthetical Comments

Parenthetical comments, also known as *parentheticals*, include description, expression, or direction that lets the actor or director know what you intend. There are two types of parentheticals in playwriting:

A parenthetical that appears within the dialogue lines. When the direction indicates an action or emotion to occur while the character is speaking, the parenthetical is put within lines of dialogue. If the parenthetical is used to signal the character's mood or delivery, it is placed between the character's name and the first word of dialogue. All the text is lowercase.

FLOYD
(exasperated)

Then what are you talking about? Huh?

The second type is a parenthetical that falls between or outside spoken lines. When there are more detailed directions (often physical directions), the parenthetical will be set apart from the dialogue by a line break. Put the direction in parentheses and indent four tabs in. The text is both upper- and lowercase, and is single-spaced within the parenthetical.

FLOYD

Then what are you talking about? Huh?

(Floyd gets up and pushes his chair over.)

The Act Ending

To end an act, simply type "Curtain Falls" or "Lights Down" (in italics or underlined), centered, at the bottom of the page.

Formatting Specs

- Use 1" margins on all sides.

- Place character cues centered above the line of dialogue.

- The dialogue should be single-spaced with a double space before a new character starts to speak.

- When a character's name is used in an action parenthetical, it should appear in all caps.

- When a character enters a room, the character's name should appear in all caps.

- The act and scene identifications should be centered, bold, and underlined.

Other Dos and Don'ts

- Do number all your script pages and put a period after the number.

- Don't overuse action. Directors want to interpret the movement onstage and make the play "their own." Actors, too. The less parenthetical emotions and directions you can include, the better.

- Don't submit your script via e-mail unless specifically requested by the publisher.

The Snowflake Theory   *Page I – I – I*

Header with the title

This line designates the page, the act, and the scene (in that order).

ACT I
Scene 1

Act and scene identification is bold, centered, and underlined.

SETTING:	MARGE's kitchen. Only a table and chairs are needed. On the table are two sets (different colors) of plastic unbreakable dishes and two sets of flatware. It's Wednesday, Feb. 26, 2003.
BEFORE RISE:	Sounds of MARGE removing dishes and flinging them to the floor.
AT RISE:	Action continues. Nothing is breaking. MARGE becomes more and more frustrated. She throws the flatware at the dishes. Finally, Marge gives up and sits.

Explain the setting and props. This is your chance to set the details of the scene. You can explain at length, if necessary. If a scene must have certain furniture, or a certain lighting scheme, say so—but don't over-detail a scene just for the sake of writing.

What happens before the lights come up? This is a place to name background music, if any, for example.

Explain what's going on when the lights come up.

MARGE

You are where you are. That's what Manny always said.

(MARGE opens a garbage bag and starts throwing everything in. REBECCA enters in a coat.)

Dialogue is flushed left and wraps all the way across.

REBECCA

It's not garbage night.

MARGE

Why are you checking on me?

Action and stage directions are indented and in parentheses.

REBECCA

You're on my way home.

Character names centered for dialogue

MARGE

Another item on your To Do List.

REBECCA

Let me help with that. ... What's in here, a dead body?

One line after each character's dialogue

MARGE

In a manner of speaking.

Character names all caps.

REBECCA

Mom?

The Snowflake Theory   *Page II – I – I*

Header with
the title

This line designates
the page, the act,
and the scene (in
that order).

                    MARGE
The kosher dishes.

                    REBECCA
You're going to eat out every night?

                    MARGE
I'm going to eat on my new hot pink dishes with my new forks,
knives, and spoons.

Dialogue is single-
spaced.

                    REBECCA
Hot pink for dairy or meat?

                    MARGE
Neither ... both!

                    REBECCA
I better sit down.

                    <u>Curtain Falls / Lights Down</u>

Show when the act is
finished.

                        ***

CHAPTER 21

POETRY

The poetry market consists mostly of magazines, literary journals, and online sites. While poems can vary greatly in length and style, all publications are concerned with two things: 1) the quality of the work; and 2) a professional presentation—especially if you're sending multiple submissions.

COVER LETTER

Submission Tips

Until recent years, most editors didn't expect or want cover letters along with a poetry submission; however, now many editors do specify that they want cover letters.

The best approach is to look up the publication's listing in *Poet's Market* or to request a copy of its submission guidelines.

Formatting Specs

- The cover letter should be no longer than one page, and not a tightly packed page.

- Use a standard font, 12-point type. Avoid bold or italics except for titles.

- Use 1" margins on all sides.

- Use block format (no indentations, an extra space between paragraphs).

- Put your name and contact information at the top of your letter, centered, or in your letterhead.

- Introduce the work you are submitting (Enclosed are three poems …).

- Provide a brief biography that includes listing some of your published work if you have any and your background, including occupation, hobbies, interests, or other life events that have bearing on your work.

- Note why you think the poetry you're submitting would be appropriate for the publication (giving you a chance to show your familiarity with the publication).

- Mention if the work you are submitting has been previously published or if you are making simultaneous submissions. Check to make sure the publication accepts simultaneous submissions before sending them.

Other Dos and Don'ts

- Do address your letter to a specific editor. Call to get the appropriate name and gender.

- Don't request guidelines in the cover letter of your submission. It's too late at this point.

- Don't ask for criticism. It's not the editor's job to coach you.

- Don't submit handwritten poems.

- Do take note if a journal specifically requests poems that either have not been previously published or poems that were previously published.

ELECTRONIC COVER LETTER

Submission Tips

Before you send a cover letter and poems to a publication via e-mail, make sure the editor accepts electronic submissions by contacting the publication directly or checking out their writers guidelines. Never send poems via e-mail unless you have permission from the editor or if the publication's submission guidelines say it is acceptable.

Formatting Specs

- Include the same information that goes into a paper cover letter, including your name and contact information. With e-mail letters, put your contact information at the lower left under your signature. It's not necessary to include your e-mail address in the body of the e-mail, since the editor can easily click "Reply" to respond.

- Use a subject line that introduces the theme or concept of your poems, unless the publisher's guidelines indicate what you should type there.

- Follow the same format you would with a paper cover letter, including the date, salutation, and block paragraph format. Read submission guidelines to determine how many poems a publication wants at one time.

Other Dos and Don'ts

- Don't use all caps or exclamation points in the subject line.

- Don't insert clip art graphics or other images in your cover letter. Keep it simple.

- Do use a formal tone as you would in a paper cover letter.

John Q. Writer
123 Author Lane
Writerville, CA 95355
(323) 555-0000
johnqwriter@email.com

August 15, 2009

Dominick Saddlestaple, editor
The Squiggler's Digest
Double-Toe Press
P.O. Box 54X
Submission Junction, AZ 86753

Dear Mr. Saddlestaple:

Enclosed are three poems for your consideration for *The Squiggler's Digest*: "The Diamond Queen," "The Boy Who Was Gromit," and "The Maker of Everything."

Although this is my first submission to your journal, I am a long-time reader of *The Squiggler's Digest* and enjoy the scope of narrative poetry you feature. I especially enjoyed Sydney Dogwood's poetry cycle in Issue 4.

My own poetry has appeared recently in *The Bone-Whittle Review*, *Bumper-Car Reverie*, and *Stock Still*.

Thank you for considering my manuscript. I look forward to hearing from you.

Sincerely,

John Q. Writer

Encl.: Three poems
SASE

Contact information at the top, centered

Date flushed right

Address the correct editor.

Brief and to the point

Single-spaced text, block format

Signature

List enclosures. Include an SASE if mailing your work.

List the poems you're submitting for consideration. Submit up to three poems.

If you are familiar with the publication, say so.

If you have poetry credits, list a few quickly and humbly.

John Q. Writer
(323) 555-0000

Poetry Editor
Poetry Review
444 Canal St.
St. Louis, MO 55435

Dear Sir or Madam,

I am sending you a collection of my poems—there are fifty-six of them in all. They cover all sorts of issues, from global politics to deep personal feelings of love and loss. I hope you'll publish at least one or two of my poems in your magazine.

I've been writing poems since I was a child and would give anything to have them published.

If you don't want to publish them, please return them to me.

Sincerely,

John Q. Writer

Don't send your submission to "Poetry Editor"; find out the name of a specific editor.

Don't send more than a few poems at a time. Read submission guidelines to find out how many poems a publication wants you to send.

Provide some background information on yourself.

Be polite—thank the editor for her time and indicate that you look forward to hearing back.

Include all of your contact information here—name, address, phone number, and e-mail.

Most publications have a specific focus, and you should note why you think your poems would be appropriate.

Your passion is appreciated, but don't veer off into unprofessionalism.

Don't ask for your poems to be returned to you—you should be sending neatly typed copies, not your originals.

Don't forget to include an SASE, unless you're sending your submission via e-mail.

329

Poetry

POETRY SUBMISSION

Submission Tips

In poetry, above all other forms, substance supersedes format. Your submissions should be neat and correspond to the rules of the medium. You don't get any points for fancy fonts or colored paper. In fact, your submission is likely to be viewed less favorably if you garnish it in such ways.

Generally, you will submit three to five poems at a time, though some editors prefer seven or more poems from a feature poet. Again, the publication's guidelines will help here.

Formatting Specs

- Use standard white bond, laser, or ink-jet paper.
- Submit each poem on a separate page, except for haiku.
- Center a title in all caps above the poem. If there is a subtitle, use uppercase and lowercase and underline it. Skip one line and center below the title.
- Include your name and contact information.
- If your poem continues to a second sheet, start the second page with a new stanza whenever possible or applicable.
- Editor preferences vary on whether submissions should be double- or single-spaced. Check the publication's guidelines. Unless otherwise directed, single-space.
- If the line of poetry extends beyond the margin, indent the second line. If you are double-spacing the entire poem, single-space the continuation of a line.
- Put in an extra line space (or two, when double-spacing) before the beginning of a stanza.
- Margins will vary, depending on the poem, but generally run at least 2" to 2.5" on the sides, with the poem roughly centered top to bottom on the page. These margins do not apply to electronic submissions.
- If you don't use a cover letter, find out if the publication wants biographical information and include such information on a separate sheet under the centered, capitalized heading "BIOGRAPHICAL INFORMATION" or "ABOUT THE POET."
- If your poem runs more than one page, use a header (generally the title or your last name) in the top left corner and a page number in the top right corner on the second and subsequent pages.
- Fold the poems together into thirds for insertion into the envelope. Fold the cover letter separately and place it on top of the poems. Better yet, use a large envelope and don't fold your cover letter or submission at all.
- Paper clip pages of the same poem together, but submit one-page poems loose leaf.

Other Dos and Don'ts

- Do enclose an SASE, which makes it easier for the editor to respond.

- Don't handwrite your poems.

- Don't use onion skin, colored, or erasable paper.

- Don't put copyright information on your poem. It's copyrighted regardless of this, and you'll likely insult the editor's intelligence or intentions.

- Do address your submission and cover letter by name to the poetry editor or other editor who routinely reviews poetry submission.

- Don't submit previously published work or make simultaneous submissions unless you know the publication accepts them and you note it in a cover letter.

ELECTRONIC POETRY SUBMISSIONS

Submission Tips

Never send poems via e-mail unless you have permission from the editor or if their submission guidelines say it is acceptable. Don't forget to include your cover letter in the body of your e-mail.

Formatting Specs

- Before you send the poems, find out how the editor prefers to receive files. He may want the poems attached as separate files or included in the body of the e-mail. A lot of editors don't like to open attachments, especially from unfamiliar people.

- Follow the same formatting specs as for a paper manuscript submission.

- If the editor doesn't specify a particular file format for an attached file, save it as a text file. Most word processing programs can read basic text files.

Other Dos and Don'ts

- Don't use all caps in your subject line.

- Do ask for specific file format guidelines to make sure the editor can open your files.

- Don't justify text or align the right margin.

- Don't put any copyright information on your poem. It's copyrighted when you write it, and the editor is aware of this.

John Q. Writer
123 Author Lane
Writerville, CA 95355
(323) 555-0000
johnqwriter@email.com

Contact information goes in upper left corner.

A cover letter should accompany the poem in a regular mail submission.

MIRACLES

Title centered, in all caps

Five lines between title and poem

Why, who makes much of a miracle?
As to me I know of nothing else but miracles,
Whether I walk the streets of Manhattan,
Or dart my sight over the roofs of houses to-
     ward the sky,
Or wade with naked feet along the beach just
     in the edge of the water,
Or stand under the trees in the woods,
Or talk by day with anyone I love, or sleep in
the bed at night with anyone I love,
Or sit at the table at dinner with the rest,
Or look at strangers opposite me riding in
     the ar,
Or watch honeybees busy around the hive of a
     summer forenoon,
Or animals feeding in the fields,
Or birds, or the wonderfulness of insects in
     the air,
Or the wonderfulness of the sundown, or of
stars shining so quiet and bright,
Or the exquisite delicate thin curve of the new
     moon in spring;
These with the rest, on and all, are to me
     miracles,
The whole referring, yet each distinct and in
     its place.
To me every hour of the light and dark is a
     miracle,
Every cubic inch of space is a miracle,
Every square yard of the surface of the earth is
     spread with the same,
Every foot of the interior swarms with the
     same.
To me the sea is a continual miracle,
The fishes that swim–the rocks–the motion of
the waves–the ships with men in them,
What stranger miracles are there?

Indent a line if it runs over.

2–2.5″ margins on both sides

2–2.5″ margins on both sides

Single-spaced poem (unless otherwise directed by publisher's guidelines)

PART III: MINDING YOUR BUSINESS

CHAPTER 22

EXPANDING YOUR OPTIONS: FREELANCING FOR CORPORATIONS

The health care industry in America spends an eight-figure number every year on printed materials. The auto industry spends nearly as much. Retailers, beverage makers, computer companies, and telecommunications firms spend billions more. "Printed material" includes brochures, newsletters, catalogs, signage, instruction manuals, press releases, speeches, new home descriptions, or employee handbooks. These days it also includes website copy, online catalogs, e-mail newsletters, online tutorials, and other electronic writing—media that are fast overtaking their traditional printed counterparts. Words are everywhere we look, and someone has to write them—which gives freelance writers an endless number of markets.

Few writers set out to become corporate copywriters, technical writers, copy editors, or ghostwriters—the tracks we discuss in this chapter. Many fall into it as a way to supplement their spotty earnings as they await a breakthrough in their own creative writing. Most discover that the corporate writing pays many times more, and is easier to break into, than creative writing. Many also find the work satisfying and varied as well as lucrative—and the hours can't be beat. Writers who work from home and can set their own schedule get used to the freedom and flexibility that comes from a freelance career. Once they are well established, they can work as much or as little as they want, depending on whether they need more money or more time. Corporate freelancing can be a marvelously elastic career path.

The trick is to find the right buyer for your work. Fortunately the opportunities have never been greater. Corporations of every type are finding that hiring freelancers cuts overhead costs. They can hire freelancers only when needed instead of hiring an employee who may be idle during slow work periods. Through e-mail, videoconferencing, and other developments, technology enables freelance writers to interact with any company regardless of location.

FINDING YOUR OWN OPPORTUNITIES

Savvy freelancers keep tabs on the local business scene to find out about new businesses in town or changes in existing businesses, such as new ownership or expansion, that may indicate a need for freelance help. As with any area of business, networking is crucial when looking for corporate assignments.

Call or e-mail all writing-related professional organizations in your area and join the active ones. The Association for Women in Communications, the Public Relations Society of

America, the International Association of Business Communicators, the Society for Technical Communication—many of these national organizations may have branches in your area. Most of them publish directories of their members, often listing the member's place of employment. This gives you an automatic contact—especially if you've involved yourself in the social networking system these organizations encourage.

Take a look at the business community in your area: Who are the ten or twenty biggest employers? The website of your local community can give you this information. Keep your eyes and ears open for listings of all kinds: Search them out in business newspapers, papers by the Chamber of Commerce or tourism bureau, and directories of every type.

To get an idea of just how far you can take this game of "who needs writers?" try this exercise today: Take a conscious look around you at written copy wherever you are—a calendar that has photo captions, signs on the backs of benches or high up on billboards, corporate websites, catalogs, alumni donation appeals, even your junk mail. These were all written by someone, somewhere, who presumably collected a paycheck for his trouble. Of course, not all of these were written by freelancers, but it's safe to assume that any of them could have been. There are few communications areas left that exclude work-for-hire as a possibility. Sometimes, you will be alerted to the need for a professional writer by the absence of good copy. Anyone who has ever laughed at terribly written real estate listings has to wonder how much better the listing could be—and how much more quickly a house might sell—if a trained writer had been hired to play up the right features.

It's usually not practical to be a freelance generalist and hire yourself out for any kind of writing. As with most professions, specialization is the key to success. In fact, before you approach any organization, learn everything you can about its history, culture, products or services, and customer base. Only then can you find your niche and successfully sell yourself as the right person for the job.

Once you've located organizations that might need your help, send a cover letter with a good sales pitch, a short bio, and writing samples to the appropriate person in the communications, public relations, or marketing department. Make sure you send your material to a specific person and that you've spelled her name correctly. It's fine, and may actually be preferable, to use e-mail.

The person to contact at some of the larger companies and organizations may go by any number of titles. She may be a director of publications, corporate communications, or public relations. If the company has a sophisticated operation, it may have borrowed the term creative services director from the advertising industry, particularly if it uses both print and audiovisual media. It may also be the marketing director or the director of human services.

When you do find work, be sure to get everything in writing. The amount of detail will vary with the complexity and size of the project. At the very least, make sure the assignment, deadline, and payment terms are clearly outlined in a letter of agreement. In the business world especially, these kinds of agreements are a sign of professionalism and are appreciated on all sides.

ADVERTISING AND PR

One way to sell your writing is to target the kind of company that depends on writers and may frequently use freelance writers: advertising and public relations firms. These are the experts to whom many companies turn for help in developing their various communications-related projects. In fact, if you go to a company on your own to vie for a freelance assignment, you may compete against advertising and PR agencies. But for now, let's look at how to get an assignment from such a firm and the advantages of selecting this route.

The biggest advantage to freelancing through an advertising or PR agency is that the agency finds the clients; all you have to do is complete the work. This can be attractive if you tire of freelance hustling, especially if you can become a regular in an agency's stable of freelancers. You may assure yourself a steady source of income, and if it's a quality firm, you enhance your own reputation by association.

If you already have some experience with a specific kind of assignment (you've designed and written brochures in your last job) or you're well grounded in a certain area of expertise (you're a volunteer or a past employee in an organization that caters to senior citizens), sell yourself as an expert in this area.

There are two main reasons public relations firms might hire freelance help. Sometimes special expertise is needed, such as in writing about engineering, medicine, or accounting. Secondly, because they must produce a large volume of collateral material, firms sometimes find themselves in need of freelance help when the workload gets too heavy, such as during a special project, time of year, or the summer months when regular staff go on vacation. This collateral material can take the form of a postcard, a brochure, or even a direct-mail piece. Sometimes a company will be looking for someone who can creatively shepherd a project from conceptualization to production. Other times they may only need simple copywriting.

In addition to corporations, here are some other possibilities to consider:

- **Hospital freelance writers.** Federal cutbacks and outside competition have forced many hospitals to walk a financial tightrope while producing even more written copy. It's no coincidence that hospitals have increased their use of freelancers to supplement or take the place of in-house employees.

- **Grant writers.** Some nonprofits, especially arts organizations, can no longer afford to have in-house grant writers. If you have grant-writing experience and skill, you could be very marketable indeed in the nonprofit sector.

- **Speechwriters.** Freelancers with skill in speechwriting are especially in demand. Executives don't hire speechwriters the way a politician does. Someone from the public relations department is usually assigned the job on top of her normal duties. As a freelancer, speechwriting may be something you can do a few times a year, along with numerous other assignments. So if you have a particular knack for speechwriting, serve it up as an area of expertise.

Books

102 Ways to Make Money Writing 1,500 Words or Less by I.J. Schecter. This guide has an extensive section on corporate writing.

The Wealthy Writer: How to Earn a Six-Figure Income as a Freelance Writer (No Kidding!) by Michael Meanwell. Meanwell reveals how to launch a freelance career—and be successful at it long-term. The book includes case studies and sample documents.

The Well-Fed Writer: Financial Self-Sufficiency as a Freelance Writer in Six Months or Less by Peter Bowerman. With an engaging style, Bowerman discusses different kinds of corporate freelance jobs (brochures, ad copy, etc.), writers' rates, dealing with difficult clients, finding new clients, and more.

Professional Organizations

American Marketing Association. Has forty thousand members and provides marketing information through research, case studies, and journals that stay on top of emerging trends. www.marketingpower.com

The Association for Women in Communications. Promotes advancement of women in communication fields by recognizing excellence, advocating leadership, and positioning members at the forefront of communications. www.womcom.org

Public Relations Society of America. World's largest organization of PR professionals. Offers continuing education, information exchange forums, and more. www.prsa.org

TECHNICAL WRITING

While the goal of creative writing is to entertain and that of advertising writing is to sell, the primary goal of technical writing is the accurate transmission of information. Technical writing, then, can be described as putting complicated information into plain language in a format that is easy to understand. The tone is objective and favors content over style. (This does not mean, however, that you should present the subject in a formal, stunted style.) Above all, technical writing should be concise, complete, clear, and consistent. The best way to achieve all these is to make sure your writing is well organized.

By far the biggest area for technical writers is in the computer industry, though there are a wide variety of possible assignments, including preparation of customer letters, utility bills, owner manuals, insurance benefit packages, and even contracts (some states have "plain language" laws requiring contracts and insurance policies to be written in simple English). In any technical field, writers who can bridge the gap between engineers who design things and the customers who use them are in high demand.

Technical writers do not necessarily need formal training in the areas they cover. To the contrary, one of the greatest talents a technical writer brings to a project is the ability to take a step back from the technical details and see the subject from a different perspective than the engineers, scientists, and experts. Thus, a technical writer becomes familiar with a subject by interviewing experts, reading journals and reports, reviewing drawings, studying specifications, and examining product samples.

Technical writers themselves often shy away from the term freelance writer, preferring to be known instead as independent contractors or consultants. This probably has a lot to do with the fact that technical writers work mostly with corporations, where the term independent contractor sounds more professional. It's very important to establish and maintain a high degree of credibility when working with firms.

The number of ways to enter the technical writing field are as varied as the people entering it. If you're cold-calling large companies, you'll want to contact the manager of technical communications or manager of documentation. Local employment agencies may also be of service. The easiest way, of course, is to have been at a company full-time in the past and have all of those connections and freelance possibilities in hand when you leave to start your own business.

For this initial contact you will want to send a cover letter, resume, and some samples of your work. Be very clear about the kind of work you're seeking; although it seems counterintuitive, writers who present themselves as having particular areas of experience and expertise come across as more professional than those who claim to be generalists who can do any brand of corporate writing. Target each cover letter to the specific company in question, emphasizing its products or services, and highlighting those brochures and writing samples that are most relevant to the work you're seeking. If you're contacting the regional ballet about writing their fund-raising material, include the donor letters you penned for the cash-strapped symphony last year. If you're contacting a hospital about writing patient brochures about how to manage diabetes, send in any other clips you've written on consumer health.

What if you don't have such clips and writing samples? If you lack the experience, build a portfolio by volunteering to write material for a nonprofit organization or offer to help your colleagues prepare reports and presentations. If you are interested in pursuing this type of work, it is probably a good idea to join the Society for Technical Communication (www.stc.org), where you can network to gain contacts in the industry. Many businesses hire writers from the STC talent pool.

338

Professional Organizations

American Medical Writers Association. Provides educational sources for biomedical writers and offers networking opportunities. www.amwa.org

Council of Science Editors. Offers networking opportunities and cutting-edge information for those who work in science writing, editing, or publishing. www.councilscienceeditors.org

Society for Technical Communication. The STC supports the arts and sciences of technical writing with networking and learning opportunities. It has over fourteen thousand members and is available to anyone whose work makes technical information available. www.stc.org

Books

Handbook of Technical Writing, ninth edition by Gerald J. Alred, Charles T. Brusaw, and Walter E. Oliu. This alphabetically organized manual is an industry standard, now updated with new information on integrating visuals, handling copyright law, and addressing ethical issues.

Kaplan Technical Writing: A Resource for Technical Writers at All Levels by Diane Martinez, Tanya Peterson, Carrie Wells, Carrie Hannigan, and Carolyn Stevenson. This book teaches technical writing for user manuals, intranet teaching, and even e-mail. It's also available for download on the Amazon Kindle.

Opportunities in Technical Writing by Jay Gould. Looking to get started as a technical writer? This book teaches you how to market yourself, deepen your technical expertise, and find jobs, while also discussing career details like starting salaries and possibilities for specialization.

CATALOG COPY

Ever pick up the J. Crew catalog and wonder who writes their descriptions of stylish khakis and heather-gray sweaters? Have you ever read through the Trader Joe's catalog and wondered how they came up with such tantalizing and adventurous portrayals of avocados? Remember: Someone has to write the copy you read as you're paging through the catalogs in your mailbox. Why can't it be you?

It's not terribly difficult to break into writing catalog copy, even if you don't have any experience in advertising. You will need to start small with niche businesses and work your way up. It helps if you begin with products you know. This could mean creating a flyer for a local farmer's market or a catalog of a regional stationer—anything to get your foot in the door. Once you have some of those under your belt, you will be ready to start pitching larger accounts.

Begin with the creative director of the company you're interested in; if there is no such person, try the marketing director. Your pitch letter will need to demonstrate that (1) you have experience, (2) you already know and like their product line, and (3) you write well. Study their existing catalog or website copy to become familiar with the style in use. Every company has its own history and way of communicating its product to customers, and you want to show that you can be creative while also respecting the existing style. Note that most very large companies utilize an advertising agency for their accounts, so you may be referred to a middleman.

Catalog copywriters are kind of the original Twitterers: They have learned to make every character count. Catalog copy must be snappy and short. Most products are introduced by a quick but memorable headline that creates a feeling for the product but doesn't merely spit out the product's name (e.g., "Weekend comfort. Workweek style" for a women's oxford cloth shirt from Lands' End). This is followed by an ultra-short description of the product and its specs. More companies have gone to bullet points in recent years with the idea that people don't really read anymore—especially when they shop online.

Many catalog copywriters do "B2B" catalogs: business-to-business catalogs, rather than consumer or trade catalogs. In other words, they are helping one company sell their goods or services to another company, not directly to Joe or Jane Shopper. One of the hazards of typical B2B copy is that it can be overly technical and boring. If you can write sharp copy and be both entertaining and informative, you will get jobs.

RESOURCES

Books

88 Money-Making Writing Jobs by Robert Bly. Robert Bly claims to make $600,000 a year as a writer. Some will find this claim difficult to swallow, but the book contains great tips on starting a writing business, including suggestions for catalog copywriting.

The Complete Guide to Writing Web-Based Advertising Copy to Get the Sale: What You Need to Know Explained Simply by Vickie Taylor. Writing web-based copy is not the same skill set as writing print catalogs. Taylor discusses pitfalls to avoid and also dissects trends in Web advertising.

Start & Run a Copywriting Business by Steve Slaunwhite. This book has tips for creating your business from the ground up, including how to get clients, how and how much to bill them, and how to tackle different kinds of projects.

COPYEDITING AND PROOFREADING

The real heroes of the writing profession are the copyeditors and proofreaders who labor to make the rest of us look good. If you've ever known someone who excels at copyediting and proofreading, you know that both take real talent. For those who possess the unique ability, copyediting and proofreading can be a good source of additional income.

To get work you will almost certainly have to pass a test. To do this, study the stylebook for your chosen field or publication (most likely The Associated Press Stylebook, The Chicago Manual of Style, or the MLA Style Manual and Guide to Scholarly Publishing). Also memorize a list of most commonly misspelled words. You'll most likely out-test most of the competition.

Once you have the credentials, you're ready to start selling yourself. The traditional route, of course, is to e-mail your resume to magazines, publishing companies, newspapers—any place that routinely hires copy editors. Sometimes a more assertive approach works as well. We know one enterprising proofreader who got frustrated with a regional magazine that didn't pay nearly enough attention to apostrophes, dangling modifiers, and Oxford commas as she would wish. Photographs were mislabeled and interviewees' names were inconsistently spelled. Rather than merely getting annoyed, she sent a corrected, marked-up copy of the magazine to the editor-in-chief, offering her services as an experienced and eagle-eyed proofreader. She got freelance work from that magazine right away.

What's the Difference Between a Copy Editor and a Proofreader?

Although some people use the terms interchangeably, *copyediting* and *proofreading* are not the same. Here's the difference.

- Copyediting: The writer's direct supervisor or editor usually edits stories for content and organization. The role of the copy editor, then, is to look for additional spelling errors and typos. He may raise questions about conflicting statements and may be charged with smoothing awkward text transitions and ensuring uniform style. In some cases, a copy editor may even rewrite portions of copy to improve the flow of text or to maintain a uniform tone. A copy editor may also be expected to keep an eye out for libel. At newspapers and magazines, it is often the copy editor's job to write headlines and photo captions. Copy editors are sometimes also called upon to design pages. This may involve deciding which stories, photos, and graphics will run and which will be featured most prominently. (Before beginning any job, freelance editors should determine the level of work expected and base their fees accordingly.)

- Proofreading: Proofreaders are charged with looking for typographical and mechanical errors after all other editing is complete. A proofreader may check typeset copy word for word against a manuscript and identify any deviations. They look for misspellings, missing copy, typos, misnumbering, mislabeling, and incorrect cross-references. Proofreaders may also check copy for conformity to type specifications and ensure attractive typography by checking letter or word spacing, margins, and repetitive word breaks.

The extent to which a copy editor or proofreader must verify facts varies widely. In the past, this has traditionally been the job of a separate fact-checker. A fact-checker does not make editorial changes but simply verifies accuracy. One client may request that the fact-checker verify all statements, while another client may request the verification of addresses and trademarks only. However, cutbacks at many companies have meant that some no longer hire a separate fact-checker, so you will do yourself a favor if you can include fact-checking in your standard services.

Copy editors and proofreaders are in high demand, so if you look hard enough and are willing to start small enough you are likely to find work. Smaller newspapers frequently need help. The pay may not be great, but jobs like that can build a resume and provide an extra source of income. Keep in mind that there is plenty of copyediting and proofreading work at places other than publications. So don't overlook nonprofit organizations and big companies—any place that publishes anything.

RESOURCES

Correspondence and Online Courses

The American Copy Editors Society (www.copydesk.org). Has links to various training opportunities for people who wish to become accredited copyeditors.

Editcetera (www.editcetera.com). Offers courses in developmental editing, copyediting, proofreading, and more either in the San Francisco Bay area or via mail correspondence.

The New School Online University (www.newschool.edu/online). Offers coursework, information, class discussions, and research links all online.

University of California Berkeley Extension Online (http://learn.berkeley.edu). Has a variety of interactive courses online for professionals, including a four-course editorial track.

INDEXING

The indexes in the back of most nonfiction books are another source of income for freelance wordsmiths. While the index is sometimes the responsibility of the book's author, few actually do it themselves because frankly, it can be a royal pain. Freelance indexers hired by the author or publisher usually do the work.

There are two basic kinds of indexing:

1. Conventional indexing. To do this job, an indexer will typically receive a set of actual hardcopy page proofs, which are exact images of how pages will appear in the book, complete with page numbers. The indexer reads these proofs and compiles a list of subject headings, subheads, and the location of each key reference. Upon completing a rough draft of the index, the indexer then edits, organizes, and proofreads it.

2. Embedded indexing. Increasingly, powerful computer programs have made the old slog of hardcopy indexing obsolete. In Microsoft Word and other programs, the indexer can tag certain terms and phrases as items they want in the final index. The code for this is not visible in the printed version, but the document will automatically generate a final index with the information arranged alphabetically. The advantage of this system is that it updates the index's page numbers automatically if the author makes last-minute changes to the page proofs or if there is ever a new and expanded edition of the book.

Since indexing is one of the last steps in completing a book, indexers frequently work under intense pressure and time constraints. Indexing cannot be started until final page proofs are available. By that time the printer wants to get the job on the press and the publisher is clamoring for a finished product. As a result, skilled indexers must possess more than good language skills, attention to detail, patience, and an analytical mind—they must also be able to work well under pressure.

Probably the best way to break into the business is to send resumes with cover letters to publishers. You can find their addresses in *Literary Market Place*, *Writer's Market*, and *Books in Print*. It is hard to get established in the indexing business, but once you do get work—and do it well—it is easier to get jobs through word of mouth and a little networking.

RESOURCES

Professional Groups

The American Society for Indexing. The only professional organization in the United States devoted to the advancement of indexing. www.asindexing.org

National Federation of Abstracting and Information Services. Serves groups that aggregate, organize, and facilitate access to information. They address common interests through education and advocacy. www.nfais.org

Books

Indexing Books, second edition by Nancy C. Mulvany. Written by a professional indexer, this book covers the indexing process from start to finish. The second edition has new information about software programs and technological developments.

The Indexing Companion by Glenda Browne and Jon Jermey. This award-winning guide covers different types of indexes, how to index from PDF files, and various software programs.

GHOSTWRITING

When a book is ghostwritten, the person whose name appears on the book as primary author has done little or none of the actual writing. He is merely a source of information—providing content, background information, and, hopefully, credibility. Typically this person is a celebrity or someone well respected in his field of expertise. While he has the experience and the name recognition that can make for a best-selling book, he lacks professional writing credentials. As a result, the so-called author relies on a more experienced writer—a ghostwriter—to put his ideas into book form.

The ghostwriter gathers information for the book by interviewing the author and will often conduct her own research and interview several other sources as well for background material. While each collaboration is different, the author usually will review the manuscript and possibly even edit it for content. For their part, ghostwriters may be credited as co-authors or get no visible credit at all. (Their motivation is often a five- or six-figure check and the opportunity to get even more lucrative work either as authors or as ghostwriters.)

The arrangement that a ghostwriter walks into is inherently more complex than the typical relationship between a writer and publisher (which is complex enough). It's easy for misunderstandings to arise between the so-called author and publisher, with the ghostwriter being caught in the middle. In one sense, the ghostwriter is a translator, taking what the author has to offer and trying to deliver what the publisher expects. The best way to diffuse some of this conflict is to clearly map out in writing what each party expects from the arrangement. When all is said and done there may still be misunderstandings, but at least the ghostwriter can justify what he has done.

There are a number of ways to break into ghostwriting. One is to seek out a rising star in sports, entertainment, business, or politics. Publishers are often in search of new talent and new celebrities. Armed with a collaboration agreement and the right amount of talent, you can sell your services to a publisher.

As you gain experience and become specialized in a certain subject area, you will find it easier to sell your talents to publishers who are looking for ghostwriters in that field of expertise. Along the way you can build your resume by collaborating on magazine articles with celebrities or experts in your chosen field of specialization. Magazines do not knowingly accept ghostwritten articles, but they would accept, for instance, an article on the modern history of baseball, "as told to" John Doe.

Very often, successful executives or entrepreneurs are looking for writers who can help them self-publish a book of their own. The finished books are then distributed through their businesses to clients, co-workers, and relatives. This is a great way to get work and hone your talents, and possibly even make a name for yourself.

RESOURCES

Books

Ghostwriting: For Fun & Profit by Eva Shaw. Shaw, who has been a professional ghostwriter for thirty years, discusses breaking into the business, how to capture clients' stories, how much to charge, and how to negotiate a contract.

CHAPTER 23

A CRASH COURSE IN MARKETING & PUBLICITY

It's great to write a book, and if you've published one, either with a traditional publisher or on your own steam, you deserve congratulations. However, just because you've written it doesn't mean your work is done. In fact, it's probably not even half done in terms of the hours you should be putting in. Even if you are lucky enough to have a professional publicist assigned to your case, you are going to have to work very hard to promote it. This book can't emphasize enough how much book promotion is your responsibility—so this section has been created to show you how to get started.

After a short foray into book marketing, the bulk of this chapter deals with book publicity—as does the chapter after that. Don't wait until your book is already published to read these chapters; by then, some of the best kinds of publicity are already next to impossible.

WHAT IS MARKETING?

We're going to get book marketing out of the way first because less of it is up to you than publicity is. Although people sometimes assume that publicity and marketing are the same thing—and they are certainly complementary—they serve different functions.

In the words of Jacqueline Deval, author of *Publicize Your Book!*, marketing is, "quite simply, how to sell books as fast as possible to as many people as possible." Book marketers determine who the readers of a particular book might be—which is often the easy part—and how to reach them successfully—which is the hard part. Is your Southern novel going to appeal to middle-aged women who enjoy middlebrow contemporary Southern fiction, like fans of Anne Rivers Siddons, or are you aiming toward more of a comic chick-lit Southern audience, such as readers who enjoy Joshilyn Jackson? Are your readers liberal or conservative? Gen-Xers or baby boomers? Dog lovers, nature lovers, bikers? All of these questions are relevant. As an author, you won't be privy to most of the marketing meetings that happen on behalf of your book, but you can help your cause tremendously by having some detailed information about the potential audience in your book proposal from Day One.

Here are some issues that a marketing director at a publishing house might deal with:

- **Format and binding.** The marketing team helps to decide whether your book will be hardcover or a "paperback original" (meaning one that debuts in trade paper without a hardcover edition first). Size is also important. They might feel that a Christmas novella needs to be bound as a smaller gift book, perhaps with a ribbon marker. Size, binding, and format all help to set the tone for what type of book yours will be—and what audience will desire it.

- **Book titles.** The right title is paramount in reaching the market for your book. Although some authors resist an audience-specific, niche-oriented title, these often sell better than generic titles. For example, the book *Eat Well, Lose Weight While Breastfeeding* is not terribly catchy, but it successfully identifies its target market right off the bat: new mothers who are nursing and want to lose some of their pregnancy weight. Some titles can be funny and memorable (e.g., *Don't Just Do Something, Sit There*, a book about Zen meditation), while others are serious (e.g., Fareed Zakaria's *The Post-American World*), and still others are gently evocative, which is the case for most fiction titles (for example, *Seducing an Angel*). At a publishing house, people on a titling committee actually hold meetings to find just the right title for your book's market. The title you suggested in your book proposal may or may not be the one that winds up on the book's cover. And unless you are already famous and title approval is part of your negotiated contract, you probably won't have much say in the matter. Even if you are famous, you may still be overruled: F. Scott Fitzgerald wanted to call his third novel *Trimalchio* and was shepherded instead to the title *The Great Gatsby*. Sometimes, publishers really do know what they're doing.

- **Book covers.** The right cover is enormously important for your book. It's not just that consumers make purchasing decisions based on whether they find a cover enticing, it's that store buyers do as well. One sales representative explains that when he gets his coveted biannual meeting with the fiction buyer at a major chain, he has about thirty minutes to present the entire season's list—which may include fifteen or twenty novels. Store buyers place their orders after a cursory description of each novel and its author, along with a good look at the cover art. Needless to say, a bad cover can defeat a book before it even gets out of the gate, so publishers usually invest a good deal of time and money in getting the right design.

- **Catalog placement.** The marketing team is responsible for preparing a publishing house's seasonal and topical catalogs. Where a book goes in the catalog is often a significant indicator of its prominence on that season's list. The most important books tend to appear at the front of the catalog (or at the beginning of that month's releases, if the catalog is in chronological order), and the oldest books—the backlist—appear in the back. (Get it?)

- **Advertising.** Whether, where, and when to advertise is a nagging question for folks in the marketing department. National book ads are very expensive—thousands of dollars for a small black-and-white placement in *The New York Times* or *The New Yorker*, and many thousands more for a fifteen-second recurring spot on NPR, for example. As it happens,

347

many studies have shown that ads are one of the least consistent or effective ways of selling books. Many ads don't give enough of a sense of the book for its target audience to get excited. Some of the more useful (and cheaper) advertising is actually done in niche publications, like small magazines that target a particular demographic. An ad for a new book about Google's founding is more likely to appeal to the specialized readers of *Wired* than it is to all of the readers of the *San Francisco Chronicle*.

- **In-store placement.** Ever walked into a Borders or a Barnes & Noble and gotten immediately sidetracked by the new or recommended books on the front table? Ever thought, "Hey! This book must be outstanding if it was recommended by the smart people who work at this store"? Well, the truth is that those books actually got "table placement" because their publishers paid for them to be there for a limited period of time, not because a chain store buyer actually read them and thought they were brilliant. That also goes for whether a book is placed on an endcap (an end-of-row display) or a specialized table further back in the store (for example, "holiday reads" or "book club favorites"). One of the discussions that goes on in the marketing department up to a year in advance is whether to pony up the considerable cash (at least four figures, and often five) that is required for advantageous store placement. Along the same lines, they discuss whether to get a book into stores such as airport shops, which charge publishers for placement on the shelves.

YOUR MARKETING PLAN

Although you will not be in control of most marketing decisions, especially the ones regarding store placement, catalog placement, and advertising plans, you can and should take the lead in establishing the audience for your book. Do this as early as the book proposal, where you will lay out exactly what the target audience can be and where to find them. Throughout the process, keep the marketing team alert for niche opportunities they might not normally hear about. For example, one author of a book about Buffy the Vampire Slayer got hooked into Slayage, the online international journal of Whedon Studies, and learned that there would be the first-ever "Buffy Studies" conference right around the time her book was launching. Once she notified her publishing house, the marketing and publicity people got together to actually launch the book at that conference, where the author was a featured speaker. Due to the uniqueness of a "Buffy Studies" conference (yes, there really is such a thing), some major media, including CNN, covered the gathering and interviewed the author. It was a super launch to the book and couldn't have happened if the author had not alerted the publishing house to this unusual opportunity.

You know your book better than anyone, and you should be able to come up with a list of niche publications, conferences, and organizations that could help sell your book. Stay in touch with the marketing director throughout the prepublication months and be sure to let her know about any sales leads you have.

WHAT IS PUBLICITY?

Remember when we quoted from Jacqueline Deval's statement that marketing is trying to sell as many books as fast as possible to as many people as possible? Well, the role of publicity is to help people know about those books and their authors. Whereas much of marketing is paid for by the publisher—advertising, the right placement in the store, the perfect cover—publicity is aimed at getting free media coverage. Well, it's sort of free. Authors can't simply pay journalists to interview them, but getting their attention can take a lot of expert time and follow-up, so in that sense good publicity can be costly indeed. Here are some helpful things to remember about publicity:

- Advertising is not publicity. As we learned in the marketing section, when you see a commercial on television, or a book ad in the incredible shrinking book pages of America's newspapers, someone paid for those—usually the company that is pushing the product. In the case of books, that's usually the publisher, though sometimes the author digs deep into his pockets and buys ad time. Although it's a great stroke to authors' egos to see their books advertised in prominent places so their family and friends can see them (as well as any high school bullies who once taunted them), advertising is actually a weak way to generate interest in books. Book consumers are smart people. People who buy books know where advertising comes from, who pays for it, and why it exists. They've seen ads for plenty of books that turned out to be a waste of trees, so they're not usually going to buy a book just because of an ad. The best that an ad can do is create what's called an impression, and it actually can take several of these before something might actually register on a consumer's radar.

- The best publicity campaigns succeed in generating word of mouth. After a book's cover design, the second most effective means of driving sales is word-of-mouth recommendations. Basically, this means that the book needs to be fodder for general conversations:

TED: "Did you hear Thomas Friedman on *The Daily Show* last night? That's the book I was recommending to you about climate change."

CINDY: "I sure did, and after work I'm going out to buy his book!"

Most people trust the opinions of their friends, moms, spouses, and colleagues about what is good to read. And as we just learned, sometimes it takes multiple "impressions" of a product before consumers are ready to actually buy: In the above example, Ted had already told Cindy that *Hot, Flat, and Crowded* was a book she would enjoy, so she was predisposed to listen to the author when she was channel surfing one night and found him chatting with Jon Stewart. Ted's mentioning it to her the next day was a third "impression," and for Cindy, the third time was the charm. Publicity (in the form of an author interview on national television) worked hand-in-hand with grassroots word of mouth to close the deal. The goal of a publicist is to garner enough media coverage to get people talking about a book and recommending it.

- Publicity capitalizes heavily on what is in the news. One of the genius aspects of publicity is its timeliness. In the Thomas Friedman example above, we know that *Hot, Flat, and Crowded* became a *New York Times* bestseller, but timing played a role in that success. The book released in September of 2008, just after the highest-ever spike in gasoline prices to around $4.50 a gallon and just before the election of President Barack Obama. Everyone was talking about energy, oil, the Middle East, and politics; the situation was perfect for Friedman's book. Good publicity works in tandem with the news and helps connect potential readers with books that can help them understand timely issues. Of course, this works most seamlessly for nonfiction, but savvy fiction authors do it, too, connecting their novels to items in the headlines. (Sometimes novelists also succeed when people long to get away from the news: In late 2008, during the worst economic recession in half a century, sales at Harlequin, the nation's largest romance publisher, rose 9 percent.)

PUBLICIZING YOUR BOOK

As you can see, it's your job to create the kind of word-of-mouth discussions that can drive sales of your book. Success as a writer often depends on speeches, book signings, newsletters, blog posts, TV appearances, radio interviews, websites, visits to groups, campus talks, and more. Who else knows your book better? Who else is as dedicated to its success? Who else can talk about it as ardently?

In fact, even though you may have a wonderfully written nonfiction book, oftentimes, good writing isn't all that is needed to make it a success. How much you are willing to talk about your book is essential because many publishers are not able to give each book the promotional attention

350

it needs to make it a success. That is up to you, the writer. If you have a book with a wide national audience, the promotion plan is equally, if not more important, than the actual contents of the book. Even well-known authors go on the road, give talks, and do interviews to promote their works. Writers reconize that self-promotion is a technique as much a part of writing success as knowing the difference between active and passive voice.

Speak Up

While public speaking is frightening to some writers, it is important to take advantage of any opportunity that allows you to speak about your work to an audience. Not only should you be willing to speak when asked, but you should also seek out speaking opportunities. Speaking gives you the chance to create excitement about your work in a personal way. You are forming a memorable relationship with the audience if you are prepared and enthusiastic. Getting to hear about an author and his work firsthand will prompt many people in an audience to be interested in your book. They will also be likely to tell someone else about it. If you can walk away with even just a handful of people interested in your book, you have created more potential sales than would have otherwise occurred.

Be imaginative about what groups to address. You'll know some of the best venues in your own area, but there are general resources around to help you. The Encyclopedia of Associations, available at libraries, is a compendium of organizations around the world. It can help you find audiences. If you write about nursing, for example, you can find dozens of nursing associations, each of which may have newsletters for members and meetings where you may be permitted to give a presentation. Look up local businesses, churches, and groups that may agree to let you promote your work to their members.

When you speak, it helps to use visual aids. Whitney Otto created a slide show to promote *The Passion Dream Book*, a novel that explores the relationship between art and the lives of artists. The slides also helped her add originality to her tour and broaden it to include libraries and art schools. Visuals are a great way to make your presentation more interesting and engaging, and even more importantly, more memorable.

Go Visit

Remember, part of your job as a writer is also to be a publicist. One way to publicize and promote is to make a point of visiting local bookstores to meet the staff and talk about your book. If bookstore staff know you, they're more likely to put your book in the window (if they get to decide which books belong there). They also may be more likely to recommend your book to customers interested in your topic because your book will stand out in their minds above the others.

Jeanne M. Dams used the *Deadly Directory*, which she calls an indispensable reference for mystery writers, to find mystery bookstores. (Unfortunately, that publication closed in 2008 by the brutal economy.) Dams visited every store within driving distance to supplement the book tour arranged by her publisher. "Even when I drew very few people, I established a personal relationship with the bookseller," she says. "That really matters because mystery bookstores hand-sell their books."

If your publisher doesn't spring for book tours (and few will), don't be afraid to plan your own. Some writers have combined book tours with family vacations, hauling the kids and sometimes even the dog along as they traverse the country. Libraries and bookstores often welcome visiting authors who wish to speak or give readings; call or e-mail several months in advance of your planned visit to set things up. E-mail a JPEG or PDF of a flyer about your visit and ask the library or bookstore to please post it widely in the community two to three weeks beforehand.

Once you plan your tour, send a news release to media outlets in every city you'll visit, then follow up with a phone call before you arrive. This will help you get some media coverage and publicity. Remember that you primarily are responsible for getting people to attend signings and readings. Such events succeed or fail based on the author's ability to mobilize her own network.

News Releases

If your publisher doesn't do it for you, write a news release and send it to your media and to any other publication or electronic news organization you want to visit. If you've written a speech, it should be easy to adapt into a brief news release, focusing on whatever major aspect of your work is most useful to a general audience. For tips on how to do this, see Jodee Blanco's *The Complete Guide to Book Publicity*.

Send your release to the editor of the appropriate department at a newspaper, and also to the book editor if the newspaper employs one. For example, releases about books on management go to the business editor; those on relationships go to the features editor. Send your release to the producer of any TV shows you are pitching.

Radio and Television

In some ways, radio is a medium made for authors. You get the chance to talk about your book and even read aloud from it, which is one of the strongest ways to hook a reader. You also may get the opportunity to interact with readers and potential readers who call in to a radio show to ask questions of the author. And you don't even have to worry about how you look! Seek out radio opportunities whenever you can; if you feel nervous, begin with a few podcasting forays as described.

Directories such as Bradley's *Guide to the Top National TV Talk & Interview Shows*, *Talk Shows and Hosts on Radio*, or *Talk Show Selects* also are helpful in finding hosts on radio and television. Television demands different skills than radio or print interviews, because your appearance is critical. If you're going to be on a TV show and can't afford a media coach, try role playing an interview and then watching a tape of it. Are any of your mannerisms distracting? Are your answers clear? Can you speak in sound bites of thirty seconds or so? Is your voice expressive? Are you entertaining? And, despite all those questions, do you seem relaxed?

Television can be an intimidating medium, so it's best to start small with your local cable station. Your chances of scheduling a TV interview will be better with a local station, and it won't be as overwhelming. These stations aren't as hectic and will be able to make you feel more comfortable about your experience. They may be more encouraging because they know you are a beginner. Knowing that the audience for these stations is smaller should also help to calm some of your public speaking fears.

If you're still intimidated and can afford it, consider hiring a media coach, who can help you learn how to do interviews. Don't feel like this is necessary, though, because as long as you are passionate about your topic, even if you aren't perfect, you will still be successful.

Write

Another way to promote your work involves writing about it. You are already a writer, so this avenue should appeal to you.

- Newsletters can be highly effective ways of finding and keeping readers, especially as you build a career over many years. You could do your own newsletter or team up with other writers you know who are looking to promote their work as well. Jeanne Dams and three other mystery writers, Barbara D'Amato, Hugh Holton, and Mark Zubro, started a newsletter to promote their books. They started their mailing list by asking their publishers to slip a postcard for a subscription into their books. They mail their newsletter to anyone who responds to the postcard, in addition to anyone they think might be interested. Into it goes an article by each author, mystery quizzes, even recipes for foods mentioned in their books. Most importantly, the newsletter always includes a list of the authors' appearances and their books in print. It can be a time-consuming and expensive promotional tool, but if you team up with other authors, you can split the costs and still reap the rewards.

- Instead of mailing print newsletters, consider doing an e-mail newsletter. The cost for this is significantly less. If you have a website or blog (which you should; see the following chapter), you can add a link asking people to subscribe to your free e-mail newsletter. Include information about your books, appearances, and anything else that might interest people who enjoy your work or the topics you write about.

- Op-ed pieces are another great way for writers to build enthusiasm for a book, especially with more serious nonfiction, where an author's expertise is a critical component of selling the book.

Network

Everyone was a beginner once, and many successful authors remember how difficult it was to become established. These authors are often a tremendous resource to beginners. The book you're reading now wouldn't exist without the generosity of writers, agents, and editors who took time to share their expertise.

Joining a writers association and attending writers conferences can help you learn how to write and sell your work, but more importantly, these networks help you meet people who may be able to help you—and whom you may be able to help. You must be sincerely willing to help others and unafraid to ask for help yourself. You never know what someone else is willing to do for you until you ask.

Writers' groups also can help their members promote their work. C.J. Songer, author of the Meg Gillis crime novel series, used a list published by Sisters in Crime, a group for mystery writers, to reach independent bookstores. Through the group, she also bought a discounted ad in *Publishers Weekly*. "Although it was a fair amount of money, *Bait* was my first-ever book and it was a treat to myself," Songer says. Because she had taken that ad, she also earned a discount on a promotional page for her book on the *Publishers Weekly* website. "It was very gratifying to be able to go online and see my own book, plus it was accessible for family and friends (and acquaintances) all across the country," she says.

Networking is infinitely easier now in the age of social media, which we cover in the next chapter. Online affinity groups and public forums like Facebook have made it easier than ever to reach thousands of like-minded readers with a single click.

RESOURCES

The Complete Guide to Book Publicity by Jodee Blanco. This book is actually geared for professional publicists, teaching them how to pitch to the media, find multiple story angles for the same book, and handle PR disasters. But authors should read it, too, to learn how publicists think and glean ideas for successful book promotion.

Get Known Before the Book Deal: Use Your Personal Strengths to Grow an Author Platform by Christina Katz. This excellent book focuses on the platform-building and networking that happen before you even submit a book proposal to an editor or agent. Much of the advice is also applicable to the crucial months just before and after your book is published.

Publicize Your Book!: An Insider's Guide to Getting Your Book the Attention It Deserves by Jacqueline Deval. This how-to guide puts authors in the driver's seat and empowers them to create pitches, develop a press kit, prepare for interviews, and more. The author also has a helpful website at www.publicizeyourbook.com.

CHAPTER 24

WEBSITES, BLOGS, PODCASTS, & SOCIAL NETWORKING

Let's take a little walk through literary history, shall we? It used to be that authors' main connection with readers, if it existed at all, was through touring and correspondence. In the nineteenth century, famous novelists like Charles Dickens and Mark Twain went on tour, often for months at a time, filling great lecture halls and taking questions from readers. In the twentieth century, with the advent of radio and then television, authors could communicate with thousands or even millions of readers at a time through interviews and readings on the air. This was an enormous leap forward for book publicists, who worked tremendously hard to maximize exposure for authors and get them booked on the most popular programs.

Now, however, it is the twenty-first century, and the rules are changing once again. According to Penny Sansevieri, author of *Red Hot Internet Publicity*, the advent of blogs and podcasts has meant that "the TV programs we would have traded a kidney for in the past are not even skimming the surface of the media that really drives readers to books, and consequently, to sales." Nowadays the Internet has brought us an unprecedented democratization in how books are publicized.

What makes the difference is peer groups: Whereas traditional print, TV, and radio publicity hit a broad audience in a shallow way, these new online media target a narrower audience in a deeper way. Blogs, podcasts, and social networks tap into word-of-mouth book recommendations, which have always been a powerful means of driving sales. Potential customers who might just breeze by an ad or even a well-placed radio interview will give serious thought to buying a book that's recommended by a blogger they trust or given five stars on www.goodreads.com by people they trust.

What's marvelous about the Internet is that it has the potential to link you directly to like-minded readers who might be interested in your book. You have the chance to get direct access to your target audience. And best of all, it's basically free.

YOUR WEBSITE

Five years ago, it was enough for an author just to have a nicely designed, professional-quality website. It was the end-all destination, with an author biography, a page for each book the author had to her credit, and maybe a few links to media articles.

Nowadays, you need to change the way you think about your author website. It is no longer a destination or end goal, but a portal. As Internet publicity has exploded, a website has become a starting point in driving sales, but it is not the last word. Here are some things your website might have:

- A place to buy. The fanciest author sites allow customers to buy the book right from the site, but this can be difficult and expensive to do. Others link directly to Amazon.com through the Amazon Associates program so customers can click through to buy the book, and the author gets a small kickback from the sale.

- A very obvious connection to your blog. Some writers make the front page of their website be their blog; others prefer to have the "official" site be more formal but have a clear place where visitors can click to get to the regularly updated blog. We'll explore blogging in a moment, but for now just know that if you decide to have a blog, you need to integrate it seamlessly with your author website.

- A clear connection to your podcast, if you have one.

- A place to sign up for your e-mail newsletter. As we saw in the last chapter, an electronic newsletter (preferably HTML and not just text) can be a great way to communicate with your readers. Make sure your website is designed to capture the names and e-mail addresses of readers who want to keep abreast of your writing and speaking engagements.

- Links to related sites. Add links to other websites that will be relevant to anyone interested in your work. If you write about science, for example, include links to scientific websites.

BUILDING YOUR WEBSITE

If you don't already have a website, you need to reserve your domain name immediately. Preferably, this is your own name as it will appear on all your books (e.g., www.AmyMarie-Author.com). If that domain name has been taken, either by another person with your same name or an entrepreneurial computer program that is looking to make a buck, you need to decide what to do. If you haven't published your first book yet, change your author name. Seriously. Use a pen name or another version of your real name (James instead of Jim, Kathy and not Katherine) if your name's site has already been taken, or try your first and middle initials with your last name. If that's not an option, you can try to buy the real domain name from the current user.

Once you have registered a domain name, it's time to build your site. Most authors tend to hire a professional for this; a clunky, unprofessional, or ugly site is actually worse than having no site at all. If you can't afford to hire an experienced web designer, try a student, whose rates will be much cheaper. If you can't afford to hire a student, you can go it alone with template software and then upgrade the site after your career is better established. Remember that the website is a portal, not a destination, so your links are crucial. So whether you hire a designer or try the DIY method, make sure your site is accessible and interactive.

SEO: Search Engine Optimization

It's great to set up a beautiful website, but what if you build it and they don't come? What if it's like that old Brady Bunch episode where Peter throws himself a hero party and none of his friends show up?

That's why you have to let technology work for you—to invite others to your party. You can do this through SEO (search engine optimization). Try a little experiment right now and Google yourself. (Yes, it seems immodest, but it's really okay.) Ideally, what you want to find on the first page of the Google search results, in roughly this order, are:

1. Your book's website or author website.

2. The Amazon.com page for your book so these prospects can easily "convert" into becoming paying customers.

3. Various media interviews or blog reviews of your book.

If your book isn't out yet, or you don't even have a publisher yet, you're not going to see those last two items, but you at least want your author site to be one of the top things that comes up whenever someone Googles your name. If you are already published, you will probably also see some library results, too, plus any op-eds you've written about your topic (you have been working on those, right?).

You'll probably notice that your author site will slowly climb the Google rankings in the weeks surrounding your book's release, especially if your site has an active blog. You can actually use your blog to generate a higher Google ranking by linking, linking, linking. For more tips on optimizing your Google ranking, go to www.smartzville.com/google-homepage.htm. One key element of success, especially for nonfiction, is getting your name so associated with your topic so your name comes up very high on the list when someone Googles your topic. There are many ways to do this: by writing and blogging so often about the topic that other people link to your page, which will help your Google ranking; by getting multiple media interviews about your topic; and by focusing on popular keywords and metatags on your site.

BLOGGING

If you are serious about your writing—and especially if you plan a career in this rather than just one book—you need to create a blog. A blog, short for *weblog*, can be anything from a public diary about your life to a running commentary about a specific topic: figure skating, science fiction movies, celebrity gossip, whatever interests you. There's even a wildly popular blog devoted to cakes gone wrong, where every day the owner posts photos of a different cake disaster.

As an author, your blog needs to be devoted to things that are relevant to your book. Now, listen up for a very important distinction (which will also come into play in this chapter's section on podcasting): The sole purpose of your blog cannot be to advertise yourself or your books.

People lose interest very quickly when they feel they're being subjected to an endless round of "Look at me!" promotions.

What people want instead is good information. If they've looked you up and have thought about buying your book, it's because they're interested in the topic you write about (for nonfiction) or the genre you write in (for fiction). As an example, let's take the hypothetical case of a popular romance novelist we'll call Amara Love. Amara updates her blog about five times a week with fresh content, sometimes discussing trends in the romance writing business, sometimes revealing where she is with a forthcoming book, sometimes making movie recommendations for the latest romantic comedy to hit theaters. She has book giveaways every once in a while to drive traffic to her site (both her own novels and other favorite writers), and she takes reader questions all the time by publicly answering some of the e-mails she receives via the "Contact Ce" button on the blog.

Some novelists have taken blogging a step further by actually blogging as their characters. Meg Cabot, author of the YA Princess Diaries series, blogs in the voice of Princess Mia at www.miathermopolis.com. Teen readers love the free extra content they're getting via the blog, and the blog helps document Mia's life in real time as teens are experiencing it themselves: spring break, summer break, holidays, etc. You don't have to go to the extreme of blogging as a character, but you do need to create a community and give useful information.

Getting Started

From a tech standpoint, blogging is quite easy. While we suggest hiring a real web designer for your author portal site, even a neophyte can create a blog in about half an hour using the templates on Blogger, TypePad, or WordPress. You'll pay some sites a monthly fee for administration, though others are free and offer free templates online. Some authors have a blog professionally designed, and if you can afford this, knock yourself out. But know that you don't have to unless you expect the audience for your book to be exceptionally tech savvy.

The things your blog must have are links, contact information, and a tagline up top that succinctly describes what your blog is about. A tagline could be "There's an App for That" for an iPhone-news related blog, or "Cats Say the Darndest Things" if you wrote a book about how felines communicate and want your blog to be a meeting place for fellow cat lovers.

TEN HOT TIPS FOR YOUR NEW BLOG

1. Be sure to enable "trackbacks," which will help to drive traffic to your site. Also, set it up so your posts are stamped with the date so readers will be able to recognize fresh content.

2. When you post, learn how to link to almost anything you can—other blogs in your field, the pages of books and movies you write about in your posts, or articles

you find interesting. Every time you do this, you help Google to "spider" your blog. On the Internet, a spider is actually a good thing: It's a web of incoming and outgoing links, all of which help to drive up your Google ranking and generate traffic.

3. Let friends, family, and acquaintances know about your new blog. If they are bloggers, politely ask if they would mind linking to your blog from theirs. These incoming links are even more valuable for your blog's Google ranking than your outgoing ones.

4. Allow reader comments. Sometimes authors worry about editorial control issues with blog comments, but as the site's owner you can choose to remove any individual comments if they should ever be offensive. Ninety-nine percent of comments should be welcome, though, so open the doors!

5. Don't be afraid to be opinionated. Some of the liveliest blog discussions happen when you take issue with something or persuasively express a strong opinion. Always be respectful, however.

6. Periodically search Google for your blog's topic, and follow those links to other people's blogs. If they are discussing something you have just posted about, leave a comment about their discussion and also a link to your own blog. This is a great way to find blog readers who are already interested in your topic.

7. Try to blog five to seven times a week. You can do this by keeping your posts short (say, 200 to 500 words) and by having some of your posts simply link to articles and questions under discussion. You can also invite guest bloggers to write or post interviews with other people in your field. If doing multiple posts a week is unrealistic, commit to blogging twice a week on the same days—say, Monday and Thursday. You will build more of a following when readers know when to expect your new posts.

8. Make sure you enable "pinging" with each blog post. This is what alerts blog directories that you have published a new post.

9. Allow your blog to utilize RSS (really simple syndication), which is a subscriber feed that people can sign up for when they're interested in your blog. This alerts readers automatically whenever you've updated your content.

10. Have a contest or giveaway every few months. You can hold trivia contests, haiku competitions, whatever you like. Readers who normally "lurk" (read but don't comment) will come out of the woodwork when there's free merchandise on the table.

Websites, Blogs, Podcasts, & Social Networking

The Secret, Most Important Reason Why You Should Blog

Still not convinced you need to start a blog? Here's the real reason why you must, especially if you are a nonfiction author trying to establish yourself as an expert on some topic: A blog is now the expected vehicle through which members of the media will find sources. Not only will they cyberstalk you on your own author website and blog, they will also monitor how often your book and blog are mentioned on other people's blogs using services like Technorati (www.technorati .com). How often other people cite you as an expert or favorably review your book increases your stature in the eyes of the media.

Journalists also trawl blogs to get a feel for how hot a topic is, which is one of the reasons you want to encourage comments on your blog. They often want to see how so-called ordinary people might be experiencing a particular topic. For example, if you've just written a book about a double-digit fall in housing prices, a journalist will be interested to see that forty people have commented on your most recent post about new housing legislation, some of them sharing personal tales of foreclosure.

Be sure to have a "Contact Me" button on your blog. Your e-mail address won't be on it for readers, so it's one-way communication and you don't have to worry about mad fans showing up at your house. (As if.)

Remember that for members of the media, time is of the essence. They might only have a couple of hours before they need to turn in their copy or book a radio interview for the end-of-day rush hour, and they're going to want to hear back from you right away. If you're lucky enough to have generated media interest, don't blow it by not checking your messages. Arrange to have the "Contact Me" messages from your blog sent to an e-mail account you check several times a day.

MANAGING THE FLOW—MAKE THAT AVALANCHE—OF INFORMATION

Many writers complain that they just don't have the time to blog or follow other people's blogs, and it's true that the blogosphere can be an enormous time sink. To help you manage the flow of information, sign up for Google Reader, a tool that customizes your blog reading and keeps you up-to-date with new posts from other people. (www. google.com/reader)

With Google Reader, and other services like it, you can subscribe to any blog you like or want to keep up with, and it will customize a sort of home page for you and chart which posts you have and have not read. You don't have to click on each post to go to it; the posts appear right on Google Reader so you can quickly scroll through them. It's like having a personalized newspaper just for you.

PODCASTING

It's safe to say that many successful authors are now blogging and that blogging is all but required if you want to have a strong career and regular interaction with readers. Admittedly, that's not yet the case with podcasting, which hasn't yet hit the mainstream author community as strongly (yet), but is still a powerful tool for you as an author. So think of it as an optional, but potentially influential, path for you. If you are already a talented oral communicator and feel comfortable in chatty conversation, a podcast may be just the ticket.

What Is a Podcast?

A podcast is a new-fashioned kind of radio show. It's all on the Internet, and listeners can either hear the show online or download it to their MP3 players or iPods. One advantage of podcasting is that the start-up costs are quite low and you don't have to worry about attracting advertisers. (Though you can certainly sell ads if you want to.) You do have to worry about attracting listeners, though. A podcast isn't like a traditional radio show where some listeners just stumble onto the content because it happens to be on the air. With podcasting, listeners have to know to look for your show.

Luckily, that is getting easier all the time as podcasting becomes more mainstream. You can syndicate your podcast through a site like Google FeedBurner (http://feedburner.google.com), which works like a blog's RSS feed in alerting your listeners whenever there's a new episode of your show.

Unlike blogging, which is easy to set up, podcasting requires a little more technical expertise. You're going to need either an external microphone for your computer or a site like AudioAcrobat (www.audioacrobat.com), which permits you to record your show by phone or via Skype from anywhere in the world. (Skype is an online service that allows users to make phone calls and conduct video conferences, often for free, over the Internet. See www.skype.com.)

What Kind of Podcast?

You may be wondering what a good podcast might sound like. Really, the Skype's the limit (pun intended); think of your podcast like an audio blog. There are as many different kinds of podcasts as there are authors, but here are three basic types.

1. The interview podcast. This is the one that most closely resembles a traditional radio show. Say you've written a book about minor league baseball. Your weekly podcast might involve interviews with present and former minor league players, umpires, fans, and the like. You'd be surprised how easy it is to get guests on your podcast, especially if you give them a good idea of what to expect and keep the interview under fifteen minutes. (By the way, always encourage your guests to link to the podcast on their own sites and blogs to help drive traffic to your podcast.)

2. The commentary podcast. This is a talking-heads type show, where you are the expert giving commentary on your topic. For example, in the minor league baseball example

above, you would offer opinions on new draft picks, spring training observations, bad umpire calls, and the like. Be sure to keep it short and have the length of your podcasts be fairly consistent. Ten to twenty minutes of commentary is plenty.

3. The call-in podcast. From a technical standpoint this is the hardest type of show to produce, because you have to worry about the audio quality not only for yourself and your guest but also for the callers, but it's potentially the most riveting in terms of interactions with interested callers.

As you've probably noticed, there's no law that says your podcast can't combine these elements. Some of the most compelling shows are the ones that mix your opinion and your guests' expertise with your callers' questions, *Talk of the Nation* style.

Be creative but consistent with your content; you are building a brand, and listeners should know what to expect. Link to your podcast from your website and/or blog. Ask listeners and blog readers which guests they would like to hear you interview or which issues they'd like to have you cover. Remember: It's all about community.

SOCIAL NETWORKING

If blogging and podcasting are steps toward building a community, social networking is like an enormous potluck: You never quite know who is bringing what or how many people will be there, but you're pretty much guaranteed to get a good meal.

Social networking is still recent enough that many people are just learning the ropes, and no one is quite sure of the best methods for using it to sell books. This means that authors have a great opportunity ahead as they try different things to see what works with their particular audience. In this section we'll explore three of the most popular kinds of social media, but be aware that there are many more already and will undoubtedly be dozens of niche sites in the future, including some focused on books.

MySpace

MySpace, which according to *The Wall Street Journal* has consistently had between 100 million and 120 million users, has been eclipsed recently by Facebook, which had that number in early 2008 but had grown to 300 million users by the middle of 2009. Still, MySpace is one of the most important social media sites. Billed as "a place for friends," MySpace emphasizes interpersonal relationships and the accumulation of contacts. Most authors are not on MySpace, and this is fine unless you fall into either one of these two categories:

• YA. If you are a YA novelist or even if you write nonfiction books for teens, you absolutely need a MySpace page. That's because the site remains the most important social networking medium for teens and young adults. Everyone who is anyone is going be there—which means you should be, too.

- You write about music. MySpace has become the "it site" for bands and those who love them. All types of music are represented on MySpace, from classical and pop to rap and hip-hop. Artists can post streaming video of performances, upload digital audio files, and enlist fans and friends. If you write about popular culture and the music scene, you need to create a presence on MySpace.

It's easy to set up a MySpace account, post pictures, and find friends. When you set up your account, use a couple of author photos and also your book cover(s) among your "top eight" photographs. You want potential friends—who are also potential customers—to be exposed to your book visually as well as in any blog posts or updates you do on MySpace.

Facebook

Facebook, now the top social networking site in the world, grew 127 percent in 2008 and as of press time had surpassed 300 million users. It vaulted past MySpace so suddenly in part because Facebook's ads were less obnoxious and obtrusive; many adult MySpace customers began switching loyalties when they discovered that Facebook might be less aggressive about constant sales pitches.

This should tell us something. No one joins Facebook to become fodder for sales pitches. They join because they want to connect with old or distant friends they never get to see. If authors (or companies) exploit Facebook as a sales tool in too obvious a way, people will simply tell Facebook to block that person.

TEN HOT TIPS FOR USING FACEBOOK

1. "Friend" promiscuously. Yes, you'll be hearing from some people you never imagined you would see again (and weren't terribly sorry to lose in the first place), but you'll be amazed at how much most of us have grown up since high school. Old friends and acquaintances can turn out to be among the strongest supporters of your writing. Once you get a name established as a writer, you'll also start getting friend requests from readers you've never met. Some writers friend everyone who asks but set parameters on Facebook for which ones will appear in their news feed; others create separate accounts for their work and personal lives.

2. Comment widely on other people's links and status updates. Facebook is all about community, so don't just stand on a platform and shout about your work with a megaphone. Get involved in conversations about other people's status updates, links, and photographs. It's fun in its own right, and it makes people more likely to pay attention to your posts.

Websites, Blogs, Podcasts, & Social Networking

3. Don't just promote yourself. All work and no play make Facebook a very dull place indeed. While you don't want to overwhelm Facebook friends with details about the fight you just had with your teen or the bills you're struggling to pay, it's great to post status updates and photographs about your life and family outside of work. What movies are you seeing? Who do you think should win on American Idol? Writers are people, too, and readers like to see that they are interested in sports, volunteer opportunities, and the like.

4. Alert friends to new releases, book signings, and works in progress. When there's something concrete and specific going on with your book, don't be afraid to shout about it. Friends who stay with you through all the steps between "An agent finally wrote back and said she wants to represent me!" to "I got a good review in *Library Journal*!" want to know these things. Let them know about upcoming author appearances and speaking engagements. Link to reviews or discussions about your latest book.

5. Push your blog posts and tweets to Facebook. One way to cut down on the tendency many people have to feel overwhelmed by social media is to arrange your various accounts to talk to each other. For example, most blog programs have a tools section to help you automatically update the blog with any new tweets. The reverse is true if you also use Twitterfeed, which pushes any new blog entries to all of your Twitter followers.

6. Become a fan of your publishing house. Most publishing houses now have a presence on Facebook, and you'll want to show your support for your press (and also receive any important general updates about products and breaking news) by becoming a fan.

7. Create a fan page for yourself or your book. It's easy to create a fan page, but some people feel awkward or conspicuous doing this. It can be a bit much for friends to receive a news update that says, "Amy Marie Author became a fan of Amy Marie Author," inviting them to also become a fan. If you don't feel comfortable creating your own book or author fan pages, ask a friend to do it for you. You can send this friend any updates or announcements to post.

8. Create a Facebook "event" for the month of your book's launch. Ask friends to RSVP if they will buy the book during that window of time, and make them eligible for special giveaways if they also blog about it then, review it on Amazon.com, link to the book or its trailer in their status update, etc. (You can choose to hide the guests who are not attending, and only show the ones who are definitely or maybe attending.)

9. Follow other authors on Red Room (www.redroom.com). Launched in 2008, Red Room, another social media site, claims it has an "author centric" mission to connect authors with readers. It works with publishers to sell authors' works on the site, and with Facebook to upload member-writers' Red Room blog posts to their social media profiles. Red Room is selective about the authors it represents, but it costs nothing to become a follower, and you can learn a lot about promotion this way.

10. Remember the three Ps: Public + Permanent = Privacy Settings. The default mode on Facebook is always open sharing. Unless you tell Facebook otherwise, almost anyone—and not just designated friends—can have access to your friend list, profile, and even your photographs. And unless you tell Facebook otherwise, absolutely anyone in your "default network" (which would be your hometown, high school or college, or city of residence) can see your status updates. All this openness can lead, and has led, to some very embarrassing situations for people who didn't realize that information or photos they thought were private were in fact in the public eye. Remember Miss New Jersey 2007, who was publicly disgraced when her humiliating Facebook photos made the national news? Learn from those mistakes and adjust your privacy settings to allow your photos, videos, and status updates to be seen by the friends you approve. Even after doing this, just work under the assumption that everything you post will be both public and permanent, and exercise appropriate caution.

Twitter

(Note: If we were being true to form, then this section would only be 140 characters. We're already more than halfway there!)

Think of Twitter as "microblogging." It's only been around since 2006, and really just took off at the end of 2008, so it's still untried—and has yet to make a profit for its creators. And yet Twitter is exploding in users. We won't venture any statistics, because by the time you read this book those numbers will be hopelessly out of date. Millions of people are now following other people on Twitter, some of whom they have met, and many they have not. Followers read these people's 140-character "tweets," often "retweeting" them to others—i.e., forwarding them on. Once people have signed up to read your tweets, they can follow you on their smart phone, on Facebook, on your blog, or online at www.twitter.com.

Some adventurous authors have begun to use Twitter to keep in touch with readers—even before their books are published. According to *Publishers Weekly,* author Rebecca Skloot began tweeting about her 2010 science book *The Immortal Life of Henrietta Lacks* in early 2009. She assembled an audience for the book by building her tweets around similar content that science readers would care about. "I treat my Twitter feed like a mini-publication, a place where I tell readers about things I think they'd be interested in, as in, 'if-you-like-my-stuff-you-should-definitely-read-this,'" Skloot told PW. "I interact a lot with readers there, but I very rarely post personal stuff, except for occasional posts about the progress of my book, which let people know that it's coming."

Other authors tweet about their signings, appearances, and media interviews, as well as what they're thinking about national issues and things in the news. Since Twitter is so new, publishers and authors are just now learning strategies that work successfully. In 2009 Chelsea Green Publishing made news by having a contest for readers to "Tweet This Book" for one of their new releases. During the four-minute contest time, they had twenty-seven contestants and forty-five total entries of people who tweeted about the book to their own followers. Now, that doesn't sound like much, but according to tech blogger Chris Webb (www.ckwebb.com), that doesn't account for how many people actually saw the forty-five tweets from these twenty-seven people: 14,216 Twitter users. As a bonus, *The Huffington Post* picked up one of the funniest entries, which further expanded the network of people who had been exposed to that book title. So here's the breakdown:

Potential customers reached: Fourteen thousand plus

Time spent: Less than five minutes

Cost to publisher: One book given away to the winner

That sounds like a pretty decent promotion to us. As you can see, the possibilities of using Twitter to generate word of mouth are endless.

GETTING STARTED ON TWITTER

If you're thinking of beginning to Twitter, spend a week or two as a follower first. Sign up for some of the wonderful tweets about writing that Writer's Digest Books puts out every Friday. Like Facebook, Twitter is free to users, so you have nothing to lose except time. Go to www.twitter.com to learn more.

You'll need to decide what kind of Twitterer you're going to be. Your followers don't want to be pitched your book constantly. They want to get an author's take on a subject they're passionate about—or in the case of fiction, characters they love. In fact, some novelists actually use Twitter as if they were microblogging as their characters.

You'll want to decide how much information is too much information. Most of the people who follow you on Twitter want to know about your work, not what you're grilling out on the deck tonight. (There are exceptions, of course, but most followers get annoyed if your tweets are often frivolous. Some authors have two Twitter accounts: one for friends and family, and one for readers. This may be more trouble than it's worth, so try to keep your Twittering professional. Ask yourself what information will be truly useful to your followers. A restaurant that tweets out its daily pie and soup specials each morning is useful to patrons; a restaurant that tweets about the &*!@*$$ coffeemaker being on the fritz again is just irritating.

RESOURCES

The Facebook Era: Tapping Online Social Networks to Build Better Products, Reach New Audiences, and Sell More Stuff by Clara Shih. Although this is not specifically about book marketing, it does have excellent information about how to use Facebook to your advantage, with examples from established retail companies.

Plug Your Book! Online Book Marketing for Authors by Steve Weber. This guide deals with search engine optimization, Google rankings, tags, and click ads as well as social networking sites, especially MySpace.

Podcasting for Dummies by Tee Morris, Chuck Tomasi, and Evo Terra. How to envision, create, and promote your podcast.

Red Hot Internet Publicity by Penny Sansevieri. This book focuses on how to use the Internet to create word-of-mouth success, with chapters on blogging, podcasting, virtual book events, and Amazon.com.

Twitter Power: How to Dominate Your Market One Tweet at a Time by Joel Comm. Though this focuses on how businesses can use Twitter to build brands and provide better customer service, there are lots of tips that apply to authors.

CHAPTER 25

FINANCES FOR FREELANCERS

Each year, thousands of writers fail in their dream of becoming freelancers. Sadly, many fail not because they couldn't write well enough but because they never mastered the business side of the profession.

While just as important to success, the business side of freelancing is often a lot less appealing. So it's easy to shove business matters into the bottom drawer, where they slowly kindle into a blaze of uncollected bills and overdue taxes. If you take the right approach, however, the details of business need not consume much of your hard work and talent. A few hours a week keeping your business matters well organized and up-to-date is all it really takes.

This chapter focuses on what you need to know to keep the business side of freelancing from overwhelming you—so your success as a writer is unfettered by the mundane details of business and taxes.

SETTING UP YOUR BUSINESS

Creating a simple budget is not only essential for business, it can make your life easier as well. For our purposes we'll assume you are a full-time freelancer or are about to become one. If this is not the case, you can still benefit from having a more complete understanding of the business side of the trade. Keeping your budget, however large or small, in order will help your life run smoother month to month and will spare you panic-stricken moments come tax time.

As with any budget, what you're trying to create is only a rough representation of what's likely to happen. As you go through the steps, keep in mind that it will get easier each year. Once you are established as a freelancer you'll have the previous year's income and expenses as a basis for planning. You'll also have a regular base of clients to make your income more predictable.

The best way to start the budgeting process is to estimate your costs. Monthly overhead (what you must pay whether you work or not) should be the first category. This includes any payments on your computer or other equipment, office rent, publications, Internet service, and an estimate of auto expenses. Whenever possible, you'll need to keep track of business expenses separately from home expenses. Some budget items are used for both work and home (e.g., your car), so the IRS expects you to keep track of things like work-related mileage separately. Later in this chapter, we'll discuss how to use that information to your advantage at tax time.

After figuring overhead, take a look at your household budget and calculate the minimum amount you'll need for living expenses. Include your rent, mortgage, car payment, other consumer debt, groceries, utilities, and the like. Then, subtract from this amount any take-home pay from your spouse or other sources of steady income.

Financial planners recommend freelancers have three to six months of overhead and living expenses available when they start their business. Even if you start with as much work as you can handle, still count on two to three months for the checks to appear in your mailbox. One survey by the Editorial Freelancers Association found that freelancers waited anywhere from a week to a year to get paid, with one or two months being typical.

Ideally, your capital reserve will be your savings account. Realistically, the start-up costs for a freelance writing business are small enough that most can get by without borrowing. If you need to borrow money, it makes sense to apply for a separate credit card for business use. (It can still be in your name.) It's a lot easier to maintain your books with a separate business account. If your card has a grace period and you pay your balance every month, your card works like a rolling line of credit with no interest cost whatsoever—but be careful not to carry debt from month to month.

PLANNING YOUR EARNINGS

The overhead calculation you did earlier is important in figuring how much you should charge for your services. Different freelancers' websites post information about typical fees, so launch a Google search about what freelancers are charging so you at least know the ballpark rates.

To calculate an hourly rate, figure the amount you hope to earn. That may be what you used to make at your old job or what you dream of making at your new one. Then, add in your annual overhead expenses. Divide that figure by the number of billable hours you expect to work in a year. (Count on spending a quarter of your time marketing your services, maintaining your records, and reading professional publications. These are not billable hours, but they are necessary ones if you want to run a successful long-term business.)

Most magazines and clients won't pay by the hour but by the word, inch, or article. You can, however, estimate how long an assignment will take and multiply that by your hourly rate. Factor in writing time, of course, but also the time you'll spend researching and revising your piece. Remember to consider expenses, too. Try to estimate your costs for phone charges, mileage, research, and other expenses. Add these to the fee you negotiate.

Always keep in mind what the market will bear when making your calculations. Check with other freelance writers in your area to find out what they charge. Don't charge more than you can get, but don't underestimate yourself, either. Lowball pricing may get you a few jobs. But it will hurt your image with clients and editors, and often, your self-esteem. It won't do your bank account any good, either.

RECORDS AND ACCOUNTS

Nobody becomes a freelance writer to do bookkeeping, but freelancers quickly find it becomes an important part of their jobs. Again, it need not be cumbersome. Ideally, record keeping should take no more than two hours each week.

Your record-keeping system can be as simple as a daily log of income and expenses. If you're more comfortable keeping records on your personal computer, your local computer store should have a wide array of software that can do the job. Quicken Home & Business, for example, is a program that enables you to create estimates and invoices, generate business reports, record mileage, track accounts payable, and watch your cash flow. Financial planners recommend that you set up a separate checking account for your business. This will keep you from tapping your business funds for personal needs, and it will provide clearer documentation of your income and business expenses.

Some tips on record keeping:

- Save and file your receipts from every business expense—travel, books purchased, blog fees, office supplies, postage, etc.

- The IRS strongly recommends you keep expense records for as long as the period of limitations for audits. In most cases, that's three years from the date the return was filed or two years from when the tax was paid, whichever is later.

- Keep income records for six years after each tax return is filed. That's the IRS period for going after unreported income.

- You'll need records for the cost of your home or improvements for as long as you own the home, if you take the home-office deduction.

- Also, you must keep records of items for which you claim depreciation, such as cars, for as long as you depreciate them, plus the three years after you file your return.

Though costly and time-consuming, audits are relatively rare. The IRS audits less than 1 percent of tax returns each year. Among businesses and the self-employed the chances are about 4 percent. Even if you're audited you won't necessarily owe money. About a fifth of those audited don't owe any additional taxes, and some even get refunds.

Your Income

Expenses are only half of what you'll be tracking. You'll also need to record income as you receive it and keep pay stubs that document your earnings. Each source that pays you more than six hundred dollars a year must report your earnings to the IRS and send you a 1099 form showing the amount. Income records are important for comparing to the amounts reported on each 1099.

If you've been bartering with other businesses (receiving goods or services rather than cash), the law requires you to report the fair market dollar value.

Cash Flow

That first big check you receive for your writing will be a thrill, but don't rush out and spend it. There's going to be a lean period. With the right strategy you can minimize the ups and downs.

The best way to avoid cash-flow problems is to continually work on developing new clients. That means sending out queries or contacting potential clients even when you're busy. Try to set aside a couple days each month for such marketing.

Never rely too much on any one source of income. Developing a few key accounts, preferably large and reliable enough to cover your overhead and basic living expenses, is important. But don't become complacent. Nothing lasts forever, so don't let any single account become more than a third of your business.

Meticulously track what your clients owe you. Record who owes you money, how much, and when it's due. As best as possible, arrange payment on your terms. Remember, book authors are not the only ones who get paid some money in advance. You may be able to get money up front for copywriting or even expense money from magazines.

For article writers, publications that pay on acceptance are obviously more desirable than those that pay on publication. If you're getting paid on publication, you could wait months for your article to be published, and at least a month after that to get paid. If paid on acceptance, you should get paid within a month of your final rewrite. Some tips:

- Fast action is the key to good cash flow. To maximize your income, incorporate billing into your weekly schedule.

- Tabulate your phone or other expenses as soon as the bill comes due.

- Bill clients as soon as payment is due.

Don't let a new, unproven account run up huge tabs before you get paid. In most cases, you won't know how good a publisher's or client's payment practices are until they owe you money.

GETTING PAID

Waiting for checks is one of the most nerve-racking parts of being a writer. Let's face it: As writers we rely heavily on the creative side of our brain. Business and finances are not something most of us enjoy dealing with. So we like to think that our creative efforts will always be rewarded fairly. Yet even when our rights are carefully spelled out in a contract, there's no guarantee that payment will arrive when it's due.

For sure, one skill that writers acquire is patience. But we needn't be too patient. No matter how bad the publisher's cash flow, it's usually better than ours. So when the wait gets too long (i.e., thirty days past due), call or e-mail immediately. You need not be confrontational. Simply send a late notice, or call to check on the status of payment or to make sure your invoice wasn't lost. If you call, be sure to get a commitment from the editor or accounting office on when the payment will be sent. If that doesn't work, your next step is to deal with the accounting department directly and find out when the check was cut or mailed. If that still doesn't work, you can consider legal action such as arbitration or small claims court.

TAX ISSUES FOR WRITERS

Becoming a freelancer means saying goodbye to those carefree days when you spent thirty minutes filling out your annual taxes. As soon as you make any money freelancing, you'll have to fill out the long form 1040 and Schedule C for business profit or loss. If you plan to deduct car or equipment expenses, you'll have another even more complex form to fill out.

Estimated Taxes

Freelancers don't have any tax withheld from their income. Doesn't that sound great?

Unfortunately, it isn't. Any self-employed person must pay estimated taxes on earnings, not just annually but quarterly. You can use IRS form 1040-ES to calculate and make your estimated payments, which are due on the 15th of January, April, June, and September. For more information, go to www.irs.gov and type in "estimated tax" in the search field.

Writers do well to plan ahead. If you can't estimate this year's income accurately, you will usually be safe from penalties if you base your quarterly taxes on what you owed the prior year. Your state and city may also require you to withhold taxes. To be safe, put aside at least 33 percent of your net earnings to cover your federal, state, and local taxes. It is better to be prepared than to be surprised.

Self-Employment Tax

If you thought the news about quarterly taxes was bad, you're going to want to sit down before reading this section. Writers and other self-employed people get to pay more tax than most other people. Don't you feel special? That's because in addition to ordinary income tax, freelancers must pay a self-employment tax to cover Social Security and Medicare. Employees pay Social Security tax, too, but the self-employed pay roughly twice as much (about 15 percent), because they're expected to cover both the "employee" half and the "employer" portion. When you look at your tax bill, you'll find that's one of the strongest motivations for taking every deduction you're allowed, which we'll cover in the next few sections.

AUTO EXPENSES

If you work from home, you can deduct mileage from home and back to any interview, trips to the library for research, or travel for any business function. This is true even if you don't qualify for the home office deduction. If you work from an office outside the home, however, you can't deduct mileage for commuting to the office.

You can calculate auto expenses using the standard mileage rate or the actual-cost method. To use the standard mileage rate, multiply the mileage driven by the current mileage rate (fifty-five cents in 2009). The rate frequently changes but is stated each year in the instructions that come with Schedule C, the IRS form for reporting business income and expenses. Using the standard mileage rate is the easiest method in terms of record keeping.

As the name implies, the actual-cost method measures what it really costs you to operate your car. For this method you'll have to keep receipts for all automobile expenses, including gas, maintenance and repairs, insurance, taxes, loan interest, and depreciation of the car's cost.

If you use the car for both business and personal reasons, calculate the percentage of business miles each year and deduct that percentage of your costs. There are limits to how much of your car's value you may write off each year. For details, you'll need a current copy of IRS publication 917.

Home-Office Expenses

Qualifying for the home-office deduction means jumping through regulatory hoops (learning what the rules are) and increasing your risk of an audit. But the tax savings can be worth it. You may be able to deduct a percentage of your mortgage interest or rent, utilities, and upkeep for your home each year.

To qualify for the deduction you must use an area of your home regularly and exclusively for business. Occasional or incidental use of your home office won't cut it, even if you don't use the space for anything else. The most accurate way to calculate the business portion of your home is to divide the square feet of the work area by the total square feet of your home. Expenses you can deduct include the business percentage of:

- Mortgage interest.

- Utilities and services, such as electricity, heat, trash removal, and cleaning services.

- Depreciation of the value of your house.

- Home security systems.

- Repairs, maintenance, and permanent improvement costs for your house.

- All costs of repairs, painting, or modifications of your home office. (You can write off repairs the first year. Permanent improvements are considered capital expenditures and subject to depreciation over several years.).

One other word of caution—you can't use home-office expenses to put you in the red. They can't be used to help create a tax loss.

Before you take any home-office deductions, figure out what the tax savings will be. If the savings are minor, you may not want to bother. What you lose in taxes, you may gain in peace of mind because you'll be saving yourself extra work. You can get more information from IRS Publication 587.

Other Expenses

The IRS applies the "ordinary" and "necessary" rules in judging the validity of a business expense. This means the expenses should be ordinary for your profession and necessary for carrying out your business.

Office equipment is a necessary—and often major—expense for freelance writers. Computers, desks, chairs, shelves, filing cabinets, and other office furnishings are deductible expenses if you use them in your business. These can be deducted even if you don't opt for the home-office deduction. IRS publication 534 provides more details on how to depreciate business property.

Among the largest costs for freelancers are phone and Internet expenses. The IRS prohibits deductions for your personal phone line, even if you use it for business. But you can still deduct the cost of long-distance business calls, even if they're from a personal line.

If you entertain sources or clients you can deduct 50 percent of that expense. You must keep a log of the date, location, person entertained, and business purpose of the entertainment for every item you deduct. If you travel in connection with your writing, you can deduct the cost of transportation, lodging, and meals.

Other deductible expenses include the cost of:

- Dues to professional organizations.

- Newspapers, magazines, and journals used for your business.

- Research, copying services, and online databases.

- Books used for research or comparison.

- Office supplies.

- Postage for business use.

- Cleaning supplies for your office.

- Legal, accounting, and other professional services.

- Business licenses.

If publishers or clients reimburse you for some of your expenses, remember to keep records of those payments and either report them as income or subtract them from the expenses you report.

Schedule C Pointers

Schedule C is a catchall form for all businesses, so much of it can be meaningless and mysterious for a freelancer. Here are a few things to remember if you fill out the form yourself:

- You'll probably be checking the "cash" box for accounting method. That just means you record income when you get the check and expenses when you pay them. Few freelancers will use the more complicated methods.

- Check the "does not apply" box for method used to value closing inventory. You don't have any. Unpublished manuscripts don't count.

- The office expense category is a catchall that includes office supplies, postage, etc.

- You only fill out the pension and profit-sharing portion if you have employees participating in a plan. Your own plan contribution, if any, is reported on form 1040.

- The tax and license expenses that you can deduct include real estate and personal property taxes on business assets, and employer social security and federal unemployment taxes.

- A big total in the "other expenses" column can make the IRS very suspicious. Break these items down as much as you can in the space provided.

- Your principal business or professional activity code will most likely be 711510 (the category for independent artists, writers, and performers) unless you work in advertising or related services (541800), the publishing industry (511000), or Internet publishing (516110).

Professional Help

As you've figured out by now, business tax forms are a lot more complicated than ordinary tax forms. So you may want professional help. If so, your options include tax preparation services and accountants.

If you're incorporated or face particularly complex business issues, you may need help from a certified public accountant (CPA). Small or medium-size CPA firms are most likely to be familiar with issues that concern you. Franchise tax services provide a consistent, mass-produced product. They're the cheapest option, but they may be less familiar with some of the unusual situations of freelancers.

Don't overlook the possibility of the DIY method through tax accounting software, which is easy to use, very accurate, and updated annually to reflect changes in the tax code. For example, TurboTax Deluxe is an excellent program for freelancers who need to file a Schedule C, and it can be much cheaper than hiring an accountant. Moreover, if you track your business's finances with Quicken or QuickBooks, which are designed by the same company that created TurboTax, you can have the program automatically input all of your business expenses and income into TurboTax.

SAVING FOR THE FUTURE

While you may be able to write in your retirement years, you still will need some other savings if you hope to maintain your standard of living. For many people, this means investing in some kind of Individual Retirement Account (IRA).

The SEP-IRA

An IRA is a personal savings plan that provides income tax advantages to individuals saving money for retirement. Most people who invest in a traditional IRA can claim an income tax deduction for the year in which the funds are contributed into the account. These contributions, as well as any gains, accumulate tax-free until you withdraw the money. You can therefore accumulate greater earnings each year the funds remain in the account. Withdrawals are subject to income tax, generally in the year in which you receive them. Since the goal of a traditional IRA is to provide retirement income, the government assesses a tax penalty of 10 percent if you withdraw money from an IRA prior to age 59½, unless certain exceptions apply.

For freelance writers, the best traditional IRA choice is the SEP-IRA, which is specifically designed for self-employed individuals. The contribution limits are much higher ($49,000 in 2009) than are allowed with a traditional IRA ($5,000 for people under age fifty and $6,000 for people over age fifty), because the government expects that self-employed workers don't have employers pitching in matching funds, pension plans, and other goodies.

The Roth IRA

A Roth IRA is a different type of sheltered retirement account, and it is the best choice for most people if their income at retirement age is expected to be higher than their income is now. (This is true for most of us.) The Roth has a tax structure different from any other IRA in that contributions are posttax, so you don't get an immediate tax deduction. However, this strategy pays off in the long run: Since you have already paid taxes on any money you place into a Roth IRA, your earnings at retirement are tax-free. Moreover, the Roth is the only type of IRA you can pass on to your heirs tax-free.

As with traditional IRAs, you can open a Roth account through a stockbroker or other provider of investment accounts. As with all IRAs, there are restrictions on your eligibility. You can stay up-to-date on the rules with IRS Publication 590 or at www.irs.gov.

INSURANCE

It's not enough just to save for a rainy day—you also have to prepare for disaster. This means having enough insurance.

Health Insurance

Health insurance will be one of the biggest expenses you'll face as a freelancer. If you're leaving a job with health benefits, federal law requires employers to continue your coverage for up to eighteen months (at your expense) through the pricey COBRA program. Beyond that you can choose from other group plans or individual coverage. Whatever route you choose, expect it to cost no less than several thousand dollars a year—and more if you have a pre-existing condition.

Many business or writers' organizations offer group health insurance, including The Authors Guild. Some even offer choices, including major medical plans with a range of deductibles and health maintenance organizations (HMOs). But membership in one of these organizations does-not guarantee you'll be accepted for coverage.

Check with the organization or its insurance carrier for details of the plan. Most are perfectly acceptable. But some organizations provide only a fixed amount of coverage based on the number of days in the hospital and cover no expenses for physician treatment outside a hospital.

Depending on your state, an individual plan may leave you vulnerable to cancellation or steep rate increases should you develop a lengthy illness. Also, most independent coverage will have a waiting period of several months.

A less costly approach is to opt for an individual plan with relatively high deductibles and co-payments. It will still do what insurance is supposed to do, which is to keep you from getting wiped out by a huge medical bill. No matter what type of plan you have, most hospitals and doctors will let you pay off what you owe over time if you ask.

One of the best cheap insurance options, if you can find it, is an HMO that offers a high deductible in exchange for low premiums. This way your deductible may still be cheaper than the rates charged to those people who have traditional coverage.

Other Insurance

Going in business for yourself should not mean neglecting disability insurance. To the contrary, seek out a plan that covers the highest possible percentage of income for as long as possible. No insurance company will underwrite a policy that pays 100 percent of your income, because that would provide no incentive for you to go back to work. But policies may go as high as 80 percent and last as long as ten years or to age sixty-five.

Many writers' organizations offer group disability coverage. The groups may also offer relatively inexpensive group life insurance that can cover such items as your mortgage. But it's important to look at disability plans closely. Some plans cover only a fixed period, so you'd be out of luck and money in the event of long-term disability.

If you work from home, also check with your home or renter's insurance carrier to make sure your business equipment is covered. Professional liability is another coverage to consider. Your largest liability exposure is for libel. If your work seems likely to involve you in libel litigation somewhere down the road, you may want to take out a separate policy through a group like the National Writers Union.

CHAPTER 26

THE PRICE IS RIGHT: WHAT TO CHARGE FOR YOUR WORK

As a group, writers are underpaid. Surveys by organizations such as The Authors Guild and the National Writers Union show that income growth for most writers lags behind that of most other professions. The question for you, then, is how do you maximize your earning potential either as a full-time or a part-time writer? In actuality, freelance writing is similar to other creative fields like art, photography, and music. You can either earn hobby rates or you can earn a professional wage. The difference is in how seriously you take your work.

Freelancers who command top dollar are experienced professionals who have spent years perfecting their skills either as freelancers or as writers employed in journalism, advertising, public relations, or publishing. Beyond being talented writers, they are reliable professionals who respect deadlines and have mastered the fine details of running an independent business. They are especially good at marketing themselves. A freelancer, like any independent business person, must also set goals and develop a business plan. The plan doesn't have to be as formal as those for bigger businesses, but at the very least you have to decide what writing skills you have to sell, who might buy them, and how you will prove you are the best person for the job.

KNOWING WHAT TO CHARGE

While producers of other products can check out the competition's prices at malls and markets, writers are lonely souls, left to negotiate individually with publishers and clients. Joining a writers group can broaden your perspective on pay rates, particularly a national group, such as the Editorial Freelancers Association or the National Writers Union, which publish data about how much their members earn for jobs. Reading books like *Writer's Market*, which annually publishes lists of pay scales for dozens of types of writing, can also help you determine what to charge. Joining a bulletin board discussion at websites like www.everywritersresource.com allows you to simply post your rates and ask plugged-in counterparts, "Am I charging enough?"

Freelancers find most of their work networking with other writers, editors, and potential clients. Other good leads come through e-mail and/or hard-copy queries, or networking through Chambers of Commerce and similar organizations. But the best referrals come from satisfied clients who tell others about your work.

As is the case in most professions, beginning writers also earn less than those who have been in the business longer. In addition, asking for more money is never easy. Some clients may be more willing to negotiate with writers who have already produced materials that meet their needs, but many are not willing to do so when dealing with a new freelancer. To get your feet wet, you may have to settle for less—at first. The trick is to raise your prices as your reputation grows. Remember: The best client is one who is willing to pay you more than once.

HOURLY RATE CALCULATION

It is important to know the hourly rate you need to earn in order to meet your needs. Follow these steps to calculate what your earnings must be in order for you to be a successful freelance writer.

1. Covering expenses. To figure out how much you'll have to earn per hour to pay for expenses, first decide how much time you'll have to devote to writing per month. To calculate the break-even hourly rate, divide your monthly expenses by the number of hours you plan to work. In the example below, if you can work 160 hours each month on your writing, the hourly rate would be $1,488/160 = $9.50 per hour.

Consider this your bare minimum hourly rate, because it does not include any remuneration for your expertise or any profit. If you use this figure to give an estimate for a job, you'd be valuing your time and talent at zero.

2. Setting fees. One way to make sure you are paid market rates is to estimate how much a company would pay an employee to do similar work. Remember that a company may also pay for health insurance, retirement funds, unemployment insurance, vacation time, holidays, and sick days. These costs can range from 25 to 45 percent of an employee's annual salary, depending on which perks the employee gets and where she lives. Use a 35 percent estimate to get a rough idea.

- Estimated yearly salary: $40,000 divided by 2,000 (40 hours per week for 50 weeks) equals an hourly pay rate of $20. (This formula assumes you will take two weeks of vacation a year. Adjust the formula as needed.)

- Adding fringe benefit costs of 35 percent ($7) gives you an hourly rate of $27.

- Add to this amount your minimum rate to cover overhead ($9.50) and you have a total hourly rate of $36.50.

- In addition, you might want to add another 20 percent of profit ($7.30) to cover things like self-employment tax, the additional costs of insuring yourself, etc. This makes for a total hourly fee of $43.80, which you would round up to $45 or $50.

A rate of $50 or more an hour may be high for a particular type of writing or may be quite reasonable depending on your level of experience, the perceived value of your work, the going rate for your geographical area, and the prevailing rates available to the client. In determining the prices you will charge for various types of work you must first conduct research. This includes talking to other writers about what they charge.

When calculating the hours you invest in your work you also need to consider the time spent writing queries and making calls to find jobs, billing, filing tax returns, driving to the post office, shopping for office supplies, and maintaining your computer. To be successful, at least one-fifth of your time should be spent marketing yourself. Your hourly rate for all these activities needs to be recouped somewhere—either in higher fees or additional hours that you bill your clients.

None of the above calculations includes reimbursement for expenses for specific jobs, such as travel, overnight mail, or long-distance telephone calls. These should be added to the bill and paid by the client. It's best to have a written contract spelling out what work you are expected to do at what rate.

PROJECT RATE CALCULATION

An alternative way of pricing is to charge by the project. The advantage of project pricing is that if you work quickly, you can earn a high hourly rate. If you quote a price of three hundred dollars for a piece and manage to turn it around in three hours, well, you do the math. If you decide to work more slowly, that's your option, too. But with a project rate, you've set your ceiling and a client probably won't pay you more.

The disadvantage of accepting a project price is that if you estimate too low, you may discover you could have earned better wages elsewhere. You can always try negotiating for more, but you'll have to convince your client why your original estimate was wrong, which is difficult and, if it's your fault, embarrassing.

Some clients will tell you the pay rate up front. Others may ask what you charge. If asked, don't be evasive. It's not very professional to show uncertainty about something as basic and important as your price. Since they're asking, feel free to quote your full fee. Remember, you can always adjust downward, but it's hard to negotiate upward after you have already quoted a price.

Seasoned writers have an easier time figuring out an acceptable price for a project. Almost by instinct they can discern the amount of time and effort that will go into a project. Beginners typically fare better by focusing on an hourly fee. This way they not only learn which types of projects are best suited for them but they also can keep better track of the gains they make in skill and efficiency. Unfortunately most clients want a fixed price, especially if they are not familiar with your work. The solution is to negotiate a set price based on the number of hours you expect to spend on the project. If you are going to earn a set fee, it is important to detail up front precisely what the work will entail. Once you have talked this over with the client or editor, estimate how many hours you expect to spend on the project including research, interviews, editing, and proofreading. (It helps to look at similar projects completed for the client in the past.) Then multiply the number of hours by your hourly rate to get the amount of money you expect to earn.

When starting out as a freelance writer, you won't be able to command the same fee as someone with several years of experience. This does not mean, however, that you are at the mercy of the client. If you are qualified as a writer, you are producing a professional product and should be compensated fairly. Decide early on the lowest figure you will accept and stick to it.

Early in your career, you might not make out as well charging by the project. But as you gain experience—enabling you to work faster and to estimate your time better—you will do quite well. Publications and most other businesses are time sensitive. To your pleasant surprise, clients and editors will be willing to pay you more for getting work done more quickly. As your proficiency and efficiency improve you will, in effect, earn more money for less work.

KEEP TRACK OF TIME

Keeping track of how long it takes to finish a project might feel as if you're attaching a meter to your mind. But it is vitally important, whether you are charging by the hour or by the project. By keeping good records for specific types of projects, you will eventually discern patterns. You can use the insight you gain to improve your work flow, cut out unnecessary steps, and set fees that maximize your income while still keeping you competitive. Even so, many writers do not closely track how much time they spend on a project. Even if they know how much time they spend at the keyboard, they often underestimate the hours spent researching, interviewing, billing, and corresponding with their clients.

It need not be this way. Keeping track of your time doesn't take as much effort as you might think. And the payoff far outweighs the investment of time you put into it. The insight you gain into your work habits can help you better use your time in the future—giving you more free time down the road. You will also improve your ability to accurately bid your services.

One easy method is to watch the clock and keep a log book by your computer or in your briefcase. Some people even use a stopwatch. They simply start the watch when they begin work, turn it off whenever they step away, and turn it on again when they resume work. The watch keeps an accurate tally of their cumulative time.

Ironically it's sometimes the small projects that reveal the most about our work habits. Bigger projects get spread over weeks or even months, making it harder to get a clear picture of all the work involved. A small project that lasts just a couple days is easier to track and analyze. You might be surprised by what you learn.

NEGOTIATING FOR MORE

Few of us like to haggle over the price of goods or services. When you land a writing job, however, you are in a good negotiating position: You have something your client wants.

A good rule to consider in wrangling over fees is to imagine a triangle with three points: good, fast, and inexpensive. Most people want things done well, inexpensively, and fast. But most times, they will only get two of the three. For example, you might be able to write something cheaply and fast, but you probably won't be able to do it well. Or you can do it fast and make it good, but it won't be inexpensive. By this reasoning, if a client asks for a quick turnaround time, you should expect to be paid extra for it.

Once you work with a client or editor and prove you can deliver, it will be easier to negotiate for more money. While many editors are understandably reluctant to invest large amounts in unknown writers, they may be able to find more in their budgets for someone they have come to know and trust.

It may be easier for beginning writers to quote a range of pay they would like to earn. You could tell the client the job would cost between one and two hundred dollars, for example, depending on how much time it involves. If you can do it for less, they may be grateful for a smaller bill and be more willing to give you another assignment. But never undervalue your work, for if you do, you can be sure that others will, too.

Negotiation doesn't have to be confrontational. After all, an editor often doesn't hold the purse strings and may be sympathetic to polite requests for more money. Before you ask for more (or ask to retain certain rights to resell your work), decide which things you sincerely want and which you can give up. First, state everything you would like. Then be prepared to adopt a position that gets you most of what you want. If you've kept a log of how long previous projects have taken and what types of work they entailed, your arguments will be more persuasive. Be realistic, however. A publication that pays ten cents a word is hardly likely to increase tenfold.

Keep in mind that business people talk money all the time, and writing is a business. If you ask for more, usually the worst that could happen is you'll be told no. At that point, it's up to you to decide whether you'll take the job or move on.

RAISING YOUR RATES

A freelancer, like any business person, eventually faces the day when he needs to raise prices. Maybe it is because inflation has cut into your profit margin or your living standard. Perhaps you feel the value of your services has increased. Or maybe you have discovered that you have been pricing your services below the market value. In any of these cases, don't be reluctant to ask for what you think is fair and justified.

Other businesses consistently raise their rates. Price increases are a fact of life. So don't keep your prices artificially low when an increase is justified. Underpricing your services can produce an image that you lack the skill and experience to command professional fees. It can also suggest that your work is of lower quality.

If you decide to raise your rates, avoid being erratic. If you change prices often—whether raising or lowering them—you may create the impression that you have no basis for your fee. When you do raise your price, make the increases small and base the change on a sound business decision you can justify. Keep in mind that an increase of just a few percent in your overall price can raise your profit margin substantially.

Of course, you don't always have to raise your rates to bring in extra income. If you really can't justify a rate increase, examine your work for instances where you give services to clients for free. While you don't want to nickel-and-dime your clients with petty fees, neither do you want to give away vital services, especially when the client receives a direct benefit. If you keep good track of your time, you can also look for ways that you may be wasting time. Improving your work habits can have the same effect as raising your rates. You can increase your earning potential by being more efficient.

You can also base your price on speed of delivery. If you are asked to turn a project around in half the time, charge 10 to 20 percent extra for this value-added service. Chances are you have to put other projects on hold and work extra hard to accomplish a last-minute request. Be fair, but charge extra for the added effort. Most businesses and consumers realize the added value of convenience, which is why we pay more for quick oil changes, overnight shipments, and eyeglasses that are ready "in about an hour."

If you are questioned about a price change, explain how you have incorporated extra value into your services and how your work has helped the client win business or helped a publication gain readership. Explain how your fee is a bargain given the benefits provided or the service received.

As a final word, consider this: A client who does not want you to earn a fair wage is not a client worth having. Is it worth losing some low-profit clients in return for earning extra income from your more profitable clients? Raising your prices may be a way to do a profitable business in a forty-hour week—to work smarter instead of working longer hours.

SAMPLE FEES

The following prices are culled from the *2010 Writer's Market* survey and represent a range of prices charged by freelance writers across North America. Use the prices only as general guidelines because the fees writers charge can vary greatly depending on location, size, complexity of the project, and the writer's own experience or expertise. The prices do not include additional expenses that are typically paid by the client. You can learn more about the going rates charged in your area by networking with other writers or by joining professional writers organizations near you. The benefits you receive will likely be more than offset the annual fees charged by most groups.

Advertising, Copywriting, and PR

Ad copywriting: $40 to $125 per hour, avg. $1.59 per word
News release: $40 to $100 per hour, avg. $440 per page
Speechwriting: $43 to $150 per hour, $2,700 to $10,000 per 30-minute speech

Audiovisual

Copyediting: $35 to $90 per hour
Film script for business: $50 to $150 per hour
Radio editorials: $50 to $70 per hour
Screenplay: $56,500 to $106,070 per screenplay
TV commercial/PSA: $60 to $85 per hour
TV movie: $100 to $500 per run minute
TV news feature: $70 to $100 per hour
TV scripts (teleplay): $100 to $500 per run minute

Book Publishing

Abstracting and abridging: $30 to $125 per hour
Book proposal consultation/writing: $30 to $125 per hour

Book query critique: $50 to $100 per hour

Book query writing: $120 to $500 per project, $200 average per project

Content editing: $29 to $100 per hour

Copyediting: $25 to $100 per hour

Ghostwriting, uncredited: $30 to $100 per hour

Indexing: $2.75 to $6 per page

Manuscript evaluation and critique: $23 to $100 per hour

Proofreading: $19 to $55 per hour, $2 to $5 per page

Research: $20 to $100 per hour, avg. $53 per hour

Rewriting: $30 to $100 per hour

Translation: 6¢ to 12¢ per target word, $7,000 to $10,000 per book

Business and Government

Annual reports: $45 to $150 per hour, $1,000 to $15,000 per project

Brochures/fliers: $50 to $200 per hour, avg. $2,777 per project

Business plan: $35 to $125 per hour

Catalogs: $50 to $80 per hour, avg. $5,000 per project

Corporate periodicals, writing: $35 to $125 per hour, $83 average per hour; $1.75 per word

Grant proposal: $30 to $125 per hour

Computer and Technical

Computer manual writing: $43 to $125 per hour

Online editing: $25 to $100 per hour; avg. $38 per hour

Technical writing: $40 to $125 per hour; avg. $65 per hour

Web page writing/editing: $40 to $125 per hour

Magazines and Trade Journals

Book/arts reviews: $25 to $900 per project

Content editing: $30 to $100 per hour, avg. $3,167 per issue

Copyediting: $20 to $60 per hour, $39 average per hour

Fact-checking: $25 to $100 per hour

Feature articles: $100 to $10,000 per project; avg. $3,597

Proofreading: $17 to $60 per hour

Newspapers

Book/art reviews: $15 to $200 high per review

Copyediting: $15 to $35 per hour; $26 per hour avg.

Feature story: $125 to $1,040 per project; $350 avg.

Local column: avg. $171 per column

Obituary: $35 to $225 per story; avg. $112 per story

Proofreading: $15 to $25 per hour; avg. $19 per hour

Stringing: $50 to $1,000 high per story; avg. $290 per story

Websites

Anne Wallingford, WordSmith (www.aw-wrdsmth.com). Anne Wallingford's Freelancer's FAQs offers useful information about setting fees, taxes, and other aspects of finance.

National Writers Union (www.nwu.org). In a section for members, includes a database of magazine rates paid to NWU members.

Society for Technical Communication (www.stc.org). The STC publishes a survey for members detailing salaries and benefits in the United States and Canada for technical writers and editors.

WritersMarket.com (www.writersmarket.com). Offers members a link to the detailed results of its annual rate survey.

Books

The Wealthy Writer by Michael Meanwell. Includes suggested pricing for high-paying freelance writing work.

Writer's Market. Includes typical pay rates, updated annually, for a variety of writing and publishing work. *Writer's Market Deluxe Edition* includes access to Writers Market.com, the regularly updated online component of the book.

PART IV:
EVERYTHING
AGENTS

CHAPTER 27

WHAT AGENTS DON'T WANT TO SEE IN CHAPTER 1

Ask any literary agent what they're looking for in a first chapter and they'll all say the same thing: "Good writing that hooks me in." Agents appreciate the same elements of good writing that readers do. They want action; they want compelling characters and a reason to read on; they want to see your voice come through in the work and feel an immediate connection with your writing style.

Sure, the fact that agents look for great writing and a unique voice is nothing new. But, for as much as you know about what agents want to see in chapter one, what about all those things they don't want to see? Obvious mistakes such as grammatical errors and awkward writing aside, writers need to be conscious of chapter one clichés and agent pet peeves—either of which, when included in your writing, can sink a manuscript and send a form rejection letter your way.

Have you ever begun a story with a character waking up from a dream? Or opened chapter one with a line of salacious dialogue? Both clichés! Chances are, you've started a story with a cliché or touched on a pet peeve (or many!) in your writing and you don't even know it—and nothing turns an agent off like what agent Cricket Freeman of the August Agency calls "nerve-gangling, major turn-off, ugly-as-sin, nails-on-the-blackboard pet peeves."

To help compile a grand list of these poisonous chapter one no-no's, dozens of established literary agents (and even one editor) were more than happy to chime in and vent about everything that they can't stand to see in that all-important first chapter. Here's what they had to say.

DESCRIPTION

"I dislike endless 'laundry list' character descriptions. For example: 'She had eyes the color of a summer sky and long blonde hair that fell in ringlets past her shoulders. Her petite nose was the perfect size for her heart-shaped face. Her azure dress—with the empire waist and long, tight sleeves—sported tiny pearl buttons down the bodice and ivory lace peeked out of the hem in front, blah, blah, blah.' Who cares! Work it into the story."

—*Laurie McLean, Larsen-Pomada Literary Agents*

"Slow writing with a lot of description will put me off very quickly. I personally like a first chapter that moves quickly and draws me in so I'm immediately hooked and want to read more."

—*Andrea Hurst, Andrea Hurst & Associates Literary Management*

"I hate seeing a 'rundown list.' Names, hair color, eye color, height, even weight sometimes. I also dislike when a writer overdescribes the scenery or area where the story starts."

—*Miriam Hees, editor, Blooming Tree Press*

"Avoid any description of the weather."

—*Denise Marcil, Denise Marcil Literary Agency*

VOICE AND POINT-OF-VIEW

"A pet peeve of mine is ragged, fuzzy point-of-view. How can a reader follow what's happening? I also dislike beginning with a killer's POV. Who would want to be in such an ugly place? I feel like a nasty voyeur."

—*Cricket Freeman, The August Agency*

"An opening that's predictable will not hook me in. If the average person could have come up with the characters and situations, I'll pass. I'm looking for a unique outlook, voice, or character and situation."

—*Debbie Carter, Muse Literary Management*

"Avoid the opening line is 'My name is …,' introducing the narrator to the reader so blatantly. There are far better ways in chapter one to establish an instant connection between narrator and reader."

—*Michelle Andelman, Lynn C. Franklin Associates*

"I don't like having a character immediately tell me how much he/she hates the world for whatever reason. In other words, tell me your issues on politics, the environment, etc., through your character. That is a real turnoff."

—*Miriam Hees (editor), Blooming Tree Press*

"I hate reading purple prose, taking the time to set up—to describe something so beautifully hat has nothing to do with the actual story. I also hate when an author starts something and then says '(the main character) would find out later.' I hate gratuitous sex and violence anywhere in the manuscript. If it is not crucial to the story then I don't want to see it in there, in any chapters."

—*Cherry Weiner, Cherry Weiner Literary*

"I recently read a ms when the second line was something like, 'Let me tell you this, Dear Reader ...' What do you think of that?"

—*Sheree Bykofsky, Sheree Bykofsky Literary*

ACTION (OR LACK THEREOF)

"I don't really like 'First day of school' beginnings, or the 'From the beginning of time,' or 'Once upon a time' starts. Specifically, I dislike a chapter one where nothing happens."

—*Jessica Regel, Jean V. Naggar Literary Agency*

"'The Weather' is always a problem—the author feels he has to set up the scene and tell us who the characters are, etc. I like starting a story in medias res."

—*Elizabeth Pomada, Larsen-Pomada Literary Agents*

"I want to feel as if I'm in the hands of a master storyteller, and starting a story with long, flowery, overly descriptive sentences (kind of like this one) makes the writer seem amateurish and the story contrived. Of course, an equally jarring beginning can be nearly as off-putting, and I hesitate to read on if I'm feeling disoriented by the fifth page. I enjoy when writers can find a good balance between exposition and mystery. Too much accounting always ruins the mystery of a novel, and the unknown is what propels us to read further. It is what keeps me up at night saying, 'Just one more chapter, then I'll go to sleep.' If everything is explained away in the first chapter, I'm probably putting the book down and going to sleep."

—*Peter Miller, Peter Miller Literary*

"Characters that are moving around doing little things, but essentially nothing. Washing dishes and thinking, staring out the window and thinking, tying shoes, thinking ... Authors often do this to transmit information, but the result is action in a literal sense but no real energy in a narrative sense. The best rule of thumb is always to start the story where the story starts."

—*Dan Lazar, Writers House*

CLICHÉS AND FALSE BEGINNINGS

"I hate it when a book begins with an adventure that turns out to be a dream at the end of the chapter."

—*Mollie Glick, Jean V. Naggar Literary Agency*

"Anything cliché such as 'It was a dark and stormy night' will turn me off. I hate when a narrator or author addresses the reader (e.g., "Gentle reader")."

—Jennie Dunham, Dunham Literary

"Sometimes a reasonably good writer will create an interesting character and describe him in a compelling way, but then he'll turn out to be some unimportant bit player. I also don't want to read about anyone sleeping, dreaming, waking up or staring at anything. Other annoying, unoriginal things I see too often: Some young person going home to a small town for a funeral, someone getting a phone call about a death, a description of a psycho lurking in the shadows, or a terrorist planting a bomb."

—Ellen Pepus, Signature Literary Agency

"I don't like it when the main character dies at the end of chapter one. Why did I just spend all this time with this character? I feel cheated."

—Cricket Freeman, The August Agency

"1. Squinting into the sunlight with a hangover in a crime novel. Good grief—been done a million times. 2. A sci-fi novel that spends the first two pages describing the strange landscape. 3. A trite statement ("Get with the program" or "Houston, we have a problem" or "You go girl" or "Earth to Michael" or "Are we all on the same page?"), said by a weenie sales guy, usually in the opening paragraph. 4. A rape scene in a Christian novel, especially in the first chapter. 5. 'Years later, Monica would look back and laugh ...' 6. "The [adjective] [adjective] sun rose in the [adjective] [adjective] sky, shedding its [adjective] light across the [adjective] [adjective] [adjective] land."

—Chip MacGregor, MacGregor Literary

"A cheesy hook drives me nuts. I know that they say 'Open with a hook!'—something to grab the reader. While that's true, there's a fine line between a hook that's intriguing and a hook that's just silly. An example of a silly hook would be opening with a line of overtly sexual dialogue. Or opening with a hook that's just too convoluted to be truly interesting."

—Dan Lazar, Writers House

"Here are things I can't stand: Cliché openings in fantasy can include an opening scene set in a battle (and my peeve is that I don't know any of the characters yet so why should I care about this battle?) or with a pastoral scene where the protagonist is gathering herbs (I didn't realize how common this is). Opening chapters where a main protagonist is in the middle of a bodily function (jerking off, vomiting, peeing, or what have you) is usually a firm NO right from the get-go. Gross. Long prologues that often don't have anything to do with the story. So common in fantasy again. Opening scenes that are all dialogue without any context. I could probably go on …"

—*Kristin Nelson, Nelson Literary*

CHARACTERS AND BACKSTORY

"I don't like descriptions of the characters where writers make the characters seem too perfect. Heroines (and heroes) who are described physically as being virtually unflawed come across as unrelatable and boring. No 'flowing, windswept golden locks'; no 'eyes as blue as the sky'; no 'willowy, perfect figures.' "

—*Laura Bradford, Bradford Literary Agency*

"Don't use inauthentic dialogue to tell the reader who the characters are, instead of showing who the characters are."

—*Jennifer Cayea, Avenue A Literary*

"Many writers express the character's backstory before they get to the plot. Good writers will go back and cut that stuff out and get right to the plot. The character's backstory stays with them—it's in their DNA—even after the cut. To paraphrase Bruno Bettelheim: 'The more the character in a fairy tale is described, the less the audience will identify with him … The less the character is characterized and described the more likely the reader is to identify with him.' "

—*Adam Chromy, Artists and Artisans*

"I'm really turned off by a protagonist named Isabelle who goes by 'Izzy.' No. Really. I am. I'm also turned off when a writer feels the need to fill in all the backstory before starting the story; a story that opens on the protagonist's mental reflection of their situation is (usually) a red flag."

—*Stephany Evans, FinePrint Literary Management*

"One of the biggest problems I encounter is the 'information dump' in the first few pages, where the author is trying to tell us everything we supposedly need to know to understand the story. Getting to know characters in a story is like getting to know people in real life. You find out their personality and details of their life over time."

—*Rachelle Gardner, Wordserve Literary*

(AND FINALLY ...) PROLOGUES

"Most of us hate prologues—just make the first chapter relevant and well written."

—*Andrea Brown, Andrea Brown Literary Agency*

"Prologues are usually a lazy way to give backstory chunks to the reader and can be handled with more finesse throughout the story. Damn the prologue, full speed ahead!"

—*Laurie McLean, Larsen-Pomada Literary Agents*

CHAPTER 28

HOW NOT TO GET AN AGENT

BY JEAN DAIGNEAU

You've finished your first manuscript (or your second or third)—so what's the next step you should take? Start preparations for a book tour? Nope. Search for the right publicist? Nope. Call your mom with the news? Maybe.

But really, if you're ready to venture into the world of publishing, the first thing to do is get an agent. Any serious writer knows agents can magically open doors that some of us only dream about. In a market as tight as the current one, however, even getting an agent can be challenging. Which means this is the time to really put your creativity to work—forget the rules, ignore the experts, and listen to what they're not telling you.

1. WATTS A FEW TYPOS AMONG FRIENDS

Prior to submitting to an agent, you've no doubt read your manuscript until you could almost recite it verbatim. Why worry then about those last few thousand words you just revised? That's what spelling and grammar check tools are for. Sew watts the wurst that mite hap pen if ewe have knot red yore man yew script won Moor thyme? If an agent can't overlook a few mistakes, she's probably not very flexible or easy to get along with, right? Who wants to work with someone like that? Besides, isn't that an agent's job? To take an unpolished manuscript and turn it into a best-seller? Your job is to write. You may as well leave the editing to the experts.

2. GIMMICKS, GIMMICKS, GIMMICKS

Cute sells. Think Beanie Babies and dyed baby chicks. (Okay, you probably weren't even born when people could buy baby chicks in a rainbow of colors, but they were cute.) So enhancing your manuscript with clip art will certainly add an interesting element. Or consider using colored stationery or perhaps an unusual font. Something like Bradley Hand ITC is definitely eye-catching. Remember, it's all about making it to the top of the slush pile, or at least getting an agent's attention.

Besides, agents are people driven by the same human emotions as the rest of us—mostly greed. What agent in his or her right mind would turn down chocolate? Or football tickets? Or cash? Okay, I'm just kidding about the cash, but don't think it can't work.

Anything that makes your submission stand out is worth trying. Steven Chudney, principal of the Steven Chudney Agency, will attest to that fact. "Twice I've received 8 by 10 glossies from prospective clients," he said. "That certainly told me a lot about their writing and them." See? From the hundreds of submittals he's received, which ones does he remember? The two authors who sent glossies. I told you gimmicks work.

3. NO TIME TO BE HUMBLE

One thing most successful people have is confidence. What better way to show it than by letting an agent know that your spouse, best friend, grandchildren, or fellow inmates all love your story? Any agent will be thrilled to know that you're the next Dr. Seuss, especially when you tell her that, while your manuscript may seem very similar to *How the Grinch Stole Christmas*, it's actually much better. So remember, you can't say enough about what a great writer you are. That agent will be so impressed with you she'll probably mention your approach during a conference presentation—as one of the most unforgettable she's encountered.

4. SHOW OFF YOUR BEST FEATURE

Relax. This has nothing to do with thong bathing suits (which is a good thing since some men don't look good in them anyway—and neither do some women). When an agent asks for the first three chapters and a synopsis, who says that's what you should send? Let's say your story really kicks into high gear in chapter five. By all means, send chapter five! Once an agent gets a taste for how talented you are, he'll be begging for the rest of your manuscript anyway.

Then, too, some agents change their submittal policies like my Uncle Jerome changes his underwear—once a week, whether he needs to or not. Just trying to keep those guidelines straight is a full-time job. Why bother? Writing is hard enough as it is.

5. ONE SIZE FITS ALL

Some so-called experts will say it's important to find out which agent is the best fit for your style of writing. Don't you believe it! Just because an agent doesn't rep a certain genre doesn't mean you shouldn't send it. After all, there are plenty of successful writers who have found their niche. If horror works for Stephen King, it stands to reason any agent will want your latest chiller. Once an agent reads it, she'll be more than delighted to change her entire business focus just to sign you up. Well, unless she's a loser. But then who wants to sign with an agent who would pass up the next Stephen King?

6. CUT TO THE CHASE

We all know that agents are busy people. But, hey, you're busy, too. Why waste time waiting to hear back from an agent? The best thing to do if you don't get an answer right away is to pick up the phone. After all, any agent will appreciate the fact that he or she doesn't have to call you back. Is there such a thing as calling too often? I'd let the agent worry about that if I were you.

Serendipity Literary Agency founder Regina Brooks deals with her share of persistent authors all the time. "Some authors call and call again and often it's not just about the book project," she said. Brooks, however, has no complaints. "I always wanted to be a therapist. And since agents border on practicing law without a license when we review contracts, what's the harm in practicing psychiatry without one, too?" Should you ever sign with her, you'll be glad to know that her diagnoses are free. Well, only if you're committed. Or perhaps need to be.

7. LOOK OUT FOR NUMERO UNO

Once you're lucky enough to have gotten to an agent who is interested in your work, this is your opportunity to question how she runs her business. You might not know everything there is about being an agent, but you certainly know what's best for you. Getting her to lower her commission rates is only a matter of telling her how outrageous they are. No amount of nitpicking is too much; when you get to this stage, it's all about you.

Then, too, you surely have some idea of what publisher you want handling your masterpiece and, therefore, where it should be sent. Don't be afraid to let an agent know exactly what you expect. And, once you're on your way to sealing the deal, you'll want to let her know that PR is her responsibility. After all, you've done the hard part; your work is done.

8. IT'S NEVER TOO EARLY

But let's say you haven't finished your first novel yet. Contrary to what you might think, that makes you one of the lucky ones. Why bother even writing something if the chances of it getting published are so slim? If you sign up with an agent before you've finished your first novel, or even started it for that matter, think of the aggravation you'll save yourself. You can pitch your idea, an agent will fall in love with it, he'll give you plenty of direction on where to go with it, and you can write with the knowledge that an adoring public and an even more grateful agent are awaiting your every word.

9. DON'T OVERLOOK ANY OPPORTUNITY

Fate, too, can sometimes play a part in your success in getting an agent. Say you're at a writers conference and you happen to follow an agent to the bathroom and into the stall next to her. If you see a hand waving at you from underneath the divider, you, my friend, are golden. I'm not suggesting you shouldn't help a person in need. Just wrap the toilet paper around your manuscript and pass it on over—or in this case, under.

After all, agents go to conferences, retreats, and workshops to meet clients, right? As the author of a future *New York Times* bestseller, the only obstacle between you and instant fame and fortune is getting your manuscript into an agent's hands so she knows it, too. Once she does, chances are good she'll whip out a contract and sign you on the spot.

10. DRAW ATTENTION TO YOURSELF

It's especially important during a tough publishing market to shed that high school wallflower persona and let the world know you're interested in finding an agent. It's all about getting the word out that you're available. Of course, for some of you, thoughts of high school and "being available" might conjure up different images—like your phone number on a few restroom walls. Which is okay, I guess, since you might pick up an agent that way. Or vice versa.

When it comes to getting noticed, children's author Cinda Chima shared this advice, gleaned from a conference she recently attended: "If you're unhappy with your agent, attend a writing conference with editors and agents and complain loudly to anyone who will listen about what an idiot your agent is. No doubt other agents will hear about it and know you're in the market and will contact you about representation." Chima, whose young adult Heir trilogy did make it onto *The New York Times* bestseller list, unfortunately did things the hard way. Prior to publication she wrote her manuscript to near perfection, then researched and queried agents until she found one that was a good fit. How that got her an agent, I'll never know. Some people are just lucky, I guess.

IN THE END

What happens, though, if you've tried all of these things and for some unknown reason, they haven't worked? My advice is simple—don't worry. Who says you need an agent in the first place? You don't really believe everything you read in *Guide to Literary Agents*, do you? Besides, between you and me, a person has to be pretty lame to read the kind of book that claims to give advice on something as simple as getting an agent. We both know you are way beyond that.

Jean Daigneau is a writer living in Kent, Ohio.

CHAPTER 29

WHEELING & DEALING AT A WRITERS CONFERENCE

Writing is a solitary task. It means a lot of time sitting at the computer, researching facts online, checking your e-mail, and staring at that first chapter you've rewritten eighteen times but still doesn't seem to work. If you want to be a writer, you're going to spend plenty of time alone, but at the same time, you need to understand the importance of networking and making friends who are fellow scribes. That's where writers conferences come in.

Conferences are your rare and invaluable opportunities to simply get out there—to mingle, network, have fun, and meet new contacts that can help further your career. There are plenty of conferences all across the country and beyond. Now you just need to know how to maximize a conference's worth, and you'll be all set.

CONFERENCES: THE BASICS

Conferences are events where writers gather to meet one another and celebrate the craft and business of writing. Attendees listen to authors and publishing professionals who present on various topics of interest. Each day is filled with sessions regarding all aspects of writing, and attendees will likely have a choice of which sessions to attend. For example, you can attend the "Query Letter Writing" session versus other panels on "The Secrets of Mystery Writing" and "The Secrets of Successful Book Proposals" held at the same time. To find out what speakers and sessions will be included, check the event's official website or e-mail the coordinator.

Since they usually take place during a weekend, you may have to clear your Friday schedule to see all speakers. Also, conferences are not to be confused with *retreats*, which are longer outings that include a lot of writing assignments. Retreats typically have small attendance and cost more because of the personal attention.

Some conferences are long-standing, while others are brand-new. Most are not out to make money and few could, even if they wanted to. A regional writers group usually organizes them, and the organizers are likely all volunteers. For example, the Southeast Mystery Writers of America hosts Killer Nashville, while the Space Coast Writers' Guild organizes the Space Coast Writers' Conference in Cocoa Beach.

HOW DO YOU FIND CONFERENCES?

Conferences are all over the place. With approximately two hundred per year in the United States, you can find them in practically every state and area of the country—and then there are even more in Canada. Some areas are hot spots, such as New York, Texas, and California, whereas other states may not have a lot of choices, but still have at least one annual event nearby.

To find a conference, you can use print directories, online directories, or simply a search engine. *Guide to Literary Agents* lists a whole smorgasbord of conferences in its back section, while *GLA*'s sister publications, such as *Children's Writer's & Illustrator's Market*, list conferences specific to the book's target readers. Also, conferences advertise in magazines (such as *Writer's Digest*) and are featured in writing-related newsletters, such as Absolute Write and Writer Gazette. Subscribe to free newsletters to get conference alerts along with plenty of other helpful info.

Helpful online directories exist especially for genre fiction writers. Look online for the web sites of the Romance Writers of America, the Mystery Writers of America, or the Society of Children's Book Writers and Illustrators, and you will find lists of upcoming conferences that are great value to scribes of those categories.

Another option is to simply use Google. The results are usually incomplete but helpful enough. Try searching for "writers conference (month and year)" and see what comes up. You won't find a ton of gatherings that way, but searches will provide a few promising leads. Since conferences sometimes pop up out of nowhere without a whole lot of hubbub, this can be a good way to find newer events.

No matter where you find a conference listing, you will want to check out the conference website, where updated lists of speakers, time, dates and registration forms can be found.

WHO WILL YOU MEET?

Perhaps the most valuable aspect of a conference is writers' ability to meet the power players and decision makers in the publishing world. In addition, they can make contacts and form partnerships with their fellow writers. Here are three different types of people you will meet.

Peers and Writers

This is where the schmoozing comes in. Besides classes and presentations, there are usually dinners as well as meet-and-greet opportunities, not to mention simply banding together at night and hitting the hotel lobby or nearby bar to relax and talk. Perhaps you didn't even know the regional writers' group in charge existed, and you may be able to get involved with the organization.

Editors

Editors spend a lot of time at conferences meeting with writers one-on-one and essentially answering any and all questions that they. Editors specialize in presenting sessions and workshops, teaching everything from craft and characters to book proposal writing and the basics of agents.

Agents

Perhaps the biggest draw, agents attend conferences for a specific reason: to find potential clients. They are bombarded with pitches and request writing samples from those attendees who dazzle them with a good idea or pitch. Short of an excellent referral, conferences are the best way to snag an agent, so take advantage of meeting one.

Usually it works like this: You will schedule a short amount of time to pitch your idea to an agent. Your "elevator pitch" should be relatively short, and then there's some time for the agent to ask questions. If the agent is interested in seeing some of your work, she will pass you a business card and request a "partial" (a sample of the manuscript, such as the first thrity pages or the first three chapters). If the agent is not interested, she will say so. When an agent requests your manuscript, you can send it in and put "Requested Material" on the envelope (or in the e-mail) so it gets past the slush pile.

While there are designated times to pitch agents, it should be said that agents are usually ready for pitches at all times from all sides. However, beware crossing the line into "annoying." Don't pitch agents in the restroom. Don't interrupt them if they're having a conversation. If an agent is sitting down with fellow agents and trying, for a brief moment, not to talk business, don't hover around waiting for eye contact so you can step in and pitch.

The simple fact that you're *at* a conference shows that you're dedicated and professional. That in itself is enough to get agents' attention. Though writers still find in-person pitching quite nerve-racking, the good news is that agents are not the mean stereotypes you may have in mind. They are almost all friendly book lovers like you.

HOW TO MAXIMIZE THE VALUE

If you want to make the most out of a conference, you have to stay busy and get involved. Go to presentations; hang out at late-night fiction readings; and make sure to stay for the whole shebang. Sign up for pitch slams and meet the power players in attendance. A little face time can pay off down the line. If you're involved with the sponsoring organization, offer to volunteer. If you pick up an agent from the airport, for example, that's plenty of one-on-one time in the car to slip in a pitch or two.

Make sure you schmooze. When you sit down at the dinner banquet, ask people what they're working on. Networking can be as simple as "I'll pass your name on to so-and-so, and I'd be appreciative if you could give me a referral to such-and-such." If you don't have business cards, make some basic ones just so others can know your contact info.

An unfortunate truth about conferences is that they can be a hit on the wallet. Some are affordable ($100-200) while others not so much ($700+). It all depends on how long the conference is, what is included, the price the conference paid to fly in speakers, etc. There are conferences where the crowd gathered at a Days Inn and others where the event was hosted in a posh hotels. Can you guess which event cost more? In addition to the basic conference cost, you have to budget money for extras. Sometimes, the little things at a conference, such as ten-minute pitch sessions with agents or an editor's personal critique of your work, will mean an additional cost. If you want to truly make the most of a conference, you will need to indulge in some extras. When all is said and done, you may have to take a day off work and spend a chunk of money on costs and hotels. Think of it as an annual writing vacation for you and budget money early in the year. If you gain contacts that lead to writing assignments down the line, the conference will pay for itself before you know it.

KNOW WHICH ONE IS RIGHT FOR YOU

With so many to choose from, how can you know which one is the best investment? Obviously proximity will play a factor, as we can't all afford a ticket to the Maui Writers' Conference. Look for events in your area and start from there. Some locations, such as Tennessee and Colorado, have a surprisingly large number of gatherings each year.

Ask yourself: "What do I want to get out of this?" Is it simply to recharge your batteries and get motivated? Because a general goal like that can be accomplished by most conferences. Do you have a polished and ready manuscript that needs an agent? Look for conferences with not only agents in attendance but agents (or acquiring editors, as they function basically the same) in attendance that handle your specific area of work, be it science fiction, medical nonfiction, or whatever else.

Conferences usually have either a general focus on all subjects of writing, or a more narrow purpose. By doing some research, you can find conferences devoted to screenwriting, playwriting, romance, mysteries, fantasy, science fiction, medical thrillers, and more.

GET OUT THERE!

Now that you know the ins and outs of a writers conference, all that's left is for you to hunt down an event and sign up. Going to a gathering and pitching agents may seem intimidating, especially if you're going alone, but the payoff is definitely worth it, and you're likely to make several friends who can ensure you don't go to a conference alone again. At the very least, you'll get some tips on how to start the befuddling first chapter that never seems to click.

CHAPTER 30

RESEARCHING YOUR OPTIONS & LOOKING OUT FOR SCAMS

Once you've received an offer of representation, you must determine if the agent is right for you. As flattering as any offer may be, you need to be confident that you are going to work well with the agent and that she is going to work hard to sell your manuscript.

EVALUATE THE OFFER

You need to know what to expect once you enter into a business relationship. You should know how much editorial input to expect from your agent, how often she gives updates about where your manuscript has been and who has seen it, and what subsidiary rights the agent represents.

More importantly, you should know when you will be paid. The publisher will send your advance and any subsequent royalty checks directly to the agent. After deducting her commission—usually 10 to 15 percent—your agent will send you the remaining balance. Most agents charge a higher commission of 20 to 25 percent when using a co-agent for foreign, dramatic, or other specialized rights. As you enter into a relationship with an agent, have her explain her specific commission rates and payment policy.

Some agents offer written contracts and some do not. If your prospective agent does not, at least ask for a "memorandum of understanding" that details the basic relationship of expenses and commissions. If your agent does offer a contract, be sure to read it carefully, and keep a copy for yourself. Since contracts can be confusing, you may want to have a lawyer or knowledgeable writer friend check it out before signing anything.

The National Writers Union (NWU) has drafted a Preferred Literary Agent Agreement and a pamphlet, *Understand the Author-Agent Relationship*, which is available to members. The union suggests clauses that delineate such issues as:

- the scope of representation (One work? One work with the right of refusal on the next? All work completed in the coming year? All work completed until the agreement is terminated?)

- the extension of authority to the agent to negotiate on behalf of the author

- compensation for the agent and any co-agent, if used

- manner and time frame for forwarding monies received by the agent on behalf of the client

- termination clause, allowing client to give about thirty days to terminate the agreement

- the effect of termination on concluded agreements as well as ongoing negotiations

- arbitration in the event of a dispute between agent and client.

If you have any concerns about the agency's practices, ask the agent about them before you sign. Once an agent is interested in representing you, she should be willing to address any questions or concerns that you have. If the agent is rude or unresponsive, or tries to tell you that the information is confidential or classified, the agent is uncommunicative at best and, at worst, is already trying to hide something from you.

AVOID GETTING SCAMMED

The number of literary agents in the country, as well as the world, is increasing. This is because each year, aspiring authors compose an increasing number of manuscripts, while publishing houses continue to merge and become more selective as well as less open to working directly with writers. With literary agents providing the crucial link between writers and publishers, it's no wonder dozens of new agencies sprout up each year in the United States alone.

While more agencies may seem like a good thing, writers who seek to pair up with a successful agent must beware when navigating the murky waters of the Internet. Because agents are such a valuable part of the process, many unethical persons are floating around the online publishing world, ready to take advantage of uninformed writers who desperately want to see their work in print.

To protect yourself, you must familiarize yourself with common agent red flags and keep your radar up for any other warning signs. First of all, it can't be stressed enough that you should never pay agents any fees just so they consider your work. Only small fees (such as postage and copying) are acceptable, and those miniscule costs are administered *after* the agent has contacted you and signed you as a client.

A typical scam goes something like this: You send your work to an agency and they reply with what seems like a form letter or e-mail, telling you they love your story. At some point, they ask for money, saying it has to do with distribution, production, submissions, analysis, or promotion. By that point, you're so happy with the prospect of finding an agent (you probably already told family and friends) that you nervously hand over the money. Game over. You've just been scammed. Your work may indeed end up in print, but you're likely getting very little if any money. To be a successful author, publishers must pay you to write; you must never pay them.

When a deal seems too good to be true, it likely is. If you want to learn more about a particular agent, look at his website. Google her name: You'll likely find a dozen writers just like you discussing this agent on an Internet forum asking questions such as "Does anyone know anything about agent so-and-so?" These writer-oriented websites exist so writers like you can meet similar persons and discuss their good/bad experiences with publications, agents, and publishing houses.

Protect yourself from scams by getting questions answered before you make any deals. When an abundance of research material is not available, you must be cautious. Ask around, ask questions, and never pay up-front fees.

IF YOU'VE BEEN SCAMMED

If you have trouble with your agent and you've already tried to resolve it to no avail, it may be time to call for help. Please alert the writing community to protect others. If you find agents online, in directories or in this book who aren't living up to their promises or are charging you money when they're listed as non-fee-charging agents, please let the Web master or editor of the publication know. Sometimes they can intervene for an author, and if no solution can be found, they can at the very least remove a listing from their directory so that no other authors will be scammed in the future. All efforts are made to keep scam artists out, but in a world where agencies are frequently bought and sold, a reputation can change overnight.

If you have complaints about any business, consider contacting The Federal Trade Commission, The Council of Better Business Bureaus, or your state's attorney general. Legal action may seem like a drastic step, but sometimes people do it. You can file a suit with the attorney general and try to find other writers who want to sue for fraud with you. The Science Fiction & Fantasy Writers of America's website offers sound advice on recourse you can take in these situations. For more details, visit www.sfwa.org/beware/.

If you live in the same state as your agent, it may be possible to settle the case in small claims court. This is a viable option for collecting smaller damages and a way to avoid lawyer fees. The jurisdiction of the small claims court includes cases in which the claim is $5,000 or less. (This varies from state to state, but should still cover the amount for which you're suing.) Keep in mind that suing takes a lot of effort and time. You'll have to research all the necessary legal steps. If you have lawyers in the family, that could be a huge benefit if they agree to help you organize the case, but legal assistance is not necessary.

Above all, if you've been scammed, don't waste time blaming yourself. It's not your fault if someone lies to you. Respect in the literary world is built on reputation, and word gets around about agents who scam, cheat, lie, and steal. Editors ignore their submissions and writers avoid them. Without clients or buyers, a swindling agent will find her business collapsing.

Meanwhile, you'll keep writing and believing in yourself. One day, you'll see your work in print, and you'll tell everyone what a rough road it was to get there, but how you wouldn't trade it for anything in the world.

WHAT SHOULD I ASK?

The following is a list of topics the Association of Authors' Representatives suggests authors discuss with literary agents who have offered to represent them. Please bear in mind that most agents are not willing to spend time answering these questions unless they have already read your material and wish to represent you.

1. Are you a member of the Association of Authors' Representatives or do you adhere to their basic canon of ethics?

2. How long have you been in business as an agent?

3. Do you have specialists at your agency who handle movie rights and television rights? Foreign rights?

4. Do you have subagents or corresponding agents in Hollywood and overseas?

5. Who in your agency will actually be handling my work? Will the other staff members be familiar with my work and the status of my business at your agency?

6. Will you oversee, or at least keep me apprised of, the work that your agency is doing on my behalf?

7. Do you issue an agent/author agreement? May I review the language of the agency clause that appears in contracts you negotiate for your clients?

8. How do you keep your clients informed of your activities on their behalf?

9. Do you consult with your clients on any and all offers?

10. What are your commission rates? What are your procedures and time frames for processing and disbursing client funds? Do you keep different bank accounts separating author funds from agency revenue? What are your policies about charging clients for expenses incurred by your agency?

11. When you issue 1099 tax forms at the end of each year, do you also furnish clients—upon request—with a detailed account of their financial activity, such as gross income, commissions, and other deductions and net income for the past year?

12. In the event of your death or disability, what provisions do you or your firm have for my continued representation?

13. If we should part company, what is your policy about handling any unsold subsidiary rights to my work?

Reprinted with the permission of the Association of Authors' Representatives (www.aar-online.org).

REPORTING A COMPLAINT

If you feel you've been cheated or misrepresented, or you're trying to prevent a scam, the following resources should be of help.

- The Federal Trade Commission, Bureau of Consumer Protection. While the FTC won't resolve individual consumer problems, it does depend on your complaints to help them investigate fraud, and your speaking up may even lead to law enforcement action. Visit www.ftc.gov.

- Volunteer Lawyers for the Arts is a group of volunteers from the legal profession who assist with questions of law pertaining to the arts. Visit www.vlany.org.

- The Council of Better Business Bureau is the organization to contact if you have a complaint or if you want to investigate a publisher, literary agent, or other business related to writing and writers. Contact your local BBB or visit www.bbb.org.

- Your state's attorney general. Don't know your attorney general's name? Go to www.attorney general.gov. This site provides a wealth of contact information, including a complete list of links to each state's attorney general website.

CHAPTER 31

NEGOTIATING YOUR CONTRACT

BY THE AUTHORS GUILD

Even if you're working with an agent, it's crucial to understand the legal provisions associated with book contracts. After all, you're the one ultimately responsible for signing off on the terms set forth by the deal. Below are nine clauses found in typical book contracts. Reading the explanation of each clause, along with the negotiating tips, will help clarify what you are agreeing to as the book's author.

1. GRANT OF RIGHTS

The Grant of Rights clause transfers ownership rights in, and therefore control over, certain parts of the work from the author to the publisher. Although it's necessary and appropriate to grant some exclusive rights (e.g., the right to print, publish and sell print-book editions), don't assign or transfer your copyright and use discretion when granting rights in languages other than English and territories other than the United States, its territories and Canada. Also, limit the publication formats granted to those that your publisher is capable of exploiting adequately.

- Never transfer or assign your copyright or "all rights" in the work to your publisher.

- Limit the languages, territories, and formats in which your publisher is granted rights.

2. SUBSIDIARY RIGHTS

Subsidiary rights are uses that your publisher may make of your manuscript other than issuing its own hardcover or paperback print book editions. Print-related subsidiary rights include book club and paperback reprint editions, publication of selections, condensations or abridgments in anthologies and textbooks, and first and second serial rights (that is, publication in newspapers or magazines either before or after publication of the hardcover book). Subsidiary rights not related to print include motion picture, television, stage, audio, animation, merchandising, and electronic rights.

Subsidiary rights may be directly exploited by your publisher or licensed to third parties. Your publisher will share licensing fees with you in proportion to the ratios set forth in your contract. You should receive at least 50 percent of the licensing proceeds.

- Consider reserving rights outside the traditional grant of primary print book publishing rights, especially if you have an agent.

- Beware of any overly inclusive language, such as "in any format now known or hereafter developed," used to describe the scope of the subsidiary rights granted.

- Make sure you are fairly compensated for any subsidiary rights granted. Reputable publishers will pay you at least 50 percent of the proceeds earned from licensing certain categories of rights, much higher for others.

3. DELIVERY AND ACCEPTANCE

Most contracts stipulate that the publisher is only obligated to accept, pay for, and publish a manuscript that is "satisfactory to the publisher in form and content." It may be difficult to negotiate a more favorable, objective provision, but you should try. Otherwise the decision as to whether your manuscript is satisfactory, and therefore publishable, will be left to the subjective discretion of your publisher.

- If you cannot do better, indicate that an acceptable manuscript is one which your publisher deems editorially satisfactory.

- Obligate your publisher to assist you in editing a second corrected draft before ultimately rejecting your manuscript.

- Negotiate a nonrefundable advance or insert a clause that would allow you to repay the advance on a rejected book from re-sale proceeds paid by a second publisher.

4. PUBLICATION

Including a publication deadline in your contract will obligate your publisher to actually publish your book in a timely fashion. Be sure that the amount of time between the delivery of the manuscript and the publication of the book isn't longer than industry standard.

- Make sure you're entitled to terminate the contract, regain all rights granted, and keep the advance if your publisher fails to publish on or before the deadline.

- Carefully limit the conditions under which your publisher is allowed to delay publication.

5. COPYRIGHT

Current copyright law doesn't require authors to formally register their copyright in order to secure copyright protection. Copyright automatically arises in written works created in or after 1978. However, registration with the Copyright Office is a prerequisite to infringement lawsuits and important benefits accrue when a work is registered within three months of initial publication.

- Require your publisher to register your book's copyright within three months of initial publication.

- As previously discussed in Grant of Rights, don't allow your publisher to register copyright in its own name.

6. ADVANCE

An advance against royalties is money that your publisher will pay you prior to publication and subsequently deduct from your share of royalty earnings. Most publishers will pay, but might not initially offer, an advance based on a formula which projects the first year's income.

- Research past advances paid by your publisher in industry publications such as *Publishers Weekly*.

7. ROYALTIES

You should earn royalties for sales of your book that are in line with industry standards. For example, many authors are paid 10 percent of the retail price of the book on the first five thousand copies sold, 12.5 percent of the retail price on the next five thousand copies sold, and 15 percent of the retail price on all copies sold thereafter.

- Base your royalties on the suggested retail list price of the book, not on net sales income earned by your publisher. Net-based royalties are lower than list-based royalties of the same percentage, and they allow your publisher room to offer special deals or write off bad debt without paying you money on the books sold.

- Limit your publisher's ability to sell copies of your book at deep discounts—quantity discount sales of more than 50 percent—or as remainders.

- Limit your publisher's ability to reduce the percentage of royalties paid for export, book club, mail order, and other special sales.

8. ACCOUNTING AND PAYMENTS

Your accounting clause should establish the frequency with which you should expect to receive statements accounting for your royalty earnings and subsidiary rights licensing proceeds. If you are owed money in any given accounting period, the statement should be accompanied by a check.

- Insist on at least a bi-annual accounting.

- Limit your publisher's ability to withhold a reserve against returns of your book from earnings that are otherwise owed to you.

- Include an audit clause in your contract which gives you or your representative the right to examine the sales records kept by the publisher in connection with your work.

9. OUT OF PRINT

Your publisher should only have the exclusive rights to your work while it is actively marketing and selling your book (i.e., while your book is "in print"). An out-of-print clause will allow you to terminate the contract and regain all rights granted to your publisher after the book stops earning money.

It is crucial to actually define the print status of your book in the contract. Stipulate that your work is in print only when copies are available for sale in the United States in an English language hardcover or paperback edition issued by the publisher and listed in its catalog. Otherwise, your book should be considered out of print and all rights should revert to you.

- Don't allow the existence of electronic and print-on-demand editions to render your book in print. Alternatively, establish a floor above which a certain amount of royalties must be earned or copies must be sold during each accounting period for your book to be considered in print. Once sales or earnings fall below this floor, your book should be deemed out of print and rights should revert to you.

- Stipulate that as soon as your book is out of print, all rights will automatically revert to you regardless of whether or not your book has earned out the advance.

Copyright © 2005 The Authors Guild. Reprinted with the permission of The Authors Guild (www.authorsguild.org).

CHAPTER 32

SO YOU HAVE AN AGENT ... NOW WHAT?

We've told you all about contacting and securing agents. But should your hard work and passion pay off in a signed deal with a big-shot agent, the journey isn't over. Now it's time to learn what lies in store after the papers are signed.

LET YOUR AGENT WORK

In the time leading up to signing a contract, you may have bantered around plenty with your agent—realizing you both love the New York Yankees and Kung Pao Chicken. But don't let this camaraderie allow you to forget that the relationship is a business one first and foremost. Does this mean you can't small talk occasionally and ask your agent how her children are doing? No. But don't call every day complaining about the traffic and your neighbor's habit of mowing his lawn before the sun comes up.

Your agent is going to read your work again (and again ...) and likely suggest possible changes to the manuscript. "When you sign with an agent, you should go over next steps, and talk about what the agent expects from you," says Sorche Fairbank, principal of the Fairbank Literary Agency. "This can vary with each author-agent relationship, and on the type of book project. We (at the Fairbank agency) are fairly hands-on with shaping and polishing a proposal or manuscript, and there often is quite a bit of work to be done before we and the author feel it's ready to send out.

"If you have a nonfiction project, there is certain to be some final tweaking of the proposal and sample chapter(s)," Fairbank says. "If you have a novel, then I hope you would be ... taking any agent advice on tightening and polishing it. Go through it one more time and weed out extraneous words, overused pet words and phrases, and stock descriptions."

KEEP WRITING

If you're not working with your agent on rewrites and revisions, it's your responsibility to continue creating. One challenge is over—another begins. As your agent is trying hard to sell your work and bring home a nice paycheck, you're expected to keep churning out material for her to sell. Keep her informed of what you're working on and when it'll be ready.

Stay passionate. Once you've convinced yourself that your first book was not a fluke, you've convinced yourself that you're a capable writer—and a capable writer needs to keep writing and always have material to sell. Continue to consider new projects and work on new things, but give preference to the first work that got you a contract. Rewrites and revisions—wanted by agents and editors alike—will likely take months and become somewhat tedious, but all that frustration will melt away when you have that first hardcover book in your hands.

SELLING THE BOOK

When the book is as perfect as can be, it's time for your agent to start shopping it to her publishing contacts. During this process, she'll likely keep you abreast of all rejections. Don't take these to heart—instead, learn from each one, especially those with editors who have kindly given a specific reason as to why they don't want the book. "When the project is being shopped around, discuss rejections with your agent. There may be patterns that point to a fixable weak spot," Fairbank says.

Your book may be bought in a preempt. That's when a publishing house tries to beat other potential buyers to your work and offers a solid price in the hopes of securing your book early and avoiding a bidding war. An actual bidding war—or *auction*—happens when a work is so stunningly marvelous that every house in town wants it bad enough to compete against each other, offering different perks such as a large advance and guaranteed ad dollars. Traditionally, the best deal (read: most money and enthusiasm) wins and signs. After the auction was finished for Elizabeth Kostova's *The Historian*, her advance was a cool $2 million. (Note: First-time novelists will likely get an advance of $20,000 to $60,000, but hey, anything can happen!)

Your agent will submit the work to publishers (either exclusively or simultaneously, depending on her opinion) and hold a private auction if need be to secure the best deal possible. Fairbank says it's important for writers to relax during the auction process and not call every 30 minutes for an update. "In an auction, everything should go through the agent, but writers may be called upon to do a few things," she says. "I have had some cases where it made sense to bring the author around to meet with the various interested houses, usually to drive home the author's expertise and promotability. There have also been times where a particular house asked for more specifics on something, and I needed my author ready to respond ASAP."

PROMOTE YOURSELF

Besides continuing to write and revise, the most important thing a writer needs to focus on is promotion. It's likely your work will not have the benefit of countless publicists setting up interviews for you. How you want to promote your work is up to you.

According to Regina Brooks, president of Serendipity Literary Agency, "It's always a great time to research who you might want on your team once the book is published (e.g., publicists, Web developers, graphic artists). Oftentimes, authors wait until the last minute to start researching these options. The more lead time a publicist has to think about your project, the better. This is also an ideal time to attend conferences to network and workshops to tighten your writing skills."

GO WITH THE FLOW

An agent's job is to agent. That means knowing which people are buying what, and where they're headed if a move is in the works. Throughout the editing process, you'll work hand in hand with your agent and editor to revise and polish the manuscript. But let's say the editor makes the not-so-uncommon decision to switch jobs or switch houses. Ideally an agent will shepherd you through the change.

"It happens more often than we'd like," says Brooks. "When it does, you hope that someone in-house will be as excited about the project as the acquiring editor initially was, but there's no guarantee." Fairbank agrees: "The most important thing the author and agent can do in that case is take a deep breath, pick up the phone, and wholeheartedly welcome the new editor to the book team."

In addition to switching editors at publishing houses, a writer must concern himself with the possibility of his agent hitting the lottery and quitting (or just quitting without hitting the lottery, which is more probable). To protect yourself, make sure that this scenario is clearly addressed in your contract with the agent. "It really depends on the initial written agreement between the agent and the author," says Brooks. "It's important that the agreement cover such situations in their termination language. This assures that all parties including the publishing company know how to proceed with royalty statements, notices, etc."

AND WHAT IF ...?

A difficult question that may come up is this: What should you do if you think your agent has given up on you or isn't fulfilling her end of the bargain? (In other words, how do you get out? Can you get out?) First, consider that if an agent is trying and failing to sell your manuscript, then at least the trying part is there. It could just be an unfortunate instance where you and an agent both love a work but can't find anyone else who feels the same. This is no one's fault. As far as simply quitting an agent is concerned, you can't opt out of a contract until the contract says so.

A similar dilemma involves authors who have a satisfactory agent but want out in favor of one perceived to be better. If you already have an agent, but others are calling in hopes to work with you, the new agents likely don't know you already have representation. Obviously you need to tell them you are currently represented. That said, you most likely can't just switch agents because you're under contract. When the time comes when you can legally opt out of a contract (and you think your agent has had ample time to make a sale), consider your options then.

GET READY FOR YOUR RIDE

Hopefully you'll never need to experience the difficulty and confusion of switching agents and/ or editors. Hopefully your work will smoothly find a house and then a large audience once it's published. Just remember that the smoother things go, the less excuses exist for you not to keep writing ,then promote the heck out of your work. Simply do what you do best (write) and continue to learn what you can about the publishing world. As Fairbank puts it so simply, "Be available, willing, and ready to help your agent."

PART V: LISTINGS

CHAPTER 33

AGENTS OPEN TO UNSOLICITED WORK

DOMINICK ABEL LITERARY AGENCY, INC.

146 W. 82nd St., #1A, New York NY 10024. (212)877-0710. **Fax:** (212)595-3133. **E-mail:** agency@dalainc.com. Member of AAR. **Represents:** 100 clients. **Currently Handles:** adult fiction and nonfiction. **How to Contact:** Query via e-mail. **Terms:** Agent receives 15% commission on domestic sales. Agent receives 20% commission on foreign sales.

ADAMS LITERARY

7845 Colony Road C4, #215, Charlotte NC 28226. (704)542-1440. **Fax:** (704)542-1450. **E-mail:** info@adamsliterary.com. **Website:** www.adamsliterary.com. **Contact:** Tracey Adams, Josh Adams, Quinlan Lee. Member of AAR. Other memberships include SCBWI and WNBA. **Member Agents:** Tracey Adams; Josh Adams; Quinlan Lee. Adams Literary is a full-service literary agency exclusively representing children's book authors and artists. **How to Contact:** "Guidelines are posted (and frequently updated) on our website."

MIRIAM ALTSHULER LITERARY AGENCY

53 Old Post Road N., Red Hook NY 12571. (845)758-9408. **Website:** www.miriamaltshulerliteraryagency.com. **Contact:** Miriam Altshuler. Estab. 1994. Member of AAR. **Represents:** 40 clients. **Currently Handles:** nonfiction books 45%, novels 45%, story collections 5%, juvenile books 5%. Ms. Altshuler has been an agent since 1982. **Represents:** Nonfiction books, novels, short story collections, juvenile. **Considers These Nonfiction Areas:** biography, ethnic, history, language, memoirs, multicultural, music, nature, popular culture, psychology, sociology, film, women's. **Considers These Fiction Areas:** literary, mainstream, multicultural, some selective children's books. Looking for literary commercial fiction and nonfiction. Does not want self-help, mystery, how-to, romance, horror, spiritual, fantasy, poetry, screenplays, science fiction or techno-thriller, western. **How to Contact:** Send Query; If we want to see your ms we will respond via email (if you do not have an email address, please send an SASE. We will only respond if interested in materials. Submit contact info with e-mail address. Prefers to read materials exclusively. Accepts simultaneous submissions. Responds in 3 weeks to mss. Obtains most new clients through recommendations from others. **Terms:** Agent receives 15% commission on domestic sales. Agent receives 20% commission on foreign sales. Charges clients for overseas mailing, photocopies, overnight mail when requested by author. **Writers Conferences:** Bread Loaf Writers' Conference; Washington Independent Writers

Conference; North Carolina Writers' Network Conference. **Tips:** See the website for specific submission details.

BETSY AMSTER LITERARY ENTERPRISES

P.O. Box 27788, Los Angeles CA 90027-0788. **Contact:** Betsy Amster. Estab. 1992. Member of AAR. **Represents:** more than 65 clients. 35% of clients are new/unpublished writers. **Currently Handles:** nonfiction books 65%, novels 35%. Prior to opening her agency, Ms. Amster was an editor at Pantheon and Vintage for 10 years, and served as editorial director for the Globe Pequot Press for 2 years. **Represents:** Nonfiction books, novels. **Considers These Nonfiction Areas:** art & design, biography, business, child guidance, cooking/nutrition, current affairs, ethnic, gardening, health/medicine, history, memoirs, money, parenting, popular culture, psychology, science/technology, self-help, sociology, travelogues, social issues, women's issues. **Considers These Fiction Areas:** ethnic, literary, women's, high quality. "Actively seeking strong narrative nonfiction, particularly by journalists; outstanding literary fiction (the next Richard Ford or Jhumpa Lahiri); witty, intelligent commercial women's fiction (the next Elinor Lipman or Jennifer Weiner); mysteries that open new worlds to us; and high-profile self-help and psychology, preferably research based." Does not want to receive poetry, children's books, romances, Western, science fiction, action/adventure, screenplays, fantasy, techno thrillers, spy capers, apocalyptic scenarios, or political or religious arguments. **How to Contact:** For adult titles: b.amster.assistant@gmail.com. See submission requirements online at website. The requirements have changed and only e-mail submissions are accepted. Accepts simultaneous submissions. Responds in 1 month to queries. Responds in 2 months to mss. Obtains most new clients through recommendations from others, solicitations, conferences. **Terms:** Agent receives 15% commission on domestic sales. Agent receives 20% commission on foreign sales. Offers written contract, binding for 1 year; 3-month notice must be given to terminate contract. Charges for photocopying, postage, long distance phone calls, messengers, galleys/books used in submissions to foreign and film agents and to magazines for first serial rights. **Writers Conferences:** USC Masters in Professional Writing; San Diego State University Writers' Conference; UCLA Extension Writers' Program; Los Angeles Times Festival of Books; The Loft Literary Center.

ARCADIA

31 Lake Place N., Danbury CT 06810. **E-mail:** arcadialit@sbcglobal.net. **Contact:** Victoria Gould Pryor. Member of AAR. **Represents:**

Nonfiction books, literary and commercial fiction. **Considers These Nonfiction Areas:** biography, business, current affairs, health, history, psychology, science, true crime, women's, investigative journalism; culture; classical music; life transforming self-help. "I'm a very hands-on agent, which is necessary in this competitive marketplace. I work with authors on revisions until whatever we present to publishers is as strong as possible. I represent talented, dedicated, intelligent and ambitious writers who are looking for a long-term relationship based on professional success and mutual respect." Does not want to receive science fiction/fantasy, horror, humor or children's/YA. "We are only able to read fiction submissions from previously published authors." **How to Contact:** Query with SASE. This agency accepts e-queries (no attachments).

THE AXELROD AGENCY

55 Main St., P.O. Box 357, Chatham NY 12037. (518)392-2100. **E-mail:** steve@axelrodagency.com. **Contact:** Steven Axelrod. Member of AAR. **Represents:** 15-20 clients. 1% of clients are new/unpublished writers. **Currently Handles:** novels 95%. Prior to becoming an agent, Mr. Axelrod was a book club editor. **Represents:** Novels. **Considers These Fiction Areas:** mystery, romance, women's. **How to Contact:** Query with SASE. Accepts simultaneous submissions. Responds in 3 weeks to queries. Responds in 6 weeks to mss. Obtains most new clients through recommendations from others. **Terms:** Agent receives 15% commission on domestic sales. Agent receives 20% commission on foreign sales. No written contract. **Writers Conferences:** RWA National Conference.

THE BALKIN AGENCY, INC.

P.O. Box 222, Amherst MA 01004. Phone/**Fax:** (413)322-8697. **E-mail:** rick62838@crocker.com. **Contact:** Rick Balkin, president. Member of AAR. **Represents:** 50 clients. 10% of clients are new/unpublished writers. **Currently Handles:** nonfiction books 85%, 5% reference books. Prior to opening his agency, Mr. Balkin served as executive editor with Bobbs-Merrill Company. **Represents:** Nonfiction books. **Considers These Nonfiction Areas:** animals, anthropology, current affairs, health, history, how-to, nature, popular culture, science, sociology, translation, biography, et alia. This agency specializes in adult nonfiction. Does not want to receive fiction, poetry, screenplays, children's books or computer books. **How to Contact:** Query with SASE. Submit proposal package, outline. Responds in 1 week to queries. Responds in 2 weeks to mss. Obtains most new clients through recommendations from others. **Terms:** Agent receives 15% commission on domestic sales. Agent receives 20% commission on foreign sales. Offers written contract, binding for 1 year. This agency charges clients for photocopying and express or foreign mail. **Tips:** "I do not take on books described as bestsellers or potential bestsellers. Any nonfiction work that is either unique, paradigmatic, a contribution, truly witty, or a labor of love is grist for my mill."

LORETTA BARRETT BOOKS, INC.

220 E. 23rd St., 11th Floor, New York NY 10010. (212)242-3420. **E-mail:** query@lorettabarrettbooks.com. **Website:** www.loretta barrettbooks.com. **Contact:** Loretta A. Barrett, Nick Mullendore. Estab. 1990. Member of AAR. **Currently Handles:** nonfiction books 50%, novels 50%. Prior to opening her agency, Ms. Barrett was vice president and executive editor at Doubleday and editor-in-chief of Anchor Books. **Member Agents:** Loretta A. Barrett; Nick Mullendore. **Represents:** Nonfiction books, novels. **Considers These Nonfiction Areas:** biography, child guidance, current affairs, ethnic, government, health/nutrition, history, memoirs, money, multicultural, nature, popular culture, psychology, religion, science, self help, sociology, spirituality, sports, women's, young adult, creative nonfiction. **Considers These Fiction Areas:** contemporary, psychic, adventure, detective, ethnic, family, fantasy, historical, literary, mainstream, mystery, thriller, young adult. "The clients we represent include both fiction and non-fiction authors for the general adult trade market. The works they produce encompass a wide range of contemporary topics and themes including commercial thrillers, mysteries, romantic suspense, popular science, memoirs, narrative fiction and current affairs." No children's, juvenile, cookbooks, gardening, science fiction, fantasy novels, historical romance. **How to Contact:** See guidelines online. Use email or if by post, query with SASE. Accepts simultaneous submissions. Responds in 3-6 weeks to queries. **Terms:** Agent receives 15% commission on domestic sales. Agent receives 20% commission on foreign sales. Offers written contract. Charges clients for shipping and photocopying.

MEREDITH BERNSTEIN LITERARY AGENCY

2095 Broadway, Suite 505, New York NY 10023. (212)799-1007. **Fax:** (212)799-1145. Member of AAR. **Represents:** 85 clients. 20% of clients are new/unpublished writers. **Currently Handles:** nonfiction books 50%, other 50% fiction. Prior to opening her agency, Ms. Bernstein served at another agency for 5 years. **Represents:** Nonfiction books, novels. **Considers These Fiction Areas:** literary, mystery, romance, thriller, young adult. "This agency does not specialize. It is very eclectic." **How to Contact:** Query with SASE. Accepts simultaneous submissions. Obtains most new clients through recommendations from others, conferences, developing/packaging ideas. **Terms:** Agent receives 15% commission on domestic sales. Agent receives 20% commission on foreign sales. Charges clients $75 disbursement fee/year. **Writers Conferences:** Southwest Writers' Conference; Rocky Mountain Fiction Writers' Colorado Gold; Pacific Northwest Writers' Conference; Willamette Writers' Conference; Surrey International Writers' Conference; San Diego State University Writers' Conference.

BOOKENDS, LLC

136 Long Hill Rd., Gillette NJ 07933. **Website:** www.bookends-inc.com; bookendslitagency.blogspot.com. **Contact:** Jessica Faust, Kim Lionetti. Member of AAR. RWA, MWA **Represents:** 50+ clients. 10% of clients are new/unpublished writers. **Currently Handles:** nonfiction books 50%, novels 50%. **Member Agents:** Jessica Faust (fiction: romance, erotica, women's fiction, mysteries and suspense; nonfiction: business, finance, career, parenting, psychology, women's issues, self-help, health, sex); Kim Lionetti

(women's fiction, mystery, true crime, pop science, pop culture, and all areas of romance)." **Represents:** Nonfiction books, novels. **Considers These Nonfiction Areas:** business, child, ethnic, gay, health, how-to, money, psychology, religion, self help, sex, true crime, women's. **Considers These Fiction Areas:** detective, cozies, mainstream, mystery, romance, thriller, women's. "BookEnds is currently accepting queries from published and unpublished writers in the areas of romance (and all its sub-genres), erotica, mystery, suspense, women's fiction, and literary fiction. We also do a great deal of nonfiction in the areas of self-help, business, finance, health, pop science, psychology, relationships, parenting, pop culture, true crime, and general nonfiction." BookEnds does not want to receive children's books, screenplays, science fiction, poetry, or technical/military thrillers. **How to Contact:** Review website for guidelines, as they change.

BOOKS & SUCH LITERARY AGENCY

52 Mission Circle, Suite 122, PMB 170, Santa Rosa CA 95409. **E-mail:** representation@booksandsuch.biz. **Website:** www.booksandsuch.biz. **Contact:** Janet Kobobel Grant, Wendy Lawton, Etta Wilson, Rachel Zurakowski. Member of AAR. Member of CBA (associate), American Christian Fiction Writers. **Represents:** 150 clients. 5% of clients are new/unpublished writers. **Currently Handles:** nonfiction books 50%, novels 50%. Prior to becoming an agent, Ms. Grant was an editor for Zondervan and managing editor for Focus on the Family; Ms. Lawton was an author, sculptor and designer of porcelein dolls. Ms. Wilson emphasizes middle grade children's books. Ms. Zurakowski concentrates on material for 20-something or 30-something readers. **Represents:** Nonfiction books, novels, juvenile books. **Considers These Nonfiction Areas:** child, humor, religion, self help, women's. **Considers These Fiction Areas:** contemporary, family, historical, mainstream, religious, romance, African American adult. This agency specializes in general and inspirational fiction, romance, and in the Christian booksellers market. Actively seeking well-crafted material that presents Judeo-Christian values, if only subtly. **How to Contact:** Query via e-mail only, no attachments. Accepts simultaneous submissions. Responds in 1 month to queries. "If you don't hear from us asking to see more of your writing within 30 days after you have sent your email, please know that we have read and considered your submission but determined that it would not be a good fit for us." Obtains most new clients through recommendations from others, conferences. **Terms:** Agent receives 15% commission on domestic sales. Agent receives 20% commission on foreign sales. Offers written contract; 2-month notice must be given to terminate contract. No additional charges. **Writers Conferences:** Mount Hermon Christian Writers' Conference; Society of Childrens' Writers and Illustrators Conference; Writing for the Soul; American Christian Fiction Writers' Conference; San Francisco Writers' Conference. **Tips:** "The heart of our agency's motivation is to develop relationships with the authors we serve, to do what we can to shine the light of success on them, and to help be a caretaker of their gifts and time."

GEORGES BORCHARDT, INC.

136 E. 57th St., New York NY 10022. Member of AAR. **Member Agents:** Anne Borchardt; Georges Borchardt; Valerie Borchardt. This agency specializes in literary fiction and outstanding nonfiction. **How to Contact:** No unsolicited mss. Obtains most new clients through recommendations from others. **Terms:** Agent receives 15% commission on domestic sales. Agent receives 20% commission on foreign sales. Offers written contract.

THE HELEN BRANN AGENCY, INC.

94 Curtis Road, Bridgewater CT 06752. **Fax:** (860)355-2572. Member of AAR. **How to Contact:** Query with SASE.

CURTIS BROWN, LTD.

10 Astor Place, New York NY 10003-6935. (212)473-5400. **Website:** www.curtisbrown.com. Alternate address: Peter Ginsberg, president at CBSF, 1750 Montgomery St., San Francisco CA 94111. (415)954-8566. Member of AAR. Signatory of WGA. **Member Agents:** Ginger Clark; Katherine Fausset; Holly Frederick; Emilie Jacobson, senior vice president; Elizabeth Hardin; Ginger Knowlton, vice president; Timothy Knowlton, CEO; Laura Blake Peterson; Maureen Walters, senior vice president; Mitchell Waters. San Francisco Office: Nathan Bransford, Peter Ginsberg (President). **Represents:** Nonfiction books, novels, short story collections, juvenile. **Considers These Nonfiction Areas:** agriculture horticulture, Americana, crafts, interior, juvenile, New Age, young, animals, anthropology, art, biography, business, child, computers, cooking, current affairs, education, ethnic, gardening, gay, government, health, history, how to, humor, language, memoirs, military, money, multicultural, music, nature, philosophy, photography, popular culture, psychology, recreation, regional, religion, science, self help, sex, sociology, software, spirituality, sports, film, translation, travel, true crime, women's, creative nonfiction. **Considers These Fiction Areas:** contemporary, glitz, new age, psychic, adventure, comic, confession, detective, erotica, ethnic, experimental, family, fantasy, feminist, gay, gothic, hi lo, historical, horror, humor, juvenile, literary, mainstream, military, multicultural, multimedia, mystery, occult, picture books, plays, poetry, regional, religious, romance, science, short, spiritual, sports, thriller, translation, western, young, women's. **How to Contact:** Prefers to read materials exclusively. No unsolicited mss. Responds in 3 weeks to queries. Responds in 5 weeks to mss. Obtains most new clients through recommendations from others, solicitations, conferences. **Terms:** Offers written contract. Charges for some postage (overseas, etc.)

BROWN LITERARY AGENCY

410 Seventh St. NW, Naples FL 34120. **Website:** www.brownliteraryagency.com. **Contact:** Roberta Brown. Member of AAR. Other memberships include RWA, Author's Guild. **Represents:** 45 clients. 5% of clients are new/unpublished writers. **Represents:** Novels. **Considers These Fiction Areas:** erotica, romance, women's, single title and category. "This agency is selectively reading material at this time." **How to Contact:** Query via e-mail only. Send synop-

sis and two chapters in Word attachment. Response time varies. **Terms:** Agent receives 15% commission on domestic sales. Agent receives 20% commission on foreign sales. Offers written contract; 30-day notice must be given to terminate contract. **Writers Conferences:** RWA National Conference. **Tips:** "Polish your manuscript. Be professional."

SHEREE BYKOFSKY ASSOCIATES, INC.

PO Box 706, Brigantine NJ 08203. **E-mail:** submitbee@aol.com. **Website:** www.shereebee.com. **Contact:** Sheree Bykofsky. Member of AAR. Other memberships include ASJA, WNBA. **Currently Handles:** nonfiction books 80%, novels 20%. Prior to opening her agency, Ms. Bykofsky served as executive editor of The Stonesong Press and managing editor of Chiron Press. She is also the author or co-author of more than 20 books, including *The Complete Idiot's Guide to Getting Published.* Ms. Bykofsky teaches publishing at NYU and SEAK, Inc. **Member Agents:** Janet Rosen, associate. **Represents:** Nonfiction books, novels. **Considers These Nonfiction Areas:** Americana, crafts, interior, new age, animals, art, biography, business, child, cooking, current affairs, education, ethnic, gardening, gay, government, health, history, how to, humor, language, memoirs, military, money, personal finance, multicultural, music, nature, philosophy, photography, popular culture, psychology, recreation, regional, religion, science, self help, sex, sociology, spirituality, sports, film, translation, travel, true crime, women's, anthropology; creative nonfiction. **Considers These Fiction Areas:** literary, mainstream, mystery. This agency specializes in popular reference nonfiction, commercial fiction with a literary quality, and mysteries. "I have wide-ranging interests, but it really depends on quality of writing, originality, and how a particular project appeals to me (or not). I take on fiction when I completely love it - it doesn't matter what area or genre." Does not want to receive poetry, material for children, screenplays, westerns, horror, science fiction, or fantasy. **How to Contact:** E-mail short queries to submitbee@aol.com. Please, no attachments, snail mail, or phone calls. Accepts simultaneous submissions. Responds in 3 weeks to queries with SASE. Responds in 1 month to requested mss. Obtains most new clients through recommendations from others. **Terms:** Agent receives 15% commission on domestic sales. Agent receives 20% commission on foreign sales. Offers written contract, binding for 1 year. Charges for postage, photocopying, fax. **Writers Conferences:** ASJA Writers Conference; Asilomar; Florida Suncoast Writers' Conference; Whidbey Island Writers' Conference; Florida First Coast Writers' Festibal; Agents and Editors Conference; Columbus Writers' Conference; Southwest Writers' Conference; Willamette Writers' Conference; Dorothy Canfield Fisher Conference; Maui Writers' Conference; Pacific Northwest Writers' Conference; IWWG. **Tips:** "Read the agent listing carefully and comply with guidelines."

MARIA CARVAINIS AGENCY, INC.

1270 Avenue of the Americas, Suite 2320, New York NY 10019. (212)245-6365. **Fax:** (212)245-7196. **E-mail:** mca@mariacarvainis agency.com. **Contact:** Maria Carvainis, Chelsea Gilmore. Member of AAR. Signatory of WGA. Other memberships include Authors Guild, Women's Media Group, ABA, MWA, RWA. **Represents:** 75 clients. 10% of clients are new/unpublished writers. **Currently Handles:** nonfiction books 35%, novels 65%. Prior to opening her agency, Ms. Carvainis spent more than 10 years in the publishing industry as a senior editor with Macmillan Publishing, Basic Books, Avon Books, and Crown Publishers. Ms. Carvainis has served as a member of the AAR Board of Directors and AAR Treasurer, as well as serving as chair of the AAR Contracts Committee. She presently serves on the AAR Royalty Committee. Ms. Gilmore started her publishing career at Oxford University Press, in the Higher Education Group. She then worked at Avalon Books as associate editor. She is most interested in women's fiction, literary fiction, young adult, pop culture, and mystery/suspense. **Member Agents:** Maria Carvainis, president/literary agent; Chelsea Gilmore, literary agent. **Represents:** Nonfiction books, novels. **Considers These Nonfiction Areas:** biography, business, history, memoirs, science, pop science, women's. **Considers These Fiction Areas:** historical, literary, mainstream, mystery, thriller, young, women's, middle grade. Does not want to receive science fiction or children's picture books. **How to Contact:** Query with SASE. Responds in up to 3 months to mss and to queries. Obtains most new clients through recommendations from others, conferences, query letters. **Terms:** Agent receives 15% commission on domestic sales. Agent receives 20% commission on foreign sales. Offers written contract. Charges clients for foreign postage and bulk copying. **Writers Conferences:** BookExpo America; Frankfurt Book Fair; London Book Fair; Mystery Writers of America; Thrillerfest; Romance Writers of America.

CASTIGLIA LITERARY AGENCY

1155 Camino Del Mar, Suite 510, Del Mar CA 92014. (858)755-8761. **Fax:** (858)755-7063. **Website:** home.earthlink.net/~mwgconference/id22.html. Member of AAR. Other memberships include PEN. **Represents:** 50 clients. **Currently Handles:** nonfiction books 55%, novels 45%. **Member Agents:** Julie Castiglia; Winifred Golden; Sally Van Haitsma; Deborah Ritchken. **Represents:** Nonfiction books, novels. **Considers These Nonfiction Areas:** animals, anthropology, biography, business, child, cooking, current affairs, ethnic, health, history, language, memoir, money, multi-cultural, narrative, nature, politics, psychology, religion, science, self-help, women's issues. **Considers These Fiction Areas:** commercial, literary, thrillers, young adult. Does not want to receive horror, screenplays, poetry or academic nonfiction. **How to Contact:** Query with SASE. Obtains most new clients through recommendations from others, solicitations, conferences. **Terms:** Agent receives 15% commission on domestic sales. Agent receives 25% commission on foreign sales. Offers written contract; 6-week notice must be given to terminate contract. **Writers Conferences:** Santa Barbara Writers' Conference; Southern California Writers' Conference; Surrey International Writers' Conference; San Diego State University Writers' Conference; Willamette Writers'

Conference. **Tips:** "Be professional with submissions. Attend workshops and conferences before you approach an agent."

FRANCES COLLIN, LITERARY AGENT

P.O. Box 33, Wayne PA 19087-0033. **Website:** www.francescollin. com. **Contact:** Sarah Yake, Associate Agent. Member of AAR. **Represents:** 90 clients. 1% of clients are new/unpublished writers. **Currently Handles:** nonfiction books 50%, fiction 50%. **Represents:** Nonfiction books, fiction, young adult. Does not want to receive cookbooks, craft books, poetry, screenplays, or books for young children. **How to Contact:** Query via e-mail describing project (text in the body of the e-mail only, no attachments) to queries@francescollin. com. "Please note that all queries are reviewed by both agents." No phone or fax queries. Accepts simultaneous submissions. **Terms:** Agent receives 15% commission on domestic sales. Agent receives 20% commission on foreign sales. Offers written contract.

DH LITERARY, INC.

P.O. Box 805, Nyack NY 10960-0990. **Contact:** David Hendin. Member of AAR. **Represents:** 10 clients. **Currently Handles:** nonfiction books 80%, novels 10%, scholarly books 10%. Prior to opening his agency, Mr. Hendin served as president and publisher for Pharos Books/World Almanac, as well as senior VP and COO at sister company United Feature Syndicate. Not accepting new clients. Please do not send queries or submissions. **Terms:** Agent receives 15% commission on domestic sales. Agent receives 20% commission on foreign sales. Offers written contract, binding for 1 year. Charges for out-of-pocket expenses for overseas postage specifically related to the sale.

SANDRA DIJKSTRA LITERARY AGENCY

1155 Camino del Mar, PMB 515, Del Mar CA 92014. (858)755-3115. **Fax:** (858)794-2822. **E-mail:** elise@dijkstraagency.com. **Website:** www.dijkstraagency.com. Member of AAR. Other memberships include Authors Guild, PEN West, Poets and Editors, MWA. **Represents:** 100+ clients. 30% of clients are new/unpublished writers. **Currently Handles:** nonfiction books 50%, novels 45%, juvenile books 5%. **Member Agents:** Sandra Dijkstra; Jill Marsal; Kevan Lyon; Elise Capron; Kelly Sonnack. **Represents:** Nonfiction books, novels. **Considers These Nonfiction Areas:** Americana, juvenile, animals, pets, anthropology, business, cooking, ethnic, gay, government, health, history, language, memoirs, military, money, nature, psychology, regional, religion, science, self help, sociology, travel, women's, Asian studies; art; accounting; biography; environmental studies; technology; transportation. **Considers These Fiction Areas:** erotica, ethnic, fantasy, juvenile, YA, middle grade, literary, mainstream, mystery, science, thriller, graphic novels. Does not want to receive Western, screenplays, short story collections or poetry. **How to Contact:** "Please see guidelines on our website. Due to the large number of unsolicited submissions we receive, we are now ONLY able to respond those submissions in which we are interested. Unsolicited submissions in which we are not interested will receive no response. (Therefore, please do

not enclose a self addressed stamped envelope [SASE], and do not send any pages or material you need returned to you. In your materials, please be sure to include all your contact information, including your email address. We accept hard copy submissions only, and will not read or respond to emailed submissions." Responds in 6 weeks to queries. Obtains most new clients through recommendations from others, solicitations, conferences. **Terms:** Agent receives 15% commission on domestic sales. Agent receives 20% commission on foreign sales. Offers written contract. Charges clients for expenses for foreign postage and copying costs if a client requests a hard copy submission to publishers. **Tips:** Be professional and learn the standard procedures for submitting your work. Be a regular patron of bookstores, and study what kind of books are being published and will appear on the shelves next to yours. Read! Check out your local library and bookstores—you'll find lots of books on writing and the publishing industry that will help you. At conferences, ask published writers about their agents. Don't believe the myth that an agent has to be in New York to be successful. We've already disproved it!

THE JONATHAN DOLGER AGENCY

49 E. 96th St., Suite 9B, New York NY 10128. **Fax:** (212)369-7118. Member of AAR. **Represents:** Nonfiction books, novels. **Considers These Nonfiction Areas:** biography, history, women's, cultural/social. **Considers These Fiction Areas:** women's, commercial. **How to Contact:** Query with SASE. No e-mail queries. **Terms:** Agent receives 15% commission on domestic sales. Agent receives 25% commission on foreign sales. **Tips:** "Writers must have been previously published if submitting fiction. We prefer to work with published/established authors, and work with a small number of new/previously unpublished writers."

DONADIO & OLSON, INC.

121 W. 27th St., Suite 704, New York NY 10001. (212)691-8077. **Fax:** (212)633-2837. **E-mail:** mail@donadio.com. **Contact:** Neil Olson. Member of AAR. **Member Agents:** Neil Olson (no queries); Edward Hibbert (no queries); Carrie Howland (query via snail mail or e-mail). **Represents:** Nonfiction books, novels. a This agency **Represents:** mostly fiction, and is very selective. **How to Contact:** Query by snail mail is preferred; for e-mail use mail@donadio.com; only send submissions to open agents. Obtains most new clients through recommendations from others.

DUNHAM LITERARY, INC.

156 Fifth Ave., Suite 625, New York NY 10010-7002. (212)929-0994. **Website:** www.dunhamlit.com. **Contact:** Jennie Dunham. Member of AAR. **Represents:** 50 clients. 15% of clients are new/unpublished writers. **Currently Handles:** nonfiction books 25%, novels 25%, juvenile books 50%. Prior to opening her agency, Ms. Dunham worked as a literary agent for Russell & Volkening. The Rhoda Weyr Agency is now a division of Dunham Literary, Inc. **Represents:** Nonfiction books, novels, short story collections, juvenile. **Considers These Nonfiction Areas:** anthropology, biography, ethnic,

government, health, history, language, nature, popular culture, psychology, science, women's. **Considers These Fiction Areas:** ethnic, juvenile, literary, mainstream, picture books, young adult. **How to Contact:** Query with SASE. Responds in 1 week to queries. Responds in 2 months to mss. Obtains most new clients through recommendations from others, solicitations. **Terms:** Agent receives 15% commission on domestic sales. Agent receives 20% commission on foreign sales.

DYSTEL & GODERICH LITERARY MANAGEMENT

1 Union Square W., Suite 904, New York NY 10003. (212)627-9100. **Fax:** (212)627-9313. **E-mail:** mbourret@dystel.com. **Website:** www.dystel.com. **Contact:** Michael Bourret and Jim McCarthy. Member of AAR. SCBWI **Represents:** 617 clients. 50% of clients are new/unpublished writers. **Currently Handles:** nonfiction books 65%, novels 35%. Dystel & Goderich Literary Management recently acquired the client list of Bedford Book Works. **Member Agents:** Jane Dystel; Stacey Glick; Michael Bourret; Jim McCarthy; Jessica Papin; Lauren Abramo; Chasya Milgrom; Rachel Oakley. **Represents:** Nonfiction books, novels, cookbooks. **Considers These Nonfiction Areas:** new age, animals, anthrolpology, biography, business, cooking, current affairs, education, ethnic, gay, government, health, history, humor, military, money, popular culture, psychology, religion, science, true crime, women's, child guidance. **Considers These Fiction Areas:** adventure, detective, ethnic, family, gay, literary, mainstream, mystery, thriller. "This agency specializes in cookbooks and commercial and literary fiction and nonfiction." **How to Contact:** Query with SASE. Please include the first 3 chapters in the body of the email. Email queries preferred (Michael Bourret only accepts email queries); will accept mail. See website for full guidelines. Accepts simultaneous submissions. Responds in 6 to 8 weeks to queries. Responds within 8 weeks to mss. Obtains most new clients through recommendations from others, solicitations, conferences. **Terms:** Agent receives 15% commission on domestic sales. Agent receives 19% commission on foreign sales. Offers written contract. **Writers Conferences:** Backspace Writers' Conference; Pacific Northwest Writers' Association; Pike's Peak Writers' Conference; Writers League of Texas; Love Is Murder; Surrey International Writers Conference; Society of Children's Book Writers and Illustrators; International Thriller Writers; Willamette Writers Conference; The South Carolina Writers Workshop Conference; Las Vegas Writers Conference; Writer's Digest; Seton Hill Popular Fiction; Romance Writers of America; Geneva Writers Conference. **Tips:** "DGLM prides itself on being a full-service agency. We're involved in every stage of the publishing process, from offering substantial editing on mss and proposals, to coming up with book ideas for authors looking for their next project, negotiating contractsand col, cting molenies for our clients. We follow a book from its inception through its sale to a publisher, its publication, and beyond. Our commitment to our writers does not, by any means, end when we have collected our commission. This is one of the many things that makes us unique in a very competitive business."

ANNE EDELSTEIN LITERARY AGENCY

20 W. 22nd St., Suite 1603, New York NY 10010. (212)414-4923. **Fax:** (212)414-2930. **E-mail:** info@aeliterary.com. **Website:** www.aeliterary.com. Member of AAR. **Member Agents:** Anne Edelstein; Krista Ingebretson. **Represents:** Nonfiction books, fiction. **Considers These Nonfiction Areas:** narrative history, memoirs, psychology, religion. **Considers These Fiction Areas:** literary. This agency specializes in fiction and narrative nonfiction. **How to Contact:** Query with SASE; submit 25 sample pages.

THE LISA EKUS GROUP, LLC

57 North St., Hatfield MA 01038. (413)247-9325. **Fax:** (413)247-9873. **E-mail:** LisaEkus@lisaekus.com. **Website:** www.lisaekus.com. **Contact:** Lisa Ekus-Saffer. Member of AAR. **Represents:** Nonfiction books. **Considers These Nonfiction Areas:** cooking, occasionally health/well-being and women's issues. **How to Contact:** Submit a one-page query via e-mail or submit your complete hard copy proposal with title page, proposal contents, concept, bio, marketing, TOC, etc. Include SASE for the return of materials. **Tips:** "Please do not call. No phone queries."

ANN ELMO AGENCY, INC.

305 Seventh Avenue, # 1101, New York NY 10001. (212)661-2880. **Fax:** (212)661-2883. **E-mail:** aalitagent@sbcgobal.net. **Contact:** Lettie Lee. Member of AAR. Other memberships include Authors Guild. **Member Agents:** Lettie Lee; Mari Cronin (plays); A.L. Abecassis (nonfiction). **Represents:** Nonfiction books, novels. **Considers These Nonfiction Areas:** biography, current affairs, health, history, how to, popular culture, science. **Considers These Fiction Areas:** ethnic, family, mainstream, romance, contemporary, gothic, historical, regency, thriller, women's. **How to Contact:** Only accepts mailed queries with SASE. Do not send full ms unless requested. Responds in 3 months to queries. Obtains most new clients through recommendations from others. **Terms:** Agent receives 15% commission on domestic sales. Agent receives 20% commission on foreign sales. Offers written contract. **Tips:** "Query first, and only when asked send a double-spaced, readable manuscript. Include a SASE, of course."

THE ELAINE P. ENGLISH LITERARY AGENCY

4710 41st St. NW, Suite D, Washington DC 20016. (202)362-5190. **Fax:** (202)362-5192. **E-mail:** elaine@elaineenglish.com; naomi@elaineenglish.com. **Website:** www.elaineenglish.com. **Contact:** Elaine English or Naomi Hackenberg for YA fiction. Member of AAR. **Represents:** 20 clients. 25% of clients are new/unpublished writers. **Currently Handles:** novels 100%. Ms. English has been working in publishing for more than 20 years. She is also an attorney specializing in media and publishing law. **Represents:** Novels. **Considers These Fiction Areas:** historical, multicultural, mystery, romance, single title, historical, contemporary, romantic, suspense, chick lit, erotic, thriller, general women's fiction. The agency is slowly but steadily acquiring in all mentioned areas. Actively seeking women's fiction, including single-title romances, and young adult fiction. Does not want to receive any science fiction, time travel, or picture books. **How to Contact:** Generally prefers e-queries sent to queries@elaineenglish.

com or YA sent to naomi@elaineenglish.com. If requested, submit synopsis, first 3 chapters, SASE. Please check website for further details. Responds in 4-8 weeks to queries; 3 months to requested submissions Obtains most new clients through recommendations from others, conferences, submissions. **Terms:** Agent receives 15% commission on domestic sales. Agent receives 20% commission on foreign sales. Offers written contract; 30-day notice must be given to terminate contract. Charges only for shipping expenses; generally taken from proceeds. **Writers Conferences:** RWA National Conference; Novelists, Inc.; Malice Domestic; Washington Romance Writers Retreat, among others.

FELICIA ETH LITERARY REPRESENTATION

555 Bryant St., Suite 350, Palo Alto CA 94301-1700. (650)375-1276. **Fax:** (650)401-8892. **E-mail:** feliciaeth@aol.com. **Contact:** Felicia Eth. Member of AAR. **Represents:** 25-35 clients. **Currently Handles:** nonfiction books 85%, novels 15% adult. **Represents:** Nonfiction books, novels. **Considers These Nonfiction Areas:** animals, anthropology, biography, business, child, current affairs, ethnic, government, health, history, nature, popular culture, psychology, science, sociology, true crime, women's. **Considers These Fiction Areas:** literary, mainstream. This agency specializes in high-quality fiction (preferably mainstream/contemporary) and provocative, intelligent, and thoughtful nonfiction on a wide array of commercial subjects. **How to Contact:** Query with SASE. Accepts simultaneous submissions. Responds in 3 weeks to queries. Responds in 4-6 weeks to mss. **Terms:** Agent receives 15% commission on domestic sales. Agent receives 20% commission on foreign sales. Agent receives 20% commission on film sales. Charges clients for photocopying and express mail service. **Writers Conferences:** "Wide Array - from Squaw Valley to Mills College." **Tips:** "For nonfiction, established expertise is certainly a plus—as is magazine publication—though not a prerequisite. I am highly dedicated to those projects I represent, but highly selective in what I choose."

FOLIO LITERARY MANAGEMENT, LLC

505 Eighth Ave., Suite 603, New York NY 10018. **Website:** www.foliolit.com. Alternate address: 1627 K St. NW, Suite 1200, Washington DC 20006. Member of AAR. **Represents:** 100+ clients. Prior to creating Folio Literary Management, Mr. Hoffman worked for several years at another agency; Mr. Kleinman was an agent at Graybill & English; Ms. Wheeler was an agent at Creative Media Agency; Ms. Fine was an agent at Vigliano Associates and Trident Media Group; Ms. Cartwright-Niumata was an editor at Simon & Schuster, HarperCollins, and Avalon Books; Ms. Becker worked as a copywriter, journalist and author. **Member Agents:** Scott Hoffman; Jeff Kleinman; Paige Wheeler; Celeste Fine; Erin Cartwright-Niumata; Laney K. Becker; Rachel Vater (fantasy, young adult, women's fiction). **Represents:** Nonfiction books, novels, short story collections. **Considers These Nonfiction Areas:** animals, equestrian, business, child, history, how to, humor, memoirs, military, nature, popular culture, psychology, religion, science, self help, women's, narrative nonfiction; art; espionage; biography; crime; politics; health/fitness;

lifestyle; relationship; culture; cookbooks. **Considers These Fiction Areas:** erotica, fantasy, literary, mystery, religious, romance, science, thriller, psychological, young, women's, Southern; legal; edgy crime. **How to Contact:** Query via e-mail only (no attachments). Read agent bios online for specific submission guidelines. Responds in 1 month to queries. **Tips:** "Please do not submit simultaneously to more than one agent at Folio. If you're not sure which of us is exactly right for your book, don't worry. We work closely as a team, and if one of our agents gets a query that might be more appropriate for someone else, we'll always pass it along. It's important that you check each agent's bio page for clear directions as to how to submit, as well as when to expect feedback."

GELFMAN SCHNEIDER LITERARY AGENTS, INC.

250 W. 57th St., Suite 2122, New York NY 10107. (212)245-1993. **Fax:** (212)245-8678. **E-mail:** mail@gelfmanschneider.com. **Contact:** Jane Gelfman, Deborah Schneider. Member of AAR. **Represents:** 300+ clients. 10% of clients are new/unpublished writers. **Represents:** Fiction and nonfiction books. **Considers These Fiction Areas:** literary, mainstream, mystery, women's. Does not want to receive romance, science fiction, westerns, or children's books. **How to Contact:** Query with SASE. Send queries via snail mail only. Responds in 1 month to queries. Responds in 2 months to mss. **Terms:** Agent receives 15% commission on domestic sales. Agent receives 20% commission on foreign sales. Agent receives 15% commission on film sales. Offers written contract. Charges clients for photocopying and messengers/couriers.

GOODMAN ASSOCIATES

500 West End Ave., New York NY 10024-4317. (212)873-4806. Member of AAR. Accepting new clients by recommendation only.

IRENE GOODMAN LITERARY AGENCY

27 W. 24th Street, Suite 700B, New York NY 10010. **E-mail:** queries@irenegoodman.com. **Website:** www.irenegoodman.com. **Contact:** Irene Goodman, Miriam Kriss. Member of AAR. **Member Agents:** Irene Goodman; Miriam Kriss; Barbara Poelle; Jon Sternfeld. **Represents:** Nonfiction books, novels. **Considers These Nonfiction Areas:** narrative nonfiction dealing with social, cultural and historical issues; an occasional memoir and current affairs book, parenting, social issues, francophilia, anglophilia, Judaica, lifestyles, cooking, memoir. **Considers These Fiction Areas:** historical, intelligent literary, modern urban fantasies, mystery, romance, thriller, women's. "Specializes in the finest in commercial fiction and nonfiction. We have a strong background in women's voices, including mysteries, romance, women's fiction, thrillers, suspense. Historical fiction is one of Irene's particular passions and Miriam is fanatical about modern urban fantasies. In nonfiction, Irene is looking for topics on narrative history, social issues and trends, education, Judaica, Francophilia, Anglophilia, other cultures, animals, food, crafts, and memoir." Barbara is looking for commercial thrillers with strong female protagonists; Miriam is looking for urban fantasy and edgy sci-fi/young adult.

How to Contact: Query. Submit synopsis, first 10 pages. E-mail queries only! See the website submission page. No e-mail attachments. Responds in 2 months to queries. **Tips:** "We are receiving an unprecedented amount of email queries. If you find that the mailbox is full, please try again in two weeks. Email queries to our personal addresses will not be answered. Emails to our personal in-boxes will be deleted."

SANFORD J. GREENBURGER ASSOCIATES, INC.
55 Fifth Ave., New York NY 10003. (212)206-5600. **Fax:** (212)463-8718. **E-mail:** queryHL@sjga.com. **Website:** www.greenburger.com. Member of AAR. **Represents:** 500 clients. **Member Agents:** Heide Lange; Faith Hamlin; Dan Mandel; Matthew Bialer; Courtney Miller-Callihan, Michael Harriot, Brenda Bowen, Lisa Gallagher. **Represents:** Nonfiction books and novels. **Considers These Nonfiction Areas:** agriculture horticulture, Americana, crafts, interior, juvenile, new age, young adult, animals, anthropology, art, biography, business, child, computers, cooking, current affairs, education, ethnic, gardening, gay, government, health, history, how-to, humor, language, memoirs, military, money, multicultural, music, nature, philosophy, photography, popular culture, psychology, recreation, regional, religion, science, self-help, sex, sociology, software, sports, film, translation, travel, true crime, women's. **Considers These Fiction Areas:** glitz, psychic, adventure, detective, ethnic, family, feminist, gay, historical, humor, literary, mainstream, mystery, regional, sports, thriller. No romances or Westerns. **How to Contact:** Submit query, first 3 chapters, synopsis, brief bio, SASE. Accepts simultaneous submissions. Responds in 2 months to queries and mss. Responds to mss. Obtains most new clients through recommendations from others. **Terms:** Agent receives 15% commission on domestic sales. Agent receives 20% commission on foreign sales. Charges for photocopying and books for foreign and subsidiary rights submissions.

THE JOY HARRIS LITERARY AGENCY, INC.
156 Fifth Ave., Suite 617, New York NY 10010. (212)924-6269. **Fax:** (212)924-6609. **Website:** joyharrisliterary.com. **Contact:** Joy Harris. Member of AAR. **Represents:** more than 100 clients. **Currently Handles:** nonfiction books 50%, novels 50%. **Represents:** Nonfiction books, novels, and young adult. **Considers These Fiction Areas:** glitz, ethnic, experimental, family, feminist, gay, hi lo, historical, humor, literary, mainstream, multicultural, multimedia, mystery, regional, short, spiritual, translation, young adult, women's. No screenplays. **How to Contact:** Visit our website for guidelines. Query with sample chapter, outline/proposal, SASE. Accepts simultaneous submissions. Responds in 2 months to queries. Obtains most new clients through recommendations from clients and editors. **Terms:** Agent receives 15% commission on domestic sales. Agent receives 20% commission on foreign sales. Charges clients for some office expenses.

JOHN HAWKINS & ASSOCIATES, INC.
71 W. 23rd St., Suite 1600, New York NY 10010. (212)807-7040. **Fax:** (212)807-9555. **E-mail:** jha@jhalit.com. **Website:** www.jhalit.com. **Contact:** Moses Cardona (moses@jhalit.com). Member of AAR. **Represents:** over 100 clients. 5-10% of clients are new/unpublished writers. **Currently Handles:** nonfiction books 40%, novels 40%, juvenile books 20%. **Member Agents:** Moses Cardona; Anne Hawkins (ahawkins@jhalit.com); Warren Frazier (frazier@jhalit.com); William Reiss (reiss@jhalit.com). **Represents:** Nonfiction books, novels, young adult. **Considers These Nonfiction Areas:** agriculture horticulture, Americana, interior, young, anthropology, art, biography, business, current affairs, education, ethnic, gardening, gay, government, health, history, how-to, language, memoirs, money, multicultural, nature, philosophy, popular culture, psychology, recreation, science, self-help, sex, sociology, software, film, travel, true crime, music, creative nonfiction. **Considers These Fiction Areas:** glitz, psychic, adventure, detective, ethnic, experimental, family, feminist, gay, gothic, hi lo, historical, literary, mainstream, military, multicultural, multimedia, mystery, religious, short, sports, thriller, translation, western, young, women's. **How to Contact:** Submit query, proposal package, outline, SASE. Accepts simultaneous submissions. Responds in 1 month to queries. Obtains most new clients through recommendations from others. **Terms:** Agent receives 15% commission on domestic sales. Agent receives 20% commission on foreign sales. Charges clients for photocopying.

HEACOCK HILL LITERARY AGENCY, INC.
West Coast Office, 1020 Hollywood Way #439, Burbank CA 91505. (505)585-0111 - NM office. **E-mail:** agent@heacockhill.com. **Website:** www.heacockhill.com. **Contact:** Catt LeBaigue. Member of AAR. Other memberships include SCBWI. Prior to becoming an agent, Ms. LeBaigue spent 18 years with Sony Pictures and Warner Bros. **Member Agents:** Tom Dark (adult fiction, nonfiction); Catt LeBaigue (juvenile fiction, adult nonfiction including arts, crafts, anthropolgy, astronomy, nature studies, ecology, body/mind/spirit, humanities, self-help). **Represents:** Nonfiction, fiction. **Considers These Nonfiction Areas:** hiking. **How to Contact:** E-mail queries only. No unsolicited manuscripts. No e-mail attachments. Obtains most new clients through recommendations from others, solicitations. **Terms:** Offers written contract. **Tips:** "Write an informative original e-query expressing your book idea, your qualifications, and short excerpts of the work. No unfinished work, please."

RICHARD HENSHAW GROUP
22 West 23rd St., Fifth Floor, New York NY 10010. (212)414-1172. **Fax:** (212)414-1182. **E-mail:** submissions@henshaw.com. **Website:** www.rich.henshaw.com. **Contact:** Rich Henshaw. Member of AAR. Other memberships include SinC, MWA, HWA, SFWA, RWA. **Represents:** 35 clients. 20% of clients are new/unpublished writers. **Currently Handles:** nonfiction books 35%, novels 65%. Prior to opening his agency, Mr. Henshaw served as an agent with Richard Curtis Associates, Inc. **Represents:** Nonfiction books, novels. **Considers These Nonfiction Areas:** animals, biography, business, computers, cooking, current affairs, gay, government, health, humor, military, money, music, nature, New Age, popular culture, psychology, science, sociology, sports, true crime. **Considers These Fiction Areas:** glitz, psychic, adventure, detective, ethnic, family, fantasy, historical, horror, humor, literary, mainstream, mystery, romance,

science, sports, thriller. This agency specializes in thrillers, mysteries, science fiction, fantasy and horror. **How to Contact:** Query with SASE. Responds in 3 weeks to queries. Responds in 6 weeks to mss. Obtains most new clients through recommendations from others, solicitations, conferences. **Terms:** Agent receives 15% commission on domestic sales. Agent receives 20% commission on foreign sales. No written contract. Charges clients for photocopying and book orders. **Tips:** "While we do not have any reason to believe that our submission guidelines will change in the near future, writers can find up-to-date submission policy information on our website. Always include a SASE with correct return postage."

KIRCHOFF/WOHLBERG, INC., AUTHORS' REPRESENTATION DIVISION

897 Boston Post Road, Madison CT 06443. (203)245-7308. **Fax:** (203)245-3218. **E-mail:** trade@kirchoffwohlberg.com. **Contact:** Ronald Zollshan. Member of AAR. Other memberships include SCBWI, AAP, Society of Illustrators, SPAR, Bookbuilders of Boston, New York Bookbinders' Guild, AIGA. 10% of clients are new/unpublished writers. **Currently Handles:** nonfiction books 5%, novels 25%, other 5% young adult. Kirchoff/Wohlberg has been in business for over 60 years. This agency specializes in juvenile fiction and non-fiction through Young Adult. **How to Contact:** Submit by mail to address above. Include SASE. Accepts simultaneous submissions. **Terms:** Offers written contract, binding for at least 1 year. Agent receives standard commission, depending upon whether it is an author only, illustrator only, or an author/illustrator book.

HARVEY KLINGER, INC.

300 W. 55th St., Suite 11V, New York NY 10019. (212)581-7068. **E-mail:** queries@harveyklinger.com. **Website:** www.harveyklinger.com. **Contact:** Harvey Klinger. Member of AAR. **Represents:** 100 clients. 25% of clients are new/unpublished writers. **Currently Handles:** nonfiction books 50%, novels 50%. **Member Agents:** David Dunton (popular culture, music-related books, literary fiction, young adult, fiction, and memoirs); Sara Crowe (children's and young adult authors, adult fiction and nonfiction, foreign rights sales); Andrea Somberg (literary fiction, commercial fiction, romance, sci-fi/fantasy, mysteries/thrillers, young adult, middle grade, quality narrative nonfiction, popular culture, how-to, self-help, humor, interior design, cookbooks, health/fitness). **Represents:** Nonfiction books, novels. **Considers These Nonfiction Areas:** biography, cooking, health, psychology, science, self help, spirituality, sports, true crime, women's. **Considers These Fiction Areas:** glitz, adventure, detective, family, literary, mainstream, mystery, thriller. This agency specializes in big, mainstream, contemporary fiction and nonfiction. **How to Contact:** Query with SASE. No phone or fax queries. Don't send unsolicited manuscripts or e-mail attachments. Responds in 2 months to queries and mss Obtains most new clients through recommendations from others. **Terms:** Agent receives 15% commission on domestic sales. Agent receives 25% commission on foreign sales. Offers written contract. Charges for photocopying mss and overseas postage for mss.

LINDA KONNER LITERARY AGENCY

10 W. 15th St., Suite 1918, New York NY 10011-6829. (212)691-3419. **E-mail:** ldkonner@cs.com. **Website:** www.lindakonnerliterary agency.com. **Contact:** Linda Konner. Member of AAR. Signatory of WGA. Other memberships include ASJA. **Represents:** 85 clients. 30-35% of clients are new/unpublished writers. **Currently Handles:** nonfiction books 100%. **Represents:** Nonfiction books. **Considers These Nonfiction Areas:** biography (celebrity only), gay, health, diet/nutrition/fitness, how to, money, personal finance, popular culture, psychology, pop psychology, self help, women's issues; African American and Latino issues; business; parenting; relationships. This agency specializes in health, self-help, and how-to books. Authors/co-authors must be top experts in their field with a substantial media platform. **How to Contact:** Query with SASE, synopsis, author bio, sufficient return postage. Prefers to read materials exclusively for 2 weeks. Accepts simultaneous submissions. Obtains most new clients through recommendations from others, occasional solicitation among established authors/journalists. **Terms:** Agent receives 15% commission on domestic sales. Agent receives 25% commission on foreign sales. Offers written contract. Charges one-time fee for domestic expenses; additional expenses may be incurred for foreign sales. **Writers Conferences:** ASJA Writers Conference, Harvard Medical School's "Publishing Books, Memoirs, and Other Creative Nonfiction" Annual Conference.

BARBARA S. KOUTS, LITERARY AGENT

P.O. Box 560, Bellport NY 11713. (631)286-1278. **Fax:** (631) 286-1538. **Contact:** Barbara S. Kouts. Member of AAR. **Represents:** 50 clients. 10% of clients are new/unpublished writers. **Represents:** Juvenile. This agency specializes in children's books. **How to Contact:** Query with SASE. Accepts simultaneous submissions. Responds in 1 week to queries. Responds in 2 months to mss. Obtains most new clients through recommendations from others, solicitations, conferences. **Terms:** Agent receives 10% commission on domestic sales. Agent receives 20% commission on foreign sales. This agency charges clients for photocopying. **Tips:** "Write, do not call. Be professional in your writing."

STUART KRICHEVSKY LITERARY AGENCY, INC.

381 Park Ave. S., Suite 914, New York NY 10016. (212)725-5288. **Fax:** (212)725-5275. **E-mail:** query@skagency.com. **Website:** www.sk agency.com. Member of AAR. **Member Agents:** Stuart Krichevsky; Shana Cohen (science fiction, fantasy); Jennifer Puglisi (assistant). **Represents:** Nonfiction books, novels. **How to Contact:** Submit query, synopsis, 1 sample page via e-mail (no attachments). Snail mail queries also acceptable. Obtains most new clients through recommendations from others, solicitations.

MICHAEL LARSEN/ELIZABETH POMADA, LITERARY AGENTS

1029 Jones St., San Francisco CA 94109-5023. (415)673-0939. **E-mail:** larsenpoma@aol.com. **Website:** www.larsen-pomada.com. **Contact:** Mike Larsen, Elizabeth Pomada. Member of AAR. Other memberships include Authors Guild, ASJA, PEN, WNBA, California

Writers Club, National Speakers Association. **Represents:** 100 clients. 40-45% of clients are new/unpublished writers. **Currently Handles:** nonfiction books 70%, novels 30%. Prior to opening their agency, Mr. Larsen and Ms. Pomada were promotion executives for major publishing houses. Mr. Larsen worked for Morrow, Bantam and Pyramid (now part of Berkley); Ms. Pomada worked at Holt, David McKay and The Dial Press. Mr. Larsen is the author of the 4th edition of *How to Write a Book Proposal* and *How to Get a Literary Agent* as well as the coauthor of *Guerilla Marketing for Writers: 100 Weapons for Selling Your Work*, which was republished in September 2009. **Member Agents:** Michael Larsen (nonfiction); Elizabeth Pomada (fiction & narrative nonfiction). **Represents: Considers These Nonfiction Areas:** anthropology, art, biography, business, current affairs, ethnic, film, foods, gay, health, history, humor, memoirs, money, music, nature, , popular culture, psychology, science, sociology, sports, travel, futurism. **Considers These Fiction Areas:** adventure, detective, ethnic, feminist, gay, glitz, historical, humor, literary, mainstream, mystery, romance, paranormal adventure, chick lit. We have diverse tastes. We look for fresh voices and new ideas. We handle literary, commercial and genre fiction, and the full range of nonfiction books. Actively seeking commercial, genre and literary fiction. Does not want to receive children's books, plays, short stories, screenplays, pornography, poetry or stories of abuse. **How to Contact:** Query with SASE. Responds in 8 weeks to pages or submissions. **Terms:** Agent receives 15% commission on domestic sales. Agent receives 20% (30% for Asia) commission on foreign sales. May charge for printing, postage for multiple submissions, foreign mail, foreign phone calls, galleys, books, legal fees. **Writers Conferences:** This agency organizes the annual San Francisco Writers' Conference (www.sfwriters.org). **Tips:** "We love helping writers get the rewards and recognition they deserve. If you can write books that meet the **Needs:** of the marketplace and you can promote your books, now is the best time ever to be a writer. We must find new writers to make a living, so we are very eager to hear from new writers whose work will interest large houses, and nonfiction writers who can promote their books. For a list of recent sales, helpful info, and three ways to make yourself irresistible to any publisher, please visit our website."

SARAH LAZIN BOOKS

126 Fifth Ave., Suite 300, New York NY 10011. (212)989-5757. **Fax:** (212)989-1393. **Contact:** Sarah Lazin. Member of AAR. **Represents:** 75+ clients. **Currently Handles:** nonfiction books 80%, novels 20%. **Member Agents:** Sarah Lazin; Rebecca Ferreira. **Represents:** Nonfiction books, novels. **Considers These Nonfiction Areas:** biography, ethnic, gay, history, memoirs, music, popular culture, religious, Works with companies who package their books; handles some photography. **How to Contact:** Query with SASE. No e-mail queries. **Terms:** Agent receives 15% commission on domestic sales. Agent receives 20% commission on foreign sales.

LESCHER & LESCHER, LTD.

346 E. 84th St., New York NY 10028. (212)396-1999. **Fax:** (212)396-1991. **Contact:** Robert Larson; Carolyn Larson. Member of AAR. **Represents:** 150 clients. **Currently Handles:** nonfiction books 80%, novels 20%. **Represents:** Nonfiction books, novels. **Considers These Nonfiction Areas:** current affairs, history, memoirs, popular culture, biography; cookbooks/wines; law; contemporary issues; narrative nonfiction. **Considers These Fiction Areas:** literary, mystery, commercial. Does not want to receive screenplays, science fiction or romance. **How to Contact:** Query with SASE. Obtains most new clients through recommendations from others. **Terms:** Agent receives 15% commission on domestic sales. Agent receives 10% commission on foreign sales.

LITERARY AND CREATIVE ARTISTS, INC.

2123 Paris Metz Rd., Chattanooga TN 37421. **E-mail:** southernlitagent@aol.com. **Contact:** Muriel Nellis. Member of AAR. Other memberships include Authors Guild, American Bar Association. **Currently Handles:** nonfiction books 50%, novels 50%. **Member Agents:** Prior to becoming an agent, Mr. Powell was in sales and contract negotiation. **Represents:** Nonfiction books, novels, art, biography, business, photography, popular culture, religion, self help, literary, regional, religious, satire. **Considers These Nonfiction Areas:** biography, business, cooking, government, health, how to, memoirs, philosophy, human drama; lifestyle. "We focus on authors that live in the Southern United States. We have the ability to translate and explain complexities of publishing for the Southern author. Actively seeking quality projects by authors with a vision of where they want to be in 10 years and a plan of how to get there." Does not want to receive unfinished, unedited projects that do not follow the standard presentation conventions of the trade. No Romance. **How to Contact:** Query via e-mail first and include a synopsis. Accepts simultaneous submissions. Responds in 2-3 months to queries. Responds in 1 week mss. Through recommendations from others. **Terms:** Agent receives 15% commission on domestic sales. Agent receives 25% commission on foreign sales. Offers written contract. Charges clients for long-distance phone/fax, photocopying, shipping. **Tips:** "If you are an unpublished author, join a writers group, even if it is on the Internet. You need good honest feedback. Don't send a manuscript that has not been read by at least five people. Don't send a manuscript cold to any agent without first asking if they want it. Try to meet the agent face to face before signing. Make sure the fit is right."

NANCY LOVE LITERARY AGENCY

250 E. 65th St., New York NY 10065-6614. (212)980-3499. **Fax:** (212)308-6405. **E-mail:** nloveag@aol.com. **Contact:** Nancy Love. Member of AAR. **Represents:** 60-80 clients. 25% of clients are new/unpublished writers. **Currently Handles:** nonfiction books 100%. **Member Agents:** This agency is not taking on any new fiction writers at this time. **Represents:** Nonfiction books. **Considers These Nonfiction Areas:** biography, cooking, current affairs, ethnic, government, health, history, how-to, nature, popular culture, psychology,

science, sociology, women's issues. This agency specializes in adult nonfiction. Actively seeking narrative nonfiction. **How to Contact:** Query with SASE. No fax queries. Accepts simultaneous submissions. Responds in 3 weeks to queries. Responds in 6 weeks to mss. Obtains most new clients through recommendations from others, solicitations. **Terms:** Agent receives 15% commission on domestic sales. Agent receives 20% commission on foreign sales. Offers written contract. **Tips:** "Nonfiction authors and/or collaborators must be an authority in their subject area and have a platform. Send an SASE if you want a response."

LYONS LITERARY, LLC

27 West 20th St., Suite 10003, New York NY 10011. (212)255-5472. **Fax:** (212)851-8405. **E-mail:** info@lyonsliterary.com. **Website:** www.lyonsliterary.com. **Contact:** Jonathan Lyons. Member of AAR. Other memberships include The Author's Guild, American Bar Association, New York State Bar Association, New York State Intellectual Property Law Section. **Represents:** 37 clients. 15% of clients are new/unpublished writers. **Currently Handles:** nonfiction books 60%, novels 40%. **Represents:** Nonfiction books, novels. **Considers These Nonfiction Areas:** crafts, animals, biography, cooking, current affairs, ethnic, gay, government, health, history, how to, humor, memoirs, military, money, multicultural, nature, popular culture, psychology, science, sociology, sports, translation, travel, true crime, women's. **Considers These Fiction Areas:** psychic, detective, fantasy, feminist, gay, historical, humor, literary, mainstream, mystery, regional, science, sports, thriller, women's, chick lit. "With my legal expertise and experience selling domestic and foreign language book rights, paperback reprint rights, audio rights, film/TV rights and permissions, I am able to provide substantive and personal guidance to my clients in all areas relating to their projects. In addition, with the advent of new publishing technology, Lyons Literary, LLC is situated to address the changing nature of the industry while concurrently handling authors' more traditional **Needs:**." **How to Contact:** Only accepts queries through online submission form. Accepts simultaneous submissions. Responds in 8 weeks to queries. Responds in 12 weeks to mss. Obtains most new clients through recommendations from others. **Terms:** Agent receives 15% commission on domestic sales. Agent receives 20% commission on foreign sales. Offers written contract. **Writers Conferences:** Agents and Editors Conference. **Tips:** "Please submit electronic queries through our website submission form."

CAROL MANN AGENCY

55 Fifth Ave., New York NY 10003. (212)206-5635. **Fax:** (212)675-4809. **E-mail:** eliza@carolmannagency.com. **Website:** www.carolmannagency.com/. **Contact:** Eliza Dreier. Member of AAR. **Represents:** roughly 200 clients. 15% of clients are new/unpublished writers. **Currently Handles:** nonfiction books 90%, novels 10%. **Member Agents:** Carol Mann (health/medical, religion, spirituality, self-help, parenting, narrative nonfiction); Laura Yorke; Gareth Esersky, Myrsini Stephanides. **Represents:** Nonfiction books, novels. **Considers These Nonfiction Areas:** anthropology, art, biography, business, child, current affairs, ethnic, government, health, history, money, popular culture, psychology, self help, sociology, sports, womens, music. **Considers These Fiction Areas:** literary, commercial. This agency specializes in current affairs, self-help, popular culture, psychology, parenting, and history. Does not want to receive genre fiction (romance, mystery, etc.). **How to Contact:** Keep initial query/contact to no more than two pages. Responds in 4 weeks to queries. **Terms:** Agent receives 15% commission on domestic sales. Agent receives 20% commission on foreign sales. Offers written contract.

THE DENISE MARCIL LITERARY AGENCY, INC.

156 Fifth Ave., Suite 625, New York NY 10010. (212)337-3402. **Fax:** (212)727-2688. **Website:** www.DeniseMarcilAgency.com. **Contact:** Denise Marcil, Anne Marie O'Farrell. Member of AAR. Prior to opening her agency, Ms. Marcil served as an editorial assistant with Avon Books and as an assistant editor with Simon & Schuster. **Member Agents:** Denise Marcil (women's commercial fiction, thrillers, suspense, popular reference, how-to, self-help, health, business, and parenting. This agency is currently not taking on new authors. **Terms:** Agent receives 15% commission on domestic sales. Agent receives 20% commission on foreign sales. Offers written contract, binding for 2 years. Charges $100/year for postage, photocopying, long-distance calls, etc.

THE EVAN MARSHALL AGENCY

Six Tristam Place, Pine Brook NJ 07058-9445. (973)882-1122. **Fax:** (973)882-3099. **E-mail:** evanmarshall@optonline.net. **Contact:** Evan Marshall. Member of AAR. Other memberships include MWA, Sisters in Crime. **Currently Handles:** novels 100%. **Represents:** novels. **Considers These Fiction Areas:** adventure, erotica, ethnic, historical, horror, humor, literary, mainstream, mystery, religious, romance, contemporary, gothic, historical, regency, science, western. **How to Contact:** Query first with SASE; do not enclose material. No e-mail queries. Responds in 1 week to queries. Responds in 3 months to mss. Obtains most new clients through recommendations from others. **Terms:** Agent receives 15% commission on domestic sales. Agent receives 20% commission on foreign sales. Offers written contract.

MARTIN LITERARY MANAGEMENT

321 High School Rd., Suite D3 #316, Bainbridge Island WA 98110. **E-mail:** sharlene@martinliterarymanagement.com. **Website:** www.MartinLiteraryManagement.com. **Contact:** Sharlene Martin. 75% of clients are new/unpublished writers. Prior to becoming an agent, Ms. Martin worked in film/TV production and acquisitions. **Member Agents:** Sharlene Martin (nonfiction). NEW: Bree Ogden (Children's books and Graphic Novels only) Bree@MartinLiteraryManagement.com. **Represents: Considers These Nonfiction Areas:** biography, business, child, current affairs, health, history, how-to, humor, memoirs, popular culture, psychology, religion, self-help, true crime, women's. This agency has strong ties to film/TV. Actively seeking nonfiction that is highly commercial and that can be adapted to film. "We are being inundated with queries and

submissions that are wrongfully being submitted to us, which only results in more frustration for the writers." **How to Contact:** Query via e-mail with MS Word only. No attachments on queries; place letter in body of e-mail. Accepts simultaneous submissions. Responds in 2 weeks to queries. Responds in 3-4 weeks to mss. Obtains most new clients through recommendations from others. **Terms:** Agent receives 15% commission on domestic sales. Agent receives 25% commission on foreign sales. Offers written contract, binding for 1 year; 1-month notice must be given to terminate contract. Charges author for postage and copying if material is not sent electronically. 99% of materials are sent electronically to minimize charges to author for postage and copying. **Tips:** "Have a strong platform for nonfiction. Please don't call. I welcome e-mail. I'm very responsive when I'm interested in a query and work hard to get my clients materials in the best possible shape before submissions. Do your homework prior to submission and only submit your best efforts. Please review our website carefully to make sure we're a good match for your work. If you read my book, Publish Your Nonfiction Book: Strategies For Learning the Industry, Selling Your Book and Building a Successful Career (Writer's Digest Books) you'll know exactly how to charm me."

THE MCCARTHY AGENCY, LLC

7 Allen St., Rumson NJ 07660. **Phone/Fax:** (732)741-3065. **E-mail:** mccarthylit@aol.com. **Contact:** Shawna McCarthy. Member of AAR. **Currently Handles:** nonfiction books 25%, novels 75%. **Member Agents:** Shawna McCarthy. **Represents:** Nonfiction books, novels. **Considers These Nonfiction Areas:** biography, history, philosophy, science. **Considers These Fiction Areas:** fantasy, juvenile, mystery, romance, science, womens. **How to Contact:** Query via e-mail only. Accepts simultaneous submissions.

MENDEL MEDIA GROUP, LLC

115 West 30th St., Suite 800, New York NY 10001. (646)239-9896. **Fax:** (212)685-4717. **E-mail:** scott@mendelmedia.com. **Website:** www.mendelmedia.com. Member of AAR. **Represents:** 40-60 clients. Prior to becoming an agent, Mr. Mendel was an academic. "I taught American literature, Yiddish, Jewish studies, and literary theory at the University of Chicago and the University of Illinois at Chicago while working on my PhD in English. I also worked as a freelance technical writer and as the managing editor of a healthcare magazine. In 1998, I began working for the late Jane Jordan Browne, a long-time agent in the book publishing world." **Represents:** Nonfiction books, novels, scholarly, with potential for broad/popular appeal. **Considers These Nonfiction Areas:** Americana, animals, anthropology, art, biography, business, child, cooking, current affairs, education, ethnic, gardening, gay, government, health, history, how to, humor, language, memoirs, military, money, multicultural, music, nature, philosophy, popular culture, psychology, recreation, regional, religion, science, self help, sex, sociology, software, spirituality, sports, true crime, women's, Jewish topics; creative nonfiction. **Considers These Fiction Areas:** contemporary, glitz, adventure, detective, erotica, ethnic, feminist, gay,

historical, humor, juvenile, literary, mainstream, mystery, picture books, religious, romance, sports, thriller, young, Jewish fiction. "I am interested in major works of history, current affairs, biography, business, politics, economics, science, major memoirs, narrative nonfiction, and other sorts of general nonfiction." Actively seeking new, major or definitive work on a subject of broad interest, or a controversial, but authoritative, new book on a subject that affects many people's lives." I also represent more lighthearted nonfiction projects, such as gift or novelty books, when they suit the market particularly well." Does not want "queries about projects written years ago that were unsuccessfully shopped to a long list of trade publishers by either the author or another agent. I am specifically not interested in reading short, category romances (regency, time travel, paranormal, etc.), horror novels, supernatural stories, poetry, original plays, or film scripts." **How to Contact:** Query with SASE. Do not e-mail or fax queries. For nonfiction, include a complete, fully-edited book proposal with sample chapters. For fiction, include a complete synopsis and no more than 20 pages of sample text. Responds in 2 weeks to queries. Responds in 4-6 weeks to mss. Obtains most new clients through recommendations from others. **Terms:** Agent receives 15% commission on domestic sales. Agent receives 20% commission on foreign sales. **Writers Conferences:** BookExpo America; Frankfurt Book Fair; London Book Fair; RWA National Conference; Modern Language Association Convention; Jerusalem Book Fair. **Tips:** "While I am not interested in being flattered by a prospective client, it does matter to me that she knows why she is writing to me in the first place. Is one of my clients a colleague of hers? Has she read a book by one of my clients that led her to believe I might be interested in her work? Authors of descriptive nonfiction should have real credentials and expertise in their subject areas, either as academics, journalists, or policy experts, and authors of prescriptive nonfiction should have legitimate expertise and considerable experience communicating their ideas in seminars and workshops, in a successful business, through the media, etc."

HOWARD MORHAIM LITERARY AGENCY

30 Pierrepont St., Brooklyn NY 11201. (718)222-8400. **Fax:** (718)222-5056. **Website:** www.morhaimliterary.com/. Member of AAR. **Member Agents:** Howard Morhaim, Kate McKean, Katie Menick. Actively seeking fiction, nonfiction and young-adult novels. **How to Contact:** Query via e-mail with cover letter and three sample chapters. See each agent's listing for specifics.

NELSON LITERARY AGENCY

1732 Wazee St., Suite 207, Denver CO 80202. (303)292-2805. **E-mail:** query@nelsonagency.com. **Website:** www.nelsonagency.com. **Contact:** Kristin Nelson, president and seniorn literary agent; Sara Megibow, associate literary agent. Member of AAR. RWA, SCBWI, SFWA. Prior to opening her own agency, Ms. Nelson worked as a literary scout and subrights agent for agent Jody Rein. **Represents:** Novels, select nonfiction. **Considers These Nonfiction Areas:** memoirs. **Considers These Fiction Areas:** literary, romance, includes fantasy with romantic elements, science fiction, fantasy, young adult, women's, chick lit (includes mysteries); commercial/mainstream. NLA specializes in representing commercial fiction and high caliber literary fiction. Actively seeking Latina writers who tackle contemporary issues in a modern voice (think Dirty Girls Social Club). Does not want short story collections, mysteries (except chick lit), thrillers, Christian, horror, or children's picture books. **How to Contact:** Query by e-mail only.

HAROLD OBER ASSOCIATES

425 Madison Ave., New York NY 10017. (212)759-8600. **Fax:** (212)759-9428. **Website:** www.haroldober.com. **Contact:** Craig Tenney. Member of AAR. **Represents:** 250 clients. 10% of clients are new/unpublished writers. **Currently Handles:** nonfiction books 35%, novels 50%, juvenile books 15%. Mr. Elwell was previously with Elwell & Weiser. **Member Agents:** Phyllis Westberg; Pamela Malpas; Craig Tenney (few new clients, mostly Ober backlist); Jake Elwell (previously with Elwell & Weiser. **How to Contact:** Submit concise query letter addressed to a specific agent with the first five pages of the manuscript or proposal and SASE. No fax or e-mail. Does not handle scripts. Responds as promptly as possible. Obtains most new clients through recommendations from others. **Terms:** Agent receives 15% commission on domestic sales. Agent receives 20% commission on foreign sales. Charges clients for photocopying and express mail/package services.

THE RICHARD PARKS AGENCY

Box 693, Salem NY 12865. (518)854-9466. **Fax:** (518)854-9466. **E-mail:** rp@richardparksagency.com. **Website:** www.richardparks agency.com. **Contact:** Richard Parks. Member of AAR. **Currently Handles:** nonfiction books 55%, novels 40%, story collections 5%. **Represents:** Nonfiction books, novels. **Considers These Nonfiction Areas:** crafts, animals, anthropology, art, biography, business, child, cooking, current affairs, ethnic, gardening, gay, government, health, history, how to, humor, language, memoirs, military, money, music, nature, popular culture, psychology, science, self help, sociology, film, travel, women's. Actively seeking nonfiction. Considers fiction by referral only. Does not want to receive unsolicited material. **How to Contact:** Query with SASE. Other Responds in 2 weeks to queries. Obtains most new clients through recommendations/referrals. **Terms:** Agent receives 15% commission on domestic sales. Agent receives 20% commission on foreign sales. Charges clients for photocopying or any unusual expense incurred at the writer's request.

L. PERKINS ASSOCIATES

5800 Arlington Ave., Riverdale NY 10471. (718)543-5344. **Fax:** (718)543-5354. **E-mail:** lperkinsagency@yahoo.com. **Contact:** Lori Perkins, Sandy Lu (Sandy@lperkinsagency@com). Member of AAR. **Represents:** 90 clients. 10% of clients are new/unpublished writers. Ms. Perkins has been an agent for 20 years. She is also the author of *The Insider's Guide to Getting an Agent*, as well as three other nonfiction books. She has also edited 12 erotic anthologies,

and is also the Editorial Director of Ravenousromance.com, an epublisher. **Represents:** Nonfiction books, novels. **Considers These Nonfiction Areas:** popular culture. **Considers These Fiction Areas:** erotica, fantasy, horror, literary, paranormal romance, dark, science, urban fantasy. "Most of my clients write both fiction and nonfiction. This combination keeps my clients publishing for years. I am also a published author, so I know what it takes to write a good book." Actively seeking a Latino Gone With the Wind and Waiting to Exhale, and urban ethnic horror. Does not want to receive anything outside of the above categories (westerns, romance, etc.). **How to Contact:** E-queries only. Accepts simultaneous submissions. Responds in 12 weeks to queries. Responds in 3-6 months to mss. Obtains most new clients through recommendations from others, solicitations, conferences. **Terms:** Agent receives 15% commission on domestic sales. Agent receives 20% commission on foreign sales. No written contract. Charges clients for photocopying. **Writers Conferences:** NECON; Killercon; BookExpo America; World Fantasy Convention, RWA, Romantic Times. **Tips:** "Research your field and contact professional writers' organizations to see who is looking for what. Finish your novel before querying agents. Read my book, *An Insider's Guide to Getting an Agent*, to get a sense of how agents operate. Read agent blogs agentinthe-middle.blogspot.com and ravenousromance.blogspot.com."

SUSAN ANN PROTTER, LITERARY AGENT

320 Central Park West, Suite 12E, New York NY 10025. **Website:** SusanAnnProtter.com. **Contact:** Susan Protter. Member of AAR. Other memberships include Authors Guild. Prior to opening her agency, Ms. Protter was associate director of subsidiary rights at Harper & Row Publishers. **How to Contact:** "We are currently not accepting new unsolicited submissions."

JODIE RHODES LITERARY AGENCY

8840 Villa La Jolla Drive, Suite 315, La Jolla CA 92037-1957. **Website:** jodierhodesliterary.com. **Contact:** Jodie Rhodes, president. Member of AAR. **Represents:** 74 clients. 60% of clients are new/unpublished writers. **Currently Handles:** nonfiction books 45%, novels 35%, juvenile books 20%. Prior to opening her agency, Ms. Rhodes was a university-level creative writing teacher, workshop director, published novelist, and vice president/media director at the N.W. Ayer Advertising Agency. **Member Agents:** Jodie Rhodes; Clark McCutcheon (fiction); Bob McCarter (nonfiction). **Represents:** Nonfiction books, novels. **Considers These Nonfiction Areas:** biography, child, ethnic, government, health, history, memoirs, military, science, women's. **Considers These Fiction Areas:** ethnic, family, historical, literary, mainstream, mystery, thriller, young adult, women's. "Actively seeking witty, sophisticated women's books about career ambitions and relationships; edgy/ trendy YA and teen books; narrative nonfiction on groundbreaking scientific discoveries, politics, economics, military and important current affairs by prominent scientists and academic professors." Does not want to receive erotica, horror, fantasy, romance, science fiction, religious/inspirational, or children's books (does accept young adult/teen). **How to Contact:** Query with brief synopsis, first 30-50 pages, SASE. Do not call. Do not send complete ms unless requested. This agency does not return unrequested material weighing a pound or more that requires special postage. Include e-mail address with query. Accepts simultaneous submissions. Responds in 3 weeks to queries. Obtains most new clients through recommendations from others, agent sourcebooks. **Terms:** Agent receives 15% commission on domestic sales. Agent receives 20% commission on foreign sales. Offers written contract; 1-month notice must be given to terminate contract. Charges clients for fax, photocopying, phone calls, postage. Charges are itemized and approved by writers upfront. **Tips:** "Think your book out before you write it. Do your research, know your subject matter intimately, and write vivid specifics, not bland generalities. Care deeply about your book. Don't imitate other writers. Find your own voice. We never take on a book we don't believe in, and we go the extra mile for our writers. We welcome talented new writers."

ANGELA RINALDI LITERARY AGENCY

P.O. Box 7877, Beverly Hills CA 90212-7877. (310)842-7665. **Fax:** (310)837-8143. **E-mail:** amr@rinaldiliterary.com. **Website:** www.rinaldiliterary.com. **Contact:** Angela Rinaldi. Member of AAR. **Represents:** 50 clients. **Currently Handles:** nonfiction books 50%, novels 50%. Prior to opening her agency, Ms. Rinaldi was an editor at NAL/Signet, Pocket Books and Bantam, and the manager of book development for The Los Angeles Times. **Represents:** Nonfiction books, novels, TV and motion picture rights (for clients only). **Considers These Nonfiction Areas:** biography, business, health books that address specific issues, career, personal finance, self help, true crime, women's issues/studies, current issues, psychology, popular reference, prescriptive and proactive self help,, books by journalists, academics, doctors and therapists, based on their research, motivational. **Considers These Fiction Areas:** commercial/literary fiction, upmarket contemporary women's fiction, suspense, literary historical thrillers like Elizabeth Kostova's *The Historian*, gothic suspense like Diane Setterfield's *The Thirteenth Tale* and Matthew Pearl's *The Dante Club*, women's book club fiction—novels where the story lends itself to discussion like Kim Edwards' *The Memory Keeper's Daughter*. Actively seeking commercial and literary fiction. Does not want to receive humor, techno thrillers, KGB/CIA espionage, drug thrillers, Da Vinci-code thrillers, category romances, science fiction, fantasy, horror, westerns, film scripts, poetry, category romances, magazine articles, religion, occult, supernatural. **How to Contact:** For fiction, send first 3 chapters, brief synopsis, SASE or brief email inquiry with the first 10 pages pastsed into the email—no attachments unless asked for. For nonfiction, query with detailed letter or outline/proposal, SASE or email—no attachments unless asked for. Do not send certified or metered mail. Other Responds in 6 weeks to queries that are posted; email queries 2-3 weeks. **Terms:** Agent receives 15% commission on domestic sales. Agent receives 25% commission on foreign sales. Offers written contract.

ANN RITTENBERG LITERARY AGENCY, INC.

30 Bond St., New York NY 10012. (212)684-6936. **Fax:** (212)684-6929. **Website:** www.rittlit.com. **Contact:** Ann Rittenberg, President and Penn Whaling, Associate. Member of AAR. **Currently Handles:** fiction 75%, nonfiction 25%. **Represents: Considers These Fiction Areas: Considers These Fiction Areas:** Upmarket women's novels and thrillers, literary. This agent specializes in literary fiction and literary nonfiction. Does not want to receive screenplays, straight genre fiction, poetry, self-help. **How to Contact:** Query with SASE. Submit outline, 3 sample chapters, SASE. Query via postal mail only. Accepts simultaneous submissions. Responds in 6 weeks to queries. Responds in 2 months to mss. Obtains most new clients through referrals from established writers and editors. **Terms:** Agent receives 15% commission on domestic sales. Agent receives 20% commission on foreign sales. Offers written contract. This agency charges clients for photocopying only.

RLR ASSOCIATES, LTD.

Literary Department, 7 W. 51st St., New York NY 10019. (212)541-8641. **Fax:** (212)262-7084. **E-mail:** sgould@rlrassociates.net. **Website:** www.rlrliterary.net. **Contact:** Scott Gould. Member of AAR. **Represents:** 50 clients. 25% of clients are new/unpublished writers. **Currently Handles:** nonfiction books 70%, novels 25%, story collections 5%. **Represents:** Nonfiction books, novels, short story collections, scholarly. **Considers These Nonfiction Areas:** interior, animals, anthropology, art, biography, business, child, cooking, current affairs, education, ethnic, gay, government, health, history, humor, language, memoirs, money, multicultural, music, nature, photography, popular culture, psychology, religion, science, self help, sociology, sports, translation, travel, true crime, women's. **Considers These Fiction Areas:** adventure, comic, detective, ethnic, experimental, family, feminist, gay, historical, horror, humor, literary, mainstream, multicultural, mystery, sports, thriller. "We provide a lot of editorial assistance to our clients and have connections." Actively seeking fiction, current affairs, history, art, popular culture, health and business. Does not want to receive screenplays. **How to Contact:** Query by either e-mail or mail. Accepts simultaneous submissions. Responds in 4-8 weeks to queries. Obtains most new clients through recommendations from others. **Terms:** Agent receives 15% commission on domestic sales. Agent receives 20% commission on foreign sales. Offers written contract.
Tips: "Please check out our website for more details on our agency."

B.J. ROBBINS LITERARY AGENCY

5130 Bellaire Ave., North Hollywood CA 91607-2908. **E-mail:** Robbins literary@gmail.com. **Contact:** (Ms.) B.J. Robbins. Member of AAR. **Represents:** 40 clients. 50% of clients are new/unpublished writers. **Currently Handles:** nonfiction books 50%, novels 50%. **Represents:** Nonfiction books, novels. **Considers These Nonfiction Areas:** biography, current affairs, ethnic, health, humor, memoirs, music, popular culture, psychology, self help, sociology, sports, film, travel, true crime, women's. **Considers These Fiction Areas:** detective, ethnic, literary, mainstream, mystery, sports, thriller. **How to Contact:** Query with SASE. Submit outline/proposal, 3 sample chapters, SASE. Accepts e-mail queries (no attachments). Accepts simultaneous submissions. Responds in 2-6 weeks to queries. Responds in 6-8 weeks to mss. Obtains most new clients through conferences, referrals. **Terms:** Agent receives 15% commission on domestic sales. Agent receives 20% commission on foreign sales. Offers written contract; 3-month notice must be given to terminate contract. This agency charges clients for postage and photocopying (only after sale of ms). **Writers Conferences:** Squaw Valley Writers Workshop; San Diego State University Writers' Conference.

RITA ROSENKRANZ LITERARY AGENCY

440 West End Ave., Suite 15D, New York NY 10024-5358. (212)873-6333. **Contact:** Rita Rosenkranz. Member of AAR. **Represents:** 35 clients. 30% of clients are new/unpublished writers. **Currently Handles:** nonfiction books 99%, novels 1%. Prior to opening her agency, Ms. Rosenkranz worked as an editor at major New York publishing houses. **Represents:** Nonfiction books. **Considers These Nonfiction Areas:** animals, anthropology, art, autobiography, biography, business, child guidance, computers, cooking, crafts, cultural interests, current affairs, dance, decorating, economics, ethnic, film, gay, government, health, history, hobbies, how-to, humor, inspirational, interior design, language, law, lesbian, literature, medicine, military, money, music, nature, parenting, personal improvement, photography, popular culture, politics, psychology, religious, satire, science, self-help, sports, technology, theater, war, women's issues, women's studies. "This agency focuses on adult nonfiction, stresses strong editorial development and refinement before submitting to publishers, and brainstorms ideas with authors." Actively seeks authors who are well paired with their subject, either for professional or personal reasons. **How to Contact:** Send query letter only (no proposal) via regular mail or e-mail. Submit proposal package with SASE only on request. No fax queries. Accepts simultaneous submissions. Responds in 2 weeks to queries. Obtains most new clients through directory listings, solicitations, conferences, word of mouth. **Terms:** Agent receives 15% commission on domestic sales. Agent receives 20% commission on foreign sales. Offers written contract, binding for 3 years; 3-month written notice must be given to terminate contract. Charges clients for photocopying. Makes referrals to editing services. **Tips:** "Identify the current competition for your project to make sure the project is valid. A strong cover letter is very important."

HAROLD SCHMIDT LITERARY AGENCY

415 W. 23rd St., #6F, New York NY 10011. (212)727-7473. **Fax:** (212)807-6025. **Contact:** Harold Schmidt. Member of AAR. **Represents:** 3 clients. **Represents:** Nonfiction, fiction. **Considers These Fiction Areas:** contemporary issues, gay, literary, original fiction with unique narrative voices, high quality psychological suspense and thrillers, likes offbeat/quirky. Seeking novels. **How to Contact:** Query with SASE; do not send material without being asked. No telephone or e-mail queries.

THE SEYMOUR AGENCY

475 Miner St., Canton NY 13617. (315)386-1831. **E-mail:** marysue@twcny.rr.com. **Website:** www.theseymouragency.com. **Contact:** Mary Sue Seymour. Member of AAR. Signatory of WGA. Other memberships include RWA, Authors Guild. **Represents:** 50 clients. 5% of clients are new/unpublished writers. **Currently Handles:** nonfiction books 50%, other 50% fiction. Ms. Seymour is a retired New York State certified teacher. **Represents:** Nonfiction books, novels. **Considers These Nonfiction Areas:** business, health, how-to, self-help, Christian books; cookbooks; any well-written nonfiction that includes a proposal in standard format and 1 sample chapter. **Considers These Fiction Areas:** religious, Christian books, romance, any type. **How to Contact:** Query with SASE, synopsis, first 50 pages for romance. Accepts e-mail queries. Accepts simultaneous submissions. Responds in 1 month to queries. Responds in 3 months to mss. **Terms:** Agent receives 12-15% commission on domestic sales.

DENISE SHANNON LITERARY AGENCY, INC.

20 W. 22nd St., Suite 1603, New York NY 10010. (212)414-2911. **Fax:** (212)414-2930. **E-mail:** info@deniseshannonagency.com. **Website:** www.deniseshannonagency.com. **Contact:** Denise Shannon. Estab. 2002. Member of AAR. Prior to opening her agency, Ms. Shannon worked for 16 years with Georges Borchardt and International Creative Management. **Represents:** Nonfiction books, novels. **Considers These Nonfiction Areas:** biography, business, health, narrative nonfiction; politics; journalism; memoir; social history. **Considers These Fiction Areas:** literary. "We are a boutique agency with a distinguished list of fiction and nonfiction authors." **How to Contact:** Query by email to: submissions@deniseshannonagency.com, or mail with SASE. Submit query with description of project, bio, SASE. See guidelines online. **Tips:** "Please do not send queries regarding fiction projects until a complete manuscript is available for review. We request that you inform us if you are submitting material simultaneously to other agencies."

WENDY SHERMAN ASSOCIATES, INC.

27 W. 24th St., New York NY 10010. (212)279-9027. **Website:** www.wsherman.com. **Contact:** Wendy Sherman. Member of AAR. **Represents:** 50 clients. 30% of clients are new/unpublished writers. **Currently Handles:** nonfiction books 50%, novels 50%. Prior to opening the agency, Ms. Sherman served as vice president, executive director, associate publisher, subsidiary rights director, and sales and marketing director for major publishers. **Member Agents:** Wendy Sherman (board member of AAR). **Represents:** Nonfiction, fiction. **Considers These Nonfiction Areas:** memoirs, psychology, narrative; practical. **Considers These Fiction Areas:** literary, women's, suspense. "We specialize in developing new writers, as well as working with more established writers. My experience as a publisher has proven to be a great asset to my clients." **How to Contact:** Query via e-mail to submissions@wsherman.com Accepts simultaneous submissions. Responds in 1 month to queries. Obtains most new clients through recommendations from others. **Terms:** Agent receives 15% commission on domestic sales. Agent receives 20% commission on foreign

and film sales. Offers written contract. **Tips:** "The bottom line is: Do your homework. Be as well prepared as possible. Read the books that will help you present yourself and your work with polish. You want your submission to stand out."

ROSALIE SIEGEL, INTERNATIONAL LITERARY AGENCY, INC.

1 Abey Dr., Pennington NJ 08543. (609)737-1007. **Fax:** (609)737-3708. **Contact:** Rosalie Siegel. Member of AAR. **Represents:** 35 clients. 10% of clients are new/unpublished writers. **Currently Handles:** nonfiction books 45%, novels 45%, other 10% young adult books; short story collections for current clients. **How to Contact:** Obtains most new clients through referrals from writers and friends. **Terms:** Agent receives 15% commission on domestic sales. Agent receives 20% commission on foreign sales. Offers written contract; 2-month notice must be given to terminate contract. Charges clients for photocopying.

SPENCERHILL ASSOCIATES

P.O. Box 374, Chatham NY 12037. (518)392-9293. **Fax:** (518)392-9554. **E-mail:** submissions@spencerhillassociates.com. **Website:** www.spencerhillassociates.com. **Contact:** Karen Solem or Jennifer Schober (and please refer to our website for the latest information). Member of AAR. **Represents:** 96 clients. 10% of clients are new/unpublished writers. Prior to becoming an agent, Ms. Solem was editor-in-chief at HarperCollins and an associate publisher. **Member Agents:** Karen Solem; Jennifer Schober. **Represents:** Novels. **Considers These Fiction Areas:** detective, historical, literary, mainstream, religious, romance, thriller, young adult. "We handle mostly commercial women's fiction, historical novels, romance (historical, contemporary, paranormal, urban fantasy), thrillers, and mysteries. We also represent Christian fiction only—no nonfiction." No nonfiction, poetry, science fiction, children's picture books, or scripts. **How to Contact:** Query submissions@spencerhillassociates.com with synopsis and first three chapters attached as a .doc or .rtf file. Please note we no longer accept queries via the mail. Responds in 6-8 weeks to queries if we are interested in pursuing. **Terms:** Agent receives 15% commission on domestic sales. Agent receives 20% commission on foreign sales. Offers written contract; 3-month notice must be given to terminate contract.

PHILIP G. SPITZER LITERARY AGENCY, INC

50 Talmage Farm Ln., East Hampton NY 11937. (631)329-3650. **Fax:** (631)329-3651. **E-mail:** luc.hunt@spitzeragency.com. **Website:** www.spitzeragency.com. **Contact:** Luc Hunt. Member of AAR. **Represents:** 60 clients. 10% of clients are new/unpublished writers. **Currently Handles:** nonfiction books 35%, novels 65%. Prior to opening his agency, Mr. Spitzer served at New York University Press, McGraw-Hill, and the John Cushman Associates literary agency. **Represents:** Nonfiction books, novels. **Considers These Nonfiction Areas:** Biography, History, Travel, Politics, Current Events. **Considers These Fiction Areas:** general fiction, detective, literary, mainstream, mystery, sports, thriller. This agency specializes in mystery/suspense, literary fiction, sports and general nonfiction (no

how-to). **How to Contact:** Query with SASE. Responds in 2 weeks to queries. Responds in 6 weeks to mss. Obtains most new clients through recommendations from others. **Terms:** Agent receives 15% commission on domestic sales. Agent receives 20% commission on foreign sales. Charges clients for photocopying. **Writers Conferences:** London Bookfair, Frankfurt, BookExpo America.

STEELE-PERKINS LITERARY AGENCY

26 Island Ln., Canandaigua NY 14424. (585)396-9290. **Fax:** (585)396-3579. **E-mail:** pattiesp@aol.com. **Contact:** Pattie Steele-Perkins. Member of AAR. Other memberships include RWA. **Currently Handles:** novels 100%. **Represents:** Novels. **Considers These Fiction Areas:** romance, women's, All genres: category romance, romantic suspense, historical, contemporary, multi-cultural, and inspirational. **How to Contact:** Submit synopsis and one chapter via e-mail (no attachments) or snail mail. Snail mail submissions require SASE. Accepts simultaneous submissions. Responds in 6 weeks to queries. Obtains most new clients through recommendations from others, queries/solicitations. **Terms:** Agent receives 15% commission on domestic sales. Offers written contract, binding for 1 year; 1-month notice must be given to terminate contract. **Tips:** "Be patient. E-mail rather than call. Make sure what you are sending is the best it can be."

STIMOLA LITERARY STUDIO, INC.

306 Chase Court, Edgewater NJ 07020. Phone/**Fax:** (201)945-9353. **E-mail:** info@stimolaliterarystudio.com. **Website:** www.stimolaliterarystudio.com. **Contact:** Rosemary B. Stimola. Member of AAR. **How to Contact:** Query via e-mail (no unsolicited attachments). Responds in 3 weeks to queries "we wish to pursue further." Responds in 2 months to requested mss. Obtains most new clients through referrals. Unsolicited submissions are still accepted. **Terms:** Agent receives 15% commission on domestic sales. Agent receives 20% (if subagents are employed) commission on foreign sales.

THE STROTHMAN AGENCY, LLC

Six Beacon St., Suite 810, Boston MA 02108. (617)742-2011. **Fax:** (617)742-2014. **E-mail:** info@strothmanagency.com. **Website:** www.strothmanagency.com. **Contact:** Wendy Strothman, Lauren MacLeod. Member of AAR. Other memberships include Authors' Guild. **Represents:** 50 clients. **Currently Handles:** nonfiction books 70%, novels 10%, scholarly books 20%. Prior to becoming an agent, Ms. Strothman was head of Beacon Press (1983-1995) and executive vice president of Houghton Mifflin's Trade & Reference Division (1996-2002). **Member Agents:** Wendy Strothman; Lauren MacLeod. **Represents:** Nonfiction books, novels, scholarly, young adult and middle grade. **Considers These Nonfiction Areas:** current affairs, government, history, language, nature. **Considers These Fiction Areas:** literary, young adult, middle grade. "Because we are highly selective in the clients we represent, we increase the value publishers place on our properties. We specialize in narrative nonfiction, memoir, history, science and nature, arts and culture, literary travel, current affairs, and some business. We have a highly selective practice in literary fiction, young adult and middle grade fiction, and nonfiction. We are now opening our doors to more commercial fiction but ONLY from authors who have a platform. If you have a platform, please mention it in your query letter." "The Strothman Agency seeks out scholars, journalists, and other acknowledged and emerging experts in their fields. We are now actively looking for authors of well written young-adult fiction and nonfiction. Browse the Latest News to get an idea of the types of books that we represent. For more about what we're looking for, read Pitching an Agent: The Strothman Agency on the publishing website www.strothmanagency.com." Does not want to receive commercial fiction, romance, science fiction or self-help. **How to Contact:** Open to email (strothmanagency@gmail.com) and postal submissions. See submission guidelines. Accepts simultaneous submissions. Responds in 4 weeks to queries. Responds in 6 weeks to mss. Obtains most new clients through recommendations from others. **Terms:** Agent receives 15% commission on domestic sales. Agent receives 20% commission on foreign sales. Offers written contract; 30-day notice must be given to terminate contract.

EMMA SWEENEY AGENCY, LLC

245 East 80th St., Suite 7E, New York NY 10075. **E-mail:** queries@emmasweeneyagency.com. **Website:** www.emmasweeneyagency.com. **Contact:** Eva Talmadge. Member of AAR. Other memberships include Women's Media Group. **Represents:** 80 clients. 5% of clients are new/unpublished writers. **Currently Handles:** nonfiction books 50%, novels 50%. Prior to becoming an agent, Ms. Sweeney was director of subsidiary rights at Grove Press. Since 1990, she has been a literary agent. **Member Agents:** Emma Sweeney, president; Eva Talmadge, rights manager and agent. **Represents:** literary fiction, young adult novels, and narrative nonfiction. **Considers These Nonfiction Areas:** popular science, pop culture and music history, biography, memoirs, cooking, and anything relating to animals. **Considers These Fiction Areas:** literary (of the highest writing quality possible), young adult. eva@emmasweeneyagency.com); Justine Wenger, junior agent/assistant (justine@emmasweeneyagency.com). **Represents:** Nonfiction books, novels. "We specialize in quality fiction and non-fiction. Our primary areas of interest include literary and women's fiction, mysteries and thrillers; science, history, biography, memoir, religious studies and the natural sciences." Does not want to receive romance and westerns or screenplays. **How to Contact:** Send query letter and first ten pages in body of e-mail (no attachments) to queries@emmasweeneyagency.com. No snail mail queries. **Terms:** Agent receives 15% commission on domestic sales. Agent receives 10% commission on foreign sales. **Writers Conferences:** Nebraska Writers' Conference; Words and Music Festival in New Orleans.

TESSLER LITERARY AGENCY, LLC

27 W. 20th St., Suite 1003, New York NY 10011. (212)242-0466. **Fax:** (212)242-2366. **E-mail:** michelle@tessleragency.com. **Website:** www.tessleragency.com. **Contact:** Michelle Tessler. Member of AAR. Prior to forming her own agency, Ms. Tessler worked at Carlisle & Co. (now a part of Inkwell Management). She has also worked at the William Morris Agency and the Elaine Markson Literary Agency. **Represents:** Nonfiction books, novels. "The Tessler Agency is a full-service boutique agency that **Represents:** writers of literary fiction and high quality nonfiction in the following categories: popular science, reportage, memoir, history, biography, psychology, business and travel." **How to Contact:** Submit query through website only.

RALPH M. VICINANZA LTD.

303 W. 18th St., New York NY 10011. (212)924-7090. **Fax:** (212)691-9644. Member of AAR. **Member Agents:** Ralph M. Vicinanza; Chris Lotts; Christopher Schelling, Matthew Mahoney. **How to Contact:** This agency takes on new clients by professional recommendation only. **Terms:** Agent receives 15% commission on domestic sales. Agent receives 20% commission on foreign sales.

WALES LITERARY AGENCY, INC.

P.O. Box 9426, Seattle WA 98109-0426. (206)284-7114. **E-mail:** waleslit@waleslit.com. **Website:** www.waleslit.com. **Contact:** Elizabeth Wales, Neal Swain. Member of AAR. Other memberships include Book Publishers' Northwest, Pacific Northwest Booksellers Association, PEN. **Represents:** 60 clients. 10% of clients are new/unpublished writers. **Currently Handles:** nonfiction books 60%, novels 40%. Prior to becoming an agent, Ms. Wales worked at Oxford University Press and Viking Penguin. **Member Agents:** Elizabeth Wales; Neal Swain. This agency specializes in quality fiction and nonfiction. Does not handle screenplays, children's literature, genre fiction, or most category nonfiction. **How to Contact:** Accepts queries sent with cover letter and SASE, and email queries with no attachments. No phone or fax queries. Accepts simultaneous submissions. Responds in 2 weeks to queries, 2 months to mss. **Terms:** Agent receives 15% commission on domestic sales. Agent receives 20% commission on foreign sales. **Tips:** "We are especially interested in work that espouses a progressive cultural or political view, projects a new voice, or simply shares an important, compelling story. We also encourage writers living in the Pacific Northwest, West Coast, Alaska, and Pacific Rim countries, and writers from historically underrepresented groups, such as gay and lesbian writers and writers of color, to submit work (but does not discourage writers outside these areas). Most importantly, whether in fiction or nonfiction, the agency is looking for talented storytellers."

TED WEINSTEIN LITERARY MANAGEMENT

307 Seventh Ave., Suite 2407, Dept. GLA, New York NY 10001. **Website:** www.twliterary.com. **Contact:** Ted Weinstein. Member of AAR. **Represents:** 75 clients. 50% of clients are new/unpublished writers. **Currently Handles:** nonfiction books 100%. **Represents: Considers These Nonfiction Areas:** biography, business, current affairs, government, health, history, popular culture, science, self help, travel, true crime, lifestyle, narrative journalism, popular science. **How to Contact:** Please visit website for detailed guidelines before submitting. E-mail queries only.

Other Responds in 3 weeks to queries. **Terms:** Agent receives 15% commission on domestic sales. Agent receives 20% commission on foreign sales. Agent receives 20% commission on film sales. Offers written contract, binding for 1 year. Charges clients for photocopying and express shipping. **Tips:** "Accepts email queries ONLY; paper submissions are discarded. See agency's Web site (www.twliterary.com) for full guidelines."

WOLGEMUTH & ASSOCIATES, INC

8600 Crestgate Circle, Orlando FL 32819. (407)909-9445. **Fax:** (407)909-9446. **E-mail:** ewolgemuth@wolgemuthandassociates. com. **Contact:** Erik Wolgemuth. Member of AAR. **Represents:** 60 clients. 10% of clients are new/unpublished writers. **Currently Handles:** nonfiction books 90%, novella 2%, juvenile books 5%, multimedia 3%. "We have been in the publishing business since 1976, having been a marketing executive at a number of houses, a publisher, an author, and a founder and owner of a publishing company." **Member Agents:** Robert D. Wolgemuth; Andrew D. Wolgemuth; Erik S. Wolgemuth. **Represents:** Material used by Christian families. "We are not considering any new material at this time." **Terms:** Agent receives 15% commission on domestic sales. Offers written contract, binding for 2-3 years; 30-day notice must be given to terminate contract.

CHAPTER 34

PUBLISHERS OPEN TO UNSOLICITED WORK

FICTION PUBLISHERS

ACADEMY CHICAGO PUBLISHERS

363 W. Erie St., Suite 4W, Chicago IL 60610-3125. (312)751-7300. **Fax:** (312)751-7306. **E-mail:** info@academychicago.com. **Website:** www.academychicago.com. **Contact:** Anita Miller, editorial director/ senior editor. "We publish quality fiction and nonfiction. Our audience is literate and discriminating." Publishes hardcover and some paperback originals and trade paperback reprints. **Needs:** We look for quality work, but we do not publish experimental, avant-garde novels. No novelized biography, history, or science fiction. **How to Contact:** Submit proposal package, clips, 3 sample chapters. **Tips:** "No fax queries, no disks. No electronic submissions. We are always interested in reprinting good out-of-print books."

ALONDRA PRESS, LLC

10122 Shadow Wood Dr. #19, Houston TX 77043. **E-mail:** lark@alondra press.com. **Website:** www.alondrapress.com. **Contact:** Kathleen Palmer, chief editor. Publishes trade paperback originals and reprints. **Needs:** "Just send us a few pages, or the entire manuscript in an e-mail attachment. We will look at it quickly and tell you if it interests us." **How to Contact:** Submit complete ms. **Tips:** "We will be looking for unusual stories, similar to *The Wind Thief*. Send your submissions in an e-mail attachment only."

ALPHA WORLD PRESS

530 Oaklawn Ave., Green Bay WI 54304. (866)855-3720. **E-mail:** office@alphaworldpress.com. **Website:** www.alphaworldpress.com. **Contact:** Tracey Vandeveer, owner. "Our press is dedicated to publishing high-quality work by, for and about lesbians from all walks of life. We publish fiction, nonfiction and poetry. We welcome all manuscripts from lesbians. We want the voices and perspectives of lesbians from all across the world to be heard through the books that we publish. We work very closely with our authors in all aspects of publishing—from editing and graphic design, to actual production, promotion and marketing." Publishes trade paperback originals and mass-market paperback originals. Receives 120 queries/year; 12 mss/year. **Needs:** We publish only lesbian-themed books for the lesbian market. **How to Contact:** Submit proposal package, 3 sample chapters, clips. Send it via e-mail in PDF. **Tips:** Our audience is lesbians only.

BKMK PRESS

University of Missouri-Kansas City, 5101 Rockhill Rd., Kansas City MO 64110-2499. (816)235-2558. **Fax:** (816)235-2611. **E-mail:** bkmk@ umkc.edu. **Website:** www.umkc.edu/bkmk. **Contact:** Ben Furnish, managing editor. "BkMk Press publishes fine literature. Reading period January–June." Publishes trade paperback originals. **How to Contact:** Query with SASE. **Tips:** "We skew toward readers of literature, particularly contemporary writing. Because of our limited number of titles published per year, we discourage apprentice writers or 'scattershot' submissions."

BLACK ROSE WRITING

P.O. Box 1540, Castroville TX 78009. **E-mail:** creator@blackrose writing.com. **Website:** www.blackrosewriting.com. **Contact:** Reagan Rothe, owner (all queries). Publishes hardcover, trade paperback, mass-market paperback and electronic originals. Receives 1,000+ queries/year; 120 mss/year. **Needs:** All genre fiction: action, horror, suspense, romance, fantasy, etc. "Black Rose Writing prefers clean, edited work that requires only minor editing checks. We believe the writer should take great pride in their work and truly look through their manuscript before submitting something in its raw, unedited form." **How to Contact:** Submit query letter via e-mail or with SASE before sending entire ms. **Tips:** "Black Rose Writing welcomes all writers but truly focuses on new, talented authors who are seeking their first big recognition and publication. We promise to give you personal feedback on every piece, dedicating ourselves to avoid automated responses or negative outlooks on an individual's subjective work. Please follow our submission guidelines online."

BLACK VELVET SEDUCTIONS PUBLISHING

1350-C W. Southport, Box 249, Indianapolis IN 46217. (888)556-2750. **E-mail:** LaurieSanders@fusemail.com. **Website:** www.black-velvetseductions.com. **Contact:** Laurie Sanders, acquisitions editor. "We only publish romance novels, romantic short story collections and romantic erotic stories. If the piece is not a romance, we will not accept it. We do not accept mainstream fiction. We look for well-crafted stories with a high degree of emotional impact. We do not accept material written in first person. All material must be in third person point of view." Publishes trade paperback and electronic originals and reprints. Receives 500 queries/year; 1,000 mss/year. **Needs:** All books must have a strong romance element. "We are particularly interested in acquiring stories with rounded and/or curvy heroines who find love with wonderful erotic men who love their rounder curvier figures. Do not be afraid to hit us with a nontraditional character or plot. We like quirky, interesting and offbeat." **How to Contact:** Prefers complete ms with cover letter and synopsis. **Tips:** "We publish romance and erotic romance. We look for books written in very deep point of view."

BOLD STROKES BOOKS, INC.

P.O. Box 249, Valley Falls NY 12185. (518)753-6642. (518)753-6648. **E-mail:** publisher@boldstrokesbooks.com. **Website:** www.boldstrokesbooks.com. **Contact:** Len Barot, acq. director (general/genre gay/lesbian fiction). Publishes trade paperback originals and reprints; electronic originals and reprints. Receives 300 queries/year; 300 mss/year. **Fiction:** "Submissions should have a gay, lesbian, transgendered, or bisexual focus and should be positive and life-affirming." **How to Contact:** Submit completed ms with bio, cover letter and synopsis—electronically only. **Tips:** "We are particularly interested in authors who are interested in craft enhancement, technical development, and exploring and expanding traditional genre definitions and boundaries and are looking for a long-term publishing relationship."

BRONZE MAN BOOKS

Bronze Man Books, Millikin Univ., 1184 W. Main, Decatur IL 62522. (217)424-6264. **Website:** www.bronzemanbooks.com. **Contact:** Dr. Randy Brooks, editorial board (areas of interest: children's books, fiction, poetry, nonfiction). Publishes hardcover, trade paperback and mass-market paperback originals. Receives 45 queries/year; 25 mss/year. **Needs:** "Literary chapbooks intended for readers of contemporary fiction, drama and poetry." **How to Contact:** Submit completed ms.

CELLAR DOOR PUBLISHING, LLC

3439 NE Sandy Blvd., Suite 309, Portland OR 97232-1959. **E-mail:** info@cellardoorpublishing.com. **Website:** www.cellardoorpublishing.com. "Cellar Door Publishing specializes in the publication of high-quality illustrated literature and graphic novels." Publishes hardcover originals, trade paperback originals and electronic originals. **Fiction:** "We are looking for all genres and age groups. We encourage creators to experiment with format and content, though it is not required. We do accept a limited number of submissions for books without illustrations. This is generally reserved for books that are either unique in content or controversial in nature, or literary projects that can be released in a serialized format." **How to Contact:** "We currently accept unsolicited submissions via online submission form and comic-book conventions only. We no longer accept unsolicited submissions through traditional mail. To submit book proposals for consideration, please use the online submission form." **Tips:** "Nonfiction submissions will also be considered if they fall into one of our categories. Submit online."

CLEIS PRESS

Cleis Press & Viva Editions, 2246 Sixth St., Berkeley CA 94710. (510)845-8000 or (800)780-2279. **Fax:** (510)845-8001. **E-mail:** cleis@cleispress.com. **Website:** www.cleispress.com. **Contact:** Brenda Knight, associate publisher. "Cleis Press publishes provocative, intelligent books in the areas of sexuality, gay and lesbian studies, erotica, fiction, gender studies and human rights." Publishes trade paperback originals and reprints. **Fiction:** "We are looking for high quality fiction by women and men. No romances." **How to Contact:** Submit complete ms. (*Writer's Market* recommends sending a query with SASE first.) **Tips:** "Be familiar with publishers' catalogs; be absolutely aware of your audience; research potential markets; present fresh new ways of looking at your topic; avoid 'PR' language and include publishing history in query letter."

COVENANT COMMUNICATIONS, INC.

920 E. State Rd., American Fork UT 84003. (801)756-9966. **Fax:** (801)756-1049. **E-mail:** info@covenant-lds.com. **Website:** www.covenant-lds.com. **Contact:** Kathryn Jenkins, managing editor. "Currently emphasizing inspirational, doctrinal, historical, biography. "Receives 350 queries/year; 1,200 mss/year. **Needs:** Our fiction is expanding, and we are looking for new approaches to Later Day Saints literature and storytelling. **How to Contact:** Submit complete ms. **Tips:** "Our audience is exclusively LDS (Latter-day Saints, 'Mormon')."

DANIEL & DANIEL PUBLISHERS, INC.

P.O. Box 2790, McKinleyville CA 95519. (707)839-3495. **Fax:** (707)839-3242. **E-mail:** dandd@danielpublishing.com. **Website:** www.danielpublishing.com. **Contact:** John Daniel, publisher. Publishes hardcover originals and trade paperback originals. Publishes poetry, fiction and nonfiction. **Fiction:** "We seldom publish books over 70,000 words. Other than that, we're looking for books that are important and well written." **How to Contact:** Query with SASE. **Tips:** "Audience includes literate, intelligent general readers. We are very small and very cautious, and we publish fewer books each year, so any submission to us is a long shot. But we welcome your submissions, by mail or e-mail only, please. We don't want submissions by phone, fax or disk."

DAW BOOKS, INC.

Distributed by Penguin Group (USA), 375 Hudson St., New York NY 10014-3658. (212)366-2096. **Fax:** (212)366-2090. **Website:** www.dawbooks.com. **Contact:** Peter Stampfel, submissions editor. Publishes hardcover and paperback originals and reprints. **Needs:** DAW Books publishes science fiction and fantasy. We do not want any nonfiction. **How to Contact:** Submit entire ms, cover letter, SASE.

DEMONTREVILLE PRESS, INC.

P.O. Box 835, Lake Elmo MN 55042-0835. **E-mail:** publisher@demontrevillepress.com. **Website:** www.demontrevillepress.com. **Contact:** Kevin Clemens, publisher (automotive fiction and nonfiction). Publishes trade paperback originals and reprints. Receives 150 queries/year; 100 mss/year. **Needs:** "We want novel-length automotive or motorcycle historicals and/or adventures." **How to Contact:** Submit proposal package, 3 sample chapters, clips, bio. **Tips:** "Automotive and motorcycle enthusiasts, adventurers, environmentalists and history buffs make up our audience."

ELLORA'S CAVE PUBLISHING, INC.

1056 Home Ave., Akron OH 44310. **E-mail:** service@ellorascave.com. **Website:** www.ellorascave.com. **Contact:** Raelene Gorlinsky, managing editor; Kelli Collins, editor-in-chief. Publishes electronic originals and reprints; print books. **Needs:** All must be under genre romance. All must have erotic content or author must be willing to add sex during editing. **How to Contact:** Submit query letter, full synopsis, first three chapters and last chapter. **Tips:** "Our audience is romance readers who want explicit sexual detail. They come to us because we offer not erotica, but Romantica™—sex with romance, plot, emotion. In addition to erotic romance with happy-ever-after endings, we also publish pure erotica, detailing sexual adventure, experimentation, and coming of age."

GAUTHIER PUBLICATIONS, INC.

Frog Legs Ink, P.O. Box 806241, Saint Clair Shores MI 48080. (586)279-1515. **E-mail:** info@gauthierpublications.com. **Website:** www.gauthierpublications.com. **Contact:** Elizabeth Gauthier, creative director (Children's/Fiction). Publishes hardcover originals and trade paperback originals. **Needs:** "We are particularly interested in mystery, thriller, graphic novels and young adult areas for the upcoming year. We do, however, consider most subjects if they are intriguing and well written." **How to Contact:** Query with SASE.

GENESIS PRESS, INC.

P.O. Box 101, Columbus MS 39701. (888)463-4461. **Fax:** (662)329-9399. **E-mail:** books@genesis-press.com. **Website:** www.genesis-press.com. Genesis Press is the largest privately owned African American book publisher in the country. Genesis has steadily increased its reach and now brings its readers everything from suspense and science fiction to Christian-oriented romance and nonfiction. Publishes hardcover and trade paperback originals and reprints. **How to Contact:** Submit clips, 3 sample chapters, SASE. If you would like your ms returned, you must follow all the rules on our website. Please use Priority or First Class mail—no Media Mail, Fed Ex or metered mail. We cannot return partials or manuscripts outside the U.S. No International Reply Coupons, please. **Tips:** Be professional. Always include a cover letter and SASE. Follow the submission guidelines posted on our website or send SASE for a copy.

GIVAL PRESS

Gival Press, LLC, P.O. Box 3812, Arlington VA 22203. (703)351-0079. **E-mail:** givalpress@yahoo.com. **Website:** www.givalpress.com. **Contact:** Robert L. Giron, editor-in-chief. Publishes trade paperback, electronic originals and reprints. Receives 200+ queries/year; 60 mss/year. **Needs:** Literary. **How to Contact:** Always query first via e-mail; provide description, author's bio and supportive material. Submit between October–December only. **Tips:** "Our audience is those who read literary works with depth to the work. Visit our website; there is much to be read/learned from the numerous pages."

GOODMAN BECK PUBLISHING

P.O. Box 253, Norwood N J07648-2428. (201)403-3097. E-mal: info@goodmanbeck.com. **Website:** www.goodmanbeck.com. **Contact:** David Michael, editor. "Our primary interest at this time is mental health, personal growth, aging well, positive psychology, accessible spirituality and self-help." Publishes trade paperback originals and reprints; mass-market paperback originals and reprints. **Needs:** "Fiction: books should be able to generate a passionate response from our adult readers." No science fiction, romance novels. **How to Contact:** Query with SASE. **Tips:** "Your book should be enlightening and marketable. Be prepared to have a comprehensive marketing plan. You will be very involved."

GRAYWOLF PRESS

250 Third Avenue North, Suite 600, Minneapolis MN 55401. **Website:** www.graywolfpress.org. **Contact:** Katie Dublinski, editorial manager (nonfiction, fiction). "Graywolf Press is an independent, nonprofit publisher dedicated to the creation and promotion of thoughtful and imaginative contemporary literature essential to a vital and diverse culture." Publishes trade cloth and paperback originals. Receives 3,000 queries/year. **Needs:** "Familiarize yourself with our list first." No genre books (romance, western, science fiction, suspense). **How to Contact:** Query with SASE. Please do not fax or e-mail.

HAMPTON ROADS PUBLISHING CO., INC.

500 Third Street, Suite 230, San Francisco CA 94107. **E-mail:** submissions@hrpub.com. **Website:** www.hamptonroadspub.com. **Contact:** Chris Nelson, acquisitions manager. "Our reason for being is to impact, uplift and contribute to positive change in the world. We publish books that will enrich and empower the evolving consciousness of mankind. Though we are not necessarily limited in scope, we are most interested in manuscripts on the following subjects: Body/Mind/Spirit, Health and Healing, Self-Help. Please be advised that at the moment we are not accepting: **Fiction** or novelized material that does not pertain to body/mind/spirit, channeled writing." Publishes and distributes hardcover and paperback originals on subjects including metaphysics, health, complementary medicine, visionary fiction and other related topics. Receives 1,000 queries/year; 1,500 mss/year. **Needs: Fiction** should have 1 or more of the following themes: spiritual, inspirational, metaphysical, i.e., past-life recall, out-of-body experiences, near-death experience, paranormal. **How to Contact:** Query with SASE. Submit outline, 2 sample chapters, clips. No longer accepting electronic submissions.

HIGHLAND PRESS PUBLISHING

P.O. Box 2292, High Springs FL 32655. (386)454-3927. **Fax:** (386)454-3927. **E-mail:** The.Highland.Press@gmail.com. **Website:** www.highlandpress.org. **Contact:** Leanne Burroughs, CEO (fiction); she will forward all mss to appropriate editor. "With our focus on historical romances, Highland Press Publishing is known as your 'Passport to Romance.' We focus on historical romances and our award-winning anthologies. Our short stories/novellas are heart warming. As for our historicals, we publish historical novels like many of us grew up with and loved. History is a big part of the story and is tactfully woven throughout the romance." Publishes paperback originals. **Needs:** We have recently opened our submissions up to all genres, with the exception of erotica. Our newest lines are inspirational, Regency and young adult. **How to Contact:** Send query letter. Query with outline/synopsis and sample chapters. Accepts queries by snail mail, e-mail. Include estimated word count, target market. **Tips:** Special interests: Children's ms must come with illustrator. "We will always be looking for good historical manuscripts. In addition, we are actively seeking inspirational romances and Regency period romances." Numerous romance anthologies are planned. Topics and word count are posted on the website. Writers should query with their proposal. After the submission deadline has passed, editors select the stories.

JOURNEYFORTH
Imprint of BJU Press, 1700 Wade Hampton Blvd., Greenville SC 29614. (864)242-5100, ext. 4350. (864)298-0268. **E-mail:** jb@bjup. com. **Website:** www.bjupress.com. **Contact:** Suzette Jordan, adult acquisitions editor. "Small independent publisher of trustworthy novels and biographies for readers pre-school through high school from a conservative Christian perspective, Christian living books and Bible studies for adults." Publishes paperback originals and reprints. .**Fiction:** Our fiction is all based on a moral and Christian worldview. **How to Contact:** Submit 5 sample chapters, synopsis, SASE. **Tips:** "Study the publisher's guidelines. No submissions by e-mail."

KITSUNE BOOKS
P.O. Box 1154, Crawfordville FL 32326-1154. **E-mail:** contact@kitsune books.com. **Website:** www.kitsunebooks.com. **Contact:** Lynn Holschuh, assistant editor. Publishes trade paperback originals and reprints. Receives 600+ queries/year; 70 mss/year. **Needs:** "We are looking for carefully written fiction that's slightly off the beaten path—interesting novels that don't fit easily into any one category. Graceful command of the language is a plus; technical command of grammar/language mechanics a must. Our latest short story collection is in the Raymond Carver tradition. Looking for authors with a unique voice and style." No children's picture books, crime thrillers, mystery, romance, war, westerns, juvenile fiction. **How to Contact:** Query via e-mail. No hardcopy submissions; no previously published material. **Tips:** "Our readership is eclectic, with a taste for the unusual, the artistic and the unexpected. Kitsune Books caters to lovers of literature, poetry and well-designed and researched nonfiction. We prefer to deal with mss electronically rather than receiving printouts (saves trees). Please read our category guidelines carefully. Although we do accept some genre fiction, please look carefully at what we don't accept before you submit. Interesting novels that don't fit easily into any one category are considered. No self-published material."

LEUCROTA PRESS
40485 Murrieta Hot Springs Rd., Suite B-4 #131, Murrieta CA 92562. (619)534-8169. **E-mail:** submissions@leucrotapress.com. **Website:** www.leucrotapress.com. **Contact:** Jessica Dall, acquisitions editor. Leucrota publishes in two seasons: Spring and Fall. Their submission reading periods are Spring (January 1–April 30) and Fall (August 1–December 31). If accepted for publication, your book will be slotted for the following season in which it was read (if you submit in Spring and are accepted, your book will be released the following Spring season). Publishes hardcover, trade paperback and electronic originals. Receives 400 queries/year; 450–600 mss/year. **Needs:** "Characterization should be your number one goal. We are looking for character-driven plots, unique settings, established worlds and histories, believable dialogue and new twists on old scenarios. Wow us with something different, something far out of the ordinary." **How to Contact:** Submit proposal package, three sample chapters, publishing history, cover letter and SASE. Do not submit complete ms unless requested. **Tips:** "Visit our website to get a feel for our editors, our **Needs:** and our overall style and attitude."

LUCKY PRESS, LLC
P.O. Box 754, Athens OH 45701-0754. **Website:** www.luckypress. com. **Contact:** Janice Phelps Williams, editor-in-chief. "Lucky Press is a small, independent publisher and a good option for hard-working, talented writers. Our books are sold primarily online, and authors must be comfortable maintaining a blog and creating social networks to promote their book." Publishes trade paperback originals. Receives 100 queries/year; 25 mss/year. **Fiction:** "We'll consider any well-written ms. We are looking for literary fiction, particularly by Ohio authors. Mss should be 30,000–95,000 words, but query with only the first 3 chapters." Does not want horror, erotica, vampires or psycho-killer mysteries. **How to Contact:** Submit query letter, synopsis and bio via e-mail to submissions@luckypress.com. **Tips:** "The author is the biggest key to success in our book sales and our best-selling books are by authors with a strong web presence."

LOON IN BALLOON INC.
133 Weber St. N., Suite #3-513 Waterloo ON N2J 3G9 Canada. **E-mail:** info@looninballoon.com. **Website:** www.looninballoon.com. Publishes trade paperback originals. Receives 100 mss/year. **Needs:** Looking for stories that could translate into film. Please only novels; no short stories, poetry or children's books. **How to Contact:** E-mail proposal package: author bio, short summary, first 2 chapters. **Tips:** "We publish adult popular fiction. We are small but aggressive."

MCBOOKS PRESS
ID Booth Building, 520 N. Meadow St., Ithaca NY 14850. (607)272-2114. **Fax:** (607)273-6068. **E-mail:** jackie@mcbooks.com. **Website:** www.mcbooks.com. **Contact:** Jackie Swift, editorial director. Publishes trade paperback and hardcover originals and reprints. **Needs:** "We will consider any type of fiction except sci-fi, fantasy, religious and children's." **How to Contact:** E-mail queries preferred. If querying by mail, include SASE. Send excerpt as RTF file attachment. **Tips:** "Give us a general outline of your book. Let us know how your book differs from what is currently on the market and what your qualifications are for writing it. Give us an idea how you would go about promoting/marketing your book."

MILKWEED EDITIONS
1011 Washington Ave. S., Minneapolis MN 55415. (612)332-3192. **E-mail:** editor@milkweed.org. **Website:** www.milkweed.org. Publishes hardcover, trade paperback and electronic originals; trade paperback

and electronic reprints. **Fiction:** For adult readers: literary fiction, nonfiction, poetry, essays. Translations welcome. No romance, mysteries, science fiction. **How to Contact:** Please consider our previous publications when considering submissions to Milkweed Editions. Query or submit complete ms with SASE. Milkweed strongly encourages digital submissions through our website. **Tips:** "We are looking for excellent writing with the intent of making a humane impact on society. Please read submission guidelines before submitting and acquaint yourself with our books in **Terms:** of style and quality before submitting. Many factors influence our selection process, so don't get discouraged."

MOUNTAINLAND PUBLISHING, INC.

P.O. Box 150891, Ogden UT 84415. **E-mail:** editor@mountain landpublishing.com. **Contact:** Michael Combe, managing editor (fiction, nonfiction). Publishes hardcover, mass-market paperback and electronic originals. Submissions are accepted by e-mail only as of January 2010. **Fiction:** "Fiction should be able to grab readers and hold their attention with dynamic writing, interesting characters and compelling plot." **How to Contact:** Submit synopsis, 1 sample chapter via e-mail. **Tips:** "Our audience is a new generation of readers who enjoy well-told stories and who want to be entertained. They want characters they can feel close to and/or love to hate. Make sure your ms is ready for print. Publishing companies will not wait for you to finish editing your story. Be confident that the work you are submitting is your best work. Please submit all ms electronically. Submissions received by mail may be returned unopened."

OAK TREE PRESS

140 E. Palmer, Taylorville IL 62568. (217)824-6500. **E-mail:** oaktreepub@aol.com. **Website:** www.oaktreebooks.com. **Contact:** Acquisitions Editor. "Oak Tree Press is an independent publisher that celebrates writers and is dedicated to the many great unknowns who are just waiting for the opportunity to break into print. We're looking for mainstream, genre fiction. Sponsors 3 contests annually: Dark Oak Mystery, Timeless Love Romance and CopTales for true crime and other stories of law enforcement professionals." Publishes trade paperback and hardcover books. **Needs:** "No science fiction or fantasy, or stories set far into the future. Next, novels substantially longer than our stated word count are not considered, regardless of genre. We look for manuscripts of 70,000–90,000 words. If the story really charms us, we will bend some on either end of the range." **How to Contact:** Query by e-mail. **Tips:** "Perhaps my most extreme pet peeve is receiving queries on projects that we've clearly advertised we don't want: science fiction, fantasy, epic tomes, bigoted diatribes and so on. Second to that is a practice I call 'over-taping,' or the use of yards and yards of tape, or worse yet, the filament tape so that it takes forever to open the package. Finding story pitches on my voice mail is also annoying."

ONEWORLD PUBLICATIONS

185 Banbury Rd., Oxford OX2 7AR United Kingdom. (44)(1865)310597. **Fax:** (44)(1865)310598. **E-mail:** submissions@oneworld-publications.com. **Website:** www.oneworld-publications.com. "We publish accessible but authoritative books, mainly by academics or experts for a general readership and cross-over student market. Authors must be well qualified. Currently emphasizing current affairs, popular science, history and psychology; de-emphasizing self-help." Publishes hardcover and trade paperback originals and trade paperback reprints. Receives 200 queries/year; 50 mss/year. **Needs:** Focusing on well-written literary and commercial fiction from a variety of cultures and periods, many exploring interesting issues and global problems. **How to Contact:** Submit through online proposal form. **Tips:** "We don't require agents—just good proposals with enough hard information."

PALARI PUBLISHING

P.O. Box 9288, Richmond VA 23227-0288. (866)570-6724. **Fax:** (866)570-6724. **E-mail:** dave@palaribooks.com. **Website:** www.palaribooks.com. **Contact:** David Smitherman, publisher/editor. Publishes hardcover and trade paperback originals. **Needs:** "Fiction with an emphasis on intelligence and quality." **How to Contact:** "We accept solicited and unsolicited manuscripts, however we prefer a query letter and SASE, describing the project briefly and concisely. This letter should include a complete address and telephone number." **Terms:** Promotes titles through book signings, direct mail and the Internet. **Tips:** "Tell why your idea is unique or interesting. Make sure we are interested in your genre before submitting. Send a good bio. I'm interested in a writer's experience and unique outlook on life."

PARADISE CAY PUBLICATIONS

P.O. Box 29, Arcata CA 95518-0029. (800)736-4509. **Fax:** (707)822-9163. info@paracay.com. **Website:** www.paracay.com. **Contact:** Matt Morehouse, publisher. "Paradise Cay Publications, Inc. is a small independent publisher specializing in nautical books, videos and art prints. Our primary interest is in manuscripts that deal with the instructional and technical aspects of ocean sailing. We also publish and will consider fiction if it has a strong nautical theme." Publishes hardcover and trade paperback originals and reprints. Receives 360–480 queries/year; 240–360 mss/year. **Needs:** All fiction must have a nautical theme. **How to Contact:** Query with SASE. Submit proposal package, clips, 2–3 sample chapters. Include a cover letter containing a story synopsis and a short bio, including any plans to promote your work. The cover letter should describe the book's subject matter, approach, distinguishing characteristics, intended audience, author's qualifications, and why the author thinks this book is appropriate for Paradise Cay. Call first. **Tips:** Audience is recreational sailors. Call Matt Morehouse (publisher).

PAULIST PRESS

997 Macarthur Blvd., Mahwah NJ 07430. (201)825-7300. **Fax:** (201)825-8345. **E-mail:** info@paulistpress.com. **Website:** www.paulistpress.com. **Contact:** Lawrence Boadt, editorial director for all fields; Paul McMahon, managing editor, all fields. "Paulist Press publishes 'ecumenical theology, Roman Catholic studies and books on scripture, liturgy, spirituality, church history and philosophy, as well as works on faith and culture.' Our publishing is oriented toward adult-level nonfiction. We do not publish poetry." Publishes

hardcover and electronic originals and electronic reprints. **Needs:** Accepts unsolicited fiction mss, but most of our novels have been commissioned. **How to Contact:** Submit resume, ms, SASE. **Tips:** "Our typical reader is probably Roman Catholic and wants the content to be educational about Catholic thought and practice, or else the reader is a spiritual seeker who looks for discovery of God and spiritual values which churches offer but without the church connection."

POCOL PRESS

6023 Pocol Dr., P.O. Box 411, Clifton VA 20124-1333. (703)830-5862. **E-mail:** chrisandtom@erols.com. **Website:** www.pocolpress.com. **Contact:** J. Thomas Hetrick, editor. Publishes trade paperback originals. Receives 90 queries/year; 20 mss/year. **Needs:** "We specialize in thematic short fiction collections by a single author and baseball fiction. Expert storytellers welcome." **How to Contact:** Query with SASE. **Tips:** "Our audience is aged 18 and over."

POSSIBILITY PRESS

One Oakglade Circle, Hummelstown PA 17036-9525. (717)566-0468. **Fax:** (717)566-6423. **E-mail:** info@possibilitypress.com. **Website:** www.possibilitypress.com. **Contact:** Mike Markowski, publisher. Our mission is to help the people of the world grow and become the best they can be, through the written and spoken word. Publishes trade paperback originals. **Needs:** Parables that teach lessons about life and success. **How to Contact:** Prefers submissions to be mailed. Include SASE. "Our focus is on co-authoring and publishing short (15,000–30,000 words) bestsellers. We're looking for kind and compassionate authors who are passionate about making a difference in the world and will champion their mission to do so, especially by public speaking. Our dream author writes well, knows how to promote, will champion their mission, speaks for a living, has a following and a platform, is cooperative and understanding, humbly handles critique and direction, is grateful, intelligent and has a good sense of humor."

RED HEN PRESS

P.O. Box 3537, Granada Hills CA 91394. (818)831-0649. **Fax:** (818)831-6659. **E-mail:** redhenpressbooks.com. **Website:** www.redhen.org. **Contact:** Mark E. Cull, publisher/editor (fiction). Publishes trade paperback originals. Receives 2,000 queries/year; 500 mss/year. **Needs:** We prefer high-quality literary fiction. **How to Contact:** "Red Hen Press is not currently accepting unsolicited material. At this time, the best opportunity to be published by Red Hen is by entering one of our contests. Please find more information in our award submission guidelines." **Tips:** "Audience reads poetry, literary fiction, intelligent nonfiction. If you have an agent, we may be too small since we don't pay advances. Write well. Send queries first. Be willing to help promote your own book."

RED SAGE PUBLISHING, INC.

P.O. Box 4844, Seminole FL 33775. (727)391-3847. **Website:** www.redsagepub.com. **Contact:** Alexandria Kendall, publisher; Theresa Stevens, managing editor. **Needs:** Romance fiction, written for the adventurous woman. **How to Contact:** Submit a one-page synopsis showing conflict, plot resolution and sensuality, as well as the first 10 pages of the completed manuscript (double-spaced). Submit samples in a digital Rich Text Format (RTF) or inline text. Please include writing credentials, if you have any. See more guidelines online. **Tips:** "We define romantic erotica. Sensuous, bold, spicy, untamed, hot and sometimes politically incorrect, *Secrets* stories concentrate on the sophisticated, highly intense adult relationship. We look for character-driven stories that concentrate on the love and sexual relationship between a hero and the heroine. Red Sage expanded into single-title books in 2004. Author voice, excellent writing and strong emotions are all important ingredients in the fiction we publish."

SOHO PRESS, INC.

853 Broadway, New York NY 10003. **E-mail:** soho@sohopress.com. **Website:** www.sohopress.com. **Contact:** Bronwen Hruska, publisher; Katie Herman, editor. Soho Press publishes primarily fiction, as well as some narrative literary nonfiction and mysteries set abroad. Publishes hardcover and trade paperback originals; trade paperback reprints. **Needs:** Literary. **How to Contact:** Submit 3 sample chapters and cover letter with synopsis, author bio, SASE. No electronic submissions, only queries by e-mail. **Tips:** "Soho Press publishes discerning authors for discriminating readers, finding the strongest possible writers and publishing them. Before submitting, look at our website for an idea of the types of books we publish, and read our submission guidelines."

SOUTHERN METHODIST UNIVERSITY PRESS

P.O. Box 750415, Dallas TX 75275-0415. (214)768-1436. **Fax:** (214)768-1428. **Website:** www.tamupress.com. **Contact:** Diana Vance. Known nationally as a publisher of the highest quality scholarly works and books for the "educated general reader," SMU Press publishes in the areas of ethics and human values, literary fiction, medical humanities, performing arts, Southwestern studies and sports. Publishes hardcover and trade paperback originals and reprints. Receives 500 queries/year; 500 mss/year. **Needs:** We are willing to look at 'serious' or 'literary' fiction. No mass market, science fiction, formula, thriller, romance. **How to Contact:** Query with SASE.

SWITCHGRASS BOOKS

Northern Illinois University Press, Switchgrass Books, 2280 Bethany Rd., DeKalb IL 60115. **Website:** www.switchgrass.niu.edu. **Needs:** "We publish only full-length novels set in or about the Midwest. Switchgrass authors must be from the Midwest, current residents of the region, or have significant ties to it. Briefly tell us in your cover letter why yours is an authentic Midwestern voice." We will not consider memoirs, short stories, novellas, graphic novels, poetry or juvenile/YA literature. **How to Contact:** Agented mss will not be considered. Send your complete ms via U.S.mail. E-mail submissions will not be considered. No queries, calls, or e-mails, please. Please include a resume or CV.

TORQUERE PRESS

P.O. Box 2545, Round Rock TX 78680. (512)586-6921. **Fax:** (866)287-4860. **E-mail:** submissions@torquerepress.com. **Website:** www.

torquerepress.com. **Contact:** Shawn Clements, submissions editor (homoerotica, suspense, gay/lesbian); Lorna Hinson, senior editor (gay/lesbian romance, historicals). Publishes trade paperback originals and electronic originals and reprints. Receives 500 queries/year; 200 mss/year. **Needs:** "We are a gay and lesbian press focusing on romance and genres of romance. We particularly like paranormal and western romance." **How to Contact:** Submit proposal package, 3 sample chapters, clips. **Tips:** "Our audience is primarily people looking for a familiar romance setting featuring gay or lesbian protagonists. Please read guidelines carefully and familiarize yourself with our lines."

UNBRIDLED BOOKS

200 North 9th Street, Suite A, Columbia MO 65201. 2000 Wadsworth Blvd. #195, Lakewood CO 80214. **Website:** http://unbridledbooks.com. **Fiction:** "Unbridled Books is a premier publisher of works of rich literary quality that appeal to a broad audience." **How to Contact:** No electronic manuscripts accepted without querying first: Send a brief description of your work, a brief description of your publishing history, a short biography, 30–50 pages of the manuscript. Send to either of the publishers, but not both, at: Greg Michalson, Co-Publisher, 200 N. 9th Street, Ste A, Columbia, MO 65201—OR—Fred Ramey, Co-Publisher, 2000 Wadsworth Blvd., #195, Lakewood, CO 80214. **Tips:** "We try to read each ms that arrives, so please be patient."

UNTAPPED TALENT LLC

P.O. Box 396, Hershey PA 17033-0396. (717)707-0720. **E-mail:** rena@unt2.com. **Website:** www.unt2.com. **Contact:** Rena Wilson Fox (areas of interest: nonfiction, children's lit, fiction, middle grade). "As a new publishing company, we only have published four titles, not enough for a catalog. Please feel free to view the books at our website." Publishes hardcover, trade & mass-market paperbacks, electronic originals. Receives 2,000 queries, 400 mss/yr. **Fiction:** "We have a strong interest in historical fiction. We are looking for books that are current and fully formulated, modern interpretations—even if the story takes place in the past." **How to Contact:** Submit proposal package with synopsis, 4 sample chapters and any background information pertinent to the story. **Tips:** Follow website instruction, make query brief; if 4 chapters are not many pages, add more; submit to acquisitions editor only.

WHITAKER HOUSE

1030 Hunt Valley Circle, New Kensington PA 15068. **E-mail:** publisher @whitakerhouse.com. **Website:** www.whitakerhouse.com. **Contact:** Tom Cox, managing editor. Publishes hardcover, trade paperback and mass-market originals. Receives 600 queries/year; 200 mss/year. **Needs:** Accepts submissions on topics with a Christian perspective. Subjects include Christian living, prayer, spiritual warfare, healing, gifts of the spirit, etc. **How to Contact:** Query with SASE. **Tips:** "Audience includes those seeking uplifting and inspirational fiction and nonfiction."

WILSHIRE BOOK CO.

9731 Variel Ave., Chatsworth CA 91311-4315. (818)700-1522. **Fax:** (818)700-1527. **E-mail:** mpowers@mpowers.com. **Website:** www. mpowers.com. Contact: Rights Department. Publishes trade paperback originals and reprints. Receives 1,200 queries/year. **Needs:** Adult allegories that teach principles of psychological growth or offer guidance in living. Minimum 30,000 words. No standard fiction. **How to Contact:** Submit 3 sample chapters or complete ms. Include outline, author bio, analysis of book's competition and SASE. No e-mail or fax submissions. **Tips:** "We are vitally interested in all new material we receive. Just as you are hopeful when submitting your manuscript for publication, we are hopeful as we read each one submitted, searching for those we believe could be successful in the marketplace. Writing and publishing must be a team effort. We need you to write what we can sell. We suggest you read the successful books similar to the one you want to write. Analyze them to discover what elements make them winners. Duplicate those elements in your own style, using a creative new approach and fresh material, and you will have written a book we can catapult onto the bestseller list. You are welcome to telephone or e-mail us for immediate feedback on any book concept you may have. To learn more about us and what we publish—and for complete manuscript guidelines—visit our website."

ZONDERVAN

Division of HarperCollins Publishers, 5300 Patterson Ave. SE, Grand Rapids MI 49530-0002. (616)698-6900. **Fax:** (616)698-3454. **Website:** www.zondervan.com. **Contact:** Manuscript Review Editor. "Our mission is to be the leading Christian communications company meeting the **Needs:** of people with resources that glorify Jesus Christ and promote biblical principles." Publishes hardcover and trade paperback originals and reprints. **Needs:** Inklings-style fiction of high literary quality. Christian relevance in all cases. Will not consider collections of short stories or poetry. **How to Contact:** Submit TOC, curriculum vitae, chapter outline, intended audience.

ZUMAYA PUBLICATIONS, LLC

3209 S. Interstate 35, #1086, Austin TX 78741. **E-mail:** acquisitions@ zumayapublications.com. **Website:** www.zumayapublications.com. **Contact:** Elizabeth Burton, executive editor. Publishes trade paperback and electronic originals and reprints. 1,000 queries received/ year. 100 mss received/year. **Fiction:** "We are currently oversupplied with speculative fiction and are reviewing submissions in SF, fantasy and paranormal suspense by invitation only. We are much in need of GLBT and YA/middle grade, historical and western, New Age/ inspirational (no overtly Christian materials, please), non-category romance, thrillers. As with nonfiction, we encourage people to review what we've already published so as to avoid sending us more of the same, at least, insofar as the plot is concerned. While we're always looking for good specific mysteries, we want original concepts rather than slightly altered versions of what we've already published." **How to Contact:** Electronic query only. **Tips:** "We're catering to readers who may have loved last year's best seller but not enough to want to read 10 more just like it. Have something different. If it does not fit standard pigeonholes, that's a plus. On the other hand, it has to have an audience. And if you're not prepared to work with us on promotion and marketing, it would be better to look elsewhere."

NONFICTION PUBLISHERS

ACADEMY CHICAGO PUBLISHERS

363 W. Erie St., Suite 4W, Chicago IL 60610-3125. (312)751-7300. **Fax:** (312)751-7306. **E-mail:** info@academychicago.com. **Website:** www.academychicago.com. **Contact:** Anita Miller, editorial director/senior editor. "We publish quality fiction and nonfiction. Our audience is literate and discriminating." Publishes hardcover and some paperback originals and trade paperback reprints. **Needs:** Currently emphasizing quality nonfiction. No religion or self-help. **How to Contact:** Submit proposal package, outline, bio, 3 sample chapters. **Tips:** "No fax queries, no disks. No electronic submissions. We are always interested in reprinting good out-of-print books."

ALLWORTH PRESS

10 E. 23rd St., Suite 510, New York NY 10010-4402. (212)777-8395. **Fax:** (212)777-8261. **E-mail:** pub@allworth.com. **Website:** www.allworth.com. **Contact:** Bob Porter, associate publisher. "Allworth Press publishes business and self-help information for artists, designers, photographers, authors and film and performing artists, as well as books about business, money and the law for the general public. The press also publishes the best of classic and contemporary writing in art and graphic design. Currently emphasizing photography, graphic & industrial design, performing arts, fine arts and crafts, et al." Publishes hardcover and trade paperback originals. **Needs:** "We are currently accepting query letters for practical, legal and technique books targeted to professionals in the arts, including designers, graphic and fine artists, craftspeople, photographers and those involved in film and the performing arts." **How to Contact:** Query. **Tips:** We are helping creative people in the arts by giving them practical advice about business and success.

ALPHA WORLD PRESS

530 Oaklawn Ave., Green Bay WI 54304. (866)855-3720. **E-mail:** office@alphaworldpress.com. **Website:** www.alphaworldpress.com. **Contact:** Tracey Vandeveer, owner. "Our press is dedicated to publishing high-quality work by, for and about lesbians from all walks of life. We publish fiction, nonfiction and poetry. We welcome all manuscripts from lesbians. We want the voices and perspectives of lesbians from all across the world to be heard through the books that we publish. We work very closely with our authors in all aspects of publishing—from editing and graphic design, to actual production, promotion and marketing." Publishes trade paperback originals and mass-market paperback originals. Receives 120 queries/year; 12 mss/year. **Needs:** Only submit nonfiction if it is written by or relates to lesbians. **How to Contact:** Submit proposal package, outline. Send it via e-mail in pdf. **Tips:** Our audience is lesbians only.

AMERICAN QUILTER'S SOCIETY

Schroeder Publishing, P.O. Box 3290, Paducah KY 42002-3290. (270)898-7903. **Fax:** (270)898-1173. **E-mail:** editor@aqsquilt.com. **Website:** www.americanquilter.com. **Contact:** Andi Reynolds, executive book editor. "American Quilter's Society publishes how-to and pattern books for quilters (beginners through intermediate skill level). We are not the publisher for non-quilters writing about quilts." Publishes trade paperback originals. Receives 100 queries/year. Multiple submissions okay. **Needs:** "Primarily how-to and patterns, but other quilting books sometimes published, including quilt-related fiction." **How to Contact:** No queries; proposals only. Note: 1 or 2 completed quilt projects must accompany proposal.

BALL PUBLISHING

P.O. Box 1660, West Chicago IL 60186. (630)231-3675. **Fax:** (630)231-5254. **E-mail:** cbeytes@ballpublishing.com. **Website:** www.ballpublishing.com. **Contact:** Chris Beytes. "We publish for the book trade and the horticulture trade. Books on both home gardening/landscaping and commercial production are considered." Publishes hardcover and trade paperback originals. **Needs:** Actively looking for photo books on specific genera and families of flowers and trees. **How to Contact:** Query with SASE. Submit proposal package, outline, 2 sample chapters. **Tips:** "We are expanding our book line to home gardeners, while still publishing for green industry professionals. Gardening books should be well thought out and unique in the market."

BANTER PRESS

561 Hudson St., Suite 57, New York NY 10014. (718)864-5080. **Fax:** (718)965-3603. **E-mail:** info@banterpress.com. **Website:** www.banterpress.com. **Contact:** David McClintock, president. Publishes trade paperback and electronic originals and reprints. Receives 25 queries/year; 12 mss/year. **Needs:** "We seek authors who are active speakers within their industry, especially those who do seminars or consulting. We're small but very experienced and selective. We are relaunching with an emphasis on business communication, online marketing and social media." **How to Contact:** Submit proposal package, outline, sample chapters, bio, analysis of competing books, author's plan for promoting the book. **Tips:** "Our readers are curious, technologically savvy professionals who need inspiring, up-to-date business information. Please don't mail us manuscripts! E-mail them as PDFs or as plain text files (.txt). Best yet, paste text into a giant e-mail."

BARRON'S EDUCATIONAL SERIES, INC.

250 Wireless Blvd., Hauppauge NY 11788. (800)645-3476. **Fax:** (631)434-3723. **Website:** www.barronseduc.com. **Contact:** Wayne Barr, acquisitions manager. "Barron's tends to publish series of books, both for adults and children." Publishes hardcover, paperback and mass-market originals and software. Receives 2,000 queries/year. **Needs:** "We are always on the lookout for creative nonfiction ideas for children and adults. No adult fiction." **How to Contact:** Query with SASE. Submit outline, 2–3 sample chapters. **Tips:** "Audience is

mostly educated self-learners and students. Try to fit into one of our series. Children's books have less chance for acceptance because of the glut of submissions. SASE must be included for the return of all materials. Please be patient for replies."

BASIC HEALTH PUBLICATIONS, INC.

28812 Top of the World Dr., Laguna Beach CA 92651. (949)715-7327. **Fax:** (949)715-7328. **Website:** www.basichealthpub.com. **Contact:** Norman Goldfind, publisher. Publishes hardcover, trade paperback and mass-market paperback originals and reprints. **Needs:** "We are very highly focused on health, alternative medicine, nutrition and fitness. Must be well researched and documented with appropriate references. Writing should be aimed at lay audience but also be able to cross over to professional market." **How to Contact:** Submit proposal package, outline, 2–3 sample chapters, introduction. **Tips:** "Our audience is over 30, well educated, middle to upper income. We prefer writers with professional credentials (MDs, PhDs, NDs, etc.), or writers with backgrounds in health and medicine."

BETTERWAY HOME BOOKS

Imprint of F+W Media, Inc., 4700 E. Galbraith Rd., Cincinnati OH 45236. (513)531-2690, ext. 11467. **E-mail:** Jacqueline.Musser@ fwmedia.com. **Website:** www.fwmedia.com. **Contact:** Jacqueline Musser, acquisitions editor. Publishes trade paperback and hardcover originals. Receives 6 queries/year; 6 mss/year. **How to Contact:** Query with SASE. Submit proposal package, outline, 1 sample chapter. **Tips:** Audience comprised of new and first time homeowners, those who take the 'weekend warrior' approach to home improvement/nesting. "We're looking for authors who bring a fresh, unique approach to home skills. We prefer authors who already have established marketing platforms for their work."

BETWEEN THE LINES

720 Bathurst St., Suite 404, Toronto ON M5S 2R4 Canada. (416)535-9914. **Fax:** (416)535-1484. **E-mail:** btlbooks@web.ca. **Website:** www.btlbooks.com. **Contact:** Amanda Crocker, editorial coordinator. "Between the Lines publishes nonfiction books in the following subject areas: politics and public policy issues, social issues, development studies, history, education, the environment, health, gender and sexuality, labour, technology, media and culture. Please note that we do not publish fiction or poetry." Publishes trade paperback originals. Receives 350 queries/year; 50 mss/year. **How to Contact:** We prefer to receive proposals rather than entire manuscripts for consideration. Submit proposal package, outline, resume, 2–3 sample chapters, cover letter, SASE. No e-mail or fax submissions at this time.

BKMK PRESS

University of Missouri-Kansas City, 5101 Rockhill Rd., Kansas City MO 64110-2499. (816)235-2558. **Fax:** (816)235-2611. **E-mail:** bkmk@ umkc.edu. **Website:** www.umkc.edu/bkmk. **Contact:** Ben Furnish, managing editor. "BkMk Press publishes fine literature. Reading period January–June." Publishes trade paperback originals. **How to Contact:** Submit 25-50 pp. sample and SASE. **Tips:** "We skew toward readers of literature, particularly contemporary writing. Because

of our limited number of titles published per year, we discourage apprentice writers or `scattershot' submissions."

BLACK ROSE WRITING

P.O. Box 1540, Castroville TX 78009. **E-mail:** pr@blackrosewriting. com. **Website:** www.blackrosewriting.com. **Contact:** Reagan Rothe, owner (all queries). Publishes hardcover, trade paperback, mass-market paperback and electronic originals. Receives 1,000+ queries/year; 120 mss/year. **Needs:** War, autobiography/biography. "Black Rose Writing prefers clean, edited work that requires only minor editing checks. We believe the writer should take great pride in their work and truly look through their manuscript before submitting something in its raw, unedited form." **How to Contact:** Submit query letter via e-mail or with SASE before sending entire ms. **Tips:** "Black Rose Writing welcomes all writers but truly focuses on new, talented authors who are seeking their first big recognition and publication. We promise to give you personal feedback on every piece, dedicating ourselves to avoid automated responses or negative outlooks on an individual's subjective work. Please follow our submission guidelines online."

BREWERS PUBLICATIONS

Imprint of Brewers Association, 736 Pearl St., Boulder CO 80302. (303)447-0816. **Fax:** (303)447-2825. **E-mail:** kristi@brewers association.org. **Website:** http://beertown.org. **Contact:** Kristi Switzer, publisher. "Brewers Publications is the largest publisher of books on beer-related subjects." Publishes hardcover and trade paperback originals. **Needs:** "We only publish nonfiction books of interest to amateur and professional brewers. Our authors have many years of brewing experience and in-depth practical knowledge of their subject. We are not interested in fiction, drinking games or beer/bar reviews. If your book is not about how to make beer, then do not waste your time or ours by sending it. Those determined to fit our **Needs:** will subscribe to and read *Zymurgy* and *The New Brewer*." **How to Contact:** Query first with proposal and sample chapter.

BROADVIEW PRESS, INC.

P.O. Box 1243, Peterborough ON K9J 7H5 Canada. (705)743-8990. **Fax:** (705)743-8353. **E-mail:** customerservice@broadviewpress.com. **Website:** www.broadviewpress.com. **Contact:** See Editorial Guidelines online. "We publish in a broad variety of subject areas in the arts and social sciences. We are open to a broad range of political and philosophical viewpoints, from liberal and conservative to libertarian and Marxist and including a wide range of feminist viewpoints." Receives 500 queries/year; 200 mss/year. **Needs:** Our focus is very much on English studies and philosophy, but within those two core subject areas we are open to a broad range of academic approaches and political viewpoints. We welcome feminist perspectives, and we have a particular interest in addressing environmental issues. Our publishing program is internationally oriented, and we publish for a broad range of geographical markets—but as a Canadian company we also publish a broad range of titles with a Canadian emphasis. **How to Contact:** Query with SASE. Submit proposal package. **Tips:** "Our titles often appeal to a broad readership; we have many books that are as much of interest to the general reader as they are to academics and students."

CELLAR DOOR PUBLISHING, LLC

3439 NE Sandy Blvd., Suite 309, Portland OR 97232-1959. **E-mail:** info@cellardoorpublishing.com. **Website:** www.cellardoorpublishing. com. "Cellar Door Publishing specializes in the publication of high-quality illustrated literature and graphic novels." Publishes hardcover originals, trade paperback originals and electronic originals. **Needs:** "We are looking for all genres and age groups. We encourage creators to experiment with format and content, though it is not required. We do accept a limited number of submissions for books without illustrations. This is generally reserved for books that are either unique in content or controversial in nature, or literary projects that can be released in a serialized format." **How to Contact:** "We currently accept unsolicited submissions via online submission form and comic book conventions only. We no longer accept unsolicited submissions through traditional mail. To submit book proposals for consideration, please use the online submission form."

CLEIS PRESS

Cleis Press & Viva Editions, 2246 Sixth St., Berkeley CA 94710. (510)845-8000 or (800)780-2279. **Fax:** (510)845-8001. **E-mail:** cleis@cleispress.com. **Website:** www.cleispress.com. **Contact:** Brenda Knight, associate publisher. "Cleis Press publishes provocative, intelligent books in the areas of sexuality, gay and lesbian studies, erotica, fiction, gender studies and human rights." Publishes trade paperback originals and reprints. **Needs:** "We are interested in books on topics of sexuality, human rights and women's and gay and lesbian literature. Please consult our website first to be certain that your book fits our list." **How to Contact:** Query or submit outline and sample chapters. **Tips:** "Be familiar with publishers' catalogs; be absolutely aware of your audience; research potential markets; present fresh new ways of looking at your topic; avoid 'PR' language and include publishing history in query letter."

CONIFER BOOKS, LLC

9599 S. Turkey Creek Rd., Morrison CO 80465. **Website:** www. sleuthguides.com. **Contact:** David Peterka, editor. "We publish reference and how-to books for the 55+ reader. This includes a large range of readers—from working Baby Boomers, retired Seniors and the active Elderly." Publishes trade paperback and electronic originals. Receives 100 queries/year; 10 mss/year. **Needs:** "We are interested in educating seniors on modern topics and promoting active lifestyles. We are looking for informative, easy-to-read nonfiction books written for the curious senior citizen. Our goal is to provide a trusted resource for investigations into a variety of senior topics, including technology, travel, family, fitness, health, finances and many more." **How to Contact:** Submit proposal package, including outline, 1 sample chapter, brief list of competing titles and author bio. **Tips:** "Visit our website for an up-to-date list of current titles and our topic wish-list. Your book should address topics specifically relevant to the 55+ reader. Our books are positive, funny and inspire an active lifestyle. Your submission should reflect this tone."

DANIEL & DANIEL PUBLISHERS, INC.

P.O. Box 2790, McKinleyville CA 95519. (707)839-3495. **Fax:** (707)839-3242. **E-mail:** dandd@danielpublishing.com. **Website:** www.danielpublishing.com. **Contact:** John Daniel, publisher. Publishes hardcover originals and trade paperback originals. Publishes poetry, fiction and nonfiction. **Needs:** "We seldom publish books over 70,000 words. Other than that, we're looking for books that are important and well written." **How to Contact:** Submit proposal package, clips, 5 pages. **Tips:** "Audience includes literate, intelligent general readers. We are very small and very cautious, and we publish fewer books each year, so any submission to us is a long shot. But we welcome your submissions, by mail or e-mail only, please. We don't want submissions by phone, fax or disk."

DEMONTREVILLE PRESS, INC.

P.O. Box 835, Lake Elmo MN 55042-0835. **E-mail:** publisher@ demontrevillepress.com. **Website:** www.demontrevillepress.com. **Contact:** Kevin Clemens, publisher (automotive fiction and nonfiction). Publishes trade paperback originals and reprints. Receives 150 queries/year; 100 mss/year. **Needs:** "Environmental, energy and transportation nonfiction works are now being accepted." **How to Contact:** Submit proposal package, 3 sample chapters, clips, bio. **Tips:** "Automotive and motorcycle enthusiasts, adventurers, environmentalists and history buffs make up our audience."

ENTREPRENEUR PRESS

2445 McCabe Way, Suite 400, Irvine CA 92614. (949)261-2325. **Fax:** (949)261-7729. **E-mail:** press@entrepreneur.com. **Website:** www. entrepreneurpress.com. **Contact:** Jere L. Calmes, publisher. "We are an independent publishing company that publishes titles focusing on starting and growing a business, personal finance, real estate and careers." Publishes quality hardcover and trade paperbacks. Receives 1,200 queries/year; 600 mss/year. **Needs:** We are currently seeking proposals covering sales, small business, startup, real estate, online businesses, marketing, etc. **How to Contact:** When submitting work to us, please send as much of the proposed book as possible. Proposal should include: cover letter, preface, marketing plan, analysis of competition and comparative titles, author bio, TOC, 2 sample chapters. Go to website for more details.

EXCALIBUR PUBLICATIONS

P.O. Box 89667, Tucson AZ 85752-9667. (520)575-9057. **E-mail:** excalibureditor@earthlink.net. **Contact:** Alan M. Petrillo, editor. "Excalibur Publications publishes nonfiction historical and military works from all time periods. We do not publish fiction." Publishes trade paperback originals. **Needs:** "We are seeking well-researched and documented works. Unpublished writers are welcome." **How to Contact:** Query with synopsis, first chapter, SASE. Include notes on photos, illustrations and maps. Accepts e-mail pitches. **Tips:** "New writers are welcome, especially those who have a fresh approach to a subject. In addition to a synopsis or proposal, we also like to see a brief bio that indicates any related experience you have, as well as information on particular marketing strategies for your work."

FACTS ON FILE, INC.

Infobase Publishing, 132 W. 31st St., 17th Floor, New York NY 10001. (212)967-8800. **Fax:** (212)339-0326. **E-mail:** llikoff@factsonfile.com. **Website:** www.factsonfile.com. **Contact:** Laurie Likoff, editorial director (science, fashion, natural history); Frank Darmstadt (science & technology, nature, reference); Owen Lancer, senior editor (American history, women's studies); James Chambers, trade editor (health, pop culture, true crime, sports); Jeff Soloway, acquisitions editor (language/literature). Facts on File produces high-quality reference materials on a broad range of subjects for the school library market and the general nonfiction trade. Publishes hardcover originals and reprints. **Needs:** No computer books, technical books, cookbooks, biographies (except YA), pop psychology, humor, fiction or poetry. **How to Contact:** Query or submit outline and sample chapter with SASE. No submissions returned without SASE. **Tips:** "Our audience is school and public libraries for our more reference-oriented books and libraries, schools and bookstores for our less reference-oriented informational titles."

FAIRVIEW PRESS

2450 Riverside Ave., Minneapolis MN 55454. (612)672-4774. **Fax:** (612)672-4980. **E-mail:** press@fairview.org. **Website:** www.fairview press.org. **Contact:** Steve Deger, acquisitions and marketing. "Fairview Press publishes books dedicated to the physical, emotional and spiritual health of children, adults and seniors—specializing in books on: Aging and Eldercare, Grief and Bereavement, Health and Wellness, Inspiration, Parenting and Childcare." Publishes hardcover and trade paperback originals and reprints. Receives 3,000 queries/year; 1,500 mss/year. **Needs:** "At this time we are particularly interested in acquiring mss on the following topics: pregnancy and childbirth, health issues for young adults, complementary/holistic/integrative medicine, diet & exercise and inspiration & mindfulness. We are de-emphasizing our former focus on end-of-life issues but will consider proposals on any topic pertaining to physical, emotional or spiritual wellness." **How to Contact:** Submit proposal package with cover letter, outline, sample chapter(s), marketing plan, SASE. "Please take the time to study our catalog and the guidelines before submitting a proposal. We prefer that you mail your proposal rather than submitting it by phone, fax, or e-mail." **Tips:** "We publish practical books written for a lay audience, often by educated professionals who are active within their disciplines. We are not interested in fiction, poetry, children's picture books, or personal memoirs about coping with illness."

FLORICANTO PRESS

Inter American Development, 650 Castro St., Suite 120-331, Mountain View CA 94041-2055. (415)552-1879. **Fax:** (702)995-1410. **E-mail:** editor@floricantopress.com. **Website:** www.floricantopress.com. **Contact:** Roberto Cabello-Argandona. "Floricanto Press is dedicated to promoting Latino thought and culture." Publishes hardcover and trade paperback originals and reprints. **Needs:** "We are looking primarily for nonfiction popular (but serious) titles that appeal to the general public on Hispanic subjects." **How to Contact:** Submit ms with word count, author bio, SASE. **Tips:** "Audience is general public interested in Hispanic culture. We need authors who are willing to promote their work heavily."

GOODMAN BECK PUBLISHING

P.O. Box 253, Norwood NJ 07648-2428. (201)403-3097. E-mal: info@goodmanbeck.com. **Website:** www.goodmanbeck.com. **Contact:** David Michael, editor. "Our primary interest at this time is mental health, personal growth, aging well, positive psychology, accessible spirituality and self-help." Publishes trade paperback originals and reprints; mass-market paperback originals and reprints. **Needs:** At this time, we are not interested religious or political works, textbooks, or how-to books. **How to Contact:** Query with SASE. **Tips:** "Your book should be enlightening and marketable. Be prepared to have a comprehensive marketing plan. You will be very involved."

GRAYWOLF PRESS

250 Third Avenue North, Suite 600, Minneapolis MN 55401. **Website:** www.graywolfpress.org. **Contact:** Katie Dublinski, editorial manager (nonfiction, fiction). "Graywolf Press is an independent, nonprofit publisher dedicated to the creation and promotion of thoughtful and imaginative contemporary literature essential to a vital and diverse culture." Publishes trade cloth and paperback originals. Receives 3,000 queries/year. **Needs:** "Familiarize yourself with our list first." **How to Contact:** Query with SASE. Please do not fax or e-mail.

GROUP PUBLISHING, INC.

1515 Cascade Ave., Loveland CO 80538. (970)669-3836. **Fax:** (970)679-4370. **E-mail:** kloesche@grouppublishing.com. **Website:** www.group.com. **Contact:** Kerri Loesche, contract & copyright administrator. "Our mission is to equip churches to help children, youth and adults grow in their relationship with Jesus." Publishes trade paperback originals. Receives 500 queries/year, 500 mss/year. **Needs:** "We're an interdenominational publisher of resource materials for people who work with adults, youth or children in a Christian church setting. We also publish materials for use directly by youth or children (such as devotional books, workbooks or Bibles stories). Everything we do is based on concepts of active and interactive learning as described in *Why Nobody Learns Much of Anything at Church: And How to Fix It*, by Thom and Joani Schultz. We need new, practical, hands-on, innovative, out-of-the-box ideas—things that no one's doing .. yet." **How to Contact:** Query with SASE. Submit proposal package, outline, 3 sample chapters, cover letter, introduction to book, and sample activities if appropriate. **Tips:** "Our audience consists of pastors, Christian education directors, youth leaders and Sunday school teachers."

GUN DIGEST BOOKS

An imprint of F+W Media, Inc., 700 East State St., Iola WI 54990. (888)457-2873. **E-mail:** dan.shideler@fwmedia.com. **Website:** www.krause.com. **Contact:** Dan Shideler, editor (all aspects of firearms history, scholarship, nonpolitical literature). Publishes hardcover, trade paperback, mass-market paperback and electronic originals.

Receives 75 submissions/year. **Needs:** "Must have mainstream appeal and not be too narrowly focused." **How to Contact:** Submit proposal package, including outline, 2 sample chapters and author bio, or submit completed manuscript. **Tips:** "Our audience is shooters, collectors, hunters, outdoors enthusiasts. We prefer not to work through agents."

HAMPTON ROADS PUBLISHING CO., INC.

500 Third Street, Suite 230, San Francisco CA 94107. **E-mail:** submissions@hrpub.com. **Website:** www.hamptonroadspub.com. **Contact:** Chris Nelson, acquisitions manager. "Our reason for being is to impact, uplift and contribute to positive change in the world. We publish books that will enrich and empower the evolving consciousness of mankind. Though we are not necessarily limited in scope, we are most interested in manuscripts on the following subjects: Body/Mind/Spirit, Health and Healing, Self-Help." Publishes and distributes hardcover and paperback originals on subjects including metaphysics, health, complementary medicine, visionary fiction and other related topics. Receives 1,000 queries/year; 1,500 mss/year. **Needs:** Body/mind/spirit, health and healing, self-help. **How to Contact:** Query with SASE. Submit outline, 2 sample chapters, clips. No longer accepting electronic submissions.

THE HARVARD COMMON PRESS

535 Albany St., 5th Floor, Boston MA 02118-2500. (617)423-5803. **Fax:** (617)695-9794. **E-mail:** info@harvardpress.com. **Website:** www. harvardcommonpress.com. **Contact:** Valerie Cimino, executive editor. "We want strong, practical books that help people gain control over a particular area of their lives. Currently emphasizing cooking, child care/parenting, health. De-emphasizing general instructional books, travel." Publishes hardcover and trade paperback originals and reprints. **Needs:** "A large percentage of our list is made up of books about cooking, child care and parenting; in these areas we are looking for authors who are knowledgeable, if not experts, and who can offer a different approach to the subject. We are open to good nonfiction proposals that show evidence of strong organization and writing and clearly demonstrate a need in the marketplace. First-time authors are welcome." **How to Contact:** Submit outline. Potential authors may also submit a query letter or e-mail of no more than 300 words, rather than a full proposal; if interested, we will ask to see a proposal. Queries and questions may be sent via e-mail. We will not consider e-mail attachments containing proposals. No phone calls, please. **Tips:** "We are demanding about the quality of proposals; in addition to strong writing skills and thorough knowledge of the subject matter, we require a detailed analysis of the competition."

HISTORY PUBLISHING COMPANY, INC.

P.O. Box 700, Palisades NY 10964. (845)231-6167. **E-mail:** history publish@aol.com. **Website:** www.historypublishingco.com. **Contact:** Leslie Hayes, editorial director. Publishes hardcover and trade paperback originals and reprints, also electronic reprints. **Needs:** "We focus on an audience interested in the events that shaped the world we live in and the events of today that continue to shape that world. Focus on interesting and serious events that will appeal to the contemporary reader who likes easy-to-read history that flows from one page to the next." **How to Contact:** Query with SASE, or submit proposal package, outline, 3 sample chapters.

HOW BOOKS

Imprint of F+W Media, Inc., 4700 E. Galbraith Rd., Cincinnati OH 45236. (513)531-2690. **E-mail:** megan.patrick@fwmedia.com. **Website:** www.howdesign.com. **Contact:** Megan Patrick, acquisitions editor. Publishes hardcover and trade paperback originals. Receives 50 queries/year; 5 mss/year. **Needs:** "We look for material that reflects the cutting edge of trends, graphic design and culture. Nearly all HOW Books are intensely visual, and authors must be able to create or supply art/illustration for their books." **How to Contact:** Query with SASE. Submit proposal package, outline, 1 sample chapter, sample art or sample design. **Tips:** "Audience comprised of graphic designers. Your art, design, or concept."

IDYLL ARBOR, INC.

39129 264th Ave. SE, Enumclaw WA 98022. (360)825-7797. **Fax:** (360)825-5670. **E-mail:** editors@idyllarbor.com. **Website:** www.idyll arbor.com. **Contact:** Tom Blaschko. "Idyll Arbor publishes practical information on the current state and art of healthcare practice. Currently emphasizing therapies (recreational, aquatic, occupational, music, horticultural) and resources for activity directors in long-term care facilities. Issues Press looks at problems in society, from video games to returning veterans and their problems reintegrating into the civilian world." Publishes hardcover and trade paperback originals and trade paperback reprints. **Needs:** "Idyll Arbor is currently developing a line of books under the imprint Issues Press, which treats emotional issues in a clear-headed manner. The latest books are *Female Sex Offenders: What Therapists, Law Enforcement and Child Protective Services Need to Know* and *Situational Mediation: Sensible Conflict Resolution.* Another series of *Personal Health* books explains a condition or a closely related set of medical or psychological conditions. The target audience is the person or the family of the person with the condition. We want to publish a book that explains a condition at the level of detail expected of the average primary care physician so that our readers can address the situation intelligently with specialists. We look for manuscripts from authors with recent clinical experience. Good grounding in theory is required, but practical experience is more important." **How to Contact:** Query preferred with outline and 1 sample chapter. **Tips:** "The books must be useful for the health practitioner who meets face to face with patients, or the books must be useful for teaching undergraduate and graduate-level classes. We are especially looking for therapists with a solid clinical background to write on their area of expertise."

IMPACT BOOKS

Imprint of F+W Media, Inc., 4700 E. Galbraith Rd., Cincinnati OH 45236. **Fax:** (513)531-2686. **E-mail:** pam.wissman@fwmedia.com. **Website:** www.northlightshop.com. **Contact:** Pamela Wissman, editorial director. Publishes trade paperback originals and reprints. Receives 50 queries/year; 10–12 mss/year. **Needs:** Art instruction for fantasy, comics, manga, anime, popular culture, graffiti, cartooning, body art. **How to Contact:** Submit proposal package, outline, 1 sample chapter, at least 1 example of sample art. **Tips:** "Audience comprised primarily of 12- to 18-year-old beginners along the lines of comic buyers, in general—mostly teenagers—but also appealing to a broader audience of young adults 19–30 who need basic techniques. Art must appeal to teenagers and be submitted in a form that will reproduce well. Authors need to know how to teach beginners step-by-step. A sample step-by-step is important."

JIST PUBLISHING

7321 Shadeland Station, Suite 200, Indianapolis IN 46256-3923. (317)613-4200. **Fax:** (317)845-1052. **E-mail:** spines@jist.com. **Website:** www.jist.com. **Contact:** Susan Pines, associate publisher (career and education reference and library titles, assessments, videos, e-products); Lori Cates Hand, product line manager, trade and workbooks (career, job search and education trade and workbook titles). "Our purpose is to provide quality job search, career development, occupational and life skills information, products and services that help people manage and improve their lives and careers—and the lives of others. Publishes practical, self-directed tools and training materials that are used in employment and training, education, and business settings. Whether reference books, trade books, assessment tools, workbooks, or videos, JIST products foster self-directed job-search attitudes and behaviors." Publishes hardcover and trade paperback originals. Receives 40 submissions/year. **Needs:** Specializes in job search, career development, occupational information, character education and domestic abuse topics. We want text/workbook formats that would be useful in a school or other institutional setting. We also publish trade titles for all reading levels. Will consider books for professional staff and educators, appropriate software and videos. **How to Contact:** Submit proposal package, including outline, 1 sample chapter, author resume, competitive analysis, marketing ideas. **Tips:** "Our audiences are students, job seekers and career changers of all ages and occupations who want to find good jobs quickly and improve their futures. We sell materials through the trade as well as to institutional markets like schools, colleges and one-stop career centers."

THE JOHNS HOPKINS UNIVERSITY PRESS

2715 N. Charles St., Baltimore MD 21218. (410)516-6900. **Fax:** (410)516-6968. **E-mail:** tcl@press.jhu.edu. **Website:** www.press.jhu.edu. **Contact:** Trevor Lipscombe, editor-in-chief (physics and mathematics; tcl@press.jhu.edu); Jacqueline C. Wehmueller, executive editor (consumer health and history of medicine; jwehmueller@press.jhu.edu); Henry Y.K. Tom, executive editor (social sciences; htom@press.jhu.edu); Wendy Harris, senior acquisitions editor (clinical medicine, public health, health policy; wharris@press.jhu.edu); Robert J. Brugger, senior acquisitions editor (American history, history of science and technology, regional books; rbrugger@press.jhu.edu); Vincent J. Burke, senior acquisitions editor (biology; vjb@press.jhu.edu); Matthew McAdam, acquisitions editor (humanities, classics, ancient studies; mlonegro@press.jhu.edu); Ashleigh McKown, assistant acquisitions editor (higher education; amckown@press.jhu.

edu). Publishes hardcover originals and reprints and trade paperback reprints. **How to Contact:** Submit proposal package, outline, 1 sample chapter, curriculum vita.

JOSEPH HENRY PRESS

National Academies Press, 500 5th St., NW Lockbox 285, Washington DC 20055. (202)334-3336. **Fax:** (202)334-2793. **E-mail:** tsmith@nas.edu. **Website:** www.nap.edu/about.html. **Contact:** Terrell Smith, project editor. "The Joseph Henry Press seeks manuscripts in general science and technology that will appeal to young scientists and established professionals or to interested lay readers within the overall categories of science, technology and health. We'll be looking at everything from astrophysics to the environment to nutrition." Publishes hardcover and trade paperback originals. Receives 200 queries/year; 60 mss/year. **How to Contact:** Submit proposal package, bio, TOC, prospectus (via mail or e-mail), SASE.

JOURNEYFORTH

Imprint of BJU Press, 1700 Wade Hampton Blvd., Greenville SC 29614. (864)242-5100, ext. 4350. (864)298-0268. **E-mail:** jb@bjup.com. **Website:** www.bjupress.com. **Contact:** Suzette Jordan, adult acquisitions editor. "Small independent publisher of trustworthy novels and biographies for readers pre-school through high school from a conservative Christian perspective, Christian living books and Bible studies for adults." Publishes paperback originals and reprints. **Needs:** Christian living, Bible studies, church and ministry, church history. "We produce books for the adult Christian market that are from a conservative Christian worldview." **How to Contact:** Submit 5 sample chapters, synopsis, SASE. **Tips:** "Study the publisher's guidelines. No submissions by e-mail."

KALMBACH PUBLISHING CO.

21027 Crossroads Circle, P.O. Box 1612, Waukesha WI 53187-1612. (262)796-8776. **Fax:** (262)798-6468. **E-mail:** books@kalmbach.com. **Website:** corporate.kalmbach.com. **Contact:** Mark Thompson, editor-in-chief (hobbies). Publishes paperback originals and reprints. **Needs:** "Focus on beading, wirework and one-of-a-kind artisan creations for jewelry-making and crafts, as well as model railroading, plastic modeling and toy train collecting/operating hobbies." **How to Contact:** Query with 2–3 page detailed outline, sample chapter with photos, drawings and how-to text. **Tips:** "Our how-to books are highly visual in their presentation. Any author who wants to publish with us must be able to furnish good photographs and rough drawings before we'll consider his or her book."

KITSUNE BOOKS

P.O. Box 1154, Crawfordville FL 32326-1154. **E-mail:** contact@kitsunebooks.com. **Website:** www.kitsunebooks.com. **Contact:** Lynn Holschuh, assistant editor. Publishes trade paperback originals and reprints. Receives 600+ queries/year; 70 mss/year. **Needs:** Write for the general reader, but demonstrate a thorough, authoritative knowledge of your subject. No cookbooks, how-to, specific religion books. **How to Contact:** Query via e-mail only. If you insist on sending a postal letter, you must include SASE. No hardcopy submissions unless requested. **Tips:** "Our readership is eclectic, with a taste for the unusual, the artistic and the unexpected. Kitsune Books caters to lovers of literature, poetry and well-designed and researched nonfiction. We prefer to deal with mss electronically rather than receiving printouts (saves trees). Please read our category guidelines carefully. "

KRAUSE PUBLICATIONS

A Division of F+W Media, Inc., 700 E. State St., Iola WI 54990. (715)445-2214. **Fax:** (715)445-4087. Websites: www.krausebooks. com. **Contact:** Paul Kennedy (antiques and collectibles, music); Corrina Peterson (firearms/outdoors); Candy Wiza (simple living); Debbie Bradley (numismatics). "We are the world's largest hobby and collectibles publisher." Publishes hardcover and trade paperback originals. Receives 300 queries/year; 40 mss/year. **How to Contact:** Submit proposal package, including outline, table of contents, a sample chapter and letter explaining your project's unique contributions. **Tips:** Audience consists of serious hobbyists. "Your work should provide a unique contribution to the special interest."

LADYBUGPRESS

NewVoices, Inc. 16964 Columbia River Dr., Sonora CA 95370-9111. (209)694-8340. **E-mail:** georgia@ladybugbooks.com. **Website:** www.ladybugbooks.com. **Contact:** Georgia Jones, editor-in-chief. Publishes trade paperback and electronic originals. Receives 50 queries/year; 30 mss/year. **Needs:** "Our tastes are eclectic. Our primary interest is in women's issues and peace." **How to Contact:** Submit proposal package, including synopsis. "We prefer electronic submissions, sent to georgia@ladbugbooks.com." **Tips:** "We have a lot of information on our website and have several related sites that give an overview of who we are and what we like to see. Take advantage of this and it will help you make good decisions about submissions."

LOVING HEALING PRESS INC.

5145 Pontiac Trail, Ann Arbor MI 48105-9627. (888)761-6268. **E-mail:** info@lovinghealing.com. **Website:** www.lovinghealing.com. **Contact:** Victor R. Volkman, sr. editor (psychology, self-help, personal growth, trauma recovery). Publishes hardcover originals and reprints; trade paperback originals and reprints. Receives 200 queries/year; 100 mss/year. **Needs:** We are primarily interested in self-help books that are person-centered and non-judgmental. **How to Contact:** Submit proposal package, including outline and 3 sample chapters, or submit completed ms.

LUCKY PRESS, LLC

P.O. Box 754, Athens OH 45701-0754. **Website:** www.luckypress. com. **Contact:** Janice Phelps Williams, editor-in-chief. "Lucky Press is a small, independent publisher and a good option for hard-working, talented writers. Our books are sold primarily online, and authors must be comfortable maintaining a blog and creating social networks to promote their book." Publishes trade paperback originals. Receives 100 queries/year; 25 mss/year. **Needs:** "We are interested in the following subjects: pets (i.e., relationship with one's pet; memoirs of a vet; pet rescue stories; parrot stories), inspiration (small books

that encourage readers to live positively and consciously; not religious), living with or parenting children with special needs, nonfiction of interest to women over 50. Also stories about people who took their lives in a completely different direction and what they learned along the way." **How to Contact:** Submit proposal package, including outline, 2 sample chapters, author bio, 1-page synopsis, list of comparative/competitive titles. **Tips:** "The author is the biggest key to success in our book sales, and our best-selling books are by authors with a strong web presence."

MCFARLAND & CO., INC., PUBLISHERS

Box 611, Jefferson NC 28640. (336)246-4460. **Fax:** (336)246-5018. **E-mail:** info@mcfarlandpub.com. **Website:** www.mcfarlandpub. com. **Contact:** Steve Wilson, editorial director (automotive, general); David Alff, editor (general); Gary Mitchem, acquisitions editor (general, baseball). "McFarland publishes serious nonfiction in a variety of fields, including general reference, performing arts, popular culture, sports (particularly baseball), women's studies, librarianship, literature, Civil War, history and international studies." Publishes hardcover and quality paperback originals; a nontrade publisher. **Needs:** Currently emphasizing medieval history, automotive history. De-emphasizing memoirs. Reference books are particularly wanted—fresh material (i.e., not in head-to-head competition with an established title). We prefer manuscripts of 250 or more double-spaced pages or at least 75,000 words. No fiction, New Age, exposés, poetry, children's books, devotional/inspirational works, Bible studies, or personal essays. **How to Contact:** Query with SASE. Submit outline, sample chapters. **Tips:** "We want well-organized knowledge of an area in which there is not information coverage at present, plus reliability so we don't feel we have to check absolutely everything. Our market is worldwide and libraries are an important part. McFarland also publishes six journals: the *Journal of Information Ethics, North Korean Review, Base Ball: A Journal of the Early Game, Black Ball: A Negro Leagues Journal, Clues: A Journal of Detection* and *Minerva: Journal of Women and War.*"

MAGNUS PRESS

P.O. Box 2666, Carlsbad CA 92018. (760)806-3743. **Fax:** (760)806-3689. **E-mail:** magnuspres@aol.com. **Website:** www.magnuspress. com. **Contact:** Warren Angel, editorial director. Publishes trade paperback originals and reprints. Receives 200 queries/year; 220 mss/year. **Needs:** "Writers must be well grounded in Biblical knowledge and must be able to communicate effectively with the lay person." **How to Contact:** Submit proposal package, outline, sample chapters, bio. **Tips:** "Magnus Press's audience is mainly Christian lay persons but also includes anyone interested in spirituality and/or Biblical studies and the church. Study our listings and catalog; learn to write effectively for an average reader; read any one of our published books."

MEADOWBROOK PRESS

5451 Smetana Dr., Minnetonka MN 55343. (952)930-1100. **Fax:** (952)930-1940. **E-mail:** info@meadowbrookpress.com. **Website:** www.meadowbrookpress.com. **Contact:** Submissions Editor.

"Meadowbrook is a family-oriented press. We specialize in pregnancy, baby care, child care, humorous poetry for children, party planning and children's activities. We are also the number one publisher of baby-name books in the country, with eight baby-naming books in print." Publishes trade paperback originals and reprints. Receives 1,500 queries/year. **Needs:** No children's fiction, academic or biography. **How to Contact:** "We prefer a query first; then we will request an outline and/or sample material. Send for guidelines." **Tips:** "Always send for guidelines before submitting material. Always submit nonreturnable copies; we do not respond to queries or submissions unless interested."

MERIWETHER PUBLISHING, LTD.

P.O. Box 7710, Colorado Springs CO 80903. (719)594-9916. **E-mail:** editor@meriwether.com. **Contact:** Theodore Zape, assoc. editor. "We are specialists in theater arts books and plays for middle grades, high schools and colleges. We publish textbooks for drama courses of all types. We also publish for mainline liturgical churches—drama activities for church holidays, youth activities and fundraising entertainment. These may be plays, musicals or drama-related books." Publishes paperback originals and reprints. **Needs:** "Most of the plays we publish are one-acts, 15–45 min. in length. We also publish full-length two-act musicals or three-act plays, 90 min. in length. We prefer comedies. Musical shows should have large cast for 20–25 performers. Comedy sketches, monologues and plays are welcome. We prefer simple staging appropriate to middle school, high school, college or church performance. We like playwrights who see the world with a sense of humor. Offbeat themes and treatments are accepted if the playwright can sustain a light touch. In documentary or religious plays, we look for good research and authenticity. We are publishing many scenebooks for actors (which can be anthologies of great works excerpts), scenebooks on special themes, and speech and theatrical arts textbooks. We also publish many books of monologs for young performers. We are especially interested in authority-books on a variety of theater-related subjects. Contemporary Drama Service is now looking for plays or musical adaptations of classic stories by famous authors and playwrights. Also looking for parodies of famous movies or historical and/or fictional characters (i.e., Robin Hood, Rip Van Winkle, Buffalo Bill, Huckleberry Finn)." **How to Contact:** Query with synopsis or submit complete script. Include SASE. **Terms:** Obtains either amateur or all rights. **Tips:** "Contemporary Drama Service is looking for creative books on comedy, monologs, staging amateur theatricals, and Christian youth activities. Our writers are usually highly experienced in theatre as teachers or performers. We welcome books that reflect their experience and special knowledge. Any good comedy writer of monologs and short scenes will find a home with us."

MOUNTAINLAND PUBLISHING, INC.

P.O. Box 150891, Ogden UT 84415. **E-mail:** editor@mountainland publishing.com. **Contact:** Michael Combe, managing editor (fiction, nonfiction). Publishes hardcover, mass-market paperback and electronic originals. Submissions are accepted by e-mail only as of January 2010. **Needs:** "Nonfiction should read like fiction. It should be captivating to the audience and on an intriguing subject." **How to Contact:** Query via e-mail. Submit proposal package, including outline, 3 sample chapters. **Tips:** "Our audience is a new generation of readers who enjoy well-told stories and who want to be entertained. They want characters they can feel close to and/or love to hate. Make sure your ms is ready for print. Publishing companies will not wait for you to finish editing your story. Be confident that the work you are submitting is your best work. Please submit all ms electronically. Submissions received by mail may be returned unopened."

NAVAL INSTITUTE PRESS

US Naval Institute, 291 Wood Rd., Annapolis MD 21402-5034. (410)268-6110. **Fax:** (410)295-1084. **E-mail:** cparkinson@usni.org; books@usni.org. **Website:** www.usni.org. **Contact:** Tom Cutler, senior acquisitions editor. **Needs:** "The Naval Institute Press publishes trade and scholarly nonfiction. We are interested in national and international security, naval, military, military jointness, intelligence and special warfare, both current and historical." **How to Contact:** Submit proposal package with outline, author bio, TOC, description/synopsis, sample chapter(s), page/word count, number of illustrations, ms completion date, intended market; or submit complete ms. Send SASE with sufficient postage for return of ms. Send by postal mail only. No email submissions, please.

NEWMARKET PRESS

18 E. 48th St., 15th Floor, New York NY 10017. (212)832-3575. **Fax:** (212)832-3629. **E-mail:** mailbox@newmarketpress.com. **Website:** www.newmarketpress.com. **Contact:** Editorial Department. Publishes hardcover and trade paperback originals and reprints. **Needs:** Currently emphasizing movie tie-in/companion books, health, psychology, child care & parenting, film & performing arts, health & nutrition, biography, history, business & personal finance and popular self-help & reference. De-emphasizing fiction. **How to Contact:** Submit proposal package, complete ms, or 1–3 sample chapters, TOC, marketing info, author credentials, SASE.

NORTH LIGHT BOOKS

Imprint of F+W Media, Inc., 4700 E. Galbraith Rd., Cincinnati OH 45236. **Website:** www.fwmedia.com. "North Light Books publishes art and craft books, including watercolor, drawing, mixed media and decorative painting, knitting, jewelry making, sewing and needle arts that emphasize illustrated how-to art instruction." Publishes hardcover and trade paperback how-to books. **Needs:** Currently emphasizing drawing including traditional, fantasy art and Japanese-style comics as well as creativity and inspiration. Interested in books on acrylic painting, basic drawing, pen and ink, colored pencil, decorative painting and beading. Do not submit coffee table art books without how-to art instruction. **How to Contact:** Query with SASE. Submit outline.

OAK TREE PRESS

140 E. Palmer, Taylorville IL 62568. (217)824-6500. **E-mail:** oaktreepub@aol.com. **Website:** www.oaktreebooks.com. **Contact:**

Acquisitions Editor. "Oak Tree Press is an independent publisher that celebrates writers and is dedicated to the many great unknowns who are just waiting for the opportunity to break into print. We're looking for narrative nonfiction, how-to. Sponsors CopTales contest for true crime and other stories of law enforcement professionals." Publishes trade paperback and hardcover books. **Needs:** "No right-wing political or racist agenda, gratuitous sex or violence, especially against women, or depicting of harm of animals." **How to Contact:** Query by e-mail. **Tips:** "Perhaps my most extreme pet peeve is receiving queries on projects that we've clearly advertised we don't want: science fiction, fantasy, epic tomes, bigoted diatribes and so on. Second to that is a practice I call 'over-taping,' or the use of yards and yards of tape, or worse yet, the filament tape so that it takes forever to open the package. Finding story pitches on my voice mail is also annoying."

ORANGE FRAZER PRESS, INC.

P.O. Box 214, 37 W. Main St., Wilmington OH 45177. (937)382-3196. **Fax:** (937)383-3159. **Website:** www.orangefrazer.com. **Contact:** John Baskin, editor (sports/history). "Orange Frazer Press accepts nonfiction only: corporate histories, town celebrations, anniversary books." Publishes hardcover and trade paperback originals. Receives 50 queries/year; 35 mss/year. **Needs:** Sports and personalities are our main focus. **How to Contact:** Submit proposal package, outline, 3 sample chapters and marketing plan. **Tips:** "For our commercial titles, we focus mainly on sports and biographies. Our readers are interested in sports or curious about famous persons/personalities."

PALADIN PRESS

7077 Winchester Circle, Boulder CO 80301. (303)443-7250. **Fax:** (303)442-8741. **E-mail:** editorial@paladin-press.com. **Website:** www.paladin-press.com. "Paladin Press publishes the Action Library of nonfiction in military science, police science, weapons, combat, personal freedom, self-defense, survival." Publishes hardcover originals and paperback originals and reprints, videos. **Needs:** "We need lucid, instructive material aimed at our market and accompanied by sharp, relevant illustrations and photos. As we are primarily a publisher of how-to books, a manuscript that has step-by-step instructions, written in a clear and concise manner (but not strictly outline form) is desirable. No fiction, first-person accounts, children's, religious, or joke books. We are also interested in serious, professional videos and video ideas (contact Michael Rigg)." **How to Contact:** To submit a book proposal to Paladin Press, send an outline or chapter description along with 1–2 sample chapters (or the entire ms) to the address below. If applicable, samples of illustrations or photographs are also useful. Do not send a computer disk at this point, and be sure keep a copy of everything you send us. We are not accepting mss as electronic submissions at this time. Please allow 2–6 weeks for a reply. If you would like your sample material returned, SASE with proper postage is required. Editorial Department, Paladin Press, Gunbarrel Tech Center, 7077 Winchester Circle, Boulder, CO 80301, or email us at editorial@paladin-press.com. Submitting a proposal for a video project is not much different than a book proposal. See guidelines online and send to David Dubrow, Video Production Manager.

PALARI PUBLISHING

P.O. Box 9288, Richmond VA 23227-0288. (866)570-6724. **Fax:** (866)570-6724. **E-mail:** dave@palaribooks.com. **Website:** www.palaribooks.com. **Contact:** David Smitherman, publisher/editor. Publishes hardcover and trade paperback originals. **Needs:** "Authoritative, well-written nonfiction that addresses topical consumer needs." **How to Contact:** "We accept solicited and unsolicited manuscripts, however we prefer a query letter and SASE, describing the project briefly and concisely. This letter should include a complete address and telephone number." **Terms:** Promotes titles through book signings, direct mail and the Internet. **Tips:** "Tell why your idea is unique or interesting. Make sure we are interested in your genre before submitting. Send a good bio. I'm interested in a writer's experience and unique outlook on life."

PARADISE CAY PUBLICATIONS

P.O. Box 29, Arcata CA 95518-0029. (800)736-4509. **Fax:** (707)822-9163. info@paracay.com. **Website:** www.paracay.com. **Contact:** Matt Morehouse, publisher. "Paradise Cay Publications, Inc. is a small independent publisher specializing in nautical books, videos and art prints. Our primary interest is in manuscripts that deal with the instructional and technical aspects of ocean sailing. We also publish and will consider fiction if it has a strong nautical theme." Publishes hardcover and trade paperback originals and reprints. Receives 360–480 queries/year; 240–360 mss/year. **Needs:** Instructional and technical mss on aspects of ocean sailing. **How to Contact:** Query with SASE. Submit proposal package, clips, 2–3 sample chapters. Include a cover letter containing a story synopsis and a short bio, including any plans to promote your work. The cover letter should describe the book's subject matter, approach, distinguishing characteristics, intended audience, author's qualifications, and why the author thinks this book is appropriate for Paradise Cay. Call first. **Tips:** Audience is recreational sailors. Call Matt Morehouse (publisher).

PAULIST PRESS

997 Macarthur Blvd., Mahwah NJ 07430. (201)825-7300. **Fax:** (201)825-8345. **E-mail:** info@paulistpress.com. **Website:** www.paulistpress.com. **Contact:** Lawrence Boadt, editorial director for all fields; Paul McMahon, managing editor, all fields. "Paulist Press publishes 'ecumenical theology, Roman Catholic studies, and books on scripture, liturgy, spirituality, church history and philosophy, as well as works on faith and culture.' Our publishing is oriented toward adult-level nonfiction. We do not publish poetry." Publishes hardcover and electronic originals and electronic reprints. **Needs:** "It should deal with traditional Catholic spirituality, sacraments, church doctrine or practical aids for ministry and prayer, or be intended as a textbook in religion classes in college or high school. Children's books should have strong religious (not just spiritual) or moral content, or deal with learning to be Catholic." **How to Contact:** Submit proposal package, including outline, 1 sample chapter, or submit completed ms. **Tips:** "Our typical reader is

probably Roman Catholic and wants the content to be educational about Catholic thought and practice, or else the reader is a spiritual seeker who looks for discovery of God and spiritual values which churches offer but without the church connection."

POPULAR WOODWORKING BOOKS

Imprint of F+W Media, Inc., 4700 Galbraith Rd., Cincinnati OH 45236. (513)531-2690. **Website:** popularwoodworking.com/books andmore/. **Contact:** David Thiel, executive editor. "Popular Woodworking Books is one of the largest publishers of woodworking books in the world. From perfecting a furniture design to putting on the final coat of finish, our books provide step-by-step instruction and trusted advice from the pros that make them valuable tools for both beginning and advanced woodworkers." Publishes trade paperback and hardcover originals and reprints. Receives 30 queries/year; 10 mss/year. **Needs:** Currently emphasizing woodworking jigs and fixtures, furniture and cabinet projects, smaller finely crafted boxes, all styles of furniture. De-emphasizing woodturning, woodcarving, scroll saw projects. **How to Contact:** Query with SASE, or electronic query. Proposal package should include an outline and digital photos. **Tips:** "Our books are for beginning to advanced woodworking enthusiasts."

QUEST BOOKS

Imprint of Theosophical Publishing House, 306 W. Geneva Rd., P.O. Box 270, Wheaton IL 60187. **E-mail:** submissions@questbooks.net. **Website:** www.questbooks.net. **Contact:** Richard Smoley, editor. "Quest Books is the imprint of the Theosophical Publishing House, the publishing arm of the Theosophical Society in America. Since 1965, Quest books has sold millions of books by leading cultural thinkers on such increasingly popular subjects as transpersonal psychology, comparative religion, deep ecology, spiritual growth, the development of creativity, and alternative health practices." Publishes hardcover and trade paperback originals and reprints. Receives 150 ms; 350 queries/year. **Needs:** Our specialty is high-quality spiritual nonfiction with a self-help aspect. Great writing is a must. We seldom publish 'personal spiritual awakening' stories. No submissions accepted that do not fit the **Needs:** outlined above. No fiction, poetry, children's books, or any literature based on channeling or personal psychic impressions. **How to Contact:** Submit proposal package, including outline, 1 sample chapter. Prefer online submissions; attachments must be sent as a single file in Microsoft Word, Rich Text, or PDF formats. Reviews artwork/photos. Hard copies of mss and artwork will not be returned. **Tips:** "Our audience includes readers interested in spirituality, particularly the world's mystical traditions. Read a few recent Quest titles and submission guidelines before submitting. Know our books and our company goals. Explain how your book or proposal relates to other Quest titles. Quest gives preference to writers with established reputations/successful publications. Please be advised that proposals or manuscripts will not be accepted if they fall into any of the following categories: works intended for or about children, teenagers, or adolescents; fiction or literary works (novels, short stories, essays or poetry); autobiographical material

(memoirs, personal experiences or family stories); works received through mediumship, trance or channeling; works related to UFOs or extraterrestrials; works related to self-aggrandizement (e.g., "how to make a fortune"); or how-to books."

RUKA PRESS

P.O. Box 1409, Washington DC 20013. **E-mail:** contact@rukapress. com. **Website:** www.rukapress.com. **Contact:** Daniel Kohan, owner. **Needs:** "We publish nonfiction books with a strong information-design component for a general audience. We are looking for books that explain things, that make an argument, that demystify. We are interested in economics, science, the arts, climate change and sustainability, but we're open to other areas, too—surprise us. We like building charts and graphs, tables and timelines. Our politics are progressive, but our books need not be political." Publishes trade paperback originals, ebooks. **How to Contact:** Submit proposal package, including outline, resume or CV, bio and one sample chapter. **Tips:** "We appeal to an audience of intelligent, educated readers with broad interests. Be sure to tell us why your proposal is unique and why you are especially qualified to write this book. We are looking for originality and expertise."

SEAWORTHY PUBLICATIONS, INC.

626 W. Pierre Lane, Port Washington WI 53074. (262)268-9250. **Fax:** (262)268-9208. **E-mail:** queries@seaworthy.com **Website:** www. seaworthy.com. **Contact:** Joseph F. Janson, publisher. "Seaworthy Publications is a nautical book publisher that primarily publishes books of interest to recreational boaters and bluewater cruisers, including cruising guides, how-to books about boating. Currently emphasizing cruising guides." Publishes trade paperback originals, hardcover originals and reprints. Receives 150 queries/year; 40 mss/ year. **Needs:** Regional guide books, first-person adventure, reference, technical—all dealing with boating. **How to Contact:** Query with SASE. Submit 3 sample chapters, TOC. Prefers electronic query via e-mail. **Tips:** "Our audience consists of sailors, boaters and those interested in the sea, sailing or long-distance cruising."

SOHO PRESS, INC.

853 Broadway, New York NY 10003. **E-mail:** soho@sohopress.com. **Website:** www.sohopress.com. **Contact:** Bronwen Hruska, publisher; Katie Herman, editor. Soho Press publishes primarily fiction, as well as some narrative literary nonfiction and mysteries set abroad. Publishes hardcover and trade paperback originals; trade paperback reprints. **Needs:** Narrative literary nonfiction. No self-help, how-to, or cookbooks. "We do not publish books with color art or photographs or a lot of graphical material." **How to Contact:** "We do not buy books on proposal. We always need to see a complete ms before we buy a book, though we prefer an initial submission of 3 sample chapters." Submit 3 sample chapters and a cover letter with a synopsis and author bio; SASE. **Tips:** "Soho Press publishes discerning authors for discriminating readers, finding the strongest possible writers and publishing them. Before submitting, look at our website for an idea of the types of books we publish, and read our submission guidelines."

SOUTHERN METHODIST UNIVERSITY PRESS

P.O. Box 750415, Dallas TX 75275-0415. (214)768-1436. **Fax:** (214)768-1428. **Website:** www.tamupress.com. **Contact:** Diana Vance. Known nationally as a publisher of the highest quality scholarly works and books for the "educated general reader." Publishes hardcover and trade paperback originals and reprints. Receives 500 queries/year; 500 mss/year. **Needs:** SMU Press publishes in the areas of ethics and human values, medical humanities, performing arts, Southwestern studies and sports. **How to Contact:** Proposals may be submitted in hard copy or as attachments to e-mails addressed to the appropriate acquisitions editor. To determine who that is, send a brief description of your ms to the acquisitions assistant, Diana Vance. Query with SASE. Submit outline, bio, 3 sample chapters, TOC.

STERLING PUBLISHING

387 Park Ave. S., 11th Floor, New York NY 10016-8810. (212)532-7160. **Fax:** (212)213-2495. **Website:** www.sterlingpub.com. **Contact:** Category Editor (i.e., Children's Editor). Publishes hardcover and paperback originals and reprints. **Needs:** "Sterling publishes highly illustrated, accessible, hands-on, practical books for adults and children. At present we do not publish fiction." **How to Contact:** "Proposals on subjects such as crafting, decorating, outdoor living and photography should be sent directly to Lark Books at their Asheville, North Carolina offices. Complete guidelines can be found on the Lark site: www.larkbooks.com/submissions. Submit outline, publishing history, 1 sample chapter (typed and double-spaced), SASE. Explain your idea. Send sample illustrations where applicable. We do not accept electronic (e-mail) submissions. Be sure to include information about yourself with particular regard to your skills and qualifications in the subject area of your submission. It is helpful for us to know your publishing history—whether or not you've written other books and, if so, the name of the publisher and whether those books are currently in print."

TRANSPERSONAL PUBLISHING

P.O. Box 7220, Kill Devil Hills NC 27948. (540)997-0325. **E-mail:** allenchips@holistictree.com. **Website:** www.transpersonalpublishing.com. **Contact:** Dr. Allen Chips, acquisitions/publishing director (holistic health texts and metaphysical/near death research). Publishes hardcover originals and reprints, trade paperback originals and reprints, electronic originals and reprints and mass-market paperback reprints. Receives 35 queries/year. **Needs:** "We are looking for textbooks and self-help, how-to books with a holistic health or transpersonal therapy orientation." **How to Contact:** Query, then submit TOC with 2 sample chapters. **Tips:** "Audience is people desiring to learn about mind-body-spirit oriented therapies/practices that lead to healing and/or enlightenment. The best authors are engaged in regular travel and seminars/workshops, demonstrating dedication, self-motivation and a people orientation. Do not phone the company with book ideas; if interested, the publisher will e-mail, then phone you."

UPPER ACCESS, INC.

87 Upper Access Rd. Hinesburg VT 05461. (802)482-2988. **Fax:** (802)304-1005. **E-mail:** info@upperaccess.com. **Website:** www.upperaccess.com. **Contact:** Steve Carlson, publisher. "Publishes nonfiction to improve the quality of life." Publishes hardcover and trade paperback originals; hardcover and trade paperback reprints. Receives 200 queries/year; 40 mss/year. **Needs:** "We are open to considering almost any nonfiction topic that has some potential for national general trade sales. Please do not submit fiction, even if it relates to nonfiction subjects. We cannot take novels or poetry of any kind at this time." **How to Contact:** Query with SASE. "We strongly prefer an initial e-mail describing your proposed title. No attachments please. We will look at paper mail if there is no other way, but e-mail will be reviewed much more quickly and thoroughly." **Tips:** "We target intelligent adults willing to challenge the status quo, who are interested in more self-sufficiency with respect to the environment. Most of our books are either unique subjects or unique or different ways of looking at major issues or basic education on subjects that are not well understood by most of the general public. We make a long-term commitment to each book that we publish, trying to find its market as long as possible."

VOYAGEUR PRESS

400 First Ave., Suite 300, Minneapolis MN 55401. (651)430-2210. **Fax:** (651)430-2211. **E-mail:** mdregni@voyageurpress.com; jleventhal@voyageurpress.com; dpernu@mbipublishing.com; kcornell@voyageurpress.com. **Contact:** Michael Dregni, publisher; Kari Cornell, acquisitions editor (crafts and cookbooks); Dennis Pernu, senior editor (music titles); Josh Leventhal, publisher (sports books). "Voyageur Press (and its sports imprint MVP Books) is internationally known as a leading publisher of quality music, sports, country living, crafts, natural history and regional books. No children's or poetry books." Publishes hardcover and trade paperback originals. Receives 1,200 queries/year; 500 mss/year. **How to Contact:** Query with SASE. Submit outline. **Tips:** "We publish books for an audience interested in regional, natural and cultural history on a wide variety of subjects. We seek authors strongly committed to helping us promote and sell their books. Please present as focused an idea as possible in a brief submission (1-page cover letter; 2-page outline or proposal). Note your credentials for writing the book. Tell all you know about the market niche and marketing possibilities for proposed book."

WHITAKER HOUSE

1030 Hunt Valley Circle, New Kensington PA 15068. **E-mail:** publisher@whitakerhouse.com. **Website:** www.whitakerhouse.com. **Contact:** Tom Cox, managing editor. Publishes hardcover, trade paperback and mass-market originals. Receives 600 queries/year; 200 mss/year. **Needs:** Accepts submissions on topics with a Christian perspective. Subjects include Christian living, prayer, spiritual warfare, healing, gifts of the spirit, etc. **How to Contact:** Query with SASE. **Tips:** "Audience includes those seeking uplifting and inspirational fiction and nonfiction."

WOODBINE HOUSE

6510 Bells Mill Rd., Bethesda MD 20817. (301)897-3570. **Fax:** (301)897-5838. **E-mail:** ngpaul@woodbinehouse.com. **Website:** www.woodbinehouse.com. **Contact:** Nancy Gray Paul, acquisitions editor. "Woodbine House publishes books for or about individuals with disabilities to help those individuals and their families live fulfilling and satisfying lives in their homes, schools and communities." Publishes trade paperback originals. **Needs:** Receptive to stories re: developmental and intellectual disabilities, e.g., autism and cerebral palsy. No personal accounts or general parenting guides. **How to Contact:** Submit complete ms with SASE, or submit outline and 3 sample chapters. **Tips:** "Do not send us a proposal on the basis of this description. Examine our catalog or website and a couple of our books to make sure you are on the right track. Put some thought into how your book could be marketed (aside from in bookstores). Keep cover letters concise and to the point; if it's a subject that interests us, we'll ask to see more."

WRITER'S DIGEST BOOKS

Imprint of F+W Media, Inc., 4700 E. Galbraith Rd., Cincinnati OH 45236. **E-mail:** writersdigest@fwmedia.com. **Website:** www.writers digest.com. **Contact:** Kelly Messerly, acquisitions editor. "Writer's Digest Books is the premiere source for instructional books on writing and publishing for an audience of aspirational writers." Publishes hardcover originals and trade paperbacks. Receives 300 queries/year; 50 mss/year. **Needs:** "Our instruction books stress results and how specifically to achieve them. Should be well researched, yet lively and readable. We do not want to see books telling readers how to crack specific nonfiction markets: *Writing for the Computer Market* or *Writing for Trade Publications*, for instance. We are most in need of fiction-technique books written by published authors. Be prepared to explain how the proposed book differs from existing books on the subject." No fiction or poetry. Typical mss are 80,000 words. **How to Contact:** Query with SASE. Submit outline, sample chapters. E-mail queries strongly preferred; no phone calls please. **Tips:** "Most queries we receive are either too broad (how to write fiction) or too niche (how to write erotic horror) and don't reflect a knowledge of our large backlist of 150 titles. We rarely publish new books on journalism, freelancing, magazine article writing or marketing/promotion. We are actively seeking fiction- and nonfiction-writing technique books with fresh perspectives; interactive and visual writing instruction books, similar to *Pocket Muse*, by Monica Wood; and general reference works that appeal to an audience beyond writers."

ZUMAYA PUBLICATIONS, LLC

3209 S. Interstate 35, #1086, Austin TX 78741. **E-mail:** acquisitions@zumayapublications.com. **Website:** www.zumayapublications.com. Contact: Elizabeth Burton, executive editor. Publishes trade paperback and electronic originals and reprints. 1,000 queries received/year. 100 mss received/year. **Needs:** "The easiest way to figure out what I'm looking for is to look at what we've already done. Our main nonfiction interests are in collections of true ghost stories, ones that have been investigated or thoroughly documented, memoirs that address specific regions and eras, and books on the craft of writing. That doesn't mean we won't consider something else." **How to Contact:** Electronic query only. **Tips:** "We're catering to readers who may have loved last year's bestseller but not enough to want to

read 10 more just like it. Have something different. If it does not fit standard pigeonholes, that's a plus. On the other hand, it has to have an audience. And if you're not prepared to work with us on promotion and marketing, it would be better to look elsewhere."

CHILDREN'S PUBLISHERS

BAREFOOT BOOKS

2067 Massachusetts Ave., Cambridge MA 02140. **Website:** www.barefootbooks.com. **Contact:** Submissions Editor. "We are a small, independent publishing company that publishes high-quality picture books for children of all ages and specializes in the work of artists and writers from many cultures. We focus on themes that support independence of spirit, encourage openness to others, and foster a lifelong love of learning. Prefers full manuscript." Publishes hardcover and trade paperback originals. Receives 2,000 queries/year; 3,000 mss/year. **Fiction:** "Barefoot Books only publishes children's picture books and anthologies of folktales. We do not publish novels." **How to Contact:** "We encourage authors to send their full manuscript. Always include SASE. **Tips:** "Our audience is made up of children and parents, teachers and students of many different ages and cultures. Since we are a small publisher, and we definitely publish for a 'niche' market, it is helpful to look at our books and our website before submitting, to see if your book would fit into the type of book we publish."

BARRON'S EDUCATIONAL SERIES, INC.

250 Wireless Blvd., Hauppauge NY 11788. (800)645-3476. **Fax:** (631)434-3723. **Website:** www.barronseduc.com. **Contact:** Wayne Barr, acquisitions manager. "Barron's tends to publish series of books, both for adults and children." Publishes hardcover, paperback and mass-market originals and software. Receives 2,000 queries/year. **Needs:** "We are always on the lookout for creative nonfiction ideas for children and adults." **How to Contact:** Query with SASE. Submit outline, 2–3 sample chapters. **Tips:** "Audience is mostly educated self-learners and students. Try to fit into one of our series. On children's stories, better to send query e-mail without attachments. SASE must be included for the return of all materials. Please be patient for replies."

BENCHMARK BOOKS

99 White Plains Rd., Tarrytown NY 10591. Phone/**Fax:** (914)332-8888. **E-mail:** mbisson@marshallcavendish.com. **Website:** www.marshallcavendish.us. Publishes about 300 young reader, middle reader and young adult books/year. "We look for interesting treatments of only nonfiction subjects related to elementary, middle school and high school curriculum." **Contact:** Michelle Bisson. Most nonfiction topics should be curriculum related. Average word length: 4,000-20,000. All books published as part of a series. "Please read our catalog or view our website before submitting proposals. We only publish series. We do not publish individual titles." **How to Contact:** Submit outline/synopsis and 1 or more sample chapters. Responds to queries/mss in 3 months. Publishes a book 2 years after acceptance.

Will consider simultaneous submissions. **Terms:** Buys work outright. Sends galleys to authors. Book catalog available online. All imprints included in a single catalog.

BICK PUBLISHING HOUSE

307 Neck Rd., Madison CT 06443. (203)245-0073. **Fax:** (203)245-5990. **Website:** www.bickpubhouse.com. "We publish psychological, philosophical, scientific information on health and recovery, wildlife rehabilitation, living with disabilities, teen psychology and science for adults and young adults." **Fiction:** Looking for YA books on nature/environment, religion, science, self-help, social issues, special needs. Average word length: 60,000. **How to Contact: Fiction:** Submit outline/synopsis and 3 sample chapters. **Nonfiction:** Submit outline/synopsis or outline/synopsis and 3 sample chapters. Responds to queries/mss in 2 weeks. Publishes book 1 year after acceptance. Will consider simultaneous submissions and previously published work. **Terms:** Pays authors royalty of 5-10%. Sends galleys to authors. Book catalog available for SASE with 1 first-class stamp; writer's guidelines available for SAE. Catalog available on website. **Tips:** "Read our books!"

CANDLEWICK PRESS

99 Dover S., Somerville MA 02144. (617)661-3330. **Fax:** (617)661-0565. **E-mail:** bigbear@candlewick.com. **Website:** www.candlewick.com. Publishes 160 picture books/year; 15 middle readers/year; 15 young adult titles/year. 5% of books by first-time authors. "Our books are truly for children, and we strive for the very highest standards in the writing, illustrating, designing and production of all of our books. And we are not averse to risk." **Contact:** Karen Lotz, publisher; Liz Bicknell, editorial director and associate publisher; Joan Powers, editorial director; Mary Lee Donovan, executive editor; Sarah Ketchersid, senior editor; Deborah Wayshak, executive editor; Andrea Tompa, associate editor; Katie Cunningham, associate editor; Kaylan Adair, associate editor; Kate Fletcher, associate editor; Jennifer Yoon, associate editor. **Fiction:** Picture books: animal, concept, contemporary, fantasy, history, humor, multicultural, nature/environment, poetry. Middle readers, young adults: contemporary, fantasy, history, humor, multicultural, poetry, science fiction, sports, suspense/mystery. **Nonfiction:** Picture books: concept, biography, geography, nature/environment. Young readers: biography, geography, nature/environment. **Terms:** Pays authors royalty of 2–10% based on retail price. Offers advances. Sends galleys to authors.

CELLAR DOOR PUBLISHING, LLC

3439 NE Sandy Blvd., Suite 309, Portland OR 97232-1959. **E-mail:** info@cellardoorpublishing.com. **Website:** www.cellardoorpublishing.com. "Cellar Door Publishing specializes in the publication of high-quality illustrated literature and graphic novels." Publishes hardcover originals, trade paperback originals and electronic originals. **Fiction:** "We are looking for all genres and age groups. We encourage creators to experiment with format and content, though it is not required. We do accept a limited number of submissions for books without illustrations. This is generally reserved for books that are either unique in content or controversial in nature, or literary projects that can be released in a serialized format." **How to Contact:** "We currently accept unsolicited submissions via online submission form and comic-book conventions only. We no longer accept unsolicited submissions through traditional mail. To submit book proposals for consideration, please use the online submission form." **Tips:** "Nonfiction submissions will also be considered if they fall into one of our categories. Submit online."

CHRISTIAN FOCUS PUBLICATIONS

Geanies House, Tain Ross-shire IV20 1TW, Scotland, UK. Estab. 1975. 44 (0) 1862 871 011. **Fax:** 44 (0) 1862 871 699. **E-mail:** info@christianfocus.com. **Website:** www.christianfocus.com. Specializes in Christian material, nonfiction, fiction, educational material. **Contact:** Catherine Mackenzie. Publishes 4–6 picture books/year; 4–6 young readers/year; 10–15 middle readers/year; 4–6 for young adult books/year. 2% of books by first-time authors. **Fiction:** Picture books, young readers, adventure, history, religion. Middle readers: adventure, problem novels, religion. Young adult/teens: adventure, history, problem novels, religion. Average word length: young readers-5,000; middle readers-max 10,000; young adult/teen-max 20,000. **Nonfiction:** All levels: activity books, biography, history, religion, science. Average word length: picture books-5,000; young readers-5,000; middle readers-5,000-10,000; young adult/teens-10,000-20,000. **How to Contact: Fiction**/nonfiction: Query or submit outline/synopsis and 3 sample chapters. Responds to queries in 2 weeks/mss in 3 months. Publishes 1 year after acceptance. Will consider electronic submissions and previously published work. **Terms:** "We do not discuss financial details of this type in public. Contracts can vary depending on the needs of author/publisher." For catalog visit our website at www.christianfocus.com. Writers guidelines are available for SASE. **Tips:** "Be aware of the international market as regards writing style/topics as well as illustration styles. Our company sells rights to European as well as Asian countries. **Fiction** sales are not as good as they were. Christian fiction for youngsters is not a product that is performing well in comparison to nonfiction, such as Christian biography/bible stories/church history etc."

CHRONICLE BOOKS

680 Second St., San Francisco CA 94107. **Website:** www.chroniclekids.com. **Contact:** Victoria Rock, founding publisher & editor-at-large; Andrea Menotti, senior editor; Julie Romeis, editor; Melissa Manlove, editor; Naomi Kirsten, assistant editor; Mary Colgan, assistant editor. Publishes 90 (both fiction and nonfiction) books/year; 5–10% middle readers/year. 10–25% of books by first-time authors; 20–40% of books from agented writers. **Fiction:** Picture books, young readers, middle readers, young adults: "We are open to a very wide range of topics." **Nonfiction:** Picture books, young readers, middle readers, young adults: "We are open to a very wide range of topics." **How to Contact:** Fiction/nonfiction: Submit complete ms (picture books); submit outline/synopsis and 3 sample chapters (for older readers). Responds to queries in 1 month; will not respond to submissions unless interested. Publishes a book 1-3 years after acceptance. Will consider simultaneous submissions, as long as they are marked "multiple submissions." Will not consider submissions

by fax, e-mail or disk. Do not include SASE; do not send original materials. No submissions will be returned; to confirm receipt, include a SASP. **Terms:** Generally pays authors in royalties based on retail price, "though we do occasionally work on a flat fee basis." Advance varies. Sends proofs to authors. Book catalog for 9 x 12 SAE and 8 first-class stamps; ms guidelines for #10 SASE. **Tips:** "Chronicle Books publishes an eclectic mixture of traditional and innovative children's books. We are interested in taking on projects that have a unique bent to them—be it subject matter, writing style, or illustrative technique. As a small list, we are looking for books that will lend us a distinctive flavor. We are also interested in growing our fiction program for older readers, including chapter books, middle grade and young adult projects."

CLEAR LIGHT PUBLISHERS

823 Don Diego, Santa Fe NM 87505. **Website:** www.clearlightbooks. com. **Contact:** Harmon Houghton, publisher. Publishes 4 middle readers/year; 4 young adult titles/year. **Fiction:** Middle readers and young adults: multicultural, American Indian and Hispanic only. **Nonfiction:** Middle readers and young adults: multicultural, American Indian and Hispanic only. **How to Contact:** Submit complete ms with SASE. "No e-mail submissions. Authors supply art. Manuscripts not considered without art or artist's renderings." Will consider simultaneous submissions. Responds in 3 months. Only send *copies*. **Terms:** Pays authors royalty of 10% based on wholesale price. Offers advances (average amount: up to 50% of expected net sales within the first year). Sends galleys to authors. **Tips:** "We're looking for authentic American-Indian art and folklore."

COTTONWOOD PRESS, INC.

109-B Cameron Drive, Fort Collins CO 80525. Estab. 1986. (970)204-0715. **Fax:** (970)204-0761. **E-mail:** cottonwood@cotton woodpress.com. **Website:** www.cottonwoodpress.com. Specializes in educational material for the English/language arts classroom. **President:** Cheryl Thurston. Cottonwood Press strives "to publish materials that are effective in the classroom and help kids learn without putting them to sleep, specializing in materials for grades 5–12." No picture books. Publishes 4 middle reader and young adult books/year. 60% of books by first-time authors. **Nonfiction:** Middle readers: textbooks. Young Adults/Teens: textbooks. **How to Contact:** Submit complete manuscript. Responds to queries in 2 weeks; mss in 2 months. Publishes a book 6 months–1 year after acceptance. Will consider simultaneous submissions if notified. **Terms:** Pay royalty of 10–15% based on net sales. **Tips:** "It is essential that writers familiarize themselves with our website to see what we do. The most successful of our authors have used our books in the classroom and know how different they are from ordinary textbooks."

CREATIVE EDUCATION

P.O. Box 227, Mankato MN 56002. Imprint of The Creative Company. (800)445-6209. **Fax:** (507)388-2746. **Contact:** Aaron Frisch. Publishes 40 young readers/year; 70 young adult titles/year. 5% of books by first-time authors. **Nonfiction:** Young readers, young adults: animal, arts/crafts, biography, careers, geography, health,

history, hobbies, multicultural, music/dance, nature/environment, religion, science, social issues, special needs, sports. Average word length: young readers-500; young adults-6,000. **How to Contact:** Submit outline/synopsis and 2 sample chapters, along with division of titles within the series. Responds to queries in 3 months; mss in 3 months. Publishes book 2 years after acceptance. **Tips:** "We are accepting nonfiction, series submissions only. Fiction submissions will not be reviewed or returned. Nonfiction submissions should be presented in series (4, 6, or 8 titles) rather than single."

MAY DAVENPORT, PUBLISHERS

26313 Purissima Rd., Los Altos Hills CA 94022-4539. (650)947-1275. **Fax:** (650)947-1373. **E-mail:** mdbooks@earthlink.net. **Website:** www.maydavenportpublishers.com. **Contact** May Davenport, editor/publisher. Publishes 1–2 picture books/year; 2–3 young adult titles/year. 99% of books by first-time authors. Seeks books with literary merit. "We like to think that we are selecting talented writers who have something humorous to write about today's unglued generation in 30,000–50,000 words for teens and young adults in junior/senior high school before they become tomorrow's 'functional illiterates.' We are interested in publishing literature that teachers in middle and high schools can use in their Language Arts, English and Creative Writing courses. There's more to literary fare than the chit-chat Internet dialog and fantasy trips on television with cartoons or humanoids." **Fiction:** Young readers, young adults: contemporary, humorous fictional literature for use in English courses in junior-senior high schools in U.S. Average word length: 40,000–60,000. Teens: Shocking pathway choices. **How to Contact:** Query. Responds to queries/mss in 3 weeks. Mss returned with SASE. Publishes a book 6–12 months after acceptance. **Terms:** Pays authors royalty of 15% based on retail price; negotiable. Pays "by mutual agreement, no advances." Guidelines free on request with SASE. **Tips:** "Write literary fare with a sense of humor. Bits of laughter may amuse 'reluctant' readers. Our focus: to read and to write English. Try it!"

DAWN PUBLICATIONS

12402 Bitney Springs Rd., Nevada City CA 95959. (530)274-7775. **Website:** www.dawnpub.com. **Co-Publishers:** Muffy Weaver and Glenn J. Hovemann. **Contact:** Glenn J. Hovemann. Publishes works with holistic themes dealing with nature. "Dawn Publications is dedicated to inspiring in children a deeper appreciation and understanding of nature." **Fiction:** Picture books exploring relationships with nature. No fantasy or legend. **Nonfiction:** Picture books: animal, nature/environment. Prefers "creative nonfiction." **How to Contact:** Query or submit complete ms by mail (enclose SASE for reply) or by e-mail (go to the website for e-mail address and instructions). Responds to queries/mss in 3 months. **Terms:** Pays authors royalty based on net sales. Offers advance. Book catalog and ms guidelines available online. **Tips:** Looking for "picture books expressing nature awareness with inspirational quality leading to enhanced self-awareness. Does not publish anthropomorphic works; no animal dialogue."

DIAL BOOKS FOR YOUNG READERS

Penguin Young Readers Group, 345 Hudson St., New York NY 10014. **Website:** http://us.penguingroup.com. President and Publisher: Lauri Hornik. **Contact:** Kathy Dawson, associate publisher; Kate Harrison, senior editor; Liz Waniewski, editor; Alisha Niehaus, editor; Jessica Garrison, editor. Publishes 20 picture books/year; 3 young readers/year; 12 middle readers/year; 15 young adult titles/year. **How to Contact:** "Due to the overwhelming number of unsolicited manuscripts we receive, we at Dial Books for Young Readers have had to change our submissions policy: As of August 1, 2005, Dial will no longer respond to your unsolicited submission unless interested in publishing it. Please do not include SASE with your submission. You will not hear from Dial regarding the status of your submission unless we are interested, in which case you can expect a reply from us within 4 months. We accept entire picture book manuscripts and a maximum of 10 pages for longer works (novels, easy-to-reads). When submitting a portion of a longer work, please provide an accompanying cover letter that briefly describes your manuscript's plot, genre (i.e. easy-to-read, middle grade or YA novel), the intended age group, and your publishing credits, if any." **Terms:** Pays authors in royalties based on retail price. Average advance payment varies.

DIVERSION PRESS

P.O. Box 270, Campbell Hall, New York NY 10916. **E-mail:** diversion press@yahoo.com. **Website:** www.diversionpress.com. **Attn:** Acquisition Editor. Publishes hardcover, trade and mass-market paperback originals. **Fiction/Nonfiction:** "We are currently seeking young adult book proposals and young adult reference books. We also are interested in illustrated children's books." **How to Contact:** Send query/proposal first. Mss accepted by request only. "We will not review works that are sexually explicit, religious, or put children in a bad light." **Tips:** Check out *Ellabug*, our first children's book, on Diversion Press Blog.

DUTTON CHILDREN'S BOOKS

Imprint of Penguin Group (USA), Inc. 345 Hudson St., New York NY 10014. (212)4143700. **Fax:** (212)414-3397. **Website:** http://us.penguingroup.com. **Contact:** Lauri Hornik, president and publisher; Julie Strauss-Gabel, associate publisher (literary contemporary young adult fiction); Lucia Monfried, senior editor (picture books and middle grade fiction). Estab.1852. Dutton Children's Books publishes fiction and nonfiction for readers ranging from preschoolers to young adults on a variety of subjects. Publishes hardcover originals as well as novelty formats. Averages 50 titles/year. **Needs:** Dutton Children's Books has a diverse, general-interest list that includes picture books, fiction for all ages and occasional retail-appropriate nonfiction. **How to Contact:** Query letter only; include SASE. **Terms:** Pays royalty on retail price. Offers advance.

EDCON PUBLISHING GROUP

30 Montauk Blvd., Oakdale NY 11769. (631)567-7227. **Fax:** (631)567-8745. **Website:** www.edconpublishing.com. **Contact:** Editor. Publishes 6 young readers/year, 6 middle readers/year, 6 young adult titles/year. 30% of books by first-time authors. Looking for educational games and nonfiction work in the areas of math, science, reading and social studies. **Nonfiction:** Grades 1–12, though primarily 6–12 remedial. **How to Contact:** Submit outline/synopsis and 1 sample chapter. Publishes book 6 months after acceptance. Will consider simultaneous submissions. Submission kept on file unless return is requested. Include SASE for return. **Terms:** Work purchased outright from authors for up to $1,000.

EERDMANS BOOKS FOR YOUNG READERS

An imprint of Wm. B. Eerdmans Publishing Co., 2140 Oak Industrial Dr. NE, Grand Rapids, MI 49505. (616) 459-4591. **Fax:** (616) 776-7683. **E-mail:** youngreaders@eerdmans.com. **Website:** www.eerdmans.com/youngreaders. **Contact:** Acquisitions Editor. Produces 10–12 picture books/year; 2 middle readers/year; 2 young adult books/year. 10% of books by first-time authors. "We seek to engage young minds with words and pictures that inform and delight, inspire and entertain. From board books for babies to picture books, nonfiction and novels for children and young adults, our goal is to produce quality literature for a new generation of readers. We believe in books!" **Fiction:** Picture books: animal, concept, contemporary, folktales, history, humor, multicultural, nature/environment, poetry, religion, special needs, social issues, sports, suspense. Young readers: animal, concept, contemporary, fantasy, folktales, history, humor, multicultural, poetry, religion, special **Needs:**, social issues, sports, suspense. Middle readers: adventure, contemporary, history, humor, multicultural, nature/environment, problem novels, religion, social issues, sports, suspense. Young adults/teens: adventure, contemporary, fantasy, folktales, history, humor, multicultural, nature/environment, problem novels, religion, sports, suspense. Average word length: picture books-1,000; middle readers-15,000; young adult-45,000. **Nonfiction:** Middle readers: biography, history, multicultural, nature/environment, religion, social issues. Young adults/teens: biography, history, multicultural, nature/environment, religion, social issues. Average word length: middle readers-35,000; young adult books-35,000. **How to Contact:** We only consider submissions sent exclusively to Eerdmans. **YA and middle-reader fiction:** Please send query, synopsis and 3 sample chapters. Responds to exclusive queries/mss in 3–5 months. "We no longer acknowledge or respond to unsolicited manuscripts. Exceptions will be made only for exclusive submissions marked as such on outside envelope." **Terms:** Offers advance against royalties. Author sees galleys for review. Catalog available for 8×10 SASE and 4 first-class stamps. Offers writer's guidelines for SASE or see website (www.eerdmans.com/youngreaders/submit.htm). **Tips:** "Find out who Eerdmans is before submitting a manuscript. Look at our website, request a catalog, and check out our books."

FACTS ON FILE, INC.

Infobase Publishing, 132 W. 31st St., 17th Floor, New York NY 10001. (212)967-8800. **Fax:** (212)339-0326. **E-mail:** llikoff@factsonfile.com. **Website:** www.factsonfile.com. **Contact:** Laurie Likoff, editorial director (science, fashion, natural history); Frank Darmstadt (science & technology, nature, reference); Owen Lancer, senior editor (American history, women's studies); James Chambers, trade editor (health, pop culture, true crime, sports); Jeff Soloway, acquisitions editor (language/literature). Facts on File produces high-quality reference materials on a broad range of subjects for the school library market and the general nonfiction trade. Publishes hardcover originals and reprints. **Needs:** No computer books, technical books, cookbooks, biographies (except YA), pop psychology, humor, fiction or poetry. **How to Contact:** Query or submit outline and sample chapter with SASE. No submissions returned without SASE. **Tips:** "Our audience is school and public libraries for our more reference-oriented books and libraries, schools and bookstores for our less reference-oriented informational titles."

FENN PUBLISHING CO.

34 Nixon Rd., Bolton ON L7E 1W2 Canada. (905)951-6600. **Fax:** (905)951-6601. **E-mail:** fennpubs@hbfenn.com. **Website:** www. hbfenn.com. **Manuscript/Art Contact:** C. Jordan Fenn, publisher. Publishes 35 books/year. Publishes children's and young adult fiction. **Fiction:** Picture books: adventure, animal, sports. Young adult: sports. **How to Contact:** Query or submit complete ms. Responds to queries/mss in 2 months.

FLASHLIGHT PRESS

527 Empire Blvd., Brooklyn NY 11225. (718)288-8300. **Fax:** (718)972-6307. **E-mail:** editor@flashlightpress.com. **Website:** www.flashlight press.com. Estab. 2004. **Editor:** Shari Dash Greenspan. Publishes hardcover and trade paperback originals. Publishes 2–3 picture books/year. 50% of books by first-time authors. **Fiction:** Picture books: contemporary, humor, multicultural. Average word length: 1,000. "We only publish fiction—2 picture books a year, so we're extremely selective. Looking for gems." **How to Contact:** Query by e-mail only, after carefully reading our Submission Guidelines (http://flashlightpress.com/submissionguidelines.html). No e-mail attachments. "Do not send anything by snail mail. Responds to queries in 10 days; usually responds to mss in 3–4 months. **Terms:** Pays authors and illustrators royalty of 8–10% based on wholesale price. Offers advance of $500–1,000. **Tips:** "Our audience is 4–8 years old. Follow our online submissions guide."

FLUX

An imprint of Llewellyn Worldwide, Ltd., 2143 Wooddale Drive, Woodbury MN 55125. (651)312-8613. **Fax:** (651)291-1908. **Website:** www.fluxnow.com. Imprint estab. 2005; Llewellyn estab. 1901. **Contact:** Brian Farrey, acquisitions editor. Publishes 21 young adult titles/year. 50% of books by first-time authors. "Flux seeks to publish authors who see YA as a point of view, not a reading level. We look for books that try to capture a slice of teenage experience, whether in real or imagined worlds." **Fiction:** Young adults: adventure, contemporary, fantasy, history, humor, problem novels, religion, science fiction, sports, suspense. Average word length: 50,000. **How to Contact:** Query. Responds to mss in 3–4 months. Will consider simultaneous submissions and previously published work. **Terms:** Pays royalties of 10–15% based on wholesale price. Offers advance. Authors see galleys for review. Book catalog available on Website. Writer's guidelines available for SASE or on website at www.fluxnow.com.

com/submission_guidelines.php. **Tips:** "Read contemporary teen books. Be aware of what else is out there. If you don't read teen books, you probably shouldn't write them. Know your audience. Write incredibly well. Do not condescend."

FULCRUM PUBLISHING

4690 Table Mountain Drive, Suite 100, Golden CO 80403. (303)277-1623. **Fax:** (303)279-7111. **Website:** www.fulcrum-books. com. **Contact:** T. Baker, acquisitions editor. **Nonfiction:** Middle and early readers: Western history, nature/environment, Native American. **How to Contact:** Submit complete ms or submit outline/synopsis and 2 sample chapters. "Publisher does not send response letters unless we are interested in publishing." Do not send SASE. **Terms:** Pays authors royalty based on wholesale price. Offers advances. Book catalog available for 9×12 SAE and 77¢ postage; ms submission guidelines available on website under "Authors" tab. **Tips:** "Research our line first. We look for books that appeal to the school market and trade."

GAUTHIER PUBLICATIONS, INC.

Frog Legs Ink, P.O. Box 806241, Saint Clair Shores MI 48080. (586)279-1515. **E-mail:** info@gauthierpublications.com. **Website:** www.gauthierpublications.com. **Contact:** Elizabeth Gauthier, creative director (Children's/Fiction). Publishes hardcover originals and trade paperback originals. **Needs:** "We are particularly interested in mystery, thriller, graphic novels and young adult areas for the upcoming year. We do, however, consider most subjects if they are intriguing and well written." **How to Contact:** Query with SASE.

GREENE BARK PRESS

P.O. Box 1108, Bridgeport CT 06601-1108. (610)434-2802. **Fax:** (610)434-2803. **E-mail:** greenebark@aol.com; service@greene-barkpress.com. **Website:** www.greenebarkpress.com. **Fiction:** Picture books, young readers: adventure, fantasy, humor. Average word length: picture books-650; young readers-1,400. **How to Contact:** Query by mail. Responds to queries in 3 months; mss in 6 months. No response without SASE. Publishes a book 18 months after acceptance. Will consider simultaneous submissions. Prefer to review complete mss with illustrations. **Terms:** Pays authors royalty of 10–12% based on wholesale price. No advances. Sends galleys to authors. Manuscript guidelines available for SASE or per e-mail request. **Tips:** "As a guide for future publications, look to our latest publications, do not look to our older backlist. Please, no telephone, e-mail or fax queries."

GROSSET & DUNLAP PUBLISHERS

An imprint of Penguin Group (USA), Inc. 345 Hudson St., New York NY 10014. **Website:** http://us.penguingroup.com/youngreaders. Estab. 1898. **Contact:** Francesco Sedita, vice president/publisher. Publishes approximately 140 titles/year. "Grosset & Dunlap publishes high-interest, affordable books for children ages 0–10 years. We focus on original series, licensed properties, readers and novelty books." **How to Contact:** "We do not accept e-mail submissions. Unsolicited manuscripts usually receive a response in 6–8 weeks."

GROUNDWOOD BOOKS

110 Spadina Ave., Suite 801, Toronto ON M5V 2K4 Canada. (416)363-4343. **Fax:** (416)363-1017. **Website:** www.groundwood books.com. **Contact:** Acquisitions Editor. Publishes 10 picture books/year; 3 young readers/year; 5 middle readers/year; 5 young adult titles/year, approximately 2 nonfiction titles/year. 10% of books by first-time authors. **How to Contact:** Submit synopsis and sample chapters. Responds to mss in 6–8 months. Will consider simultaneous submissions. **Terms:** Offers advances. Sends galleys to authors. Backlist available on website. **Tips:** "Try to familiarize yourself with our list before submitting to judge whether or not your work is appropriate for Groundwood. Visit our website for guidelines."

H & W PUBLISHING INC

531 Conrad Dr., Cincinnati OH 45231. Estab. 2007. (513)675-2968. **Fax:** (513)761-4221. **E-mail:** info@handwpublishing.com. **Website:** www.handwpublishing.com. Specializes in African American children's literature. Publishes 2 books/year. 90% of books by first-time authors. "Our company empowers, inspires and uplifts." **Fiction:** Picture Books: concept, contemporary, humor, poetry, religion. Young Readers: adventure, contemporary, nature/environment, poetry. Middle Readers: contemporary, problem novels. Average word length: picture books-1,200; young readers-850; middle readers-2,500. **Nonfiction:** Young Readers: biography, social issues. Average word length: picture books-700; young readers-1,200.) **How to Contact:** Submit complete manuscript or submit outline/synopsis. Responds to queries in 1 month. Responds to mss in 2 months. Publishes a book 18 months after acceptance. **Terms:** Pays authors royalty 5% and work purchased outright for $2,500–4,000. Writer's and artist's guidelines available at www.handwpublishing.com. **Tips:** "We specialize in literature for African American children. Illustrations should be detailed and reflect positive images. Story lines should either be humorous, contemporary, or teach without being preachy. No books on slavery please."

HACHAI PUBLISHING

527 Empire Blvd., Brooklyn NY 11225. (718)633-0100. **Fax:** (718)633-0103. **E-mail:** info@hachai.com; hachai1@aol.com. **Website:** www.hachai.com. Publishes 4 picture books/year; 1 young reader/year; 1 middle reader/year. 75% of books published by first-time authors. "All books have spiritual/religious themes, specifically traditional Jewish content. We're seeking books about morals and values; the Jewish experience in current and Biblical times; and Jewish observance, Sabbath and holidays." **Contact:** Devorah Leah Rosenfeld, submissions editor. **Fiction:** Picture books and young readers: contemporary, historical fiction, religion. Middle readers: adventure, contemporary, problem novels, religion. Does not want to see fantasy, animal stories, romance, problem novels depicting drug use or violence. **How to Contact:** Submit complete ms. Responds to queries/mss in 6 weeks. **Terms:** Work purchased outright from authors for $800–1,000. Book catalog, ms guidelines available for SASE. **Tips:** "Write a story that incorporates a moral, not a preachy morality tale. Originality is the key. We feel Hachai publications will

appeal to a wider readership as parents become more interested in positive values for their children."

HEALTH PRESS NA INC

P.O. Box 37470, Albuquerque NM 87176-7479. (505)888-1394 or (877)411-0707. **Fax:** (505)888-1521. **E-mail:** goodbooks@healthpress.com. **Website:** www.healthpress.com. **Contact:** Editor. Publishes 4 young readers/year. 50% of books by first-time authors. **Fiction:** Picture books, young readers: health, special needs. Average word length: young readers-1,000–1,500; middle readers-1,000–3,000. **Nonfiction:** Picture books, young readers: health, special needs:, social issues, self-help. **How to Contact:** Submit complete ms. Responds in 3 month. Publishes a book 1 year after acceptance. Will consider simultaneous submissions. **Terms:** Pays authors royalty. Sends galleys to authors. Book catalog available.

HOLIDAY HOUSE INC.

425 Madison Ave., New York NY 10017. (212)688-0085. **Fax:** (212)421-6134. **Website:** www.holidayhouse.com. Publishes 35 picture books/year; 3 young readers/year; 15 middle readers/year; 8 young adult titles/year. 20% of books by first-time authors; 10% from agented writers. Mission Statement: "To publish high-quality books for children." **Nonfiction:** All levels, but more picture books and fewer middle-grade nonfiction titles: animal, biography, concept, contemporary, geography, historical, math, multicultural, music/dance, nature/environment, religion, science, social issues. **How to Contact:** Send complete manuscript to the Acquisitions Editor. "We respond only to manuscripts that meet our current needs." **Terms:** Pays authors an advance against royalties. Book catalog, ms guidelines available for SASE. **Tips:** "We need books with strong stories, writing and art. We do not publish board books or novelties. No easy readers."

ILLUMINATION ARTS

P.O. Box 1865, Bellevue WA 98009. (425)644-7185. **Fax:** (425)644-9274. **E-mail:** liteinfo@illumin.com. **Website:** www.illumin.com. **Contact:** Ruth Thompson, editorial director. **Fiction:** Word length: Prefers under 1,000, but will consider up to 1,500 words. **How to Contact:** Submit complete ms. Responds to queries in 3 months with SASE only. No electronic or CD submissions for text or art. Publishes a book 1–2 years after acceptance. Will consider simultaneous submissions. **Terms:** Pays authors royalty based on wholesale price. Book fliers available for SASE. **Tips:** "Read our books and follow our guidelines. Be patient. The market is competitive. We receive 2,000 submissions annually and publish 2–3 books a year. Sorry, we are unable to track unsolicited submissions."

IMPACT PUBLISHERS, INC.

P.O. Box 6016, Atascadero CA 93423-6016. (805)466-5917. **E-mail:** submissions@impactpublishers.com. **Website:** www.impact publishers.com. **Contact:** Freeman Porter, submissions editor. Imprints: Little Imp Books, Rebuilding Books, The Practical Therapist Series. Publishes 1 young reader/year; 1 middle reader/year; 1 young adult title/year. 20% of books by first-time authors. "Our purpose is to make the best human-services expertise available to the widest possible audience. We publish only popular psychology and self-help materials written in everyday language by professionals with advanced degrees and significant experience in the human services." **Nonfiction:** Young readers, middle readers, young adults: self-help. **How to Contact:** Query or submit complete ms, cover letter, résumé. Responds to queries in 12 weeks; mss in 3 months. Will consider simultaneous submissions or previously published work. **Terms:** Pays authors royalty of 10–12%. Offers advances. Book catalog available for #10 SAE with 2 first-class stamps; ms guidelines available for SASE. All imprints included in a single catalog. **Tips:** "Please do not submit fiction, poetry or narratives."

JOURNEY STONE CREATIONS

3533 Danbury Rd., Fairfield OH 45014. Estab 2004. (513)860-5616. **Fax:** (513)860-0176. **E-mail:** pat@jscbookscom. **Website:** www.jscbooks.com. "We specialize in children's book publishing. Over the last five years, we have published 57 books and are now focusing on special markets and private label products. We are also creating customized books for numerous national and regional organizations. Anyone who has a message and wants that message delivered to children is our potential client. We will write, illustrate and publish a book with your message to kids. Our new clients include grocery chains, hospitals, banks, safety organizations, ecology and animal-rights organizations and the entertainment business." **Fiction:** Picture books: adventure, animal, contemporary, history, humor, multicultural, nature/environment, poetry, religion, sports. Early readers: adventure, animal, contemporary, health, history, humor, multicultural, nature/environment, poetry, religion, sports, suspense. "We are not accepting middle readers at this time." Word length: picture books-1,200 or fewer; early readers-5,000 or fewer. **How to Contact:** Query only after reviewing **Needs:** on website. Reports on queries in 4–6 weeks. Publishes a book up to 2 years after acceptance. Accepts simultaneous and electronic submissions. "At this time we are only accepting picture books and early-reader books with fewer than 5,000 words. We are reviewing books for publication 12–18 months away. However, we are seeking only specific topics and themes. *Do not submit without first checking our website.*" **Terms:** Author payment negotiable based on project price or prefers to purchase work outright. Book catalog available on website. Writer's guidelines available on website. **Tips:** "Make sure you submit only your best work. For writers, if it is not letter perfect, we don't want to see it. Review our guidelines. We cannot stress the importance of submitting only after you have read our needs. Don't waste your time and money submitting things we do not need. We are only publishing children's fiction/non-fiction, no adult or teen fiction at this time."

JOURNEYFORTH

An imprint of Bob Jones University Press. 1700 Wade Hampton Blvd., Greenville SC 29614. (803)242-5100, ext. 4350. **Fax:** (864)298-0268. **E-mail:** jb@bjupress.com. **Website:** www.bjupress.com. Specializes in trade books. **Acquisitions Editor:** Nancy Lohr. Publishes 1 picture book/year; 2 young readers/year; 4 middle readers/year; 4 young adult titles/year. 10% of books by first-time authors. "We aim to produce well-written books for readers of varying abilities and interests and fully consistent with biblical worldview." **Fiction:** Young readers, middle readers, young adults: adventure, animal, contemporary, fantasy, folktales, history, humor, multicultural, nature/environment, problem novels, suspense/mystery. Average word length: young readers-10,000–12,000; middle readers-10,000–40,000; young adult/teens-40,000–60,000. **Nonfiction:** Young readers, middle readers, young adult: biography. Average word length: young readers-10,000–12,000; middle readers-10,000–40,000; young adult/teens-40,000–60,000. **How to Contact:** Query or submit outline/synopsis and 5 sample chapters. "Do not send stories with magical elements. We are not currently accepting picture books. We do not publish: romance, science fiction, poetry or drama." Responds to queries in 4 weeks; mss in 3 months. Publishes book 12–15 months after acceptance. Will consider previously published work. **Terms:** Pays authors royalty based on wholesale price. Book catalog and writers guidelines are at www.bjupress.com/books/freelance.html. **Tips:** "Review our backlist to be sure your work is a good fit."

KAEDEN BOOKS

P.O. Box 16190, Rocky River OH 44116-6190. **E-mail:** lstenger@kaeden.com. **Website:** www.kaeden.com. **Contact:** Lisa Stenger, editor. Kaeden Books produces high-quality children's books for the educational market. **Fiction:** Stories with humor, surprise endings and interesting characters suitable for the educational market. "Must have well-developed plots with clear beginnings, middles and endings. No adult or religious themes." Word count range: 25–2,000. **Nonfiction:** Unique, interesting topics, supported with details and accurate facts. Word count range: 25–2,000. Submit complete ms; include SASE. Do not send originals. Responds within 1 year. For complete guidelines see www.kaeden.com. No phone calls, please. **Terms:** Work purchased outright from authors. Pays royalties to previous authors. **Tips:** "We are particularly interested in humorous stories with surprise endings and beginning chapter books."

KAR-BEN PUBLISHING, INC.

A division of Lerner Publishing Group, Inc., 241 First Ave. N., Minneapolis, MN 55401. (612)332-3344. **Fax:** (612)-332-7615. **E-mail:** editorial@karben.com. **Website:** www.karben.com. **Contact:** Joni Sussman, publisher. Publishes 10–15 books/year (mostly picture books). 20% of books by first-time authors. All of Kar-Ben's books are on Jewish themes for young children and families. **Fiction:** Picture books: adventure, concept, folktales, history, humor, multicultural, religion, special needs; must be on a Jewish theme. Average word length: picture books-1,000. **Nonfiction:** Picture books, young readers: activity books, arts/crafts, biography, careers, concept, cooking, history, how-to, multicultural, religion, social issues, special needs; must be of Jewish interest. **How to Contact:** Submit complete ms. Responds to queries/mss in 6 weeks. Publishes a book 24–36 months after acceptance. Will consider simultaneous submissions. **Terms:** Pays authors royalties of 3–5% of net against advance of $500–1,000; or purchased outright. Book catalog free on request.

Manuscript guidelines on website. **Tips:** Looks for books for young children with Jewish interest and content, modern, nonsexist, not didactic. **Fiction:** or nonfiction with a Jewish theme can be serious or humorous, life cycle, Bible story, or holiday related. Looking in particular for stories that reflect the ethnic and cultural diversity of today's Jewish family."

LEE & LOW BOOKS INC.

95 Madison Ave., New York NY 10016-7801. (212)779-4400. **Fax:** (212)683-1894. **E-mail:** info@leeandlow.com; lmay@leeandlow.com. **Website:** www.leeandlow.com. **Contact:** Louise May, vice president/editorial director; Emily Hazel, assistant editor. Publishes 12-14 children's books/year. 25% of books by first-time authors. Lee & Low Books publishes books with diverse themes. "One of our goals is to discover new talent and produce books that reflect the diverse society in which we live." **Fiction:** Picture books, young readers: anthology, contemporary, history, multicultural, poetry. "We are not considering folktales or animal stories." Picture book, middle reader: contemporary, history, multicultural, nature/environment, poetry, sports. Average word length: picture books-1,000-1,500. **Nonfiction:** Picture books: concept. Picture books, middle readers: biography, history, multicultural, science and sports. Average word length: picture books-1,500-3,000. **How to Contact:** Submit complete ms. No e-mail submissions. Responds within 6 months, only if interested. Publishes a book 2-3 years after acceptance. Will consider simultaneous submissions. Guidelines on website. **Terms:** Pays authors advances against royalty. Book catalog available for 9×12 SAE and $1.68 postage; catalog and ms guidelines available via website or with SASE. **Tips:** "We strongly urge writers to visit our website and familiarize themselves with our list before submitting. Materials will only be returned with SASE."

LEGACY PRESS

P.O. Box 261129, San Diego CA 92196. (858) 277-1167. **Website:** www.legacypresskids.com. **Contact:** Editorial Department. Publishes 3 young readers/year; 3 middle readers/year; 3 young adult titles/year. Publishes nonfiction, Bible-teaching books. "We publish books that build a legacy in kids' faith, targeting kids ages 2-12. **Nonfiction:**, devotional, journals, guidebooks, young readers, middle readers, young adults. **Nonfiction:** Young readers, middle readers, young adults: reference, religion. **How to Contact:** Submit outline/synopsis and 3-5 sample chapters. Will consider simultaneous submissions and previously published work. **Terms:** Pays authors royalty or work purchased outright. Offers advances. **Tips:** "Become familiar with our products and get to know the Christian bookstore market. We are looking for innovative ways to encourage and teach children about the Christian life."

LILY RUTH PUBLISHING

P.O. Box 2067, Jacksonville TX 75766. (903)715-0740. **Fax:** (903)737-9748. **E-mail:** lilyruthpublishing@yahoo.com. **Website:** www.lilyruthpublishing.com. Estab. 2008. Specializes in fiction. **Contact:** Jennifer L. Stone. Publishes 2 middle readers/year. 75% of books by first-time authors. "Here at Lily Ruth Publishing we believe that literature

for children should be, above all, fun. Strong stories from authors with unique voices are what make reading entertaining and exciting, inspiring a love of reading that will last a lifetime." **Fiction:** Early and middle readers: adventure, fantasy, history, humor. Young adults/Teens: adventure, fantasy, humor. Average word length: middle readers-25,000; young adults-50,000. **How to Contact:** Query or submit outline/synopsis and 3 sample chapters. Responds to queries in 3 months; mss in 3 months. Publishes a book 6 months-1 year after acceptance. Will consider simultaneous submissions. **Terms:** Pays authors 10-15% based on retail price. Sends galleys to authors. Catalog available on website.

MAGICAL CHILD

Shades of White, 301 Tenth Ave., Crystal City MO 63019. (314)740-0361. **E-mail:** acquisition@magicalchildbooks.com. **Website:** www.magicalchildbooks.com. Estab. 2007. Specializes in trade books, fiction. **Contact:** Acquisitions Editor. Publishes 1-3 picture books/year; 1-3 young readers/year; 1-3 middle readers/year. 80% of books by first-time authors. "The Neo-Pagan Earth Religions Community is the fastest growing demographic in the spiritual landscape, and Pagan parents are crying out for books appropriate for Pagan kids. It is our plan to fill this small, but growing need." **Fiction:** Picture books: adventure, contemporary, nature/environment. Young Readers: adventure, contemporary, nature/environment. Middle Readers: adventure, contemporary, nature/environment. *Submit only stories appropriate for Earth Religions NOT Native American.* Average word length: picture books-500-800; young readers-500-4,500; middle readers-11,200-28,000. **Nonfiction:** Middle readers: biography, history (earth religions only for both). Average word length: middle readers-11,200-28,000. **How to Contact:** Query or submit outline/synopsis for picture books only; submit outline/synopsis and 3 sample chapters for all other categories. Responds to queries 3 weeks; mss in 3-6 months. Publishes a book 18+ months after acceptance. Will consider simultaneous submissions. **Terms:** Pays authors royalty based on retail price. Offers advances. Sends galleys to authors. Originals returned to artist at job's completion. Book catalog available for SASE (envelope size #10 and 1 first-class stamp); all imprints included in single catalog. **Tips:** "Visit our submissions guidelines on the website. Follow the information provided there. We expect our authors to take an active role in promoting their books. If you can't do that, please don't submit your manuscript. No calls, please. Our list is very specific. We only publish books for the earth religions market. Please do not send us manuscripts outside of our requested needs."

MASTER BOOKS

Imprint of New Leaf Publishing Group, Inc., P.O. Box 726, Green Forest, AR 72638. (870)438-5288. **Fax:** (870)438-5120. **E-mail:** nlp@newleafpress.net. **Website:** www.nlpg.com, www.masterbooks.net. **Contact:** Craig Froman, acquisitions editor. 3 young readers/year; 3 middle readers/year; 2 young adult titles/year. 10% of books by first-time authors. **Nonfiction:** Picture books: activity books, animal, nature/environment, creation. Young readers, middle readers, young adults: activity books, animal, Christian biography, nature/environment, science, creation. **How to Contact:** Submission guidelines at our website. Responds to queries/mss in 4 months. Publishes book 1 year after acceptance. Will consider simultaneous submissions. Must download submissions form from website. **Terms:** Pays authors royalty of 3–15% based on wholesale price. Sends galleys to authors. Book catalog and ms guidelines available on website. **Tips:** "All of our children's books are creation-based, including topics from the Book of Genesis. We look also for home-school educational material that would be supplementary to a home-school curriculum."

MEADOWBROOK PRESS

5451 Smetana Dr., Minnetonka MN 55343-9012. (952)930-1100. **Fax:** (952)930-1940. **Website:** www.meadowbrookpress.com. **Contact:** Submissions Editor. 20% of books by first-time authors; 10% of books from agented writers. Publishes children's poetry books, activity books, arts-and-crafts books and how-to books. "Meadowbrook does not accept unsolicited children's picture books, short stories or novels. We are primarily a nonfiction press. We offer specific guidelines for children's poetry. Be sure to specify the type of project you have in mind when requesting guidelines." **Nonfiction:** Publishes activity books, arts/crafts, how-to, poetry. Average word length: varies. **How to Contact:** See guidelines on website before submitting. Responds only if interested. Publishes a book 1–2 years after acceptance. Will consider simultaneous submissions. **Terms:** Pays authors royalty of 5–7% based on retail price. Offers average advance payment of $1,000–3,000. Book catalog available for 5×11 SASE and 2 first-class stamps; ms guidelines available for SASE. **Tips:** "Writers should visit our website before submitting their work to us. Writers should also ote the style and content patterns of our books. No phone calls; please-e-mail us. We work with the printed word and will respond more effectively to your questions if we have something in front of us."

MERIWETHER PUBLISHING LTD.

885 Elkton Dr., Colorado Springs CO 80907-3557. (719)594-9916. **Fax:** (719)594-9916. **E-mail:** editor@meriwether.com. **Website:** www.meriwetherpublishing.com. **Contact:** Ted Zapel, comedy plays and educational drama; Rhonda Wray, religious drama. 75% of books by first-time authors; 5% of books from agented writers. "Our niche is drama. Our books cover a wide variety of theatre subjects from play anthologies to theater craft. We publish books of monologs, duologs, short one-act plays, scenes for students, acting textbooks, how-to speech and theatre textbooks, improvisation and theatre games. Our Christian books cover worship on such topics as clown ministry, storytelling, banner-making, drama ministry, children's worship and more. We also publish anthologies of Christian sketches. We do not publish works of fiction or devotionals." **Fiction:** Middle readers, young adults: anthology, contemporary, humor, religion. "We publish plays, not prose-fiction. Our emphasis is comedy plays instead of educational themes." **Nonfiction:** Middle readers: activity books, how-to, religion, textbooks. Young adults: activity books, drama/theater arts, how-to church activities, religion. Average length: 250 pages. **How**

to Contact: Query or submit outline/synopsis and sample chapters. Responds to queries in 3 weeks; mss in 2 months or less. Publishes a book 6–12 months after acceptance. Will consider simultaneous submissions. **Terms:** Pays authors royalty of 10% based on retail or wholesale price. Book catalog for SAE and $2 postage; ms guidelines for SAE and 1 first-class stamp. **Tips:** "We are currently interested in finding unique treatments for theater arts subjects: scene books, how-to books, musical comedy scripts, monologs and short comedy plays for teens."

MILKWEED EDITIONS

1011 Washington Ave. S. Suite 300, Minneapolis MN 55415-1246. (612)332-3192. **Fax:** (612)215-2550. **E-mail:** editor@milkweed.org. **Website:** www.milkweed.org. **Contact:** Daniel Slager, publisher. Publishes 3–4 middle readers/year. 25% of books by first-time authors. "Milkweed Editions publishes with the intention of making a humane impact on society, in the belief that literature is a transformative art uniquely able to convey the essential experiences of the human heart and spirit. To that end, Milkweed Editions publishes distinctive voices of literary merit in handsomely designed, visually dynamic books, exploring the ethical, cultural and esthetic issues that free societies need continually to address." **Fiction:** Middle readers: adventure, contemporary, fantasy, multicultural, nature/environment, suspense/mystery. Does not want to see folktales, health, hi-lo, picture books, poetry, religion, romance, sports. Average length: middle readers-90–200 pages. **How to Contact:** Use Submissions Manager online at www.milkweed.org. Publishes a book 1 year after acceptance. Will consider simultaneous submissions. **Terms:** Pays authors variable royalty based on retail price. Offers advance against royalties. Sends galleys to authors. Book catalog available for $1.50 to cover postage; ms guidelines available for SASE or at website.

MIRRORSTONE

P.O. Box 707, Renton WA 98057. (425)254-2287. **Website:** www.mirrorstonebooks.com. **Contact:** Nina Hess. Publishes 6 middle readers/year; 4 young adult titles/year. 5% of books by first-time authors. "We publish fantasy novels for young readers based on the lore of the Dungeons & Dragons role-playing game." **Fiction:** Young readers, middle readers, young adult: fantasy only. Average word length: middle readers-30,000–40,000; young adults-60,000–75,000. **How to Contact:** Query with samples, writing credits. "No manuscripts, please." Responds to queries if interested. Publishes book 9–24 months after acceptance. **Terms:** Pays authors royalty of 4–6% based on retail price. Offers advances (average amount: $4,000). Ms guidelines available on our website. All imprints included in a single catalog. Catalog available on website. Editorial staff attended or plans to attend ALA Conference.

ONSTAGE PUBLISHING

190 Lime Quarry Road, Suite 106J, Madison AL 35758-8962. (256)461-0661. **E-mail:** onstage123@knology.net. **Website:** www.onstagepublishing.com. **Contact:** Dianne Hamilton. Publishes 1–2 middle readers/year; 1–2 young adult titles/year. 80% of books by first-time authors. **Fiction:** Middle readers: adventure, contempo-

rary, fantasy, history, nature/environment, science fiction, suspense/mystery. Young adults: adventure, contemporary, fantasy, history, humor, science fiction, suspense/mystery. Average word length: chapter books-4,000–6,000; middle readers-5,000 and up; young adults-25,000 and up. "We do not produce picture books." **How to Contact:** Send complete ms if under 20,000 words, otherwise send synopsis and first 3 chapters. Responds to queries/mss in 6–8 months. Publishes a book 1–2 years after acceptance. Will consider simultaneous submissions. **Terms:** Pays authors advance plus royalties. Sends galleys to authors. Catalog available on website. **Tips:** "Study our titles and get a sense of the kind of books we publish, so that you know whether your project is likely to be right for us."

OUR SUNDAY VISITOR, INC.

200 Noll Plaza, Huntington IN 46750. **Website:** www.osv.com. **Contact:** Jacquelyn Lindsey, David Dziena and Bert Ghezzi. Publishes religious, educational, parenting, reference and biographies. OSV is dedicated to providing books, periodicals and other products that serve the Catholic Church. "Our Sunday Visitor, Inc. is publishing only those children's books that tie in to sacramental preparation and Catholic identity. Contact the acquisitions editor for manuscript guidelines." **Nonfiction:** Picture books, middle readers, young readers, young adults. **How to Contact:** Query, submit complete ms, or submit outline/synopsis and 2–3 sample chapters. Responds to queries/mss in 2 months. Publishes a book 18–24 months after acceptance. Will consider simultaneous submissions, electronic submissions via disk or modem, previously published work. **Terms:** Pays authors royalty of 10–12% net. Sends page proofs to authors. Book catalog available for SASE; ms guidelines available for SASE and online at www.osv.com. **Tips:** "Stay in accordance with our guidelines."

PACIFIC PRESS

P.O. Box 5353, Nampa ID 83653-5353. (208)465-2500. **Fax:** (208)465-2531. **E-mail:** booksubmissions@pacificpress.com. **Website:** www.pacificpress.com/writers/books.htm. **Contact:** Scott Cady. Publishes 1 picture book/year; 2 young readers/year; 2 middle readers/year. 5% of books by first-time authors. "Pacific Press brings the Bible and Christian lifestyle to children." **Fiction:** Picture books, young readers, middle readers, young adults: religious subjects only. No fantasy. Average word length: picture books-100; young readers-1,000; middle readers-15,000; young adults-40,000. **Nonfiction:** Picture books, young readers, middle readers, young adults: religion. Average word length: picture books-100; young readers-1,000; middle readers-15,000; young adults-40,000. **How to Contact:** Query or submit outline/synopsis and 3 sample chapters. Responds to queries in 3 months; mss in 1 year. Publishes a book 6–12 months after acceptance. Will consider e-mail submissions. **Terms:** Pays author royalty of 6–15% based on wholesale price. Offers advances (average amount: $1,500). Sends galleys to authors. Manuscript guidelines for SASE. Catalog available on website (www.adventistbookcenter.com). **Tips:** "Pacific Press is owned by the Seventh-day Adventist Church. The Press rejects all material that is not Bible-based."

PELICAN PUBLISHING CO. INC.

1000 Burmaster St., Gretna LA 70053-2246. (504)368-1175. **Website:** www.pelicanpub.com. **Contact:** Nina Kooij, editor-in-chief. **Art Contact:** Terry Callaway, production manager. Publishes 20 young readers/year; 3 middle readers/year. 4% of books from agented writers. "Pelican publishes hardcover and trade paperback originals and reprints. Our children's books (illustrated and otherwise) include history, biography, holiday and regional. Pelican's mission is 'to publish books of quality and permanence that enrich the lives of those who read them.'" **Fiction/Nonfiction:** Young readers: history, holiday, science, multicultural and regional. Middle readers: Louisiana history. Multicultural needs include stories about African Americans, Irish Americans, Jews, Asian Americans and Hispanics. Does not want animal stories, general Christmas stories, "day at school" or "accept yourself" stories. Maximum word length: young readers-1,100; middle readers-40,000. **How to Contact:** Query. Responds to queries in 1 month; mss in 3 months. Publishes a book 9–18 months after acceptance. **Terms:** Pays authors in royalties; buys ms outright "rarely." Sends galleys to authors. Book catalog and ms guidelines available on website. **Tips:** "No anthropomorphic stories, pet stories (fiction or nonfiction), fantasy, poetry, science fiction or romance. Writers: be as original as possible. Develop characters that lend themselves to series and always be thinking of new and interesting situations for those series. Give your story a strong hook—something that will appeal to a well-defined audience. There is a lot of competition out there for general themes. We look for stories with specific hooks and audiences, and writers who actively promote their work."

PHILOMEL BOOKS

An imprint of Penguin Young Readers Group (USA), 345 Hudson St., New York NY 10014. (212)414-3610. **Website:** http://us.penguingroup.com. **Contact:** submissions editor. Publishes 8–10 picture books/year; 15–18 middle grades/year; 5 young readers/year. 5% of books by first-time authors; 80% of books from agented writers. "We look for beautifully written, engaging manuscripts for children and young adults." **Fiction:** All levels: adventure, animal, boys, contemporary, fantasy, folktales, historical fiction, humor, sports, multicultural. Middle readers, young adults: problem novels, science fiction, suspense/mystery. No concept picture books, mass-market "character" books, or series. Average word length: picture books-1,000; young readers-1,500; middle readers-14,000; young adult-20,000. **Nonfiction:** Picture books. **How to Contact:** "Philomel will no longer respond to your unsolicited submission unless interested in publishing it. Please *do not* include a self-addressed stamped envelope with your submission. You will not hear from Philomel regarding the status of your submission unless we are interested in publishing it, in which case you can expect a reply from us within approximately four months. We regret that we cannot respond personally to each submission, but rest assured that we do make every effort to consider each and every one we receive." **Terms:** Pays authors in royalties. Average advance payment "varies." Sends galleys to authors. Book catalog, ms guidelines free on request with SASE (9×12 envelope for catalog). **Tips:** Wants "unique fiction or nonfiction with a strong voice and lasting quality. Discover your own voice and own story and persevere." Looks for "something unusual, original, well written. Fine art or illustrative art that feels unique. The genre (fantasy, contemporary, or historical fiction) is not so important as the story itself and the spirited life the story allows its main character."

PIANO PRESS

P.O. Box 85, Del Mar CA 92014-0085. (619)884-1401. **Fax:** (858)755-1104. **E-mail:** pianopress@pianopress.com. **Website:** www.pianopress.com. **Contact:** Elizabeth C. Axford, M.A, editor. "We publish music-related books, either fiction or nonfiction, coloring books, songbooks and poetry." **Fiction:** Picture books, young readers, middle readers, young adults: folktales, multicultural, poetry, music. **Nonfiction:** Picture books, young readers, middle readers, young adults: multicultural, music/dance. **How to Contact:** Query. Responds to queries in 3 months; mss in 6 months. Publishes a book 1 year after acceptance. Will consider simultaneous submissions, electronic submissions via disk or modem. **Terms:** Pays authors royalty of 5–10% based on retail price. Sends galleys to authors. Book catalog available for #10 SASE and 2 first-class stamps. All imprints included in a single catalog. Catalog also available on website. **Tips:** "We are looking for music-related material only for any juvenile market. Please do not send non-music-related materials. Query first before submitting anything."

PICCADILLY PRESS

5 Castle Rd., London NW1 8PR United Kingdom. (44)(207)267-4492. **Fax:** (44)(207)267-4493. **E-mail:** books@piccadillypress. co.uk. **Website:** www.piccadillypress.co.uk. **Fiction:** Picture books: animal, contemporary, fantasy, nature/environment. Young adults: contemporary, humor, problem novels. Average word length: picture books-500–1,000; young adults-25,000–35,000. **Nonfiction:** Young adults: self-help (humorous). Average word length: young adults-25,000–35,000. **How to Contact: Fiction:** Submit complete ms for picture books or submit outline/synopsis and 2 sample chapters for YA. Enclose a brief cover letter and SASE for reply. **Nonfiction:** Submit outline/synopsis and 2 sample chapters. Responds to mss in approximately 6 weeks. **Tips:** "Keep a copy of your manuscript on file."

RAZORBILL

An imprint of Penguin Group, 345 Hudson Street, New York NY 10014. Imprint estab. 2003. (212)414-3448. **Fax:** (212)414-3343. **E-mail:** razorbill@us.penguingroup.com. Website: www.razorbill books.com. Specializes in fiction. **Contact:** Gillian Levinson, editorial assistant; Jessica Rothenberg, Brianne Mulligan, editors. Publishes about 30 middle-grade and YA titles/year. "This division of Penguin Young Readers is looking for the best and the most original of commercial contemporary fiction titles for middle grade and YA readers. A select quantity of nonfiction titles will also be considered." **Fiction:** Middle readers: adventure, contemporary, graphic novels, fantasy, humor, problem novels. Young adults/teens: adventure, contemporary, fantasy, graphic novels, humor, multicultural, suspense, paranormal, science fiction, dystopian, literary, romance.

Average word length: middle readers-40,000; young adult-60,000. **Nonfiction:** Middle readers and Young adults/teens: concept. **How to Contact:** Submit outline/synopsis and 3 sample chapters along with query and SASE. Responds to queries/mss in 1–3 months. Publishes a book 1–2 years after acceptance. Will consider e-mail submissions and simultaneous submissions. **Terms:** Offers advance against royalties. Authors see galleys for review. Catalog available online at www.razorbillbooks.com. **Tips:** "New writers will have the best chance of acceptance and publication with original, contemporary material that boasts a distinctive voice and a well-articulated world. Check out www.razorbillbooks.com to get a better idea of what we're looking for."

SEEDLING PUBLICATIONS, INC.

Continental Press, Inc., 520 E. Bainbridge St., Elizabethtown PA 17022. (800)233-0759. **E-mail:** lsalem@jinl.com. **Website:** www. continentalpress.com. **Contact:** Megan Bergonzi, managing editor. "We are an education niche publisher, producing books for beginning readers. Stories must include language that is natural to young children and story lines that are interesting to 5–7-year-olds and written at their beginning reading level. Continental Press's Seedling product line focuses on fiction and nonfiction leveled readers and other materials that support early literacy in prekindergarten through second grade. Familiarity with reading recovery, guided reading and other reading intervention programs will give you a sense of the kinds of materials needed for Seedling products." Publishes Seedling books in an 8-, 12-, or 16-page format for beginning readers. Receives 450 mss/year. **Needs:** Science, math or social studies concepts are considered. **How to Contact:** Submit complete ms. Does not accept mss or queries via fax or e-mail. **Tips:** "Follow our guidelines. Do not submit full-length picture books or chapter books. We are an education niche publisher. Our books are for children, ages 5–7, who are just beginning to read independently. We do not accept stories that rhyme or poetry at this time. Try your manuscript with young readers. Listen for text that doesn't flow when the child reads the story. Rewrite until the text sounds natural to beginning readers. Visit our website to be sure your manuscript fits our market."

STERLING PUBLISHING

387 Park Ave. S., 11th Floor, New York NY 10016-8810. (212)532-7160. **Fax:** (212)213-2495. **Website:** www.sterlingpub.com. **Contact:** Category Editor (i.e., Children's Editor). Publishes hardcover and paperback originals and reprints. **Needs:** "Sterling publishes highly illustrated, accessible, hands-on, practical books for adults and children. At present we do not publish fiction." **How to Contact:** "For children's books, please submit full manuscripts. We do not accept electronic (e-mail) submissions. Be sure to include information about yourself with particular regard to your skills and qualifications in the subject area of your submission. It is helpful for us to know your publishing history—whether or not you've written other books and, if so, the name of the publisher and whether those books are currently in print."

SYLVAN DELL PUBLISHING

976 Houston Northcutt Blvd., Suite 3, Mt. Pleasant SC 29464. **Website:** www.sylvandellpublishing.com. **Contact:** Donna German, editor. Publishes hardcover, trade paperback and electronic originals. Receives 2,000 mss/year. **Needs:** "The picture books we publish are usually, but not always, fictional stories that relate to animals, nature, the environment and science. All books should subtly convey an educational theme through a warm story that is fun to read and that will grab a child's attention. Each book has a 3–5 page *For Creative Minds* section to reinforce the educational component. This section will have a craft and/or game as well as 'fun facts' to be shared by the parent, teacher or other adult. Authors do not need to supply this information. Mss should be <1,500 words and meet all of the following criteria: (1) Fun to read (mostly fiction with nonfiction facts woven into the story); (2) National or regional in scope; (3) Must tie into early elementary school curriculum; (4) Must be marketable through a niche market such as a zoo, aquarium or museum gift shop. We are not looking for mss about pets (dogs or cats in particular), new babies, local or state-specific, magic, biographies, history-related, ABC books, poetry, series, young adult books or novels, holiday-related books. We do not consider mss that have been previously published in any way, including e-books or self-published." **How to Contact:** We only accept e-submissions. **Tips:** "We want the children excited about the books. We envision the books being used at home and in the classroom."

TANGLEWOOD BOOKS

P.O. Box 3009, Terre Haute IN 47803. **Website:** www.tanglewood books.com. **Acquisitions Editor:** Erica Bennet. Produces 2–3 picture books/year, 1–2 middle readers/year, 1–2 young adult titles/year. 20% of books by first-time authors. "Tanglewood Press strives to publish entertaining, kid-centric books." **Fiction:** Picture books: adventure, animal, concept, contemporary, fantasy, humor. Average word length: picture books-800. **How to Contact:** Accepts international submissions. Query with 3–5 sample chapters. Responds to mss in up to 18 months. Publishes book 2 years after acceptance. Considers simultaneous submissions. For ms/illustration packages: Send ms with sample illustrations. Submit ms/illustration packages to Peggy Tierney, publisher. **Terms:** Royalty of 3–5% for picture books. Author sees galleys for review. **Tips:** "Please see lengthy 'Submissions' page on our website."

TILBURY HOUSE, PUBLISHERS

103 Brunswick Ave., Gardiner ME 04345. (207)582-1899. **Fax:** (207)582-8227. **E-mail:** karen@tilburyhouse.com. **Website:** www.tilburyhouse.com. **Publisher:** Jennifer Bunting. **Children's Book Editors:** Audrey Maynard, Karen Fisk. Publishes 2–4 picture book/year. **Fiction:** Picture books, young readers, middle readers: multicultural, nature/environment. Special needs include books that teach children about tolerance and honoring diversity. **Nonfiction:** Picture books, young readers, middle readers: multicultural, nature/environment. **How to Contact:** Submit complete ms or outline/synopsis. Responds to queries/mss in 1 month. Publishes a book 1–2 years after accep-

tance. Will consider simultaneous submissions "with notification." **Terms:** Pays authors royalty based on wholesale price. Sends galleys to authors. Book catalog available for SAE and postage. **Tips:** "We are always interested in stories that will encourage children to understand the natural world and the environment, as well as stories with social justice themes. We really like stories that engage children to become problem solvers as well as those that promote respect, tolerance and compassion. We do not publish books with personified animal characters, historical fiction, chapter books or fantasy."

TRICYCLE PRESS

P.O. Box 7123, Berkeley CA 94707. **Website:** www.tenspeed.com. **Contact:** Nicole Geiger, publisher. Publishes 14–18 picture books/year; 2–4 middle readers/year; 3 board books/year. 25% of books by first-time authors. Press looks for something outside the mainstream; books that encourage children to look at the world from a different angle. "We publish high-quality trade books." **Fiction:** Board books, picture books, young readers: concept. Middle grade: literary fiction, high-quality contemporary, fantasy, history, multicultural, nature, poetry, suspense/mystery; no mass-market fiction. Average word length: picture books-500–1,000. **Nonfiction:** Picture books, middle readers: animal, arts/crafts, biography, careers, concept, cooking, history, how-to, multicultural, music/dance, nature/environment, science. **How to Contact:** All submissions must come with an SASE. Submit complete ms for picture books. Submit outline/synopsis and 2–3 sample chapters for middle grade, young adult and longer nonfiction. Responds to mss in 4–6 months. Publishes a book 1–2 years after acceptance. Welcomes simultaneous submissions. No electronic or faxed submissions. **Terms:** Pays authors royalty of 7.5% based on net receipts. Offers advances. Sends galleys of novels to authors. Book catalog for 9×12 SASE (3 first-class stamps). Manuscript guidelines for SASE (5 first-class stamps). Manuscript guidelines available at website. **Tips:** "We are looking for something a bit outside the mainstream and with lasting appeal (no one-shot-wonders)."

TWO LIVES PUBLISHING

191 Water St., Ambler PA 19002. (609)502-8147. **Fax:** (610)717-1460. **E-mail:** bcombs@twolives.com. **Website:** www.twolives.com. **Contact:** Bobbie Combs. Publishes 1 picture book/year; 1 middle reader/year. 100% of books by first-time authors. "We create books for children whose parents are lesbian, gay, bisexual or transgender. We only want stories featuring children and their gay or lesbian parents." **Fiction:** Picture books, young readers, middle readers: contemporary. **How to Contact:** Query. Responds to queries/mss in 3 months. Publishes book 2–3 years after acceptance. Will consider e-mail submissions, simultaneous submissions, previously published work. **Terms:** Pays authors royalty of 5–10% based on retail price. Offers advances (average amount: $250). Sends galleys to authors. Catalog available on website.

UNTAPPED TALENT LLC

P.O. Box 396, Hershey PA 17033-0396. (717)707-0720. **E-mail:** rena@unt2.com. **Website:** www.unt2.com. **Contact:** Rena Wilson Fox (areas of interest: nonfiction, children's lit, fiction, middle grade).

"As a new publishing company, we only have published four titles, not enough for a catalog. Please feel free to view the books at our website." Publishes hardcover, trade & mass-market paperbacks, electronic originals. Receives 2,000 queries, 400 mss/yr. **Fiction:** "We have a strong interest in historical fiction. We are looking for books that are current and fully formulated, modern interpretations—even if the story takes place in the past." **How to Contact:** Submit proposal package with synopsis, 4 sample chapters and any background information pertinent to the story. **Tips:** Follow website instruction, make query brief; if 4 chapters are not many pages, add more; submit to acquisitions editor only.

WEIGL PUBLISHERS INC.

350 5th Ave., 59th floor, New York NY 10118-0069. (866)649-3445. **Fax:** (866)449-3445. **E-mail:** linda@weigl.com. **Website:** www.weigl.com. **Contact:** Heather Hudak. Publishes 25 young readers/year; 40 middle readers/year; 20 young adult titles/year. 15% of books by first-time authors. "Our mission is to provide innovative high-quality learning resources for schools and libraries worldwide at a competitive price." **Nonfiction:** Young readers: animal, biography, geography, history, multicultural, nature/environment, science. Middle readers: animal, biography, geography, history, multicultural, nature/environment, science, social issues, sports. Young adults: biography, careers, geography, history, multicultural, nature/environment, social issues. Average word length: young readers-100 words/page; middle readers-200 words/page; young adults-300 words/page. **How to Contact:** Query by e-mail only. Publishes book 6-9 months after acceptance. Will consider simultaneous submissions. **Terms:** Work purchased outright from authors. Book catalog available for SASE or available on website.

WESTERN PSYCHOLOGICAL SERVICES

12031 Wilshire Blvd., Los Angeles CA 90025. (310)478-2061. **Fax:** (310)478-7838. **E-mail:** bthomas@wpspublish.com. **Website:** www.wpspublish.com. **Contact:** Brian Thomas, marketing manager. "Western Psychological Services publishes psychological and educational assessments that practitioners trust. Our products allow professionals to accurately screen, diagnose and treat people in need. WPS publishes practical books and games used by therapists, counselors, social workers and others in the helping professions who work with children and adults." Publishes psychological and educational assessments and some trade paperback originals. Receives 60 queries/year; 30 mss/year. **Needs:** Children's books dealing with feelings, anger, social skills, autism, family problems, etc. **How to Contact:** Submit complete ms.

WILLIAMSON BOOKS

An imprint of Ideals Publications, 2636 Elm Hill Pike, Ste. 120, Nashville TN 37214. **Website:** www.idealsbooks.com. **Manuscript and Art Contact:** Williamson Books Submission. Publishes 2-4 titles/year. 50% of books by first-time authors; 10% of books from agented authors. Publishes "very successful nonfiction series (Kids Can! series) on subjects such as history, science, arts/crafts, geog-

raphy, diversity, multiculturalism; Little Hands series for ages 2-6; Kaleidoscope Kids series (age 7 and up) and Quick Starts for Kids! series (ages 8 and up). Our goal is to help every child fulfill his/her potential and experience personal growth." **Nonfiction:** Hands-on active learning books, animals, African American, arts/crafts, Asian, biography, diversity, careers, geography, health, history, hobbies, how-to, math, multicultural, music/dance, nature/environment, Native American, science, writing and journaling. Does not want to see textbooks, picture books, fiction. "Looking for all things African American, Asian American, Hispanic, Latino and Native American, including crafts and traditions, as well as their history, biographies and personal retrospectives of growing up in U.S. for grades pre K-8th. We are looking for books in which learning and doing are inseparable." **How to Contact:** Query with annotated TOC/synopsis and 1 sample chapter. Responds to queries/mss in 4 months. Publishes book "about 1 year" after acceptance. Writers may send an SASE for guidelines or reply to submission. **Terms:** Pays authors advance against future royalties based on wholesale price or purchases outright. Sends galleys to authors. **Tips:** "Please do not send any fiction or picture books of any kind; those should go to Ideals Children's Books. Look at our books to see what we do. We're interested in interactive learning books with a creative approach packed with interesting information, written for young readers ages 3-7 and 8-14. In nonfiction children's publishing, we are looking for authors with a depth of knowledge shared with children through a warm, embracing style. Our publishing philosophy is based on the idea that all children can succeed and have positive learning experiences. Children's lasting learning experiences involve their participation."

WORDSONG

An imprint of Boyds Mills Press, Inc. 815 Church St., Honesdale PA 18431. **Website:** www.wordsongpoetry.com. Estab. 1990. 5% of books from agented writers. "We publish fresh voices in contemporary poetry." **Needs:** All levels: All types of quality children's poetry. **How to Contact:** Submit complete ms or submit through agent. Label package "Manuscript Submission" and include SASE. "Please send a book-length collection of your own poems. Do not send an initial query." Responds in 3 months. **Terms:** Authors paid royalty or work purchased outright. Offers advances. Ms guidelines available on website. **Tips:** "Collections of original poetry, not anthologies, are our biggest need at this time. Keep in mind that the strongest collections demonstrate a facility with multiple poetic forms and offer fresh images and insights. Check to see what's already on the market and on our website before submitting."

ZUMAYA PUBLICATIONS, LLC

3209 S. Interstate 35, #1086, Austin TX 78741. **E-mail:** acquisitions@zumayapublications.com. **Website:** www.zumayapublications.com. **Contact:** Elizabeth Burton, executive editor. Publishes trade paperback and electronic originals and reprints. 1,000 queries received/year. 100 mss received/year. **Fiction:** "We are currently oversupplied with speculative fiction and are reviewing submissions in SF, fantasy and paranormal suspense by invitation only. We are much in need of GLBT and YA/middle grade, historical and western, New Age/inspirational (no overtly Christian materials, please), non-category romance, thrillers. As with nonfiction, we encourage people to review what we've already published so as to avoid sending us more of the same, at least, insofar as the plot is concerned. While we're always looking for good specific mysteries, we want original concepts rather than slightly altered versions of what we've already published." **How to Contact:** Electronic query only. **Tips:** "We're catering to readers who may have loved last year's best seller but not enough to want to read 10 more just like it. Have something different. If it does not fit standard pigeonholes, that's a plus. On the other hand, it has to have an audience. And if you're not prepared to work with us on promotion and marketing, it would be better to look elsewhere."

CHAPTER 35

CONTESTS & AWARDS

FICTION

ANNUAL GIVAL PRESS NOVEL AWARD

Gival Press, LLC, P.O. Box 3812, Arlington VA 22203. (703)351-0079. **E-mail:** givalpress@yahoo.com. **Contact:** Robert L. Giron. "Offered annually for a previously unpublished original novel (not a translation). It must be in English with at least 30,000-100,000 words of literary quality. Guidelines online, via e-mail, or by mail with SASE." **Deadline:** May 30. Charges $50 (USD) reading fee. **Prize:** $3,000, plus publication of book with a standard contract.

ANNUAL GIVAL PRESS SHORT STORY AWARD

Gival Press, LLC, P.O. Box 3812, Arlington VA 22203. (703)351-0079. **E-mail:** givalpress@yahoo.com. **Website:** www.givalpress.com. **Contact:** Robert L. Giron. "Offered annually for a previously unpublished original short story (not a translation). It must be in English with at least 5,000-15,000 words of literary quality. Guidelines by mail with SASE, by e-mail, or online." **Deadline:** August 8. Charges $25 (USD) reading fee. **Prize:** $1,000, plus publication on website. The editor narrows entries to the top ten; previous winner chooses the top 5 and the winner—all done anonymously.

BARD FICTION PRIZE

Bard College, P.O. Box 5000, Annandale-on-Hudson NY 12504-5000. (845)758-7087. **E-mail:** bfp@bard.edu. Estab. 2001. Open to younger American writers. "The Bard Fiction Prize is intended to encourage and support young writers of fiction to pursue their creative goals and to provide an opportunity to work in a fertile and intellectual environment." **Deadline:** July 15. **Prize:** $30,000 and appointment as writer-in-residence at Bard College for 1 semester.

BINGHAMTON UNIVERSITY JOHN GARDNER FICTION BOOK AWARD

Binghamton University, Dept. of English, General Literature & Rhetoric, P.O. Box 6000, Binghamton NY 13902-6000. (607)777-2713. **Contact:** Maria Mazziotti Gillan, creative writing prog. director. Estab. 2001. "Contest offered annually for a novel or collection of fiction published in previous year. Offered annually for a novel or collection of short stories published that year in a press run of 500 copies or more. Each book submitted must be accompanied by an application form. Publisher may submit more than 1 book for prize consideration. Send 3 copies of each book. Guidelines available online or for SASE." **Deadline:** March 1. **Prize:** $1,000. Judged by professional writer not on Binghamton University faculty.

BONOMO MEMORIAL LITERATURE PRIZE

Italian Americana, URI/CCE, 80 Washington St., Providence RI 02908-1803. (401)277-5306. **Fax:** (401)277-5100. **E-mail:** bonomo al@etal.uri.edu or it.americana@yahoo.com. **Website:** www.italian americana.com. **Contact:** Carol Bonomo Albright, editor. Offered annually for the best fiction, essay, or memoir that is published annually by an Italian-American. Send submission of 20 pages maximum, double-spaced in duplicate to be considered for publication/prize. Acquires first North American serial rights.

THE ALEXANDER PATTERSON CAPPON FICTION AWARD

New Letters, University of Missouri-Kansas City, 5101 Rockhill Rd., Kansas City MO 64110. (816)235-1168. **Fax:** (816)235-2611. **E-mail:** newletters@umkc.edu. **Contact:** Ashley Kaine. Offered annually for unpublished work to discover and reward new and upcoming writers. Buys first North American serial rights. Open to any writer. **Deadline:** May 18. Charges $15 (includes cost of a 1-year subscription). **Prize:** 1st Place: $1,500 and publication in a volume of New Letters; runner-up will receive a complimentary copy of a recent book of poetry or fiction courtesy of BkMk Press. All entries will be given consideration for publication in future issues of New Letters.

G. S. SHARAT CHANDRA PRIZE FOR SHORT FICTION

BkMk Press, University of Missouri-Kansas City, 5100 Rockhill Rd., Kansas City MO 64110-2499. (816)235-2558. **Fax:** (816)235-2611. **E-mail:** bkmk@umkc.edu. **Website:** www.umkc.edu/bkmk. "Offered annually for the best book-length ms collection (unpublished) of short fiction in English by a living author. Translations are not eligible. Initial judging is done by a network of published writers. Final judging is done by a writer of national reputation. Guidelines for SASE, by e-mail, or on website." **Deadline:** January 15 (postmarked). Charges $25 fee. **Prize:** $1,000, plus book publication by BkMk Press.

DARK OAK MYSTERY CONTEST

Oak Tree Press, 140 E. Palmer St., Taylorville IL 62568. (217)824-6500. **E-mail:** oaktreepub@aol.com. **Contact:** Editor (prefers email contact). Offered annually for an unpublished mystery manuscript (up to 85,000 words) of any sort from police procedurals to amateur sleuth novels. Acquires first North American, audio and film rights to winning entry. Open to authors not published in the past 3 years. **Deadline:** July 31. Charges $35/mss. **Prize:** Publishing Agreement, and launch of the title.

WILLIAM F. DEECK MALICE DOMESTIC GRANTS FOR UNPUBLISHED WRITERS

Malice Domestic, P.O. Box 8007, Gaithersburg MD 20898-8007. **E-mail:** grants@malicedomestic.org. **Contact:** Harriet Sackler. Offered annually for unpublished work in the mystery field. Malice awards up to 2 grants to unpublished writers in the malice domestic genre at its annual convention in May. The competition is designed to help the next generation of malice authors get their first work published and to foster quality malice literature. Malice domestic literature is loosely described as mystery stories of the Agatha Christie type, i.e., traditional mysteries. These works usually feature no excessive gore, gratuitous violence, or explicit sex. Writers who have been published previously in the mystery field, including publication of a mystery novel, short story, ordramatic work, are ineligible to apply. Members of the Malice Domestic Board of Directors and their families are ineligible to apply. Malice encourages applications from minority candidates. Guidelines online. **Deadline:** November 15. **Prize:** $1,500, plus a comprehensive registration to the following year's convention and two nights' lodging at the convention hotel.

JACK DYER FICTION PRIZE

Crab Orchard Review, Dept. of English, Southern Illinois Univ. Carbondale, Carbondale IL 62901-4503. **E-mail:** jtribble@siu.edu. **Contact:** Jon C. Tribble, man. editor. "Offered annually for unpublished short fiction. Crab Orchard Review acquires first North American serial rights to all submitted work. Open to any writer. Open to US citizens only." March 1 - April 30. Charges $10/entry (can enter up to 3 stories, each story submitted requires a separate fee and can be up to 6,000 words), which includes one copy of Crab Orchard Review featuring the winners. **Prize:** $1,500 and publication.

THE FAR HORIZONS AWARD FOR SHORT FICTION

The Malahat Review, University of Victoria,, P.O. Box 1700, Stn CSC, Victoria BC V8W 2Y2 Canada. (250)721-8524. **Fax:** (250)472-5051. **E-mail:** malahat@uvic.ca. **Website:** www.malahatreview.ca. **Contact:** John Barton, Editor. Open to "emerging short fiction writers from Canada, the United States, and elsewhere" who have not yet published their fiction in a full-length book (48 pages or more). Submissions must be unpublished. No simultaneous submissions. Submit one piece of short fiction, 3,500 words maximum; no restrictions on subject matter or aesthetic approach. Include separate page with author's name, address, e-mail, and title; no identifying information on mss. pages. No e-mail submissions. Do not include SASE for results; mss. will not be returned. Guidelines available on website. **Deadline:** May 1 of odd-numbered years. Charges $25 CAD for Canadian entries, $30 USD for US entries; $45 USD from Mexico and outside North America; includes a one-year subscription to The Malahat Review. **Prize:** Offers $500 CAD, publication in Fall issue of *The Malahat Review* and payment at the rate of $40 per printed page upon publication. Announced in Fall on website, Facebook page, and in quarterly e-newsletter, Malahat Lite.

FAW ANGELO B. NATOLI SHORT STORY COMPETITION

Fellowship of Australian Writers, P.O. Box 973, Eltham VIC 3095 Australia. **E-mail:** president@writers.asn.au. **Contact:** Awards Coordinator. Competition for a short story up to 3,000 words long. Guidelines online or for SASE. **Deadline:** 30th November; Opening date: 1st September. Charges $10. **Prize:** $800.

FAW CHRISTINA STEAD AWARD

Fellowship of Australian Writers, P.O. Box 973, Eltham VIC 3095 Australia. **E-mail:** president@writers.asn.au. **Contact:** Awards Coordinator. Annual award for a work of fiction with an Australia theme. Guidelines for SASE or online. **Deadline:** 30th November; Opening date: 1st September. Charges $15. **Prize:** $500.

FAW JENNIFER BURBIDGE SHORT STORY AWARD

Fellowship of Australian Writers, P.O. Box 973, Eltham VIC 3095 Australia. **E-mail:** president@asn.au. **Contact:** Award Co-ordinator. Award for a short story (maximum 3,000 words) dealing with any aspect of the lives of those who suffer some form of mental disability and/or the impact on their families. Guidelines online or for SASE. **Deadline:** November 30; Opening September 1. Charges $10. **Prize:** $250.

FIRSTWRITER.COM INTERNATIONAL SHORT STORY CONTEST

Website: www.firstwriter.com, United Kingdom. **Contact:** J. Paul Dyson, managing editor. "Accepts short stories up to 3,000 words on any subject and in any style." **Deadline:** April 1. Charges $7.50 for 1 short story; $12 for 2; $15 for 3; and $20 for 5. **Prize:** total about $300. Ten special commendations will also be awarded and all the winners will be published in firstwriter magazine and receive a $30 subscription voucher, allowing an annual subscription to be taken out for free All submissions are automatically considered for publication in firstwriter magazine and may be published there online. firstwriter magazine editors.

FISH UNPUBLISHED NOVEL AWARD

Fish Publishing, Durrus, Bantry, Co. Cork Ireland. **E-mail:** info@fishpublishing.com. **Website:** www.fishpublishing.com. **Contact:** Clem Cairns. A competition for the best unpublished novel entered. **Deadline:** September 30. Charges $50 USD. **Prize:** Publication of winning novel and cash. "This is not an annual award, but is run every so often."

FLASH FICTION PRIZE

National League of American Pen Women, Nob Hill, San Francisco Branch, The Webhallow House, 1544 Sweetwood Dr., Broadmoor Village CA 94015-1717. **E-mail:** pennobhill@aol.com. **Website:** www.soulmakingcontest.us. **Contact:** Eileen Malone. "Three flash fiction (short-short) stories per entry, under 500 words. Previously published material is accepted. Indicate category on each story. Identify only with 3×5 card. Open annually to any writer." **Deadline:** November 30. Charges $5/entry (make checks payable to NLAPW, Nob Hill Branch). **Prize:** 1st Place: $100; 2nd Place: $50; 3rd Place: $25.

GLIMMER TRAIN'S FAMILY MATTERS CONTEST

Glimmer Train Press, Inc., 1211 NW Glisan St., Suite 207, Portland OR 97209. **Fax:** (503)221-0837. **E-mail:** eds@glimmertrain.org. **Website:** www.glimmertrain.org. **Contact:** Linda Swanson-Davies. Offered for unpublished stories about family. Word count should not exceed 12,000. All shorter lengths welcome. See complete writing guidelines and submit onilne at website. Open in the months of April and October. Winners will be called two months after the close of each competition, and results announced in their respective bulletins, on their website, and in a number of additional print and online publications. Charges $15 fee/story. **Prize:** 1st Place: $1,200, publication in Glimmer Train Stories, and 20 copies of that issue; 2nd Place: $500; 3rd Place: $300.

GLIMMER TRAIN'S FICTION OPEN

Glimmer Train, Inc., Glimmer Train Press, Inc., 1211 NW Glisan St., Suite 207, Portland OR 97209. (503)221-0836. **Fax:** (503)221-0837. **E-mail:** eds@glimmertrain.org. **Website:** www.glimmertrain.org. **Contact:** Linda Swanson-Davies. "Open to all writers. No theme restrictions. Word count range: 2000-20,000. See complete writing guidelines and submit online at website. Open all during the months of March, June, September and December. Winners will be called 2 months after the close of each competition and results will be announced in their respective bulletin month, on their website, and in a number of additional print and online publications." Charges $20/story. **Prize:** 1st Place: $2,000, publication in Glimmer Train Stories, and 20 copies of that issue; 2nd Place: $1,000 and consideration for publication; 3rd Place: $600.

GLIMMER TRAIN'S SHORT-STORY AWARD FOR NEW WRITERS

Glimmer Train Press, Inc., 1211 NW Glisan St., Suite 207, Portland OR 97209. (503)221-0836. **Fax:** (503)221-0837. **E-mail:** eds@glimmertrain.org. **Website:** www.glimmertrain.org. **Contact:** Linda Swanson-Davies. "Offered for any writer whose fiction hasn't appeared in a nationally distributed print publication with a circulation over 5,000. Word count: should not exceed 12,000 words. All shorter lengths welcome. Open quarterly during the months of February, May, August, and November. See complete writing guidelines and submit online at website. Winners will be called 2 months after the close of each competition, and results will be announced in their respective bulletin month, on their website, and in a number of additional print and online publications." Charges $15 fee/story. **Prize:** Winner receives $1,200, publication in Glimmer Train Stories, and 20 copies of that issue; 2nd Place: $500; 3rd Place: $300.

GLIMMER TRAIN'S VERY SHORT FICTION AWARD (JANUARY)

Glimmer Train Press, Inc., 1211 NW Glisan St., #207, Portland OR 97209. (503)221-0836. **Fax:** (503)221-0837. **E-mail:** eds@glimmertrain.org. **Website:** www.glimmertrain.org. **Contact:** Linda Swanson-Davies. "Offered to encourage the art of the very short story. Word count: 3,000 maximum. Open January 1-31. See complete writing guidelines and submit online at website. Winners will be called and results will be announced in their April bulletin and in a number of additional print and online publications." Charges $15 fee/story. **Prize:** Winner receives $1,200, publication in Glimmer Train Stories, and 20 copies of that issue; 2nd Place: $500; 3rd Place: $300.

GLIMMER TRAIN'S VERY SHORT FICTION CONTEST (JULY)

Glimmer Train Press, Inc., 1211 NW Glisan St., 207, Portland OR 97209. (503)221-0836. **Fax:** (503)221-0837. **E-mail:** eds@glimmertrain.org. **Contact:** Linda Swanson-Davies. "Offered to encourage the art of the very short story. Word count: 3,000 maximum. Open July 1-31. See complete writing guidelines and submit online at website. Winners will be called and results will be announced in their October bulletin, on their website, and in a number of additional print and online publications." Charges $15 fee/story. **Prize:** First Place: $1,200, publication in Glimmer Train Stories, and 20 copies of that issue; 2nd Place: $500; 3rd Place: $300.

LYNDALL HADOW/DONALD STUART SHORT STORY COMPETITION

Fellowship of Australian Writers (WA), P.O. Box 6180, Swanbourne WA 6911. (61)(8)9384-4771. **Fax:** (61)(8)9384-4854. **E-mail:** admin@fawwa.org.au. **Website:** www.fawwa.org.au. Annual contest for unpublished short stories (maximum 3,000 words). "We reserve the right to publish entries in an FAWWA publication or on its website." Guidelines online or for SASE. **Deadline:** June 1. Charges $10/story. **Prize:** 1st Place: $400; 2nd Place: $100; Highly Commended: $50.

BARRY HANNAH PRIZE FOR FICTION

The Yalobusha Review, Dept. of English, University of Mississippi, P.O. Box 1848, University MS 38677-1848. (662)915-3175. **E-mail:** yrfiction@yahoo.com. **Contact:** Fiction Editor. Annual contest for great unpublished short fiction. No online submissions. Include cover letter and SASE for results only. Name should not appear on manuscript itself. Manuscripts should not be returned. **Deadline:** November 15. Charges $10. **Prize:** $500 and publication in Yalobusha Review. Retains first North American rights. Judged by the John and Renee Grisham visiting writer. Past judges have included Tom Franklin, Padget Powell, and Jack Pendarvis.

TOM HOWARD/JOHN H. REID SHORT STORY CONTEST

c/o Winning Writers, 351 Pleasant St., PMB 222, Northampton MA 01060-3961. (866)946-9748. **E-mail:** johnreid@mail.qango.com. **Website:** www.winningwriters.com. **Contact:** John Reid. Estab. 1993. "Both unpublished and published work accepted (maximum 5,000 words). Guidelines for SASE or online." **Deadline:** March 31. Charges $15 USD/story/essay/prose work. **Prize:** 1st Place: $3,000; 2nd Place: $1,000; 3rd Place: $400; 4th Place: $250; and 6 most highly commended awards of $150 each. The top 10 entries will be published on the Winning Writers website. Judged by John H. Reid; assisted by Dee C. Konrad.

L. RON HUBBARD'S WRITERS OF THE FUTURE CONTEST

P.O. Box 1630, Los Angeles CA 90078. (323)466-3310. **E-mail:** contests@authorservicesinc.com. **Contact:** Contest Administrator. "Offered for unpublished work to find, reward, and publicize new speculative fiction writers so they may more easily attain professional writing careers." Open to new and amateur writers who have not professionally published a novel or short novel, more than 1 novelette, or more than 3 short stories. Eligible entries are short stories or novelettes (under 17,000 words) of science fiction or fantasy. Guidelines for SASE, online, or via e-mail. No entry fee. Entrants retain all rights to their stories. **Deadline:** December 31, March 31, June 30, September 30. **Prize:** Awards quarterly 1st Place: $1,000; 2nd Place: $750; and 3rd Place: $500. **Prize:** $5,000. Judged by professional writers only.

INDIANA REVIEW FICTION CONTEST

Indiana Review, Ballantine Hall 465, Indiana University, Bloomington IN 47405-7103. (812)855-9535. **Fax:** (812)855-4253. **E-mail:** inreview@indiana.edu. **Website:** www.indianareview.org. "Submit only 1 story per entry fee, 35 double-spaced pages maximum. 12 pt. font. Offered annually for unpublished work. Guidelines on website and with SASE request." **Deadline:** October. Charges $15 fee (includes a 1-year subscription). **Prize:** $1,000 Judged by guests; 2009 prize judged by Ron Carlson.

THE INNERMOONLIT AWARD FOR BEST SHORT-SHORT STORY

E-mail: timescythe11@yahoo.com. **Contact:** Brian Agincourt Massey. "Annual contest for unpublished short-short stories that do not exceed 500 words. Guidelines available online at website. No entry fee. Open to all writers 18 years and older." **Deadline:** September 1. Charges No entry fee. **Prize:** 1st Place: $100; 2nd Place: $50; 3rd Place: $25. Brian Massey.

INTERNATIONAL 3-DAY NOVEL CONTEST

200-341 Water St., Vancouver BC V6B 1B8 Canada. **E-mail:** info@3daynovel.com. **Website:** www.3daynovel.com. **Contact:** Melissa Edwards. Estab. 1977. "Offered annually for the best novel written in 3 days (Labor Day weekend). To register, send SASE (IRC if from outside Canada) for details, or entry form available online. Open to all writers. Writing may take place in any location." **Deadline:** Friday before Labor Day weekend. Charges $50 fee (lower group rates available). **Prize:** 1st place receives publication; 2nd place receives $500; 3rd place receives $100.

JERRY JAZZ MUSICIAN NEW SHORT FICTION AWARD

Jerry Jazz Musician, 2207 NE Broadway, Portland OR 97232. **E-mail:** jm@jerryjazzmusician.com. Three times a year, Jerry Jazz Musician awards a writer who submits, in our opinion, the best original, previously unpublished work of approximately 3,000-5,000 words. The winner will be announced via a mailing of our Jerry Jazz newsletter. Publishers, artists, musicians, and interested readers are among those who subscribe to the newsletter. Additionally, the work will be published on the home page of Jerry Jazz Musician and featured there for at least 4 weeks. The Jerry Jazz Musician reader tends to have interests in music, history, literature, art, film, and theater—particularly that of the counter-culture of mid-20th century America. Guidelines available online. **Deadline:** September, January, and May. **Prize:** $100 Judged by the editors of Jerry Jazz Musician.

JESSE JONES AWARD FOR FICTION

6335 W. Northwest Hwy., #618, Dallas TX 75225. (214)363-7253. **E-mail:** dpayne@smu.edu. **Contact:** Darwin Payne, president. Offered annually by Texas Institute of Letters for work published January 1-December 31 of year before award is given to recognize the writer of the best book of fiction entered in the competition. Writers must have been born in Texas, have lived in the state for at least 2 consecutive years at some time, or the subject matter of the work should be associated with the state. President changes every two years. See website for guidelines. **Deadline:** January 1. **Prize:** $6,000.

THE LAWRENCE FOUNDATION AWARD

Prairie Schooner, 201 Andrews Hall, P.O. Box 880334, Lincoln NE 68588-0334. (402)472-0911. **Fax:** (402)472-9771. **E-mail:** jengelhardt2@unlnotes.unl.edu. **Contact:** Hilda Raz. Offered annually for the best short story published in Prairie Schooner in the previous year. **Prize:** $1,000

THE LEDGE ANNUAL FICTION AWARDS COMPETITION

The Ledge Magazine, 40 Maple Avenue, Bellport NY 11713. **E-mail:** info@theledgemagazine.com. **Contact:** Timothy Monaghan, editor-in-chief. Stories must be unpublished and 7,500 words or less. There are no restrictions on form or content. Guidelines online or for SASE. **Deadline:** March 1. Charges $10/first story; $6/additional story. $20 subscription to The Ledge Magazine gains free entry for the first story. **Prize:** 1st Place: $1,000 and publication; 2nd Place: $250 and publication; 3rd Place: $100 and publication.

LITERAL LATTÉ FICTION AWARD

Literal Latté, 200 E. 10th St., Suite 240, New York NY 10003. (212)260-5532. **E-mail:** litlatte@aol.com. **Website:** www.literal-latte.com. **Contact:** Edward Estlin, contributing editor. "Award to provide talented writers with 3 essential tools for continued success: money, publication, and recognition. Offered annually for unpublished fiction (maximum 8,000 words). Guidelines for SASE, by e-mail, or online. Open to any writer." **Deadline:** January 15. **Prize:** 1st Place: $1,000 and publication in Literal Latté; 2nd Place: $300; 3rd Place: $200; also up to 7 honorable mentions.

LONG STORY CONTEST, INTERNATIONAL

White Eagle Coffee Store Press, P.O. Box 383, Fox River Grove IL 60021. (847)639-9200. **E-mail:** wecspress@aol.com. **Contact:** Frank E. Smith, publisher. "Offered annually since 1993 for unpublished work to recognize and promote long short stories of 8,000-14,000 words (about 30-50 pages). Sample of previous winner: $6.95, including postage. Open to any writer; no restrictions on materials." **Deadline:** December 15. Charges $15 fee; $10 for second story in same envelope. **Prize:** $1,000, publication, and 25 copies of chapbook.

THE MARY MACKEY SHORT STORY PRIZE

Soul-Making Literary Competition, National League of American Pen Women, Nob Hill, San Francisco Bay Area, The Webhallow House, 1544 Sweetwood Dr., Broadmoor Village CA 94015-1717. **E-mail:** pennobhill@aol.com. **Contact:** Eileen Malone. "One story/entry, up to 5,000 words. All prose works must be typed, page numbered, and double-spaced. Identify only with 3X5 card. Open annually to any writer." **Deadline:** November 30. Charges $5/entry (make checks payable to NLAPW, Nob Hill Branch). **Prize:** 1st Place: $100; 2nd Place: $50; 3rd Place: $25.

THE MALAHAT REVIEW NOVELLA PRIZE

The Malahat Review, University of Victoria, P.O. Box 1700 STN CSC, Victoria BC V8W 2Y2 Canada. (250)721-8524. **E-mail:** malahat@uvic.ca. **Contact:** John Barton, Editor. "Held in alternate years with the Long Poem Prize. Offered to promote unpublished novellas. Obtains first world rights. After publication rights revert to the author. Open to any writer." Submit novellas between 10,000 and 20,000 words in length. Include separate page with author's name, address, e-mail, and novella title; no identifying information on mss. pages. No e-mail submissions. Do NOT include SASE for results; mss. will not be returned. Guidelines available on website. **Deadline:** February 1 (even years). Charges $35 CAD fee for Canadian entrants; $40 US for American entrants; $45 US for entrants from elsewhere (includes a 1-year subscription to Malahat). **Prize:** $500, plus payment for publication ($40/page) and one year's subscription. 2008 winner: Andrew Tibbetts. Winner and finalists contacted by e-mail. Winner published in summer issue of The Malahat Review and announced on website, Facebook page, and in quarterly e-newsletter, Malahat Lite.

MILKWEED NATIONAL FICTION PRIZE

Milkweed Editions, 1011 Washington Ave. S., Suite 300, Minneapolis MN 55415. (612)332-3192. **Fax:** (612)215-2550. **Website:** www.milkweed.org. **Contact:** The Editors. Estab. 1986. "Annual award for unpublished works. Milkweed is looking for a novel, novella, or a collection of short stories written in English. Mss should be of high literary quality. Please consult submissions guidelines on website before submitting. All mss submitted to Milkweed will automatically be considered for the prize. Submission directly to the contest is no longer necessary. Writers are recommended to have previously published a book of fiction or 3 short stories (or novellas) in magazines/journals with national distribution. Catalog available on request for $1.50." **Deadline:** Open. **Prize:** Publication by Milkweed Editions and a cash advance of $5,000 against royalties agreed upon in the contractual arrangement negotiated at the time of acceptance.

C. WRIGHT MILLS AWARD

The Society for the Study of Social Problems, 901 McClung Tower, University of Tennessee, Knoxville TN 37996-0490. (865)689-1531. **Fax:** (865)689-1534. **E-mail:** mkoontz3@utk.edu. **Website:** www.sssp1.org. **Contact:** Michele Smith Koontz, administrative officer and meeting manager. "Offered annually for a book published the previous year that most effectively critically addresses an issue of contemporary public importance; brings to the topic a fresh, imaginative perspective; advances social scientific understanding of the topic; displays a theoretically informed view and empirical orientation; evinces quality in style of writing; and explicitly or implicitly contains implications for courses of action." **Deadline:** January 15. **Prize:** $500 stipend.

THE NELLIGAN PRIZE FOR SHORT FICTION

Colorado Review/Center for Literary Publishing, 9105 Campus Delivery, Dept. of English, Colorado State University, Ft. Collins CO 80523-9105. (970)491-5449. **E-mail:** creview@colostate.edu. **Contact:** Stephanie G'Schwind, editor. Offered annually to an unpublished short story. Guidelines for SASE or online. **Deadline:** March 12. Charges $15. **Prize:** $1,500 and publication of story in Colorado Review.

FRANK O'CONNOR AWARD FOR SHORT FICTION

descant, Texas Christian University's literary journal, TCU Box 297270, Fort Worth TX 76129. (817)257-6537. **Fax:** (817)257-6239. **E-mail:** descant@tcu.edu. **Contact:** Dan Williams and Alex Lemon, editors. Offered annually for unpublished short stories. Publication retains copyright but will transfer it to the author upon request. **Deadline:** September-March. **Prize:** $500.

ONCEWRITTEN.COM FICTION CONTEST

Oncewritten.com, 1850 N. Whitley Ave., #404, Hollywood CA 90028. **E-mail:** fictioncontest@oncewritten.com. **Website:** www.oncewritten.com. **Contact:** Monica Poling. The purpose of this annual contest is to find high quality short fiction to feature on the website and in Off the Press, our monthly newsletter, which is distributed specifically to people interested in reading about new authors. **Deadline:** April 30 and October 31. Charges $5/story. **Prize:** 1st Place: $100. Judged by: editor and 1 industry professional.

PATERSON FICTION PRIZE

PCCC, Poetry Center, One College Blvd., Paterson NJ 07505-1179. (973)684-6555. **Fax:** (973)523-6085. **E-mail:** mgillan@pccc.edu. **Contact:** Maria Mazziotti Gillan, executive director. Offered annually for a novel or collection of short fiction published the previous calendar year. Guidelines for SASE or online. **Deadline:** April 1. **Prize:** $1,000.

PEN/FAULKNER AWARDS FOR FICTION

PEN/Faulkner Foundation, 201 E. Capitol St., Washington DC 20003. (202)675-0345. **Fax:** (202)675-0360. **E-mail:** jneely@penfaulkner.org. **Website:** www.penfaulkner.org. **Contact:** Jessica Neely, Executive Director. Offered annually for best book-length work of fiction by an American citizen published in a calendar year. **Deadline:** October 31. **Prize:** $15,000 (one Winner); $5,000 (4 Finalists).

THE PINCH LITERARY AWARD IN FICTION

The Univ. of Memphis/Hohenberg Foundation, Dept. of English, 435 Patterson Hall, Memphis TN 38152. (901)678-4591. **E-mail:** editor@thepinchjournal.com. Offered annually for unpublished short stories of 5,000 words maximum. Guidelines for SASE or on website. **Deadline:** March 15. Charges $20/story, which is put toward a 1-year subscription for The Pinch. **Prize:** 1st Place: $1,500 and publication; 2nd Place: possible publication and 1-year subscription.

THE KATHERINE ANNE PORTER PRIZE FOR FICTION

Nimrod International Journal, The University of Tulsa, 800 S. Tucker Dr., Tulsa OK 74104. (918)631-3080. **Fax:** (918)631-3033. **E-mail:** nimrod@utulsa.edu. **Contact:** Francine Ringold. "This annual award was established to discover new, unpublished writers of vigor and talent. Open to US residents only." **Deadline:** April 30. Charges $20 (includes a 1-year subscription to Nimrod). **Prize:** 1st Place: $2,000 and publication; 2nd Place: $1,000 and publication. Nimrod retains the right to publish any submission. the Nimrod editors select the finalists and a recognized author selects the winners.

THOMAS H. RADDALL ATLANTIC FICTION PRIZE

Writers' Federation of Nova Scotia, 1113 Marginal Rd., Halifax NS B3H 4P7 Canada. (902)423-8116. **Fax:** (902)422-0881. **E-mail:** talk@writers.ns.ca. **Contact:** Nate Crawford, executive director. Estab. 1990. "Full-length books of fiction written by Atlantic Canadians, and published as a whole for the first time in the previous calendar year, are eligible. Entrants must be native or resident Atlantic Canadians who have either been born in Newfoundland, Prince Edward Island, Nova Scotia, or New Brunswick, and spent a substantial portion of their lives living there, or who have lived in 1 or a combination of these provinces for at least 24 consecutive months prior to entry deadline date." Publishers: Send 4 copies and a letter attesting to the author's status as an Atlantic Canadian, and the author's current mailing address and telephone number. To recognize the best Atlantic Canadian adult fiction. **Deadline:** First Friday in December. Charges No fee or form. **Prize:** $15,000.

THE ROGERS WRITERS' TRUST FICTION PRIZE

The Writers' Trust of Canada, 90 Richmond St. E., Suite 200, Toronto ON M5C 1P1 Canada. (416)504-8222. **Fax:** (416)504-9090. **E-mail:** info@writerstrust.com. **Contact:** Amanda Hopkins. "Awarded annually for a distinguished work of fiction—either a novel or short story collection—published within the previous year. Presented at the Writers' Trust Awards event held in Toronto each Fall. Open to Canadian citizens and permanent residents only." **Deadline:** August 6. **Prize:** $25,000 and $2,500 to four finalists.

RROFIHE TROPHY

Open City, Open City Magazine & Books, 270 Lafayette St., #1412, New York NY 10012. **Website:** http://opencity.org/rrofihe.html. **Contact:** Rick Rofihe, editor. "Seventh annual contest for an unpublished short story (up to 5,000 words). Stories should be typed, double-spaced, on 8 1/2 × 11 paper with the author's name and contact information on the first page, and name and story title on the upper right corner of remaining pages. Limit 1 submission/author. Author must not have been previously published in Open City. Enclose SASE to receive names of winner and honorable mentions. All mss are nonreturnable and will be recycled. First North American serial rights (from winner only)." **Deadline:** October 15 (postmarked).

Charges $10 (make check payable to RRofihe). **Prize:** $500, a trophy, and publication in Open City. Judge: Rick Rofihe.

SASKATCHEWAN FICTION AWARD

Saskatchewan Book Awards, Inc., 205B-2314 11th Ave., Regina SK S4P 0K1 Canada. (306)569-1585. **Fax:** (306)569-4187. **E-mail:** director@bookawards.sk.ca. **Contact:** Jackie Lay, executive director. Offered annually for work published September 15-September 14 annually. This award is presented to a Saskatchewan author for the best book of fiction (novel or short fiction), judged on the quality of writing. **Deadline:** First deadline: July 31; Final deadline: September 14. Charges $25 (Canadian). **Prize:** $2,000.

JOANNA CATHERINE SCOTT NOVEL EXCERPT PRIZE

National League of American Pen Women, Nob Hill, San Francisco Bay Area Branch, The Webhallow House, 1544 Sweetwood Dr., Broadmoor Village CA 94015-1717. **E-mail:** pennobhill@aol.com. **Contact:** Eileen Malone. "Send first chapter or the first 20 pages, whichever comes first. Include a 1-page synopsis indicating category at top of page. Identify with 3×5 card only. Open annually to any writer." **Deadline:** November 30. Charges $5/entry (make checks payable to NLAPW, Nob Hill Branch). **Prize:** 1st Place: $100; 2nd Place: $50; 3rd Place: $25.

MICHAEL SHAARA AWARD FOR EXCELLENCE IN CIVIL WAR FICTION

Civil War Institute at Gettysburg College, 300 N. Washington St., Campus Box 435, Gettysburg PA 17325. (717)337-6590. **Fax:** (717)337-6596. **E-mail:** civilwar@gettysburg.edu. Estab. 1997. "Offered annually for fiction published for the first time in January 1-December 31 of the year of the award to encourage examination of the Civil War from unique perspectives or by taking an unusual approach. All Civil War novels are eligible. To nominate a novel, send 4 copies of the novel to the address above with a cover letter. Nominations should be made by publishers, but authors and critics can nominate as well." **Deadline:** December 31. **Prize:** $5,000.

MARY WOLLSTONECRAFT SHELLEY PRIZE FOR IMAGINATIVE FICTION

Rosebud, N3310 Asje Rd., Cambridge WI 53523. (608)423-4750. **Fax:** (608)423-9976. **E-mail:** jrodclark@smallbytes.net. **Website:** www.rsbd.net. **Contact:** J. Roderick Clark, editor. Biennial (odd years) contest for unpublished stories. Entries are welcome any time. Acquires first rights. Open to any writer. **Deadline:** October 15. Charges $10/story. **Prize:** $1,000, plus publication in Rosebud. 4 runner-ups receive $100 and publication in Rosebud.

SHORT SCIENCE FICTION STORY CONTEST

Crossquarter Publishing Group, P.O. Box 23749, Santa Fe NM 87502. (505)690-3923. **Fax:** (214)975-9715. **E-mail:** contest@crossquarter.com. **Website:** www.crossquarter.com. **Contact:** Anthony Ravenscroft. Annual contest for short science fiction (up to 7,500 words) showcasing the best in the human spirit. No horror or dystopia. Guidelines and entry form available online. **Deadline:** February 15.

Charges $15; $10/each additional entry. **Prize:** 1st Place: $250; 2nd Place: $125; 3rd Place: $75; 4th Place: $50. Winners are also combined into an anthology.

24-HOUR SHORT STORY CONTEST

WritersWeekly.com, P.O. Box 2399, Bangor ME 04402. **E-mail:** writersweekly@writersweekly.com. **Contact:** Angela Hoy. "Quarterly contest in which registered entrants receive a topic at start time (usually noon CST) and have 24 hours to write a story on that topic. All submissions must be returned via e-mail. Each contest is limited to 500 people. Guidelines via e-mail or online." **Deadline:** Quarterly—see website for dates. Charges $5. **Prize:** 1st Place: $300; 2nd Place: $250; 3rd Place: $200. There are also 20 honorable mentions and 60 door prizes. The top 3 winners' entries are posted on Writers Weekly.com (non-exclusive electronic rights only). Writers retain all rights to their work. Angela Hoy (publisher of WritersWeekly.com and Booklocker.com).

WAASMODE FICTION CONTEST

Passages North, Dept. of English, Northern Michigan University, 1401 Presque Isle Ave, Marquette MI 49855. (906)227-1203. **Fax:** (906)227-1096. **E-mail:** passages@nmu.edu. **Website:** myweb. nmu.edu/~passages. **Contact:** Kate Myers Hanson. Offered every 2 years to publish new voices in literary fiction (maximum 5,000 words). Guidelines for SASE or online. **Deadline:** Submit October 15-February 15. Charges $10 reading fee/story. Make checks payable to Northern Michigan University. Send entries to Passages North. **Prize:** $1,000 and publication for winner; 2 honorable mentions are also published; all entrants receive a copy of Passages North.

WD POPULAR FICTION AWARDS

Writer's Digest, 4700 E. Galbraith Rd., Cincinnati OH 45236. (715)445-4612; ext. 13430. **E-mail:** popularfictionawards@fwmedia.com. **Contact:** Nicole Florence. Contest for 4,000-word mss in the categories of romance, mystery/crime fiction, sci-fi/fantasy, thriller/suspense, and horror. Entries must be original, in English, unpublished, and not accepted by any other publisher at the time of submission. Writer's Digest retains one-time rights to the winning entries. **Deadline:** November 1. Charges $20. **Prize:** Grand Prize: $2,500, $100 of Writer's Digest Books, ; 1st Place: $500, $100 of Writer's Digest Books, and a ms critique and marketing advice from a Writer's Digest editor; Honoroable Mentions: promotion in Writer's Digest.

GARY WILSON SHORT FICTION AWARD

descant, Texas Christian University's literary journal, TCU, Box 297270, Fort Worth TX 76129. (817)257-6537. **Fax:** (817)257-6239. **E-mail:** descant@tcu.edu. **Website:** www.descant.tcu.edu. **Contact:** David Kuhne, editor. Offered annually for an outstanding story in an issue. **Prize:** $250.

THOMAS WOLFE FICTION PRIZE

North Carolina Writers' Network, P.O. Box 898, Davidson NC 28036. (919)336-293-8844. **Fax:** (919)929-0535. **E-mail:** toabbott@ davidson.edu. **Website:** www.ncwriters.org. **Contact:** Tony Abbott, contest coordinator. Offered annually for unpublished work "to recognize a notable work of fiction—either short story or novel excerpt—while honoring one of North Carolina's best writers—Thomas Wolfe." Past judges have included Anne Tyler, Barbara Kingsolver, C. Michael Curtis and Randall Kenan. **Deadline:** TBA, please see website for guidelines. Charges $15 fee for members of the NC Writers' Network, $25 for non-members. **Prize:** $1,000 and potential publication.

TOBIAS WOLFF AWARD IN FICTION

Bellingham Review, Mail Stop 9053, Western Washington University, Bellingham WA 98225. (360)650-4863. **E-mail:** bhreview@wwu. edu. **Contact:** Brenda Miller. Offered annually for unpublished work. Guidelines for SASE or online. **Deadline:** December 1-March 15. Charges $18 entry fee for 1st entry; $10 for each additional entry. **Prize:** $1,000, plus publication and subscription. All finalists considered for publication. All entrants receive subscription.

WOW! WOMEN ON WRITING QUARTERLY FLASH FICTION CONTEST

Wow! Women on Writing, 740 S. Van Buren St., Suite D, Placentia CA 92870. **E-mail:** contestinfo@wow-womenonwriting.com. **Website:** www.wow-womenonwriting.com/contest.php. **Contact:** Angela Mackintosh, CEO. Contest offered quarterly. "We are open to all themes and genres, although we do encourage writers to take a close look at our literary agent guest judge for the season if you are serious about winning." Entries must be 250-500 words. **Deadline:** August 31, November 30, February 29, May 31. Charges $10. **Prize:** 1st Place: $250 cash prize, 1 Year Premium-Green Writers' Markets subscription ($48 value), $25 Amazon Gift Certificate, book from our sponsor, story published on WOW! Women On Writing, interview on blog; 2nd Place: $150 cash prize, 1 Year Premium-Green Writers' Markets subscription ($48 value), $25 Amazon Gift Certificate, book from our sponsor, story published on WOW! Women On Writing, interview on blog; 3rd Place: $100 cash prize, 1 Year Premium-Green Writers' Markets Subscription ($48 value), $25 Amazon gift certificate, book from our sponsor, story published on WOW! Women On Writing, interview on blog; 15 honorable mentions: $20 gift certificate from Amazon, book from our sponsor, story title and name published on WOW! Women On Writing.

WRITER'S DIGEST SHORT SHORT STORY COMPETITION

Writer's Digest, 4700 E. Galbraith Rd., Cincinnati OH 45236. (715)445-4612; ext. 13430. **Contact:** Nicole Florence. We're looking for fiction that's bold, brilliant, and brief. Send us your best in 1,500 words or fewer. All entries must be original, unpublished, and not submitted elsewhere until the winners are announced. Writer's Digest reserves one-time publication rights to the 1st-25th winning entries. **Deadline:** December 1. Charges $20. **Prize:** 1st Place: $3,000; 2nd Place: $1,500; 3rd Place: $500; 4th-10th Place: $100; 11th-25th Place: $50 gift certificate for Writer's Digest Books.

WRITERS' JOURNAL ANNUAL FICTION CONTEST

Val-Tech Media, P.O. Box 394, Perham MN 56573. (218)346-7921. **Fax:** (218)346-7924. **E-mail:** writersjournal@writersjournal.com. **Website:** www.writersjournal.com. **Contact:** Leon Ogroske (editor@writersjournal.com). Offered annually for previously unpublished fiction. Open to any writer. Guidelines for SASE or online. Writer's name must not appear on submission. A separate cover sheet must include name of contest, title, word count, and writer's name, address, phone, and e-mail (if available). **Deadline:** January 30. Charges $15 reading fee. **Prize:** Results announced in July/August. Winners notified by mail. 1st Place: $500; 2nd Place: $200; 3rd Place: $100; plus honorable mentions. Prize-winning stories and selected honorable mentions are published in the July/August Writers' Journal. A list of winners is posted on website or available for SASE. Receives fewer than 350 entries.

WRITERS' JOURNAL ANNUAL HORROR/GHOST CONTEST

Val-Tech Media, P.O. Box 394, Perham MN 56573. (218)346-7921. **Fax:** (218)346-7924. **E-mail:** writersjournal@writersjournal.com. **Website:** www.writersjournal.com. **Contact:** Leon Ogroske. "Offered annually for previously unpublished works. Open to any writer. Guidelines for SASE or online. Guidelines available for SASE, by fax, phone, e-mail, or on website and in publication. Accepts inquiries by e-mail, phone, fax. For previously unpublished works up to 2,000 words. Cover letter should include name, address, phone, e-mail, word count, and title; just title on ms. **Deadline:** March 30. Charges $7 fee. **Prize:** 1st Place: $250; 2nd Place: $100; 3rd Place: $50; plus honorable mentions. Prize-winning stories and selected honorable mentions are published in Writers' Journal. Results announced in September. Winners notified by mail. For contest results, send SASE or visit website. Receives fewer than 250 entries.

WRITERS' JOURNAL ANNUAL ROMANCE CONTEST

Val-Tech Media, P.O. Box 394, Perham MN 56573. (218)346-7921. **Fax:** (218)346-7924. **E-mail:** writersjournal@writersjournal.com. **Contact:** Leon Ogroske. "Offered annually for previously unpublished works. Open to any writer." Receives fewer than 150 entries. **Deadline:** July 30. Charges $7 fee. **Prize:** 1st Place: $250; 2nd Place: $100; 3rd Place: $50; plus honorable mentions. Prize-winning stories and selected honorable mentions are published in Writers' Journal.

WRITERS' JOURNAL ANNUAL SHORT STORY CONTEST

Val-Tech Media, P.O. Box 394, Perham MN 56573. (218)346-7921. **Fax:** (218)346-7924. **E-mail:** writersjournal@writersjournal.com. **Website:** www.writersjournal.com. **Contact:** Leon Ogroske. "Offered annually for previously unpublished short stories. Open to any writer. Guidelines for SASE or online." Receives fewer than 250 entries. **Deadline:** May 30. Charges $10 reading fee. **Prize:** 1st Place: $350; 2nd Place: $125; 3rd Place: $75; plus honorable mentions. Prize-winning stories and selected honorable mentions are published in Writers' Journal.

NONFICTION

AMWA MEDICAL BOOK AWARDS COMPETITION

American Medical Writers Association, 30 West Gude Dr., Suite 525, Rockville MD 20850-1161. (301)294-5303. **Fax:** (301)294-9006. **E-mail:** slynn@amwa.org. **Website:** www.amwa.org. **Contact:** Awards Liaison. Offered annually to honor the best medical book published in the previous year in each of 3 categories: Books for Physicians, Books for Health Care (non-physicians) Professionals, and Public Health Care Consumers. **Deadline:** March 1. Charges $50 fee.

THE BROSS PRIZE

The Bross Foundation, Lake Forest College, 555 N. Sheridan, Lake Forest IL 60045. (847)735-5175. **Fax:** (847)735-6192. **E-mail:** rmiller@lfc.edu. **Contact:** Ron Miller. Offered every 10 years for unpublished work to award the best book or treatise on the relation between any discipline or topic of investigation and the Christian religion. Next contest in 2010. Manuscripts awarded prizes become property of the college. Open to any writer. **Deadline:** September 1 of contest year. **Prize:** Award varies depending on interest earned.

JOHN BULLEN PRIZE

Canadian Historical Association, 395 Wellington St., Ottawa ON K1A 0N4 Canada. (613)233-7885. **Fax:** (613)567-3110. **E-mail:** cha-shc@lac-bac.gc.ca. Offered annually for an outstanding historical dissertation for a doctoral degree at a Canadian university. Open only to Canadian citizens or landed immigrants. **Deadline:** November 30. **Prize:** $500.

CANADIAN AUTHORS ASSOCIATION LELA COMMON AWARD FOR CANADIAN HISTORY

74 Mississaga St. E., Orillia ON L3V 1A5 Canada. (705)719-3926. **Fax:** 1(866)393-1401. **E-mail:** admin@canauthors.org. **Contact:** Anita Purcell. Offered annually for a work of historical nonfiction on a Canadian topic by a Canadian author. Entry form required. Obtain entry form from contact name or download from website. **Deadline:** December 15. Charges $35 (Canadian) entry fee. **Prize:** $2,500 and a silver medal. The CAA Awards Chair appoints a trustee for this award. That trustee selects two judges. The identities of the trustee and judges are confidential throughout the judging process. Decisions of the trustee and judges are final, and they may choose not to award a prize. A shortlist of the best three entries in each category will be announced in April 2010. The winners will be announced at the gala awards banquet during the annual CanWrite! conference in Victoria in June 2010.

CANADIAN LIBRARY ASSOCIATION STUDENT ARTICLE CONTEST

Canadian Library Association, 328 Frank St., Ottawa ON K2P 0X8 Canada. (613)232-9625, ext. 301. **Fax:** (613)563-9895. **Contact:** Valerie Delrue. Offered annually to unpublished articles discussing, analyzing, or evaluating timely issues in librarianship or information science. Open to all students registered in or recently graduated from a Canadian library school, a library techniques program, or faculty of education library program. Submissions may be in English or French. **Deadline:** March 31. **Prize:** 1st Place: $150 and trip to CLA's annual conference; 1st runner-up: $150 and $75 in CLA publications; 2nd runner-up: $100 and $75 in CLA publications.

THE DOROTHY CHURCHILL CAPPON CREATIVE NONFICTION AWARD

New Letters, University of Missouri-Kansas City, 5101 Rockhill Rd., Kansas City MO 64110. (816)235-1168. **Fax:** (816)235-2611. **E-mail:** newletters@umkc.edu. **Contact:** Ashley Kaine. Contest is offered annually for unpublished work to discover and reward emerging writers and to give experienced writers a place to try new genres. Acquires first North American serial rights. Open to any writer. Guidelines for SASE or online. **Deadline:** Third week of May. Charges $15 fee (includes cost of a 1-year subscription). **Prize:** 1st Place: $1,500 and publication in a volume of New Letters; runner-up will receive a copy of a recent book of poetry or fiction courtesy of BkMk Press. All entries will receive consideration for publication in future editions of New Letters.

MORTON N. COHEN AWARD

Modern Language Association of America, 26 Broadway, 3rd Floor, New York NY 10004-1789. (646)576-5141. **Fax:** (646)458-0030. **E-mail:** awards@mla.org. **Contact:** Coordinator of Book Prizes. Estab. 1989. Awarded in odd-numbered years for a distinguished edition of letters. At least 1 volume of the edition must have been published during the previous 2 years. Editors need not be members of the MLA. **Deadline:** May 1. **Prize:** A cash award and a certificate to be presented at the Modern Language Association's annual convention in January.

A THE SHAUGHNESSY COHEN PRIZE FOR POLITICAL WRITING

The Writers' Trust of Canada, 90 Richmond St. E., Suite 200, Toronto ON M5C 1P1 Canada. (416)504-8222. **Fax:** (416)504-9090. **E-mail:** info@writerstrust.com. **Contact:** Amanda Hopkins, program coordinator. "Awarded annually for a nonfiction book of outstanding literary merit that enlarges our understanding of contemporary Canadian political and social issues. Presented at the Politics & the Pen event each spring in Ottawa. Open to Canadian citizens and permanent residents only." **Deadline:** November 5. **Prize:** $25,000 and $2,500 to four finalists.

CARR P. COLLINS AWARD FOR NONFICTION

The Texas Institute of Letters, 6335 W. Northwest Hwy., #618, Dallas TX 75225. (214)363-7253. **E-mail:** dpayne@smu.edu. **Website:** texasinstituteofletters.org/. **Contact:** Darwin Payne. Offered annually for work published January 1-December 31 of the previous year to recognize the best nonfiction book by a writer who was born in Texas, who has lived in the state for at least 2 consecutive years at one point, or a writer whose work has some notable connection with Texas. See website for guidelines. **Deadline:** January 3. **Prize:** $5,000.

COMPETITION FOR WRITERS OF BC HISTORY

British Columbia Historical Federation, P.O. Box 5254, Station B, Victoria BC V8R 6N4 Canada. **E-mail:** info@bchistory.ca. **Website:** www.bchistory.ca. "Offered annually to nonfiction books containing a facet ofnonfiction books about BC history and published during contest year. Books become the property of BC Historical Federation." **Deadline:** December 31. **Prize:** Cash, a certificate, and an invitation to the BCHF annual conference. The contest winner receives the Lieutenant-Governor's Medal for Historical Writing.

CREATIVE NONFICTION PRIZE

National League of American Pen Women, Nob Hill, San Francisco Branch, The Webhallow House, 1544 Sweetwood Dr., Broadmoor Village CA 94015-1717. **E-mail:** pennobhill@aol.com. **Contact:** Eileen Malone. All prose works must be typed, page numbered, and double-spaced. Each entry up to 3,000 words. Identify only with 3×5 card. Open annually to any writer. **Deadline:** November 30. Charges $5/entry (make checks payable to NLAPW, Nob Hill Branch). **Prize:** 1st Place: $100; 2nd Place: $50; 3rd Place: $25.

A CUP OF COMFORT

Adams Media F+W Media,, 57 Littlefield St., Avon MA 02322. **Fax:** (508)427-6790. **E-mail:** cupofcomfort@adamsmedia.com. **Website:** www.cupofcomfort.com. "A Cup of Comfort is the best-selling book series featuring inspiring true stories about the relationships and experiences that deeply affect our lives. Stories must be true, written in English, uplifting, and appropriate for a mainstream audience. This prize includes publication in an anthology. Contest is offered 1-2 times/year. Deadline is 6-12 months prior to publication. Call for submissions and guidelines on website. Open to aspiring and published writers. Limited rights for a specified period of time; applies only to those stories selected for publication. **Prize:** $500 grand prize; $100 for all other stories published in each book (50 stories/anthology).

ANNIE DILLARD AWARD IN CREATIVE NONFICTION

Bellingham Review, Mail Stop 9053, 516 High St., Western Washington University, Bellingham WA 98225. (360)650-4863. **E-mail:** bhreview@cc.wwu.edu. **Contact:** Brenda Miller. Offered annually for unpublished essays on any subject and in any style. Guidelines for SASE or online. **Deadline:** December 1-March 15. Charges $18/1st entry, $10/additional entry. **Prize:** 1st Place: $1,000, plus publication and copies. All finalists considered for publication. All entrants receive subscription.

GORDON W. DILLON/RICHARD C. PETERSON MEMORIAL ESSAY PRIZE

American Orchid Society, Inc., 16700 AOS Ln., Delray Beach FL 33446-4351. (561)404-2040. **Fax:** (561)404-2045. **E-mail:** jmengel@aos.org;lstewart@aos.org. **Website:** www.aos.org. **Contact:** Lindsay Stewart. Estab. 1985. "Annual contest open to all writers. The theme is announced each May in Orchids magazine. All themes deal with an aspect of orchids, such as repotting, growing, hybridizing, etc. Unpublished submissions only. Themes in past years have included Orchid Culture, Orchids in Nature, and Orchids in Use. Acquires one-time rights." **Deadline:** November 30. **Prize:** Cash award and a certificate. Winning entry usually published in the May issue of Orchids magazine.

THE DONNER PRIZE

The Award for Best Book on Canadian Public Policy, The Donner Canadian Foundation, 349 Carlaw Ave., Toronto ON M4M 2T1 Canada. (416)368-8253 or (416)368-3763. **E-mail:** sherry@mdgassociates. com. **Website:** www.donnerbookprize.com. **Contact:** Sherry Naylor. "Offered annually for nonfiction published January 1-December 31 that highlights the importance of public policy and to reward excellent work in this field. Entries must be published in either English or French. Open to Canadian citizens." **Deadline:** November 30. **Prize:** $30,000; 5 shortlist authors get $5,000 each.

EDUCATOR'S AWARD

The Delta Kappa Gamma Society Intma Society Internationernational, P.O. Box 1589, Austin TX 78767-1589. (888)762-468. **Fax:** (512)478-3961. **Website:** www.deltakappagamma.net. **Contact:** Educator's Award Committee. "Offered annually for quality research and nonfiction published January-December of previous year. This award recognizes educational research and writings of female authors whose work may influence the direction of thought and action necessary to meet the needs of today's complex society. The book must be written by 1 or 2 women who are citizens of any country in which The Delta Kappa Gamma Society International is organized: Canada, Costa Rica, Denmark, Estonia, Finland, Germany, Great Britain, Guatemala, Iceland, Mexico, The Netherlands, Norway, Puerto Rico, Sweden, US. Guidelines (required) for SASE. **Deadline:** February 1. **Prize:** $2,500.

EVERETT E. EDWARDS MEMORIAL AWARD

Agricultural History, P.O. Box 5075, Minard Hall 203, NDSU, Fargo ND 58105-5075. (701)231-5831. **Fax:** (701)231-5832. **E-mail:** ndsu. agricultural.history@ndsu.nodak.edu. **Contact:** Claire Strom. Offered annually for best graduate paper written during the calendar year on any aspect of agricultural and rural studies (broadly interpreted). Open to submission by any graduate student. **Deadline:** December 31. **Prize:** $200 and publication of the paper in the scholarly journal, Agricultural History.

EVANS BIOGRAPHY & HANDCART AWARDS

Mountain West Center for Regional Studies, Utah State University, 0700 Old Main Hill, Logan UT 84322-0700. (435)797-3630. **Fax:** (435)797-3899. **E-mail:** mwc@cc.usu.edu. Estab. 1983. Offered to encourage the writing of biography about people who have played a role in Mormon Country (not the religion, the region—Intermountain West with parts of Southwestern Canada and Northwestern Mexico). Publishers or authors may nominate books. Criteria for consideration: Work must be a biography or autobiography on someone who lived in our significantly contributed to the history of the Interior West; must be submitted for consideration for publication year's award; new editions or reprints are not eligible; mss are not accepted. Submit 5 copies. **Deadline:** January 1. **Prize:** $10,000 and $1,000.

EVENT NONFICTION CONTEST

Event, The Douglas College Review, P.O. Box 2503, New Westminster BC V3L 5B2 Canada. (604)527-5293. **Fax:** (604)527-5095. **E-mail:** event@douglas.bc.ca. Offered annually for unpublished creative nonfiction. Maximum length: 5,000 words. Acquires first North American serial print rights and limited non-exclusive digital rights for the 3 winning entries. Open to any writer, except Douglas College employees. **Deadline:** April 15. Charges $29.95 entry fee, which includes 1-year subscription; American and overseas residents pay in U.S. funds. **Prize:** 3 winners will each receive $500, plus payment for publication.

DINA FEITELSON RESEARCH AWARD

International Reading Association, Division of Research & Policy, 800 Barksdale Rd., Newark DE 19714-8139. (302)731-1600, ext. 423. **Fax:** (302)731-1057. **E-mail:** research@reading.org. **Contact:** Marcella Moore. "This is an award for an exemplary work published in English in a refereed journal that reports on an empirical study investigating aspects of literacy acquisition, such as phonemic awareness, the alphabetic principle, bilingualism, or cross-cultural studies of beginning reading. Articles may be submitted for consideration by researchers, authors, et al. Copies of the applications and guidelines can be downloaded in pdf format from the website." **Deadline:** September 1. **Prize:** Monetary award and recognition at the International Reading Association's annual convention.

WALLACE K. FERGUSON PRIZE

Canadian Historical Association, 395 Wellington St., Ottawa ON K1A 0N4 Canada. (613)233-7885. **Fax:** (613)567-3110. **E-mail:** cha-shc@ lac-bac.gc.ca. **Contact:** Michel Duquet, executive coordinator. Offered to a Canadian who has published the outstanding scholarly book in a field of history other than Canadian history. Open to Canadian citizens and landed immigrants only **Deadline:** December 2. **Prize:** $1,000.

GEORGE FREEDLEY MEMORIAL AWARD

Theatre Library Association, Benjamin Rosenthal Library, Queens College, CUNY, 65-30 Kissena Blvd., Flushing NY 11367. (718)997-3672. **Fax:** (718)997-3753. **E-mail:** svallillo@comcast.net. **Contact:** Stephen M. Vallillo, book awards committee chair. Estab. 1968. Offered for a book published in the US within the previous calendar year on a subject related to live theatrical performance (including cabaret, circus, pantomime, puppetry, vaudeville, etc.). Eligible books may include biography, history, theory, criticism, reference, or related fields. **Deadline:** March 15 of year following eligibility. **Prize:** $500 and a certificate to the winner; $200 and certificate for honorable mention.

LIONEL GELBER PRIZE

Munk Center for International Studies, University of Toronto, 1 Devonshire Place, Toronto ON M5S 3K7 Canada. (416)946-8901. **Fax:** (416)946-8915. **E-mail:** gelberprize.munk@utoronto.ca. **Contact:** Prize Manager. Estab. 1989. Offered annually for the year's most outstanding work of nonfiction in the field of international relations. Books must be published in English or English translation between January 1 and December 31 of the current year, and submitted by the publisher. Publishers should submit 6 copies of each title (up to 3 titles can be submitted). **Deadline:** October 31. **Prize:** $15,000 (Canadian funds).

GOVERNOR GENERAL'S LITERARY AWARD FOR LITERARY NON-FICTION

Canada Council for the Arts, 350 Albert St., P.O. Box 1047, Ottawa ON K1P 5V8 Canada. (613)566-4414, ext. 5573. **Fax:** (613)566-4410. **Website:** www.canadacouncil.ca/prizes/ggla. **Contact:** Lori Knoll. Offered annually for the best English-language and the best French-language work of literary nonfiction by a Canadian. **Deadline:** depends on the book's publication date: Books in English: March 15, June 1 or August 7. Books in French: March 15 or July 15. **Prize:** Each laureate receives $25,000; non-winning finalists receive $1,000.

JOHN GUYON LITERARY NONFICTION PRIZE

Crab Orchard Review, English Department, Southern Illinois Univ. Carbondale, Carbondale IL 62901-4503. **E-mail:** jtribble@siu.edu. **Contact:** Jon C. Tribble, managing editor. "Offered annually for unpublished work. This competition seeks to reward excellence in the writing of creative nonfiction. This is not a prize for academic essays. Crab Orchard Review acquires first North American serial rights to submitted works. Open to US citizens only." March 1 - April 30. Charges $10/essay (limit of 3 essays of up to 6,500 words each), which includes one copy of Crab Orchard Review featuring the winners. **Prize:** $1,500 and publication.

ALBERT J. HARRIS AWARD

International Reading Association, Division of Research and Policy, 800 Barksdale Rd., Newark DE 19714-8139. (302)731-1600, ext. 423; (800)336-7323. **Fax:** (302)731-1057. **E-mail:** research@reading.org. **Contact:** Marcella Moore. "Offered annually to recognize outstanding published works focused on the identification, prevention, assessment, or instruction of learners experiencing difficulty learning to read. Articles may be nominated by researchers, authors, and others. Copies of the applications and guidelines can be downloaded in PDF format from the website." **Deadline:** September 1. **Prize:** Monetary award and recognition at the International Reading Association's annual convention.

ALEXANDER HENDERSON AWARD

Australian Institute of Genealogical Studies, 41 Railway Rd., Blackburn VIC 3130. (61)(3)9877-3789. **E-mail:** info@aigs.org. au. Award presented to the person who produced the best family history published in Australia. Each entry will remain the property of the institute and will become a part of its library collection. **Deadline:** November 30. **Prize:** Certificate and trophy. The award is judged by a panel comprised a genealogist, librarian, literary critic, and historian.

THE KIRIYAMA PRIZE

Pacific Rim Voices, 300 Third St., Suite 822, San Francisco CA 94107. (415)777-1628. **Fax:** (415)777-1646. **E-mail:** admin@kiriyamaprize.org. **Contact:** Jeannine Stronach, prize manager. Offered for work pub-lished from January 1 through December 31 of the current prize year to promote books that will contribute to greater mutual understanding and increased cooperation throughout the Pacific Rim and South Asia. Guidelines and entry form on request, or may be downloaded from the website. Books must be submitted for entry by the publisher. Proper entry forms must be submitted. **Deadline:** late Fall each year. **Prize:** $30,000 to be divided equally between the author of 1 fiction and 1 nonfiction book.

KATHERINE SINGER KOVACS PRIZE

Modern Language Association of America, 26 Broadway, 3rd Floor, New York NY 10004-1789. (646)576-5141. **Fax:** (646)458-0030. **E-mail:** awards@mla.org. **Contact:** Coordinator of Book Prizes. Estab. 1990. Offered annually for a book published during the previous year in English or Spanish in the field of Latin American and Spanish literatures and cultures. Books should be broadly interpretive works that enhance understanding of the interrelations among literature, the other arts, and society. Author must be a current member of the MLA. **Deadline:** May 1. **Prize:** A cash award and a certificate to be presented at the Modern Language Association's annual convention in January.

LINCOLN PRIZE AT GETTYSBURG COLLEGE

Gettysburg College and Lincoln & Soldiers Institute, 300 N. Washington St., Campus Box 435, Gettysburg PA 17325. (717)337-6590. **Fax:** (717)337-6596. **E-mail:** lincolnprize@gettysburg.edu. Offered annually for the "finest scholarly work in English on the era of the American Civil War. The award will usually go to a book published in the previous year; however articles, essays, and works of fiction may be submitted." Guidelines for SASE or online. **Deadline:** November 1. **Prize:** $50,000.

TONY LOTHIAN PRIZE

under the auspices of the Biographers' Club, 119a Fordwych Rd., London NW2 3NJ United Kingdom. (44)(20)8452 4993. **E-mail:** anna@annaswan.co.uk. **Contact:** Anna Swan. "Entries should consist of a 10-page synopsis and 10 pages of a sample chapter for a proposed biography. Open to any biographer who has not previously been published or commissioned or written a book." **Deadline:** August 1. Charges Entry fee: £10. **Prize:** £2,000. Judges have included Michael Holroyd, Victoria Glendinning, Selina Hastings, Frances Spalding, Lyndall Gordon, Anne de Courcy, Nigel Hamilton, Anthony Sampson, and Mary Lovell. Further details at www.bio graphersclub.co.uk.

WALTER D. LOVE PRIZE

North American Conference on British Studies, History Department, 0119 Sutherland Bldg., Penn State University, Abington PA 19001. **E-mail:** dmhirst@wustl.edu. **Contact:** Derek Hirst. "Offered annually for best article in any field of British Studies. Open to American or Canadian writers." **Deadline:** April 1. **Prize:** $150.

JAMES RUSSELL LOWELL PRIZE

Modern Language Association of America, 26 Broadway, 3rd Floor, New York NY 10004-1789. (646)576-5141. **Fax:** (646)458-0030.

E-mail: awards@mla.org. **Contact:** Coordinator of Book Prizes. Offered annually for literary or linguistic study, or critical edition or biography published in previous year. Open to MLA members only. **Deadline:** March 1. **Prize:** A cash award and a certificate to be presented at the Modern Language Association's annual convention in January.

SIR JOHN A. MACDONALD PRIZE

Canadian Historical Association, 395 Wellington St., Ottawa ON K1A 0N4 Canada. (613)233-7885. **Fax:** (613)567-3110. **E-mail:** cha-shc@lac-bac-gc.ca. **Contact:** Michel Duquet, executive coordinator. Offered annually to award a previously published nonfiction work of Canadian history judged to have made the most significant contribution to an understanding of the Canadian past. Open to Canadian citizens only. **Deadline:** December 2. **Prize:** $1,000

RICHARD J. MARGOLIS AWARD

c/o Margolis & Bloom, LLP, 535 Boylston St., 8th floor, Boston MA 02116. (617)267-9700, ext. 517. **E-mail:** harry@margolis.com. **Contact:** Harry S. Margolis. Sponsored by the Blue Mountain Center, this annual award is given to a promising new journalist or essayist whose work combines warmth, humor, wisdom, and concern with social justice. Submit 3 copies of 2 examples of your published or unpublished work (maximum 30 pages) and a short biographical note. **Deadline:** July 1. **Prize:** $5,000 and a 1-month residency at the Blue Mountain Center—a writers and artists colony in the Adirondacks in Blue Mountain Lake, New York.

HOWARD R. MARRARO PRIZE

Modern Language Association of America, 26 Broadway, 3rd Floor, New York NY 10004-1789. (646)576-5141. **Fax:** (646)458-0030. **E-mail:** awards@mla.org. **Contact:** Coordinator of Book Prizes. Offered in even-numbered years for a scholarly book or essay on any phase of Italian literature or comparative literature involving Italian, published in previous year. Authors must be members of the MLA. **Deadline:** May 1. **Prize:** A cash award and a certificate to be presented at the Modern Language Association's annual convention in January.

KENNETH W. MILDENBERGER PRIZE

Modern Language Association of America, 26 Broadway, 3rd Floor, New York NY 10004-1789. (646)576-5141. **Fax:** (646)458-0030. **E-mail:** awards@mla.org. **Contact:** Coordinator of Book Prizes. Offered annually for a publication from the previous year in the field of language culture, literacy, or literature with a strong application to the teaching of languages other than English. Author need not be a member. **Deadline:** May 1. **Prize:** A cash award, and a certificate, to be presented at the Modern Language Association's annual convention in January and a year's membership in the MLA.

MLA PRIZE FOR A DISTINGUISHED BIBLIOGRAPHY

Modern Language Association of America, 26 Broadway, 3rd Floor, New York NY 10004-1789. (646)576-5141. **Fax:** (646)458-0030. **E-mail:** awards@mla.org. **Contact:** Coordinator of Book Prizes. Offered in even-numbered years for enumerative and descriptive bibliographies published in monographic, book, or electronic format in the 2 years prior to the competition. Open to any writer or publisher. **Deadline:** May 1. **Prize:** A cash prize and a certificate to be presented at the Modern Language Association's annual convention in January.

MLA PRIZE FOR A DISTINGUISHED SCHOLARLY EDITION

Modern Language Association of America, 26 Broadway, 3rd Floor, New York NY 10004-1789. (646)576-5141. **Fax:** (646)458-0030. **E-mail:** awards@mla.org. **Contact:** Coordinator of Book Prizes. Offered in odd-numbered years. To qualify for the award, an edition should be based on an examination of all available relevant textual sources; the source texts and the edited text's deviations from them should be fully described; the edition should employ editorial principles appropriate to the materials edited, and those principles should be clearly articulated in the volume; the text should be accompanied by appropriate textual and other historical contextual information; the edition should exhibit the highest standards of accuracy in the presentation of its text and apparatus; and the text and apparatus should be presented as accessibly and elegantly as possible. Editor need not be a member of the MLA. **Deadline:** May 1. **Prize:** A cash award and a certificate to be presented at the Modern Language Association's annual convention in January.

MLA PRIZE FOR A FIRST BOOK

Modern Language Association of America, 26 Broadway, 3rd Floor, New York NY 10004-1789. (646)576-5141. **Fax:** (646)458-0030. **E-mail:** awards@mla.org. **Contact:** Coordinator of Book Prizes. Offered annually for the first book-length scholarly publication by a current member of the association. To qualify, a book must be a literary or linguistic study, a critical edition of an important work, or a critical biography. Studies dealing with literary theory, media, cultural history, and interdisciplinary topics are eligible; books that are primarily translations will not be considered. **Deadline:** April 1. **Prize:** A cash award and a certificate to be presented at the Modern Language Association's annual convention in January.

MLA PRIZE FOR INDEPENDENT SCHOLARS

Modern Language Association of America, 26 Broadway, 3rd Floor, New York NY 10004-1789. (646)576-5141. **Fax:** (646)458-0030. **E-mail:** awards@mla.org. **Contact:** Coordinator of Book Prizes. Offered annually for a book in the field of English, or another modern language, or literature published in the previous year. Authors who are enrolled in a program leading to an academic degree or who hold tenured or tenure-track positions in higher education are not eligible. Authors need not be members of MLA. Guidelines and application form for SASE. **Deadline:** May 1. **Prize:** A cash award, a certificate, and a year's membership in the MLA.

LINDA JOY MYERS MEMOIR PRIZE

National League of American Pen Women, Nob Hill, San Francisco Branch, Webhallow House, 1544 Sweetwood Dr., Broadmoor Village CA 94015-1717. **E-mail:** pennobhill@aol.com. **Contact:** Eileen Malone. "One memoir/entry, up to 3,000 words, double spaced.

Previously published material is acceptable. Indicate category on first page. Identify only with 3X5 card. Open annually to any writer." **Deadline:** November 30. Charges $5/entry (make checks payable to NLAPW, Nob Hill Branch). **Prize:** 1st Place: $100; 2nd Place $50; 3rd Place $25.

GEORGE JEAN NATHAN AWARD FOR DRAMATIC CRITICISM

Cornell University, Department of English, Goldwin Smith Hall, Ithaca NY 14853. (607)255-6801. **Fax:** (607)255-6661. **Contact:** Chair, Department of English. Offered annually to the American who has written the best piece of drama criticism during the theatrical year (July 1-June 30), whether it is an article, essay, treatise, or book. Only published work may be submitted; author must be an American citizen. **Prize:** The annual award now amounts to $10,000. In addition, the winner receives a trophy symbolic of, and attesting to, the award. **Tips:** See guidelines and entry form online at website.

NATIONAL WRITERS ASSOCIATION NONFICTION CONTEST

The National Writers Association, 10940 S. Parker Rd., #508, Parker CO 80134. (303)841-0246. **Fax:** (303)841-2607. **E-mail:** natlwritersassn@hotmail.com. **Contact:** Sandy Whelchel, director. "Annual contest to encourage writers in this creative form and to recognize those who excel in nonfiction writing." **Deadline:** December 31. Charges $18 fee. **Prize:** 1st Place: $200; 2nd Place: $100; 3rd Place: $50.

THE FREDERIC W. NESS BOOK AWARD

Association of American Colleges and Universities, 1818 R St. NW, Washington DC 20009. (202)387-3760. **Fax:** (202)265-9532. **E-mail:** info@aacu.org. **Contact:** Bethany Sutton. Offered annually for work published in the previous year. Each year the Frederic W. Ness Book Award Committee of the Association of American Colleges and Universities recognizes books which contribute to the understanding and improvement of liberal education. Guidelines for SASE or online. "Writers may nominate their own work; however, we send letters of invitation to publishers to nominate qualified books." **Deadline:** May 1. **Prize:** $2,000 and a presentation at the association's annual meeting—transportation and 1 night hotel for meeting are also provided.

OUTSTANDING DISSERTATION OF THE YEAR AWARD

International Reading Association, 800 Barksdale Rd., P.O. Box 8139, Newark DE 19714-8139. (302)731-1600, ext. 423; (800)336-7323. **Fax:** (302)731-1057. **E-mail:** research@reading.org. **Contact:** Marcella Moore. "This award is offered annually to recognize dissertations in the field of reading and literacy. Applicants must be members of the International Reading Association. Copies of the applications and guidelines can be downloaded in PDF format from the website." **Deadline:** October 1.

FRANK LAWRENCE AND HARRIET CHAPPELL OWSLEY AWARD

Southern Historical Association, Dept. of History, University of Georgia, Athens GA 30602-1602. (706)542-8848. **Fax:** (706)542-

2455. **Contact:** Southern Historical Association. Estab. 1934. Offered in odd-numbered years for recognition of a distinguished book in Southern history published in even-numbered years. Publishers usually submit the books. **Deadline:** March 1.

PRESERVATION FOUNDATION CONTESTS

The Preservation Foundation, Inc., 2213 Pennington Bend, Nashville TN 37214. **E-mail:** preserve@storyhouse.org. **Website:** www. storyhouse.org. **Contact:** Richard Loller. "Contest offered annually for unpublished nonfiction. General nonfiction category (1,500-5,000 words)—any appropriate nonfiction topic. Travel nonfiction category (1,500-5,000 words)—must be true story of trip by author or someone known personally by author. E-mail entries only (no mss). First entry in each category is free; $10 fee for each additional entry (limit 3 entries/category). Open to any previously unpublished writer. Defined as having made no more than $750 by creative writing in any previous year." **Deadline:** August 31. **Prize:** 1st Place: $100 in each category; certificates for finalists.

JAMES A. RAWLEY PRIZE

Organization of American Historians, P.O. Box 5457, 112 N. Bryan Ave., Bloomington IN 47408-5457. (812)855-7311. **Fax:** (812)855-0696. **Contact:** Award and Prize Committee Coordinator. "Offered annually for a book dealing with the history of race relations in the US. Books must have been published in the current calendar year. Guidelines available online." **Deadline:** October 1; books to be published after October 1 of the calendar year may be submitted as page proofs. **Prize:** $1,000.

PHILLIP D. REED MEMORIAL AWARD FOR OUTSTANDING WRITING ON THE SOUTHERN ENVIRONMENT

Southern Environmental Law Center, 201 W. Main St., Suite 14, Charlottesville VA 22902-5065. (434)977-4090. **Fax:** (434)977-1483. **E-mail:** cmccue@selcva.org. **Website:** www.SouthernEnvironment. org/phil_reed. **Contact:** Cathryn McCue, writing award coor. Offered annually for nonfiction pieces that most effectively tell stories about the South's environment. Categories include Journalism and Book. Entries must have been published during the previous calendar year and have a minimum of 3,000 words. Guidelines online or for SASE. **Deadline:** early January. **Prize:** $1,000 for winner in each category. See www.southernenvironment.org/about/reed_award/.

EVELYN RICHARDSON NONFICTION AWARD

Writers' Federation of Nova Scotia, 1113 Marginal Rd., Halifax NS B3H 4P7 Canada. (902)423-8116. **Fax:** (902)422-0881. **E-mail:** talk@writers.ns.ca. **Contact:** Nate Crawford, executive director. "This annual award is named for Nova Scotia writer Evelyn Richardson, whose book We Keep a Light won the Governor General's Literary Award for nonfiction in 1945. There is no entry fee or form. Full-length books of nonfiction written by Nova Scotians, and published as a whole for the first time in the previous calendar year, are eligible. Publishers: Send 4 copies and a letter attesting to the author's status as a Nova Scotian, and the author's current mailing address and telephone number." **Deadline:** First Friday in December. **Prize:** $2,000.

SASKATCHEWAN NONFICTION AWARD

Saskatchewan Book Awards, Inc., 205B-2314 11th Ave., Regina SK S4P 0K1 Canada. (306)569-1585. **Fax:** (306)569-4187. **E-mail:** director@bookawards.sk.ca. **Contact:** Jackie Lay, executive director. Offered annually for work published September 15-September 14. This award is presented to a Saskatchewan author for the best book of nonfiction, judged on the quality of writing. **Deadline:** First deadline: July 31; Final deadline: September 14. Charges $25 CAD. **Prize:** $2,000 CAD.

SASKATCHEWAN SCHOLARLY WRITING AWARD

Saskatchewan Book Awards, Inc., 205B-2314 11th Ave., Regina SK S4P 0K1 Canada. (306)569-1585. **Fax:** (306)569-4187. **E-mail:** director@bookawards.sk.ca. **Contact:** Jackie Lay, executive director. Offered annually for work published September 15-September 14 annually. This award is presented to a Saskatchewan author for the best contribution to scholarship. The work must recognize or draw on specific theoretical work within a community of scholars, and participate in the creation and transmission of knowledge. **Deadline:** First deadline: July 31; Final deadline: September 14. Charges $25 (Canadian). **Prize:** $2,000.

ALDO AND JEANNE SCAGLIONE PRIZE FOR COMPARATIVE LITERARY STUDIES

Modern Language Association of America, 26 Broadway, 3rd Floor, New York NY 10004-1789. (646)576-5141. **Fax:** (646)458-0030. **E-mail:** awards@mla.org. **Contact:** Coordinator of Book Prizes. Offered annually for outstanding scholarly work published in the preceding year in the field of comparative literary studies involving at least 2 literatures. Author must be a member of the MLA. Works of scholarship, literary history, literary criticism, and literary theory are eligible; books that are primarily translations are not eligible. **Deadline:** May 1. **Prize:** A cash award and a certificate to be presented at the Modern Language Association's annual convention in January.

ALDO AND JEANNE SCAGLIONE PRIZE FOR FRENCH AND FRANCOPHONE STUDIES

Modern Language Association of America, 26 Broadway, 3rd Floor, New York NY 10004-1789. (646)576-5141. **Fax:** (646)458-0030. **E-mail:** awards@mla.org. **Contact:** Coordinator of Book Prizes. Offered annually for work published in the preceding year that is an outstanding scholarly work in the field of French or francophone linguistic or literary studies. Author must be a member of the MLA. Works of scholarship, literary history, literary criticism, and literary theory are eligible; books that are primarily translations are not eligible. **Deadline:** May 1. **Prize:** A cash award and a certificate to be presented at the Modern Language Association's annual convention in January.

ALDO AND JEANNE SCAGLIONE PRIZE FOR ITALIAN STUDIES

Modern Language Association of America, 26 Broadway, 3rd Floor, New York NY 10004-1789. (646)576-5141. **Fax:** (646)458-0030. **E-mail:** awards@mla.org. **Contact:** Coordinator of Book Prizes. Offered in odd-numbered years for a scholarly book on any phase of Italian literature or culture, or comparative literature involving Italian, including works on literary or cultural theory, science, history, art, music, society, politics, cinema, and linguistics, preferably but not necessarily relating other disciplines to literature. Books must have been published in year prior to competition. Authors must be members of the MLA. **Deadline:** May 1. **Prize:** A cash award and a certificate to be presented at the Modern Language Association's annual convention in January.

ALDO AND JEANNE SCAGLIONE PRIZE FOR STUDIES IN GERMANIC LANGUAGES & LITERATURE

Modern Language Association of America, 26 Broadway, 3rd Floor, New York NY 10004-1789. (646)576-5141. **Fax:** (646)458-0030. **E-mail:** awards@mla.org. **Contact:** Coordinator of Book Prizes. Offered in even-numbered years for outstanding scholarly work appearing in print in the previous 2 years and written by a member of the MLA on the linguistics or literatures of the Germanic languages. Works of literary history, literary criticism, and literary theory are eligible; books that are primarily translations are not eligible. **Deadline:** May 1. **Prize:** A cash award, and a certificate to be presented at the Modern Language Association's annual convention in January.

ALDO AND JEANNE SCAGLIONE PRIZE FOR STUDIES IN SLAVIC LANGUAGES AND LITERATURES

Modern Language Association of America, 26 Broadway, 3rd Floor, New York NY 10004-1789. (646)576-5141. **Fax:** (646)458-0030. **E-mail:** awards@mla.org. **Contact:** Coordinator of Book Prizes. Offered in odd-numbered years for books published in the previous 2 years. Membership in the MLA is not required. Works of literary history, literary criticism, philology, and literary theory are eligible; books that are primarily translations are not eligible. **Deadline:** May 1. **Prize:** A cash award and a certificate to be presented at the Modern Language Association's annual convention in January.

ALDO AND JEANNE SCAGLIONE PUBLICATION AWARD FOR A MANUSCRIPT IN ITALIAN LITERARY STUDIES

Modern Language Association, 26 Broadway, 3rd Floor, New York NY 10004-1789. (646)576-5141. **Fax:** (646)458-0030. **E-mail:** awards@mla.org. **Contact:** Coordinator of Book Prizes. Awarded annually to an author of a ms dealing with any aspect of the languages and literatures of Italy, including medieval Latin and comparative studies, or intellectual history if main thrust is clearly related to the humanities. Materials from ancient Rome are eligible if related to postclassical developments. Also translations of classical works of prose and poetry produced in Italy prior to 1900 in any language (i.e., neo-Latin, Greek) or in a dialect of Italian (i.e., Neapolitan, Roman, Sicilian). Work can be in English or Italian. Authors must be members of the MLA and currently reside in the US or Canada. **Deadline:** August 1. **Prize:** A cash award and a certificate to be presented at the Modern Language Association's annual convention in January.

MINA P. SHAUGHNESSY PRIZE

Modern Language Association of America, 26 Broadway, 3rd Floor, New York NY 10004-1789. (646)576-5141. **Fax:** (646)458-0030. **E-mail:** awards@mla.org. **Contact:** Coordinator of Book Prizes. Offered annually for a scholarly book in the fields of language, culture, literacy or literature with strong application to the teaching of English published during preceding year. Authors need not be members of the MLA. **Deadline:** May 1. **Prize:** A cash prize, a certificate, to be presented at the Modern Language Association's annual convention in January, and a one-year membership in the MLA.

FRANCIS B. SIMKINS AWARD

Southern Historical Association, Dept. of History, University of Georgia, Athens GA 30602-1602. (706)542-8848. **Fax:** (706)542-2455. **Contact:** John B. Boles, editor. Estab. 1934. "The award is sponsored jointly with Longwood College. Offered in odd-numbered years for recognition of the best first book by an author in the field of Southern history over a 2-year period." **Deadline:** March 1.

CHARLES S. SYDNOR AWARD

Southern Historical Association, Dept. of History, University of Georgia, Athens GA 30602. (706)542-8848. **Fax:** (706)542-2455. **Contact:** Southern Historical Association. Offered in even-numbered years for recognition of a distinguished book in Southern history published in odd-numbered years. Publishers usually submit books. **Deadline:** March 1.

THE AMAURY TALBOT PRIZE FOR AFRICAN ANTHROPOLOGY

Royal Anthropological Institute, 50 Fitzroy St., London England W1T 5BT United Kingdom. (44)(207)387-0455. **Fax:** (44)(207)388-8817. **E-mail:** admin@therai.org.uk. Annual award for nonfiction on anthropological research relating to Africa. Only works published the previous calendar year are eligible. Preference is given to those relating first to Nigeria and then West Africa. Guidelines online or for SASE. **Deadline:** March 31. **Prize:** 500£.

WESTERN WRITERS OF AMERICA

MSC06 3770, 1 University of New Mexico, Albuquerque NM 87131-0001. (505)277-5234. **Fax:** (505)277-5275. **E-mail:** wwa@unm.edu. **Contact:** Paul Hutton, exec. director. Estab. 1953. "17 Spur Award categories in various aspects of the American West." Send entry form with your published work. "The nonprofit Western Writers of America has promoted and honored the best in Western literature with the annual Spur Awards, selected by panels of judges. Awards, for material published last year, are given for works whose inspirations, image and literary excellence best represent the reality and spirit of the American West." Charges No fee. Today, Spurs are offered for the best western novel (short novel), best novel of the west (long novel), best original paperback novel, best short story, best short nonfiction. Also, best contemporary nonfiction, best biography, best history, best juvenile fiction and nonfiction, best TV or motion picture drama, best TV or motion picture documentary, best western song, and best first novel. Accepts multiple submissions, each with its own entry form.

WRITERS' JOURNAL ANNUAL SCIENCE FICTION/FANTASY CONTEST

Val-Tech Media, P.O. Box 394, Perham MN 56573. (218)346-7921. **Fax:** (218)346-7924. **E-mail:** writersjournal@writersjournal.com. **Website:** www.writersjournal.com. **Contact:** Leon Ogroske. Offered annually for unpublished work (maximum 2,000 words). No e-mail submissions accepted. Guidelines for SASE or online. Receives fewer than 200 entries. **Deadline:** November 30. Charges $7 fee. **Prize:** 1st Place: $250; 2nd Place: $100; 3rd Place: $50, plus honorable mentions. Prize-winning stories and selected honorable mentions will be published in Writers' Journal magazine.

A THE WRITERS' TRUST NONFICTION PRIZE

The Writers' Trust of Canada, 90 Richmond St. E., Suite 200, Toronto ON M5C 1P1 Canada. (416)504-8222. **Fax:** (416)504-9090. **E-mail:** info@writerstrust.com. **Contact:** Amanda Hopkins. "Offered annually for a work of nonfiction published in the previous year. Award presented at The Writers' Trust Awards event held in Toronto each Fall. Open to Canadian citizens and permanent residents only." **Deadline:** August 6th. **Prize:** $25,000 (Canadian), and $2,500 to four finalists.

WRITING FOR CHILDREN & YOUNG ADULTS

AUSTIN PUBLIC LIBRARY FRIENDS FOUNDATION AWARDS FOR BEST CHILDREN'S BOOK ($500) AND BEST YOUNG ADULT BOOK ($500)

6335 W. Northwest Hwy, #618, Dallas TX 75225. (214)363-7253. **E-mail:** dpayne@smu.edu. **Contact:** Darwin Payne. Offered annually for work published January 1-December 31 of previous year to recognize the best book for children and young people. Writer must have been born in Texas, have lived in the state for at least 2 consecutive years at one time, or the subject matter must be associated with the state. See website for judges and further information. **Deadline:** First week of January. **Prize:** $500 for each award winner.

THE GEOFFREY BILSON AWARD FOR HISTORICAL FICTION FOR YOUNG PEOPLE

The Canadian Children's Book Centre, 40 Orchard View Blvd., Suite 101, Toronto ON M4R 1B9 Canada. (416)975-0010. **Fax:** (416)975-8970. **Website:** www.bookcentre.ca. "Created in Geoffrey Bilson's memory in 1988. Open to Canadian citizens and residents of Canada for at least 2 years." Awarded annually to reward excellence in the writing of an outstanding work of historical fiction for young readers, by a Canadian author, published in the previous calendar year. **Deadline:** mid-December. **Prize:** $5,000.

THE NORMA FLECK AWARD FOR CANADIAN CHILDREN'S NON-FICTION

The Canadian Children's Book Centre, 40 Orchard View Blvd., Suite 101, Toronto ON M4R 1B9 Canada. (416)975-0010. **Fax:** (416)975-8970. **E-mail:** info@bookcentre.ca. **Website:** www.bookcentre.ca.

"The Norma Fleck Award was established by the Fleck Family Foundation and the Canadian Children's Book Centre in 1999 to recognize and raise the profile of exceptional Canadian nonfiction books for young people." Presented annually for books published between January 1 and December 31 of the previous calendar year. Open to Canadian citizens or landed immigrants. Please visit website for submission guidelines and eligibility criteria, as well as specific submission deadline. **Deadline:** mid-December. **Prize:** $10,000.

INTERNATIONAL READING ASSOCIATION CHILDREN'S AND YOUNG ADULTS' BOOK AWARDS

International Reading Association, P.O. Box 8139, Newark DE 19714-8139. (302)731-1600, ext. 229. **Fax:** (302)731-1057. **Website:** www.reading.org. "Offered annually for an author's first or second published book in fiction and nonfiction in 3 categories: primary (pre-school-age 8), intermediate (ages 9-13), and young adult (ages 14-17). Recognizes newly published authors who show unusual promise in the children's book field. Guidelines and deadlines are on the website." **Prize:** $1,000, and a medal for each category.

THE VICKY METCALF AWARD FOR CHILDREN'S LITERATURE

The Writers' Trust of Canada, 90 Richmond St. E., Suite 200, Toronto ON M5C 1P1 Canada. (416)504-8222. **Fax:** (416)504-9090. **E-mail:** info@writerstrust.com. **Contact:** Amanda Hopkins. "The Metcalf Award is presented to a Canadian writer for a body of work in children's literature at The Writers' Trust Awards event held in Toronto each Fall. Open to Canadian citizens and permanent residents only." **Prize:** $20,000.

MILKWEED PRIZE FOR CHILDREN'S LITERATURE

Milkweed Editions, 1011 Washington Ave. S., Suite 300, Minneapolis MN 55415. (612)332-3192. **Fax:** (612)215-2550. **E-mail:** editor@milkweed.org. **Contact:** The Editors. Estab. 1993. Annual prize for unpublished works. The Milkweed Prize for Children's Literature will be awarded to the best ms for children ages 8-13 that Milkweed accepts for publication during each calendar year by a writer not previously published by Milkweed Editions. Mss should be of high literary quality and must be double-spaced, 90-200 pages in length. All mss submitted to Milkweed will automatically be considered for the prize. Submission directly to the contest is not necessary, and there is no deadline. Manuscripts are accepted on a rolling basis. Must review guidelines online; Milkweed strongly encourages digital submissions through our Submission Manager. **Prize:** $10,000 advance on royalties agreed upon at the time of acceptance.

PATERSON PRIZE FOR BOOKS FOR YOUNG PEOPLE

The Poetry Center at Passaic County Community College, One College Blvd., Paterson NJ 07505-1179. (973)523-6085. **Fax:** (973)523-6085. **E-mail:** mgillan@pccc.edu. **Website:** www.pccc.edu/poetry. **Contact:** Maria Mazziotti Gillan, exec. director. At above address or visit www.pccc.edu/poetry and go to prizes." Offered annually for books published the previous calendar year. Three categories: pre-kindergarten-grade 3; grades 4-6; grades 7-12. Open to any writer." **Deadline:** March 15. **Prize:** $500 in each category.

SASKATCHEWAN CHILDREN'S LITERATURE AWARD

Saskatchewan Book Awards, Inc., 205B-2314 11th Ave., Regina SK S4P 0K1 Canada. (306)569-1585. **Fax:** (306)569-4187. **E-mail:** director@bookawards.sk.ca. **Website:** www.bookawards.sk.ca. **Contact:** Jackie Lay, executive director. Offered annually for work published September 15-September 14. This award is presented to a Saskatchewan author for the best book of children's or young adult's literature, judged on the quality of writing. **Deadline:** First **Deadline:** July 31; Final **Deadline:** September 14. Charges $25 CAN. **Prize:** $2,000 CAN

SYDNEY TAYLOR MANUSCRIPT COMPETITION

Association of Jewish Libraries, Sydney Taylor Manuscript Award Competition, 204 Park St., Montclair NJ 07042. **E-mail:** stmacajl@aol.com. **Contact:** Aileen Grossberg. Material should be a work of fiction in English, with universal appeal of Jewish content for readers aged 8-11 years. "It should deepen the understanding of Judaism for all children, Jewish and nonJewish, and reveal positive aspects of Jewish life." No poems or plays. Length: 64-200 pages. Rules, entry forms available at website: www.jewishlibraries.org. Judged by 5 AJL member librarians. Open to any writer. Must be unpublished. **Deadline:** December 15. **Prize:** $1,000.

RITA WILLIAMS YOUNG ADULT PROSE PRIZE

National League of American Pen Women, Nob Hill, San Francisco Branch, Category of the Soul-Making Literary Competition, The Webhallow House, 1544 Sweetwood Dr., Broadmoor Vig. CA 94015-1717. **E-mail:** pennobhill@aol.com. **Contact:** Eileen Malone. "Up to 3,000 words in story, essay, journal entry, creative nonfiction, or memoir by writer in grades 9-12. Indicate age and category on each first page. Identify with 3×5 card only. Open annually to young adult writers." **Deadline:** November 30. Charges $5/entry (make checks payable to NLAPW, Nob Hill Branch). **Prize:** 1st Place: $100; 2nd Place: $50; 3rd Place: $25.

PAUL A. WITTY SHORT STORY AWARD

Executive Office, International Reading Association, P.O. Box 8139, Newark DE 19714-8139. (302)731-1600, ext. 229. **Fax:** (302)731-1057. **E-mail:** committees@reading.org. "Offered to reward author of an original short story published in a children's periodical during 2010 which serves as a literary standard that encourages young readers to read periodicals. Write for guidelines or download from website." **Deadline:** December 1. **Prize:** $1,000.

WORK-IN-PROGRESS GRANT

Society of Children's Book Writers and Illustrators (SCBWI), 8271 Beverly Blvd., Los Angeles CA 90048. (323)782-1010. **E-mail:** scbwi@scbwi.org. **Website:** www.scbwi.org. Four grants—one designated specifically for a contemporary novel for young people, one for nonfiction, one for an unpublished writer, one general fiction—to assist SCBWI members in the completion of a specific project. Open to SCBWI members only. Applications received only between February 15 and March 15.

WRITE A STORY FOR CHILDREN COMPETITION

Academy of Children's Writers, P.O. Box 95, Huntingdon Cambridgeshire PE28 5RL England. Phone/**Fax:** (44)(148)783-2752. **E-mail:** enquiries@childrens-writers.co.uk. **Contact:** Contest Director. Annual contest for the best unpublished short story writer for children. Guidelines and entry forms online or send SAE/IRC. Open to any unpublished writer over the age of 18. **Deadline:** March 31. Charges $10 (US) Bill. No checks; £2.70 (UK). **Prize:** 1st Place: £2,000; 2nd Place: £300; 3rd Place: £200. Judgesd by a panel appointed by the Academy of Children's Writers.

WRITERS' LEAGUE OF TEXAS
CHILDREN'S BOOK AWARDS

Writers' League of Texas, 611 S. Congress, Ste 130, Austin TX 78704. (512)499-8914. **Fax:** (512)499-0441. **E-mail:** wlt@writersleague.org. **Website:** www.writersleague.org. **Contact:** Jan Baumer, program manager. Offered annually for work published January 1-December 31. Honors 2 outstanding books for children. Writer's League of Texas dues may accompany entry fee. **Deadline:** March 1. Charges $35 fee. **Prize:** Two prizes of $1,000 and trophies.

POETRY

ACORN-PLANTOS AWARD
FOR PEOPLES POETRY

Acorn-Plantos Award Committee, 36 Sunset Ave., Hamilton ON L8R 1V6 Canada. **E-mail:** jeffseff@allstream.net. **Contact:** Jeff Seffinga. "Annual contest for work that appeared in print in the previous calender year. This award is given to the Canadian poet who best (through the publication of a book of poems) exemplifies populist or peoples poetry in the tradition of Milton Acorn, Ted Plantos, et al. Work may be entered by the poet or the publisher; the award goes to the poet. Entrants must submit 5 copies of each title. Poet must be a citizen of Canada or a landed immigrant. Publisher need not be Canadian." **Deadline:** June 30. Charges $25 (CDN)/title. **Prize:** $500 (CDN) and a medal. Judged by a panel of poets in the tradition who are not entered in the current year.

ANHINGA PRIZE FOR POETRY

Anhinga Press, Drawer W, P.O. Box 10595, Tallahassee FL 32302. (850)442-1408. **Fax:** (850)442-6323. **E-mail:** info@anhinga.org. **Website:** www.anhinga.org. Estab. 1983. Offered annually for a book-length collection of poetry by an author who has not published more than 1 book of poetry. Guidelines for SASE or on website. Open to any writer writing in English. **Deadline:** February 15-May 1. Charges $25 fee. **Prize:** $2,000, and publication.

ANNUAL GIVAL PRESS OSCAR WILDE AWARD

Gival Press, LLC, P.O. Box 3812, Arlington VA 22203. (703)351-0079. **E-mail:** givalpress@yahoo.com. **Contact:** Robert L. Giron. "Award given to the best previously unpublished original poem—written in English of any length, in any style, typed, double-spaced on 1 side only—which best relates gay/lesbian/bisexual/transgendered life, by a poet who is 18 or older. Entrants are asked to submit their poems without any kind of identification (with the exception of titles) and with a separate cover page with the following information: name, address (street, city, and state with zip code), telephone number, e-mail address (if available) and a list of poems by title. Checks drawn on American banks should be made out to Gival Press, LLC." **Deadline:** June 27 (postmarked). Charges $5 (USD) reading fee per poem. **Prize:** $100 (USD), and the poem, along with information about the poet, will be published on the Gival Press website.

ATLANTIC POETRY PRIZE

Writers' Federation of Nova Scotia, 1113 Marginal Rd., Halifax NS B3H 4P7 Canada. (902)423-8116. **Fax:** (902)422-0881. **E-mail:** talk@writers.ns.ca. **Contact:** Nate Crawford, executive director. Full-length books of adult poetry written by Atlantic Canadians, and published as a whole for the first time in the previous calendar year, are eligible. Entrants must be native or resident Atlantic Canadians who have either been born in Newfoundland, Prince Edward Island, Nova Scotia, or New Brunswick, and spent a susbstantial portion of their lives living there, or who have lived in one or a combination of these provinces for at least 24 consecutive months prior to entry deadline date. Publishers: Send 4 copies and a letter attesting to the author's status as an Atlantic Canadian and the author's current mailing address and telephone number. **Deadline:** First Friday in December. **Prize:** $2,000.

THE BASKERVILLE PUBLISHERS POETRY AWARD &
THE BETSY COLQUITT POETRY AWARD

descant, Texas Christian University's literary journal, TCU, Box 297270, Fort Worth TX 76129. (817)257-6537. **Fax:** (817)257-6239. **E-mail:** descant@tcu.edu. **Contact:** Dan Williams and Alex Lemon. "Annual award for an outstanding poem published in an issue of descant." **Deadline:** September - April. **Prize:** $250 for Baskerville Award; $500 for Betsy Colquitt Award. Publication retains copyright, but will transfer it to the author upon request.

THE BINGHAMTON UNIVERSITY
MILT KESSLER POETRY BOOK AWARD

Binghamton Center for Writers, Dept. of English, General Literature & Rhetoric, Library North, Room 1149, Vestal Parkway E., P.O. Box 6000, Binghamton NY 13902-6000. (607)777-2713. **E-mail:** cwpro@binghamton.edu. **Contact:** Maria Mazziotti Gillan, creative writing program director. Estab. 2001. Offered annually for work published that year. Books must be 48 pages or more with a press run of 500 copies or more. Each book submitted must be accompanied by an application form available online. Poet or publisher may submit more than 1 book for prize consideration. Send 3 copies of each book. Guidelines available online or for SASE. Open to any writer over the age of 40. **Deadline:** March 1. **Prize:** $1,000. Judged by professional poet not on Binghamton University faculty.

BLUE MOUNTAIN ARTS/SPS STUDIOS POETRY CARD CONTEST

P.O. Box 1007, Boulder CO 80306. (303)449-0536. **Fax:** (303)447-0939. **E-mail:** poetrycontest@sps.com. **Website:** www.sps.com. "We're looking for original poetry that is rhyming or non-rhyming, although we find no-rhyming poetry reads better. Poems may also be considered for possible publication on greeting cards or in book anthologies. Contest is offered biannually. Guidelines available online." **Deadline:** December 31 and June 30. **Prize:** 1st Place: $300; 2nd Place: $150; 3rd Place: $50. Blue Mountain Arts editorial staff.

THE FREDERICK BOCK PRIZE

Poetry, Poetry, 444 North Michigan Ave., Suite 1850, Chicago IL 60610. (312)787-7070. **E-mail:** poetry@poetrymagazine.org. Estab. 1981. Offered annually for poems published in Poetry during the preceding year (October through September). Poetry buys all rights to the poems published in the magazine. Copyrights are returned to the authors on request. Any writer may submit poems to Poetry. **Prize:** $500.

M. AND S. BONOMO FICTION AWARD

Italian Americana, URI/CCE, 80 Washington St., Providence RI 02903-1803. **E-mail:** bonomoal@etal.uri.edu or it.americana@yahoo. com. **Website:** www.italianamericana.com. **Contact:** Carol Bonomo Albright, editor. Offered annually as an honorific. **Prize:** $1,000.

THE BORDIGHERA ITALIAN-AMERICAN POETRY PRIZE

Sonia Raiziss-Giop Foundation, Bordighera Press @ John D. Calandra Italian American Institute, Graduate Center, The City University of New York, 25 West 43rd St., 17th Floor, New York NY 10036. **E-mail:** daniela@garden.net. **Contact:** Daniela Gioseffi. "Offered annually to find the best unpublished manuscripts of poetry in English, by an American of Italian descent, to be translated into quality Italian and published bilingually. No Italian-American themes required, just excellent poetry. Guidelines for SASE or see online. Judges change every 2 years. Former judges include Daniela Gioseffi, Felix Stefanile, Dorothy Barresi, W.S. DePiero, Donna Masini, Michael Palma, Patricia Fargnoli." **Deadline:** May 31. **Prize:** $2,000 and bilingual book publication to be divided between poet and consigned translator.

BARBARA BRADLEY PRIZE

New England Poetry Club, P.O. Box 190076, Boston MA 02119. **E-mail:** contests@nepoetryclub.org. **Contact:** NEPC Contest Coordinator. Offered annually for a poem under 21 lines, written by a woman. It must be submitted only in April and May contests. **Deadline:** May 31. Charges $10 is entry fee for every 3 poems, for 3 contests. **Prize:** $200.

BRIGHT HILL PRESS ANNUAL POETRY BOOK COMPETITION

Bright Hill Press, P.O. Box 193, Treadwell NY 13846. Phone/**Fax:** (607)829-5055. **E-mail:** wordthur@stny.rr.com. **Contact:** Bertha Rogers, editor. Send 48-65 pages, bio, TOC, acknowledgments

page, and 2 title pages (1 with name, address, etc.; 1 with title only). Poems can be published in journals or anthologies. Guidelines online, for SASE, or via e-mail. **Deadline:** November 30. Charges $22 fee. **Prize:** $1,000, publication, and 25 copies of the winning book.

BRITTINGHAM PRIZE IN POETRY; FELIX POLLAK PRIZE IN POETRY

University of Wisconsin Press, Dept. of English, 600 N. Park St., University of Wisconsin, Madison WI 53706. **E-mail:** rwallace@wisc.edu. **Contact:** Ronald Wallace, contest director. Estab. 1985. "Offered for unpublished book-length mss of original poetry. Submissions must be received by the press during the month of September, accompanied by a required SASE for contest results. Does not return mss. One entry fee covers both prizes. Guidelines for SASE or online." Charges $25 fee (payable to Univ. of Wisconsin Press). **Prize:** $2,500 ($1,000 cash prize and $1,500 honorarium for campus reading) and publication of the 2 winning mss.

GERALD CABLE BOOK AWARD

Silverfish Review Press, P.O. Box 3541, Eugene OR 97403. (541)344-5060. **E-mail:** sfrpress@earthlink.net. **Website:** www.silverfish reviewpress.com. **Contact:** Rodger Moody, series editor. "Purpose is to publish a poetry book by a deserving author who has yet to publish a full-length book collection. For guidelines send SASE, or request by e-mail." **Deadline:** October 15. Charges $20 reading fee. **Prize:** $1,000, 25 copies, and publication by the press for a book-length ms of original poetry.

THE CENTER FOR BOOK ARTS POETRY CHAPBOOK COMPETITION

The Center for Book Arts, 28 W. 27th St., 3rd Floor, New York NY 10001. (212)481-0295. **Fax:** (866)708-8994. **E-mail:** info@center forbookarts.org. **Website:** www.centerforbookarts.org. **Contact:** Sarah Nicholls. Offered annually for unpublished collections of poetry. Individual poems may have been previously published. Collection must not exceed 500 lines or 24 pages. **Deadline:** December 1 (postmarked). Charges $25 fee. **Prize:** $500 award, $500 honorarium for a reading, publication, and 10 copies of chapbook.

JOHN CIARDI PRIZE FOR POETRY

BkMk Press, University of Missouri-Kansas City, 5100 Rockhill Rd., Kansas City MO 02903-1803. (816)235-2558. **E-mail:** bkmk@umkc. edu. **Website:** www.umkc.edu/bkmk. "Offered annually for the best book-length collection (unpublished) of poetry in English by a living author. Translations are not eligible. Initial judging is done by a network of published writers. Final judging is done by a writer of national reputation. Guidelines for SASE, by e-mail, or on website." **Deadline:** January 15 (postmarked). Charges $25 fee. **Prize:** $1,000, plus book publication by BkMk Press.

CLEVELAND STATE UNIVERSITY POETRY CENTER PRIZES

Cleveland State University Poetry Center, 2121 Euclid Ave., Cleveland OH 44115-2214. (216)687-3986. **Fax:** (216)687-6943. **E-mail:** poetrycenter@csuohio.edu. **Contact:** Rita Grabowski, poetry center manager. Estab. 1987. Offered annually to identify, reward, and publish the best unpublished book-length poetry ms (minimum 48 pages) in 2 categories: First Book Award and Open Competition (for poets who have published at least one collection with a press run of 500). Submission implies willingness to sign standard contract for publication if manuscript wins. Does not return mss. Guidelines for SASE or online. **Deadline:** Submissions accepted November 1-February 15. Charges $25 fee. **Prize:** First Book and Open Book Competitions award publication and a $1000 advance against royalties for an original manuscript of poetry in each category.

THE COLORADO PRIZE FOR POETRY

Colorado Review/Center for Literary Publishing, Dept. of English, Colorado State University, 9105 Campus Delivery, Ft. Collins CO 80523-9105. (970)491-5449. **E-mail:** creview@colostate.edu. **Contact:** Stephanie G'Schwind, editor. Estab. 1995. "Offered annually to an unpublished collection of poetry. Guidelines available for SASE or online at website." To connect writers and readers by publishing exceptional writing. **Deadline:** January 14. Charges $25 fee (includes subscription). **Prize:** $1,500 and publication of book.

CRAB ORCHARD SERIES IN POETRY OPEN COMPETITION

1000 Faner Dr., Southern Illinois University, Carbondale IL 62901-4503. **Contact:** Jon C. Tribble, series editor. "Offered annually for collections of unpublished poetry. Open to US citizens and permanent residents." Visit website for current deadlines. Charges $25 fee. **Prize:** Two winners selected: both receive $3,500 and publication.

T.S. ELIOT PRIZE FOR POETRY

Truman State University Press, 100 E. Normal St., Kirksville MO 63501-4221. (660)785-7336. **Fax:** (660)785-4480. **E-mail:** tsup@truman.edu. **Website:** tsup.truman.edu. **Contact:** Nancy Rediger. Annual competition for unpublished poetry collection. Guidelines for SASE, online, or by e-mail. **Deadline:** October 31 (postmarked). Charges $25 fee. **Prize:** $2,000 and publication.

JANICE FARRELL POETRY PRIZE

The Soul-Making Literary Competition, National League of American Pen Women, Nob Hill, San Francisco Branch, The Webhallow House, 1544 Sweetwood Dr., Broadmoor Village CA 94015-1717. **E-mail:** pennobhill@aol.com. **Contact:** Eileen Malone. "Poetry may be double- or single-spaced. One-page poems only, and only 1 poem/page. All poems must be titled. 3 poems/entry. Indicate category on each poem. Identify with 3X5 card only. Open annually to all writers." **Deadline:** November 30. Charges $5/entry (make checks payable to NLAPW, Nob Hill Branch). **Prize:** 1st Place: $100; 2nd Place: $50; 3rd Place: $25. Judged by a local San Francisco successfully published poet.

FIELD POETRY PRIZE

Oberlin College Press/FIELD, 50 N. Professor St., Oberlin OH 44074-1091. (440)775-8408. **Fax:** (440)775-8124. **E-mail:** oc.press@oberlin.edu. **Website:** www.oberlin.edu/ocpress/prize.htm. **Contact:** Linda Slocum, managing editor. "Offered annually for unpublished work. Contest seeks to encourage the finest in contemporary poetry writing. Open to any writer." **Deadline:** Submit in May only. Charges $25 fee, which includes a 1-year subscription to FIELD. **Prize:** $1,000 and the book is published in Oberlin College Press's FIELD Poetry Series.

ALLEN GINSBERG POETRY AWARDS

The Poetry Center at Passaic County Community College, One College Blvd., Paterson NJ 07505-1179. (973)684-6555. **Fax:** (973)684-5843. **E-mail:** mgillan@pccc.edu. **Contact:** Maria Mazziotti Gillan, exec. director. "Offered annually for unpublished poetry to honor Allen Ginsberg's contribution to American literature. The college retains first publication rights. Open to any writer." **Deadline:** April 1. Charges $18, which includes the cost of a subscription to The Paterson Literary Review. **Prize:** First: $1,000; Second: $200; Third: $100.

GIVAL PRESS POETRY AWARD

Gival Press, LLC, P.O. Box 3812, Arlington VA 22203. (703)351-0079. **E-mail:** givalpress@yahoo.com. **Contact:** Robert L. Giron, editor. "Offered annually for a previously unpublished poetry collection as a complete ms, which may include previously published poems; and previously published poems must be acknowledged & poet must hold rights. The competition seeks to award well-written, original poetry in English on any topic, in any style. Guidelines for SASE, by e-mail, or online. Entrants are asked to submit their poems without any kind of identification (with the exception of the titles) and with a separate cover page with the following information: name, address (street, city, state, and zip code), telephone number, e-mail address (if available), short bio, and a list of the poems by title. Checks drawn on American banks should be made out to Gival Press, LLC." **Deadline:** December 15 (postmarked). Charges $20 reading fee (USD). **Prize:** $1,000, publication, and 20 author's copies. The editor narrows entries to the top 10; previous winner selects top 5 and the winner—all done anonymously.

GOVERNOR GENERAL'S LITERARY AWARD FOR POETRY

Canada Council for the Arts, 350 Albert St., P.O. Box 1047, Ottawa ON K1P 5V8 Canada. (613)566-4414, ext. 5573. **Fax:** (613)566-4410. **E-mail:** lori.knoll@canadacouncil.ca. **Website:** www.canadacouncil.ca/prizes/ggla. Offered for the best English-language and the best French-language work of poetry by a Canadian. Publishers submit titles for consideration. Deadline depends on the book's publication date in English: March 15, June 1, or August 7. Books in French: March 15 or July 15. **Prize:** Each laureate receives $25,000; non-winning finalists receive $1,000.

GREEN ROSE PRIZE IN POETRY

New Issues Poetry & Prose, Western Michigan University, 1903 W. Michigan Ave., Kalamazoo MI 49008-5463. (269)387-8185. **Fax:** (269)387-2562. **E-mail:** william.olsen@wmich.edu. **Contact:** William Olsen, editor. Offered annually for unpublished poetry.

The university will publish a book of poems by a poet writing in English who has published 1 or more full-length collections of poetry. Guidelines for SASE or online. New Issues Poetry & Prose obtains rights for first publication. Book is copyrighted in the author's name. **Deadline:** May 1-September 30. **Charges** $20 fee. **Prize:** $2,000 and publication of book. Author also receives 10% of the printed edition.

THE GRIFFIN POETRY PRIZE

The Griffin Trust for Excellence in Poetry, 363 Parkridge Crescent, Oakville ON L6M 1A8 Canada. (905)618-0420. **E-mail:** info@griffinpoetryprize.com. **Contact:** Ruth Smith. Offered annually for work published between January 1 and December 31. **Deadline:** December 31. **Prize:** Two $50,000 (Canadian) prizes. One prize will go to a living Canadian poet or translator, the other to a living poet or translator from any country, which may include Canada. a panel of qualified English-speaking judges of stature. Judges are chosen by the Trustees of The Griffin Trust For Excellence in Poetry.

KATHRYN HANDLEY PROSE POEM PRIZE

National League of American Pen Women, Nob Hill, San Francisco Branch, The Webhallow House, 1544 Sweetwood Dr., Colma CA 94015-1717. **E-mail:** pennobhill@aol.com. **Contact:** Eileen Malone. Poetry may be double- or single-spaced. 1-page poems only, and only 1 prose poem/page. 3 poems/entry. Indicate category on each poem. Identify only with 3X5 card. Open annually to all writers. **Deadline:** November 30. **Charges** $5/entry (make checks payable to NLAPW, Nob Hill Branch). **Prize:** 1st Place: $100; 2nd Place: $50; 3rd Place: $25.

THE BEATRICE HAWLEY AWARD

Alice James Books, 238 Main St., Farmington ME 04938. Phone/**Fax:** (207)778-7071. **E-mail:** ajb@umf.maine.edu. **Website:** www.alicejamesbooks.org. **Contact:** Julia Bouwsma, associate managing editor. "Offered annually for unpublished full-length poetry collection. Open to US residents only. Guidelines online or for SASE." **Deadline:** December 1. **Charges** $25. **Prize:** $2,000 and publication

THE BESS HOKIN PRIZE

Poetry, 444 North Michigan Ave. Suite 1850, Chicago IL 60611. (312)787-7070. **E-mail:** poetry@poetrymagazine.org. **Website:** www.poetrymagazine.org. Estab. 1947. Offered annually for poems published in Poetry during the preceding year (October-September). Poetry buys all rights to the poems published in the magazine. Copyrights are returned to the authors on request. **Prize:** $1,000.

FIRMAN HOUGHTON PRIZE

New England Poetry Club, P.O. Box 19007, Boston MA 02119. **E-mail:** contests@nepoetryclug.org. **Website:** www.nepoetryclub.org/contests.htm. **Contact:** NEPC Contest Coordinator. Offered annually for a lyric poem under 200 lines. Submitted only in April or May to New England Poetry Club. **Deadline:** May 31. **Charges** $10 fee for 3 contest entries, payable to New England Poetry Club. Members free. **Prize:** $250.

INDIANA REVIEW POETRY PRIZE

Indiana Review, Ballantine Hall 465, Indiana University, Bloomington IN 47405-7103. (812)855-3439. **Fax:** (812)855-9535. **Website:** www.indianareview.com. **Contact:** Alessandra Simmons, Editor. Offered annually for unpublished work. Judged by guest judges; 2009 prize judged by Natasha Trethewey. Open to any writer. Send no more than 3 poems per entry. Guidelines on web site and with SASE request. **Deadline:** Late March or Early April. **Charges** $15 fee (includes a 1-year subscription). **Prize:** $1,000.

IOWA POETRY PRIZES

University of Iowa Press, 100 Kuhl House, Iowa City IA 52242. (319)335-2000. **Fax:** (319)335-2055. Offered annually to encourage poets and their work. Submissions must be postmarked during the month of April; put name on title page only. Open to writers of English (US citizens or not). Manuscripts will not be returned. Previous winners are not eligible. **Charges** $20 reading fee. **Deadline:** April 30.

RANDALL JARRELL POETRY COMPETITION

North Carolina Writers' Network, Appalachian State University, Department of English, Box 32052, Boone NC 28608. **E-mail:** mailtlkenned@uncg.edu. **Contact:** Terry L. Kennedy. Offered annually for unpublished work "to honor Randall Jarrell and his life at UNC-Greensboro by recognizing the best poetry submitted." Competition is open any writer who is a legal resident of North Carolina or a member of the NC Writers Network. **Deadline:** February 15. **Charges** $10 (NCWN members); $15 (nonmembers) entry fee. **Prize:** The contest awards the winner publication in The Crucible literary journal and $200.

THE ROBINSON JEFFERS TOR HOUSE 2010 PRIZE FOR POETRY

The Robinson Jeffers Tor House Foundation, P.O. Box 2137, Carmel CA 93921. (831)624-1813. **Fax:** (831)624-3696. **E-mail:** thf@torhouse.org. **Contact:** Poetry Prize Coordinator. The 2010 Prize includes a reading in Chicago on June 9 sponsored by the Poetry Center as part of "The Big Read: The Poetryof Robinson Jeffers." Included is round-trip air (economy), one night's lodging, and a $500 honorarium. The Big Read is an initiative of the National Endowment for the Arts in partnership with the Institute of Museum and Library Services and Arts Midwest. Open to well-crafted poetry in all styles, ranging from experimental work to traditionalforms, including short narrative poems. Each poem should be typed on 81/2" by 11" paper, and no longer than three pages. On a cover sheet only, include: name, mailing address, telephone number and email; titles of poems; bio optional. Multiple and simultaneous submissions welcome. The annual Tor House Prize for Poetry is a living memorial to American poet Robinson Jeffers (1887-1962) **Deadline:** March 15. **Charges** $10 for first 3 poems; $15 for up to 6 poems; $2.50 for each additional poem. Checks and money orders should be made out to Tor House Foundation. **Prize:** $1,000 for an original, non-published poem not to exceed three pages in length; $200 for Honorable Mention. Final judging by Mark Doty.

JUNIPER PRIZE FOR POETRY
University of Massachusetts Press, Amherst MA 01003. (413)545-2217. **Fax:** (413)545-1226. **E-mail:** info@umpress.umass.edu. **Contact:** Carla J. Potts. Estab. 1964. The University of Massachusetts Press offers the annual Juniper Prize for Poetry, awarded in alternate years for the first and subsequent books. Considers simultaneous submissions, "but if accepted for publication elsewhere, please notify us immediately. Manuscripts by more than 1 author, entries of more than 1 mss simultaneously or within the same year, and translations are not eligible." **Deadline:** August 1 - September 29 (postmark). Winners announced online in April on the press website. Charges $25 fee. **Prize:** Includes publication and $1,500 in addition to royalties. In even-numbered years (2010, etc.), only "subsequent" books will be considered: mss whose authors have had at least 1 full-length book or chapbook (of at least 30 pages) of poetry published or accepted for publication. Self-published work is not considered to lie within this "books and chapbooks" category. In odd-numbered years (2011, etc.), only "first books" will be considered: mss by writers whose poems may have appeared in literary journals and/or anthologies but have not been published or accepted for publication in book form.

THE LEDGE ANNUAL POETRY CHAPBOOK CONTEST
The Ledge Magazine, 40 Maple Ave., Bellport NY 11713. **E-mail:** info@theledgemagazine.com. **Contact:** Timothy Monaghan, Editor-in-Chief. Offered annually to publish an outstanding collection of poems. No restrictions on form or content. Send 16-28 pages, titles page, bio, acknowledgments, SASE. Guidelines online or for SASE. Open to any writer. **Deadline:** October 31. Charges $18 fee. All entrants receive a copy of the winning chapbook upon its publication. **Prize:** $1,000 and publication and 25 copies of the chapbook.

THE LEDGE POETRY AWARDS COMPETITION
The Ledge Magazine & Press, 40 Maple Ave., Bellport NY 11713. **E-mail:** info@theledgemagazine.com. **Contact:** Timothy Monaghan, editor-in-chief. "Offered annually for unpublished poems of exceptional quality and significance. No restrictions on form or content. All poems are considered for publication in the magazine. Guidelines online or for SASE. Open to any writer." **Deadline:** April 30. Charges $10/first 3 poems; $3/additional poem. $20 subscription to The Ledge Magazine gains free entry for the first three poems. **Prize:** 1st Place: $1,000 and publication in The Ledge Magazine; 2nd Place: $250 and publication; 3rd Place: $100 and publication.

THE LEVINSON PRIZE
Poetry, 444 North Michigan Ave., Suite 1850, Chicago IL 60611. (312)787-7070. **Fax:** (312)787-6650. **E-mail:** poetry@poetrymagazine. org. **Website:** www.poetrymagazine.org. Estab. 1914. Offered annually for poems published in Poetry during the preceding year (October-September). Poetry buys all rights to the poems published in the magazine. Copyrights are returned to the authors on request. **Prize:** $500.

LEVIS READING PRIZE
Virginia Commonwealth Univ., Dept. of English, P.O. Box 842005, Richmond VA 23284-2005. (804)828-1329. **Fax:** (804)828-8684. **E-mail:** tndidato@vcu.edu. **Contact:** Thom Didato. "Offered annually for books of poetry published in the previous year to encourage poets early in their careers. The entry must be the writer's first or second published book of poetry. Previously published books in other genres, or previously published chapbooks or self-published material, do not count as books for this purpose." **Deadline:** January 15. **Prize:** $1,000 honorarium and an expense-paid trip to Richmond to present a public reading.

THE RUTH LILLY POETRY PRIZE
The Modern Poetry Association, 444 North Michigan Ave., Suite 1850, Chicago IL 60610. **E-mail:** poetry@poetrymagazine.org. Estab. 1986. Offered annually to a poet whose accomplishments in the field of poetry warrant extraordinary recognition. No applicants or nominations are accepted. **Deadline:** Varies. **Prize:** $100,000.

LITERAL LATTÉ POETRY AWARD
Literal Latté, 200 E. 10th St., Suite 240, New York NY 10003. (212)260-5532. **E-mail:** LitLatte@aol.com. **Contact:** Jenine Gordon Bockman, editor. "Offered annually to any writer for unpublished poetry (maximum 2,000 words per poem). All styles welcome. Winners published in Literal Latté." Acquires first rights. **Deadline:** July 15. Charges $10/up to 6 poems; $15/set of 10 poems. **Prize:** 1st Place: $1,000; 2nd Place: $300; 3rd Place: $200.

FRANCES LOCKE MEMORIAL POETRY AWARD
The Bitter Oleander Press, 4983 Tall Oaks Dr., Fayetteville NY 13066-9776. (315)637-3047. **Fax:** (315)637-5056. **E-mail:** info@bitter oleander.com. **Contact:** Paul B. Roth. Offered annually for unpublished, imaginative poetry. Open to any writer. **Deadline:** June 15. Charges $10 for 5 poems; $2/additional poem. **Prize:** $1,000, publication in the autumn issue, and 5 copies of that issue.

LOUISE LOUIS/EMILY F. BOURNE STUDENT POETRY AWARD
Poetry Society of America, 15 Gramercy Park S., New York NY 10003. (212)254-9628. **Fax:** (212)673-2352. **Website:** www.poetry society.org. **Contact:** Programs Associate. Offered annually for unpublished work to promote excellence in student poetry. Open to American high school or preparatory school students (grades 9-12). Guidelines for SASE and online. Judged by prominent American poets. It is strongly encouraged that applicants read the complete contest guidelines before submitting. **Deadline:** October 1-December 22. Charges $5 for a student submitting a single entry; $20 for a high school submitting unlimited number of its students' poems. **Prize:** $250.

THE MACGUFFIN NATIONAL POET HUNT
The MacGuffin, 18600 Haggerty Rd., Livonia MI 48152. **E-mail:** macguffin@schoolcraft.edu. **Website:** www.macguffin.org. **Contact:** Managing Editor. Work is judged blindly by a renowned, published

poet. Offered annually for unpublished work. Guidelines available by mail, e-mail, or on the website. Acquires first rights (if published). Once published, all rights revert to the author. **Deadline:** April 3-June 3 (postmarked). Charges $15 for a 5-poem entry. **Prize:** 1st Place: $500; 2 Honorable Mentions will be published. 2010 Judge: Jim Daniels. Past judges include Thomas Lynch, Vivian Shipley, Molly Peacock, Bob Hicok, Laurence Lieberman, Thomas Lux, and Conrad Hilberry.

NAOMI LONG MADGETT POETRY AWARD
Lotus Press, Inc., P.O. Box 21607, Detroit MI 48221. **E-mail:** lotus press@comcast.net. **Contact:** Constance Withers. "Offered annually to recognize an unpublished poetry ms by an African American. Guidelines for SASE, by e-mail, or online." **Deadline:** January 2 - March 31. **Prize:** $500 and publication by Lotus Press.

MORTON MARR POETRY PRIZE
Southwest Review, P.O. Box 750374, Dallas TX 75275-0374. (214)768-1037. **Fax:** (214)768-1408. **E-mail:** swr@mail.smu.edu. **Contact:** Willard Spiegelman. "Annual award given to a poem by a writer who has not yet published a first book of poetry. Contestants may submit no more than 6 poems in a traditional form (i.e., sonnet, sestina, villanelle, rhymed stanzas, blank verse, etc.). A cover letter with name, address, and other relevant information may accompany the poems which must be printed without any identifying information. Guidelines for SASE or online. Open to any writer who has not yet published a first book of poetry." **Deadline:** September 30. Charges $5/poem. **Prize:** 1st Place: $1,000; 2nd Place: $500; publication in The Southwest Review.

SHEILA MOTTON AWARD
New England Poetry Club, 2 Farrar St., Cambridge MA 02138. **Website:** www.nepoetryclub.org. **Contact:** NEPC Contest Coordinator. Checks for all contests should be made to New England Poetry Club. All entries should be sent in duplicate with name, address, phone, and email of writer on only one copy. (Judges receive copies without names). **Deadline:** May 31. **Prize:** $500.

NATIONAL WRITERS ASSOCIATION POETRY CONTEST
The National Writers Association, 10940 S. Parker Rd. #508, Parker CO 80134. (303)841-0246. **Fax:** (303)841-2607. **E-mail:** natlwriters assn@hotmail.com. **Contact:** Sandy Whelchel, director. Annual contest to encourage the writing of poetry, an important form of individual expression but with a limited commercial market. Email Sandy for a form until new website is formed. **Deadline:** Oct. 1. Charges $10 fee. **Prize:** 1st Place: $100; 2nd Place: $50; 3rd Place: $25.

THE PABLO NERUDA PRIZE FOR POETRY
Nimrod International Journal, 800 S. Tucker Dr., Tulsa OK 74104. (918)631-3080. **Fax:** (918)631-3033. **E-mail:** nimrod@utulsa.edu. **Contact:** Francine Ringold. Annual award to discover new writers of vigor and talent. Open to US residents only. **Deadline:** April 30. Charges $20 (includes a 1-year subscription). **Prize:** 1st Place: $2,000 and publication; 2nd Place: $1,000 and publication. Nimrod retains the right to publish any submission. the Nimrod editors (finalists). A recognized author selects the winners.

NEW ISSUES FIRST BOOK OF POETRY PRIZE
New Issues Poetry & Prose, Dept. of English, Western Michigan University, 1903 W. Michigan Ave., Kalamazoo MI 49008-5331. (269)387-8185. **Fax:** (269)387-2562. **E-mail:** william.olsen@wmich. edu. **Contact:** William Olsen, editor. Offered annually for publication of a first book of poems by a poet writing in English who has not previously published a full-length collection of poems in an edition of 500 or more copies. New Issues Poetry & Prose obtains rights for first publication. Book is copyrighted in author's name. Guidelines for SASE or online. **Deadline:** November 30. Charges $15. **Prize:** $2,000 and publication of book. Author also receives 10% of the printed edition.

THE JOHN FREDERICK NIMS MEMORIAL PRIZE
Poetry, 444 North Michigan Ave., Suite 1850, Chicago IL 60611. (312)787-7070. **E-mail:** poetry@poetrymagazine.org. **Website:** www.poetrymagazine.org. Offered annually for poems published in Poetry during the preceding year (October-September). Judged by the editors of Poetry. Poetry buys all rights to the poems published in the magazine. Copyrights are returned to the authors on request. **Prize:** $500.

ONCEWRITTEN.COM POETRY CONTEST
Oncewritten.com, 1850 N. Whitley Ave., #404, Hollywood CA 90028. **E-mail:** editor@oncewritten.com. **Website:** www.once written.com. **Contact:** Monica Poling, editor. "The purpose of this annual contest is to find high quality, previously unpublished poetry to feature on the website and in Off the Press, our monthly newsletter, which is distributed specifically for people interested in reading about new authors." **Deadline:** March 31. Charges $15. **Prize:** 1st Prize: $500; Runner-Up: $100. Judged by the editor and industry professionals.

THE OPEN WINDOW
Hidden Brook Press, 109 Bayshore Rd., RR#4, Brighton ON K0K 1H0 Canada. (613)475-2368. **E-mail:** writers@hiddenbrookpress. com. An annual poetry anthology contest. A wide open window theme including family, nature, death, rhyming, city, country, war and peace, social—long, short haiku, or any other genre. Send sets of 3 poems with short bio (35-40 words) and a SASE. Electronic and hard copy submissions required. Previously published and simultaneous submissions are welcome. **Deadline:** November 30. Charges $15/3 poems. **Prize:** 1st Place: $100; 2nd Place: $75; 3rd Place: $50; 4th Place: $40; 5th Place: $30; 6th Place: $25; 7th Place: $20; 8th Place: $15; 9th-10th Place: $10; plus up to 12 honorable mentions. All winners, honorable mentions, and runners up receive 1 copy of the book for each published poem. Authors retain copyright.

THE OPEN WINDOW
Hidden Brook Press, 109 Bayshore Rd., RR#4, Brighton ON K0K 1H0 Canada. (613)475-2368. **E-mail:** writers@hiddenbrookpress.

com. The Open Window International Poetry Chapbook Anthology Contest is interested in all types and styles of poetry. See The Hidden Brook Press website for examples of the type of poetry we have published in the past. Previously published and multiple submissions are welcome. **Deadline:** Annually. Charges $15/3 poems. **Prize:** 1st Place: $100; 2nd Place: $75; 3rd Place: $50; 4th Place: $40; 5th Place: $30; 6th Place: $25; 7th Place: $20; 8th Place: $15; 9th-10th Place: $10; plus 15-25 Honorable Mentions. Winning poems published in The Open Window International Poetry Chapbook Anthology. All winning and honorable mention submissions receive 1 copy of the book for each published poem. Authors retain copyright.

GUY OWEN AWARD

Southern Poetry Review, Dept. of Languages, Literature, and Philosophy, Armstrong Atlantic State University, 11935 Abercorn St., Savannah GA 31419-1997. (912)344-3196. **Fax:** (912)344-3494. **E-mail:** james.smith@armstrong.edu. **Website:** www.spr.armsrong.edu. **Contact:** James Smith. Send 3-5 unpublished poems (maximum 10 pages) and SASE for response only. Include contact information on cover sheet only. All entries considered for publication. Please indicate simultaneous submissions. **Deadline:** March 1-June 15 (postmarked). Charges $15 entry fee (includes 1-year subscription). **Prize:** $1,000 and publication of winning poem in Southern Poetry Review. Final judge will be a distinguished poet.

THE PATERSON POETRY PRIZE

The Poetry Center at Passaic County Community College, One College Blvd., Paterson NJ 07505-1179. **Fax:** (973)523-6085. **E-mail:** mgillan@pccc.edu. **Contact:** Maria Mazziotti Gillan, Exec. Director. "Offered annually for a book of Poetry 48 pages or more, with a print run of 500 or more, published in the previous year. Guidelines available online or send SASE to above address." **Deadline:** February 1. **Prize:** $1,000.

PAUMANOK POETRY AWARD

English Department, Knapp Hall, Farmingdale State College of New York, 2350 Broadhollow Rd., Route 110, Farmingdale NY 11735. **Fax:** (631)420-2051. **E-mail:** brownml@farmingdale.edu. **Contact:** Margery L. Brown, director, Visiting Writers Program. "Offered annually for published or unpublished poems. Send cover letter, 1-paragraph bio, 3-5 poems (name and address on each poem). Include SASE for notification of winners. (Send photocopies only; mss will not be returned.)" **Deadline:** September 15. Charges $25 fee, payable to Farmingdale State University VWP. **Prize:** 1st Place: $1,500, plus expenses for a reading in series; Runners-up (2): $750, plus expenses for a reading in series.

PEARL POETRY PRIZE

Pearl Editions, 3030 E. Second St., Long Beach CA 90803. (562)434-4523. **Fax:** (562)434-4523. **E-mail:** pearlmag@aol.com. **Contact:** Marilyn Johnson, editor/publisher. "Offered annually to provide poets with further opportunity to publish their poetry in book-form and find a larger audience for their work. Mss must be original works written in English. Guidelines for SASE or online. Open to all writers."

Deadline: June 30. Charges $20. **Prize:** $1,000 and publication by Pearl Editions.

PERUGIA PRESS PRIZE

Perugia Press, Celebrating Poetry by Women since 1997, P.O. Box 60364, Florence MA 01062. (413)587-2646. **E-mail:** info@perugia press.com. **Contact:** Susan Kan. "The contest is for first or second poetry books by women. Some poems in the submission may be previously published, but the ms as a whole must be unpublished. Send SASE or visit our website for guidelines. The contest is open to women poets who are US residents and who have not published more than 1 book." **Deadline:** Nov. 15. Charges $25. **Prize:** $1,000 and publication.

PHILBRICK POETRY AWARD

Providence Athenaeum, 251 Benefit St., Providence RI 02903. (401)421-6970. **Fax:** (401)421-2860. **E-mail:** smarkley@providence athenaeum.org. **Contact:** Sandy Markley. Offered annually for New England poets who have not yet published a book. Previous publication of individual poems in journals or anthologies is allowed. Judged by nationally-known poets. Guidelines for SASE or online. July 15-October 15. Charges $10 fee (includes copy of previously published chapbook). **Prize:** $500, publication of winning ms as a chapbook, and a public reading at Providence Athenaeum with the final judge/award presenter.

THE PINCH LITERARY AWARD IN POETRY

The Univ. of Memphis/Hohenberg Foundation, Dept. of English, 435 Patterson Hall, Memphis TN 38152. (901)678-4591. **E-mail:** editor@ thepinchjournal.com. "Offered annually for unpublished poems and fiction. Guidelines for SASE or on website." **Deadline:** March 15. Charges $20 fee for up to 3 poems or 5,000/word fiction. **Prize:** 1st Place: $1,500 for fiction and $1,000 for poetry and publication; 2nd and 3rd Place: Publication and a 1-year subscription.

THE POETRY CENTER BOOK AWARD

The Poetry Center, San Francisco State University, 1600 Holloway Ave., San Francisco CA 94132-9901. (415)338-2227. **Fax:** (415)338-0966. **Website:** www.sfsu.edu/~poetry. Estab. 1980. Offered annually for books of poetry and chapbooks, published in year of the prize. "Prize given for an extraordinary book of American poetry written in English." Please include a cover letter noting author name, book title(s), name of person issuing check, and check number. Will not consider anthologies or translations. **Deadline:** January 31 for books published and copywrited in the previous year. Charges $10 reading fee/entry. **Prize:** $500 and an invitation to read in the Poetry Center Reading Series.

POETS OUT LOUD PRIZE

Poets Out Loud, Fordham University at Lincoln Center, 113 W. 60th St., Room 924-I, New York NY 10023. (212)636-6792. **Fax:** (212)636-7153. **E-mail:** pol@fordham.edu. Annual competition for an unpublished, full-length poetry ms (50-80 pages). **Deadline:** November 15. Charges $25 entry fee. **Prize:** $2,000 book publication, and book launch in POL reading series

MARGARET REID POETRY CONTEST
FOR TRADITIONAL VERSE

c/o Winning Writers, 351 Pleasant St., PMB 222, Northampton MA 01060-3961. **E-mail:** johnreid@mail.qango.com. **Website:** www. winningwriters.com. **Contact:** John Reid. Estab. 2004. "Seeks poems in traditional verse forms, such as sonnets." Both unpublished and published work accepted. Guidelines for SASE or on website. **Deadline:** June 30. Charges $7 for every 25 lines of poetry. **Prize:** 1st Place: $3,000; 2nd Place: $1,000; 3rd Place: $400; 4th Place: $250; plus 6 Most Highly Commended awards of $150 each. The top 10 entries will be published on the Winning Writers website. Judged by John H. Reid and Dee C. Konrad.

SASKATCHEWAN POETRY AWARD

Saskatchewan Book Awards, Inc., 205B-2314 11th Ave., Regina SK S4P 0K1 Canada. (306)569-1585. **Fax:** (306)569-4187. **E-mail:** director@bookawards.sk.ca. **Contact:** Jackie Lay, executive director. Offered annually for work published September 15-September 14. This award is presented to a Saskatchewan author for the best book of poetry, judged on the quality of writing. **Deadline:** First deadline: July 31; Final deadline: September 14. Charges $25 (Canadian). **Prize:** $2,000

SILVER WINGS ANNUAL POETRY CONTEST

Silver Wings, P.O. Box 2340, Clovis CA 93613. (559)347-0194. **E-mail:** cloviswings@aol.com. **Contact:** Jackson Wilcox. Estab. 1983. "The annual contest is sponsored by Silver Wings, a small bimonthly poetry magazine." "We would like to encourage new writers of poetry with a Christian message or thought." **Deadline:** December 31. Charges $3. **Prize:** 1st Place: $100; 2nd Place: $50; 3rd Place: $35; 4th Place: $30; 5th Place: $25; 6th Place: $20; 7th Place: $15. A few Honorable Mentions are also published with no cash prize. Accepts first rights with permission to publish in Silver Wings. Poetry on Wings Board in February.

SLIPSTREAM ANNUAL POETRY
CHAPBOOK COMPETITION

Slipstream, Box 2071, Niagara Falls NY 14301. **E-mail:** editors@slip-streampress.org. **Website:** www.slipstreampress.org. **Contact:** Dan Sicoli, co-editor. "Offered annually to help promote a poet whose work is often overlooked or ignored. Open to any writer." Winner is featured prominently on the Slipstream website for one year, as well as in all Slipstream catalogs, press releases, and promotional material. Winning chapbooks are submitted by Slipstream for review by various national and international poetry/writing pubications and may also be featured in the Grants & Awards section of Poets & Writers magazine. **Deadline:** December 1. Charges $20. **Prize:** $1,000 and 50 copies of published chapbook. (Everyone who enters receives a copy of the winning chapbook plus one complimentary issue of Slipstream magazine.

HELEN C. SMITH MEMORIAL AWARD FOR POETRY

The Texas Institute of Letters, 6335 W. Northwest Hwy., #618, Dallas TX 75225. (214)363-7253. **E-mail:** dpayne@smu.edu. **Contact:** Dar-win Payne. Offered annually for the best book of poems published January 1-December 31 of previous year. Poet must have been born in Texas, have lived in the state at some time for at least 2 consecutive years, or the subject matter must be associated with the state. See website for guidelines. **Deadline:** January 1. **Prize:** $1,200.

THE SOW'S EAR CHAPBOOK PRIZE

The Sow's Ear Poetry Review, P.O. Box 127, Millwood VA 22646. (540)955-3955. **E-mail:** rglesman@gmail.com. **Contact:** Robert G. Lesman, managing editor. Estab. 1988. Offered for poetry mss of 22-26 pages. Guidelines for SASE, by e-mail, or on website. **Deadline:** Submit March-April (May 1 postmark). Charges $27 fee; $30 for Canadian addresses, $40 elsewhere; includes subscription. **Prize:** $1,000, 25 copies, and distribution to subscribers.

THE SOW'S EAR POETRY PRIZE

The Sow's Ear Poetry Review, P.O. Box 127, Millwood VA 22646-0127. (540)955-3955. **E-mail:** rglesman@gmail.com. **Website:** sows-ear. kitenet.net. **Contact:** Robert G. Lesman, managing editor. Estab. 1988. Offered for previously unpublished poetry. Guidelines on website, for SASE or by e-mail. All finalists' submissions considered for publication. Entries are not returned. Include SASE or e-mail address for notification. **Deadline:** November 1 postmark. Submit September-October. Charges $27, covering up to 5 poems. **Prize:** $1,000, publication of winner and some finalists. Contestants receive a year's subscription.

THE EDWARD STANLEY AWARD

Prairie Schooner, 201 Andrews Hall, P.O. Box 880334, Lincoln NE 68588-0334. (402)472-0911. **Fax:** (402)472-9771. **E-mail:** jengelhardt2@unlnotes.unl.edu. **Contact:** Hilda Raz. Offered annually for poetry published in Prairie Schooner in the previous year. **Prize:** $1,000.

THE ELIZABETH MATCHETT STOVER MEMORIAL AWARD

Southwest Review, Southern Methodist University, P.O. Box 750374, Dallas TX 75275-0374. (214)768-1037. **Fax:** (214)768-1408. **E-mail:** swr@mail.smu.edu. **Contact:** Jennifer Cranfill, Senior Editor and Willard Spiegelman, Editor-In-Chief. "Offered annually to the best works of poetry that have appeared in the magazine in the previous year. Please note that mss are submitted for publication, not for the prizes themselves. Guidelines for SASE and online." **Prize:** $300 Jennifer Cranfill and Willard Spiegelman.

STROKESTOWN INTERNATIONAL
POETRY COMPETITION

Strokestown International Poetry Festival, Bawn St., Strokestown, County Roscommon Ireland. (+353) 71 9633759. **E-mail:** director@ strokestownpoetry.org. **Website:** www.strokestownpoetry.com. **Contact:** Director. This annual competition was established to promote excellence in poetry, and participation in the reading and writing of it. Acquires first publication rights. **Deadline:** February 6. Charges Charges $5 (4 euros, £4). **Prize:** 1st **Prize:** 4,000 euros (approximately $3,900) for a poem in English of up to 70 lines, plus others totalling about $3,000 dollars. Up to 10 shortlisted po-ets will be invited to read at the Strokestown International Poetry Festival and paid a reading fee. Lawrence Sail, Mary O'Donnell, and Peter Denman.

TRANSCONTINENTAL POETRY AWARD
Pavement Saw Press, 321 Empire Street, Montpelier OH 43543. (419)485-0524. **E-mail:** info@pavementsaw.org. **Website:** pavement saw.org. **Contact:** David Baratier, editor. "Offered annually for a first book of poetry. Judged by the editor and a guest judge. Guidelines available online." **Deadline:** August 15. Charges $20 fee. **Prize:** $1,000, 50 copies for judge's choice, and standard royalty contract for editor's choice. All writers receive 2 free books for entering.

UTMOST CHRISTIAN POETRY CONTEST
Utmost Christian Writers Foundation, 121 Morin Maze, Edmonton AB T6K 1V1 Canada. (780)461-0221. The purpose of this annual contest is "to promote excellence in poetry by poets of Christian faith. All entries are eligible for most of the cash awards, but there is a special category for rhyming poetry with prizes of $300 and $100. All entries must be unpublished." **Deadline:** February 28. Charges $20/poem (maximum 5 poems). **Prize:** 1st Place: $1,000; 2nd Place: $600; ten prizes of $100 are offered for honorable mention. Rights are acquired to post winning entries on the organization's website. Judged by a committee of the Directors of Utmost Christian Writers Foundation (who work under the direction of Barbara Mitchell, chief judge).

DANIEL VAROUJAN AWARD
New England Poetry Club, 2 Farrar Street, Cambridge MA 02138. **E-mail:** contests@nepoetryclub.org. **Website:** www.nepoetryclub. org/contests.htm. **Contact:** NEPC Contest Coordinator. "One-thousand dollars for a poem in English worthy of the Armenian poet executed by the Ottoman Turks in the 1915 genocide that destroyed three-fourths of the Armenian population. Send poems in duplicate, with name and address of poet on one copy only. **Deadline:** May 31. Charges $10/up to 3 entries; made payable to New England Poetry Club. Members free. **Prize:** $1,000.

CHAD WALSH POETRY PRIZE
Beloit Poetry Journal, P.O. Box 151, Farmington ME 04938. (207)778-0020. **E-mail:** bpj@bpj.org. **Contact:** Lee Sharkey and John Rosen-wald, editors. "Offered annually to honor the memory of poet Chad Walsh, a founder of the Beloit Poetry Journal." The editors select an outstanding poem or group of poems from the poems published in the journal that year. Charges No entry fee. **Prize:** $3,500 in 2009

WAR POETRY CONTEST
Winning Writers, 351 Pleasant St., PMB 222, Northampton MA 01060-3961. (866)946-9748. **Fax:** (413)280-0539. **E-mail:** adam@winningwriters.com. **Contact:** Adam Cohen. Estab. 2002. "This an-nual contest seeks outstanding, unpublished poetry on the theme of war. Up to 3 poems can be submitted, with a maximum total of 500 lines. English language only; translations accepted if you wrote the

original poem." Submit online or by mail. Guidelines for SASE or see website. Nonexclusive right to publish submissions on Winning Writers.com, in e-mail newsletter, and in press releases. **Deadline:** November 15-May 31. Charges $15. **Prize:** 1st Place: $2,000 and publication on WinningWriters.com; 2nd Place: $1,200 and publica-tion; 3rd Place: $600 and publication; Honorable Mentions (12): $100 and publication. 2009 winner was Robert Hill Long for Wolverine and White Crow, Motivations, and Insurrection. Final Judge: award-winning poet Jendi Reiter.

THE WASHINGTON PRIZE
Dearlove Hall, Adirondack Community College, 640 Bay Rd., Queensbury NY 12804. **E-mail:** editor@wordworksdc.com. **Web-site:** www.wordworksdc.com. **Contact:** Nancy White, Washington Prize Admin. Estab. 1981. Offered annually "for the best full-length poetry manuscript (48-64 pp.) submitted to The Word Works each year. The Washington Prize contest is the only forum in which we con-sider unsolicited manuscripts." Acquires first publication rights. Open to any American writer. **Deadline:** January 15-March 1. Charges $25 fee. **Prize:** $1,500, book publication and 100 author copies; all en-trants receive a copy of the winning book.

WERGLE FLOMP HUMOR POETRY CONTEST
Winning Writers, 351 Pleasant St., PMB 222, Northampton MA 01060-3961. (866)946-9748. **Fax:** (413)280-0539. **E-mail:** adam@winningwriters.com. **Website:** www.winningwriters.com. **Contact:** Adam Cohen. Estab. 2002. "This annual contest seeks today's best humor poems. One poem of any length should be submitted, along with the name of the vanity contest that was spoofed. The poem should be in English. Inspired gibberish is also accepted. See website for guidelines, examples, and to submit your poem. nonexclusive right to publish submissions on WinningWriters.com, in e-mail news-letter, and in press releases." **Deadline:** August 15-April 1. Charges No fee to enter. **Prize:** 1st Place: $1,500; 2nd Place: $800; 3rd Place: $400. Twelve Honorable Mentions get $75 each. All prize winners receive publication at WinningWriters.com. Non-US winners will be paid in US currency (or PayPal) if a check is inconvenient. Final judge is Jendi Reiter.

WHITE PINE PRESS POETRY PRIZE
White Pine Press, P.O. Box 236, Buffalo NY 14201. **E-mail:** wpine@whitepine.org. **Contact:** Dennis Maloney, editor. Offered annually for previously published or unpublished poets. Manuscript: Up to 80 pages of original work; translations are not eligible. Poems may have appeared in magazines or limited-edition chapbooks. Open to any US citizen **Deadline:** November 30 (postmarked). Charges $20 fee. **Prize:** $1,000 and publication. Final Judge is a poet of national reputation. All entries are screened by the editorial staff of White Pine Press.

STAN AND TOM WICK POETRY PRIZE
Wick Poetry Center, 301 Satterfield Hall, Kent State University, P.O. Box 5190, Kent OH 44242-0001. (330)672-2067. **Fax:** (330)672-3333. **E-mail:** wickpoet@kent.edu. **Contact:** David Hassler, director. Open

to anyone writing in English who has not previously published a full-length book of poems (a volume of 50 pages or more published in an edition of 500 or more copies). Send SASE or visit the website for guidelines. **Deadline:** May 1. Charges $20 reading fee. **Prize:** $2,000 and publication by the Kent State University Press.

WILLIAM CARLOS WILLIAMS AWARD

Poetry Society of America, 15 Gramercy Park S., New York NY 10003. (212)254-9628. **Fax:** (212)673-2352. **Website:** www.poetrysociety.org. **Contact:** Programs Associate. Offered annually for a book of poetry published by a small press, nonprofit, or university press. Winning books are distributed to PSA Lyric Circle members while supplies last. Books must be submitted directly by publishers. Entry forms are required. It is strongly encouraged that applicants read the complete contest guidelines on the PSA website before submitting. **Deadline:** October 1-December 22. Charges $20 fee. **Prize:** $500-1,000.

THE J. HOWARD AND BARBARA M.J. WOOD PRIZE

Poetry, 444 North Michigan Ave., Suite 1850, Chicago IL 60611. (312)787-7070. **E-mail:** poetry@poetrymagazine.org. **Website:** www.poetrymagazine.org. Estab. 1994. Offered annually for poems published in Poetry during the preceding year (October-September). Poetry buys all rights to the poems published in the magazine. Copyrights are returned to the authors on request. **Prize:** $5,000.

WRITECORNER PRESS $500 POETRY AWARD

Writecorner Press, P.O. Box 140310, Gainesville FL 32614. (352)338-7778. **Website:** www.writecorner.com. **Contact:** Mary Sue Koeppel, Robert B. Gentry, coeditors. "Offered annually for unpublished poetry. Poetry may be in any style and on any subject. Maximum poem length is 40 lines. Only unpublished poems are eligible. No limit on number of poems entered by any 1 poet. The winning poem is published, as are the editors' choices poems. Copyright then returns to the authors. Guidelines for SASE or online." **Deadline:** March 31, 2010. Submit between Oct. 1 - March 31 annually. Charges $5/poem; $3 each additional poem. **Prize:** $500 First prize, $100 Editor's Choices, and publication on www.writecorner.com. Judged by Mary Sue Koeppel and Robert B. Gentry, editors.

WRITERS' JOURNAL POETRY CONTEST

Val-Tech Media, P.O. Box 394, Perham MN 56573. (218)346-7921. **Fax:** (218)346-7924. **E-mail:** writersjournal@writersjournal.com. **Website:** www.writersjournal.com. **Contact:** Esther M. Leiper-Estabrooks. "Offered for previously unpublished poetry. Receives fewer than 300 entries. Guidelines for SASE or online." **Deadline:** April 30, August 30, December 30. Charges $3/poem. **Prize:** 1st Place: $50; 2nd Place: $25; 3rd Place: $15. First, second, third, and selected honorable mention winners will be published in Writers' Journal magazine.

ZONE 3 POETRY AWARDS

ZONE 3, Austin Peay State University, P.O. Box 4565, Clarksville TN 37044. (931)221-7031. **Fax:** (931)221-7149. **E-mail:** wallacess@apsu.edu. **Contact:** Susan Wallace, managing editor. "Offered annually for unpublished poetry. Previous judges include Carolyn Forché, Margie Piercy, Maxine Kumin, Stephen Dunn, Mark Jarman, and Michael Collier. Open to any poet." Charges $10 fee (includes 1-year subscription). **Prize:** 1st Place: $500; 2nd Place: $300; 3rd Place: $100.

CHAPTER 36

CONFERENCES & WORKSHOPS

AMERICAN INDEPENDENT WRITERS (AIW)
SPRING WRITERS CONFERENCE

1001 Connecticut Ave. NW, Suite 701, Washington DC 20036. (202)775-5150. **Fax:** (202)775-5810. **E-mail:** info@amerindywriters. org. **Website:** www.amerindywriters.org. **Contact:** Taryn Carrino. Estab. 1975. Annual conference held in June. **Average attendance:** 350. Focuses on fiction, nonfiction, screenwriting, poetry, children's writing, and technical writing. Gives participants the chance to hear from and talk with dozens of experts on book and magazine publishing, as well as on the craft, tools, and business of writing. Speakers have included Erica Jong, John Barth, Kitty Kelley, Vanessa Leggett, Diana McLellan, Brian Lamb, and Stephen Hunter. New York and local agents attend the conference. **Additional Information:** See the website or send a SASE in mid-February for brochures/guidelines and fees information.

ANHINGA WRITERS' STUDIO WORKSHOPS

P.O. Box 357154, Gainesville FL 32635. (352) 379-8782. **Fax:** (352) 380-0018. **E-mail:** info@anhingawriters.org. **Website:** www.anhinga writers.org. Estab. 1997. Formerly Writing the Region. Annual conference held in summer. **Conference duration:** 4 days. **Average attendance:** 250. Conference concentrates on fiction, narrative non-fiction, poetry, and consultations with agents, edtitors, and publishers. **Costs:** available online. Lower costs for half-day and one-day registration.

ASJA WRITERS CONFERENCE

American Society of Journalists and Authors, 1501 Broadway, Suite 302, New York NY 10036. (212)997-0947. **Fax:** (212)937-2315. **E-mail:** asjaoffice@asja.org; director@asja.org. **Website:** www.asja. org/wc. **Contact:** Alexandra Owens, exec. director. Estab. 1971. Annual conference held in April. **Conference duration:** 2 days. **Average attendance:** 600. Covers nonfiction and screenwriting. Held at the Grand Hyatt in New York. Speakers have included Arianna Huffington, Kitty Kelley, Barbara Ehrenreich, Stefan Fatsis. Largest gathering of nonfiction freelance authors in the country. **Costs:** $200+, depending on when you sign up (includes lunch). Check website for updates. **Accommodations:** The hotel holding our conference always blocks out discounted rooms for attendees. **Additional Information:** Brochures available in February. Registration form is on the website. Inquire by e-mail or fax. Sign up for conference updates on website.

AUSTRALIAN POETRY FESTIVAL

Poets Union and the Australian Poetry Centre, P.O. Box 755, Potts Point NSW 1335 Australia. (61)(2)9357 6602. **Fax:** (61)(2)9818-5377. **E-mail:** info@poetsunion.com; martinlangford@bigpond.com. **Website:** www.poetsunion.com. Estab. 1998. "The Australian Poetry Festival is a joint festival to be hosted by the Poets Union and the Australian Poetry Centre on September 3, 4 and 5, 2010, in Sydney, and in other locations." The Australian Poetry Festival is a joint festival to be hosted by the Poets Union and the Australian Poetry Centre.

BLOODY WORDS

64 Shaver Ave., Toronto ON M9B 3T5 Canada. **E-mail:** carosoles@ rogers.com; cheryl@freedmanandsister.com; amummenhoff@rogers.com; info@bloodywords.com. **Website:** www.bloodywords.com. **Contact:** Caro Soles. Estab. 1999. Annual conference usually held in June. 2010 dates: May 28-30. **Conference duration:** 3 days. **Average attendance:** 250. Focuses on mystery fiction and aims to provide a showcase for Canadian mystery writers and readers, as well as provide writing information to aspiring writers. We will present 3 tracks of programming: Just the Facts, where everyone from coroners to toxicologists to tactical police units present how things are done in the real works; and What's the Story - where panelists discuss subjects of interest to readers; and the Mystery Cafe, where 12 authors read and discuss their work. Bloody Words is Canada's oldest and largest gathering of mystery readers and authors. The conference has become the June event to look forward to for people who enjoy genre conventions. **Costs:** $175. Includes banquet. **Accommodations:** A special rate will be available at The Downtown Hilton Hotel in Toronto, Ontario. **Additional Information:** Registration is available online. Send inquiries via e-mail.

BLUE RIDGE "AUTUMN IN THE MOUNTAINS" NOVEL RETREAT

(800)588-7222. **E-mail:** ylehman@bellsouth.net. **Website:** www. lifeway.com/novelretreat. **Contact:** Yvonne Lehman, director. Estab. 2007. Annual retreat held in October at Ridgecrest/LifeWay Conference Center near Asheville NC. Retreat duration: Sunday through lunch on Thursday. **Average attendance:** 55. All areas of novel writing is included. For beginning and advanced novelists. Site: LifeWay/Ridgecrest Conference Center, 20 miles east of Asheville, NC. Faculty: Dr. Dennis Hensley, Dr. Angela Hunt, Jeff Gerke, Deborah Raney, DiAnn Mills, Ray Blackstock, Ann Tatlock, Yvonne Lehman. No editors or agents. Mornings: large group class.

Afternoons: writing time and workshops. Evening: discussion and faculty panel. **Costs:** Retreat Fee: $375. **Accommodations:** $84 in Mountain Laurel Hotel on campus. Meals: $96.

BRISBANE WRITERS FESTIVAL

P.O. Box 3453, 12 Merivale St., South Brisbane QLD 4101 Australia. (61)(7)3255-0254. **Fax:** (61)(7)3255-0362. **E-mail:** info@brisbane writersfestival.com.au. **Website:** www.brisbanewritersfestival.com. au. **Contact:** Jane O'Hara, Artistic Director. Annual festival held in September. This event draws on local, national, and international guests for an eclectic mix of panels, discussions, debates, launches and interviews.

BYRON BAY WRITERS FESTIVAL

Northern Rivers Writers' Centre, P.O. Box 1846, 69 Johnson St., Byron Bay NSW 2481 Australia. 040755-2441. **E-mail:** jeni@nrwc. org.au. **Website:** www.byronbaywritersfestival.com. **Contact:** Jeni Caffin, director. Estab. 1997. Annual festival held the first weekend in August at Byron's Bay Belongil Fields. Festival duration: 3 days. Celebrate and reflect with over 100 of the finest writers from Australia and overseas. Workshops, panel discussions, and literary breakfasts, lunches, and dinners will also be offered. The Byron Bay Writers Festival is organised by the staff and Committee of the Northern Rivers Writers' Centre, a member based organisation receiving core funding from Arts NSW. **Costs:** See costs online under Tickets. Early bird, NRWC members and students, kids. **Additional Information:** "2010 Festival dates are August 6-8 with workshops beginning August 2 and discounted Early Bird 3 day passes are on sale from March 26 at our website or through Jetset Byron Bay on 02 6685 6262. Full program on sale June 4.

CALIFORNIA CRIME WRITERS CONFERENCE

cosponsored by Sisters in Crime/Los Angeles and the Southern California Chapter of Mystery Writers of America, No public address available, **E-mail:** sistersincrimela@yahoo.com. **Website:** www. sistersincrimela.com. Estab. 1995. Annual conference held June, 2011. TBO. **Average attendance:** 150. Conference on mystery and crime writing. Offers craft and forensic sessions, a keynote speaker, a luncheon speaker, author and agent panels, and book signings. **Additional Information:** Conference information is available on the website. Website might be down temporarily.

CLARION WEST WRITERS WORKSHOP

P.O. Box 31264, Seattle WA 98101-1264. (206)322-9083. **E-mail:** info@clarionwest.org. **Website:** www.clarionwest.org. Clarion West is an intensive 6-week workshop for writers preparing for professional careers in science fiction and fantasy, held annually in Seattle, Washington, USA. Usually goes from mid-June through end of July. **Conference duration:** 6 weeks. **Average attendance:** 18. Held near the University of Washington. Deadline for applications is March 1. Instructors are well-known writers and editors in the field. This year's workshop will be held from June 21 - July 31, 2009. **Costs:** $3,200 (for tuition, housing, most meals). $100 discount if application received prior to February 1. Limited scholarships are available based

on financial need. **Additional Information:** This is a critique-based workshop. Students are encouraged to write a story every week; the critique of student material produced at the workshop forms the principal activity of the workshop. Students and instructors critique mss as a group. Students must submit 20-30 pages of ms to qualify for admission. Conference guidelines are available for a SASE. Visit the website for updates and complete details.

DESERT DREAMS

Phoenix Desert Rose Chapter No. 60, PO Box 27407, Tempe AZ 85285. (866)267-2249. **E-mail:** info@desertroserwa.org; desert dreams@desertroserwa.org. **Website:** www.desertroserwa.org. Estab. 1986. Conference held every other April. **Conference duration:** 3 days. **Average attendance:** 250. Covers marketing, fiction, screen-writing, and research. Keynote speakers: New York Times Bestselling Author Linda Lael Miller and Brad Schreiber VP of Storytech (The Writer's Journey with Chris Vogler). **Costs:** $218+ (includes meals, seminars, appointments with agents/editors). **Accommodations:** Discounted rates for attendees is negotiated at the Crowne Plaza San Marcos Resort in Chandler, Ariz. **Additional Information:** Send inquiries via e-mail. Visit website for updates and complete details.

EAST OF EDEN WRITERS CONFERENCE

P.O. Box 3254, Santa Clara CA 95055. **E-mail:** eastofeden@south baywriters.com; press@southbaywriters.com. **Website:** www.south baywriters.com. Estab. 1987. Biennial conference held in September of even years. **Average attendance:** 300. Writers of all levels are welcome. Pitch-sessions to agents and publishers are available, as are meetings with authors and editors. Workshops address the craft and the business of writing and publishing. Location: Salinas, Calif. - Steinbeck Country. **Costs:** Costs vary. The full conference (Friday through Sunday noon) is approximately $350; Saturday only is approximately $200. The fee includes meals, workshops and pitch/meeting sessions. Contests require attendance and additional nominal fee. **Accommodations:** Negotiated rates at local hotels - $85-110 per night, give or take. **Additional Information:** The East of Eden conference is run by writers/volunteers from the nonprofit California Writers Club, South Bay Branch. The Salinas Community Center's Sherwood Hall has been reserved for September 24-26, 2010. Luis Valdez heads the list of seven keynote speakers. Some thirty-five professional presenters will lead workshops touching 2010 theme "Why do I write?" For details, please visit our website or send an SASE.

EAST TEXAS CHRISTIAN WRITERS CONFERENCE

The School of Humanities, Dr. Jerry L. Summers, Dean, Scarborough Hall, East Texas Baptist Univ., 1209 N. Grove, Marshall TX 75670. (903)923-2269. **E-mail:** jhopkins@etbu.edu. **Website:** www. etbu.edu/News/CWC. Estab. 2002. Annual conference held 2nd weekend of April. **Average attendance:** 125. Conference offers: contact, conversation, and exchange of ideas with other aspiring writers; outstanding presentations and workshop experiences with established authors, agents, editors, and publishers; potential publishing and writing opportunities; networking with other writers with related interests; promotion of both craft and faith; and one-on-one consultations with agents, editors, and publishers. Speakers have included Vickie Phelps, Terry Burns, Robert Darden, Bill Keith, Miriam Hees, Lenora Worth, Donn Taylor, and Mary Lou Redding. Offers an advanced track and teen track beginner, intermediate, and advanced level contest. Partial scholarships available for students only. **Costs:** Visit website. **Accommodations:** Visit website for a list of local hotels offering a discounted rate.

ENVIRONMENTAL WRITERS' CONFERENCE & WORKSHOP IN HONOR OF RACHEL CARSON

New-Cue, Inc., Methodist College, Clark Hall, 5300 Ramsey St., Fayetteville NC 28311. (845)630-7047 or (910)630-7046. **Fax:** (910)630-7221. **E-mail:** info@new-cue.org. **Website:** www.new-cue.org. Estab. 1999. Biennial conference held in June. Next one will be in 2010. **Conference duration:** 4 days. **Average attendance:** 100. This interdisciplinary event is a blend of scholarly presentations, readings, informal discussions, and writing workshops. Held at The Spruce Point Inn in Boothbay Harbor, Maine. Speakers have included Lawrence Buell, Bill McKibben, Carl Safina, Linda Lear and Verlyn Klinkenborg. **Costs:** Registration costs include sessions, meals and keynote reception. **Accommodations:** Special rates are available for participants at the Spruce Point Inn. Transportation and area information is available through the Boothbay Harbor Chamber of Commerce.

FESTIVAL OF FAITH AND WRITING

Department of English, Calvin College, 1795 Knollcrest Circle SE, Grand Rapids MI 49546. (616)526-6770. **E-mail:** ffw@calvin.edu. **Website:** www.calvin.edu/festival. Estab. 1990. Biennial festival held in April. **Conference duration:** 3 days. The festival brings together writers, editors, publishers, musicians, artists, and readers to discuss and celebrate insightful writing that explores issues of faith. Focuses on fiction, nonfiction, memoir, poetry, drama, children's, young adult, academic, film, and songwriting. Past speakers have included Joyce Carol Oates, Salman Rushdie, Patricia Hampl, Thomas Lynch, Leif Enger, Marilynne Robinson and Michael Chabon. Agents and editors attend the festival. **Costs:** Consult website. **Accommodations:** Shuttles are available to and from local hotels. Shuttles are also available for overflow parking lots. A list of hotels with special rates for conference attendees is available on the festival website. High school and college students can arrange on-campus lodging by e-mail. **Additional Information:** Online registration opens in October. Accepts inquiries by e-mail and phone

FLATHEAD RIVER WRITERS CONFERENCE

P.O. Box 7711, Kalispell MT 59904-7711. **E-mail:** answers@authors oftheflathead.org. **Website:** www.authorsoftheflathead.org. Estab. 1990. Annual conference held in early mid-October. **Average attendance:** 100. We provide several small, intense 3-day workshops before the general weekend conference. Workshops, panel discussions, and speakers focus on novels, nonfiction, screenwriting, short stories, magazine articles, and the writing industry. Formerly held at the Grouse Mountain Lodge in Whitefish, Montana. Past speakers have included Sam Pinkus, Randy Wayne White, Donald Maass,

Ann Rule, Cricket Pechstein, Marcela Landres, Amy Rennert, Ben Mikaelsen, Esmond Harmsworth, Linda McFall, and Ron Carlson. Agents will be speaking and available for meetings with attendees. **Accommodations:** Rooms are available at a discounted rate. **Additional Information:** "Our 20th Annual Flathead River Writers' Conference will be reduced in scope and duration. It will be a one-day conference on October 2nd and 3rd, 2010 at Flathead Valley Community College. There will be no pre-conference workshops this year. It is our hope that by doing this we can relieve some of the pressures on your pocketbooks and still make it possible for you to enjoy and learn from top-notch speakers. We will soon announce the agenda for our conference and the particulars. Watch our website for details. Send inquiries via e-mail."

FLORIDA CHRISTIAN WRITERS CONFERENCE

2344 Armour Ct., Titusville FL 32780. (321)269-5831. **Fax:** (321)264-0037. **E-mail:** billiewilson@cfl.rr.com. **Website:** www.flwriters.org. Estab. 1988. Annual conference held in March. **Conference duration:** 4 days. **Average attendance:** 275. Covers fiction, nonfiction, magazine writing, marketing, Internet writing, greeting cards, and more. Conference is held at the Christian Retreat Center in Brandenton, Florida. **Costs:** $575 (includes tuition, meals). **Accommodations:** We provide a shuttle from the Orlando airport. $725/double occupancy; $950/single occupancy. **Additional Information:** "Each writer may submit 2 works for critique. We have specialists in every area of writing. Brochures/guidelines are available online or for a SASE."

GOTHAM WRITERS' WORKSHOP

WritingClasses.com, 555 Eighth Ave., Suite 1402, New York NY 10018. (212)974-8377. **Fax:** (212)307-6325. **E-mail:** dana@write. org. **Website:** www.writingclasses.com. Estab. 1993. Online classes are held throughout the year. There are four terms of NYC classes, beginning in January, April, June/July, and September/October. Offers craft-oriented creative writing courses in general creative writing, fiction writing, screenwriting, nonfiction writing, article writing, stand-up comedy writing, humor writing, memoir writing, novel writing, children's book writing, playwriting, poetry, songwriting, mystery writing, science fiction writing, romance writing, television writing, article writing, travel writing, business writing and classes on freelancing, selling your screenplay, hot to blog, nonfiction book proposal, and getting published. Also, the Workshop offers a teen program, private instruction, mentoring program, and classes on selling your work. Classes are held at various schools in New York City as well as online at www.writingclasses.com. Agents and editors participate in some workshops. **Costs:** $395/10-week workshops; $125 for the four-week online selling seminars and 1-day intensive courses; $295 for 6-week creative writing and business writing classes.

THE GREAT AMERICAN PITCHFEST & SCREENWRITING CONFERENCE

Twilight Pictures, 12400 Ventura Blvd. #735, Studio City CA 91604. (877)255-2528. **E-mail:** info@pitchfest.com. **Website:** pitchfest. com/index.shtml. **Conference duration:** 2 days (one day conference, one day pitchfest). "Our companies are all carefully screened, and only the most credible companies in the industry are invited to hear pitches. They include: agents, managers, and production companies." Annual **Costs:** Saturday is free, with a full day of industry classes, workshops, and panels, all led by industry professionals. The Sunday Pitchfest is $250. **Accommodations:** All activities will be held at the Burbank Marriott Hotel & Convention Center, 2500 N. Hollywood Way, Burbank, CA 91505. **Additional Information:** June 26-27, 2010.

GREEN MOUNTAIN WRITERS CONFERENCE

47 Hazel St., Rutland VT 05701. (802)236-6133. **E-mail:** ydaley@sbcglobal.net. **Website:** www.vermontwriters.com. Estab. 1999. "Annual conference held in the summer; 2010 dates are Aug. 2 - Aug. 6. Covers fiction, creative nonfiction, poetry, journalism, nature writing, essay, memoir, personal narrative, and biography. Held at an old dance pavillion on on a remote pond in Tinmouth, Vermont. Speakers have included Stephen Sandy, Grace Paley, Ruth Stone, Howard Frank Mosher, Chris Bohjalian, Joan Connor, Yvonne Daley, David Huddle, David Budbill, Jeffrey Lent, Verandah Porche, Tom Smith, and Chuck Clarino." **Costs:** $500 before July 1; $525 after July 1. Partial scholarships are available. **Accommodations:** "We have made arrangements with a major hotel in nearby Rutland and 3 area bed and breakfast inns for special accommodations and rates for conference participants. You must make your own reservations."

HEART TALK

Women's Center for Ministry, Western Seminary, 5511 SE Hawthorne Blvd., Portland OR 97215-3367. (800)517-1800, ext. 1931. **Fax:** (503)517-1889. **E-mail:** wcm@westernseminary.edu. **Website:** www.westernseminary.edu/women. Estab. 1998. Biannual conference held in March. Conference alternates between writing one year and speaking the next. Provides inspirational training for beginning and advanced writers/speakers. Workshops may include writing fiction, nonfiction, children's books, publishing, trends, dialogue, book proposals, websites, blogs, etc. Editors/publicists available for one-on-one consultations. Past speakers have included Robin Jones Gunn, Deborah Hedstrom-Page, Patricia Rushford, Sally Stuart, and many more. **Additional Information:** Conference information is available online, by e-mail, phone, or fax.

HIGHLAND SUMMER CONFERENCE

Box 7014, Radford University, Radford VA 24142-7014. (540)831-5366. **Fax:** (540)831-5951. **E-mail:** rbderrick@radford.edu; jasbury@radford.edu. **Website:** www.radford.edu/~arsc. **Contact:** Ruth Derrick. Estab. 1978. Annual conference held in June. 2010 date: June 7-18. **Conference duration:** 2 weeks. **Average attendance:** 25. Covers fiction, nonfiction, poetry, and screenwriting. This year's Highland Summer Conference will be conducted the first week by Pamela Duncan. The second week of the Conference will be conducted by author George Ella Lyon. Special evening readings by Dot Jackson and Charles Swanson. Go to website for more information. **Costs:** The cost is based on current Radford tuition for 3 credit hours, plus an additional conference fee. On-campus meals and housing are

available at additional cost. In 2009, conference tuition was $815/in-state undergraduates, $1,944/for out-of-state undergraduates, $900/in-state graduates, and $1,728/out-of-state graduates. **Accommodations:** We do not have special rate arrangements with local hotels. We do offer accommodations on the Radford University campus in a recently refurbished residence hall. The 2009 cost was $26-36/night. **Additional Information:** Conference leaders typically critique work done during the 2-week conference, but do not ask to have any writing submitted prior to the conference. Conference brochures/guidelines are available in March for a SASE.

HIGHLIGHTS FOUNDATION WRITERS WORKSHOP AT CHAUTAUQUA

814 Court St., Honesdale PA 18431. (570)253-1192. **Fax:** (570)253-0179. **E-mail:** contact@highlightsfoundation.org. **Website:** www.highlightsfoundation.org. Estab. 1985. Annual conference held July 16-23, 2011. **Average attendance:** 100. Workshops are geared toward those who write for children at the beginner, intermediate, and advanced levels. Offers seminars, small group workshops, and one-on-one sessions with authors, editors, illustrators, critics, and publishers. Workshop site is the picturesque community of Chautauqua, New York. Speakers have included Bruce Coville, Candace Fleming, Linda Sue Park, Jane Yolen, Patricia Gauch, Jerry Spinelli, Eileen Spinelli, Joy Cowley and Pam Munoz Ryan. **Costs:** 2009 was $2,400 (includes all meals, conference supplies, gate pass to Chautauqua Institution). **Accommodations:** We coordinate ground transportation to and from airports, trains, and bus stations in the Erie, Pennsylvania and Jamestown/Buffalo, New York area. We also coordinate accommodations for conference attendees. **Additional Information:** "We offer the opportunity for attendees to submit a manuscript for review at the conference. Workshop brochures/guidelines are available upon request."

INTERNATIONAL MUSEUM PUBLISHING SEMINAR

University of Chicago, Graham School of General Studies, 1427 E. 60th St., Chicago IL 60637. (773)702-1682. **Fax:** (773)702-6814. **E-mail:** spesin@uchicago.edu. kjaffe@uchicago.edu. **Website:** grahamschool.uchicago.edu. Sarah Pesin **Contact:** Kineret Jaffe. Estab. 1988. Biennial conference. **Conference duration:** 2 1/2 days. **Average attendance:** 250. Primarily covers nonfiction, writing, and editing in museums. Recent themes have included selecting an attractive books cover, artful strategies for cutting costs, digital imaging, a survival guide, and more. The conference moves to a new city each year and is co-sponsored by the university with different museums. **Costs:** $600-650 **Accommodations:** See website for hotel options. **Additional Information:** Send a SASE in January for brochure/guidelines. Inquire via e-mail or fax.

IWWG EARLY SPRING IN CALIFORNIA CONFERENCE

International Women's Writing Guild, P.O. Box 810, Gracie Station, New York NY 10028-0082. (212)737-7536. **Fax:** (212)737-9469. **E-mail:** iwwg@iwwg.org. **Website:** www.iwwg.org. Estab. 1982. Annual conference held the second week in March. **Average attendance:** 50. Conference promotes creative writing, personal growth, and voice. Site is a redwood forest mountain retreat in Santa Cruz, California. **Costs:** $350/members; $380/nonmembers for weekend program with room and board; $125 for weekend program without room and board. **Accommodations:** All participants stay at the conference site or may commute. **Additional Information:** Brochures/guidelines are available online or for a SASE. Inquire via e-mail or fax.

JACKSON HOLE WRITERS CONFERENCE

PO Box 1974, Jackson WY 83001. (307)413-3332. **E-mail:** tim@ jacksonholewritersconference.com. **Website:** www.jacksonhole writersconference.com. Estab. 1991. Annual conference held in June. For 2010: June 24-27. **Conference duration:** 4 days. **Average attendance:** 110. Covers fiction, creative nonfiction, and young adult and offers ms critiques from authors, agents, and editors. Agents in attendance will take pitches from writers. Paid manuscript critique programs are available. **Costs:** $355-385, includes all workshops, speaking events, cocktail party, BBQ, and goodie bag with dining coupons. **Additional Information:** Held at the Center for the Arts in Jackson, Wyoming, and online.

KARITOS CHRISTIAN ARTS CONFERENCE

1122 Brentwood Ln., Wheaton IL 60189. (847)925-8018. **E-mail:** bob@karitos.com. **Website:** www.karitos.com. Estab. 1996. Annual conference held each summer in July. 2010: July 15-17. **Average attendance:** 200-300. Karitos is a celebration and teaching weekend for Christian artists and writers. Literary arts track focuses on practical instruction in the craft of writing. Site for this year's conference is Living Waters Community Church in the Chicago suburb of Bolingbrook. Past faculty has included Lori Davis, John DeJarlais, Eva Marie Everson, Lin Johnson, Patricia Hickman, Elma Photikarm, Rajendra Pillai, Jane Rubietta, Travis Thrasher and Chris Wave. **Costs:** See website for costs.

KILLER NASHVILLE

P.O. Box 680686, Franklin TN 37068-0686. (615)599-4032. **E-mail:** contact@killernashville.com. **Website:** www.killernashville.com. Estab. 2006. Annual conference held in August. **Conference duration:** 3 days. **Average attendance:** 180+. Conference designed for writers and fans of mysteries and thrillers, including fiction and nonfiction authors, playwrights, and screenwriters. There are many opportunities for authors to sign books. 2010 guest of honor is Jeffery Deaver. Authors/panelists have included Michael Connelly, Bill Bass, J.A. Jance, Carol Higgins Clark, Hallie Ephron, Greg Hurwitz, Chris Grabenstein, Rhonda Pollero, P.J. Parrish, Reed Farrel Coleman, Kathryn Wall, Mary Saums, Don Bruns, Bill Moody, Richard Helms, Brad Strickland and Steven Womack. Literary agents and acquisitions editors attend and take pitches from writers. The conference is sponsored by American Blackguard, Barnes and Noble, Mystery Writers of America, Sisters in Crime and the Nashville Scene, among others. Representatives from the FBI, TBI, ATF, police department and sheriff's department present on law enforcement procedures to the general public.

THE MACDOWELL COLONY

100 High St., Peterborough NH 03458. (603)924-3886. **Fax:** (603)924-9142. **E-mail:** admissions@macdowellcolony.org. **Website:** www.macdowellcolony.org. Estab. 1907. Open to writers, playwrights, composers, visual artists, film/video artists, interdisciplinary artists and architects. Applicants send information and work samples for review by a panel of experts in each discipline. Application form submitted online at www.macdowellcolony.org/apply.html. Work samples and completed application forms must still be mailed. See application guidelines for details. **Costs:** Travel reimbursement and stipends are available for participants of the residency, based on need. There are no residency fees.

MARYMOUNT MANHATTAN COLLEGE WRITERS' CONFERENCE

Marymount Manhattan College, 221 E. 71st St., New York NY 10021. (212)774-4810. **E-mail:** lfrumkes@mmm.edu. Estab. 1993. "Annual conference held in June. Keynote speakers for this year's conference held on June 3rd 2010 will be David Baldacci and Cathy Black. **Conference duration:** 1 day. **Average attendance:** 200. We present workshops on several different writing genres and panels on fiction and nonfiction, literary agents, memoir and more. Over 60 distinguished authors, agents, and publicists attend. Keynote speakers have included Lewis Lapham and Joyce Carol Oates." **Costs:** $165 before June 1; $185 after June 1 (includes lunch, reception).

MONTROSE CHRISTIAN WRITERS' CONFERENCE

5 Locust St., Montrose PA 18801. (570)278-1001 or (800)598-5030. **Fax:** (570)278-3061. **E-mail:** mbc@montrosebible.org. **Website:** www.montrosebible.org. Estab. 1990. "Annual conference held in July. Offers workshops, editorial appointments, and professional critiques. We try to meet a cross-section of writing needs, for beginners and advanced, covering fiction, poetry, and writing for children. It is small enough to allow personal interaction between attendees and faculty. Speakers have included William Petersen, Mona Hodgson, Jim Fletcher, and Terri Gibbs." **Costs:** $150/tuition; $35/critique for 2008. **Accommodations:** Housing and meals are available on site.

MOUNT HERMON CHRISTIAN WRITERS CONFERENCE

37 Conference Drive, Mount Hermon CA 95041. **E-mail:** info@ mounthermon.org. **Website:** www.mounthermon.org/writers. Estab. 1970. Annual professional conference (always held over the Palm Sunday weekend, Friday noon through Tuesday noon. 2011 dates are April 15-19). **Average attendance:** 450. Sponsored by and held at the 440-acre Mount Hermon Christian Conference Center near San Jose, California in the heart of the coastal redwoods, we are a broad-ranging conference for all areas of Christian writing, including fiction, nonfiction, fantasy, children's, teen, young adult, poetry, magazines, inspirational and devotional writing. This is a working, how-to conference, with Major Morning tracks in all genres (including a track especially for teen writers), and as many as 20 optional workshops each afternoon. Faculty-to-student ratio

is about 1 to 6. The bulk of our more than 70 faculty members are editors and publisher representatives from major Christian publishing houses nationwide. Speakers have included T. Davis Bunn, Debbie Macomber, Jerry Jenkins, Bill Butterworth, Dick Foth and others. **Accommodations:** Registrants stay in hotel-style accommodations. Meals are buffet style, with faculty joining registrants. **Additional Information:** "The residential nature of our conference makes this a unique setting for one-on-one interaction with faculty/staff. There is also a decided inspirational flavor to the conference, and general sessions with well-known speakers are a highlight. Registrants may submit 2 works for critique in advance of the conference, then have personal interviews with critiquers during the conference. All conference information is online by December 1 of each year. All conference information is online by December 1 of each year. Send inquiries via e-mail. Tapes of past conferences are also available online."

NATCHEZ LITERARY AND CINEMA CELEBRATION

P.O. Box 1307, Natchez MS 39121-1307. (601)446-1208. **Fax:** (601)446-1214. **E-mail:** carolyn.smith@colin.edu. **Website:** www.colin.edu/NLCC. Estab. 1990. Annual conference held in February. **Conference duration:** 5 days. Conference focuses on all literature, including film scripts. Each year's conference deals with some general aspect of Southern history. Speakers have included Eudora Welty, Margaret Walker Alexander, William Styron, Willie Morris, Ellen Douglas, Ernest Gaines, Elizabeth Spencer, Nikki Giovanni, Myrlie Evers-Williams, and Maya Angelou.

NATIONAL WRITERS ASSOCIATION
FOUNDATION CONFERENCE

P.O. Box 4187, Parker CO 80134. (303)841-0246. **Fax:** (303)841-2607. **E-mail:** natlwritersassn@hotmail.com. **Website:** www.nationalwriters. com. **Contact:** Sandy Whelchel. Estab. 1926. Annual conference held the second week of June in Denver. **Conference duration:** 1 day. **Average attendance:** 100. Focuses on general writing and marketing. **Costs:** Approximately $100. **Additional Information:** Awards for previous contests will be presented at the conference. Brochures/guidelines are online, or send a SASE.

NEW JERSEY ROMANCE WRITERS PUT
YOUR HEART IN A BOOK CONFERENCE

P.O. Box 513, Plainsboro NJ 08536. **E-mail:** njrwconfchair@yahoo. com; njrw@njromance writers.org. **Website:** www.njromancewriters. org. Estab. 1984. Annual conference held in October. **Average attendance:** 500. Workshops are offered on various topics for all writers of romance, from beginner to multi-published. Speakers have included Nora Roberts, Kathleen Woodiwiss, Patricia Gaffney, Jill Barnett and Kay Hooper. Appointments are offered with editors/agents. Annual. **Accommodations:** Special rate available for conference attendees at the Sheraton at Renaissance Woodbridge Hotel in Iselin, New Jersey. **Additional Information:** Conference brochures, guidelines, and membership information are available

for SASE. Massive bookfair is open to the public with authors signing copies of their books.

NIMROD AWARDS CELEBRATION &
WRITING WORKSHOP

University of Tulsa, 800 S. Tucker Drive, Tulsa OK 74104-3189. (918)631-3080. **Fax:** (918)631-3033. **E-mail:** nimrod@utulsa.edu. **Website:** www.utulsa.edu/nimrod. Estab. 1978. Annual conference held in October. **Conference duration:** 1 day. Offers one-on-one editing sessions, readings, panel discussions, and master classes in fiction, poetry, nonfiction, memoir, and fantasy writing. Speakers have included Myla Goldberg, B.H. Fairchild, Colleen McElroy, Gina Ochsner, Kelly Link, Rilla Askew, Matthew Galkin, and A.D. Coleman. **Additional Information:** Full conference details are online in August.

NORTH CAROLINA WRITERS'
NETWORK FALL CONFERENCE

P.O. Box 954, Carrboro NC 27510-0954. (919)251-9140. **Fax:** (919)929-0535. **E-mail:** mail@ncwriters.org. **Website:** www.nc writers.org. Estab. 1985. "Annual conference held in November in different NC venues. **Average attendance:** 250. This organization hosts two conferences: one in the spring and one in the fall. Each conference is a weekend full of workshops, panels, book signings, and readings (including open mic). There will be a keynote speaker, along with sessions on a variety of genres, including fiction, poetry, creative nonfiction, journalism, children's book writing, screenwriting, and playwriting. We also offer craft, editing, and marketing classes. We hold the event at a conference center with hotel rooms available. Speakers have included Donald Maass, Noah Lukeman, Joe Regal, Jeff Kleinman, and Evan Marshall. Some agents will teach classes and some are available for meetings with attendees." **Costs:** Approximately $250 (includes 2 meals). **Accommodations:** Special rates are usually available at the Conference Hotel, but conferees must make their own reservations. **Additional Information:** Brochures/guidelines are available online or by sending your street address to mail@ncwriters.org. You can also register online.

ODYSSEY FANTASY WRITING WORKSHOP

P.O. Box 75, Mont Vernon NH 03057. **E-mail:** jcavelos@sff.net. **Website:** www.odysseyworkshop.org. Estab. 1996. Annual workshop held in June (through July). **Conference duration:** 6 weeks. **Average attendance:** 16. A workshop for fantasy, science fiction, and horror writers that combines an intensive learning and writing experience with in-depth feedback on students' mss. Held on the campus of Saint Anselm College in Manchester, New Hampshire. Speakers have included George R.R. Martin, Elizabeth Hand, Jane Yolen, Harlan Ellison, Melissa Scott and Dan Simmons. **Costs:** $1,900/tuition; $775-1,550/on-campus apartment; approximately $500/on-campus meals. **Additional Information:** Prospective students must include a 4,000 word writing sample with their application. Accepts inquiries by SASE, e-mail, fax and phone. Application deadline April 8.

WILLIAM PATERSON UNIVERSITY
SPRING WRITER'S CONFERENCE
English Department, Atrium 232, 300 Pompton Rd., Wayne NJ 07470. (973)720-3067. **Fax:** (973)720-2189. **E-mail:** parrasj@wpunj. edu. **Website:** http://euphrates.wpunj.edu/writersconference. Annual conference held in April. **Conference duration:** 1 day. **Average attendance:** 100-125. Small writing workshops and panels address topics such as writing from life, getting your work in print, poetry, playwriting, fiction, creative nonfiction, and book and magazine editing. Sessions are led by William Paterson faculty members and distinguished guest writers and editors of verse and prose. Speakers have included Alison Lurie, Russell Banks, Terese Svoboda, and Anthony Swofford. **Costs:** $50 (includes lunch).

PIKES PEAK WRITERS CONFERENCE
Pikes Peak Writers, 427 E. Colorado Ave., #116, Colorado Springs CO 80903. (719)531-5723. **E-mail:** info@pikespeakwriters.com. **Website:** www.pikespeakwriters.com. Estab. 1993. Annual conference held in April. **Conference duration:** 3 days. **Average attendance:** 400. Workshops, presentations, and panels focus on writing and publishing mainstream and genre fiction (romance, science fiction/fantasy, suspense/thrillers, action/adventure, mysteries, children's, young adult). Agents and editors are available for meetings with attendees on Saturday. **Costs:** $300-500 (includes all meals). **Accommodations:** Marriott Colorado Springs holds a block of rooms at a special rate for attendees until late March. **Additional Information:** Readings with critiques are available on Friday afternoon. Also offers a contest for unpublished writers; entrants need not attend the conference. Deadline: November 1. Registration and contest entry forms are online; brochures are available in January. Send inquiries via e-mail.

PNWA SUMMER WRITERS CONFERENCE
PMB 2717, 1420 NW Gilman Blvd., Issaquah WA 98027. (425)673-2665. **E-mail:** pnwa@pnwa.org. **Website:** www.pnwa.org. Estab. 1955. All conferences are held in July. **Conference duration:** 4 days. **Average attendance:** 400. Attendees have the chance to meet agents and editors, learn craft from authors and uncover marketing secrets. Speakers have included J.A. Jance, Sheree Bykofsky, Kimberley Cameron, Jennie Dunham, Donald Maass, Jandy Nelson, Robert Dugoni and Terry Brooks. Annual. **Accommodations:** The conference is held at the Hilton Seattle Airport & Conference Center. **Additional Information:** "PNWA also holds an annual literary contest every February with more than $12,000 in prize money. Finalists' manuscripts are then available to agents and editors at our summer conference. Visit the website for further details."

REMEMBER THE MAGIC
International Women's Writing Guild, P.O. Box 810, Gracie Station, New York NY 10028-0082. (212)737-7536. **Fax:** (212)737-9469. **E-mail:** iwwg@iwwg.org. **Website:** www.iwwg.org. Estab. 1978. Annual conference held in July-August. **Average attendance:** 400. Conference to promote creative writing and personal growth, professional know-how and contacts, and networking. Over 50 workshops

are offered each day. Conferees have the freedom to make their own schedule. **Costs:** $1,399 single for members; $1,419 double for nonmembers. These fees include the 7-day program and room and board for the week. Rates for a 5-day stay and a weekend stay, as well as commuter rates, are also available. **Additional Information:** Conference brochures/guidelines are available online or for a SASE. Inquire via e-mail or fax.

RETREAT FROM HARSH REALITY
Mid-Michigan RWA, P.O. Box 2725, Kalamazoo MI 49003-2725. **E-mail:** retreat@midmichiganrwa.org. **Website:** www.mid michiganrwa.org/retreat.html. Estab. 1985. Annual conference held in April **Average attendance:** 50. Conference focusing on romance and fiction writing. Speakers have included Rosanne Bittner, Debra Dixon, Bettina Krahn, Ruth Ryan Langan, Elizabeth Bevarly, Julie Kistler, Merline Lovelace, and Elizabeth Grayson.

RT BOOKLOVERS CONVENTION
55 Bergen St., Brooklyn NY 11201. (718)237-1097 or (800)989-8816, ext. 12. **Fax:** (718)624-2526. **E-mail:** jocarol@rtconvention.com. **Website:** www.rtconvention.com. Annual conference held in April. Features 125 workshops, agent and editor appointments, a book fair, and more. **Costs:** See website for pricing and other information.

SANDHILLS WRITERS CONFERENCE
Augusta State University, Department of Communications and Professional Writing, 2500 Walton Way, Augusta GA 30904-2200. **E-mail:** akellman@aug.edu. **Website:** www.sandhills.aug.edu. Annual conference held the fourth weekend in March. Covers fiction, poetry, children's literature, nonfiction, plays, and songwriting. Located on the campus of Augusta State University in Georgia. Agents and editors will be speaking at the event. **Accommodations:** Several hotels are located near the university.

SAN FRANCISCO WRITERS CONFERENCE
1029 Jones St., San Francisco CA 94109. (415)673-0939. **Fax:** (415)673-0367. **E-mail:** sfwriterscon@aol.com. **Website:** www.sf writers.org. **Contact:** Michael Larsen, director. Estab. 2003. "Annual conference held President's Day weekend in February. **Average attendance:** 400+. Top authors, respected literary agents, and major publishing houses are at the event so attendees can make face-to-face contact with all the right people. Writers of nonfiction, fiction, poetry, and specialty writing (children's books, cookbooks, travel, etc.) will all benefit from the event. There are important sessions on marketing, self-publishing, technology, and trends in the publishing industry. Plus, there's an optional 4-hour session called Speed Dating for Agents where attendees can meet with 20+ agents. Speakers have included Jennifer Crusie, Richard Paul Evans, Jamie Raab, Mary Roach, Jane Smiley, Debbie Macomber, Firoozeh Dumas, Zilpha Keatley Snyder, Steve Berry, Jacquelyn Mitchard. More than 20 agents and editors participate each year, many of whom will be available for meetings with attendees." **Costs:** $600+ with price breaks for early registration (includes all sessions/workshops/keynotes, Speed Dating with Editors, opening gala at the Top of the Mark, 2 continental

breakfasts, 2 lunches). Optional Speed Dating for Agents is $50. **Accommodations:** The Intercontinental Mark Hopkins Hotel is a historic landmark at the top of Nob Hill in San Francisco. Elegant rooms and first-class service are offered to attendees at the rate of $159/night. The hotel is located so that everyone arriving at the Oakland or San Francisco airport can take BART to either the Embarcadero or Powell Street exits, then walk or take a cable car or taxi directly to the hotel. **Additional Information:** "Present yourself in a professional manner and the contact you will make will be invaluable to your writing career. Brochures and registration are online."

SCBWI SOUTHERN BREEZE FALL CONFERENCE

P.O. Box 26282, Birmingham AL 35260. **E-mail:** jskittinger@bell south.net. **Website:** www.southern-breeze.org. Estab. 1992. Annual conference held on the third Saturday in October (2010: Oct. 16). **Conference duration:** 1 day. The Society of Children's Book Writers and Illustrators is geared toward the production and support of quality children's literature. Offers approximately 28 workshops on craft and the business of writing, including a basic workshop for those new to the children's field. Manuscript and portfolio critiques are offered. Speakers typically include editors, agents, art directors, authors and illustrators. **Accommodations:** "We have a hotel room block with a conference rate. The conference is held at a nearby school. Pre-registration is required."

SCENE CONFERENCE

Kansas Writers Association, P.O. Box 2236, Wichita KS 67201. **E-mail:** info@kwawriters.org. **Website:** www.kwawriters.org/ sceneofthecrime.htm. Biennual conference held in April. Features agent/editor consultations, banquet and speaker sessions with editors, agents and authors. A full list of each year's speakers is available on the website. **Accommodations:** Wichita Airport Hilton.

THE SCHOOL FOR WRITERS SUMMER WORKSHOP

The Humber School for Writers, Humber Institute of Technology & Advanced Learning, 3199 Lake Shore Blvd. W., Toronto ON M8V 1K8 Canada. (416)675-6622. **E-mail:** antanas.sileika@ humber.ca; hilary.higgins@humber.ca. **Website:** www.creativeandperformingarts.humber.ca/content/writers.html. Annual workshop held second week in July. **Conference duration:** 1 week. **Average attendance:** 100. New writers from around the world gather to study with faculty members to work on their novel, short stories, poetry, or creative nonfiction. Agents and editors participate in conference. Include a work-in-progress with your registration. Faculty has included Martin Amis, David Mitchell, Rachel Kuschner, Peter Carey, Roddy Doyle, Tim O'Brien, Andrea Levy, Barry Unsworth, Edward Albee, Ha Jin, Mavis Gallant, Bruce Jay Friedman, Isabel Huggan, Alistair MacLeod, Lisa Moore, Kim Moritsugu, Francine Prose, Paul Quarrington, Olive Senior, and D.M. Thomas, Annabel Lyon, Mary Gaitskill, M. G. Vassanji. **Costs:** $949/Canadian residents before June 12; $1,469/non-Canadian residents before June 12; $999/Canadian residents after June 12; $1,519/non-Canadian residents after June 12 (includes panels, classes, lunch). Scholarships are available. Ac-

commodations: Approximately $60/night. See www.conference. humber.ca for a modest college dorm room. Nearby hotels are also available. **Additional Information:** Accepts inquiries by e-mail, phone, and fax.

SEAK FICTION WRITING FOR PHYSICIANS CONFERENCE

P.O. Box 729, Falmouth MA 02541. (508)548-7023. **Fax:** (508)540-8304. **E-mail:** mail@seak.com. **Website:** www.seak.com. Estab. 1980. Annual conferences held on Cape Cod. The medical seminar is taught by *New York Times* bestselling authors Michael Palmer, MD and Tess Gerritsen, MD. Session topics include writing fiction that sells, screenwriting, writing riveting dialogue, creating memorable characters, getting your first novel published, and more. Agents will be speaking and available for one-on-one meetings. 11th Annual Conference is Oct. 22-24, 2010

SLEUTHFEST

MWA Florida Chapter, **E-mail:** sleuthfestlinda@gmail.com. **Website:** www.mwa-florida.org/sleuthfest.htm. **Contact:** Linda Hengerer, chairperson. Annual conference held in Feb/March, at the Deerfield Beach Hilton, Florida. **Conference duration:** 4 days. Hands-on workshops, 4 tracks of writing and business panels, and 2 keynote speakers for writers of mystery and crime fiction. 2010 Guests of Honor were David Morrell and Stephen J. Cannell. Also offers agent and editor appointments and paid ms critiques. A full list of attending speakers as well as agents and editors is online. This event is put on by the local chapter of the Mystery Writers of America. Email www. sleuthfest.com for information about 2011. **Accommodations:** The Deerfield Beach Hilton.

SOCIETY OF CHILDREN'S BOOK WRITERS & ILLUSTRATORS ANNUAL SUMMER CONFERENCE ON WRITING AND ILLUSTRATING FOR CHILDREN

8271 Beverly Blvd., Los Angeles CA 90048-4515. (323)782-1010. **Fax:** (323)782-1892. **E-mail:** scbwi@scbwi.org. **Website:** www.scbwi.org. Estab. 1972. Annual conference held in early August. **Conference duration:** 4 days. **Average attendance:** 1,000. Held at the Century Plaza Hotel in Los Angeles. Speakers have included Andrea Brown, Steven Malk, Scott Treimel, Ashley Bryan, Bruce Coville, Karen Hesse, Harry Mazer, Lucia Monfried, and Russell Freedman. Agents will be speaking and sometimes participate in ms critiques. **Costs:** Approximately $400 (does not include hotel room). **Accommodations:** Information on overnight accommodations is made available. **Additional Information:** Ms and illustration critiques are available. Brochure/guidelines are available in June online or for SASE.

SOUTH COAST WRITERS CONFERENCE

Southwestern Oregon Community College, P.O. Box 590, 29392 Ellensburg Avenue, Gold Beach OR 97444. (541)247-2741. **Fax:** (541)247-6247. **E-mail:** scwc@socc.edu. **Website:** www.socc.edu/ scwriters. Estab. 1996. Annual conference held President's Day weekend in February. **Conference duration:** 2 days. Covers fiction, historical, poetry, children's, nature, and marketing. John Daniel is the next scheduled keynote speaker and presenters include John Daniel,

Linda Barnes, Jayel Gibson, Kim Griswell, Diane Hammond, Leigh Anne Jasheway, Marianne Monson, Rebecca Olson, Dennis Powers, Keith Scales, Erica Wheeler, Jaimal Yogis. **Additional Information:** See website for cost and additional details.

SPACE COAST WRITERS GUILD ANNUAL CONFERENCE

No public address available, (321)956-7193. **E-mail:** scwg-jm@cfl.rr.com. **Website:** www.scwg.org/conference.asp. Annual conference held last weekend of January along the east coast of central Florida. **Conference duration:** 2 days. **Average attendance:** 150+. This conference is hosted each winter in Florida and features a variety of presenters on all topics writing. Critiques are available for a price, and agents in attendance will take pitches from writers. Previous presenters have included Debra Dixon, Davis Bunn (writer), Ellen Pepus (agent), Jennifer Crusie, Mike Resnick, Christina York, Ben Bova, Elizabeth Sinclair. Annual. **Accommodations:** The conference is hosted on a beachside hotel, with special room rates available.

STEAMBOAT SPRINGS WRITERS CONFERENCE

Steamboat Springs Arts Council, P.O. Box 774284, Steamboat Springs CO 80477. (970)879-8138. **E-mail:** info@steamboatwriters.com. **Website:** www.steamboatwriters.com. **Contact:** Susan de Wardt. Estab. 1982. Annual conference held in mid-July. **Conference duration:** 1 day. **Average attendance:** approximately 35. Attendance is limited. Featured areas of instruction change each year. Held at the restored train depot. Speakers have included Carl Brandt, Jim Fergus, Avi, Robert Greer, Renate Wood, Connie Willis, Margaret Coel and Kent Nelson. **Costs:** $50 prior to May 21; $60 after May 21 (includes seminars, catered lunch). A pre-conference dinner is also available. **Additional Information:** Brochures are available in April for a SASE. Send inquiries via e-mail.

STONY BROOK SOUTHAMPTON SCREENWRITING CONFERENCE

Stony Brook Southampton, 239 Montauk Highway, Southampton NY 11968. (631)632-5007. **E-mail:** southamptonwriters@notes.cc.sunysb.edu. **Website:** www.sunysb.edu/writers/screenwriting/. **Contact:** Conference Coordinator. "The Southampton Screenwriting Conference welcomes new and advanced screenwriters, as well as all writers interested in using the language of film to tell a story. The five-day residential Conference will inform, inspire, challenge, and further participants' understanding of the art of the screenplay and the individual writing process. Our unique program of workshops, seminars, panel presentations, and screenings will encourage and motivate attendees under the professional guidance of accomplished screenwriters, educators, and script analysts." Annual. **Costs:** $1,200+. **Additional Information:** Space is limited.

TENNESSEE WRITERS ALLIANCE WORDFEST

Tennessee Writers Alliance, Inc., P.O. Box 120396, Nashville TN 37212. **E-mail:** inquiries@tn-writers.org. **Website:** www.tn-writers.org/Workshops.asp. Annual conference held in June near Nashville, TN. **Conference duration:** 1 day. Previous speakers have included

Robert Hicks, Tama Kieves, Richard Goodman, Ted Swindley and Carl Harris. The conference features a variety of sessions on fiction, nonfiction, playwriting, creative nonfiction, inspiring writers and more. **Costs:** Costs: Available online. **Accommodations:** Hotel accommodations available not far from the conference site.

THE WRITERS' WORKSHOP

387 Beaucatcher Rd., Asheville NC 28805. (828)254-8111. **E-mail:** writersw@gmail.com. **Website:** www.twwoa.org. Estab. 1984. Held throughout the year. Sites are in Asheville and Charlotte, North Carolina. Past facilitators: Laine Cunningham, Karen Ackerson, Anne Barnhill. Upcoming: Creative Nonfiction Workshop with Jeremy B. Jones. Techniques will be taught on making nonfiction stories come alive, such as creating a sense of place, inserting dialogue, and more. Students may bring five pages (double-spaced) to the class for review. Jones received his MFA in Nonfiction Writing from the University of Iowa. His essays have been published in various literary magazines including Crab Orchard Review, and he has recently won Honorable Mention in Best American Essays 2009. Classes are held at 387 Beaucatcher Road in Asheville. Registration is in advance only by mailing check or money order to The Writers' Workshop, 387 Beaucatcher Rd., Asheville, NC 28805. Financial aid in exchange for volunteering is available. For more information please email or call . All classes meet Saturdays, 10-4pm and cost $75 / $70 with membership, unless otherwise noted. For printable directions, go to our website. **Costs:** Vary. Financial assistance available to low-income writers. Information on overnight accommodations is made available.

THRILLERFEST

PO Box 311, Eureka CA 95502. **E-mail:** infocentral@thrillerwriters.org. **Website:** www.thrillerwriters.org/thrillerfest/. **Contact:** Shirley Kennett. Estab. 2006. 2010 conference: July 7-10 in Manhattan. **Conference duration:** 4 days. **Average attendance:** 700. Conference "dedicated to writing the thriller and promoting the enjoyment of reading thrillers." Speakers have included David Morrell, Sandra Brown, Eric Van Lustbader, David Baldacci, Brad Meltzer, Steve Martini, R.L. Stine, Katherine Neville, Robin Cook, Andrew Gross, Kathy Reichs, Brad Thor, Clive Cussler, James Patterson, Donald Maass, and Al Zuckerman. Two days of the conference is CraftFest, where the focus is on writing craft, and two days is ThrillerFest, which showcase the author-fan relationship. Also featured are AgentFest, a unique event where authors can pitch their work face-to-face to forty top literary agents; and the international Thriller Awards and Banquet. Annual. **Costs:** Price will vary from $200 to $1,000 dollars depending on which events are selected. Various package deals are available offering savings, and Early Bird pricing is offered beginning August of each year. **Accommodations:** Grand Hyatt in New York City.

UNIVERSITY OF NORTH DAKOTA WRITERS CONFERENCE

Department of English, 110 Merrifield Hall, 276 Centennial Drive, Stop 7209, Grand Forks ND 58202. (701)777-3321. **E-mail:** writers conference@und.nodak.edu. **Website:** www.undwritersconference. org. Estab. 1970. Annual conference held in March. Offers panels, readings, and films focused around a specific theme. Almost all events take place in the UND Memorial Union, which has a variety of small rooms and a 1,000-seat main hall. Past speakers include Art Spiegelman, Truman Capote, Sir Salman Rushdie, Allen Ginsberg, Alice Walker, and Louise Erdrich. **Costs:** All events are free and open to the public. Donations accepted.

VIRGINIA FESTIVAL OF THE BOOK
Virginia Festival of the Book Foundation for the Humanities, 145 Ednam Dr., Charlottesville VA 22903-4629. (434)924-7548. **Fax:** (434)296-4714. **E-mail:** vabook@virginia.edu. **Website:** www.vabook. org. **Contact:** Nancy Coble Damon, Program Director. Estab. 1995. 16th Annual Virginia Festival of the Book, March 17-21. **Average attendance:** 20,000. Festival held to celebrate books and promote reading and literacy.

WESTERN RESERVE WRITERS' CONFERENCE
Lakeland Community College, 7700 Clocktower Dr., Kirtland OH 44060-5198. (440)525-7116 or (800)589-8520. **E-mail:** deencr@ aol.com. **Website:** www.deannaadams.com. Estab. 1983. Biannual conference held in March and September. **Average attendance:** 120. Conference covers fiction, nonfiction, business of writing, children's writing, science fiction/fantasy, women's fiction, mysteries, poetry, short stories, etc. Classes take place on a community college campus. Editors and agents will be available for meetings with attendees. 19th Annual Western Reserve Spring Writers Conference - Saturday, March 27, 2010 from 8:30am to 1:30pm, Lakeland Community College - visit the College website (under Continuing Education) or contact conference coordinator Deanna Adams. Biannual. **Costs:** $69 for March mini-conference (half day); $95 for September all-day conference, including lunch if registered two weeks before the event. There is an additional fee for agent and editor consultations. **Additional Information:** Presenters are veterans in their particular genres. There will be a prestigious keynote speaker at the September conference. Check website at least 6 weeks prior to the event for guidelines and updates. Send inquiries via e-mail.

WINTER POETRY & PROSE GETAWAY IN CAPE MAY
18 N. Richards Ave., Ventnor NJ 08406. (888)887-2105. **E-mail:** info@wintergetaway.com. **Website:** www.wintergetaway.com. **Contact:** Peter Murphy. Estab. 1994. Annual conference. Join Peter E. Murphy and friends for the 18th annual Winter Poetry & Prose Getaway on the oceanfront in historica Cape May, NJ, January 14-17, 2011. This is not your typical writers' conference. Energize your writing with challenging and supportive workshos thpfocus on at starting new material. Advance your craft with feedback from our award-winning faculty including Pulitzer Prize & National Book Award winners. Thousands of people have enjoyed the getaway over the past 17 years, developing their craft as writers and making lifelong friends. The focus isn't on our award-winning faculty, it's on helping you improve and advance your skills." Features a variety of poetry and prose workshops,

each with 10 or fewer participants. Choose from poetry, memoir, creative nonfiction, novel, short story, children's market, songwriting, and more. **Accommodations:** Please see website or call for current fee information. **Additional Information:** Previous faculty has included Julianna Baggott, Christian Bauman, Laure-Anne Bosselaar, Kurt Brown, Mark Doty (National Book Award Winner), Stephen Dunn (Pulitzer Prize Winner), Carol Plum-Ucci, James Richardson, Mimi Schwartz, Terese Svoboda, and more.

WISCONSIN BOOK FESTIVAL
222 S. Bedford St., Suite F, Madison WI 53703. (608)262-0706. **Fax:** (608)263-7970. **E-mail:** alison@wisconsinbookfestival.org. **Website:** www.wisconsinbookfestival.org. Estab. 2002. Annual festival held in October. **Conference duration:** 5 days. The festival features readings, lectures, book discussions, writing workshops, live interviews, children's events, and more. Speakers have included Michael Cunningham, Grace Paley, TC Boyle, Marjane Satrapi, Phillip Gourevitch, Myla Goldberg, Audrey Niffenegger, Harvey Pekar, Billy Collins, Tim O'Brien and Isabel Allende. **Costs:** All festival events are free.

WRITE ON THE SOUND WRITERS' CONFERENCE
Edmonds Arts Commission, 700 Main St., Edmonds WA 98020. (425)771-0228. **Fax:** (425)771-0253. **E-mail:** wots@ci.edmonds.wa.us. **Website:** www.ci.edmonds.wa.us/ArtsCommission/wots.stm. Estab. 1985. Annual conference held in October. **Conference duration:** 2.5 days. **Average attendance:** 200. Features over 30 presenters, a literary contest, ms critiques, a reception and book signing, onsite bookstore, and a variety of evening activities. Held at the Frances Anderson Center in Edmonds, just north of Seattle on the Puget Sound. Speakers have included Elizabeth George, Dan Hurley, Marcia Woodard, Holly Hughes, Greg Bear, Timothy Egan, Joe McHugh, Frances Wood, Garth Stein and Max Grover. **Costs:** See website for more information. **Additional Information:** Brochures are available Aug. 1. Accepts inquiries via phone, e-mail and fax.

2010 WRITERS' LEAGUE OF TEXAS AGENTS CONFERENCE
Writers' League of Texas, 611 S. Congress Ave., Suite 130, Austin TX 78704. (512)499-8914. **Fax:** (512)499-0441. **E-mail:** wlt@ writersleague.org. **Website:** www.writersleague.org. Estab. 1982. Annual conference held in the summer. **Conference duration:** 3 days. **Average attendance:** 300. "The Writers' League of Texas Agents Conference is the place to meet agents and editors to learn the latest trends in publishing. This event provides writers iwth the opportunity to meet top literary agents and editors from New York and the West Coast. Topics include: finding and working with agents and publishers, writing and marketing fiction and nonfiction, dialogue, characterization, voice, research, basica and advanced fiction writing, the business of writing, and workshops for genres." Speakers have included Malaika Adero, Stacey Barney, Sha-Shana Crichton, Jessica Faust, Dena Fischer, Mickey Freiberg, Jill Grosjean, Anne Hawkins, Jim Hornfischer, Jennifer Joel, David Hale Smith and Elisabeth Weed. **Costs:** $309 member/$439 nonmember. **Accommodations:** 2010 event is at the Hyatt Regency Austin, 208

Barton Springs Road, Austin, TX 78704. Check back often for new information. **Additional Information:** June 25-27, 2010. Contests and awards programs are offered separately. Brochures are available upon request.

WRITERS WEEKEND AT THE BEACH

P.O. Box 877, Ocean Park WA 98640. (360)262-0160. **E-mail:** bhansen6@juno.com. **Website:** www.writersweekend.wordpress.com. Estab. 1992. Annual conference held in March. **Conference duration:** 2 days. **Average attendance:** 50-60. A retreat for writers with an emphasis on poetry, fiction, and nonfiction. Held at the Ocean Park Methodist Retreat Center & Camp. Speakers have included Wayne Holmes, Jim Whiting, Colette Tennant, and Linda Clare. **Costs:** $195-205 (includes lodging, meals, full workshop); $145/everything but lodging; $95/Saturday only (includes lunch); $25/Sunday critique session (includes brunch); $10/Saturday evening only. **Accommodations:** Offers on-site overnight lodging.

WRITERS WORKSHOP IN SCIENCE FICTION

English Department/University of Kansas, Lawrence KS 66045-2115. (785)864-3380. **Fax:** (785)864-1159. **E-mail:** jgunn@ku.edu. **Website:** www.ku.edu/~sfcenter. Estab. 1985. Annual workshop held in late June/early July (2010: July 5-16). Conference for writing and marketing science fiction. Classes meet in university housing on the University of Kansas campus. Workshop sessions operate informally in a lounge. Speakers have included Frederik Pohl, Kij Johnson, James Gunn, and Chris McKitterick. **Costs:** See website for tuition rates, dormitory housing costs, and deadlines. **Accommodations:** Housing information is available. Several airport shuttle services offer reasonable transportation from the Kansas City International Airport to Lawrence. **Additional Information:** Admission to the workshop is by submission of an acceptable story. Two additional stories should be submitted by the middle of June. These 3 stories are distributed to other participants for critquing and are the basis for the first week of the workshop. One story is rewritten for the second week. Send SASE for brochure/guidelines. This workshop is intended for writers who have just started to sell their work or need that extra bit of understanding or skill to become a published writer.

WRITE-TO-PUBLISH CONFERENCE

WordPro Communication Services, 9118 W Elmwood Dr., #1G, Niles IL 60714-5820. (847)296-3964. **Fax:** (847)296-0754. **E-mail:** lin@writetopublish.com. **Website:** www.writetopublish.com. Estab. 1971. Annual conference held June 8-11, 2011. **Conference duration:** 4 days. **Average attendance:** 250. Conference on writing fiction, nonfiction, devotions, and magazine articles for the Christian market. Held at Wheaton College in Wheaton, Illinois. Speakers have included Dr. Dennis E. Hensley, agent Chip MacGregor, David Long (Bethany House), Carol Traver (Tyndale House), Dave Zimmerman (InterVarsity Press), Ed Gilbreath (Urban Ministries), Ken Peterson (WaterBrook Multnomah). **Costs:** $475 (includes all sessions, Saturday night banquet, 1 ms evaluation); $105/meals. **Accommodations:** Campus residence halls: $260/double; $340/single. A list of area hotels is also on the website.

WRITING FOR THE SOUL

Jerry B. Jenkins Christian Writers Guild, 5525 N. Union Blvd., Suite 200, Colorado Springs CO 80918. (866)495-5177. **Fax:** (719)495-5181. **E-mail:** leilani@christianwritersguild.com. **Website:** www.christianwritersguild.com/conferences. **Contact:** Leilani Squiers, admissions manager. Annual conference held in February. Workshops and continuing classes cover fiction, nonfiction, magazine writing, children's books, and teen writing. Appointments with more than 30 agents, publishers, and editors are also available. The keynote speakers are nationally known, leading authors. The conference is hosted by Jerry B. Jenkins. **Costs:** $649/guild members; $799/nonmembers. **Accommodations:** $159/night at the Grand Hyatt in Denver.

GLOSSARY OF PUBLISHING, PRINTING, & PRODUCTION TERMS

#10 Envelope. A standard business-size envelope.

Acknowledgments Page. The page of a book on which the author credits sources of assistance—both individuals and organizations.

Acquisitions Editor. The person responsible for originating and/or acquiring new publishing projects.

Adaptation. The process of rewriting a composition (novel, story, film, article, play) into a form suitable for some other medium, such as television or the stage.

Advance. Money a publisher pays a writer prior to book publication, usually paid in installments, such as one-half upon signing the contract and one-half upon delivery of the complete, satisfactory manuscript. An advance is paid against the royalty money to be earned by the book. Agents take their percentage off the top of the advance as well as from the royalties earned.

Adventure. A genre of fiction in which action is the key element, overshadowing characters, theme, and setting.

Auction. Publishers sometimes bid for the acquisition of a book manuscript with excellent sales prospects. The bids are for the amount of the author's advance, guaranteed dollar amounts, advertising and promotional expenses, royalty percentage, etc. Auctions are conducted by agents.

Author's Copies. An author usually receives about ten free copies of his hardcover book from the publisher; more from a paperback firm. He can obtain additional copies at a discounted price (usually 50 percent of the retail price).

Autobiography. A book-length account of a person's entire life written by the subject himself.

Backlist. A publisher's list of books that were not published during the current season, but that are still in print.

Backstory. The history of what has happened before the action in your story takes place, affecting a character's current behavior.

Bio. A sentence or brief paragraph about the writer; includes work and educational experience.

Biography. An account of a person's life (or the lives of the members of a family or a close-knit group of people) written by someone other than the subject(s). The work is set within the historical framework (that is, the unique economic, social and political conditions) existing during the subject's life.

Blurb. The copy on paperback book covers or hardcover book dust jackets, either promoting the book and the author or featuring testimonials from book reviewers or well-known people in the book's field. Also called flap copy or jacket copy.

Boilerplate. A standardized publishing contract. Most authors and agents make many changes on the boilerplate before accepting the contract.

Book Doctor. A freelance editor hired by a writer, agent, or book editor who analyzes problems that exist in a book manuscript or proposal and offers solutions to those problems.

Book Packager. Someone who draws elements of a book together—from the initial concept to writing and marketing strategies—and then sells the book package to a book publisher and/or movie producer. Also known as book producer or book developer.

Bound Galleys. A prepublication, often paperbound, edition of a book, usually prepared from photocopies of the final galley proofs. Designed for promotional purposes, bound galleys serve as the first set of review copies to be mailed out. Also called bound proofs.

Category Fiction. A term used to include all types of fiction. See genre.

Climax. The most intense point in the story line of a fictional work.

Clips. Samples, usually from newspapers or magazines, of your published work. Also called tearsheets.

Commercial Fiction. Novels designed to appeal to a broad audience. These are often broken down into categories such as western, mystery, and romance. See genre.

Confession. A first-person story in which the narrator is involved in an emotional situation that encourages sympathetic reader identification, concluding with the affirmation of a morally acceptable theme.

Conflict. A prime ingredient of fiction that usually represents some obstacle to the main character's (that is, the protagonist's) goals.

Contributor's Copies. Copies of the book sent to the author. The number of contributor's copies is often negotiated in the publishing contract.

Co-Publishing. Arrangement where author and publisher share publication costs and profits of a book. Also called co-operative publishing.

Copyediting. Editing of a manuscript for writing style, grammar, punctuation, and factual accuracy.

Copyright. A means to protect an author's work. A copyright is a proprietary right designed to give the creator of a work the power to control that work's reproduction, distribution, and public display or performance, as well as its adaptation to other forms.

Cover Letter. A brief letter that accompanies the manuscript being sent to an agent or publisher.

Creative Nonfiction. Type of writing where true stories are told by employing the techniques usually reserved for novelists and poets, such as scenes, character arc, a three-act structure, and detailed descriptions. This category is also called narrative nonfiction or literary journalism.

Critiquing Service. An editing service offered by some agents in which writers pay a fee for comments on the salability or other qualities of their manuscript. Sometimes the critique includes suggestions on how to improve the work. Fees vary, as does the quality of the critique.

Curriculum Vitae (CV). Short account of one's career or qualifications.

Deadline. A specified date and/or time that a project or draft must be turned into the editor. A deadline factors into a preproduction schedule, which involves copyediting, typesetting, and production.

Deal Memo. The memorandum of agreement between a publisher and author that precedes the actual contract and includes important issues such as royalty, advance, rights, distribution, and option clauses.

Deus Ex Machina. A term meaning "God from the machine" that refers to any unlikely, contrived, or trick resolution of a plot in any type of fiction.

Dialogue. An essential element of fiction and, to some degree, memoir. Dialogue consists of conversations between two or more people, and can be used heavily or sparsely.

Division. An unincorporated branch of a publishing house/company.

Electronic Rights. Secondary or subsidiary rights dealing with electronic/multimedia formats (the Internet, CD-ROMs, electronic magazines).

El-Hi. Elementary to high school. A term used to indicate reading or interest level.

Erotica. A form of literature or film dealing with the sexual aspects of love. Erotic content ranges from subtle sexual innuendo to explicit descriptions of sexual acts.

Ethnic. Stories and novels whose central characters are African American, Native American, Italian American, Jewish, Appalachian, or members of some other specific cultural group. Ethnic fiction usually deals with a protagonist caught between two conflicting ways of life: mainstream American culture and his ethnic heritage.

Evaluation Fees. Fees an agent may charge to simply evaluate or consider material without further guarantees of representation. Paying up-front evaluation fees to agents is never recommended and strictly forbidden by the Association of Authors' Representations. An agent makes money through a standard commission—taking 15 percent of what you earn through advances and, if applicable, royalties.

Exclusive. Offering a manuscript, usually for a set period of time such as one month, to just one agent and guaranteeing that agent is the only one looking at the manuscript.

Experimental. Type of fiction that focuses on style, structure, narrative technique, setting, and strong characterization rather than plot. This form depends largely on the revelation of a character's inner being, which elicits an emotional response from the reader.

Family Saga. A story that chronicles the lives of a family or a number of related or interconnected families over a period of time.

Fantasy. Stories set in fanciful, invented worlds or in a legendary, mythic past that rely on outright invention or magic for conflict and setting.

Film Rights. May be sold or optioned by the agent/author to a person in the film industry, enabling the book to be made into a movie.

Floor Bid. If a publisher is very interested in a manuscript, he may offer to enter a floor bid when the book goes to auction. The publisher sits out of the auction, but agrees to take the book by topping the highest bid by an agreed-upon percentage (usually 10 percent).

Foreign Rights. Translation or reprint rights to be sold abroad.

Foreign Rights Agent. An agent who handles selling the rights to a country other than that of the first book agent. Usually an additional percentage (about 5 percent) will be added on to the first book agent's commission to cover the foreign rights agent.

Genre. Refers to either a general classification of writing, such as a novel, poem, or short story, or to the categories within those classifications, such as problem novels or sonnets. Genre fiction is a term that covers various types of commercial novels, such as mystery, romance, Western, science fiction, and horror.

Ghostwriting. A writer puts into literary form the words, ideas, or knowledge of another person under that person's name. Some agents offer this service; others pair ghostwriters with celebrities or experts.

Gothic. Novels characterized by historical settings and featuring young, beautiful women who win the favor of handsome, brooding heroes while simultaneously dealing with some life-threatening menace—either natural or supernatural.

Graphic Novel. Contains comiclike drawings and captions, but deals more with everyday events and issues than with superheroes.

High Concept. A story idea easily expressed in a quick one-line description.

Hi-Lo. A type of fiction that offers a high level of interest for readers at a low reading level.

Historical. A story set in a recognizable period of history. In addition to telling the stories of ordinary people's lives, historical fiction may involve political or social events of the time.

Hook. Aspect of the work that sets it apart from others and draws in the reader/viewer.

Horror. A story that aims to evoke some combination of fear, fascination, and revulsion in its readers—either through supernatural or psychological circumstances.

How-To. A book that offers the reader a description of how something can be accomplished. It includes both information and advice.

Imprint. The name applied to a publisher's specific line of books.

In Medias Res. A Latin term, meaning "into the midst of things," that refers to the literary device of beginning a narrative at a dramatic point in a story well along in the sequence of events to immediately convey action and capture reader interest.

IRC. International Reply Coupon. Buy at a post office to enclose with material sent outside the country to cover the cost of return postage. The recipient turns them in for stamps in their own country.

ISBN. This acronym stands for International Standard Book Number. ISBN is a tool used for both ordering and cataloging purposes.

Joint Contract. A legal agreement between a publisher and two or more authors that establishes provisions for the division of royalties their co-written book generates.

Juvenile. Category of children's writing that can be broken down into easy-to-read books (ages seven to nine), which run 2,000–10,000 words, and middle-grade books (ages nine to twelve), which run 20,000–40,000 words.

Libel. A form of defamation, or injury, to a person's name or reputation. Written or published defamation is called libel, whereas spoken defamation is known as slander.

Literary. A book where style and technique are often as important as subject matter. In literary fiction, character is typically more important than plot, and the writer's voice and skill with words are both very essential. Also called serious fiction.

Logline. A one-sentence description of a plot.

Mainstream Fiction. Fiction on subjects or trends that transcend popular novel categories like mystery or romance. Using conventional methods, this kind of fiction tells stories about people and their conflicts.

Marketing Fee. Fee charged by some agents to cover marketing expenses. It may be used to cover postage, telephone calls, faxes, photocopying, or any other legitimate expense incurred in marketing a manuscript. Recouping expenses associated with submissions and marketing is the one and only time agents should ask for out-of-pocket money from writers.

Mass Market Paperbacks. Softcover books, usually 4" ×7" inches, on a popular subject directed at a general audience and sold in groceries, drugstores, and bookstores.

Memoir. An author's commentary on the personalities and events that have significantly influenced one phase of his life.

Midlist. Those titles on a publisher's list expected to have limited sales. Midlist books are mainstream, not literary, scholarly or genre, and are usually written by new or relatively unknown writers.

Multiple Contract. Book contract that includes an agreement for a future book(s).

Mystery. A form of narration in which one or more elements remain unknown or unexplained until the end of the story. Subgenres include: amateur sleuth, caper, cozy, heist, malice domestic, and police procedural.

Net Receipts. One method of royalty payment based on the amount of money a book publisher receives on the sale of the book after the booksellers' discounts, special sales discounts and returned copies.

Novelization. A novel created from the script of a popular movie and published in paperback. Also called a movie tie-in.

Novella. A short novel or long short story, usually 20,000–50,000 words. Also called a novelette.

Occult. Supernatural phenomena, including ghosts, ESP, astrology, demonic possession, paranormal elements, and witchcraft.

One-Time Rights. This right allows a short story or portions of a fiction or nonfiction book to be published again without violating the contract.

Option. The act of a producer buying film rights to a book for a limited period of time (usually six months or one year) rather than purchasing said rights in full. A book can be optioned multiple times by different production companies.

Option Clause. A contract clause giving a publisher the right to publish an author's next book.

Outline. A summary of a book's content (up to fifteen double-spaced pages); often in the form of chapter headings with a descriptive sentence or two under each one to show the scope of the book.

Picture Book. A type of book aimed at ages two to nine that tells the story partially or entirely with artwork, with up to 1,000 words. Agents interested in selling to publishers of these books often handle both artists and writers.

Platform. A writer's speaking experience, interview skills, website, and other abilities that help form a following of potential buyers for his book.

Proofreading. Close reading and correction of a manuscript's typographical errors.

Proposal. An offer to an editor or publisher to write a specific work, usually a package consisting of an outline and sample chapters.

Prospectus. A preliminary written description of a book, usually one page in length.

Psychic/Supernatural. Fiction exploiting—or requiring as plot devices or themes—some contradictions of the commonplace natural world and materialist assumptions about it (including the traditional ghost story).

Query. A letter written to an agent or a potential market to elicit interest in a writer's work.

Reader. A person employed by an agent or buyer to go through the slush pile of manuscripts and scripts and select those worth considering.

Regional. A book faithful to a particular geographic region and its people, including behavior, customs, speech, and history.

Release. A statement that your idea is original, has never been sold to anyone else, and that you are selling negotiated rights to the idea upon payment. Some agents may ask that you sign a release before they request pages and review your work.

Remainders. Leftover copies of an out-of-print or slow-selling book purchased from the publisher at a reduced rate. Depending on the contract, a reduced royalty or no royalty is paid to the author on remaindered books.

Reprint Rights. The right to republish a book after its initial printing.

Romance. A type of category fiction in which the love relationship between a man and a woman pervades the plot. The story is told from the viewpoint of the heroine, who meets a man (the hero), falls in love with him, encounters a conflict that hinders their relationship, and then resolves the conflict with a happy ending.

Royalties. A percentage of the retail price paid to the author for each copy of the book that is sold. Agents take their percentage from the royalties earned and from the advance.

SASE. Self-addressed stamped envelope. It should be included with all mailed correspondence.

Scholarly Books. Books written for an academic or research audience. These are usually heavily researched, technical, and often contain terms used only within a specific field.

Science Fiction. Literature involving elements of science and technology as a basis for conflict, or as the setting for a story.

Serial Rights. The right for a newspaper or magazine to publish sections of a manuscript.

Simultaneous Submission. Sending the same query or manuscript to several agents or publishers at the same time.

Slice of Life. A type of short story, novel, play, or film that takes a strong thematic approach, depending less on plot than on vivid detail in describing the setting and/or environment, and the environment's effect on characters involved in it.

Slush Pile. A stack of unsolicited submissions in the office of an editor, agent, or publisher.

Standard Commission. The commission an agent earns on the sales of a manuscript. The commission percentage (usually 15 percent) is taken from the advance and royalties paid to the writer.

Subagent. An agent handling certain subsidiary rights, usually working in conjunction with the agent who handled the book rights. The percentage paid the book agent is increased to pay the subagent.

Subsidiary. An incorporated branch of a company or conglomerate (for example, Crown Publishing Group is a subsidiary of Random House, Inc.).

Subsidiary Rights. All rights other than book publishing rights included in a book publishing contract, such as paperback rights, book club rights, and movie rights. Part of an agent's job is to negotiate those rights and advise you on which to sell and which to keep.

Suspense. The element of both fiction and some nonfiction that makes the reader uncertain about the outcome. Suspense can be created through almost any element of a story, including the title, characters, plot, time restrictions, and word choice.

Synopsis. A brief summary of a story, novel, or play. As a part of a book proposal, it is a comprehensive summary condensed in a page or page and a half, single-spaced. Unlike a query letter or logline, a synopsis is a front-to-back explanation of the work—and will give away the story's ending. See outline.

Terms. Financial provisions agreed upon in a contract, whether between writer and agent, or writer and editor.

Textbook. Book used in school classrooms at the elementary, high school, or college level.

Theme. The point a writer wishes to make. It poses a question—a human problem.

Thriller. A story intended to arouse feelings of excitement or suspense. Works in this genre are highly sensational, usually focusing on illegal activities, international espionage, sex, and violence.

TOC. Table of Contents. A listing at the beginning of a book indicating chapter titles and their corresponding page numbers. It can also include chapter descriptions.

Trade Book. Either a hardcover or softcover book sold mainly in bookstores. The subject matter frequently concerns a special interest for a more general audience.

Trade Paperback. A softbound volume, usually 5" ×8" inches, published and designed for the general public; available mainly in bookstores.

Translation Rights. Sold to a foreign agent or foreign publisher.

Unsolicited Manuscript. An unrequested full manuscript sent to an editor, agent, or publisher.

Vet. A term used by editors when referring to the procedure of submitting a book manuscript to an outside expert (such as a lawyer) for review before publication. Memoirs are frequently vetted to confirm factual accuracy before the book is published.

Westerns/Frontier. Stories set in the American West, almost always in the nineteenth century, generally between the antebellum period and the turn of the century.

Young Adult (YA). The general classification of books written for ages twelve to fifteen. They run 40,000–80,000 words and include category novels—adventure, sports, paranormal, science fiction, fantasy, multicultural, mysteries, romance, and others.

FICTION GENRE DESCRIPTIONS

Action-Adventure. Action is the key element (overshadowing characters) and involves a quest or military-style mission set in exotic or forbidding locales such as jungles, deserts, or mountains. The conflict typically involves spies, mercenaries, terrorists, smugglers, pirates, or other dark and shadowy figures. Usually for a male audience.

Biographical Novel. A life story documented in history and transformed into fiction through the insight and imagination of the writer. This type of novel melds the elements of biographical research and historical truth into the framework of a novel, complete with dialogue, drama, and mood. A biographical novel resembles historical fiction, save for one aspect: Characters in a historical novel may be fabricated and then placed into an authentic setting; characters in a biographical novel have actually lived.

Gothic. This type of category fiction dates back to the late eighteenth and early nineteenth centuries. Contemporary gothic novels are characterized by atmospheric, historical settings and feature young, beautiful women who win the favor of handsome, brooding heroes—simultaneously dealing successfully with some life-threatening menace, either natural or supernatural. Gothics rely on mystery, peril, romantic relationships, and a sense of foreboding for their strong, emotional effect on the reader. A classic early gothic novel is Emily Brontë's *Wuthering Heights*.

Historical Fiction. A fictional story set in a recognizable period of history. As well as telling the stories of ordinary people's lives, historical fiction may involve political or social events of the time.

Horror. Howard Phillips (H.P.) Lovecraft, a master of the horror tale in the twentieth century, distinguished horror literature from fiction based entirely on physical fear and the merely gruesome. "The true weird tale has something more than secret murder, bloody bones, or a sheeted form clanking chains according to rule. A certain atmosphere of breathless and unexplainable dread of outer, unknown forces must be present; there must be a hint, expressed with a seriousness and portentousness becoming its subject, of that most terrible concept of the human brain—a malign and particular suspension or defeat of the fixed laws of Nature which are our only safeguards against the assaults of chaos and the daemons of unplumbed space." It is that atmosphere—the creation of a particular sensation or emotional level—that, according to Lovecraft, is the most important element in the creation of horror literature. Contemporary writers enjoying considerable success in horror fiction include Stephen King and Dean Koontz.

Mystery. A form of narration in which one or more elements remain unknown or unexplained until the end of the story. The modern mystery story contains elements of the serious novel: a convincing account of a character's struggle with various physical and psychological obstacles in an effort to achieve his goal, good characterization, and sound motivation.

Popular Fiction. Generally a synonym for category or genre fiction; that is, fiction intended to appeal to audiences for certain kinds of novels. Popular, or category, fiction is defined as such primarily for the convenience of publishers, editors, reviewers, and booksellers who must identify novels of different areas of interest for potential readers.

Psychological. A narrative that emphasizes the mental and emotional aspects of its characters, focusing on motivations and mental activities rather than on exterior events. The psychological novelist is less concerned about relating what happened than about exploring why it happened.

Roman À Clef. The French term for "novel with a key." This type of novel incorporates real people and events into the story under the guise of fiction. Robert Penn Warren's *All the King's Men*, in which the character Willie Stark represents Huey Long, is a novel in this genre.

Romance. The romance novel is a type of category fiction in which the love relationship between a man and a woman pervades the plot. The story is often told from the viewpoint of the heroine, who meets a man (the hero), falls in love with him, encounters a conflict that hinders their relationship, then resolves the conflict. Romance is the overriding element in this kind of story: The couple's relationship determines the plot and tone of the book, and the characters and plot both must be well-developed and realistic: Contrived situations and flat characters are unacceptable. Throughout a romance novel, the reader senses the sexual and emotional attraction between the heroine and hero.

Science Fiction and Fantasy. Science fiction can be defined as literature involving elements of science and technology as a basis for conflict, or as the setting for a story. The science and technology are generally extrapolations of existing scientific fact, and most (though not all) science fiction stories take place in the future. There are other definitions of science fiction, and much disagreement in academic circles as to just what constitutes science fiction and what constitutes fantasy. This is because in some cases the line between science fiction and fantasy is virtually nonexistent. Despite the controversy, it is generally accepted that, to be science fiction, a story must have elements of science. Fantasy, on the other hand, rarely utilizes science, relying instead on magic and mythological and neo-mythological beings.

Contemporary science fiction, while maintaining its focus on science and technology, is more concerned with the effects of science and technology on people. Since science is such an important factor in writing science fiction, accuracy with reference to science fact is important. Most of the science in science fiction is hypothesized from known facts, so in addition to being firmly based in fact, the extrapolations must be consistent. Science fiction writers make their own rules for future settings, but the field requires consistency.

Techno-Thriller. This genre utilizes many of the same elements as the thriller, with one major difference. In techno-thrillers, technology becomes a major character, such as in Tom Clancy's *The Hunt for Red October.*

Thriller. A novel intended to arouse feelings of excitement or suspense. Works in this genre are highly sensational, usually focusing on illegal activities, international espionage, sex, and violence. A thriller is often a detective story in which the forces of good are pitted against the forces of evil in a kill-or-be-killed situation.

Mystery Subgenres

Classic Mystery (Whodunit). A crime (almost always a murder or series of murders) is solved. The detective is the viewpoint character; the reader never knows any more or less about the crime than the detective, and all the clues to solving the crime are available to the reader.

Amateur Detective. As the name implies, the detective is not a professional detective (private or otherwise) but is almost always a professional something. This professional association routinely involves the protagonist in criminal cases (in a support capacity), gives her a special advantage in a specific case, or provides the contacts and skills necessary to solve a particular crime. (Examples: Jonathan Kellerman, Patricia Cornwell)

Cozy. A special class of the amateur detective category that frequently features a female protagonist (Agatha Christie's Miss Marple stories are the classic example). There is less onstage violence than in other categories, and the plot is often wrapped up in a final scene where the detective identifies the murderer and explains how the crime was solved. In contemporary stories, the protagonist can be anyone from a chronically curious housewife to a mystery-buff clergyman to a college professor, but she is usually quirky, even eccentric. (Examples: Susan Isaacs, Lillian Jackson Braun)

Private Detective. When described as hard-boiled, this category takes a tough stance. Violence is more prominent, characters are darker, the detective—while almost always licensed by the state—operates on the fringes of the law, and there is often open resentment between the detective and law enforcement. More "enlightened" male detectives and a crop of contemporary females have brought about new trends in this category. (For female P.I.s—Sue Grafton, Sara Paretsky; for male P.I.s—John D. MacDonald, Lawrence Sanders, Robert B. Parker)

Police Procedurals. The most realistic category, these stories require the most meticulous research. A police procedural may have more than one protagonist, since cops rarely work alone. Conflict between partners, or between the detective and her superiors, is a common theme. But cops are portrayed positively as a group, even though there may be a couple of bad or ineffective law enforcement characters for contrast and conflict. Jurisdictional disputes are still popular sources of conflict as well. (Example: Ridley Pearson)

Historical. May be any category or subcategory of mystery, but with an emphasis on setting, the details of which must be diligently researched. But beyond the historical details (which must never overshadow the story), the plot develops along the lines of its contemporary counterpart. (Examples: Candace Robb, Caleb Carr, Anne Perry)

Suspense/Thriller. Where a classic mystery is always a whodunit, a suspense/thriller novel may deal more with the intricacies of the crime, what motivated it, and how the villain (whose identity may be revealed to the reader early on) is caught and brought to justice. Novels in this category frequently employ multiple points of view and have a broader scope than a more traditional murder mystery. The crime may not even involve murder—it may be a threat to global economy or regional ecology; it may be technology run amok or abused at the hands of an unscrupulous scientist; it may involve innocent citizens victimized for personal or corporate gain. Its perpetrators are kidnappers, stalkers, serial killers, rapists, pedophiles, computer hackers, or just about anyone with an evil intention and the means to carry it out. The protagonist may be a private detective or law enforcement official but is just as likely to be a doctor, lawyer, military officer, or other individual in a unique position to identify the villain and bring her to justice. (Examples: James Patterson, Michael Connelly)

Espionage. The international spy novel is less popular since the end of the Cold War, but stories can still revolve around political intrigue in unstable regions. (Examples: John LeCarré, Ken Follett)

Medical Thriller. The plot can involve a legitimate medical threat (such as the outbreak of a virulent plague) or the illegal or immoral use of medical technology. In the former scenario, the protagonist is likely to be the doctor (or team) who identifies the virus and procures the antidote; in the latter, she could be a patient (or the relative of a victim) who uncovers the plot and brings down the villain. (Examples: Robin Cook, Michael Crichton)

Courtroom Drama. The action takes place primarily in the courtroom; the protagonist is generally a defense attorney out to prove the innocence of her client by finding the real culprit. (Examples: Scott Turow, John Grisham)

Woman in Jeopardy. A murder or other crime may be committed, but the focus is on the woman (and/or her children) currently at risk, her struggle to understand the nature of the danger, and her eventual victory over her tormentor. The protagonist makes up for her lack of physical prowess with intellect or special skills, and solves the problem on her own or with the help of her family (but she runs the show). Closely related to this category is the romantic suspense. But, while the heroine in a romantic suspense is certainly a woman in jeopardy, the mystery or suspense element is subordinate to the romance. (Example: Mary Higgins Clark)

Romance Subgenres

Historical. Can cover just about any historical (or even prehistorical) period. Setting in the historical is especially significant, and details must be thoroughly researched and accurately presented. Some specific historical romance categories include the following:

Gothic. Historical with a strong element of suspense and a feeling of supernatural events, although these events frequently have a natural explanation. Setting plays an important role in establishing a dark, moody, suspenseful atmosphere. (Example: Victoria Holt)

Historical Fantasy. Traditional fantasy elements of magic and magical beings, frequently set in a medieval society. (Examples: Jayne Ann Krentz, Kathleen Morgan)

Early America. Usually Revolution to Civil War, set in New England or the South, or frontier stories set in the American West.

Native American. One or both of the characters are Native Americans; the conflict between cultures is a popular theme.

Regency. Set in England during the Regency period, from 1811–1820.

Category or Series. These are published in specific lines or imprints by individual publishing houses (such as Harlequin and Silhouette); each line has its own requirements as to word length, story content, and amount of sex.

Single-Title Contemporary. Longer contemporary romances that do not necessarily conform to the requirements of a specific romance line and therefore feature more complex plots and nontraditional characters.

Erotica. Deals mainly with the characters' sex lives and features graphic descriptions.

Glitz. So called because they feature (generally wealthy) characters with high-powered positions in careers that are considered to be glamorous—high finance, modeling/acting, publishing, fashion—and are set in exciting or exotic (often metropolitan) locales such as Monte Carlo, Hollywood, London, or New York. (Examples: Judith Krantz, Jackie Collins)

Romantic Comedy. Has a fairly strong comic premise and/or a comic perspective in the author's voice or the voices of the characters (especially the heroine). (Example: Jennifer Crusie)

Romantic Suspense. With a mystery or psychological thriller subplot in addition to the romance plot. (Examples: Barbara Michaels, Tami Hoag, Nora Roberts, Catherine Coulter)

Paranormal. Containing elements of the supernatural or science fiction/fantasy. There are numerous subcategories (many stories combine elements of more than one) including:

Time Travel. One or more of the characters travels to another time—usually the past—to find love. (Examples: Jude Deveraux, Diana Gabaldon)

Science Fiction/Futuristic. Science-fiction elements are used for the story's setting: imaginary worlds, parallel universes, Earth in the near or distant future. (Examples: Jayne Ann Krentz, J.D. Robb)

Contemporary Fantasy. From modern ghost and vampire stories to New Age themes such as extraterrestrials and reincarnation. (Example: Linda Lael Miller)

Multicultural. Most currently feature African-American couples, but editors are looking for other ethnic stories as well. Multiculturals can be contemporary or historical and fall into any subcategory.

Christian. Feature an inspirational, Christian message centering on the spiritual dynamic of the romantic relationship, and faith in God as the foundation for that relationship; sensuality is played down. (Examples: Janette Oke, Karen Kingsbury)

PROFESSIONAL ORGANIZATIONS

AGENTS' ORGANIZATIONS

ASSOCIATION OF AUTHORS' AGENTS (AAA)
David Higham Associates Ltd, 5-8 Lower John Street, Golden Square, London W1F 9HA . (020) 7434 5900. **E-mail:** anthonygoff@davidhigham.co.uk. **Website:** www.agentsassoc.co.uk.

ASSOCIATION OF AUTHORS' REPRESENTATIVES (AAR)
E-mail: info@aar-online.org. **Website:** www.aar-online.org.

ASSOCIATION OF TALENT AGENTS (ATA)
9255 Sunset Blvd., Suite 930, Los Angeles CA 90069. (310)274-0628. **Fax:** (310)274-5063. **E-mail:** shellie@agentassociation.com. **Website:** www.agentassociation.com.

WRITERS' ORGANIZATIONS

ACADEMY OF AMERICAN POETS
584 Broadway, Suite 604, New York NY 10012-5243. (212)274-0343. **Fax:** (212)274-9427. **E-mail:** academy@poets.org. **Website:** www.poets.org.

AMERICAN CRIME WRITERS LEAGUE (ACWL)
17367 Hilltop Ridge Dr., Eureka MO 63205. **Website:** www.acwl.org.

AMERICAN MEDICAL WRITERS ASSOCIATION (AMWA)
30 West Gude Drive, Suite 525, Rockville MD 20850-4347. (301)294-5303. **Fax:** (301)294-9006. **E-mail:** amwa@amwa.org. **Website:** www.amwa.org.

AMERICAN SCREENWRITERS ASSOCIATION (ASA)
269 S. Beverly Dr., Suite 2600, Beverly Hills CA 90212-3807. (866)265-9091. **E-mail:** asa@goasa.com. **Website:** www.asascreenwriters.com.

AMERICAN TRANSLATORS ASSOCIATION (ATA)
225 Reinekers Lane, Suite 590, Alexandria VA 22314. (703)683-6100. **Fax:** (703)683-6122. **E-mail:** ata@atanet.org. **Website:** www.atanet.org.

EDUCATION WRITERS ASSOCIATION (EWA)
2122 P St., NW Suite 201, Washington DC 20037. (202)452-9830. **Fax:** (202)452-9837. **E-mail:** ewa@ewa.org. **Website:** www.ewa.org.

GARDEN WRITERS ASSOCIATION (GWA)
10210 Leatherleaf Ct., Manassas VA 20111. (703)257-1032. **Fax:** (703)257-0213. **E-mail:** info@gardenwriters.org. **Website:** www.gardenwriters.org.

HORROR WRITERS ASSOCIATION (HWA)
244 5th Ave., Suite 2767, New York NY 10001. **E-mail:** hwa@horror.org. **Website:** www.horror.org.

THE INTERNATIONAL WOMEN'S WRITING GUILD (IWWG)
P.O. Box 810, Gracie Station, New York NY 10028-0082. (212)737-7536. **Fax:** (212)737-9469. **E-mail:** dirhahn@aol.org. **Website:** www.iwwg.com.

MYSTERY WRITERS OF AMERICA (MWA)
1140 Broadway, Suite 1507, New York NY 10001. (212)888-8171. **Fax:** (212)888-8107. **E-mail:** mwa@mysterywriters.org. **Website:** www.mysterywriters.org.

NATIONAL ASSOCIATION OF SCIENCE WRITERS (NASW)
P.O. Box 7905, Berkeley, CA 94707. (510)647-9500. **E-mail:** LFriedmann@nasw.org. **Website:** www.nasw.org.

NATIONAL ASSOCIATION OF WOMEN WRITERS (NAWW)
24165 IH-10 W., Suite 217-637, San Antonio TX 78257. Phone/**Fax:** (866)821-5829. **Website:** www.naww.org.

ORGANIZATION OF BLACK SCREENWRITERS (OBS)
Golden State Mutual Life Insurance Bldg., 1999 West Adams Blvd., Rm. Mezzanine Los Angeles, CA 90018. **Website:** www.obswriter.com.

OUTDOOR WRITERS ASSOCIATION OF AMERICA (OWAA)
121 Hickory St., Suite 1, Missoula MT 59801. (406)728-7434. **Fax:** (406)728-7445. **E-mail:** krhoades@owaa.org. **Website:** www.owaa.org.

POETRY SOCIETY OF AMERICA (PSA)
15 Gramercy Park, New York NY 10003. (212)254-9628. **Website:** www.poetrysociety.org. Poets & Writers, 90 Broad St., Suite 2100, New York NY 10004. (212)226-3586. **Fax:** (212)226-3963. **Website:** www.pw.org.

ROMANCE WRITERS OF AMERICA (RWA)

114615 Benfer Road, Houston TX 77069. (832)717-5200. **Fax:** (832)717-5201. **E-mail:** info@rwanational.org. **Website:** www.rwa national.org.

SCIENCE FICTION AND FANTASY WRITERS OF AMERICA (SFWA)

P.O. Box 877, Chestertown MD 21620. **E-mail:** execdir@sfwa.org. **Website:** www.sfwa.org.

SOCIETY OF AMERICAN BUSINESS EDITORS & WRITERS (SABEW)

University of Missouri, School of Journalism, 30 Neff Annex, Columbia MO 65211. (602) 496-7862. **E-mail:** sabew@sabew.org. **Website:** www.sabew.org.

SOCIETY OF AMERICAN TRAVEL WRITERS (SATW)

7044 S. 13 St., Oak Creek WI 53154. (414)908-4949. **Fax:** (414)768-8001. **E-mail:** satw@satw.org. **Website:** www.satw.org.

SOCIETY OF CHILDREN'S BOOK WRITERS & ILLUSTRATORS (SCBWI)

8271 Beverly Blvd., Los Angeles CA 90048. (323)782-1010. **Fax:** (323)782-1892. **E-mail:** scbwi@scbwi.org. **Website:** www.scbwi.org.

AMERICAN INDEPENDENT WRITERS (AIW)

1001 Connecticut Ave. NW, Suite 701, Washington DC 20036. (202)775-5150. **Fax:** (202)775-5810. **E-mail:** info@aiwriters.org. **Website:** www.americanindependentwriters.org.

WESTERN WRITERS OF AMERICA (WWA)

E-mail: spiritfire@kc.rr.com. **Website:** www.westernwriters.org.

INDUSTRY ORGANIZATIONS

AMERICAN BOOKSELLERS ASSOCIATION (ABA)

200 White Plains Rd., Suite 600, Tarrytown NY 10591. (914)591-2665. **Fax:** (914)591-2720. **E-mail:** info@bookweb.org. **Website:** www.bookweb.org.

AMERICAN SOCIETY OF JOURNALISTS & AUTHORS (ASJA)

1501 Broadway, Suite 302, New York NY 10036. (212)997-0947. **Fax:** (212)937-2315. **E-mail:** director@asja.org. **Website:** www.asja.org.

ASSOCIATION FOR WOMEN IN COMMUNICATIONS (AWC)

3337 Duke St., Alexandria VA 22314. (703)370-7436. **Fax:** (703)342-4311. **E-mail:** info@womcom.org. **Website:** www.womcom.org.

ASSOCIATION OF AMERICAN PUBLISHERS (AAP)

71 5th Ave., 2nd Floor, New York NY 10003. (212)255-0200. **Fax:** (212)255-7007. Or, 50 F St. NW, Suite 400, Washington DC 20001. (202)347-3375. **Fax:** (202)347-3690. **Website:** www.publishers.org.

THE ASSOCIATION OF WRITERS & WRITING PROGRAMS (AWP)

Mail Stop 1E3, George Mason University, Fairfax VA 22030. (703)993-4301. **Fax:** (703)993-4302. **E-mail:** services@awpwriter. org. **Website:** www.awpwriter.org.

THE AUTHORS GUILD, INC.

31 E. 32nd St., 7th Floor, New York NY 10016. (212)563-5904. **Fax:** (212)564-5363. **E-mail:** staff@authorsguild.org. **Website:** www.authors guild.org.

CANADIAN AUTHORS ASSOCIATION (CAA)

P.O. Box 581, Stn. Main Orilla ON L3V 6K5 Canada. (705)653-0323. **Fax:** (705)653-0593. **E-mail:** admin@canauthors.org. **Website:** www. canauthors.org.

CHRISTIAN BOOKSELLERS ASSOCIATION (CBA)

P.O. Box 62000, Colorado Springs CO 80962-2000. (800)252-1950. **Fax:** (719)272-3510. **E-mail:** info@cbaonline.org. **Website:** www.cbaonline.org.

THE DRAMATISTS GUILD OF AMERICA

1501 Broadway, Suite 701, New York NY 10036. (212)398-9366. **Fax:** (212)944-0420. **Website:** www.dramatistsguild.com.

NATIONAL LEAGUE OF AMERICAN PEN WOMEN (NLAPW)

1300 17th St. NW, Washington DC 20036-1973. (202)785-1997. **Fax:** (202)452-8868. **E-mail:** nlapw1@verizon.net. **Website:** www. americanpenwomen.org.

NATIONAL WRITERS ASSOCIATION (NWA)

10940 S. Parker Rd., #508, Parker CO 80134. (303)841-0246. **Fax:** (303)841-2607. **E-mail:** natlwritersassn@hotmail.com. **Website:** www.nationalwriters.com

NATIONAL WRITERS UNION (NWU)

256 West 38th Street, Suite 703, New York, NY 10018. (212)254-0279. **Fax:** (212)254-0673. **E-mail:** nwu@nwu.org. **Website:** www. nwu.org.

PEN AMERICAN CENTER

588 Broadway, Suite 303, New York NY 10012-3225. (212)334-1660. **Fax:** (212)334-2181. **E-mail:** pen@pen.org. **Website:** www.pen.org.

THE PLAYWRIGHTS GUILD OF CANADA (PGC)

215 Spadina Ave., Suite #210, Toronto ON M5T 2C7 Canada. (416)703-0201. **Fax:** (416)703-0059. **E-mail:** info@playwrightsguild. ca. **Website:** www.playwrightsguild.com.

VOLUNTEER LAWYERS FOR THE ARTS (VLA)

One E. 53rd St., 6th Floor, New York NY 10022. (212)319-2787. **Fax:** (212)752-6575. **Website:** www.vlany.org.

WOMEN IN FILM (WIF)

6100 Wilshire Blvd., Suite 710, Los Angeles CA 90048. (323)935-2211. **Fax:** (323)935-2212. **E-mail:** info@wif.org. **Website:** www.wif.org.

WOMEN'S NATIONAL BOOK ASSOCIATION (WNBA)

P.O. Box 237, FDR Station, New York NY 10150. (212)208-4629. **Fax:** (212)208-4629. **E-mail:** publicity@bookbuzz.com. **Website:** www.wnba-books.org.

WRITERS GUILD OF ALBERTA (WGA)

11759 Groat Rd., Edmonton AB T5M 3K6 Canada. (780)422-8174. **Fax:** (780)422-2663. **E-mail:** mail@writersguild.ab.ca. **Website:** writersguild.ab.ca.

WRITERS GUILD OF AMERICA-EAST (WGA)

555 W. 57th St., Suite 1230, New York NY 10019. (212)767-7800. **Fax:** (212)582-1909. e-mail: info@wgaeast.org. **Website:** www.wgaeast.org.

WRITERS GUILD OF AMERICA-WEST (WGA)

7000 W. Third St., Los Angeles CA 90048. (323)951-4000. **Fax:** (323)782-4800. **Website:** www.wga.org.

WRITERS UNION OF CANADA (TWUC)

90 Richmond St. E., Suite 200, Toronto ON M5C 1P1 Canada. (416)703-8982. **Fax:** (416)504-9090. **E-mail:** info@writersunion.ca. **Website:** www.writersunion.ca.

WORD-COUNT GUIDELINES

Ask a simple question about word count, and a surprisingly heated discussion erupts. Who's right? Who gets to decide how long is too long and how short is too short? Here's the definitive information on industry standard for word count for fiction (novels, young adult, middle grade) and, for reasons I'll explain later, memoir.

The most important thing is to realize that there are always exceptions to these rules. And man, people love to point out exceptions—and they always will. However, if there is one thing I remember from when my wife dragged me kicking and screaming to watch *He's Just Not That Into You*, it's that you cannot count on being the exception; you must count on being the rule. Aiming to be the exception is setting yourself up for disappointment. What writers fail to see is that for every successful exception to the rule (for example, a first-time 175,000-word novel), there are hundreds of failures. Almost always, high word count means that the writer simply did not edit his work enough. Or it means he has actually written two or more books combined into one. With that in mind, let's break down some general word-count guidelines.

"But what about J.K. Rowling?" asks that man in the back of the room, putting his palms up in the air. Well, remember the first Harry Potter book? It wasn't that long. After J.K. made the publishing house oodles and oodles of money, she could do whatever she wanted. And because most writers haven't earned oodles, they need to stick to the rules and make sure their work gets read. The other thing that can make you an exception is absolutely brilliant writing. But let's face it: Most of our work doesn't classify as "absolutely brilliant," and that's okay.

ADULT FICTION WORD COUNTS, IN SHORT

80,000–89,999: Totally cool

90,000–99,999: Generally safe

70,000–79,999: Might be too short; probably all right

100,000–109,999: Might be too long; probably all right

Below 70,000: Too short

110,000 or above: Too long

ADULT NOVELS: COMMERCIAL AND LITERARY

Aim for between 80,000 and 89,999 words. This is a 100 percent safe range for literary, romance, mystery, suspense, thriller, and horror. Now, speaking broadly, you can get away with as few as 71,000 words and as many as 109,000 words. But when a book dips below 80K, it might be perceived as too short—not giving the reader enough. (The one exception to this rule is the "chick lit" genre, which favors shorter, faster reads. If you're writing chick lit, 65,000–75,000 is a better target range.) And while it can be permissible to go over 100,000 words if your book really warrants such length, don't cross the six-figure mark by much. Agent Rachelle Gardner of Wordserve Literary points out that more than 110K is defined as "epic or saga"—and chances are your cozy mystery or literary novel is not an epic. Gardner also mentions that passing 100,000 in word count means you've written a book that will be more costly to produce—making it a difficult sell.

SCI-FI AND FANTASY

Science fiction and fantasy books tend to run long largely because of all the descriptions and world-building involved. The thing is: Writers tend to know that these categories run long so they make them run really long and hurt their chances with an agent.

With these genres, 100,000–110,000 is an excellent range. It's six-figures long but not excessive. There's also nothing wrong with keeping it a bit shorter; it shows that you can whittle your work down.

In broader terms, anything between 85,000 and 125,000 may be acceptable when writing science fiction and fantasy.

MIDDLE-GRADE

Middle-grade fiction—that is, a novel for readers in the nine to twelve age range—usually falls within 20,000–45,000 words, depending on the subject matter and target reader age. When writing a longer book aimed at twelve-year-olds (that could be considered tween), using the term "upper middle grade" is advisable. These are books that resemble young adult fiction in matter and storytelling, but still tend to stick to middle-grade themes and avoid hot-button, YA-acceptable themes such as sex and drugs. With upper middle grade, you can aim for 32,000–40,000 words. You can stray a little over but not much.

With a simpler middle grade idea (*Football Hero* or *Jenny Jones and the Cupcake Mystery*), aim lower. Shoot for 20,000–30,000 words.

YOUNG ADULT (YA)

Perhaps more than any other, YA is the one category where word count is very flexible. For starters, 50,000–69,999 is a great range.

The word from the agent blogosphere is that these books tend to be trending longer and can top in the 80,000-word range. However, this progression is still in motion, and trends can be fickle, so you may be playing with fire the higher you go. Make sure you have a compelling reason for exceeding 70,000 words. One good reason is that your YA novel is science fiction or fantasy. Once again, these categories are expected to be a little longer because of the description and world-building they entail.

Concerning the low end, fewer than 50,000 words could be acceptable, but be sure to stay above 40,000 to remain viable in this genre.

PICTURE BOOKS

The standard for this category is text for thirty-two pages, which might mean one line per page, or more. Aim for 500–600 words; when a manuscript gets closer to 1,000, editors and agents might shy away.

WESTERNS

Marketable manuscripts in this genre can be anywhere from 50,000–80,000 words. A good target range is anywhere around the 65,000-word mark.

MEMOIR

I'm including memoir in this discussion of fiction word counts because this breed of nonfiction is queried—and evaluated by agents and editors—in much the way a novel would be, because the form relies so heavily on the writer's voice, style, approach and story arc. Memoir, after all, is the one nonfiction category where writers must complete the entire manuscript prior to submitting, rather than compose only a few sample chapters as part of a book proposal.

Concerning word count for memoir, aim for 80,000–89,999.

This is one genre where writers often have a tendency to go unnecessarily long—possibly indicating to an agent that they're too close to their own story to properly revise their work. With that in mind, lower word counts (70,000–79,999) are not a terrible thing. At the same time, you may want to consider the high end of memoir to be 99,999.

OTHER THOUGHTS

Some literary agents such as Kristin Nelson of Nelson Literary and Nathan Bransford of Curtis Brown, Ltd., say that you shouldn't think about word count, but rather you should think about pacing and telling the best story possible. While that sounds good in theory, the fact is: Not every agent feels that way and is willing to give a 129,000-word debut novel a shot. Agents receive so many queries and submissions that they are looking for reasons to say no. And if you submit a project well outside the typical length conventions, then you are giving them ammunition to reject you.

Some writers may just take their chances, cross their fingers, and hope for the best.

But I believe that we cannot count on being the exception; we must count on being the rule. That's the way to give yourself the best shot at success.

Become a
Writer's Digest VIP

Fuel your passion for writing with the Writer's Digest VIP Program. You'll have access to the best writing advice, markets, competitions, tips, prompts, and more. The program includes:

- **One-year U.S. subscription** to *Writer's Digest* magazine

- **One-year of online access to WritersMarket.com,** with updated listings for more than 8,000 book publishers, magazines, literary agents, contests, scriptwriting markets, and more

- **Access to our most important webinar:** The Essentials of Online Marketing & Promotion—a 1-hour tutorial on how to promote yourself as a writer and get the attention of editors and agents

- **Discounts on Writer's Online Workshops** course registrations and purchases made at the Writer's Digest Shop

- **And more!**

Become a Writer's Digest VIP and take your writing career to the next level!

http://www.writersdigestshop.com/product/writers-vip/

Writer's Digest University.com

Our workshops combine the best of this world-class writing instruction with the convenience and immediacy of the Web to create a state-of the-art learning environment. You get all of the benefits of a traditional workshop setting—peer review, instructor feedback, a community of writers, and productive writing practice—without any of the hassle. All courses run on an asynchronous model; you regularly check in at a day and time that works for you.

Go online and find a course that's the perfect fit for you!

GET PAID
FOR YOUR WRITING!

Whether you write poetry or children's books, magazine articles, or novels, you can make money from your passion. WritersMarket.com gives you the tools and resources to make it possible.

- ➤ Organize your markets, queries, and manuscrtipts with the unique "My Markets" tool.
- ➤ Search the latest listings updated every week
- ➤ Get advice and commentary from experts
- ➤ Find the right answers to the most commonly asked questions!

Unlock your full potential now!

WritersMarket.com
Where & How to Sell What You Write

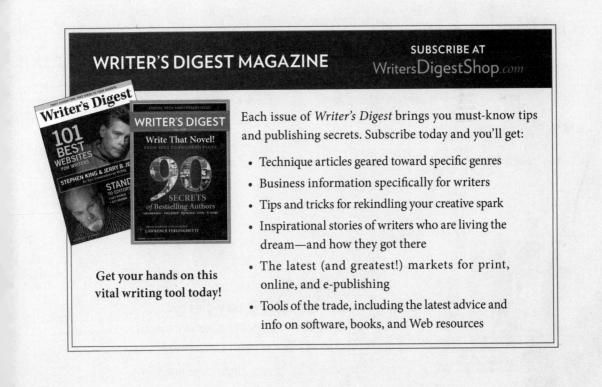

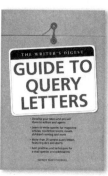